Hilary Kingsley read English at university before training as a journalist in the West Country, where she became an associate of the probation service and a Dartmoor Prison visitor. She has worked as a critic and feature writer on the *Daily Mirror*, and contributes regularly to many publications including *The Times*. She is the author of several books on television, including *Soap Box* and *Casualty* and is currently working on a political biography.

She lives in London with her journalist husband and three children.

Geoff Tibballs worked in television for fifteen years before leaving to pursue a writing career in 1989. Since then he has had sixteen books published on a wide variety of subjects ranging from television to true crime, social history to sport. With Hilary Kingsley, he wrote the widely acclaimed history of television, *Box of Delights*. His previous true crime books include *The Contract Killers* and *The Murder Guide to Great Britain*. He lives in the Midlands with his wife and two daughters.

Also by Hilary Kingsley

Box of Delights (*with Geoff Tibballs*)
Soap Box
The EastEnders' Handbook
Casualty: The Inside Story

Also by Geoff Tibballs

The Contract Killers
The Murder Guide to Great Britain
Box of Delights (*with Hilary Kingsley*)
The Encyclopedia of TV Detectives
London's Burning
Ian St John's Book of Soccer Lists
Brookside: The First Ten Years
Soldier, Soldier
Great Sporting Failures
The Big Breakfast Bowl
The Guinness Book of Innovations

No Way Out

Battered Women Who Killed

Hilary Kingsley and Geoff Tibballs

HEADLINE

Copyright © 1994 Hilary Kingsley and Geoff Tibballs

The right of Hilary Kingsley and Geoff Tibballs
to be identified as the Authors of
the Work has been asserted by them in accordance with the
Copyright, Designs and Patents Act 1988.

First published in 1994
by HEADLINE BOOK PUBLISHING

First published in paperback in 1995
by HEADLINE BOOK PUBLISHING

10 9 8 7 6 5 4 3 2

All rights reserved. No part of this publication may be
reproduced, stored in a retrieval system, or transmitted,
in any form or by any means without the prior written
permission of the publisher, nor be otherwise circulated
in any form of binding or cover other than that in which
it is published and without a similar condition being
imposed on the subsequent purchaser.

ISBN 0 7472 4340 9

Printed and bound in Great Britain by
Cox & Wyman Ltd, Reading, Berks

HEADLINE BOOK PUBLISHING
A division of Hodder Headline PLC
338 Euston Road
London NW1 3BH

No Way Out is dedicated to all women who have suffered from violent men and are waiting for understanding, safety and justice

Contents

Introduction

The scene is a labour ward in a large Liverpool hospital in 1983. A dark-haired girl of sixteen in the advanced stage of labour cries out with the waves of pain. With her is the baby's father, a tall, strong young man of eighteen. He is uneasy about being there and wants to leave. The staff are used to the qualms of first-time fathers. But this one is different. He wants her to leave with him.

He isn't patient. He reacts angrily to her yells and tells her to push harder to 'get it over' more quickly. He ignores the attempts of a nurse to calm him and when a male doctor arrives, examines the young mother and talks of using forceps for the delivery, the rage of this prospective parent explodes. He butts the doctor on the face with his head. The doctor's nose bleeds. It is cut and probably broken. The young man again insists that the girl leaves and tries to drag her to the window. Eventually he gives up. He leaves and she has the baby that night. The next day she cannot refuse him when he comes to take her home with the child, a boy. There he discovers that she needed a vaginal cut during the birth and that a male doctor later stitched up the wound. Madly jealous, he proceeds to punish her. He forces her to

1

have sexual intercourse then kicks her in the groin and crotch, splitting the stitches.

Six weeks later, the young mother tries to leave this man who says she is his. He finds her and brings her back. During the next nine years, she has two more babies, born at home, because he refuses to let her go in the ambulance a neighbour has called. She tries to leave him three more times, succeeds once but returns because he has kept the oldest child and she fears that he is being cruelly treated. During those years he hits her with an iron, sticks pins under her fingernails when he believes, wrongly, that she has been unfaithful, insists that she watch pornographic films and then copy the acts she sees and finally, to show that he means business, he holds a loaded gun to her vagina and threatens to kill her and the children if she gives him 'trouble'.

This is not a dirty, titillating fiction about sex and violence among a subspecies on the fringes of society. It is a sample of what life was like for Sandra Fleming, who finally killed Christopher Porter, that vicious and insanely possessive young man, with his own gun.

'Every time I got away from him, he brought me back and gave me hidings,' she says. 'He threatened to chop me up and spread me over England. He made sure no one ever knew where I was, so he could have got away with it.'

He might well have – because no one, not those doctors, not the police she contacted, not members of her own family or his, ever supported her or came to her aid. By the time she made it to the police station with her children in April 1992 on the night she fought back, she weighed only six stone.

At her trial at Liverpool Crown Court, Sandra was found not guilty of murder but guilty of the lesser offence of manslaughter on the grounds of diminished responsibility. Because she was said to be suffering from Battered Woman Syndrome, an American term to describe a group of symptoms, beginning to be used in courts in Britain, she was put on probation. But the judge warned that she was 'a wholly exceptional case'. He was willing to show mercy, he said, but added that no woman should get the idea that if she were ill-treated by her partner, she had the right to shoot him.

The full story of the relationship between Sandra and the good looking boy who was her neighbour and became her lover, master and torturer, isn't told in *No Way Out* because Sandra is still living under the threat of violence from former associates of the dead man and she must be protected.

The point is that Sandra's experience was anything but exceptional. The women whose stories Geoff Tibballs and I retell in *No Way Out* were exceptional only in that snapshots of their lives were exposed in courts. We have in some cases imagined lines of dialogue, guessed the reactions of onlookers. We have invented no facts, created no circumstances and assumed no motives. It is in no one's interests, certainly not women's, to encourage people to take the law into their own hands or to sanction unnecessary killings. So we do not suggest that these women are heroines, merely that they are not criminals from whom society needs protection.

They are as varied as we could make them. Many are middle class, outwardly confident and successful. They are of many nationalities, of all ages, seventeen in the case of Emma Humphries, or those who suddenly took action against their tormentors in their middle years, or like Arlene Caris, from New York, who was a grandmother when she shot and killed the husband who was bashing her and molesting their grandchild.

Sandra Fleming didn't want to kill Chris Porter, though she may often have wished him gone from her life. She is not a violent person. None of the other women referred to in this book were hitters, punchers, stabbers or shooters before they met their violent mates. None had been in trouble with the police for any serious infringement of the law before that fatal day when they decided 'it's him or me'. None was 'the kind of woman' to put up with this sort of treatment. None could 'tell' because she was ashamed. None could believe that another person could ever comprehend how it is to exist in a minefield of explosive male emotions that dragged her deeper into nothingness each day. Until that special day when something inside her snapped and made her take action, none had considered killing a human being – except herself – before. Why kill herself? Because the battered woman feels – knows – that she is somehow to blame.

So these stories are about how some women have reacted to a life of losing the war at home. Domestic violence, sociology-speak for men using women and children as things to control, is an age-old institution. We try to reflect this by reopening the cases of Kitty Byron (1902), Fanny Hyde (1872) and Marguerite Fahmy (1923). These women have in the past been included in lists of 'murderous' women but they are, we believe, closer to Sandra Fleming than the lipsmacking writers of old-style crime books imagined.

These are better times for women – though not yet nearly good enough. In Brazil, for example, thanks to the dogged campaigners who lobbied long and hard during the 1980s, some legislation which matched the country's culture of machismo has been changed. In 1991 their Supreme Court ruled that a man may no longer kill his wife and win acquittal on the ground of 'legitimate defence of honour'. Finally no woman could be murdered by her husband after an accusation of adultery and the husband walk free.

At around the same time in the United States campaigners were working to persuade the governors of several states to consider granting clemency in some of the cases where women had killed their abusers. It was long overdue. The figures on domestic violence there are mind-numbing. Take this one. More American women, rich and poor alike, are injured by the men in their lives than by car accidents, muggings and rape by strangers, combined. In 1992 the American Medical Association, backed by the Surgeon General, announced that violent men constitute a major threat to women's health. It was estimated by the National League of Cities that as many as half of all women would experience violence in their marriage at some time.

Between 22 per cent and 35 per cent of visits to the accident and emergency departments of hospitals by American women are for injuries from violence by the men in their homes. Women may start some of the arguments, but they take almost all of the violence that follows. Especially horrific is the brutal treatment reserved for pregnant women. It is responsible for more defects to the infants when they're born than all of those against which children are usually immunised.

Calls for clemency have so far not helped Brenda Clubine or Arlene Caris, who remain behind bars today. Happily for Joyce Steiner, a woman who ran her own detective agency until her disastrous second marriage, clemency was granted. She served only ten months of the five year sentence meted out to her. In the same state, Maryland, a few years later another giant step forward was taken. Previously there, as in many states, evidence of spousal abuse was not admissible in custody hearings. The 1993 television movie *Going Underground* highlighted the case of an architect's wife who lost custody of her two young children when her husband left them. The reason was that she was admitted to hospital suffering from injuries inflicted by this same man after a particularly savage beating. Only after several women defied the courts and went 'underground' with their children, was the lobbying of women's groups successful in reforming the law.

The hunger for change has spread to Britain. By 1994, women who have killed, those like Sandra Fleming and more importantly (because they are still in prison) like Emma Humphries and Sara Thornton, whose stories are told in this book, find themselves at the centre of a heated legal and political debate.

Some people, reading the short account of Sandra's story here, may conclude that she 'got off lightly'. Some who have never come across people locked into violent relationships like hers will ask, why didn't she leave, go somewhere where he couldn't find her, get help, not go back?

Those questions tend to shrivel on the tongue as soon as

you meet one woman who is a victim of the violent man she once loved and may love still. Ask her what it is like to wake up each day wondering when and how she will be knocked around? What is it like to exist in a constantly revolving cycle of anger, abuse and remorse? The reason so many can't 'just leave' is that the man, often flanked by members of his family who cannot or will not believe that he has been brutal, will come after them and the danger will be all the greater.

Many have lost all confidence that they can survive on their own. They believe at a deeper level that their suffering is what they are due as worthless individuals. Many have no money and no idea that there exist refuges or places of safety. Many have gone to the police and their tales have fallen on deaf ears. We hope these stories will give an idea why they couldn't just leave.

But should we care? Here are a couple of British statistics compiled by the Association of London Authorities (ALA) for their 'Zero Tolerance' Campaign launched in January 1994 to suggest why we should. One is that domestic violence accounts for a quarter of all reported crimes. Another is that it is estimated that only 2 per cent of violent attacks on women are reported to the police yet there is also an estimate that the number of cases reported has risen by over 1,000 per cent in the last five years.

These statements prove that it's a big problem. That you and I probably know at least one woman who is currently concealing the fact that her husband – who may be old, young, educated and successful or unskilled and unemployed – is terrorising her, and perhaps her children too, behind the closed doors of their home. Domestic violence may be physical hitting of some kind. It may be sexual – the forcing by a man of a woman to take part in sexual acts which may hurt, humiliate or disgust her. The violence may be psychological. The man may need to assert control by 'proving' how inadequate she is. He may hide things, deny that things have happened, isolate her by preventing her from mixing with her relatives and friends. He may watch and check her every movement, limiting her freedom.

The violence may be emotional by constant criticism, belittling her efforts or by threatening public embarrassment. It may also be financial. Many women who are battered have been made totally dependent on their partners, reduced to asking for every penny they need to buy essentials for the household, the children and themselves. The violence often erupts after the man has drunk alcohol. But whatever the triggers, it tends to become more and more frequent. After the fights, the man is frequently apparently desperate to be forgiven and for the woman to demonstrate her forgiveness, often with sex which she is too frightened to refuse.

It may seem obvious, but what all battered women need is to be believed, helped to a safe haven and supported through a period of wavering, often through depression. The help, practical and psychological, needs to be long-term. Children are also victims of this violence. Included in the ALA's findings was the result of research with a volunteer sample of a thousand London women victims. In 70 per cent of those cases, children had also been beaten by the violent man.

Here are a few generalisations. However many celebrities sign petitions on the matter, battered women will face this lack of understanding and support for a long time to come unless the law is changed. Women's refuges are often hopelessly stretched and as public spending is reduced, so too is the funding for them. Aggressive men are not receiving psychiatric help. Boys who grow up in violent households and learn to rage against women will, unless counselled and treated, continue to grow into men who abuse their women and children.

When the bough breaks in some women's lives and they kill the men who terrorise them, it almost always makes newspaper headlines which we read with surprise because we don't expect women to lash out. Crime is all about men. Girls learn to follow the rules, don't they?

As you might expect, the American figures on deaths from domestic violence are truly shocking. There an average of 1,500 abused women are killed annually by their mates. Each year another 400 to 800 of them hit back and kill their violent men. The British death figures may seem less alarming, but the courts' responses to them are a cause for concern.

According to Home Office records for 1982 to 1989 between 4 and 14 women a year were indicted for killing their men. Those deaths accounted for 7 per cent of homicides on male victims. Meanwhile between 8 and 109 men were indicted for killing their wives, ex-wives or lovers. On average that's 2 women a week. Those deaths make up 45 per cent of all the non-accidental deaths of British women. What is alarming, is the way the law deals with them. According to the Crown Prosecution Service 40 per cent of the men who kill their women have the conviction reduced to manslaughter on the grounds of provocation. To provoke a man to kill you isn't that difficult, it would seem. In the past, the grounds have included 'naggings', 'refusing to have sex' and in one case in 1991, refusing to move the mustard pot. When Joseph McGrail walked free from court with a suspended sentence in July 1991 after punching his 'nagging' common-law wife to death, the judge Mr Justice Popplewell said that the woman would 'try the patience of a saint'.

By comparison only 24 per cent of women who kill the men who abused them or their children have had their convictions reduced to manslaughter. The rest have been convicted of murder which carries only one sentence: life.

If it's any consolation to anyone, while the numbers of violent assaults in the home are soaring (the Metropolitan Police reported a 66 per cent rise between 1990 and 1991) the numbers of women who reach the point where they believe 'it's him or me' is not rising. So judges who fret that enlightened policies in courts would give the 'green light' to wives to reach for the breadknife when tired of husbands who leave the lavatory seat up, should relax. But tolerance of the uneven and often unfair sentences to women who kill is changing.

In 1993 a number of civil liberties' and women's groups, ranging from radical feminists to the National Federation of Women's Institutes (membership 300,000), began urging reform. They want the Home Secretary and the Lord Chancellor to review the Homicide Act and change the defence of provocation to take into account the effects of prolonged domestic violence. Lord Devlin's definition of provocation in 1949 in the case of Renee Duffy, was that it was 'an act or series of acts or words spoken . . . which would cause in any reasonable person . . . a sudden and temporary loss of control, rendering the accused so subject to passion as to make him for the moment not master of his mind'.

The point is that repeated threats of, or actual physical or mental cruelty do things to make *her* not the *mistress* of *her* mind. Furthermore, because she knows from bitter experience, what happens when the storm is raging, the time that elapses between the act of provocation and the response is not always a cooling-off period. It may be a boiling-up or brimming-over period.

Before his elevation to the Upper House, Jack Ashley MP introduced a Private Member's Bill on this subject but its passage was blocked. He is now preparing to push a similar bill through the House of Lords. Meanwhile in April 1994, the torch was passed in the Commons to Harry Cohen, Labour MP for Leyton in East London, the man who was successful in changing the law on rape within marriage. (A law commission's findings in 1992 supported his move and judges now rule accordingly, though there has as yet been no change by statute.)

The wording of his bill on provocation is slightly different from Lord Ashley's. He has added the notion that provocation could be the cumulative effect of things done, said or both. Also added is the stipulation that those things done could be any conduct of the deceased including domestic violence, violence to immediate family members or the threat of it. Another key clause removes the requirement for the loss of control to be sudden as well as temporary.

He said:

Last year there was a Home Affairs Select Committee

considering the problems of domestic violence. A lot of pressure was put on the government, but the response was pretty poor. That's why we need the lobby of women's groups to hammer home the message that it's just not acceptable. We also need to provide the necessary resources for women who are in that situation.

We must also change the law. It is unfair at the moment. It does not give women the same rights as men. Women are branded as common murderers when they are really the victims themselves. And there are a lot of women who are in prison serving life sentences who should not be there. I want to see them released. I don't want to rely on clemency. This Conservative government is such a hard-hearted lot, anyway. No, these women should not be there under the law. The courts should recognise their motivation and take it into consideration. It is not right that their freedom should depend on the mercy of a minister.

Harry Cohen bases his belief in the change of the law of provocation partly on the experience of similar changes in the law in New South Wales, Australia. 'If resistance to change is based on the fear that this would justify revenge killings,' he argues, 'it's crazy. The effect there has been that there has been no rise in killings by women, certainly not for motives of revenge.'

One of the pressure groupes, Rights of Women, has a different strategy. This is to have introduced an entirely new partial defence for murder, that of self-preservation. 'The existing defences were devised by men for men,' says

Jill Radford of Rights of Women. 'We believe that rather than trying to change existing laws in a way which may benefit men more than victims of domestic violence, that there should be a new defence structured around women's experience.'

They want reform of the defence of self-defence which includes the rule that a person may not use a weapon unless one is being used against her. They point out that women are almost always physically less strong than men and men have learned since boyhood how to overpower others. So it's no wonder that women reach for whichever weapon is at hand and use it, clumsily, desperately and sometimes, fatally.

Rights of Women members have also examined the issue of escape. 'For a woman, escaping from a violent partner in her own home raises far more complex issues than are raised for an adult man escaping from a one-off violent encounter in a public place,' Jill Radford points out. She does not, she adds, endorse the use of 'syndrome' defences such as Battered Woman Syndrome under the defence of diminished responsibility because it relies on the evidence of so-called experts and on psychiatric terms. Some women's experiences may be described easily in such terms. Those of women from ethnic minorities may not.

What Rights of Women members have come up with is the partial defence of self-preservation. It would apply when a woman has killed someone in a familial situation after that person has subjected her to continuing abuse to the extent that she honestly believes she has reached the point where she will not continue to live while the aggressor is alive.

Helena Kennedy QC, who has defended many battered women, favours changes to the definition of provocation (rather than the inclusion of a new defence) and put forward her views in the Yorkshire Television documentary *Women Who Kill*:

These laws [on homicide] weren't designed with women in mind. If in self-defence they use a knife, having been struck with a hand or fist, it may seem like excessive force. It may seem unreasonable and so they may find the plea of self-defence has failed for them because it's not been about even handed combat.

I often try to describe it to a jury as being like the fuse on dynamite where they ultimately snap and go out of control. It may take a period of time before this eventually happens and because there was a delay the correct defence was not available in the past.

She has gone on to urge the Home Secretary to order the review of the cases of around fifty women, half the total number currently in British prisons for murder.

I am now receiving letters from women who are serving life sentences having been convicted of murdering husbands who battered them and for whom, with the knowledge that we have now, the outcome might have been very different.

Some of them are well into their sentences having spent many years in prison and I think we should have a review to see whether there aren't women who shouldn't be there.

One who shouldn't be there is Sara Thornton who killed her former policeman husband Malcolm after a furious row in June 1989. Sara, thirty-three and barely five feet tall, killed strapping Thornton with a knife as he lay in a drunken stupor after he had threatened her daughter and accused Sara of whoring. She was sentenced to life. But with the aid of a pressure group, Justice For Women, she is campaigning for leave to appeal for a second time.

In tape recordings made in her cell at Bullwood prison, she talks of the humiliation of her trial and appeal. 'It really was all right for him to beat me – so long as we kept it quiet. Domestic violence is very hard to put across in a court of law because it has very little to do with law. It's about pain and power and control,' she says.

Brenda Clubine has a simple message to all women who are discovering the strength of men's anger towards them. She says, 'If he hits you once, he'll hit you again'.

Hair on the End
of a Pickaxe

Supper times were not relaxed times in the Scotlands' house in Pankhurst Crescent, Stevenage. Certainly not when Thomas Scotland was at home, which was most nights. For his family, meal times were dramas of tension and suspense which they'd rather not watch, let alone be part of. For June Scotland, his wife of twenty-two years, this particular meal was a test, the setting of a new scene in a living drama and she was by no means sure of the script. She would have to improvise. Would Thomas Scotland, then forty-eight, approve of the Chinese-style turkey and stirfry vegetables, the ingredients of which she'd bought at Tesco? He'd taken her there – it was the only place he ever took her to. He'd approved of this menu in the past, but would he examine it that evening, taste it and howl before picking up his plate and throwing it in her direction?

This wasn't a comedy. Sadly not. Whether or not the food flew would depend, June and their teenage daughter Caroline knew, on Scotland's mood on that warm night of 25 August 1987. If he hadn't had a drink, he would probably not be violent. He would, however, always need to play the leading role, show he was master of his kingdom. He

17

wouldn't put up with slacking or sloppiness. Oh no. Not that many people knew this about the compact little Scot, with his oddly unattractive brown hair and strange light eyes, each of which seemed to look in a different direction as if hiding some fear. A fear of being judged too soft, too weak, perhaps. At least his sons Alistair and Alan had turned out well; proper men. He'd had to be firm, but it had worked. Alistair was at a polytechnic in Coventry studying civil engineering. At that time he was on holiday in Corfu with student friends. Alan had been to university, gained his degree and now had a good job and a home in Manchester. No one could say Thomas Scotland had failed with them.

The neighbours hadn't given it that much thought, if the truth be known. They weren't part of the audience to the scenes the Scotlands enacted in their ordinary, decent but dowdy end-of-terrace house in the Chells district of Stevenage new town, Hertfordshire. Bert Whitford was grateful to be given a lift to work by the small Scotsman on occasion. Ted Bunce had struck up a conversation with him a few times. Others nodded when they passed. But few of them had ever stepped foot inside his home to see the strange, sparsely furnished rooms, strange because its owner worked many hours of overtime and had, at one stage, gone to Saudi Arabia to earn a tidy lump sum.

Few had ever been invited into the back garden that had never known much tending. Thomas wasn't much of a gardener. Luckily there was a weeping willow tree at the end of it which lent it grace and would for a while guard a secret. The garden would become the stage for another act in this tragic piece. But in 1987 there wasn't much going on, not so far as anyone could tell.

Thomas Scotland was an electrical engineer by training, hard-working, a bit touchy if you asked his workmates at British Aerospace in Stevenage and later Rank Xerox, Welwyn Garden City. He was a contract machine operator, independent. But he was 'sociable and amusing', the prosecution said in court at the trial and he was liked well enough.

This story really began twenty-two years before that stirfry supper when small, dark-haired June Rose married Thomas Scotland of Bo'ness near Edinburgh. He was her own age but much older in so many ways. It had to be said that her family and friends had never liked him.

People warned her that he was not the man she thought he was. They said he was sharp, abrasive and rude. June's father, James Rose, had known the boy's father. He was a disciplinarian, a nasty piece of work in his opinion. But young Thomas was industrious, determined and it seemed that a lass could have done worse. He was flattering and attentive to her and insisted to her parents that wee June was the girl for him.

The week after the wedding he changed. The sweet talk stopped. June was stunned to discover that being Mrs Thomas Scotland was going to be the beginning and end of her role. 'You are a married woman, so you don't go out,' he announced. He would not hear of her taking a job. He did not want her to see friends or spend time with her parents and relatives. He made it clear that he was her life now and what he said, what he ordered, was what was to happen. He would hold the purse strings and, when the children arrived, he would decide on the way that they would be brought up. He also began to drink heavily. Somehow June believed that she would find compensations. She

19

thought that when the children came he could not possibly dictate how she loved them and looked after them. She was wrong.

In 1971 the family came south from Linlithgow to Stevenage. Little Alan and Alistair soon began school and then Caroline was born. As they grew they were to nickname their father Mr Killjoy because fun and laughter were not on his agenda. Nor was love and affection. June was told that she must not fuss over them or pander to them. Kisses were forbidden.

When Caroline was five, her father discovered that she had scribbled on the wallpaper in her bedroom. Telling her this was wrong was not enough, he decided. His answer was to throw her teddy bears and other soft toys on the fire. She wept as she watched them burn and she never forgot.

More than twenty years later Alistair was to tell the court, 'He ruled everyone with a rod of iron. He was never loving towards anyone. He would slap mum about. He would dominate us all. He would dominate all out faults. My dad was always able to see the worst in everything we did.'

Scotland would stand over the children as they did their homework and slap them if he decided they were slacking. If they walked along the street in a way their father thought sloppy, he would prod them hard in the back. They were never allowed to leave food on their plates. They had to eat everything given them. It was different for him. He would open the fridge, inspect the provisions his wife had bought and if he decided a steak, bought for him, was substandard, he would toss it away. Dishes served to him that did not gain his approval would be thrown at the cook: June. If she challenged his behaviour in any way, she would receive 'a thump in the face'. All the children were aware that he was sometimes violent to their mother. On one occasion Alistair told the court he had seen his father hit her with a shoe. 'I remember mum saying that if it had not been for us children she would not have stayed with him. Very often I would come home from school and find mum crying because of an incident with dad.'

Neither June nor the children were encouraged to bring friends home. Alistair remembered that his father once gave his older brother Alan a bloody nose for coming home late. Caroline's friends were subject to scrutiny and were almost invariably deemed unsuitable. Pals were hurled out of the children's bedrooms causing hideous embarrassment. Later when Caroline began going out her father would wait at the end of the street until she arrived and yank her out of her friend's car.

There were times when Thomas Scotland seemed to want to improve the atmosphere at home. He would try to change his ways, Alistair reported, 'But it was a strain for him to behave normally to us'.

What the two boys did not know was that for their little sister, his abnormal behaviour was far, far more of a strain to bear. The mischievous child had grown into a pretty girl. When she was eleven, Thomas Scotland could no longer keep to his own rules banning cuddles and caresses. By then the sexual side of his marriage was less than rapturous. June had become a nervy, dispirited woman. She dreaded the slamming of the front door at night, the noise that announced her husband was home and that the reign of terror was about to recommence.

She had seen a doctor who prescribed Valium tranquillisers and antidepressants. With these she functioned. She even performed the sex act, when it was demanded, after a fashion. Doing it was less trouble than refusing, she decided. When Scotland had taken a fair amount of drink, which he often did, the business was mercifully short if never sweet. Later she was to say that she got through the hours as a 'servant, a zombie'.

June may have thought she was past feeling pain, but she was not. In 1984 she learned of something that changed her. Any slight doubt she may have had that the man she married was a monster was swept away. Caroline was suicidal. Life was too painful for her. When her mother asked what was wrong, the horrible truth came tumbling out. She told her mother that she too was serving Thomas Scotland, her own father, in bed. She too was unable to refuse because she had to obey him in this as in everything and because this abuse had started four years earlier when she was merely eleven. What started as 'touching' her intimately, progressed until full sexual intercourse was forced upon her. But so terrified was the girl, that she made her mother promise not to tackle the man about it.

June's response was to withdraw further into her shell to avoid having to confront the problem. But as Caroline matured, her mother realised they must try to escape. One solution was to take off to a caravan on a site near Welwyn, Hertfordshire. But when they managed to get away in the summer of 1987, Thomas tracked them down and insisted they return. He said he would hound them until they did so. They returned home and carried on. In June's heart, hatred was growing. In Caroline's, despair was taking over.

Somehow she soldiered on at school, studying to follow her brothers to university. There were friends at school including a Vietnamese lad she liked. But Thomas Scotland didn't approve of the boy and told her she mustn't see him.

She was eighteen and it seemed she was in prison. In June 1987 she tried to get out by killing herself. Luckily that's hard to do by drinking a bottle of Drambuie and swallowing as many aspirins as there are in the packet. After a trip to hospital, she came home and her father kept his distance. If Caroline hadn't been so wrapped up in her own problems she may have noticed that her mother was clearly heading for a crisis of her own. Would she too try to take her own life? Would she finally find a way of running off somewhere where he couldn't find her and drag her back? June Scotland was later to tell psychiatrists that she felt then that her husband Thomas was tearing the family apart and that somehow she had to find the strength to do something to stop him. If she couldn't do it she might as well give up completely.

Then came the twist in the plot. After that stirfry supper in August 1987 Stevenage lost Thomas Scotland to Saudi Arabia, where he'd worked in the 1960s. His departure didn't seem to make a great deal of difference.

June Scotland didn't dash out to the shopping centre, return looking like Joan Collins and announce she'd be throwing a party. Nothing startling was seen to happen in Pankhurst Crescent. The neighbours slowly learned that June's husband had received an offer of work and had acted on it then and there. That was how these things happen. He had made a clean break. If they wished to speculate about the state of the marriage, that was up to them.

Alistair telephoned from the airport to say he was back from Corfu and to ask his father to collect him and was told the news. June said she'd already received a card from Thomas.

She knew they'd not go short of money because Thomas Scotland had saved much of his overtime earnings and formed a nominal company called Caddenoak into which he'd deposited his money. For tax purposes, and without giving her direct access to any of it, he'd made June a director.

It was unlikely that he had ever intended her to use it, but what he hadn't checked was June's ability to forge his signature. She practised and practised and managed to convince the bank that Thomas Scotland was sending cheques from Saudi Arabia for her to cash. The bank had no cause for suspicion. The amounts were modest and the £6,800 in the account lasted for several years. The mortgage had been paid off and Caroline had a job. June wasn't an extravagant woman – she'd never been allowed to be. So they'd continue to live in the crescent, keeping themselves to themselves.

That summer June and Caroline took a short trip to Scotland to see relatives. One of them was Thomas's sister Dorothea to whom, for once, they spoke openly. Both women told Dorothea how her brother liked to dominate them and how much more relaxed life was now that he was abroad. Once back home, they tried their best to make life more comfortable. They did nothing special: Caroline found a new job and was able to use her father's car; Alistair was happy to use his father's motorbike. It wasn't as though Thomas had need of them where he was.

June was still edgy, still taking tranquillisers. But she needed fewer and her life was changing. Two years later she had something important to focus upon. Caroline's affair with a local boy had led to an unplanned pregnancy. For June this was a happy accident. Freed from fear and abuse, Caroline changed from an abused suicidal teenager into an increasingly confident, responsible and attractive young woman. In November 1989 she gave birth. Her baby, a girl called Cayleigh, filled the house with the unfamiliar sound of laughter. There was no stern voice to say, 'Let her cry. Don't pick her up, don't spoil her!' Mother and grandmother could do as they pleased. The front door would not slam to announce that they were on parade. Gradually Alan and Alistair began to realise that their parents had decided to live apart. It was no surprise and they had no regrets. As Alistair said later, it had seemed only a matter of time anyway.

But there was no formal announcement. For three Christmases June Scotland sent out cards to friends and family signed 'Best wishes from Thomas and June'. There was some concern when in August 1990 the Gulf War began. How would Thomas Scotland and his fellow workers in Saudi be affected by the great drama of Saddam Hussein's invasion of Kuwait?

Up in Scotland Dorothea, nephew Derek and the rest of Thomas's family were also worried. Thomas had never kept closely in touch, but they were used to hearing from him occasionally. On the telephone June laid their fears to rest. She had spoken to Thomas and received postcards. He was safe, far from the trouble spots.

Despite Cayleigh enjoying her first summer and crawling

around the garden, the Scotlands were still a quiet family in August 1990. It was during August that neighbour Steven Sykes called to check whether they'd have any objection to his building a conservatory onto his house, whose garden backed onto theirs. It was to be a modern, gabled conservatory and the building work that would take place during the autumn wouldn't be too noisy. It would mean temporarily taking down the boundary garden fence to allow the materials to be brought in. He would, Sykes said, make sure it was put up again afterwards and there would be no damage.

June could not think of any objections offhand. Nor could Caroline, who by then was working at the pathology department of Stevenage's Lister Hospital. So they put the matter out of their minds. The conservatory was complete by the following February and looked most pleasing. From the back of the Scotlands' house Steven's wife Margaret and their young son could be seen using it.

The trouble was that with a spanking new conservatory you need a sturdy new fence. It would be pointless to put back the dilapidated old one. Steven Sykes was again knocking at the Scotland's door a couple of months later to discuss it. This time he spoke to Alistair, then twenty-three, and the two men considered the different types of fence. They agreed to share the cost of the materials, but Steven and a friend would do the hard work of erecting it. Again June and Caroline had no objections.

Shortly after breakfast on Easter Sunday 31 March 1991, Steven and his friend and neighbour Ted Bunce began to dig the trenches they'd need to insert the posts. As the pickaxe went it, it hit something hard in the cold earth.

When Steven Sykes looked at the blade, he noticed that in the clump of earth attached to it were several matted fine strands. He knew instinctively what they were: hairs. The two men quickly raked over the soil. Only a few feet down was a large wrapped bundle. It was bound like an untidy parcel and despite the dirt they could see that the binding was a series of men's ties. Undoing a section of it, they uncovered a decomposed body. Bones protruded from part of what had been a shirt.

On the skull was a white and blue plastic carrier bag, the bag from Tesco that had once held the packets of turkey, mushrooms, green peppers, onions and tomatoes, the ingredients of the stirfry that had been eaten three-and-a-half years earlier. They called the police.

Not long after that, June Scotland went into the bedroom where her son Alistair was asleep. She had seen the police cordoning off a section of the garden. She knew there would be a ring at the door at any minute. Alistair later told Luton Crown Court that his mother was crying as she said, 'I have something terrible to tell you'. He asked if his grandfather or grandmother had died and she shook her head saying, 'I think they have found your dad'. Then she went downstairs and opened the door to the police.

When the forensic experts went to work on the bones, on soil samples and in various parts of the house, they found that Thomas Scotland had consumed an extra ingredient in that stirfry. Ground up and added to the meal had been six Valium tablets and forty-eight tablets of the travel sickness preparation, Sea Legs. June had bought them from two separate chemists on the day of the meal. She'd hoped they would fatally poison her husband, instead they merely made him feel ill, take to his bed and demand she call a doctor. She couldn't do that. She knew it. She knew she had to do something then that she would never have dreamed herself capable of. It seemed that the only solution was to send him on a journey from which he would not return. She did this by beating him over the head with a rolling pin which she later burned.

Did she dream it? Was that appalling mess of blood, saliva and vomit a vision, a scene from a horror movie she had once watched accidentally? No. There were the tiny bloodstains the police found on skirting boards on the landing and in the hall cupboard into which he'd tried to crawl at one point to cower and escape an onslaught he had never expected. But the blows were too numerous, too intensely hate filled.

Caroline was with her mother by then, calm enough and brave enough to close Scotland's eyes. She'd been in her bedroom, listening to music on her headphones, only dimly aware of the last angry rantings of her father. When the screaming started, she ran to protect her mother, who by then was in the kitchen, and was stunned at what she saw. 'Even when he was dead, he looked evil. It was like she hadn't killed him. I had to shut his eyes,' she said then and many times later.

Thomas Scotland had no need of sea or earth legs from then on. June Scotland, drained and dazed, needed all the support she could get. Caroline was stronger, calmer. As the women sat together, hearts thumping, in the living room, trying to calm themselves with glasses of Bacardi rum, it was Caroline who devised a plan that she thought could spare them all further pain.

She steeled herself to go back to the kitchen and look at the blood-drenched body with the horribly smashed head. She said later that the man she had loathed and feared was now just a disgusting mess. As she stood over him, she decided on what to do.

The first thing was to rest. Exhausted, they went to the spare room, climbed on to the bed and lay holding hands till sleep came. The following day the women wrapped their victim in a tarpaulin, first hiding his hideous head in a plastic bag. They then tied it all with a handful of his ties grabbed from the wardrobe. When darkness came, the dragged him to the garden. Caroline then dug a shallow grave for Thomas Scotland, tyrant, deceased, under the willow tree. A day after that she telephoned her father's colleagues at work and told them that he'd been made an offer he couldn't refuse. He had accepted a job in Saudi Arabia.

The final scenes of this drama were perhaps the least spectacular. They were acted out one year after Steven and Ted had dug up the earth and began the last act. June Scotland had been arrested, charged and sent on remand to Holloway Prison. She had felt a strange sense of relief on her arrest, but prison had been hard for a timid woman like her to take, deprived as she was of the support of her daughter Caroline and the hugs and chatter of her dear granddaughter.

The trial began in Luton on Friday 20 March 1992. The Crown insisted that the charge against her must be murder because of the deliberate steps she had taken to kill her husband. With Caroline, she was also charged with preventing a burial.

29

What could you say about this alleged murderess as she stood in the dock to hear that charge? It seemed it must be a mistake. A dumpy, decent little woman like that? What was her motive, then? To get her hands on his money? It was hardly a fortune, £6,800. Or to sell their house, which she tried to do, for £68,000 in order to buy a smaller one and live thriftily on the money saved? She'd failed anyway. Her attempt to forge his signature didn't work that time.

The court heard June plead not guilty to murder. It also heard that she told the police how Thomas Scotland yelled from his bed, 'You are trying to kill me, aren't you?' and how she had replied, 'I want to get rid of you. I hate you. I've hated you for years.'

And later, 'He was a pig . . . he used to kick the boys and hurt my daughter . . . I was just like a zombie really . . . when he gave up the drink, he seemed to be worse . . . he just totally humiliated everybody . . . he didn't like anybody,' she had blurted out. She also tried to explain why she had not done the sensible thing, why she had not left him. 'I did not have the nerve. I knew the kind of person he was, that he would come and get me. It just seemed impossible to get away from him.'

Caroline took the stand. She told how, as she was digging the grave her mother had cried, and suddenly said, 'I can't go through with this, I want to end it now and tell someone'. The daughter told her, 'We have to cover this up. No one will understand.'

Was she right? Would the jury believe June Scotland had had no other way out? Michael Stuart Moore QC, for the prosecution seemed not to believe it. 'A lot of people have unpleasant marriages', was his lofty comment to them. 'It is no way to end it by simply killing the partner.'

Against June were the details of the rolling pin bludgeoning, the decision to hide the body, the fact that it had worked for almost four years and worked so well: a fence a few feet further away and it would have worked to this day.

But Dr Nigel Eastman, consultant psychiatrist of St George's Hospital London, testified that after examining her, he believed that June Scotland was suffering from a depressive illness at the time of the killing. Her daughter's distress and overdose had acted as a 'watershed', which meant to her that not only was her husband controlling the family, he was tearing it apart. 'The illness made her overreactive to her impulses and more likely to act in a calculating manner.'

Helena Kennedy QC, defending told the jury that his wife could not leave her husband because of the 'terrible, horrible cycle' of violence and threats had made her 'freeze' psychologically. She may have been intelligent and sensible in 1963 when she first embarked on this marriage of misery, but she became 'meek, very passive and unable to assert herself'. She went on, 'We are not talking about murder – the mark of Cain – we are talking about manslaughter. She was someone who was abused and subjected to the most terrible behaviour. Eventually her psyche surrendered.'

The jury did believe June Scotland. The verdict was manslaughter on the grounds of diminished responsibility. Mr Justice Garland sentenced her to two years' probation on condition she live at a women's refuge in London.

'No good whatsoever would be served by seeking to punish you further,' he said. To Caroline he added, 'When you were eighteen you found yourself in a situation that must have been impossible, almost an intolerable burden on you'. As Caroline left the court and walked with her mother to freedom, she said, 'I feel great'.

But June and Caroline were punished after that. Not by the cursing of Thomas Scotland, properly buried at last. But by the pain and silence of Alistair and Alan his sons. They too suffered at his hands. But they could not bring themselves to forgive their mother and sister for what they did that night. They have not spoken to them since.

The Burning Bed

Francine Hughes was like a woman possessed. Her ex-husband James, her cruel tormentor for the past thirteen years, looked so vulnerable lying there asleep on the bed. In her hand was a can of gasoline. And she kept pouring . . . pouring . . . pouring, drenching the floor all around the bed and creating a potential ring of fire. There was no possibility of her stopping. The voices in her head told her she must carry on. The can was empty. Still the brute did not stir. Why could he not always have been so calm and relaxed, instead of beating her at every available opportunity. She backed out of the bedroom, struck a match and tossed it in.

The room was engulfed instantly in a ball of flame, the force from which sucked the door shut with awesome power. Francine rushed from the house to the car where three of her children were waiting – daughters Christy and Nicole, age twelve and six respectively, and ten-year-old Jimmy. Her other son, seven-year-old Dana, had not yet returned home from playing hockey. Francine then drove to the Ingham Country jail parking lot at Mason, Michigan. It was a journey of only seven miles, but for Francine that night, it seemed to take an eternity. By the time she arrived, she was hysterical.

The sound of the screeching tyres as the car pulled into the parking lot alerted the sheriff's police sergeant Edward Nye. As he approached the vehicle, he could see that the driver had a tight grip on the steering wheel and was sobbing loudly. 'What has happened?' he asked. Francine just carried on sobbing. 'Look, ma'am, you must tell me', he persevered. Still Francine did not reply. Instead her anguish grew louder than ever. Six or seven times in all, the Sergeant tried to elicit some clue as to the cause of the woman's misery, but to no avail. He was about to give it up as a hopeless case and adopt a fresh approach when suddenly she blurted out, 'I did it, I did it, I did it'. 'What did you do?' urged Sgt Nye, seizing the branch of opportunity. Francine paused, collected herself and turned to face her interrogator. 'He was sleeping and I set the bedroom on fire.' 'You mean it's burning now?' said Nye. 'Yes, it is,' answered Francine. Having obtained the relevant information, the emergency services headed for the Hughes' small, split-level white house in Dansville.

By the time they got there, the house was completely gutted. James Hughes was dead, having perished from inhaling the clouds of evil black smoke. Amidst the charred ruins, the police found a gasoline can with the cap missing.

The sheriff's deputies endeavoured to piece together the background to the case. Francine Hughes remained in a state of shock, but Sgt Nye managed to glean a few details from her children. One said of their father, 'He has been beating her for ten years'.

Extenuating circumstances or not, Francine was charged with first-degree murder. To the authorities in the small town of Dansville, Michigan, approximately midway between Detroit and the eastern shore of Lake Michigan, it was just another domestic quarrel that had got out of hand. The United States of the 1970s was full of such cases. But geographical considerations and the history of Francine and James Hughes meant that this local dispute was to achieve nationwide significance, providing fresh hope for battered wives throughout the nation. It even spawned its own television movie.

Francine Hughes' case may simply have passed into obscurity had it not been for the fact that Dansville is situated next to East Lansing, the home of Michigan State University. It was thus something of a reformist hotbed, containing numerous action groups committed to improving the lives of the individual. Feminist groups were particularly prevalent and within two months of Francine Hughes' arrest, they had formed the Francine Hughes Defense Committee to raise money for her defence and to increase public awareness of the case. Whilst not actually condoning murder, they maintained that women like Francine Hughes who are faced with violence should have a right to defend themselves and 'should be free from the threat of punishment'.

They circulated petitions to have the charges dropped, the committee's Kate Wilson stating, 'We believe that Francine had reached a point where she believed that she couldn't escape James and she felt the police wouldn't help her because they don't consider domestic violence a serious crime'. When it became clear that the charges would not be dropped, over $600 was raised for her legal fees. The case was gathering momentum.

Francine and James Hughes had been high school sweethearts in Jackson, Michigan. The muscular youth was the only one for brown-eyed Francine and in 1963, at the age of sixteen, she dropped out of high school and married him. They set up home some twenty-five miles north of Jackson in Dansville where James put his strength to good use by landing a job as a construction worker. Even before the marriage, it was apparent that he liked to throw his weight around at home too. If Francine thought that by walking down the aisle with him, she could change his ways – that he would somehow have greater respect for her now that she was his wife – she was sadly mistaken.

For six years he subjected his young bride to a series of vicious beatings. He regularly chased her around the house with knives, attempted to choke her to death and once tried to run her down in his car. Psychological abuse can be just as terrifying as physical abuse and when he was not actually hitting her, he was threatening her. He refused to let her use the telephone and if he thought she had made a call in his absence he would rip the wires from the wall. Apart from the sheer terror caused by such wanton demolition, it made Francine feel horribly isolated. With no link to the outside world, there was no chance of summoning help in the wake of one of his rages. Between these ritual beatings, Francine bore him four children.

Like many battered wives, she was raped repeatedly – he often forced her to have intercourse after hitting her. The children were not immune from his attacks either; she once caught him kicking the baby. The presence of children frequently makes it more difficult for a wife to walk out on her husband, no matter how appalling his behaviour. A dangerous man can use children as an emotional stick with which to beat the wife, threatening to harm them should she ever consider leaving him. Consequently, in many cases of this nature, the hardest part is making the break.

But Francine Hughes seemed to have overcome that hazardous hurdle in 1971 when she finally obtained a divorce from James and took the children back to Jackson. Yet she was not completely free of him since under the terms of the divorce, James continued to have access to the children. Some six months after the divorce was finalised, he paid one of his routine visits to Francine and the family. It culminated in a furious row between him and his former wife. He stormed out of the house, slamming the front door behind him, and drove back towards Dansville in the blackest of moods, his emotional instability heightened by an excess of alcohol.

He never made it back to town. En route, he was involved in a near-fatal car crash, the injuries from which, whilst not crippling him, supposedly made it impossible for him to work again. It may have been a serious accident, yet it does seem certain that James Hughes made the most of his injuries. He milked them for all he was worth, leading all around him to believe that he needed constant care and attention. He went out of his way to make Francine feel guilty, tugging at her heart strings.

It would have made a great story for a rock 'n' roll song. 'I need you,' he told her. 'And remember, if it hadn't been for our quarrel, I'd never have got into the car in such an angry state of mind.' Unaccountably, Francine responded. She felt guilty, not only about the argument but because he had been drinking before the accident. His mother and father asked her to return and care for him and so she brought the children back to Dansville where she moved into a house next door to James and his parents. Ultimately, she was to tell friends later, she felt she owed something to the man who was the father of her children.

Now it is not uncommon for people to get back together again after a divorce, but this had not been a divorce sparked by mutual boredom or a fleeting affair by one of the partners. This had been caused by sustained brutality over a period of six years. This man had beaten her black and blue. He had threatened, and tried, to kill her. Yet here she was moving back to be with him, to play nursemaid. Presumably, Francine had decided that Hughes' injuries would render him harmless, that he no longer presented a physical threat. How wrong she was.

James Hughes revelled in having both his mother and ex-wife on hand to look after him. He switched from house to house and, before long, got back into the old routine of kocking Francine around. Permanently unemployed, he had nothing better to do with his time than hit her. He also killed her beloved pet dog by leaving it out in the cold to freeze to death.

Francine sought help from both the police and the local prosecutor's office. The former were regular visitors to the Hughes' residence, but nothing effective was ever done. Francine held on until 1976 when she decided the only way out was to acquire a degree of financial independence which would enable her to support her children and to move away once again from Dansville and the bitter memories it had. So she enrolled at a business college in Dansville with a view to acquiring the skills necessary to obtain future employment. Her ex-husband was livid. He told her,

'If you leave me, I swear I'll hunt you down and kill you'.

Francine pressed ahead regardless, enjoying the experience of meeting new people at college and of being free from her former husband's stranglehold. She was determined to succeed, to make something of herself. For the first time in ages, she could see a purpose in life, a real future for herself and her children.

Her best friend at college was classmate Betty Cover. Francine mostly used to wear sweaters to college in order to hide the signs of James's brutality (like many wife-beaters, he was careful not to leave any telltale marks about the face), but one day Mrs Cover spotted a large bruise on Francine's arm. Then another time when Francine took her sweater off in the women's changing room, Betty noticed a series of bruises on her friend's back.

'How did you come by those?' she asked. 'They look dreadful.' 'They're from my husband,' said Francine, who remained in the habit of referring to him as such. 'He hits me. My life is miserable. I can't take much more. The reason I'm coming to school is because I want to get off ADC [Aid to Dependent Children], get a job, leave him and support the children. But I need an education before I can do that.'

On another occasion Betty Cover, Francine and another classmate, Sally Hotchkiss, were talking to a girl whose boyfriend had slapped her. Sally Hotchkiss recalled, 'We all said, "That was bad", but Francine went further, saying her husband beat her a lot and used to hit her before they were married'. The women remembered James Hughes arriving at college several times to collect Francine and noted that he clearly did not like her being with friends. This was reiterated by a neighbour of the Hughes' who said, 'If Francine was ever visiting when James was around, he'd come and order her back to the house'. Another local resident told reporters before the trial, 'James Hughes busted into my house once thinking she was here and I threw him out'.

The more Francine immersed herself in her studies, the more James Hughes resented it. He wanted to keep her down at his level, to have her at his constant beck and call. He was bitterly jealous at the thought of her bettering herself, particularly if it led to her becoming independent of him. Similarly, he hated her making new friends – or indeed having any friends – who might fill her head with ideas not strictly in accordance with his best interests. Insecure to the point of paranoia, he behaved like a child deprived of his favourite plaything, except that instead of lapsing into a major sulk, he expressed his temper tantrums in full-blown violence.

On the afternoon of 9 March 1977, Francine returned home from business college and put a frozen dinner in the oven for James. Frozen dinners were not for him. 'You should be here at home,' he screamed, 'looking after me, cooking me proper meals, not running off to school.'

He beat her up. But that afternoon he was not satisfied with yet another brutal demonstration of his physical superiority. He wanted to make sure she knew who was the boss. He tore up her business school textbooks and papers and forced her to burn them in the rubbish bin in the backyard. He forbade her to return to school. For Francine, this was the ultimate humiliation, the senseless destruction of everything she had worked so hard for.

Her world lay in ashes. There now seemed no way out –

Hughes had blocked off her only route of escape. The quarrels were so vindictive that day and the beatings so forceful and unremitting that twelve-year-old Christy Hughes who, alas, had become only too familiar with domestic brawls, felt compelled to call the police. They arrived to find the vitriol in full flow. 'I'll kill you, I'll kill you before the night is out,' James threatened Francine in full hearing of the others.

As had happened many times before when they were called out to disturbances at the house, the police chose not to arrest James Hughes. They considered his words to be nothing more than an idle threat and preferred to try and defuse the situation by calming him down. Soon James, exhausted from hitting Francine, retired to bed early. The police, deciding he posed no further threat, promptly left. Francine could not take any more. While James slept, she told the children to put their coats on and loaded them into the family car, preparing to drive away once and for all. 'Let's not come back this time, Mommy,' they pleaded. And suddenly something snapped. She asked young Jimmy to tell her the combination for a lock which James kept on the garage door. The next thing, the can of gasoline was in her hand, then the lighted match. The rest, like James Hughes, is history. After surrendering to the police, Francine Hughes spent seven months languishing in jail awaiting her trial.

The feminist campaign for her defence grew in vigour, arousing widespread public interest so that by the time the trial began, in October 1977, the sixty-four seater courtroom in Lansing City Hall, around twenty miles northwest of Dansville, was packed to the rafters. In Michigan, the maximum penalty for murder was life imprisonment. Francine's lawyer, Aryon Greydanus, realised that he was on unsteady ground with a plea of self-defence since the deceased had been asleep for two hours before Francine had set fire to his bed. It could, of course, have been rightly argued that Francine Hughes' actions were entirely in accordance with self-defence since, knowing her ex-husband to be a violent individual, she was simply reacting to his threat to kill her that night. Indeed, a neighbour who described James Hughes as 'a mean son-of-a-bitch when he got drunk – and that was a lot' went so far as to venture that 'She got him before he got her'.

But, possibly fearing that a self-defence plea could be asking a lot of even a sympathetic jury, Greydanus claimed instead that at the time of the killing, Francine had been suffering from temporary insanity. As a line of defence, this was nothing new but his suggestion for the cause of the insanity was.

For this insanity had not arisen from accepted medical facts with a solid foundation in law over the centuries, but had been born out of her years as a battered woman. He argued that it was precisely because she had been beaten and battered for so long that she temporarily lost control of her actions on the night of 9 March.

Greydanus said that Francine Hughes had been battered for such a length of time that she feared that if she tried to flee, her ex-husband would catch her and kill her. The lawyer told the jury that 'she was no longer mentally able to cope' with the beatings. Evidence of Francine's life of misery was paraded before the court. Two of her children, Jimmy and Christy, testified that their father hit mum a lot in the afternoon before the fire.

Four policeman and one former officer all testified that thirty-one-year-old James Hughes was a known trouble-maker and that they had been called to the family home on several occasions. Captain Harry Tift, the county sheriff's detective, said that he personally had attended two or three complaints at the Hughes house over the six-month period leading up to March 1977. But, he affirmed, Francine had never signed a complaint against James. Referring to the last visit, at 3pm on the day of the fire, Capt Tift said, 'There had been an argument but she told the deputies it was all over with, forget about it, they wouldn't be needed'.

The key witness was Francine herself. For three-and-a-half hours, she spoke in her own defence. She recalled how she spread the gasoline almost in a trance. It was, she said, 'Like watching myself do the things I was doing'. She said that while she was pouring, she heard something in her mind. 'It was an urgent voice or whisper, saying, "Do it, do it, do it". And I kept pouring.'

Describing the feeling of total helplessness which she experienced during her years of suffering, she told the court, 'I just felt like I was alone, and no matter what I did, it wasn't any help.'

Aryon Greydanus then asked Judge Ray C. Hotchkiss for a directed acquittal verdict, stating that the prosecution had failed to show that the defendant was guilty of pre-meditated murder. The judge rejected Mr Greydanus's motion, saying that it would be a 'Grievous error for the judge to take the case from the jury, unless the prosecution presented no evidence'. Prosecutor Martin Palus Jnr quickly discounted any lingering thoughts in the jury's minds that Francine may have been acting in self-defence. He pointed out that a claim of self-defence was not valid in this case because 'the person exercising it cannot be the aggressor'. Who was the aggressor here?' he asked. 'What honest, imminent threat was presented by James Berlin Hughes sleeping on his bed?'

In his closing speech, Aryon Greydanus painted a tragic picture of Francine Hughes to the jury of ten women and just two men. With the balance of the jury heavily stacked in such a way, he knew that if he could appeal to their feminine sensitivities, strike a familiar chord, he would have a good chance of obtaining an acquittal for his client. He had no need to embroider the facts; just the plain truth of Francine's miserable life was sufficient to touch the heart of any normal human being. Mr Greydanus said she was no 'cold-blooded killer' but rather a woman 'starved for love'. He added that throughout her time with the deceased, she had been 'raped again and again and again. . . . Francine Hughes went through thirteen years of not only beatings, of not only physical abuse, but mental abuse. I couldn't possibly make you understand the suffering, the terror that Francine Hughes went through in her life.'

The jury retired to deliberate for six-and-a-half hours. On 3 November, the eighth day of the trial, they acquitted Francine Hughes of first-degree murder by reason of insanity. Hearing the verdict, Francine, whose face had been as pale as the white sweater she wore for the final day of the proceedings, shouted, 'Oh my God' and hugged her attorney. He responded by patting her on the back as she burst into tears of joy. It was ruled that Francine would be freed provided she cleared a psychiatric examination: Michigan law required that a person found innocent by reason of insanity had to undergo psychiatric testing to determine whether treatment was needed. It was little more than a formality.

Francine Hughes was perfectly sane now that she had finally escaped the vice-like grip of her former husband. Following the acquittal, Aryon Greydanus confidently predicted that Francine 'will be free tomorrow. And,' he added poignantly, 'I think she will be free from now on'. He was right. Francine Hughes underwent a series of routine tests and was duly freed.

Reaction to the verdict was mixed. Judge Hotchkiss told journalists that the real issue in the case had never really been broached. 'All of a sudden, we realise that we have thousands of people who have had no recourse under the law. Where are we when these people are crying out loud for help? Self-defence is a real issue, but it was never really covered in the trial.' However, Hotchkiss thought it unlikely that the case would set a precedent. 'I doubt very many wives are living with unemployed, mentally ill or mentally deranged men,' he said.

Although delighted that Francine was not convicted, feminists expressed reservations about the verdict. 'We would have been happier with an outright acquittal,' admitted Linda Miller, head of Michigan's chapter of the National Organisation for Women. Nevertheless local pressure groups planned to make Francine Hughes a symbol for battered women.

Both she and Aryon Greydanus appeared on American television to discuss the case where the latter warned that unless the authorities woke up to the problem of battered women, 'The same thing is going to happen, and . . . a jury again will acquit a woman for doing the same thing.' The lawyer's words merely served to underline the fears of the nation's men that the Francine Hughes case would lead to an almighty backlash against them. A friend of James Hughes told reporters that the verdict 'means open season on men', while the dead man's own brother said in a television interview, 'I think this decision will give a lot of violent women an excuse to go out and commit violent acts – to take their revenge'.

Even a family neighbour, who had once dragged James off Francine in response to the children's screams that he was killing her in the backyard, had said before the trial that he thought Francine should be sent to prison for life. 'If she gets out of this,' he told the press, 'there'll be a lot of dead guys lying around. I don't condone woman-beating, but murder is murder and I sure don't condone murder.'

Francine Hughes was certainly not forgotten. Seven years after her trial, NBC turned her story into a television movie, *The Burning Bed*, starring the former star of *Charlie's Angels*, Farrah Fawcett.

Meanwhile, lawyers and public alike were keeping a close watch on the outcome of similar cases in the wake of Hughes' verdict. One of the most sensational was that of Diana Cervantes Barson who, in the early part of 1979, killed her common-law husband in Houston, Texas. She shot him, cut his body into five pieces, put it in a number of garbage bags, loaded it into the boot of her Cadillac and drove to California to ask relatives for help in disposing of the bags. Police found her in an orange grove in San Bernardino, her wrists slashed in a suicide attempt, and some of the bags lying nearby, complete with their grisly contents. But after recounting two years of beatings from her husband, culminating in three days of threats and abuse with loaded revolvers and an ice pick, she was acquitted.

Her defence counsel, David Berg, said afterwards, 'It was the most brutal act in recent history and it took the jury only one hour and forty minutes to acquit her!' He added that the acquittal was 'A clear-cut case of affirmation of a woman's right to physical self-defence'. The worm had turned.

'Shall I Pull the Knife Out or Leave It In?'

She was a tiny figure in the dock. As she sat there, little of her five-foot tall and less than eight stone body could be seen above the front of the dock of court number nine on the third floor of Birmingham Crown Court on the morning of Tuesday 13 February 1990.

Only the dark, wavy hair, the challenging eyes and high cheek bones that made her look older than her thirty-five years were obvious to the gathering. At that moment, though, she felt young and vulnerable, unable even to begin to understand the series of moves and countermoves about to be made by those trained in the law to determine her fate.

Later she was to tell people how she had longed to liven up the proceedings. Even the judge in his robes had what seemed to her a comic-book name: Mr Justice Igor Judge. She might have been called Mrs Sara Accused Thornton. She joked that she'd have liked to send out for pizzas and have slices of them passed round to all the solemn-looking people there. The most solemn thing was that question.

'Sara Elizabeth Thornton, you are charged with the

murder of Malcolm Thornton on Thursday 14 June 1989. How do you plead?'

'Not guilty.'

She said it in her usual unaccented voice. It was a voice that over the following nine days would surprise and worry the jury of four women and eight men. It wasn't the voice of a meek little fool. It wasn't the voice of an oversexed schemer either, much as the prosecution who would seek to give her that image might have wished it to be. Sara Thornton was middle class, well travelled and educated. Her enemies knew she gave as good as she got. Unfortunately her worst enemy, at this worst time of her life, was herself.

Sara Thornton had never denied killing her husband of ten months late on that Wednesday night, ten days before he was due in court on a charge of assaulting her. She repeatedly told the police she'd killed him and had even demonstrated how she'd done it. She showed them how she had held a kitchen knife with a sharp blade over him as he lay drunk, angry and abusive on a couch in the living room of their home at 73 Church Walk, Atherstone, Warwickshire. She'd tried to find a bigger weapon – the truncheon he'd kept since his time as a policeman – but though she'd searched the usual drawer for it, it wasn't to be found. So the knife had to do.

At some stage, the police said, she also claimed to have sharpened the knife in preparation for the deed. It wasn't true because she hadn't planned to use it but no one ever checked that detail.

She had wanted to frighten her husband with the knife, to force him to do as she asked, which was to shut up, end the row and go to bed, not to lie there any longer. Otherwise, she thought he would just go on drinking and smoking and perhaps drop his cigarette, impervious to the smell of singeing and possibly to the fire that could engulf them all. That was always her worry. She didn't want him to kill himself or his nice grown son Martin from his first marriage, who'd been staying with them for four months and helping them both.

She didn't want him to kill her. Her life may have been a mess by then but Luise, her darling daughter, the child she and others had heard Malcolm threaten to hurt, needed her too much for her to risk dying. Luise, now growing up so fast in America, was out of the house on that night.

Sara didn't want to kill him, but that's what she did. She pushed the knife down, heard him make a low noise, looked and saw it sticking out of his stomach.

There was surprisingly little blood. It seems that the next thing Sara did – though afterwards she said she remembered nothing – was to pick up the telephone. The jury was told that it was around half past midnight when the ambulance service recorded the following call:

Sara: Hello, good afternoon, I've just killed my husband. I have stuck a six-inch carving knife in his belly on the left-hand side.
Operator: Where are you, love?
Sara: I'm at 73 Church Walk, Atherstone, Warwickshire. My name is Mrs Sara Thornton, my husband is Mr Malcolm Thornton and I think he's dead.
Operator: 73 Church Walk, Atherstone.

Sara: Warwickshire.

Operator: Yes, darling, your name is, again, Mrs Thornton?

Sara: Thornton. Shall I pull the knife out or leave it in?

Operator: Leave it where it is, darling.

Sara: Leave the knife in.

Operator: That's right.

After that, Martin Thornton, then twenty-one years old and a six-footer like his father, was to tell the court that he rushed downstairs from his bedroom to find the dying man lying on the floor. He remembered he'd heard Sara rummaging in a kitchen drawer. As he looked at his mortally injured father he heard Sara announcing that she had killed him in a voice that she might use to report that she had just put the rubbish out. Calmly, she took out a dish of curry from the kitchen freezer and placed it in the microwave oven to defrost. Then she began filling the washing machine with items to be washed, apparently wondering out loud how a wash might affect the leather trimmings on a jumper. When the police arrived they recalled that she was eating the curry. Later she was in the living room with a camera, snapping Malcolm as he lay dying.

A cold, callous killer? A murderous mad woman? This behaviour may have made people think so. But it wasn't hard to make strangers think badly of Sara Thornton. She could easily be a pain in the neck to those around her as anyone who knew her would agree: her father, her former menfriends, her colleagues and neighbours.

She wasn't a 'lady', that's for sure. She liked men, liked drinking with them and arguing with them. She liked playing pool, dancing and sometimes, when she wanted to shock onlookers, she would remove bits of her clothing. To her it was a great joke.

When the two police constables arrived and found Malcolm lying there and questioned her they said she was acting strangely. One of them, PC David Gill led her upstairs to collect some things before they left for the police station. On the way up she pinched his bottom playfully. Typical of her, many would say, probably with pursed lips and in weary, superior tones. There weren't many people on Sara's wavelength in Atherstone on the Leicestershire border. The old market town, half forgotten on the road between Birmingham and Coventry, is too small, too prettily Georgian and staid.

Moyra Friend, mother to Martin and his brother Stuart, who had been married to Malcolm for fifteen years and who sat in the public gallery of court number nine with a group of relatives, was later to describe Sara to reporters as 'a dangerous and devious woman'. She would also insinuate that Sara was a heavy drinker and a slut who displayed herself to men. Friend wasn't alone in believing that.

Pat Thompson, the former landlady of the Wheatsheaf, the pub in which Sara had met Malcolm back in May 1987, had banned her from the place as had several other publicans in the area. She was later to tell the *Sun* newspaper, 'She was very attractive, well spoken and intelligent. But she was almost schizophrenic. One minute she was okay. Then she'd have one of her flare-ups. She'd become abusive and have a go at someone for no reason.

'She'd be dressed outrageously and never wore knickers. Once she came in wearing a short skirt and just a chiffon scarf wrapped round her boobs. Her favourite trick was to strip off and parade around naked. Locals ignored it, but strangers sat goggle-eyed.'

It was quite a different story where Malcolm was concerned. He was hard to dislike. Clearly intelligent he was also affable and attractive with his 1970s moustache and well-pressed suits. Meet him on the street or in a pub and he was cheerful with everyone. He could listen and observe; good policemen all do that. He was also funny. Alcoholics often are, until the need for this socially-acceptable anaesthetic becomes uncontrollable and the pain can no longer be hidden.

He certainly seemed like the man Sara needed – worldly, well set-up and in need of stimulating company. Ten years older than she, he wasn't, thank goodness, another drifter such as she'd found in the past. He had a responsible, respectable job as head of security with the transport company TNT. His fifteen years as a policeman, first with Blackpool police, then with the Met, qualified him for that. In between he'd been a publican and had worked in Saudi Arabia, swiftly teaching himself Arabic when he arrived. That's where he met and married his second wife Anne. He liked a drink and made sure he had one every day. It was only beer most of the time, the strong kind mind, and sometimes whisky – which copper doesn't like whisky? Thornton certainly didn't believe that he had a problem with drinking, not in 1987.

He was fooling himself. He'd already been convicted of drink-driving once, a conviction which threatened his job. He wouldn't have admitted to being volatile and possessively jealous either. Yet in a Coventry pub, on only the second occasion that he had met Sara, he became so angry because she had been bought a drink by another man that she eventually poured the drink in his pocket to cool him down.

Sara by comparison was the open one. She never pretended to him or anyone else that she was a goodie-goodie. She admitted she'd made many mistakes. She could lie, spin stories about herself. But most people soon twigged that despite her obvious brightness and ability, she was 'a woman with problems'.

That's how Malcolm described her to Moyra, when he decided to try marriage for a third time. Despite that there's no doubt he cared for Sara. In a letter to his younger son Stuart he wrote, 'I cannot give you and Martin back the missing years when I was not there. But if you accept me for what I am and have been, then I'm here now. I'm very much in love with Sara (yes, even at my age) and she looks after me so well and is also lots of fun.'

Problems had often arisen from the fun in Sara's life and there had certainly been plenty of them. Three psychiatrists were to tell the court about some of them though they had only bits of the jigsaw. Sara's life before she met Malcolm was a catalogue of crises in all shapes and sizes.

Sara Cooper was born in Nuneaton in 1955 to educated parents. Her father was a government administrator working in the Gilbert Islands and Fiji in the South Pacific. Her mother was a marine biologist. With her adopted sister Billy, who was three years younger than Sara, they'd moved homes and school many times before returning to Britain when an aunt died, leaving her father an estate in Cumberland. Sara was ten. Those tropical beginnings, though, had a lasting effect. Sara said it was from growing up in a hot climate that she hated wearing layers of clothes and found underwear uncomfortable. The uninhibited sexual behaviour of the islanders also made her more 'forward' than girls who'd grown up in cold, restrained 1950s Britain, the girls who became those ladies of Atherstone she was later to embarrass.

This small but feisty misfit was eventually sent to Millfield public school in Somerset, whose relaxed, progressive coeducational system made it a favourite of rich and fashionable parents. It must have been at Millfield that Sara developed an air of self-confidence and a genuine enjoyment of the company of boys. Unfortunately her social success wasn't matched by her academic achievement and feelings of failure seemed to develop, made worse at seventeen when she was abruptly taken away from the school by her parents.

According to Sara, she then ran off to London after arguing bitterly with her mother and worked as a nanny. Mrs Cooper was soon to become ill and never fully recovered. Sara was under stress and unhappy. A doctor prescribed tranquillisers and swallowing a handful of these seems to have been an early, bungled attempt at an overdose. Her mother died before the two were properly reconciled.

Then came a worse spell. After a short relationship with a man in 1976, Sara became pregnant and had an abortion. A more serious suicide attempt followed sometime later when she swallowed a quantity of antidepressants. For a few days she was admitted to a psychiatric hospital – she had been found wandering naked at night. It was the 1981 record of this that was presented to the court.

'This report reveals a serious mental history,' said the prosecuting QC, Brian Escott-Cox, and the judge adjourned the proceedings for a day while the report was considered.

Sara must have thought this was the beginning of the jury hearing her side of the story, but it was not. She didn't know it then, but the jury was never to learn of what happened between Malcolm and her. In some ways her relationship with Thornton was similar to that between Sara and Helmut Scharley, a German she had met in the 1970s.

Scharley was twenty years her senior, and he seemed to be offering her love and stability. With nothing else on her horizon, Sara went to Germany, got married and in 1978 gave birth to her daughter Luise. Scharley took a job in Venezuela the following year, leaving in March. Sara followed four months later and, discovering that she'd married someone she didn't even greatly like or understand, she decided to cut her losses. She hurried back to Britain to live with her now frail grandparents. The two years which followed were not happy ones. She and the German were divorced, her grandmother died and her grandfather's mental state declined.

The old man and the young depressed mother often argued. Her GP Dr Kenneth Farn was to state, when the trial was over, that the old man, once a JP and a successful businessman, was by then senile and tightfisted. Sara was depressed.

At one point Sara cut her wrists, he said. Two weeks later she tried feebly to cut her throat. She was admitted to a psychiatric hospital in Coventry, but managed to convince the doctors that she had merely overreacted to a few incidents and was not seriously disturbed.

By 1983 she was found a small house in Coventry by a housing association. Living on social security her volatile moods and sometimes crazy behaviour continued. Luckily she was still able to consult Dr Farn and she was surviving. When a relationship with a younger man led to pregnancy she chose not to complicate her life further and opted for a second abortion.

It was not the way she would have chosen to live. Perhaps it was no wonder then that when this not-too-stable, not-too-contented thirty-two-year-old single mother met tall, charming, seemingly solid Malcolm Thornton, then forty-two, in The Wheatsheaf in May 1987 they talked at length. They had an Indian meal and went back to her house. She felt the gods were smiling on her at last.

Other women might have spotted the danger signs, cleverer women or women whose lives had been more straightforward. Women such as well-spoken Helen Thomas, Sara's friend and colleague at the transport company TNT, the same firm for which Malcolm had worked before his drinking got the better of him and he'd had to leave. Thomas was now a witness for the prosecution.

The women had been at a conference together in Coventry a couple of weeks before the stabbing and it was planned that Thomas would tell the jury of Sara's remarks and threats made against her husband during that time. This would show that it had been a planned crime: a proper, premeditated murder.

That sales conference had been in mid-June. What Helen Thomas and the court couldn't know was that Sara, Malcolm and Luise had been through a period of hell just before then. Malcolm's drunken binges, his threats to his wife and her daughter and his terrifyingly violent lashings-out had alarmed everyone around them.

What's more they had caused Sara finally to tell the police that this time she would press charges for assault and would not be dissuaded from it by an alcoholic promising to stay sober and begging for one last chance. The case was due to be heard in July. By then, though, Malcolm Thornton was answering to a higher court.

That drink was a problem for Malcolm had become plain to Sara very soon after they had met. It's likely though that she didn't admit this to herself until fifteen months later when they were married. In the beginning, the knocks were forgivable – such was the strength of Malcolm's remorse. He'd punched her in the eye one night after getting drunk and had not remembered doing so the next morning. He'd been horrified when he found out and bought her presents to make amends.

But not drinking was not an option and Sara must bear some of the responsibility for this. Most of their social life revolved around meeting friends in pubs. Malcolm's friends were mostly policemen or former policemen like himself, and there was always whisky in the house in case they called. Malcolm was often drunk in the evenings and, Sara discovered, it wasn't by accident. He didn't just forget himself and have a few too many, he usually aimed to have too many – to get 'plastered' and stay that way.

On the day of TNT's Open Day in July 1988 Malcolm became so intoxicated that two colleagues eventually took him back home to Church Walk. When Sara opened the door and stepped out, he punched her so hard that she fell into a hedge in the garden to the horror both of Luise and Malcolm's workmates. One of them tried to help him upstairs and was himself attacked. Alarmed, he called the police. Although the incident was recorded the police chose not to remove Malcolm. Instead Sara and Luise spent the night away, in a hotel, waiting for Malcolm to return to his 'normal' civilised state.

Why didn't she see the glaringly obvious signs and leave? To outsiders this must have seemed strange. The answer was that in a civilised state Malcolm was loveable. He was good to be with, popular in a way that Sara on her own never was. The couple must also have had a strong sexual relationship – why else did he need her so much? But it was too strong perhaps. At the start of the partnership they lived in some style and comfort. Sara and Luise had a secure home and the chance of a settled middle-class life with a sober Malcolm Thornton if only the drunken rages could have been stopped.

Malcolm apparently blamed his drinking on the breakdown of his second marriage to Anne and the fact that it had cost him a home and progress in his career. His boss Ken Matthews was aware of the problems. Sara's GP, Dr Kenneth Farn, was also aware of the problems. It was he who suggested Malcolm seek the treatment of Dr Max Glatt, a much respected specialist in alcohol addiction, in London. Hours of shouting, threats, recriminations and abuse followed. Finally, when exhausted and achingly sober, Malcolm seemed to agree that he should submit himself to Dr Glatt's hands in an attempt to dry out. Arrangements were made. But when a friend came to collect him, Malcolm had disappeared to a pub.

Despite that set-back Dr Glatt's treatment seemed to work and after one month he returned to Sara, his old job and – he promised – the support of Atherstone Alcoholics Anonymous. Filled with hope, the couple married quietly in August. They were starting afresh. It seemed too good to be true and it was.

When he was in London Malcolm may have accepted Dr Glatt's rule that alcoholics must give up entirely, forever, refusing even a teaspoonful of the tea-time trifle if it's laced with sherry. Back home he told friends that he'd sorted himself out and could now control his drinking; he could not.

In October the police were again called to the house when Malcolm was thrashing Sara in a drink-sodden storm. Sara was trying to fight back, Luise had run to a neighbour in fear.

'It's difficult to explain why I didn't leave,' Sara said much later in an interview in the *Guardian*. 'I felt guilty – that if I was sexier or quieter or a better wife, he wouldn't need to drink. I wanted a home for Luise and I worried that he would commit suicide.'

Later still she was to reflect mournfully, 'I get upset when I see him described as "a violent brute" because when he was not drinking he was a lovely man. He was very funny. When he was sober he never hit me once.'

Significantly, even years after the killing, Sara Thornton showed she had come to accept beatings so completely that she seemed to assume that not being hit by a husband was unusual and that Malcolm should be appreciated for those non-violent phases.

For a few months of that winter of 1988, though, the hitting did stop. It seemed that the Thorntons were, against the odds, moving forwards. Malcolm had gained promotion at work and Sara had started to work for TNT too, on the telephone sales side. Her good clear voice helped, of course.

But in February 1989 when Sara was in hospital having an eye operation, Malcolm was stopped in his car by the police. He was breathalysed and found to be over the limit. This time he resigned from his job. Then he went drinking to wipe it all from his mind. He succeeded to the extent that neighbours remember him lying in the street in a stupor. When he eventually returned home, there was war. Furniture flew, the police arrived and Malcolm was taken to the cells.

On his return, Malcolm refused to submit himself to a second course of treatment. His response was to pack, leave Sara and go to stay with relatives in Blackpool. Sara wasn't one to concede defeat so soon, though. She found Malcolm in a pub, dragged him out and brought him home where a friend of his was waiting with an offer that could have saved his dignity and his life. The friend had acquired a shop in Atherstone and a franchise to sell Tandy electrical products. The offer was to let Malcolm run it and perhaps take it over. Malcolm agreed and within a short time he had opened a department selling records. He was keen to take over the franchise himself, arranging to repay the friend for the goodwill and stock as the business progressed.

Sadly, being his own boss meant that Malcolm felt he didn't have to appear in control of himself from Monday to Friday. Binges weren't for the weekends only any more; he could give himself permission to do things that other bosses would flatly refuse. Such as permission to eat harmless-looking oranges into which he'd injected vodka using the syringe Sara kept in the kitchen for adding brandy to the Christmas cake. Such as permission to drink Coca Cola spiked with spirits off and on throughout the day. Such as permission to close the shop at short notice in order to drink wine, strong beer, whisky or anything he could afford, and to sleep off the after-effects. Anything and everything seemed possible and, when he was drunk, he forgot that the business was going rapidly down the drain.

Malcolm's need for alcohol increased and Sara continued to bear the brunt. Tired of trying to stop him falling over in pubs and in the streets, she tried to contain his binges to their home. As a result, her sufferings increased. Policemen know about exerting force and they know which actions leave tell-tale marks and which do not. Often there were no traces of what had happened between Thornton and the woman who seemed always to ignite his furies. Often though, there were signs and several of Sara's and Malcolm's friends began noticing the bruises and cuts which she tried to ignore, feeling herself partly to blame and suffering the guilt all battered women attach to themselves. But it becomes hard to ignore it when the man you love threatens to throw you through a plate glass window, smashes a glass on your hand and yells that he'll break your child's legs.

By this time Malcolm was also noticeably paranoid about Sara, frequently accusing her of scheming to hurt him and repeatedly accusing her of having sex with other men. Sara being Sara, she did not alter the way she behaved or dress like a frump to try to convince him that sex with strangers was the last thing on her mind. It probably was, but he would not have believed it.

Between mopping up the vomit, trying to straighten the house, hiding the cigarette burns on the sofa and chairs, organising repairs to broken windows and attempting to keep the shop a going concern, Sara contacted members of Alcoholics Anonymous, the church and the social services. None could offer any practical assistance. 'Towards the end, they knew that he was beating me up,' Sara reflected later. 'The police had been called out several times. Not just by me, but by other people. I began to feel as if there was absolutely no hope because nobody cared.

'I began increasingly to feel as if there was some sort of conspiracy between Malcolm and the police. I thought they wouldn't help me because they didn't want to.'

But Malcolm was also becoming verbally abusive to Luise, who was then ten. In May he lashed out, swearing at her while cursing her mother in front of Luise's young pals and their relatives. It was because of Luise's mounting alarm that Sara decided to ask the police to charge Malcolm with assault. This time her bleeding nose, cut lip and bruised cheeks were ample evidence that he deserved it.

Perhaps it was the shock of the formal charge. Perhaps it was due to the week or so they then spent apart – she visited her now remarried father, Malcolm his sons – but for the first two weeks of June there was peace in the house in Church Walk. With his son Martin staying there and helping in the shop, Malcolm remained sober. Hoping she could trust him as he said she could, Sara decided to attend the weekend TNT sales conference with Helen Thomas and two other women colleagues. From the Coventry hotel room, Sara had telephoned the house at nine o'clock that evening. To her dismay, Luise was highly distressed. She said Malcolm was drunk and spilling food. Her mother was livid and worried. She arranged for a taxi firm she trusted to collect Luise and take her to friends and spat out her desperation over Malcolm in front of Helen Thomas.

Ms Thomas told the court, 'She left a meal to phone Malcolm and came back crying, saying he had hit her ten-year-old daughter'. Later she said that Sara had discussed her plans for a divorce claiming that she was afraid to do it in case she lost her share of Thornton's money. Her words, Ms Thomas recalled, were, 'I'm not prepared to lose everything for him'. Crucially, according to the witness, Sara clearly said in front of colleagues, 'I've got to kill him'.

Whether Malcolm had any money left by that time is doubtful. Whether Sara thought he had is even more doubtful. But others, including Moyra his first wife, seemed to believe he was solvent. What's not in doubt is that next to going to The Wheatsheaf that day in May 1987, making those remarks was the second most serious mistake of Sara Thornton's life.

Over the next weeks Sara continued to try everything to achieve the opposite of what she'd allegedly threatened: she tried to keep Malcolm alive. She had called Patrick Hanlon, a member of the local AA. She tried to hide Thornton's wallet to make it difficult for him to obtain drink. This made him rabid and he threatened her and Luise in front of Patrick Hanlon. She even tried to get him into hospital by mixing sleeping tablets into his food, hoping she could pretend he had taken an overdose. But the plot backfired. Enraged, Malcolm put a chair through the glass pane of the back door. He later told the police who arrived that his wicked wife had locked him out.

For the next two days and nights Sara and Luise lived in fear. Malcolm would not accept Sara's apology for the sleeping pill trick and told Ella Thompstone, who ran the taxi company, that he wanted to be taken to Blackpool. Sara knew deep down by then that the situation was hopeless. Luise was suffering too much. A surge of hatred for him went through her. She scrawled 'I hate you' with a lipstick on the mirror in her bedroom and she made an appointment with her solicitor to arrange an official separation. The date was to be the day after the assault case hearing, 22 June.

On the third morning Sara and Luise found Malcolm slumped on the sofa. He'd been sick and there was a new cigarette burn on a chair. The day, which included a trip to the police station for Luise to make a statement in connection with the assault charge, was long and tense. Sara sent Luise to stay with a relative for the night. Later she and her stepson Martin went to The Three Tuns pub. When Martin returned home he found his father drunk and half asleep on the sofa. He went to bed just after midnight.

Sara arrived home shortly afterwards and went directly to her bedroom. When she entered the sitting room, wearing a dressing gown, Malcolm Thornton roused himself to begin his last tirade. He said he would kill her if she'd been out with other men and he called her a whore. 'Been selling your body again?' he growled, then added, 'Get out of the house. You won't get any of my money. I'll fucking kill you while you're asleep.'

Sara went to the kitchen to calm down, cool off, collect herself. That's what she would have called it. But after so much stress for so long, what was happening was possibly the reverse. Inside the temperature was rising.

Dr Kenneth Farn has no doubt that Sara was suffering from severe depression when she went out to the living room again, this time holding a knife. 'All the symptoms were there, she was a very sick woman and as far as I know she still is. If Sara had been anyone else, she would have killed Malcolm Thornton years ago.'

Dr Farn had treated Malcolm Thornton time and again for problems relating to his addiction and knew perhaps better than any expert at the court what had been going on at 73 Church Walk. It was to his daughter's house nearby that Sara had dashed on six separate occasions to use the telephone to tell the police, 'I'm terrified, I can't stand it any more'.

But Dr Farn was not at the court in Birmingham to tell the jury this, regrettably for Sara. Prosecuting counsel Brian Escott-Cox QC was intent on proving that what made this woman push the knife into her husband's stomach was something far easier to understand. The motive, he said, was Sara Thornton's need for money. If she had simply walked out of the marriage, she would have done so with nothing. By killing him and claiming it was self-defence, she must have believed she would gain financially.

Helen Thomas also told the court that Sara herself drank heavily. Martin Thornton gave evidence that Sara had threatened his father with a knife days before the killing while she was preparing chicken. He also told of her attempt to give Thornton Mogadon sleeping pills. He was asked too to describe how she had seemed immediately after committing the crime. 'She said she had just killed him in the matter of fact way she might say she was putting out the rubbish.'

Sara was asked to tell the court about her early life, of Malcolm Thornton's violence towards her. Then she was asked about the stabbing. Why had she taken the knife? 'I didn't want to be hurt by him any more.' She said she intended 'to frighten him, to show he could not hurt me'. She was asked to demonstrate her motion with the knife.

'I thought he was going to push it away. I did not want to hurt him. I was confused. I was angry. I just wanted him to come to bed and I wanted him to see how much he was hurting me and destroying everything.'

Compared with the simple motive of greed, this did not add up to a whole lot of sense. When she returned to the stand later, Sara made even less sense. She confessed to having lied to the psychiatrists she saw about her O- and A-level results. She had presented herself as someone of greater academic achievement than she really was. What she clearly thought could establish her basic honesty, succeeded only in establishing that she was an unreliable story teller.

Brian Escott-Cox then played his trump card. He asked Sara about her lack of 'modesty' concerning her body and her habit of not wearing knickers. She did not deny it but simply explained that she had suffered from the common fungus, thrush. Wearing less underwear helped reduce it. It also helped stamp an impression of wantonness on the jury and, through the press reports, the public.

Before the judge's summing up, it was clear to many in the court that Sara's defence had been open to question. Her lawyers, led by barrister David Barker, had decided that they could not argue that Sara's actions had been accidental or in self-defence because no threat of immediate attack was provable. If they tried to plead that the crime was not murder but manslaughter due to provocation, they would be unlikely to succeed because Sara did not grab the knife in the frenzied heat of the moment and jab it into her tormentor.

To establish this defence under the law as it stands, there must be proof of a sudden loss of control. There was no sudden act here. Sara paused before she picked up the weapon. She was even on record as telling the police she had sharpened the thing first – although she was sure later that she had neither said it nor done it in reality.

The lawyers decided her best defence was diminished responsibility. Unhappily they seemed not to have convinced Sara of this. Or, if they had, she was too confused to understand exactly what the jury needed to be sure of. For when Escott-Cox put it to her that there was 'something wrong with her' when she put the knife near Malcolm Thornton's slumped body, she denied it. Everything Sara said amounted to a plea of 'I was provoked'.

The three psychiatrists who had examined Sara found evidence of a personality disorder. However, the third one, Dr Barbara Brockman, said she believed the disorder was 'stabilising'.

In his speech to the jury of eight men and four women Mr Justice Judge said the motive of monetary gain was not proven. There was no evidence that Malcolm Thornton had any money for Sara to acquire. The account for the shop was all but empty and there were considerable debts. Sara was still the owner of a house in Coventry and she had applied for a second mortgage to prop up her husband's business. He asked the jury to consider the claims about the deceased's alcoholism. He suggested they should consider that Thornton was still able to gain promotion at his job.

'There are many unhappy, indeed miserable, husbands and wives. It is a fact of life. It has to be faced,' he told them. 'But on the whole it is hardly reasonable, you may think, to stab [someone] fatally where there are other alternatives available, like walking out or going upstairs.'

The jury retired mid-morning on 22 February. By the end of the day they had not reached an agreement. They spent the evening at a hotel and returned the following day, reaching a verdict more than twenty-four hours later. The foreman told the court that theirs was a majority verdict. Ten out of the twelve of them had agreed. The verdict was, 'guilty of murder'. Mr Justice Judge had to pass the mandatory sentence for the crime: life. Sara Thornton was taken to Risley Prison, Warrington, to begin her separation from her daughter, and after three months she was moved to Durham Prison.

Meanwhile many of those who had followed the trial were pointing to obvious disappointments. The verdict might so easily have been different, it seemed to Sara's friends and a growing number of supporters. Her defence had not shown that Sara would never have gained financially from her husband's death. Their house was re-mortgaged and would have to be sold. The issue of the alleged knife sharpening had not been examined. No evidence had been offered to support claims of Malcolm Thornton's destructive behaviour caused by his alcoholism. This might have convinced the most strait-laced jury in the land that even if Sara Thornton *had* been a wanton woman, *had* walked the streets stark naked every day of her life, she was still more sinned against than sinning. Dr Farn, Dr Glatt, Patrick Hanlon, Malcolm's former boss and his second wife Anne could have borne witnesses to the fact that drink made Malcolm a beast.

After a year in Durham, Sara was moved to Bullwood Prison in Hockley, Essex. It was from there that she consulted new lawyers about an appeal. Lord Gifford QC attempted to have the conviction for murder quashed and replaced by one of manslaughter on the grounds of provocation. For this the sentence was variable. Many battered women who are judged to be no threat to society as a whole and unlikely to commit the same serious crime again, have been given suspended sentences which ensure that their children are not also made to suffer.

Sara's experience in the appeal court was no less disturbing than her trial in Birmingham. 'It was quite humiliating,' she said on a tape-recorded message to her new campaigning friends. 'When Lord Gifford started to speak on my behalf I wept and when I didn't have a tissue I had to wipe my nose on my skirt. And I thought, "Oh, they're going to think I'm a slut!" When I asked Lord Gifford to find out if someone could get me a cushion, so I could see what was happening, he asked the clerk of the court to arrange something. Nothing was done and I was told by one of the officers that if I made a fuss, I'd be taken downstairs.'

The result seems hardly surprising now. With the benefit

of hindsight to have abandoned diminished responsibility as a defence and put all Sara's eggs into the basket of provocation seemed an equally risky course, according to Gareth Pierce, the lawyer who took up her case afterwards. The three judges headed by Lord Justice Beldam refused to accept that there had been anything unsafe and unsatisfactory about the first conviction. They also stated that the concept of provocation as a 'sudden and temporary loss of self-control' was sound. Sara's action did not fit that definition, they concluded.

On learning that her hopes had been dashed Sara was deeply disappointed. On hearing that Joseph McGrail of Kingstanding, Birmingham, a man who had killed his alcoholic common-law wife, had that week been given a suspended sentence, she was enraged. She saw this as further evidence of injustice. McGrail had taken Marion Kennedy by the throat as she lay in a drunken stupor, thrown her onto the bed and kicked her to death. The judge at his trial, Mr Justice Popplewell, expressed his sympathy for McGrail and commented that Kennedy 'would have tried the patience of a saint'.

On 3 August Sara Thornton began a hunger strike that was to last for twenty days and end only on the arrival of Luise, who begged her to stay alive. Meanwhile support for a change in the legal definition of provocation was mounting. Lord Denning, who had made the original 'heat of the moment' ruling in 1949, declared: 'In the light of women's experiences I would today direct the jury that prolonged violence over the years may result in provocation.'

Jack (later Lord) Ashley, the campaigning politician for Stoke-on-Trent, moved for cross-party action to bring

Sara's case before the Law Lords. The then Home Secretary Kenneth Baker replied to Jack Ashley, 'I think that
a broader definition of provocation could let in revenge or
planned killings and I would be unhappy at that. I think it
right that strict criteria should apply.' He added that he
would intervene only when new evidence or 'some other
consideration of substance' was brought to his attention.

In prison Sara met and enjoyed the support of members
of women's groups who are campaigning on behalf of
women who are battered behind Britain's closed doors.
Sara also had a short but sweet friendship with writer and
campaigner George Delf who did much to publicise her
case and arrange that first appeal.

In January 1992 Bisla Rajinda Singh, a clothes shop
owner from Erith, Kent, was given an eighteen-month suspended sentence for manslaughter on the grounds of
provocation. He had lost his temper with his wife Abnesh
and strangled her with a cord.

In the summer of 1992 the life sentence meted out to
Kiranjit Ahluwalia for killing her violent husband was quashed on appeal. She was released after a retrial in September of that year. At least for one human punchbag, the
battering stopped.

Early in 1994 Sara Thornton was moved to Styal Prison
in Cheshire. It was perhaps a sign that the authorities no
longer thought she was a dangerous woman in need of top
security. She was further away from the London journalists
and campaigners too. From her cell there, looking longingly
at the photographs she has of Luise, Sara Thornton will
continue to harry the authorities until, like Kiranjit, she
is freed.

Death at the Savoy

Hitchcock could not have wished for a better story. The clash of Eastern and Western cultures; a fatal shooting at one of the world's most famous hotels and the final dramatic moments conducted against the spectacular backdrop of a violent thunderstorm. And at the centre of it all was a beautiful, vulnerable French woman, trapped in a world of physical and emotional degradation, forced to perform unnatural sexual acts by a slavish Egyptian playboy husband.

Never allowed out unless accompanied by her husband's personal secretary, the victim of repeated brutal assaults, one of which dislocated her jaw, yet unable to obtain a divorce, it is scarcely surprising that the only way out she could see was to rid herself of her tormentor.

It was the early hours of 10 July 1923 and Madame Marie-Marguerite Fahmy, her husband Prince Ali Kamel Fahmy Bey and his entourage were entering the ninth day of their stay at London's luxurious Savoy Hotel.

Already the air was rife with threat and counter threat, a state of affairs which had resulted in an exceedingly public row in the Savoy Grill shortly before midnight. The sparks were also flying outside, the oppressive nature of the Fahmy marriage being more than matched by the elements. The previous day, London had sweltered in tropical heat but around midnight the storm that had been threatening all day finally arrived. It was to be the capital's worst thunderstorm for years.

The *Daily Telegraph* graphically described the events:

> For over two hours the sky was illuminated by brilliant, continuous flashes that gave the buildings an eerie appearance, and at least once what seemed to be a gigantic fireball broke into a million fragments of dazzling fiery sparks. Equally dramatic were the heavy crashes of thunder which grew in a mighty crescendo, intense and majestic, and then into a diminuendo as the storm swept irresistibly over the city.

The expansive Fahmy suite was on the fourth floor of the Savoy, at the rear of the building overlooking the River Thames. The Fahmys were thus spared the noisy traffic of the Strand. That night, the river seemed to be alight, vividly reflecting the shafts of electricity in the sky.

At around 1.30am, night porter John Beattie was pushing a trolleyload of luggage along the immaculate grey carpet which lined the corridor. As he reached the door of the Fahmy suite, the Prince stepped out, wearing mauve silk pyjamas. His left cheek was slightly flushed.

'Look at my face! Look what she has done!' he raged to the disbelieving porter who was forced to stop in his tracks to inspect the damage. While he did so, a deafening clap of thunder reverberated along the corridor, coinciding with

the other door of the suite being flung open. There stood
Madame Fahmy in her white, beaded evening dress.

To put it mildly, she was in a state of high agitation. She
screamed at her husband in French which, although he had
served overseas as a soldier in the First World War, Beattie
was totally unable to translate. But the message was clearly
not one of bonhomie. Fearful for the hotel's reputation,
the porter politely suggested that, given the lateness of the
hour, the couple might be advised to return to their suite.

Bowing his farewell, Beattie hurried on his way but had
only progressed some ten yards when he heard a whistle.
He assumed that it was an impolite command made in his
direction, and turned accordingly. He saw the Prince, now
alone, snapping his fingers at something. It seemed to be a
dog although Beattie could not actually detect the presence
of any form of hound. Having just turned the corner, heading for the front of the hotel, Beattie was startled by three
loud bangs in quick succession. He knew instantly that they
were in no way connected with the storm. They sounded
like revolver shots.

He abandoned his trolley, ran back to the corner and
looked along the corridor from where the sounds had come.
Reaching the suite, he knocked on the door. A few seconds
later, it was thrown open to reveal the motionless figure of
Madame Fahmy standing in the doorway, clutching a pistol
in her right hand. Behind her, in the suite itself, lay the
crumpled body of the Prince. Blood was trickling from
his mouth.

As the porter drew nearer, Madame Fahmy tossed down
the pistol beside the body. He saw that her white dress
was spattered with blood, but the majority of spillage was

reserved for the plush carpet beneath the Prince's head. The Prince was still alive – but only just.

Clearly in a state of shock, the distraught Madame Fahmy uttered, 'What have I done? What have I done?' At least that was Beattie's interpretation, but it has to be remembered that linguistics were not his strong point.

Beattie swiftly summoned assistance. First on the scene was the night manager, Arthur Mariani, who fortunately spoke fluent French. 'What have I done? What will happen?' Madame Fahmy demanded excitedly. 'Why did you do this?' asked Mariani. She replied, 'Oh, sir, I have been married six months. They have been torture to me, and I have suffered terribly.' Mariani also believed she said something about quarrelling with her husband over divorce but a few of her words were lost in the storm which was raging towards a conclusion. While they waited for the police to arrive, Madame Fahmy used the house-phone in the suite to call her husband's devoted male secretary, Said Enani. She told him, 'Come quickly, come quickly! I have shot at Ali!'

Enani, his nerves torn to shreds, rushed to the suite, just in time to witness his master being stretchered into a luggage lift (an ignominious exit for a Prince), bound for Charing Cross Hospital. Seeing that Madame Fahmy was being attended to by the Savoy doctor, Edward Gordon, the secretary returned to his room. The curious onlookers had been gently ushered back to their rooms when the police arrived, led by Detective Inspector Edward Grosse. He was horrified to learn that Beattie, who had been told somewhat prematurely to tidy up, had stowed away the gun, three cartridge cases and a spent bullet for safe keeping. Not only therefore had vital evidence been tampered with, but by the time everything was handed over to Grosse, Beattie's fingerprints covered it. The inspector was not amused.

Madame Fahmy was taken to Bow Street Police Station. There she learned that her husband had died at 3.25am.

The case gripped the public's imagination, all the more so because it involved the wealthy. Newspaper headlines blared out the sensational events: FRENCH WIFE CHARGED WITH MURDER OF PLAYBOY EGYPTIAN HUSBAND and SAVOY SHOOTING WHILE STORM RAGES.

Little did the public know that the Prince's death was a tragedy that had been waiting to happen for some time. For Ali Fahmy Bey was no romantic Eastern hero in the mould of Rudolph Valentino's 1921 model in *The Sheik*. Instead he was an arrogant sexual pervert who made life hideously unbearable for his new bride.

Madame Fahmy was born Marie-Marguerite Alibert in a modest suburb of Paris in December 1890. Her parents were devout Roman Catholics and were not wealthy. Her father was a cab driver. Marie-Marguerite had a chequered youth. At sixteen she gave birth to a daughter, the identity of the father remaining a mystery. The child was put into the care of an aunt and, within a couple of months, its mother had become engaged to André Meller, a man twelve years her senior. The relationship was short-lived. Another proposed wedding fell through in 1913 but, despite this decidedly unpromising start to her love life, she persevered and six years later finally made it up the aisle with one Charles Laurent, an old friend with whom she had been reunited while recovering in a nursing home following an operation.

This association proved equally doomed with Laurent

quickly abandoning her to accept a post in Japan. Marie-Marguerite had no wish to leave Paris and, at this stage, even less desire to sample Eastern culture. They were duly divorced and she overcame her grief by throwing herself into a nightly ritual of partying and dining out. Laurent had generously compensated her for his desertion, including leaving her his house and car, and she was thus able to move in the city's most exclusive circles.

In January 1922 she and some friends visited Egypt where she received an invitation to attend a party on board the yacht of Prince Ali Kamel Fahmy Bey. She declined the offer but when Fahmy Bey pursued her in Paris four months later her resolve weakened.

Fahmy Bey was ten years younger than Marie-Marguerite. Educated in France and England, he acquired considerable wealth on the death of his father who, in addition to running a string of cotton plantations in Northern Egypt, also owned a large amount of property. The young Ali specialised in charitable deeds in his native land whereupon the Egyptian government rewarded him with the title of Prince. He came to the conclusion that with his money and good looks, he could have any woman he wanted. By the time he was working for the Egyptian Legation in Paris, he had decided that that woman would be the reluctant Marie-Marguerite.

He did everything possible to sweep her off her feet, wooing her with limousine outings and general displays of affection. She was intrigued by his expressive eyes although she later noted that they would suddenly harden 'into a ferocity which was positively terrifying'. But for the time being, the Prince was charm personified. However after her previous misfortunes, Marie-Marguerite was in no hurry to rush headlong into another failed liaison.

In August, she went on holiday to her villa at Deauville. Fahmy followed her. She moved on to Spain. He would only be consoled when she allowed him to accompany her. He then had to journey to Italy and insisted that she go with him. 'I will marry you. Come,' he implored.

Although she clearly enjoyed his company and viewed him as an enlightened member of the Eastern world, she was not yet ready to make that sort of commitment. So he headed for Italy alone, except for his ever-present entourage comprising half-a-dozen faithful minions.

By the end of September, he was in Egypt from where his letters became more pleading, more passionate, more desperate in their attempts to persuade her to join him. In one he wrote:

Torch of my life – you appear to me surrounded by a halo. I see your head encircled by a crown which I reserve for it here. It is a crown which I have reserved for you on your arrival in this beautiful country of my ancestors. . . . Come, come quickly, and appreciate the beautiful sun of Egypt. My only consolation is you. Believe me, I love you very much.

From your faithful Little Baba.

It seemed he liked her.

Her resistance eroded away by such flowery prose, Marie-Marguerite finally succumbed and, on 22 November, she landed at Alexandria. The immediate welcome did not disappoint. As promised, she was installed in his palace like a princess. Thinking her smitten by the opulence, Fahmy Bey pressed her on the subject of marriage. 'You are to become my wife,' he told her. 'You are my only happiness.' She resisted. 'Later, later,' she stalled. 'Let me become accustomed to the idea.'

But nowhere in his Prince's manual was there any mention of being kept waiting. A man in his position was simply not used to being strung along. He would not take 'no' or 'later' for an answer. And so, despite her reservations about marrying into the Eastern way of life, she at last agreed to become his bride.

In doing so, it should be pointed out that, lest she be accused of marrying for money, Marie-Marguerite was actually forfeiting a sizeable allowance. Under the terms of their divorce her first husband, Charles Laurent, had been paying her a handsome sum, to cease only when she remarried.

The ceremony with Prince Fahmy was conducted on 26 December. She chose to adopt the Moslem religion since an inheritance from his mother was assured only on condition that he married a woman of the faith. The future Madame Fahmy did include one proviso – that she should not have to don the Moslem veil and would be permitted to continue to wear Western clothes. The Prince raised no objections.

All went smoothly until she was suddenly asked to waive the right of divorce. This came as a complete surprise to her. Realising that Moslem husbands were allowed to take four wives if they so desired and that, without the capacity to divorce, she would be bound to him, whether she liked it or not, till death did them part, she protested vehemently.

But Prince Fahmy would not back down over this issue and the signing of the civil marriage contract was delayed for four hours by protracted negotiations. It was resolved when the Prince made her a financial offer she could not refuse. Marie-Marguerite was supposed to be paid £2,000 yet in the event received just £450 plus an IOU.

So her new husband possessed the sole right of divorce. Thus he could simply cast her aside if he wanted to or, alternatively, seek his pleasures elsewhere while remaining married to her. For her part, she was trapped. It was a decision she would bitterly regret – and soon.

On the honeymoon along the Nile on board the Prince's largest yacht, she was introduced to his peculiar sexual delights. It appears that they had not made love before the wedding but, not unreasonably, she expected her young stud to have a normal, healthy sexual appetite. Indeed there was nothing wrong with his appetite, more in the manner in which it was served. Unusually for a Prince, who one would expect to use the front door, he always chose the tradesman's entrance. This disturbed Madame Fahmy greatly, not only because her slim frame meant she was not built for such activity, but also because it made her suspect that her husband was homosexual. She recalled how in the past she had observed the Prince taking an affectionate interest in pretty Egyptian youths and concluded that while committing sodomy with her, he was secretly fantasising that her body was male. This did little for her self-esteem. And what's more, she was stuck with him for the rest of her life.

The Prince demanded his pleasures nightly. As the sheer physical pain worsened, she protested – but in vain. The more she complained, the rougher he became. Already it had developed into a marriage of hell, and the honeymoon was not yet over!

Apart from the physical humiliation, Madame Fahmy suddenly found herself publicly rebuked. So attentive and considerate before the marriage, the Prince had changed beyond all recognition. It was the turn of Mr Hyde. Once when she dared to complain about his treatment of a crew member, he screamed at her in words which implied that if she was so fond of the company of sailors, he would leave her alone with the entire crew. With that, he stormed ashore. Worse still, on another occasion he kept her locked up on the yacht for three days, guarded by his henchmen, while he tasted the fruits of the land.

Impossible though it may seem, the situation deteriorated after the honeymoon. On her return to the palace, she saw fit to send a remarkable statement to her lawyer in Paris:

> I, Marie-Marguerite Alibert, of full age, of sound mind and body, formally accuse, in the case of my death, violent or otherwise, Ali Fahmy Bey, of having contributed in my disappearance.
>
> Yesterday, 21 January 1923, at three o'clock in the afternoon, he took his Bible or Koran – I do not know how it is called – kissed it, put his hand on it, and swore to avenge himself upon me tomorrow, in eight days, a month, or three months, but I must disappear by his hand. This oath was taken without any reason, neither jealousy, bad conduct, nor a scene on my part.

I desire and demand justice for my daughter and for my family.

Done at Zamalik, at about eleven o'clock in the morning, 22 January 1923.   (M.-Marguerite Alibert)
P.S. Today he wanted to take my jewellery from me. I refused; hence a fresh scene.

By now it was evident that Prince Fahmy demanded total subservience from his wife. He treated this spirited Western woman as if he were breaking in a horse. She was never allowed out alone, unless accompanied by the mysterious Said Enani, who immediately reported her every movement to his master. Once when she sneaked off to the cinema alone, Prince Fahmy punished her by punching her in the face with such force that he dislocated her jaw. He wrote to Madame Fahmy's sister, 'Just now I am engaged in training her. Yesterday, to begin, I did not come in to lunch or to dinner, and I also left her at the theatre. This will teach her, I hope, to respect my wishes. With women one must act with energy and be severe.'

In May, Prince Fahmy accepted a diplomatic position in Paris. Longing for the familiarity of her home country, Madame Fahmy eagerly accompanied him and while in the French capital, took the opportunity of seeking medical advice. When at the start of July the Prince announced his intention to take a holiday in London, Madame Fahmy begged to be allowed to remain in Paris. Her request was rejected out of hand.

On 1 July, the Fahmy entourage booked in at the Savoy. The agony resulting from her husband's sexual proclivities worsened and she wasted no time in consulting the hotel doctor, Edward Gordon, whose surgery was situated across the Strand in Southampton Street. The doctor's visits continued on a daily basis for the next eight days. On some occasions the Prince was present but, presumably given the delicate nature of the matter under discussion, he chose to lurk silently in the background. He was conspicuous by his absence when Dr Gordon, who spoke excellent French, called on the afternoon of July 4. Madame Fahmy showed the doctor the bruises on her arms which had been inflicted during the frequent violent rows with her husband.

By now, she had also developed external haemorrhoids which were dangerously inflamed. She said that her husband had 'torn her by unnatural intercourse' and that he was 'always pestering her' for that form of sex.

Dr Gordon prescribed ointments but told her that if the condition did not respond to treatment within a few days, she should seek the advice of a specialist surgeon. Convinced that Prince Fahmy would claim that she had invented her ailment, she repeatedly asked the doctor to issue a certificate outlining her physical condition. The ointments had little effect, particularly in the heatwave that had engulfed London and which made her condition even more unbearable. So on the morning of 9 July Dr Gordon was joined on his visit by Mr Ivor Back, a consultant surgeon. Mr Back immediately recommended an operation and arranged for her to be admitted to a London nursing home the following day.

That same morning, Madame Fahmy received an unsigned note, written in French.

Please permit a friend who has travelled widely among

Orientals, and who knows the craftiness of their acts, to give you some advice.

Do not agree to return to Egypt, or even Japan, for any object. Rather abandon fortune than risk your life. Money can always be recovered by a good lawyer; but think of your life. A journey means a possible accident, a poison in the flower, a subtle weapon that is neither seen nor heard. Remain in Paris with those who love you·and will protect you.

The note made Madame Fahmy even more positive that her life was in danger. The reference to poison was particularly poignant, reminding her of various incidents at the palace in Egypt when she had been taken ill after drinking coffee. Such thoughts would have put many a lesser mortal off their lunch but, obviously confident in the Savoy's cuisine, she dined there with her husband and the ubiquitous Said Enani. Hungry for argument, the Prince bridled at Madame Fahmy's declaration that she was returning to Paris the next day for an operation. The ensuing difference of opinion was extremely public but provided excellent entertainment for those within earshot. According to accounts of the time, this could have included anybody who understood French within a mile radius of the Savoy. The row peaked at Marie-Marguerite's announcement: 'I'm going to leave you, and you'll pay dearly for it.'

The upshot of it all was that the Prince refused adamantly to pay for the operation. He proceeded to send a telegram to a jeweller's in Paris, stating: 'NOTHING TO BE DELIVERED TO MY WIFE ON MY ACCOUNT DURING MY ABSENCE. FAHMY.'

Relations between the two were now at their lowest ebb. That evening the couple, together with Said Enani, went to

Daly's Theatre in Coventry Street, just off Leicester Square. Somewhat ironically as it transpired, the production was *The Merry Widow*.

On leaving the theatre, they took supper at the Savoy Grill. As was the custom on such occasions, the leader of the orchestra came over to their table and asked Madame Fahmy whether she would care to select a tune. No sooner had he uttered the innocent words than it became apparent that she would not.

'Thank you very much,' she replied in French. 'My husband is going to kill me in twenty-four hours and I am not very anxious for music.' His training not having prepared him for such a situation, the conductor responded limply, 'I hope you will be here tomorrow, Madame'.

Other snippets of conversation emerged from the table, all of which conspired to suggest that it was not exactly a joyous gathering. At one point, Madame Fahmy seized a wine bottle and shouted at her husband, 'You shut up or I'll smash this over your head'. To which he replied, 'If you do, I'll do the same to you'.

They left the table shortly after midnight, each going their separate ways. Madame Fahmy returned to the suite while the Prince braved the storm to venture off to some unknown destiny around Piccadilly, more than likely a den of vice. Perhaps what he found was too tame for his liking since he arrived back at the Savoy not long after 1 a.m. Within thirty minutes he would be lying in a pool of blood.

The Times of 11 July reported that Madame Fahmy had been charged with the wilful murder of her husband:

By causing injuries to him by shooting him with a

Sandra Fleming – the years of terror she suffered at the hands of Christopher Porter ended with his violent death in April 1992 (*Yorkshire Television*)

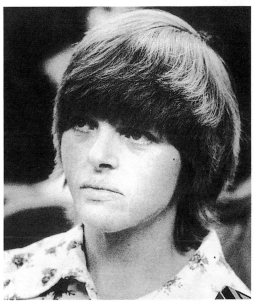

Jennifer Patri (*The Post Crescent*)

Mr Thomas Scotland
(*Fairley of Luton*)

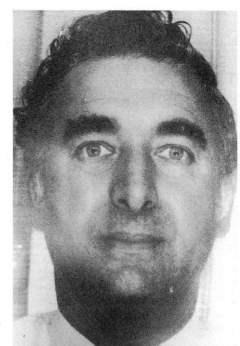

The garden where Thomas
Scotland's body was
discovered three and a half
years after he had been
bludgeoned to death with a
rolling-pin (*Fairley of
Luton*)

Caroline Scotland leaves court during her mother's trial for the murder of her father (*Fairley of Luton*)

June Scotland – since the week after her wedding she had suffered years of terror and degradation. As Helena Kennedy QC said, 'eventually her psyche surrendered' (*Fairley of Luton*)

Sara Thornton's apparently calm reaction after fatally stabbing her husband led many to label her a cold, callous murderer (*News Team International*)

Malcolm Thornton – Sara said of him, 'when he was not drinking he was a lovely man... When he was sober he never hit me once.' (*John Cole*)

revolver at about 1.30am on July 10 at the Savoy Hotel. . . . Detective Inspector Grosse said that near suite 41 in the corridor of the fourth floor on a wall at right angles to the suite, about three feet from the floor, there was a small hole, apparently caused by a bullet ricochet. A few yards further along the same corridor, part of the beading of a glass door had apparently been shot away, and a few yards farther still, there was an indent on a wooden bannister, apparently caused by a bullet ricochet.

In the bedroom, occupied by Madame Fahmy, he found a white evening gown, on the bottom of which were bloodstains. In another bedroom in the same suite were several crushed beads, similar to those on the trimming of the dressing gown.

According to the interpreter, Madame Fahmy said when charged: 'I have told the police I did it. I told the truth. It does not matter. My husband has assaulted me in front of so many people since we have been married. He has told me many times to kill him. I lost my head.'

Having been charged, Madame Fahmy was taken to Holloway Prison. It was a far cry from the palatial accommodation to which she had become accustomed but no matter how base the inmates, they could not have been any lower than the man with whom she had been locked in a loveless marriage. It seemed an open and shut case. Even allowing for the mitigating circumstances – assuming of course that the jury believed them – surely the best Madame Fahmy could hope for was a lengthy spell of imprisonment. At worst, her pretty little neck would dangle at the end of a rope. Happily, she did still have the means to afford the finest counsel that money could buy. That meant engaging the services of Sir Edward Marshall Hall, the most celebrated defender of his time and a man whose theatrical expertise would not have been out of place on the West End stage. Supported by Sir Henry Curtis-Bennett and Roland Oliver, Marshall Hall accepted the brief for the sum of 652 guineas. It was to be money well spent.

The trial began at the Old Bailey on Monday 10 September 1923 before a jury consisting of ten men and two women. Her words translated by an interpreter, Madame Fahmy pleaded 'Not guilty'. Concluding his opening speech for the Crown, Percival Clarke said of Madame Fahmy, 'From her own lips it is known that she caused the death of her husband. And in the absence of any other offence, you must find her guilty of murder.'

Therefore the priority of Marshall Hall and his colleagues was to prove that the shooting was nothing more than a tragic accident, that, menaced by her approaching husband and believing the automatic pistol to be empty, she had simply used it to frighten him. It was also necessary to prove that, at that precise moment, her own life had been in grave danger from this sadistic pervert. But to blacken the Prince's character would be no easy task since most of the witnesses to his atrocities were his own loyal employees who were unlikely to speak out against their master, no matter how incapable he now was of retaliation.

An indication of the difficulties which lay ahead came when the dapper figure of Said Enani was called to the stand. Even under the incisive probing of such a seasoned interrogator as Marshall Hall, the Prince's secretary remained economical with the truth.

The defence counsel raised an incident in Paris, which took place shortly before the ill-fated trip to London.

'Following a visit to the Folies Bergères, did Fahmy seize her by the throat?'

'I do not know that,' answered Enani elusively. 'I did see him take off a bracelet which she had given him and throw it at her.'

'On that occasion,' pressed Marshall Hall, 'I suggest that she was bleeding from the mouth from a blow given by her husband?'

'I remember a small mark near her nose,' conceded Enani.

'Do you know that he swore on the Koran to kill her?'

'No.'

'Did you know that she was in fear of her life?'

'No. I never knew.'

'Was she always crying?'

'No.'

'Was not the Madame Fahmy of 1923 a totally different person from the Madame Laurent of 1922?'

'Perhaps.'

'Had every bit of life been crushed out of her during those six months?'

'I do not know.'

'From being a gay, cheerful, entertaining and fascinating woman, did she not become sad, broken and miserable?'

'They were always quarrelling.'

'At supper on the night of the tragedy, did he say "I will

disfigure you so that no one else will want you"'?'

'I do not remember.'

Said Enani's lapses of memory conveniently continued although he did go so far as to admit that the Prince had been 'a bit unkind' to Madame Fahmy.

He would hear nothing of any stories about his master's sexual perversions, a delicate subject since Enani himself was rumoured to be one of the Prince's numerous homosexual lovers. Marshall Hall tackled this area with the final question of his cross-examination. 'I suggest,' he boomed, 'that the association between yourself and Fahmy was notorious in Egypt.' Enani resisted the temptation to answer in kind, instead choosing to reply quietly, 'That is not so'.

Having met with only limited success with Said Enani, Marshall Hall saw the opportunity to emphasise his theory of accidental shooting when questioning expert gunsmith Robert Churchill. The weapon used was a Browning .32 automatic pistol, one of a matching pair kept by the Fahmys at their bedside to ward off jewel thieves. Churchill confirmed that the pistol was, if gripped tightly, very easily triggered and that someone not familiar with automatic weapons – say a woman – might think that the only way to empty the gun was to fire the round in the barrel. He agreed that such a person might also be unaware that in an automatic, the recoil of one round lifts another out of the magazine and into the firing position. Thus Marshall Hall was able to illustrate how Madame Fahmy could have fired three shots purely by accident.

Marshall Hall made further inroads into the minds of the jury when asking Dr Gordon about a scratch mark he had observed on the back of Madame Fahmy's neck. 'Was the mark on the neck consistent with a hand clutching at her throat?' The doctor replied assuredly, 'It was. Madame Fahmy complained that her husband was very passionate, and that his conduct had made her ill. Her condition was consistent with conduct she alleged against him.'

Opening the case for the defence, Marshall Hall pulled no punches in his condemnation of the deceased. 'Fahmy Bey, shortly before he was shot, attacked his wife like a raving, lustful beast because she would not agree to an outrageous suggestion he made – a suggestion which would fill every decent-minded person with utter revulsion. Almost throughout their miserably tragic life of six months, this treacherous Egyptian beast pursued his wife with this unspeakable request, and because she – immoral though she may have been – resisted him, he heaped cruelty and brutality on her until she was changed, by fear, from a charming, attractive woman to a poor quaking creature hovering on the brink of a nervous ruin.'

When Madame Fahmy stepped falteringly into the witness box, she detailed the events of the fateful night. She said that her husband had finally agreed to pay for her operation but only on condition that she submitted to his physical desires. 'I will if you do something for me,' he said leeringly. When she refused, another furious row erupted in the corridor outside their suite. He started to tear off her dress.

Madame Fahmy testified, 'He seized me suddenly and brutally by the throat with his left hand. His thumb was on my windpipe and his fingers were pressing on my neck. I pushed him away but he crouched to spring on me and said, "I will kill you. I will kill you." '

She managed to break free from his stranglehold and

rushed into the bedroom to pick up her gun. Fahmy followed her, terrifyingly.

'I lifted my arm in front of me,' she continued, 'and without looking pulled the trigger. The next moment I saw him on the ground before me. I do not know how many times the revolver went off.' Adding that she thought the gun was empty of cartridges, she sobbed, 'I thought the sight of the pistol might frighten him.'

She went on to recount how, during their time in Egypt, her husband had placed her under the constant surveillance of six Africans who took it in turns to keep watch over her every move. One of them, a man-mountain named Costa, was even in the habit of following her into the bedroom when she wanted to change. She protested to the Prince about such an outrageous intrusion of privacy but he remained totally indifferent to her plight, simply saying, 'It is his right'.

With his taste for the theatrical, Marshall Hall sent a hush around the courtroom when asking for a pistol similar to her own to be handed to the defendant. She looked at it with horror until Marshall Hall reassured her, 'Come, Madame Fahmy, take hold of the pistol; it is harmless now.'

With that, reported the *Daily Express*, 'the small black-gloved hand of the trembling woman in the witness box closed on the pistol'.

Marshall Hall was back in more strident mood when addressing the jury at the conclusion of her testimony. 'I submit that this poor wretch of a woman, suffering the tortures of the damned, driven to desperation by the brutality and beastliness of the man whose will she dared to oppose, thought that he was carrying out the threat he had constantly made, and that when he seized her by the neck, he was indeed about to kill her.'

On the afternoon of the fourth day of the trial, Marshall Hall launched into what is generally regarded as the finest defence speech of his illustrious career. Quietly but purposefully, he entranced the jury:

> This woman made one great mistake – possibly the greatest mistake any woman of the West can make. She married an Oriental. It is common knowledge that the Oriental's treatment of women does not fit in with the idea the Western woman has of the way she should be treated by her husband. . . . The curse of this case is the atmosphere of the East which we cannot understand – the Eastern feeling of possession of the woman, the Turk in his harem. This man Fahmy was entitled to have four wives if he liked, which to us Western people, with our ideas of women, is almost unintelligible – something we cannot deal with.
>
> Picture this woman, inveigled into Egypt by false pretences – by letters which for adulatory expression could hardly be equalled. And which make one feel sick. At first, everything is honey and roses. He shows her his beautiful palace, his costly motor cars, his wonderful motor boat, his retinue of servants, his lavish luxuries, and cries, 'Ah, I am Fahmy Bey – I am a prince!'

Marshall Hall continued in a similar vein the following morning, painting a graphic portrait of the thunderstorm on the night of the shooting. 'Imagine its effect on a woman of nervous temperament who had been living such a life as she had lived for the past six months – outraged, abused, beaten, degraded. Now her degrader was advancing menacingly on her.'

As he spoke those words, Marshall Hall seized a pistol and adopted what he considered to be the crouch of a stealthy Oriental.

'In sheer desperation – as he crouched for the last time, crouched like an animal, like an Oriental, retired for the last time to get a bound forward – she turned the pistol and put it to his face.' In a dramatic movement, he levelled the gun at the foreman of the jury, then paused for a second before adding, 'And, to her horror, the thing went off.'

With that, Marshall Hall released his grip on the gun and sent it clattering to the floor – exactly as Madame Fahmy had dropped it. The silence was breathtaking.

But he was not finished yet. For his finale, he drew upon Robert Hichen's novel, *Bella Donna*. 'You will remember the final scene, where this woman goes out of the gates of the garden into the dark night of the desert. Members of the jury, I want you to open the gates where this Western woman can go out – not into the dark night of the desert but back to her friends, who love her in spite of her weaknesses; back to her friends, who will be glad to receive her; back to her child, who will be waiting for her with open arms.'

Suddenly a shaft of sunlight shone through the Old Bailey skylight. Taking his cue, Marshall Hall raised his arm aloft and implored the jury, 'You will open the gate and let this Western woman go back into the light of God's great Western sun'.

Exhausted by his own performance, he concluded, 'I don't ask you for a verdict, I demand it at your hands'.

It was a tough act to follow. In his summing up, Mr Justice Swift remarked that he had been 'shocked, sickened and disgusted' by certain aspects of the evidence. He told the jury that they had the option of three verdicts – guilty of murder, guilty of manslaughter or not guilty of both.

It took just an hour for the jury to decide. Madame Fahmy was found not guilty of murder and not guilty of manslaughter. She was a free woman at last. The verdict was greeted with wild enthusiasm inside and outside the court. Madame Fahmy herself was overcome with emotion, to the point of nearly fainting. She had to wait inside the court for a further hour, not only to recover her composure and sense of balance but also to allow the delirious crowds to disperse.

Later, meeting a representative of the *People* newspaper who had won the rights for an exclusive interview, she observed sadly, 'Marriages between East and West can hardly ever turn out happily'. And a policeman, entrusted with her detention in the hours immediately after the shooting, went on to describe Prince Ali Kamel Fahmy Bey as a 'brutal pervert who treated his wife like a white slave'. Over the next couple of days, Madame Fahmy made a point of expressing her gratitude to Marshall Hall whose closing speech, with its distinct racist overtones, drew a formal complaint from the Egyptian Bar, which accused him of insulting all Egypt and the East in general. He apologised for any unintentional injury and the matter was forgotten long before his death in 1927.

Madame Fahmy returned to Paris where she was greeted

as a heroine. But after a few years, she disappeared from public gaze just as suddenly and unexpectedly as she had entered it.

Undetected Clues

The Steiners' kitchen at their lovely home in Glen Burnie, in the state of Maryland, is the sort you see in expensive magazines. Space. Style. Nothing flimsy or cheap. It's a large, airy room with a shining tiled floor. There are cupboards filled with tasteful china and elegant dishes and worksurfaces dotted with the white and chromium machines that make modern life easier than it was for our mothers yet not so easy that culinary artistry might appear to have died. It was a busy room, a room that saw a lot.

It's a room that defined Joyce Steiner in the Reagan years of oil-rich conspicuous spending: confident, middle class, well-off and respectable. It was the hub of her life as an educated American woman who had until recently a thriving career but at the same time valued and gave great attention to her family – her daughter Kimberley and husband Robert. It was a piece of the jigsaw of the American Dream. Other women could spy on her in this setting and easily envy Joyce that kitchen. Most of the women who knew her, also envied her busy, productive life. This she knew, and the bitter irony of it sometimes made her want to scream and cry.

On Mother's Day in May 1988 the Glen Burnie Police came to this kitchen. They found Robert Steiner in a pool of blood on those immaculate tiles. He was dying from a bullet from a .38 calibre Colt revolver. Joyce had called them. She was there to unlock the doors to let them in, doors Steiner had locked. She had shot him in the head. He died later that night. Joyce heard the news as she sat in the cell in the county jail. She didn't cry. She says she felt free. 'When they told me, the weight of the world lifted off my shoulders,' she said later.

Two months after the event she was indicted for murder. On 1 December a jury of seven women and five men heard the story of what had happened that day. They studied the tall brunette in the good clothes and chic jewellery. Joyce imagined the men might think the worst. But she thought that surely the women would understand. They did not. The prosecution argued that she had killed Robert, not in self-defence during a furious fight, but as he sat innocently eating a sandwich. Here's an educated, intelligent woman with her own money. Good God, said the state's attorney, if this man had really been giving her a hard time, why the hell hadn't she left?

It seemed an unanswerable charge. Why hadn't she walked out? You don't have to plug your husband full of bullets if he slaps you around and you don't like it. Not in 1988.

No doubt the women on the jury wished to disassociate themselves from such incredible behaviour. They would never allow themselves to get into such an appalling marriage. If they did, they'd get themselves out of it and in a lawful way. Sympathy? Forget it.

Joyce Steiner was convicted and sentenced to five years which she fully expected to serve. She didn't expect to change that much in the time. It wasn't long, however, before she did something she'd never allowed herself to do before. The shame of it had stopped her. She admitted to herself and to others that she had been a battered wife for seven years.

A couple of hundred miles southwest from New York and Philadelphia is Baltimore, a bustling eastern port at the head of one of the tributaries of Chesapeake Bay. It's an old industrial city into whose safe harbour the steamships once chugged and from whose seven railway lines goods were speedily exported all over the union. Today there are still canning factories, massive steel works and an awesome shipyard. Around two million people from ethnic backgrounds of all kinds fuel the city. Whites, whose ancestors were Irish Catholics or Anglo-Saxon Protestants, are the fat cats of course. Many live right there in the city. Many more merely work in it and, to avoid the risks of street crime and pollution, live in quieter, greener surroundings, in places that are tiny dots on the map between Baltimore and Washington DC, such as the one thirty miles south, called Glen Burnie.

Joyce was the owner of a private detection agency there in the late 1970s. It grossed over $1 million a year and it was challenging, satisfying work too. She knew that what she did for her clients, many of them women seeking evidence of their husbands' duplicity, was worthwhile. She'd tested it herself. She had set up the agency after hiring a private eye to track down the necessary clues to her own first husband's affair with her best friend. Piqued by this, she was in no hurry to remarry. Her daughter Kimberley, then twelve, saw her father regularly and life was comfortable.

Joyce's powers of detection failed her, however, when she began dating Robert Steiner. He was a six-footer, handsome, strong, meticulously well dressed and well mannered. He had come through the Vietnam war to pick up his life as owner of a popular restaurant, The Old Mill Pancake House, in Annapolis, Maryland's capital twenty-five miles down the bay.

'When I met this man he was the Prince Charming that everybody was waiting for,' Joyce recalled. 'I was completely taken in. He would take me anywhere. He would do anything in the world for me. He showered me with gifts. I thought, well you are thirty-three years old. Your daughter is gonna grow up and leave in a few years. Are you going to be a successful woman with a lot of money – alone?'

Robert Steiner was not after Joyce's money. The restaurant was profitable and his father was a rich man, a property developer, from whom he had a generous allowance. Satisfied that he was also happy to live with Kim, who liked him too, Joyce married Steiner in 1981 when she was thirty-five. He was forty-two and had been married twice before.

The first year was wine and roses. Steiner continued to take her on romantic holidays and he carried on making impulsive, extravagant gestures. Joyce would be trying to decide which outfit out of dozens she'd tried on to buy only to hear him insist that she take all of them. For several Christmases, her task was to stretch out in the back of a limousine while a chauffeur took her from Annapolis to

Saks in Fifth Avenue, New York, where she would have to find enough to keep her Gold Card busy for a day.

It was less than a year later that the angry outbursts began. An argument over nothing suddenly made Steiner violent. He began beating Joyce and threw Kim across the room when she tried to intervene. The teenager hit her arm on a chair and cut it. It was the first and last time he mistreated her. It was not, alas, the same for Joyce.

Steiner had been drinking heavily that day and later he seemed so terribly, tenderly sorry. He said it had been the alcohol that did it, that it would never happen again. It did, naturally. A pattern of drink, violence, then remorse and lavish present-buying began.

But Steiner's state of mind worsened. That year he had a heated exchange with a friend over whether he would dare shoot his dog. Steiner had to rise to this, it seemed. As Joyce watched in horror, he fired a bullet into their Shetland dog, Ora, killing him.

He also began blaming his violence on Vietnam. When he remembered those times, anger welled up in him, he said. But he refused to take the advice of his friends who suggested he join veteran support groups. That would be to admit he needed support and men like Robert Steiner, from good strong stock, needed none of that. But as time went on the mere mention of Vietnam could turn him into a war-like aggressor.

Once while *Tour of Duty*, a cheaply made television action drama series supposedly set in that war, was playing in the living room he got up and left for a while. When he returned, to Joyce and Kim's dismay, his face was smeared with brown-green camouflage paint and he pounced from chair to sofa and coffee table, like a guerrilla fighter in the jungle.

By 1983 he'd become jealous of the time Joyce spent at her agency and, ominously, of the time she spent in the company of other men. He said he needed more of her time. So she sold the agency. Somewhere inside, she was flattered that he wanted her to be with him more, somewhere inside she felt guilty that she had neglected him.

She was, after all, a conventional woman whose parents and older sister Lois enjoyed happy marriages. How could she tell them what was happening in hers? How could she confess that after losing one man to another woman and becoming the first person in the whole family to get a divorce, that she was contemplating doing it again because she couldn't keep the second one content? There was no way she could do it. Bright, resourceful Joyce Steiner told no one what was happening to her. They thought she led a perfect life in a fabulous home with a beautiful daughter and a husband who showered her with presents. She denied the truth about the abuse to everyone, including herself.

The violence became more varied and more depraved. Steiner would catch her in her car and smash the windscreen as a 'reminder' that she was not free. At night, after drinking, Steiner would press a lit cigarette against her thigh to see if she was pretending to be asleep to avoid having sex with him. If she woke up it proved she was 'playing possum' and she would be beaten. If she went on pretending to be asleep, she would avoid the sex but the burns would be horrendous. And as with most abusive husbands, beatings were almost invariably followed by brutal sex, proof that he was a man and could do what men do.

Joyce reflected later, 'The first time he hit me I was just petrified. The second time . . . well, it's just like riding a bike, I guess. Each time it gets a little easier. It got to be something I got used to.'

She also got used to the tokens of his remorse – huge diamonds, rubies, rows of pearls. Robert Steiner did nothing by halves.

She went to work at The Old Mill. Her husband's drinking had progressed and he was soon incapable of working or being seen around the place. Joyce was managing it alone. What's more, she was managing it well. For him that was unforgivable. His envy of her ability inflamed his temper.

Later she sighed to recall, 'When he was drunk he would tell me how much he hated me because I had made something I could look back on. He couldn't say that about anything because his father had given him everything.'

But as the cycle of battering and begging for another chance continued, Joyce sank into the familiar trap of generations of punchbag women all over the world: she began to worry that it was her fault. Steiner's friends helped her think along those lines. If she tried to talk to them, ask their advice about his temper when they came to drink beer and play cards, many of them, who were off-duty police officers would reply that she must be saying something to spark off the rows or make him angry. What they said made her feel worse.

Experts say that women who have enjoyed absorbing, successful jobs are especially vulnerable to feeling they are failures if their marriages don't work out. Joyce felt this but she was also coming to realise that she had to leave. But towards the end of 1984 Steiner found out and became almost incandescent with rage. He was also, as ever, drunk. He barricaded himself and Joyce inside the house and said he would kill them both. The five-hour siege ended when the state police finally helped Joyce to climb out of a second storey window. They did not arrest Steiner. Instead they took him off to a mental hospital. Joyce agreed to his release from there on condition that he saw a psychiatrist on a regular basis. He agreed and saw one six times. The specialist told Joyce privately that her husband's problems went back to his childhood and he was sure to talk openly about them given time. It could mean a complete change in the way he thought about himself. Overjoyed, Joyce told her father-in-law.

It was probably her one chance and she had blown it by underestimating the fragility of the male ego. For the old man belligerently insisted that his son needed no fancy therapy, only hard work to keep his mind occupied. A week later, Steiner began running a new restaurant that his father had bought for him and the sessions with the psychiatrist stopped.

Joyce tried to escape several times. She fled to the home of a friend, but Steiner arrived there and threatened to burn the place down. To show he meant business, he set the friend's car ablaze.

On another occasion Joyce moved into her daughter Kim's college dormitory. Steiner was soon on the telephone, telling her he would be there to kill them both if she didn't get back home double quick.

One day during the summer of 1987, Steiner had drunk himself into a particularly dark mood. He told Joyce she could get out. She rushed upstairs, packed a bag and came down. 'You'll be back,' he sneered. 'No I won't,' said Joyce. Then he stunned her with a twisted smile and the promise, 'When your mother and your father and your daughter are laid out in the funeral home, you'll come back. First I'll kill them, then I'll kill you.' Not surprisingly, Joyce unpacked.

Joyce left again twice, staying at hotels. At that stage she hadn't even considered a shelter for battered women as the place for her. It did not cross the mind of this woman of the world that there were professionals who could help.

'Shelters were for poor people – they were like flop houses to me,' she said later. 'I was middle class. I had money.' She also had a husband threatening murder.

By 1988 Kim was finishing college and Joyce had decided she would set her daughter up in the business she chose. She wanted to run a beauty salon. By that time Steiner had closed The Old Mill and in his sober moments had hatched a plan to redesign it and reopen it as an Italian restaurant. But he had no more money of his own. He needed funds from Joyce. He decided that Kim should not have the salon.

It was Mother's Day and Joyce planned to be the loving mother she had always been. She wanted to tell Kim that she could definitely have her wish. Steiner had not been drinking on that Sunday in May, but he still saw red. He didn't reason, he demanded she give the money over to him and a shouting match began. She had taken control again and he couldn't bear it. He shook her and she scratched his face. He flung her onto the floor and began kicking her. He said he wouldn't finish with her until he had killed her.

'You're worth more to me dead than alive!' he yelled. 'I'll get the money and the insurance!' Then he beat her until she was all but unconscious, lying on those pristine kitchen floor tiles. He began locking the doors. Then with unnerving calm, he moved around the elegant kitchen, opened one cupboard for bread, opened another that was the cleverly concealed refrigerator, took out fillings for a sandwich and made himself a snack. As he sat eating it, Joyce was dragging herself up off the floor.

As she staggered to her feet, she saw him eating and was reminded that he was stone-cold sober, yet he was still trying to kill her. All the other times, she had made herself believe that it was the drink talking, that in reality he didn't want her dead, he hadn't meant to harm her. That wasn't the real him. But now she saw that this *was* the real him. She recalled struggling to get to the rolltop desk, grabbing the .38 Colt calibre revolver she had been issued as a means of protection when she was carrying the restaurant's takings to the deposit safe at the bank.

She began running to the back door unaware that while she had blacked out on the floor, Steiner had taken the precaution of locking her in. 'He caught me and that's when we started to struggle,' she said. 'He came at me again with his head down, which was the way he would always hit me, like a football tackle. That's when I shot him. I closed my eyes and pulled the trigger.' She released one bullet into his head. It never came out.

Under Maryland law in December 1988, a defendant in a murder trial was not permitted to offer the evidence of an expert on the likelihood of her having suffered from Battered Woman Syndrome. The condition, likened to a post-traumatic stress disorder, occurs when victims fear for their lives if they leave their abusers, eventually seeing death as the only escape. They suffer from low esteem and blame themselves for the abuse. They feel trapped. Only now is it being listed in the psychiatric reference books although it had been recognised and defined for many years before Joyce Steiner faced her jury. Even if Joyce had been able to plead not guilty because she was suffering from this syndrome it is uncertain whether it would have had an effect on the members of a jury.

When the jury found this sophisticated woman guilty of second-degree murder – homicide with no justification – she was stunned. She appealed, was allowed out on bail but when the case was heard again in April she lost. The sentence of five years was, it was pointed out to her, far from the maximum. She might have been given thirty years. She should consider herself lucky.

In a sense she was lucky. And not just because she was to serve only eleven months of her sentence. She became one of what was described as the Maryland Eight. And she understood what had happened to her.

During those eleven months at the massively over-crowded Maryland Correction Institution, though, she loathed the lack of privacy and dignity, wept at the shame she had brought on her family, worried about Kim, and flinched at the cockroaches which infested the place.

She worked in the library and also attended the Wednesday night Unity sessions where abused women met to share and support each other. It was there that she heard about the work being done by a former inmate who had just been released. Leslie Ford had served five-and-a-half years for attempting to kill her abuser. When she got out she was determined to do something to change the law and, working at a battered women's refuge in Baltimore called the House of Ruth, she managed to enlist the help of a group of lawyers. During 1990 they drew up a list of twelve women who had been jailed for criminal actions relating to abuse who had not been able to give evidence of the abuse at their trials. A campaigning organisation, the Public Justice Center, backed them.

Maryland's Governor William Donald Schaefer was sent the dossiers. He said, when he had read them, that he had been greatly moved. He said that some of the women whose lives he'd read about would have been dead had they not fought back. But he said he struggled over the moral issues involved in freeing people convicted of murder and sentenced to prison terms. 'First of all you think, they committed murder. And as a lawyer, you think, all the evidence was there, what else could happen?'

He went on to say that he weighted these thoughts with the fact that evidence of abuse is not admissible as a mitigating factor in criminal trials. He concluded that most of the twelve had 'served enough time'.

'This isn't something they made up: a long history of abuse, terrible abuse.' He added that he would support a bill going through the General Assembly the following week to allow evidence of Battered Woman Syndrome at trials.

His words had been encouraging. But words are cheap. Would Schaefer risk becoming only the second state governor to commute the sentences of battered women who had killed?

The first was Richard Celeste, Governor of Ohio, who in 1990 released twenty-six women found guilty of killing brutal partners or fathers. He brought a storm of protest hailing down. Critics accused him of giving women a licence to kill.

A month after Schaefer had met some of the women at the House Of Ruth, he announced that eight of the twelve on the list would go free. In her cell Joyce was listening to the five o'clock news. 'I heard my name, then I heard women all over the place yelling and screaming,' she said.

A few days later Joyce, along with seven fellow inmates, walked out into the crisp Maryland winter. They would remain on probation for the rest of their allotted prison terms, but they were in every other respect free.

'Of course I wish that I had walked away [from my husband],' said one of Joyce's fellow released women, Mytokia Friend, a former Baltimore police officer who shot her abusive husband with her service revolver. She had served three of a fifteen year term. 'That's why I'm here, to encourage women to walk away. It isn't worth it. They don't have to walk in our footsteps.'

Joyce told reporters as she left, 'You don't have to be poor or illiterate to have the crap beat out of you!'

Today Joyce Steiner has a new partner, a man she met during her time on bail awaiting her appeal. She has a job as an executive secretary for an environmental management firm, a position she also found in those busy three months out on appeal. Her daughter Kim is the successful business woman her mother guessed she'd be and Joyce's parents and sister are as supportive and loving as she should have known they would be when she felt she couldn't tell them the truth about her life. She doesn't cook in a palatial kitchen these days. She doesn't wear Robert Steiner's large jewels. She counsels other abused women and talks to inmates on the telephone from jail. She doesn't forget what she did, ever. When she drives out of Maryland, she makes sure to check in with the sheriff of whichever state she's visiting.

Today she can joke. 'I say, "Hi, I'm that murderer from Maryland".'

The Body in the Dam

Whilst not exactly a 'Dixon of Dock Green' figure, Major D. J. H. Botha, Chief of CID in South Africa's Orange Free State, inspired considerable confidence among the country's white population. Like all good policemen, he regularly received snippets of information. Some provided that first vital clue towards solving a hitherto baffling crime, others proved worthless.

When, on 2 August 1957 a helpful member of the public gave him information regarding the disappearance of thirty-nine-year-old garage mechanic Marthinus Johannes Laubscher, Major Botha was unsure into which category it fell. Apart from anything else, he didn't even know that Laubscher was missing.

At the time, the South African police had to rely heavily on the assistance of the Whites since they were unlikely to receive much co-operation from the Black community following a series of clashes resulting from South Africa's new policy of apartheid. In June 1955, police armed with Sten guns and rifles with bayonets fixed had broken up a three-thousand-strong anti-apartheid protest in Johannesburg. As the unrest continued, the image South African police presented to the outside world was hardly one of care and consideration.

The tip-off given to Major Botha strongly implied that there was something sinister about the disappearance of Marthinus Laubscher from his home in Wepener, a small town southeast of Bloemfontein. The informer also advised the authorities to take a keen interest in Laubscher's twenty-eight-year-old wife Maria (who preferred to be known as Miemie) and the one-time family lodger, twenty-one-year-old Jacobus Frederik van Jaarsveld.

The following day, Mrs Laubscher went to Wepener charge office and officially reported her husband missing. She said he had gone to neighbouring Basutoland the previous day but had not returned. Fearing for his safety, she added that he was a heavy drinker who had incurred mounting debts. She thought that he may have fled to escape his worries.

When the news reached Major Botha, he sought out Mrs Laubscher but his suspicions were further aroused when there was no sign of either her or van Jaarsveld at the house in Wepener. Local enquiries as to Mr Laubscher's whereabouts were inconclusive. Townsfolk revealed that Mrs Laubscher and van Jaarsveld had told them too that the husband had gone away to Basutoland. Still there was no sign of wife or lodger until 6 August when Major Botha traced Mrs Laubscher to Aliwal North, where she was staying with her mother. Miemie Laubscher tried to sow the seed in the Major's mind that her husband's disappearance could have been a suicide bid. She repeated that he had been depressed about their financial situation. But after quizzing Miemie and her mother, Botha found van

Jaarsveld walking in a nearby street and promptly took him to the police station for questioning.

Van Jaarsveld's statement was markedly different. It was tantamount to a confession to murder. He said that he and Mrs Laubscher had been out for the evening of 31 July and had planned to attack her bullying, drunken husband. Returning to the Laubscher residence, he had felled Marthinus Laubscher with a blow on the back of the head from a *jukskei* (Afrikaans for a wooden ox-yoke). Van Jaarsveld and Mrs Laubscher then carried him into the bedroom and put him on the bed. Van Jaarsveld said he then left the room and Mrs Laubscher told him to come back later when her husband was asleep. He did so and tried to strangle him with a towel. When this was unsuccessful, he said Mrs Laubscher handed him a belt to perform the final act. The body was then put under the bed in a small outside room.

According to van Jaarsveld's statement, on 2 August he and Mrs Laubscher went to Basutoland and planned how to dispose of the body. In the dead of night, he then drove the corpse in a van to Rustfontein Dam near Bloemfontein. Shaken by what he had done, he sped along the dark, quiet country roads leading back to Wepener, at times reaching speeds of up to 110mph. It was a journey of some sixty miles and not long before reaching Wepener he collided with an ox (a common hazard when driving in rural South Africa, particularly at night), damaging the van in the process.

On 8 August the police decided to search the Laubschers home. They found hanging behind the bedroom door a lady's raincoat. The belt was missing. In a baby's pram in the same room lay a *jukskei*. The evidence appeared to corroborate van Jaarsveld's story.

The next day, van Jaarsveld took detectives to a spot where the Modder River entered the Rustfontein Dam. Amidst the swirling waters, divers eventually dragged a man's body from the dam. It had been weighted down with a heavy pulley wheel. The belt from a woman's coat was tied around the neck. It was bound so tightly that it could not be loosened manually – it had to be cut.

The body was subsequently identified as that of Marthinus Laubscher, the inquest revealing that he had died of strangulation. As Major Botha and his men delved into the background to Laubscher's untimely end, the story that unfolded was one of a Jekyll and Hyde husband prone to sudden violent outbursts, an errant wife and a bizarre love triangle.

The Laubschers were married in Zastron in 1950. Marthinus, who was nicknamed 'Spokies', had a drink problem even prior to his marriage. Before agreeing to become his wife, Miemie begged him to stop drinking. He agreed but, like so many premarital promises, as a statement of intent it was no more reliable than an election manifesto. The result was that just a few weeks after the wedding, he was once again hitting the bottle with a vengeance. The more he drank, the more strained their relationship became.

They argued relentlessly, often violently. After one particularly vitriolic encounter, Laubscher threatened to shoot his wife. She called the police who took possession of a .22 rifle. No charges were pressed. It has to be pointed out that Miemie Laubscher was no shrinking violet either. She too liked a drink and, increasingly disenchanted with the state of her marriage, thought about seeking solace and affection elsewhere. One night in 1953, she and another woman were enjoying an evening out when they met the dark, stocky van Jaarsveld, then just seventeen, and his brother.

With Laubscher away in Basutoland, the two boys were invited to stay the night and Miemie ended up sleeping with Jacobus. She found out that he had left home at fourteen and that, like her husband, he was a mechanic. As far as Miemie was concerned, that was where the similarity ended. When Laubscher returned the next day, van Jaarsveld was still at the house. Not altogether surprisingly, there was an almighty row. Miemie announced that she was leaving Laubscher to live with van Jaarsveld.

She later testified that her husband gave her one hour to pack her bags before throwing her and van Jaarsveld out. He also warned her against taking their two young daughters. Possibly because of his comparative youth, van Jaarsveld appeared a bewildered onlooker to this episode of matrimonial strife and any contribution he might have wished to make to the discussion was rendered immaterial when he discovered that the impulsive Miemie had already put her belongings in his car, ready for the off. Miemie and her boyfriend headed for Ladybrand and then on to Senekal, a town some one hundred miles north of Wepener, where they lived in a boarding house as man and wife.

Miemie taught Jacobus the ways of the world – including how to drink – and they cohabited harmoniously. For a start, alcohol did not have the same adverse effect on van Jaarsveld as it did on her husband. Miemie enjoyed the novel experience of not living in constant fear of being beaten up. Meanwhile, back in Wepener Laubscher was brooding. He wanted Miemie back. One night, he set off for Senekal and arrived at the boarding house to find the couple in bed. 'Evening, my sweet,' he said, standing in the doorway. Miemie simply smiled back and said, 'Oh, you know what the trouble is'.

Once again, van Jaarsveld decided to opt out of the argument, turning his back on the proceedings while Laubscher pleaded with Miemie to come home. Receiving no encouragement, Laubscher began crying and, on his way out, sobbed, 'Well, I suppose all that remains now is divorce'.

According to van Jaarsveld, the following day Laubscher told him that if he would sign a letter, a divorce could be arranged with Miemie. The one stipulation was that Laubscher would keep the children. Van Jaarsveld duly signed and the trio returned to Wepener. But against all the odds, instead of pressing ahead for a divorce, the Laubschers effected a reconciliation. Laubscher even fixed van Jaarsveld up with a job at the same garage in which he was working and, more incredibly still, allowed him to board with them.

This was not a wise move. Maybe the amount of alcohol he regularly consumed had addled Laubscher's brain for in addition he told van Jaarsveld, 'If ever you need any money, you only have to ask'. This was a decidedly strange offer since Laubscher himself was said to be in dire straits. The temptation resulting from being under the same roof proved too great for Miemie and van Jaarsveld to resist and the affair soon started up again. Inevitably, Laubscher found out was was going on behind his back and confronted them. It seems that his request to them to desist was couched in the most polite of terms, possibly more amicable ones than the situation demanded. He suggested that it would be a good idea if van Jaarsveld were to pack his bags and made him promise never to come to the house again. Van Jaarsveld agreed. But by now, van Jaarsveld said that he was under the spell of Miemie Laubscher's haunting brown eyes.

It appeared that she did not want the affair to end and wrote him a series of love letters. Van Jaarsveld's own father warned the boy to leave her alone but his words fell on deaf ears. On 14 July 1957, the Laubschers threw a party. Unfortunately, the ensuing activity bore more resemblance to open warfare than a joyous gathering.

The couple argued so bitterly that the guests thought it diplomatic to leave somewhat earlier than planned. One male guest remained and was in the sitting room a little later when he heard a commotion and gurgling sounds coming from the bathroom. There, the guest said he found Laubscher lying on his back on the floor, with Miemie sitting astride on his stomach and choking him with both hands. Laubscher was struggling to get to his feet. By the time the guest hauled Miemie off, Laubscher was partly unconscious and had to be helped to the bedroom. Yet such was the changeable, volatile nature of the Laubschers that by 11pm, they were sitting on the sofa with their arms around each other. Within three weeks, Marthinus Laubscher was dead.

After his first statement to the police, in which he took total responsibility for the killing, van Jaarsveld changed his tune. He decided that taking all the blame was 'going to get him nowhere' and, on 14 August, dictated a second statement in which he maintained instead that while he had delivered the first blow and had later helped dispose of the body, the actual murder had been carried out by Miemie Laubscher.

As a result of this new version of events, both Jacobus Frederik van Jaarsveld and Maria Magdalena Josina Laubscher were charged with murder. They were tried separately at Bloemfontein in October 1957. First to stand trial, on 14 October before Justice A. J. Smit, was van Jaarsveld. He pleaded not guilty. The court heard that on the evening of 31 July, Marthinus Laubscher remained at home with the children while van Jaarsveld and Mrs Laubscher went out for a drink. In their absence, Laubscher became exceedingly drunk, a condition exacerbated when he joined the returning duo for further drinks later that evening.

It was the last night he was seen alive – by the following day, neighbours were told he was missing. And on 3 August, van Jaarsveld and Mrs Laubscher left Wepener, bound for Rouxville. Pieter Christian de Jager, Miemie's younger brother, said he boarded with the Laubschers in Wepener during the early part of 1957. He recalled how Laubscher often drank a lot and regularly assaulted Miemie. One day, de Jager found Miemie and van Jaarsveld in an intimate position on the bed at the house. When he confronted them, they promised that it would not happen again. A garage inspector at Fraser's Ltd of Wepener remembered asking van Jaarsveld on 2 August where Marthinus Laubscher was. Van Jaarsveld replied that he had gone away and Mrs Laubscher told other enquirers the same story. Then it was van Jaarsveld's turn to give evidence. He said that on the evening of 31 July, he and Mrs Laubscher had been to a local hotel for a number of drinks. They were both very

drunk and van Jaarsveld testified that on their way back to
the house Mrs Laubscher told him to hit her husband 'with
something' when they arrived home. Van Jaarsveld said:

I wanted to use a bottle but she brought me a *jukskei*. I
hit him with it. I then went to the kitchen for a glass of
water which I gave to Mr Laubscher. Then I went
to bed.

Later, Mrs Laubscher woke me. She said, 'We can't
leave the matter like this. He will go and tell.' She told
me to strangle him. I put my hands around his throat
but he began to struggle. 'Is he dead?' she asked. 'Yes,'
I said. She then touched her husband and said, 'No, he
is still alive.' At that point, I wanted to leave him, and
I told Mrs Laubscher I was going. But she said, 'If you
do, there will be trouble between us'.

I then put my hands around his throat again but I
didn't squeeze very hard. I told Mrs Laubscher that
my hands were tired. She then produced a belt and put
it around Mr Laubscher's neck. At that point, I went
into the kitchen for a drink of water and then into the
lounge where I played some records. I was still playing
the records when Mrs Laubscher came to me and said,
'You can come and have a look now. He is dead.' I
asked her she had used a belt. She replied that she
could see that I didn't really want to kill her husband.

The body was wrapped in a blanket and hidden
under a bed in another room. The next day, Mrs Laubscher suggested tying a weight to the body and dumping it in a dam. I said I wanted to give myself up but
she wouldn't hear of it. Later, I removed the blanket

from the body before dumping it in the water.

The jury took just an hour to reach their verdict. They found Jacobus guilty of murder, but with extenuating circumstances. Watched by his parents who were among the spectators in the packed courtroom, van Jaarsveld nervously chewed his fingernails waiting for the judge to pronounce sentence. He was sentenced to fifteen years' imprisonment; the mitigating circumstances and his comparative youth saved him from the death penalty.

Three days later, it was the turn of Miemie Laubscher. She too pleaded not guilty, laying the blame firmly at the feet of her former lover. She claimed van Jaarsveld suddenly burst into the house and attacked her husband. She said she was lying in bed with her husband on the night of 31 July when she felt a kick in the side:

> I was afraid – I thought my husband was about to assault me. It would not have been the first time he had assaulted me in bed. Then I heard a commotion. It was dark and my immediate concern was for the safety of my children. I jumped out of bed, grabbed my youngest daughter, who had woken up, and went into the sitting room. As I fled from the bedroom, I heard a sort of gurgling sound on the bed.
>
> I noticed that the front door was open. I went to get a blanket but I only got as far as the bathroom when I saw van Jaarsveld.
>
> I said, 'What are you doing here?' – because he had not been asked to spend the night at the house.
>
> He asked me to come to the bedroom and said,

'Come and see. It is all over with Spokies. He got what he asked for.' He told me he'd hit my husband and strangled him. I said, 'Oh, how cruel.'

Mrs Laubscher was clearly a mistress of the understatement. She continued, 'He asked me to come and give him a hand.' I said, "Leave me alone," and I went into the kitchen. Later he told me to say that, if anyone asked, I was to say my husband had gone missing.'

Miemie Laubscher was obsessed with the fear of being attacked by her husband. She recalled how he often used to hit her. The doctor confirmed that on 7 March 1957, he treated her for slight concussion and how, on a later occasion, he found multiple bruises on her arms and legs – injuries which, he stated, could definitely have been caused by kicks and blows. Another witness described seeing Marthinus Laubscher strike his wife with a small chair.

Despite her somewhat cavalier attitude and willingness to leave the children with her drunken husband while she enjoyed a night on the town, Miemie Laubscher cared deeply for her offspring. She not only feared for her own safety but theirs too. The court heard how Laubscher used to shout and scream at the eldest daughter.

The tale of a wife trapped in a miserable marriage – remember, it was alleged that Laubscher would only grant her a divorce provided he could have custody of the children – touched many a heart in the crowded courtroom. But there were significant flaws in Miemie Laubscher's assertion that she had nothing whatsoever to do with the killing.

On the night of 2 August, the night on which the body

was dumped in Rustfontein Dam, at least two local garage attendants testified that they saw Mrs Laubscher in the van with van Jaarsveld. Then there was the belt found around the neck of the deceased. It was of the same colour and material as Mrs Laubscher's own coat.

Nor did the events at the July party enhance her case. She stated that the scuffle in the bathroom began after her husband had suddenly grabbed her. Whoever was the instigator, one of the family's servants said that as Mrs Laubscher was pulled off her husband, she was screaming, 'Let go of me. He must die.'

The servants also recalled how, after the husband's sudden disappearance, Mrs Laubscher had told them that he had gone to Basutoland, adding, 'Now that the baas [boss] is not here, we will have a nice time.'

Even more damning was the testimony of the dead man's mother, Mrs Jacomina Laubscher. She revealed that on 10 July 1957, Miemie had come to her house and said, 'Mammy, I am going to hit Marthinus with a piece of iron. I am going to kill him. I want my children and I want to go.' The mother-in-law replied, 'Take your children and go, but don't kill my boy. He does not deserve it.'

She added that on two other occasions, she had heard Miemie threaten to kill Marthinus. Things did not look good for Miemie Laubscher. In his closing speech, her defence counsel, Mr H. R. Jacobs, told the jury that they must not try her on her morals. He said she was as entitled to her moral standards as they, or any individual, were to theirs. But this was the 1950s and women were not supposed to stray, no matter how appallingly they were treated at home. The jury found her guilty of murder but 'with extenuating circumstances'.

Pleading for her life after the verdict, Mr Jacobs told the judge, 'The accused has had a most unhappy home life. She was suffering from mental strain and shock when the crime was committed. Remember her children. Her love for them has played a great part in this sad case.'

The case had certainly captured the imagination of the Bloemfontein public and a crowd of four hundred turned up to hear the sentence pronounced. Bearing in mind the jury's recommendation for mercy, the judge, who had warned them against prejudging the issue in the light of the guilty verdict returned against van Jaarsveld, sentenced Miemie Laubscher to twelve years in prison. On hearing the sentence, she was close to fainting before the attendant matron took her arm and led her back down the stairs to the cells.

Miemie Laubscher paid a heavy price for ridding herself of her bullying husband.

Kill Her as Well

Ex-miner Tom Veitch was an enterprising soul. He had discovered that there were plentiful supplies of coke to be found buried along a footpath near his home in Seaham, a close-knit community to the south of Sunderland in the heart of Britain's industrial northeast.

The footpath had been created on the site of a disused mineral line which once carried coal trains on the three-mile journey from Murton Colliery to Seaham Harbour. Tom Veitch had started digging into the side of the old line to recover coke which had been left there from its operating days. It was an ongoing job. He had carved out a large hole, leaving it at the end of the day before returning at a later date to gather more fuel from his secret mine.

On Tuesday 8 August 1989, with eager anticipation, he arrived at the spot at Cold Hesledon, half-a-mile east of the Pemberton Arms public house, only to find that the hole had been filled in. Puzzled, he started digging but, not unreasonably, lost his appetite for the task when his excavations unearthed a human body.

The body, that of a burly, pony-tailed man, was identified as forty-one-year-old Michael Meade, a car dealer of Cliffe

Park in the Roker district of Sunderland. A length of wire was twisted around his neck. The subsequent postmortem confirmed that he had died from asphyxiation. Medical evidence pointed to the murder having been committed on or around Monday 7 August.

The first task of the police was to establish why anyone would want Michael Meade dead. As they looked into his background, it did not take them long to establish a motive. His domestic life was, to say the least, turbulent and within two days his common-law wife, thirty-three-year-old Susan Harrison, was arrested and charged with his murder. When interviewed by police, she claimed to have suffered 'ten years of sheer hell' at the hands of Meade. She went on to admit being involved in his death and even to being present when he was killed, but insisted that she herself did not murder him. And she steadfastly refused to name the person or persons responsible.

The eldest of three children, pretty ash-blonde Susan Harrison was a bright girl who attended Sunderland's Bede Grammar School. She had worked as a civil servant for the Department of Health and Social Security at Phoenix House, Sunderland, and as a nurse at Ryhope General Hospital in the town.

Susan's family and friends described her as a 'happy-go-lucky' girl. In 1979, while working as a barmaid at the Seaburn Hotel, she met Meade who was a disc jockey there. She quickly fell for his chat-up lines and smooth patter. They set up home in a flat on the upper floor of a house in Cliffe Park and enjoyed the good life with his income from a second-hand car business and money left to him by relatives. Meanwhile, she operated a little cottage industry from the flat, making women's underwear.

The future seemed rosy for Susan Harrison, but she was soon to find out how little she really knew about Michael Meade. A former public schoolboy, Meade had been devastated by the death of his mother when he was a teenager but overcame his grief by throwing himself into the business of making money. His search for wealth began when he was just seventeen. He set up his own businesses in Sunderland and started recording local rock music groups who wanted to send demonstration discs to record companies. His capital at that time was a few thousand pounds borrowed from his grandmother who owned part of a family run garage firm in the northeast.

By the time Meade closed his Wearside premises to move to Newcastle, he had not only repaid the loan but still had money in the bank. Operating from a basement office on the North Road leading out of Newcastle, he expanded his business to include a recording studio, a mobile discotheque and the manufacture of sound cabinets for rock bands.

He saw himself as a young tycoon and, in a newspaper interview in 1969 (by which time he was twenty-one), he summed up his philosophy as 'work equals success'. He boasted of monthly earnings almost four times the national average yet still he said it was not enough. He was driven to make more and more money.

Meade's financial status, allied to a wit and charm which could make him the life and soul of the party, attracted an endless stream of women to his bed. But then, at the age of twenty-two, he underwent surgery and lengthy treatment for a brain tumour. As a result, he appeared to suffer a dramatic personality change. From then on, he suddenly began to squander his hard-earned cash on gambling, expensive clothes and fast cars. By 1971, he was driving an E-type Jaguar. He was a regular customer at a petrol station on Newcastle's West Road where the forecourt attendant was an attractive twenty-two-year-old named Joan.

One day, he turned up with a glamorous girl in the passenger seat. He filled the car up, walked into the garage and threw two tickets to Tenerife down on the counter.

Joan later recalled, 'He told me that he had been planning to go on holiday with the woman in the car but he was going to finish with her and wanted to take me instead. I was absolutely amazed and I turned him down because I didn't even know him.'

When Meade returned from Tenerife, he continued visiting Joan until eventually she agreed to go out with him. They got engaged and she moved into a house in Beatrice Street, Sunderland, with Meade and his father. It was then that Meade started behaving aggressively towards her, sometimes beating her to keep her quiet. Since he was beginning to spend money at an alarming rate, he demanded that she bring her wage packet home unopened and give it to him.

He began to decide what she should wear and exactly how she should look, forcing her to go out and buy bright lipstick, short skirts and sexy tops. He even had her fitted up with tarty wigs and hairpieces, which she hated. He would fly into rages and lose his temper over minor things, regularly throwing objects about the room.

Hardly surprisingly, Joan concluded that marriage to this man was no longer a particularly appealing idea. She returned to her parents' home and sent back his ring, together with a note terminating their engagement. Meade promised faithfully that he would change his ways and managed to win her back.

On 22 December 1973, they married. By Boxing Day, she had a gashed eye after another beating. She said, 'He openly flirted with every woman in sight and even showed me lovebites and scratches on his back, which he got while having sex with other girls'.

Shortly afterwards, Joan left him and went back to her parents' house. But Meade came after her in a blinding rage and smashed all the windows of the house with bricks. He also held a knife to Joan's throat and threatened to kill her and her mother and father. Seeing no escape from Meade's evil clutches, she swallowed two bottles of his headache tablets in desperation. When she came round, she was in hospital. After Meade's grandmother had been to visit her, he agreed to allow Joan to return to her parents' home. However he grabbed Joan in the street and took her back to the flat they had shared.

Virtually a prisoner, she realised that the only way to be free of him was to flee abroad. Promising her parents that under no circumstances would she ever go back to him, she escaped to Spain where she landed a job as a holiday courier. Even there, she lived in fear of Meade at first and constantly changed jobs and locations in the hope that he would not be able to catch up with her.

She later said she definitely believed he could have tracked her down in Spain as he was capable of doing anything he had set his mind to. Such was the terrifying hold he exercised over her. In the end, Joan remained in

Spain for seven years before deciding it was safe to return to England. She sighed, 'Marrying Michael Meade was the biggest mistake of my life'. She went on to describe him as an evil man who behaved like an animal. Filled with hatred, she had often considered knifing him but although she had wished him dead many times, she had never found the courage to put her thoughts into practice.

But perhaps the biggest tragedy of all was that she had never met Susan Harrison, the woman who was to take Joan's place as Meade's punchbag. In fact, the first time they set eyes on one another was when Joan Davis, as she had become, gave evidence at Newcastle Crown Court in May 1990. And standing in the dock, jointly accused of Meade's murder, was Susan Harrison.

Back in 1979 Susan had been madly in love with Meade and, although they were not married, she soon became pregnant with their first daughter, Shelley. At first, Meade had been caring and attentive towards Susan but that all changed when she was expecting Shelley. He punched her in the stomach several times during her pregnancy, and frequently hit her with a belt or with an old police truncheon which he kept in the flat. His rages were uncontrollable.

She later recounted how he would explode at her if he found any dust in the house or, as on one occasion, if the cups were put away with the handles facing the wrong way. He grabbed all the crockery from the cupboards and hurled it at her before forcing her to clean up the mess in front of her friends. When they had gone, just to make sure she had learned her lesson, he beat her savagely.

Susan's friends often saw her sporting black eyes and

bruises but she did not dare go to her doctor about her injuries since Meade had warned her things would be worse if she did. Once, he threatened to pour boiling water over her if she complained to anyone. Even after the birth of Shelley, he maintained an attitude of undisguised malevolence.

He displayed no fatherly concern for the baby. Indeed, he showed no interest in her whatsoever, refusing to hold her or even call her by her name. Susan thought about leaving him nine times in all. 'I used to say that I would leave him,' she said, 'but he would just laugh in my face and say it wouldn't be healthy for either me or the baby if I did.'

He told Susan Harrison that the only way she would ever leave would be in a coffin. Because of the way Meade had treated little Shelley, Susan had no desire to have another child by him. But he ordered her to stop taking the pill. Fearful of the consequences if she disobeyed him, she yielded to his demands and in 1982, two years after the birth of Shelley, their second daughter, Prophecy, was born. Nothing changed. He continued to torture Susan but what really petrified her was the way he treated the children. While they were still just toddlers, they were subjected to fearful beatings and mental abuse.

He would lash them with his belt if they wandered into rooms where they were not allowed and, as a further punishment, he would make them stay in their rooms for up to three days without food. The door handles were removed so they could not escape and Susan was reduced to finding a way of sneaking food into them when Meade was not around. Meade thought nothing of leaving the children alone in the flat or of putting them outside, in all weathers, in a tiny pen measuring five feet square. When Prophecy was just two, she fell out of an upstairs window.

Susan returned home from work to find a note from a neighbour saying she had discovered the girl lying with a broken leg and had taken her to hospital. When Meade was told what had happened he replied, 'Stupid kid'. He then nailed a roof on the cot to make sure she could not get out again.

Sometimes Meade would make the children watch him and Susan having sex by shouting to them to come into the bedroom. As with his first wife, Meade controlled how Susan looked, telling her what to wear, how to wear her hair and how much make-up to apply. He would not allow her to dress in clothes he did not like and instead forced her to wear clothes which she described in court as 'tarty'.

He then delighted in publicly humiliating her by putting his hand up her skirt and calling her 'slag' and 'prostitute'. On a number of occasions, he told her he had thought about putting her and the children 'on the game'. She later told the court that when his business friends called round to their home, he ordered her to dress up in sexy underwear and then allowed his friends to fondle her in exchange for cash. She said Meade watched while this was going on and seemed to enjoy it.

Meade often used to bind her up with tape when they were having sex, frequently striking her at the same time.

He would photograph the two of them having sex by using a timing device and ordered her to take sexy satin underwear and suspenders along with her on visits to the North Sea ferry on which he worked for four months as a disc jockey. Over the last few months of his life, he also made her wear a plastic mac when they were having sex because he did not like her skin touching his. Whenever she told Meade how much she hated the things he was making her do, he coldly replied, 'Tough'.

It was from around February 1989 onwards that Meade's behaviour deteriorated even further. Banned from using his car because of drinking and driving, he started flying from Newcastle Airport to Leeds where he spent days and nights gambling in casinos and staying in top hotels. He ran up massive debts by his gambling and was only able to fund that particular habit by operating an insurance fraud.

His absences provided a merciful relief for Susan and the girls although he had forbidden her to visit her parents. When he was back in Sunderland, he was more brutally tyrannical than ever. Susan lost around two stone in weight. Her younger sister Elaine said later; 'Susan was very disturbed. She was extremely thin, haggard-looking, and nervous. She smoked all the time and ate very little.'

Meade talked openly to his friends about killing Susan and the children and of running away to the South of France where he would 'blow' his cash and spectacularly commit suicide.

It was then that Susan Harrison decided that the only way out of her and her children's nightmare was to have Michael Meade murdered. She had become friends with a woman named Rhonda Stoker to whom she recounted the graphic details of Meade's disgusting activities. Miss Stoker advised her to leave him, but Susan said that no matter where she went he would find her. And the consequences did not bear thinking about. Rhonda Stoker later testified, 'She said she wanted him killed and asked me if I knew anyone who could get rid of him'.

The court heard that a couple of months later, in June, Miss Stoker put Susan in touch with twenty-one-year-old Danny Boyes, a doorman at the Victoria public house in Sunderland. They first met at the Shipwright hostelry in the North Hylton district of the town.

After asking Susan why she wanted Meade killed, Boyes took down details about his lifestyle and asked for a photograph of him. A number of subsequent meetings took place between them and thirty-four-year-old Clifton Britton, the head doorman at the Victoria, to discuss the plan to kill Meade.

Initially, a sum of £5,000 was agreed but the price later trebled. So desperate was she to be free from Meade that Susan Harrison was not deterred by the sudden inflation, despite the fact that in order to raise the £15,000 she would have to sell the flat. The contract killing was put on hold for a while but then Meade's violence and cruelty escalated to an even more hideous level.

On Sunday 30 July, Meade held a Stanley knife against Susan's throat, telling her to watch out because the time was getting close to kill her and the children. He added that it was just a taste of things to come.

The following Saturday, 5 August, he viciously beat nine-year-old Shelley with a belt and forced her to sit in the kitchen for three hours without moving, simply because she had left a fingerprint on the lens of his precious camera. Susan was so distressed that in the afternoon she took the girls round to the home of a friend, Sandra Anderson. Susan told her that Shelley had been crying for four hours because of her ordeal at the hands of Meade. Mrs Anderson said that the girl's eyes were swollen with crying.

For Susan Harrison, that was the final nail in Meade's coffin. Bitterly upset, she told Sandra Anderson, 'This is it, it has to happen tonight'. Susan herself later admitted, 'I wanted him dead from June, but this just made me more upset than I had ever been before. I thought to myself, he is going to die.' So that night, the plan for the murder of Michael Meade was put into operation.

Susan and Meade left the Shagorika Indian Restaurant at Seaburn shortly after midnight. She drove him west in their Volkswagen Sirocco to a secluded spot down a country lane next to the River Wear. The location was not far from the busy A19 road which links Teesside, Wearside and Tyneside, but it was far enough to ensure total privacy. The couple lay on a blanket on a grassy bank, ready to have sex. As Meade became increasingly aroused, Danny Boyes stepped out of the darkness brandishing a shotgun. Meade was caught at his most vulnerable. Not only were his trousers down, his defences were too.

At gunpoint, Boyes ordered Meade into the back of Susan's car, telling him that someone wanted to see him. It was to be made to look like a kidnapping. Boyes told Susan to drive and directed her to the 'death place', a field a few miles away near Hylton Bridge next to the Wear. The car lights were turned off and Meade was ordered out. He was forced to lie face down on the ground. There, he was strangled with the wire.

Then things started to go wrong.

There was no sign of the back-up car, to be driven by Clifton Britton, and so the body had to be transported in the boot of Susan's own vehicle – hardly the best way of guaranteeing her immunity from forensic evidence. And as Meade's body was being dragged into the car, his foot smashed a brake light. On the drive back to Sunderland, the police, spotting the broken light, actually followed the car for a while but, to the immense relief of the living occupants, did not stop it.

On the Sunday morning, a friend of Meade's, Avelino Riovieros, called at the house. He was supposed to be meeting Meade to attend a car auction that day. He was to testify that Susan Harrison came to the gate and told him her husband had gone away taking £15,000, his passport and driving licence. He thought she seemed nervous. For most of the Sunday, Meade's body remained in the boot of the car on the drive outside the Cliffe Park flat. Then, shortly before 4pm, Susan drove it to nearby Roker block yard for collection.

Her friend Rhonda Stoker was to testify that later that night she received a phone call from an anxious Susan, saying that the car was still at the block yard. Nobody had been to collect it. Susan picked Stoker up and they drove there. The car was still parked where it had been left with its gruesome contents. Danny Boyes was supposed to arrange for the disposal of the body but, after the killing, he suffered post-traumatic shock syndrome and vanished for three days, going on a wild drinking spree to erase the memory of his participation.

The two women went back to Cliffe Park and waited for another nail-biting half-hour before Susan returned to the block yard. At last, the car had gone. Stoker said that Susan had told her the body would be buried by two men (each of whom were paid £500 and never traced) and it would be rendered unidentifiable.

But the mystery burial squad had reckoned without Tom Veitch and his quest for coke. For just when it seemed that Susan Harrison was free from Michael Meade, he came back to haunt her.

Two days after the body was removed, Tom Veitch dug him up again. And when Susan saw a story in the *Sunderland Echo* headed PONYTAIL MURDER she realised that despite all the careful preparations Meade had been found. She knew she would have to go to the police. The day after Susan was arrested, Boyes and Britton were picked up. A number of people had known about their involvement in the murder plot – indeed the biggest surprise was that Michael Meade had never got to hear about it.

The three were charged with murder.

When Susan Harrison appeared before Peterlee magistrates on 11 August her solicitor appealed, 'Over the last few days she has suffered a terrible trauma, but it is nothing compared to the trauma of the last ten years at the hands of Mr Meade. For a period of ten years the torture which she and her children have undergone would be difficult to explain in the short time the court has here. It has been gross, but she has always been prevented by him from obtaining any medical assistance which now makes it difficult for me to get any evidence.'

The trial began at Newcastle Crown Court on 8 May 1990. All three defendants pleaded not guilty. Prosecuting counsel, Stephen Williamson QC, said that Meade had been killed by a wire twisted round his neck with a piece of wooden dowelling. The dowel, which had been attached to the wire, was found at the scene of the crime. He alleged that while Meade lay face down, Boyes put the wire round the victim's neck, held it together behind the neck and pulled it tight. Susan Harrison told the police that she had stayed in the car and had heard the sounds of death from there, but Boyes maintained that he had been unable to finish the job and that it was Harrison who had pulled on the wire until Meade was dead.

Home Office pathologist Dr James Sunter's examination of the line left by the wire around Meade's throat showed that it had been pulled hard and steadily, suggesting that only one person had been involved. If there had been a change of hands, he said he would have expected a blurring of the line. But Mr Williamson said the Crown submitted that both Harrison and Boyes had been together at the scene and were equally guilty.

As for Britton, Mr Williamson claimed that he was to lead the way to the 'death place' in another car with Harrison following. But in fact Britton deliberately got lost on the fatal night as he had decided that he wanted no part in the proceedings.

Rhonda Stoker gave an insight into Susan Harrison's life of hell with Meade. She said that when Meade locked the children in their rooms, they would cry for their mother night after night. And even though Susan begged him, he would not allow her to see them until he thought they had been punished sufficiently. Of the murder plot, Stoker told the jury that at first Boyes gave the impression that two other people, on the run and involved with the IRA, would carry out the killing for £5,000. But then the price went up and Boyes told Susan he would be doing the killing himself as the other people had 'chickened out'.

Rhonda Stoker said, 'I didn't really believe it would come to anything. I expected Danny just to take the money and do nothing for it.' She said that the morning after the killing, Susan telephoned her and told her what had happened.

Along with two other women, Sandra Anderson and Barbara Turnbull, Rhonda Stoker went to the flat at Cliffe Park. There Susan told them that the body was in the boot of her Volkswagen car which was parked on her drive. She was concerned because Meade's body was still there but said that someone would be coming for it at 4pm. Miss Stoker said the other two women did not believe Susan's story and asked to see the body in the boot. Susan refused.

Sandra Anderson testified that on numerous occasions she had see Susan with black eyes, bruises on her arms and once with a tooth missing. She said that Susan had often complained to her that Meade beat her up and hit the children with a belt. A few months before his death, Susan had told her that she had had enough of him because he had threatened to kill her and the children. Mrs Anderson told the court that Meade was not the sort of man you could say no to.

Despite Anderson's opposition, he had used her home as a mailing address for a credit card fiddle. (The court was told that police investigations into Meade's finances showed he had debts of over £41,800 to twenty-seven credit card companies when he died. This amount had been significantly reduced prior to his death by Meade fraudulently claiming sickness insurance on the loans.) Mrs Anderson added that, even though there were guests in the house at the time, Meade would often order Susan along to the bedroom for sex. She said her friend would always do as she was told because she was so afraid of him.

'Sue always had a bad time with him, but in the last few months she was going through hell.' In the early hours of the Sunday morning Susan had telephoned her to say Meade was dead, but Mrs Anderson said that because she was still half asleep, she had not really taken her seriously.

Both Danny Boyes and Susan Harrison remained adamant that the other had carried out the actual killing. Boyes, who had split from his wife and children, was later described by friends as living in a fantasy land when he agreed to take part in the plot to kill Michael Meade. After placing the wire around Meade's neck, Boyes was said to have told police that Meade began coughing as the wire was tightened. He claimed he was unable to go through with it and told Susan Harrison that if she wanted the job doing, she would have to do it herself.

He said that Harrison, who had been watching through an open car window, then got out of the car and started tightening the wire. Boyes added that she had been shouting abuse at him. 'She said if I did not carry it out, I could end up in trouble or my family could end up being killed. She then started telling me about all sorts of people Michael knew.' As Meade lay dead, Boyes vomited violently.

When Susan Harrison took the stand, her account of life with Michael Meade prompted such lurid headlines as WIFE TELLS OF DEMAND FOR KINKY SEX and MY FONDLE-FOR-CASH SESSIONS BY ACCUSED. Alternating between outward calmness and moments when she sat sobbing with her head in her hands, she recounted the beatings and batterings inflicted on both her and the children.

On one occasion in 1984 when she had to go into hospital for an operation after a lump was found in her breast,

Meade told her he hoped she had cancer and that she would die in agony. She said she finally made up her mind to have him murdered because she could see no other way out.

She told the jury, which included four women, that she was over the moon after Meade had been killed. Attempting to explain the dead man's behaviour, a neurosurgeon revealed that Meade suffered from depression and had psychological problems because he could not come to terms with being an epileptic. He often complained of severe head pains, apparently caused by the surgery he underwent to remove the brain tumour. The pains appeared to be aggravated by alcohol.

Although there was still conflicting evidence as to who had killed Meade, Paul Worsley QC, defending Susan Harrison, told the jury that they no longer only had to decide whether or not she was guilty of murder – they could return a verdict of manslaughter on the grounds of either provocation or diminished responsibility. The public gallery was packed throughout the trial but an eerie hush fell over the courtroom when, on the eleventh day of the trial, after over three hours' deliberation, the jury delivered their verdicts.

All three defendants were cleared of murder. Clifton Britton walked free; Danny Boyes was found guilty of attempted murder and sentenced to ten years in prison; Susan Harrison was convicted of manslaughter on the grounds of provocation and sentenced to seven years' imprisonment. Sentencing her, Mr Justice Waite commented that she had been driven to 'extreme desperation' but said that there were confidential agencies she should have turned to.

Speaking to the *Daily Express* while in Low Newton

Remand Centre, County Durham, awaiting trial, Susan Harrison recalled Michael Meade's murder:

> I watched in the wing mirror of my car as a wire was pulled round his neck. I wanted to make sure he was dead and out of my life for good.
>
> His actions in the minutes before he died sums him up. We had arranged to make it look as though I was also being kidnapped. When a gun was pointed at his head and he was going to die he said, 'Kill her as well'.

After the verdict, her nineteen-year-old sister Elaine said, 'Susan was prepared for the worst. But she used to say that, even if she was given a life sentence, it could not be as bad as another ten years with him.'

Seduction at the
Hairnet Factory

George Watson was looking forward to the prospect of lunch. It presented him with the one opportunity each day to escape from the stuffy confines of the Brooklyn hairnet factory which he owned. Added to which, with a workforce composed predominantly of women, he relished the chance of being able to rest his aching eardrums for an hour or so from their idle chatter. He had nothing against women – quite the contrary in fact – but he believed that there were times when they should be seen and not heard. And that included the hours in which they worked.

So that lunchtime of 26 January 1872, Watson left his third-floor office in a buoyant mood. Wrapped up against the bitterly cold New York winter air, into which he was about to step in search of local delicacies, he began the descent of the stairs towards ground level. His progress was quickly halted, however, when on the landing he encountered one of his employees, a pretty eighteen-year-old girl named Fanny Hyde. But Fanny was more than just another of his working girls – she had been his unwilling lover for the past three years.

George Watson thought nothing untoward about

Fanny's presence on the landing – until, that is, he spotted a small gun in her hand. Before he had time to plead for his life, the young girl raised the weapon and shot him once in the head. Watson slumped to the floor. Death was as instantaneous as it was unexpected. A rivulet of blood trickled gently from the fatal wound. It seemed inconceivable that such a deadly deed could produce so little in the way of blood, that the spark of life could be extinguished so quickly. Yet it had taken Fanny Hyde just a split second to put an end to the repeated atrocities to which she had been subjected since entering George Watson's employment.

Those first eighteen years of Fanny's life had been filled with misery. As Fanny Windley, she was born in 1854 in Nottingham, the lace-making capital of England. Her first taste of tragedy came at the tender age of four when her mother died.

Fanny's education was minimal and, with the family income depleted by the loss of her mother, she was put out to work at the age of eight. Since the Act of 1833 it had been illegal to employ children under nine (except in silk factories), but employers were wont to overlook such matters. Besides, the likelihood of Fanny being able to lay her hands on her birth certificate was remote to say the least. And because her family needed the money, she was unlikely to tell anyone that she was an under-age worker. If anybody queried the situation, she simply told them that she was a young looking ten-year-old. Nobody was any the wiser.

Two years later, the Windley family left England bound for the United States. But a change of scenery brought little respite to Fanny's life of hard labour and no sooner had the ship docked than she was found work in a factory. Then when she was fifteen, she took a job with George Watson's hairnet manufacturers. Making hairnets might not have been the dream of every young girl but it was steady work and the conditions were an improvement on those she had experienced in England. And to a vulnerable lass in the big city, Watson himself seemed a suitable moral guardian.

At forty-five he was a respectable family man with a doting wife and five children. It appeared that no parent could wish for their daughter to be in safer hands than those of Mr Watson. But the hands of this pillar of New York commerce proved to be anything but safe. They had a marked tendency to wander. Some of the other girls had heard rumours to that effect. 'You ought to watch him,' they told Fanny.

'Oh surely not,' she said disbelievingly. 'He seems so decent and honourable. Anyway,' she added as an after-thought, 'I think I can take care of myself.'

It was not long before Fanny was forced to put her words into practice. She had been aware that Watson found her attractive. Indeed, most men did. But his words and actions were inoffensive at first – nothing more than the occasional affectionate smile, a paternal hand on the shoulder or a verbal compliment about her hair or clothes. At that stage, there was absolutely no hint that his designs were of a more carnal nature.

Fanny had been there for some four months when her illusions were dramatically shattered. One evening, she found herself the last to leave. All the other girls had gone home; the factory was deserted apart from herself and

Watson. 'Come into my office,' he suggested.

Fanny saw no reason to decline his invitation. She was less sure when he locked the door behind her. He then proceeded to have sex with her. Quite how compliant Fanny was remains open to question. Certainly there was no claim that Watson had raped her on this occasion so it can be assumed that she consented to a degree. It would seem that, after her initial reservations, she was flattered by the boss's attentions, intrigued by the thought of having sex with an older, experienced man.

One thing is certain however. No matter what her feelings were at the time, Fanny deeply regretted the incident afterwards. She wanted nothing more to do with Watson. As far as she was concerned it had been a momentary lapse which must not be repeated. She was determined to keep her distance from him in future.

Unfortunately, Watson had other ideas. He clearly had no intention of backing off. Perhaps he regarded ready access to his workers as a boss's perk. Hard though she tried to keep out of his way, taking particular care to make sure that she was never alone with him, he always contrived to find methods of manoeuvring her into compromising situations. He continued to pester her with even greater vigour than before. The sex sessions resumed. Fanny's protests fell on deaf ears.

She pleaded with him to leave her alone and when he refused, she realised that she had little alternative but to seek employment elsewhere. 'I don't want to go but I'm going to have to leave,' she told him. 'I can't go on like this. I can't take any more.' But it was not that simple.

'Just you try!' warned Watson. 'If you leave here, I'll make sure you never work anywhere else in this city.'

Fanny did not take his threat lightly. She knew he exerted considerable influence among New York's smaller businessmen. A wrong word from him and she could find it extremely difficult to find another job. And she could not risk the prospect of long-term unemployment. So reluctantly she stayed at George Watson's hairnet factory, forced to concede that the power and control he wielded over her was, for the time being, insurmountable.

Fanny found herself in an impossible situation. The only way she could hang on to her job and therefore help to support the family, was by having sex with a man she had grown to loathe. And she was too ashamed to tell her brother or father that she had initially succumbed to Watson's charms – that was not the sort of thing a girl did in those days, particularly one who was just fifteen years old.

Given the frequency of Watson's demands, it should have come as little surprise to Watson that Fanny eventually fell pregnant. But he was not prepared for this. The scandal could ruin him, destroy his image of respectability. It would not only seriously damage his standing in the business community but it would surely wreck his marriage. He could not allow any of these things to happen and so he slipped Fanny some mysterious medicine to induce an abortion.

Although the medicine had the desired effect, it also brought about a noticeable deterioration in Fanny's health. In no time at all, she lost in the region of 2 stone, her friends observing that 'her flesh simply fell away'. Slowly she recovered, but remained more determined than ever to free herself from the fearsome hold which Watson exercised over her.

When she was eighteen, Fanny found what appeared to

be the ideal escape route – marriage to another man. She met a young lad by the surname of Hyde. He was no means wealthy but he was sincere and she was willing to have him. But before she could contemplate marrying her new beau, she knew that she had to rid herself of the unwanted attentions of George Watson. She decided to appeal to her boss's religious instincts.

Fanny cornered Watson one day. She began, 'I want you to promise with your hand on the Bible that you will leave me alone in future'. Watson looked puzzled. 'Why?' he demanded. 'Because I am to be married soon,' replied Fanny. Watson gave the matter due consideration. 'Very well, I promise,' he said and proceeded to place his hand on the Holy Book and repeat Fanny's words.

But George Watson was not a man to keep his word – not where women were concerned. To him, swearing on the Bible was not binding. So while Fanny basked in the afterglow of her wedding, thinking all her troubles were over, Watson knew differently – she was in for a rude awakening. They were only just beginning. Like a hound pursuing a fawn, Watson renewed the hunt when Fanny returned to work and he became increasingly violent in his lust. The more she protested, the more he chased her. It became apparent that the only course of action was to do something she should have done a long time ago – tell her family.

'I have a confession to make,' she told her husband one night, 'something which has been preying on my mind for a long time but something which I have dared not tell you.'

This was not what a husband wished to hear from his new bride. She continued, 'My employer, Mr Watson, he pesters me so. He will not leave me alone – even though I beg him.'

'How long has this been going on?' asked the anxious spouse. 'Over three years,' answered Fanny. 'Ever since I went to work for him.' She then spilled out the details of the sex sessions, pleading for forgiveness.

But young Hyde was not angry with Fanny. On the contrary, he sympathised with her plight and he swore to make Watson keep his hands off her once and for all.

When the two came face to face, it was a boy versus a man. Watson not only had the advantage of years and wealth but also of education and power. Hyde was totally overshadowed. He put on a brave show, however, and made Watson promise to leave Fanny alone. Not wishing to create a scene and, perhaps a mite worried by the younger man's physical power, Watson acquiesced. But as with his previous promise, it was utterly worthless.

As he continued to maul and molest Fanny, Watson received another visit – this time from her brother. The conversation and outcome were much the same. By now, Fanny was beside herself with anguish. She saw no escape from Watson. Her husband could not afford to take her away from the hairnet factory and so she was stuck with this intolerable situation. Those closest to her had failed her. And so on that fateful January lunchtime, she took the law into her own hands.

As the police clamoured around Watson's body, wondering who could have perpetrated such a terrible deed, they did not have long to wait for the answer. Within a few hours of the killing, Fanny surrendered to the authorities. She readily admitted shooting Watson and, despite the background circumstances, deeply regretted it.

Fanny Hyde stood trial on a charge of first-degree murder in the Court of Oyer and Terminer, Brooklyn, on 15 April 1872 before Judge Tappan. District Attorney Winchester Britton conducted the prosecution while Samuel Morris appeared for the defence. The *New York Times* reported that, 'Great interest was felt in the case and the Court-room was filled with spectators, among whom were a number of ladies'.

They were all eager for a glimpse of the unfortunate Fanny. Sitting between her father and her husband, she listened intently as her defence counsel argued that the case was one of justifiable homicide, that the accused had acted in self-defence. Mr Morris told the jury that far from lying in wait for George Watson at lunchtime on 26 January, Fanny had 'met the deceased at the top of the stairs, and when she went upstairs and reached the top, he suddenly seized on her with violence, in an indecent manner and insisted upon her accompanying him to an improper place. And they had a struggle ... and then it was that she shot him.'

This account did not, of course, explain what Fanny was doing with a gun in the first place. Morris also claimed that at the time of the killing not only was Fanny acting in defence of her honour but she was suffering from temporary insanity. He said that the seeds of this insanity were sown three years previously when she had first been seduced by George Watson. He added that since then 'her health had become broken and she a wreck, that she was suffering from disease at the time, that her mind was at the time affected, under great strain, the sense of some great wrong pressing upon it, great grief, and all these things existing at the time. Add to that this assault made upon her by this man, and, like the touching of the match to the powder, it exploded, and she became irresponsible.'

According to Morris, Fanny's insanity was a condition known as transitoria mania, a disease which had the benefit, or otherwise, of coming and going as it pleased. It was a new one to most members of the jury. To further their understanding, therefore, the defence attorney arranged for a definitive description of the illness, written by medical expert Dr William Hammond, to be read to the court. In it, Dr Hammond wrote, 'There is a form of insanity, which, in its culminating act is extremely temporary in its character, and which, in all its manifestations, from beginning to end, is of that duration. . . . By authors it has been variously designated as transitoria mania, ephemeral mania, temporary insanity, and morbid impulse. It may be exhibited in the perceptional, intellectual, emotional or volitional form, or as general mania.'

Dr Hammond's piece added that the symptoms could be brought on by all manner of everyday occurrences, including air pollution, dampness and menstruation. He was leaving little room for prosecution manoeuvre.

Other eminent medical men were called to testify. As well as describing the temporary insanity, they drew attention to the peculiar mental effect exerted upon teenagers such as Fanny Hyde during menstrual periods, one which could extend to the point of manifesting itself in a series of hysterical fits. Clearly no girl in such a state would be in control of either her emotions or actions.

In addition, Morris was at pains to recount the traumatic life of young Fanny Hyde at the hands of George Watson –

how she had been seduced, aborted, physically and mentally abused, her health and sanity torn to shreds. Finally, having repeatedly sought refuge from these assaults, she was subjected to another fearful attack. She had no option but to fell her assailant. Fanny herself took the stand to relate these events with a calmness and maturity which belied her tender years. Members of the all-male jury frequently sobbed at hearing her moving evidence.

The defence seized the opportunity of invoking the jury's moral outrage, drawing comparisons with two similar case of recent years, the trials of Amelia Norman and Mary Harris.

Miss Norman had been cruelly seduced at sixteen by New York merchant Henry Ballard before being impregnated by him and dumped in a brothel. She took her revenge by stabbing him. He survived the attack but she stood trial in 1844, charged with intent to kill. She was acquitted.

From the age of nine, Mary Harris, one of a poor Irish family in Burlington, Iowa, worked at a fancy goods store. One of the customers, Adoniram Burroughs, took great pleasure in fondling the girl and stealing kisses. Many years later, he persuaded Mary to come to Chicago under the pretence that they would be married. He repeatedly postponed the nuptials until one day in 1863 Mary read that he had married another. She sought him out in Washington and shot him dead. She too was found not guilty of murder and set free.

Samuel Morris argued that Fanny Hyde came from a similar mould – poor and trusting – and that she too had been seduced and treated appallingly, even to the point of violence, by a much older man. (Watson had often pushed her around and forced her to have sex.)

Morris appealed to the jurymen's paternal nature, 'Gentlemen, if you go home tonight and your daughter tells you that some villain has ruined her, you will not wait, the instinct of your nature will not permit you to wait a moment until you have avenged her dishonour in the blood of her seducer'.

Another of her attorneys was even more forceful. 'Men whose base lust will spur them to such acts of violence are a disgrace of humanity and their destruction by the victims of their lust is a proper doom.' It was strong stuff.

George Watson had been publicly vilified. Although his widow testified that he was a kind, considerate husband, few in the courtroom were willing to accept her version of the dead man's character. They preferred the portrayal of the archetypal nineteenth-century villain who callously seduces young girls.

District Attorney Britton tried to pour scorn on the insanity defence, calling it a 'sham', but the balance had seemingly tilted very much in Fanny's favour. Nevertheless the jury were unable to agree on a verdict. After twenty-nine hours' deliberation, they were duly discharged on 21 April.

Rumours abounded that ten members of the jury had stood for acquittal and two for manslaughter in the third degree. There was even a splendid story that the ten had agreed that if the other two would consent to a verdict of manslaughter in the fourth degree, for which the penalty was a $1,000 fine, they would not only join in the verdict but would contribute the sum necessary to effect Fanny's immediate release!

The proposition was rejected but led to a stinging rebuke

in the *New York Times* which accused the majority of the jurors of being oversentimental, simply because the defendant was a pretty young girl. The newspaper worried that the jury's offer might set a precedent. It wrote, 'That 10 jurors should have been found who were ready and anxious to take the woman's punishment upon themselves was quite unprecedented. Should their intended course in this offering to undergo vicarious punishment be followed by other juries, we may look for very interesting results. If jurors will pay the fines of pretty female criminals, they will doubtless be willing to undergo punishment for the sake of the pretty pickpocket or the beautiful sneak-thief. We shall have our prisons filled with sentimental jurors undergoing confinement in the place of female criminals, while the prompt payment of fines imposed upon fascinating murderesses will be easily managed when the sum total is assessed in equal parts upon 12 men.'

The article suggested that the jury might have been less eager to volunteer to take Fanny Hyde's punishment if she was to have been condemned to the whipping-post.

Fanny Hyde was released on bail of $2,500 and her case was called for retrial in January 1873. But she failed to show up, much to the consternation of Samuel Morris who had stood her bail. Two months later, on 24 March, she was arrested in Washington, D.C., and confined to Brooklyn's Raymond Street Jail pending a fresh date for her new trial. The months ticked by until in September 1873, she was again released, this time on bail of $5,000. The *New York Times* stated, 'It is very uncertain when the case will be brought to trial'.

It was a remarkably accurate assessment, for Fanny Hyde

was never summoned again to face her murder charge. Instead, free at last from the unremitting harassment, abuse and increasingly brutal sexual torment of George Watson, she quietly slipped into anonymity.

The Battered Bride

Renee Duffy was walking along the street to the shops when she bumped into a friend. The friend could not help noticing that Renee was sporting a black eye. 'What happened to you?' she asked. 'Oh, it's nothing,' Renee replied. 'I walked into something at home.'

A few weeks later, the same thing happened. Another friend, another injury, this time a scratched face. 'How did you do that?' came the query. Once more Renee played it down. 'I can't remember,' she said. 'I think it was an accident at work – it's nothing important.' And so it went on.

Renee Duffy was only nineteen. Slim and attractive with neatly groomed fair hair, she came from a good working-class background. Her father, James, worked at Manchester's Smithfield meat market and Renee was one of four children, having two sisters and a brother. She had been married to her muscular husband George, a 28-year-old brewery worker, for just eighteen months, and already they had a nine-month-old son, also named George. The three lived together in a cramped flat in Kennet House in the Cheetham district north of Manchester city centre. It should have been a happy family home but instead that flat

159

had become a prison to Renee. The reason was all too common – George used to knock her about.

But Renee was not one to complain. She kept quiet about the numerous black eyes, scratches, bumps and bruises which covered her body. If anybody asked, she said they were caused accidentally. Her mother, Emily Russell, was less patient. Whenever she saw the results of George's handiwork, she threw him out of her house. And each time, he begged to be allowed back, promising that it would never happen again. They were empty promises. When things showed no signs of improving, Renee considered leaving him. But she knew that he would not let her take the baby. How could she condemn an innocent little child, her child, to being raised by a monster? She was trapped. She knew it, and George Duffy knew it.

Money was tight for the Duffys. They both worked but Renee was fed up with her waitressing job and wanted to spend more time with her son. She had decided to hand in her notice at work but was dreading telling George, especially as Christmas was drawing near. It seemed to take so little to anger him. The evening of Tuesday 7 December 1948 saw another outbreak of violence in the Duffy household. After being on the receiving end of a particularly savage beating, Renee decided that enough was enough.

This time she really was going to leave him. 'I'm going,' she announced. 'And I'm not coming back.' This merely served to infuriate him further and as she packed a few belongings, he launched another blistering attack on her defenceless body. In desperation, she managed to push him away. 'You're not taking the baby,' he warned. 'So you needn't think you are.'

She ran to the kitchen to find something with which to

defend herself, picked up a hammer and waited. It went quiet. To Renee's tormented mind, this did not represent peace and quiet, it was an ominous silence. She had experienced it too often in the past – the lull before the storm. She knew that this temporary tranquillity could suddenly explode into an orgy of violence. So she stayed in the kitchen for some time, not daring to come out, just in case he was lying in wait. Eventually, it became apparent that he had tired himself out and had probably fallen asleep. She ventured out of the kitchen, carrying a chopper as well as the hammer for protection.

All Renee Duffy remembered after that was hitting George twice with the hammer while he lay on the bed. She gathered up the baby and at ten o'clock that night fled through the pouring rain to her mother's home in West Gorton, three miles away. Soaked to the skin, a distraught Renee told her sister, 'I have killed George. I have hit him with a hammer. We were arguing over my chucking my job and he told me to get to work. He hit me and twisted my arm. I told him he was going too far and he started tantalising me and said, "Get it done".'

Alerted by a neighbour, a police officer found George Duffy lying unconscious on the bed with an overcoat draped over his head. The walls of the bedroom were heavily marked with blood, suggesting that a number of blows had rained down upon the victim. A hatchet and a blood-stained hammer were also found at the flat. The police later traced Renee and the baby to her sister's home. Renee told them, 'He was hitting me and twisting my wrist. I had enough of it. I went in the other room and brought the hammer and hit him with it.'

On 8 December under her real name of Doreen Duffy,

she was charged with wounding with intent to murder. She replied, 'I did not intend to murder'. But when George Duffy died in Crumpsall Hospital later that day, the charge of attempted murder became one of murder. It was 16 March 1949 when Renee Duffy stood trial at Manchester Assizes. The proceedings attracted precious little press coverage, being overshadowed by the arrest and forthcoming trial of John George Haigh who would go down in criminal history as the notorious Acid Bath Murderer.

When they were not reporting the Haigh case, the newspapers preferred to concentrate on concerns over King George VI's health following an operation; the fact that Princess Margaret wore a 'striking New Look costume of brown corduroy' to visit a nursery school in Hertfordshire; the birth of the first llama of the season at London Zoo; and the startling news that the womenfolk of Britain were turning their backs on cod, preferring instead a better class of fish such as plaice or sole. Faced with such stiff competition, the Duffy case had little chance of receiving widespread coverage.

Renee Duffy pleaded not guilty to murder, entering a plea of provocation. Despite claims of her husband's lengthy history of violence being produced as evidence of provocation, the plea was doomed to failure. The court heard that she had not acted immediately in response to his assault – she had actually waited until he had fallen asleep – and her case was further weakened when Home Office pathologist, Dr George Stewart, stated that the dead man had no fewer than nine separate scalp wounds, calling into question Mrs Duffy's claim that she had only struck her husband twice. An interesting development was the disclosure that many of the couple's arguments started over George Duffy's 'unnatural sexual demands'.

Describing the events of the night of 7 December, Renee said, 'I told him I was leaving home when we were in the bedroom and he made a flying leap at me over the bed. I pushed him away and went into the kitchen. I picked up the hammer with the idea that if he started at me again, I would hit him with it. I cannot really remember properly what happened when I went back into the bedroom. I remember hitting him twice with the hammer. Next thing I saw all blood. Then I was frightened and took the baby and went out. He used to beat me three or four times a week,' she told the court, 'and though he was a cruel husband and the marriage was unhappy, I thought the world of him and I didn't want to leave him'.

The details of George Duffy's dreadful treatment of his young bride shocked the court. Defence counsel Mr J. J. Stansfield said that Duffy had behaved more like a beast than a man. Renee herself wept while listening to some of the evidence.

Mr Justice Devlin began his summing up, 'This is a tragic story in which the husband's conduct might have contributed in a very large measure'. But he then explained to the jury the relevance of a history of violence to the provocation defence, 'A long course of cruel conduct may be more blameworthy than a sudden act provoking retaliation, but you are not concerned with blame attaching to the dead man. It does not matter how cruel he was, how much or how little he was to blame, except in so far as it resulted in the final act of the defendant.' Judge Devlin went on to define provocation as conduct 'which would cause in any reasonable person, and actually causes in the accused, a sudden and temporary loss of self-control'. It was a classic definition, one which would be heard over forty years later at the appeal of Kiranjit Ahluwalia and many other women who had fought back.

Regarding Renee Duffy, Judge Devlin added, 'What matters is whether this girl had time to say, "Whatever I have suffered, whatever I have endured, I know that Thou shalt not kill".'

The jury of ten men and two women took just over ninety minutes to find her guilty of murder at the end of a trial which had lasted barely two days, but they added a strong recommendation for mercy. Judge Devlin had no choice but to sentence Renee Duffy to die on the gallows. As he donned the dreaded black cap, Renee's mother, sitting at the back of the court, burst into tears and was led out crying uncontrollably. In the corridor outside the court baby George began to whimper. Renee herself was stoical at this most testing of times. Supported by two wardresses, she showed no emotion at the pronunciation of the death sentence.

When asked by the judge whether there was anything she wished to say, she shook her head slightly and moved her lips in an almost inaudible 'no'. Judge Devlin was not without compassion. 'I have no power to grant or withhold mercy in this case,' he said, 'but I shall see to it that the Secretary of State, whose duty it is to inform the King on these matters, shall have the recommendation. I cannot doubt that it will be carefully considered.'

There was enormous public concern over the death sentence passed on Renee Duffy. The condemned cell at Manchester Strangeways Prison, where she passed the anxious hours by playing whist with her two wardress minders, was adorned with so many flowers that it resembled an entry for a Britain in Bloom contest. So many complete strangers wanted to demonstrate their support, physically and florally. It seemed wholly unjust to the vast majority of people that a twenty-year-old girl should hang for freeing herself and her baby from a savage husband who had bullied and beaten her throughout their short married life.

An appeal was promptly lodged and heard on 4 April. The previous two-and-a-half weeks had brought enormous pressure to bear on the family. Mrs Russell, who had postponed an operation pending the appeal, said that 'Renee's cheeks were hollow with strain' waiting for the adjudication. Meanwhile Renee's brother, Terence, had obtained compassionate leave from his army posting in Cyprus to provide a shoulder for the clan to cry on.

Come the day of reckoning, the Lord Chief Justice, Mr Justice Oliver, said the only possible defence was that the appellant had acted under such provocation as would reduce the crime from murder to manslaughter. It was difficult, he continued, to see how the trial jury could have brought in a verdict of manslaughter unless they felt such intense sympathy with the appellant as would induce them to find a verdict of manslaughter instead of one of murder. 'If her husband had hit her there and then, and she happened to have a hammer in her hand, it may have been a case of manslaughter. As it was, she had armed herself with a hammer and a hatchet before she attacked her husband who was in bed.'

He noted with satisfaction that the jury had been able to

keep their minds fixed on the question which they had to decide to such an extent that, in a case in which there was enormous sympathy with the appellant, they were still able to bring in a verdict according to law. Mr Justice Oliver added that it was said that the direction by the trial judge on the subject of provocation was open to criticism but in his Lordship's view it was as good a direction as could be given and might well stand as a classic direction to be given to a jury on the subject of provocation in a case in which the whole of their sympathy must be with the accused woman rather than the dead man.

As a result, he concluded that the applicant had been properly convicted of murder according to law, and the appeal was dismissed. The bad news had no time to sink in. Immediately after the dismissal of the appeal, Renee Duffy's solicitor, Mr F. R. Johnson, took a taxi to the Home Office to present a petition containing over twelve thousand signatures pleading for a reprieve. It certainly had the desired effect, for the following day the Home Secretary, Mr Chuter Ede, recommended a reprieve.

A relieved Renee was told of the decision by Mr C. T. Cape, the governor of Strangeways Prison, at 3.45 a.m. Her immediate reaction was to smoke two cigarettes given to her by the wardresses. It was reported that a little later she asked for curlers to set her hair. But the moment to which she was really looking forward was a visit from baby George, dressed in a new velvet suit and white shoes, clothes purchased with money sent to the family by well-wishers.

It was indeed a touching reunion. However Renee's legal advisers had not yet concluded their campaign to clear her name. They were convinced that she should not be in jail at all, that she should be freed. Accordingly, on 11 May they applied for a King's pardon but thirteen days later they learned that it had been unsuccessful – the Home Secretary had refused to recommend the King to grant a pardon.

In the end, Renee Duffy, the battered bride, served just two-and-a-half years in prison. Her reputation had been partly restored, principally at the expense of the deceased, a situation which apparently angered George Duffy senior's family who refuted allegations of his brutality. They even raised a petition in an attempt to clear his name too, stating that 'he was a good, clean-living boy and bore an exemplary character'. In cases such as these, there are no winners, only losers.

A few hours before her acquittal, Francine Hughes (*left*) is escorted back to the court by Ingham County officers. Captain Harry Tift (*right*) was the chief investigator on the case (*Associated Press/Wide World Photos*)

Jill Devaughn with her brutal second husband, Michael (*News Team International*)

The beautiful Marie-Marguerite Fahmy (*The Hulton-Deutsch Collection*)

Prince Ali Kamel Fahmy Bey (*Syndication International*)

THE DAILY MIRROR, Tuesday, September 11, 1923.

GERMANY SEEKING NEW CONFERENCE WITH FRANCE

The Daily Mirror

NET SALE MUCH THE LARGEST OF ANY DAILY PICTURE NEWSPAPER

No. 6,194.   Registered at the G.P.O. as a Newspaper.   TUESDAY, SEPTEMBER 11, 1923   One Penny.

SAVOY SHOOTING: MME. FAHMY'S TRIAL OPENS

Mme. Said, sister of the dead man, with her husband, Dr. Said (centre), and Abdul Fatah Raouf Bey, an Egyptian lawyer, representing Mme. Said.

Sir Henry Curtis Bennett, K.C., one of the counsel engaged for the defence.

Mr. Cecil Whiteley, K.C., who held a watching brief arriving at the Old Bailey.

Said Enani, the dead man's secretary, said the couple were not very happy.

A new portrait, received from Paris last night, of Mme. Fahmy, who is charged with the murder of her husband, Ali Kamel Fahmy Bey (inset), a wealthy young Egyptian.

The large crowd that waited outside the Old Bailey in the hope of gaining admittance for the opening of the trial. Many fashionably-dressed women were present.

Passionate letters, descriptions of life in an Egyptian palace, and an account of frequent quarrels between the dead man and his wife, figured in the evidence and examination of Said Enani, secretary to Ali Kamel Fahmy Bey, at the opening yesterday of the trial of Mme. Marie Marguerite Fahmy on a charge of murdering her husband by shooting him at the Savoy Hotel. In his opening address, counsel for the prosecution stated that after marriage Mme. Fahmy always slept with a pistol close at hand.

The shooting at the Savoy hits the headlines (*Syndication International*)

Jim and Linda Cooney are greeted Hawaiian-style at the beginning of a night out at The Breakers hotel (*The Palm Beach Post*)

Margaret Williams leaves Bow Street Magistrates' Court (*The Hulton-Deutsch Collection*)

The Hand of Fate

Bordered to the east by the splendour of Lake Michigan
and to the west by the mighty Mississippi, the state of
Wisconsin is a quiet rural backwater in the American Mid-
west where much of the land is given over to farming.

In the heart of Wisconsin is Waupaca County, an agricul-
tural area where cattle graze while the majority of the
people set about their daily chores of making a living from
the land. The population of Waupaca County (which in
1977 stood at forty thousand) traditionally boasts a conservative attitude. They are solid, respectable citizens. As a
result it has always been a relatively peaceful haven, far
removed from the street crime of inner-city Chicago and
Milwaukee. Sure, there are disputes – tempers can run high
among farmers, sometimes with serious consequences since
they have ready access to firearms – but such incidents tend
to be isolated rather than the norm.

The focal point of Waupaca County is the small dairy
town of Waupaca itself. In March of 1977, it was home to
thirty-two-year-old Jennifer Patri and her two daughters.
Slim, blonde and hailing from a middle-class background,
Jennifer was a familiar figure about town. As well as over-

seeing a thriving pig farm, she sacrificed part of her weekends to teach at the Lutheran Sunday school. Like all responsible mothers, ensuring that her children had a sound upbringing and a good education was of vital importance to Jennifer and therefore, in the midst of her hectic schedule, she also found time to preside over a local Parent-Teacher Association. Basically, she was an active member of the community.

To her fellow parents and colleagues at the Sunday school, Jennifer seemed to be a model of cheerfulness and efficiency. But her home life boasted neither of these qualities. Since the age of eighteen, she had been married to Robert, a car body repair man. Robert Patri's major problem was one all too common in husbands who mistreat their wives – he drank to excess.

When Patri was sober he could, if the mood took him, be a perfectly normal husband. True he was lazy, insensitive, tended to drive recklessly and had been involved in a number of minor scrapes with the law, but there was nothing unduly sinister about him. No horns, no forked tail. But, particularly when under the influence of a considerable amount of alcohol, he was capable of acts of extreme violence, invariably perpetrated against his wife.

It was claimed that he repeatedly slapped Jennifer around, once causing her to miscarry, and subjected her to vicious and agonising sexual abuse. Sometimes the assaults were unrelenting. No sooner was one finished than a new wave began. Often the pain was equalled only by the humiliation. Her attorney, Alan Eisenberg, was to comment later, 'He apparently dreamed up his own sexual circus and she was the ring monkey'.

Robert Patri clearly saw himself as the ringmaster, the one who cracked the whip in the house. As if the attacks on Jennifer were not sufficiently odious in their own right, he allegedly compounded his deplorable actions by sexually molesting their twelve-year-old daughter.

Eventually, Jennifer was said to have discovered what her husband had been doing to their daughter. Given the treatment which she herself had endured from Robert and the fact that her out-of-work activities were so geared towards the welfare of children, one would have expected that Jennifer would have walked out on Patri. Or better still, she could have left him and also notified the police or the medical profession. Yet she declined either to leave him or tell the authorities, explaining later, 'I felt dutybound to my marriage vows'.

To the outsider, it is difficult to comprehend such misplaced loyalty. It can only be assumed that Jennifer thought she was rendering a greater service to her children by keeping the family together. Ultimately, her decision was immaterial. Usually in cases of wife-battering, it is the woman who seeks refuge elsewhere but here, in a novel twist, it was Robert Patri who quit the family home. He had found himself another woman who was pretty and vivacious and moved in with her in a different part of town. This finally stung Jennifer to file for divorce.

Although in a small town like Waupaca, it was inevitable that their paths would cross from time to time, Jennifer could not have anticipated encountering her estranged husband on a regular basis. It was not unreasonable for her to presuppose that, having deserted her and the children, Robert would want nothing further to do with them.

Instead Jennifer found that her hopes of being free from his threats and brutality were premature. For while Robert Patri may have been perfectly happy living apart from his wife, he still wanted to maintain contact with the children. In view of his previous behaviour, Jennifer was equally adamant in denying him access.

Predictably, Robert did not take kindly to this. 'You try and stop me seeing my kids and I'll take them far away from here,' he told her during one furious confrontation. 'Then you'll never see them again.'

Jennifer also claimed that, as well as threatening to kidnap their daughters, Robert vowed to kill her.

It was because of this that in February 1977 Jennifer went to a local store and purchased a .12 gauge shotgun. She maintained that it was purely to protect herself and her defenceless children from her viciously aggressive husband as the arguments over Robert's right to visit the children grew increasingly bitter. They reached the point where Jennifer was convinced that he would carry out his threats.

The crunch came on the evening of 25 March 1977. Robert had arranged to come over to the farmhouse and discuss the situation with a view to taking the girls out on a day trip. Jennifer said later, 'I was anticipating trouble'.

She was not disappointed. As their quarrel reached its peak, Robert suddenly produced a butcher's knife and promised to silence her for good. Fearing for her life, Jennifer made for the next room, picked up the loaded shotgun and shot Patri twice, once in the back and once in the head.

Through a murky haze, Jennifer attempted to conceal all evidence of the shooting. She cleaned up the blood, wrapped the body in sheets of plastic and buried it in a shallow grave in the smokehouse next to their farm. Realising that Robert's car might be spotted by inquisitive neighbours and the information used at a later date to prove that he had been at the house that evening, she then took steps to dispose of the vehicle.

Finally, she set the smokehouse on fire, starting no fewer than five separate blazes to make sure the body would be destroyed. Within minutes, the fire had spread to the rest of the farmhouse and the whole building was burning fiercely. Jennifer was confident of avoiding detection but had reckoned without the vigilance of the fire services.

As they sifted through the smouldering debris, one of the men called out excitedly, 'Hey, over here!' Closer inspection revealed a human hand poking through the rubble. The sheriff of Waupaca, Lawrence Schmies, was duly informed.

Once identification showed the victim to be Robert Patri, the obvious suspect, particularly given the location of the find, was his wife, Jennifer. After setting the fire she had driven to North Dakota to attend a pigbreeders' fair but had returned the next day to confess to her crime. She was charged with the first degree murder of thirty-four-year-old Robert Patri.

She remained in jail for the next three months on a bond of $100,000. Many people thought that it was wrong for her to be locked up – among them, interestingly enough, members of her late husband's family. For not only did Robert Patri's mother and brother later testify in Jennifer's defence but the brother also helped to enlist the services of Milwaukee lawyer Alan Eisenberg who rapidly secured her release pending trial.

The killing had taken place just seventeen days after

Francine Hughes had slain her husband in the neighbouring state of Michigan (see p. 33) and Eisenberg saw the opportunity of whipping up a similar campaign in support of his client. Wisconsin feminists rallied to the cause and with the trial taking place in December 1977, little more than a month after Francine Hughes' acquittal, it attracted a great deal of pre-publicity, much of it orchestrated by Alan Eisenberg. Not all of it was favourable. Sheriff Schmies said of the feminists, 'I wonder if these people know what they're doing. If they get their way, there's going to be a lot of killings.'

Although in general the residents of Waupaca disapproved of the feminists' intervention and the appointment of a big city lawyer, there was a tremendous sympathy for Jennifer among them as the tales of battery unfurled and they perceived her very much as the victim. While the police appeared content to rest on their laurels, convinced that Jennifer's signed confession would be sufficient to condemn her, Eisenberg was sure he could achieve an acquittal, boosted by the precedent of two other similar cases in Wisconsin over recent years. One woman's charge was reduced from murder to manslaughter and she was put on probation, the other was acquitted altogether.

Eisenberg noted that Wisconsin lawyers had been assisted during the previous four years by a broader interpretation of what was permissible in self-defence cases. 'Before, evidence was confined to that day in question,' he said, 'now the state law says an entire pattern of conduct is admissible.'

However the Patri trial did not go precisely as planned. The neatly groomed Jennifer was a confused witness, changing her account of where the shooting had taken place and being unable to recollect any of the events between the shooting and her arrest.

Such memory loss is not at all uncommon among battered women who kill. Many are still dazed after having at last plucked up the courage to take the life of their adversary. They are in a state of shock, not knowing what they are doing. Even when pressed by the police or a prosecutor, they often cannot recall the exact details of what happened immediately after the killing. This applies particularly to mothers, usually in a long-standing marriage. They try to blot the slaying out of their minds, still feeling guilty that – no matter how great the provocation – they have taken away the father of their children. Plus there is the added guilt of having killed the man that they once loved and, in some cases, still do.

Jennifer's claim of self-defence was treated scornfully by the prosecution who emphasised the point that Robert Patri had been shot in the back. What kind of a threat could he possibly pose with his back to her, they demanded? And apart from the testimony of Jennifer herself, witnesses struggled to cite incidents of physical abuse beyond 'a few arm twists'.

The verdict in the Patri case was unsatisfactory for both sides. Jennifer was found guilty of manslaughter and sentenced to ten years in prison. Prosecution and feminists alike were disappointed for different reasons. The former lost their murder conviction and the latter their acquittal. Nevertheless Candace Wayne, a lawyer with Chicago's Legal Center for Battered Women, attempted to find some consolation. She told *Newsweek* magazine that such cases 'raise the level of public awareness about the pervasiveness of the physical abuse of women'.

The one person who seemed happy with the outcome was attorney Eisenberg who hailed the manslaughter conviction as 'a complete and total victory'.

Although her immediate reaction to the verdict was 'I don't think I could ask for anything better', Jennifer Patri could not have shared her attorney's views as she began her long prison sentence. And things were to deteriorate still further. A year later, in December 1978, she faced a new charge, this time one of arson for having set fire to her house in the wake of killing her husband. It seemed the prosecutor was determined to get his pound of flesh.

Psychiatric experts called by the defence testified that at the time she started the fire, Jennifer was suffering from temporary insanity. The jury accepted this and found her not guilty by reason of insanity. Unfortunately, it was once again not the victory for which Jennifer's lawyers had hoped: the jury decided that the insanity was more than just temporary. They ruled that she was still insane.

Thus Jennifer Patri, active community worker, Sunday school teacher and dedicated parent, ended up in a state mental hospital.

At Jennifer Patri's murder trial, the prosecution had suggested that she was not a battered wife at all. This theory was further advanced in 1983 by author Steven Englund whose book *Manslaughter* recounted the Patri case. According to Englund, a niece whom the defence said Robert Patri had molested, later denied it.

She also told Englund that her aunt Jennifer had earlier confided that she had aborted herself in the bath with a coat hanger. The courtroom version was that her husband had beaten her until she had miscarried. Englund concluded that Mrs Patri murdered her husband out of jealousy over his relationship with a more vivacious, prettier woman. He did, however, concede that Jennifer Patri may have perceived herself to be a battered wife. To an extent, the jury certainly believed she had been.

The acknowledgement of Battered Woman Syndrome by the American courts, while a long-overdue development, did create a situation which could place judge and jury in a real dilemma. Some female defendants who killed their spouses or lovers for other reasons than self-defence or provocation – greed, revenge or just plain boredom – immediately pleaded that they too were battered women in the hope of winning an acquittal.

One case in which this plea was used was that of Kathryn England who, in January 1983, stood trial in Green County, Tennessee, for the murder of her husband Franklin.

The Englands had married young but after twenty-five years together, began to grow apart. It was rumoured that both parties had conducted affairs. Early on the morning of 6 March 1982, a neighbour was roused by a feverish banging on his front door. It was Kathryn England in a highly excitable state. 'Something's happened to my husband!' she screamed. 'Please come quickly. There's blood everywhere.'

The neighbour found Franklin England lying dead on the bathroom floor in a pool of blood. He had been shot in the chest. A .22 calibre bullet was embedded in the mattress. There were also bullet holes in the ceiling, one of which had been made by a larger calibre weapon. Mrs England claimed that the rifle had gone off accidentally while she had been shooting at blackbirds in the attic and that the bullet must have passed through the floor and into the bed below where her husband had been sleeping. He had then managed to stagger into the bathroom.

According to the police, she later told them a different story, how she had fired the .22 rifle into the mattress to wake her husband up for sex. At that stage, they said, she made no mention of her husband being anything but a considerate and affectionate man.

At the trial, she repeated the blackbird story but her defence counsel also introduced the Battered Woman Syndrome. It was claimed that Franklin England had abused his wife both physically and sexually, that she had been forced to have sex three days after a hysterectomy with the result that some of her stitches had broken. Mrs England also alleged that her husband had once hit her in the stomach while she was pregnant, causing her to lose the baby. She said that he had threatened to kill her if she ever reported him. She added that she had been subjected to twenty-five years of unnatural sex acts, humiliation and physical violence and had even tried to commit suicide.

'I never meant to kill him,' she sobbed. 'I just didn't want him to hit me any more.'

A clinical psychologist testified that the accused possessed all the symptoms of a battered wife, and two of her sons took the stand to disclose that their father had treated their mother cruelly. However a third son, who still lived at home, was not called.

The prosecution made great capital of that omission, and of the defendant's varying statements. She admitted that she had lied. As for the story about waking her husband for sex, why should anyone who claimed to have been sexually abused for so long, wish to encourage her tormentor in that direction?

She was also unable to produce any medical evidence to support her claims of mistreatment. Indeed a neighbour described them as a perfectly happy couple who often walked arm-in-arm through the tobacco fields where they worked. And Mrs England confessed under cross-examination to asking a lawyer what sum of money she could expect to receive as a widow or a divorcee.

The prosecutor drew the jury's attention to the two holes in the ceiling: one had been made by a .22 (a crude attempt had been made to cover this hole), the other, seven inches away, by a larger .270 calibre rifle. This second hole was situated directly above the spot where there had been a sizeable spillage of blood onto the bed. He claimed that the defendant had fired the .22 as a practice shot to calculate the ideal angle with which to fire the larger weapon through her husband's heart. A .270 rifle had been found in the attic. It contained a spent cartridge. The upshot was that the jury found Kathryn England guilty of first-degree murder and she was sentenced to life imprisonment.

It could be argued that the evidence against Jennifer Patri seemed just as damning as that against Kathryn England. Certainly, Steven Englund questioned whether Patri was quite the picture of innocence she presented to the court. In both cases, the verdict depended on whether or not the jury accepted that the defendant was suffering from Battered Woman Syndrome. In both cases, this was the factor that made the difference between a verdict of manslaughter or one of murder.

Death of a Trumpeter

September 1969 was a time of change and of strife. In Paris an uneasy peace held in the struggle between young and old and parts of the city still bore the scars of the student riots. Scenes of anger and police brutality there had shocked the world the year before. The old order of Charles De Gaulle was no more and Georges Pompidou, president of just three months, struggled to keep a new balance in French corridors of power in the year that a man had kept his balance on the moon.

On Tuesday 23 September, a trial was to begin in the Seine Assize Court. It was a case that might have been heard in 1869 or even 1569. For the story that was to unfold is ageless and yet entirely modern. It was of a series of events in what is usually referred to lightly as the war of the sexes. But there was nothing light about this. It was of a woman who was pushed to the limit of her endurance by a selfish, violent man. Finally she had no way out; she had to kill him.

This woman, Raymonde Heldenbergh, had been waiting in prison three years. She yearned for the truth to be told and for two of her four daughters who were charged with her, accused also of murder, to be cleared so that their lives could be mended and their reputations restored.

The man who died was Robert Heldenbergh, a Warrant Officer trumpeter with the Republican Guard. His wife Raymonde was charged with wrapping around his neck a scarf decorated with the Republican Guard emblem, a scarf that he had given her when their love was strong. Then their daughters Isoline and Martine allegedly each took an end of the scarf and pulled until their father fought no more.

The 26th of September 1966 was a doubly symbolic day for Robert. He was fifty-five years old and it was the day he retired from his life in the military. As he collected his personal items from his locker at the barracks, he invited several pals to join him later for a farewell drink. He planned to go home and pack all his belongings too. For this was also the day that he was due to leave his wife of twenty-seven years. Why choose this day to make two dramatic changes? Because divorce proceedings were already in progress and he had been ordered to continue to cohabit until the time of his retirement. He wasn't going to hang about a moment longer. If that sounded heartless, so be it.

Robert Heldenbergh was a man who blew his own trumpet in both senses. He was not a sentimental man. On that day he was a very cheerful man, looking forward to the first day of the rest of his life with his mistress in the new home they planned to make together in a quiet town in Northern France. As for the separation from his children, four daughters and one son, well, they were growing up or grown. He would see them from time to time, when they chose to visit. He'd left children before – the two daughters of his first marriage – it was no big thing.

On that same day Raymonde had just completed the first day of the rest of her life and it was wretched. At fifty-one she had been forced to take work as a cleaner. She had not had to work since her marriage and she felt a great sense of shame. She did it because she already knew what the paltry allowance that Robert was due to make for her and the children was to be, that is, if he paid it. And if he paid it would still not be nearly enough to keep them housed and fed let alone to provide some of the comforts they had enjoyed until the marriage turned sour and the beatings began.

So there they were – he, bursting with excited anticipation, she, exhausted and broken.

How different it was when they'd met in 1939. Then she was a dancer with the Concert Mayol and he was already in the Republican Guard, a First Prize winner at the Paris Conservatoire. At the dance at which she first saw him, he was performing a solo on the trumpet. He seemed young and fresh. He turned out to be twenty-eight, a divorced man with two daughters, but ready to be loved and admired.

They had a small but stylish wedding and moved into an apartment in Rue Abel-Bonnevalle in a quiet eastern suburb of the city. Only a few hundred metres away was the ring road and the busy A3 road which took drivers north to Normandy and Brittany. Very soon Raymonde was pregnant with their first daughter, Josselyne. Then came Isoline. Then came their son Christian and, after a pause, two more daughters Martine and little Régine.

Life was sweet. Thanks to his being in constant demand

to play in private bands, Robert earned a good living and Raymonde was happy to look after her children and her husband who showered her with gifts. She was, friends and relatives would agree, an excellent cook and housekeeper and an enlightened mother, 'as devoted to her children as a tigress to her cubs' the court would later hear one of her neighbours confirm.

So what went wrong? The seeds of the trouble lay in the fact that she was not musically trained and did not encourage her children to play musical instruments. To her playing an instrument was something one did as a job, not as a pleasure, not to satisfy a spiritual need. As he grew older, Robert liked to exclaim, with a dramatic flourish, that 'music is my life!'. As the requests to play at fashionable gatherings diminished, so Robert's suffering for his art increased. He needed an excuse for his suffering. He found it in Raymonde and the children. More and more he blamed them for his lack of an exciting other life and more and more he took to drinking wine and cognac to wallow in his misfortune as an artist who was not appreciated.

With the drinking and the self-pity came the violent outbursts. He began to strike Raymonde for the smallest thing and the children began to live in dread of arguments. 'You could hear the noise of the quarrels every day,' several neighbours testified at the trial. 'He was nervy, irritable. He drank, he beat me,' Raymonde said.

To escape the scenes Robert, the tortured artist, began to give trumpet lessons. He made one room in the apartment his 'library', filling it with books on musical theory, sheet music and newspaper and magazine clippings. Each night when he finally returned home, he locked himself inside. Confused and hurt, Raymonde and the children became closer, bonded by their fear of 'the enemy' they couldn't understand.

The fights and the violence raged until August 1965. At this point the Republican Guard was temporarily stationed in Northern France. It was there that fate intervened for Robert Heldenbergh. In a bar he glanced across the tables and saw a familiar face – that of an old flame, Jeanne Delmotte. They'd had a brief romance nearly thirty years before, but the Guard had moved on and eventually Jeanne had married another. Both had aged, of course, but they recognised each other immediately when they met that August. What's more, Jeanne had appealing news: she was widowed and free. Robert was immediately smitten because Jeanne, a musician, appreciated his art, his creative needs. Or so he thought. At any rate it seemed to him a sign. He visited lawyers immediately and without even consulting the mother of his five children, he began the process of divorce. When he did return he spared Raymonde no details. 'I've met the woman I truly love, the woman who understands me and my music. I can't wait to be free of you and those children I despise!' he told her.

The divorce courts were, she later realised, even more cruel although unintentionally so. They granted a legal separation in February 1966 but ruled that Robert must remain in the marital home for the remaining five months before his retirement from the Guard. That way, they loftily supposed, the couple could prepare themselves for change. Instead the bitterness and the beatings only worsened. Robert Heldenbergh felt he had nothing to lose.

He made no secret of his plans for a rosy future with

Jeanne and was off on the A3 North at every opportunity. It was also obvious that he cared nothing for his wife's future and that of their children. By then Christian was away doing his compulsory military service and could not console his mother. Josselyne was living her own life in Cannes. Isoline, then twenty-six, was married to a man called Aubut and had three young children of her own. Luckily she lived in Avenue Brement, Noisy Le Sec, only a few minutes' walk from her parents' home, in Rue Abel-Bonnevalle.

Raymonde, abandoned and soon to be in financial straits, was sinking into a depression. It was made worse by her discovery in May of that year that Robert had withdrawn 6,400F (£480) from their savings account. She knew where it had gone: into the account of Jeanne Delmotte.

On the night of 26 September Robert arrived at the apartment in Rue Abel-Bonnevalle, around 7pm. Only Régine and Martine, the youngest girls, were at home. Their father's mood alarmed them. He was puffed up with bravado and brandy from the raucous speeches and toasts at his goodbye gathering. Unsteadily, but with determination, he began to unhook pictures from the wall and to take photographs out of frames. 'I'll take this! And this! Ah, this is too good to leave. That rubbish they can keep!' he muttered to himself as he went from room to room.

He placed the chosen articles in a trunk while babbling that it wouldn't be long before he was free of them all. Little Régine watched hoping her mother would arrive. In desperation she ran out of the apartment to tell her big sister Isoline what was happening. Isoline's heart began to pound with anger. She instructed Régine to stay and mind her young children and, without stopping to take a coat she ran back to her parents' home. At the door she saw her father warmly shaking the hands of a young friend and 'disciple' in the Guard, Raphael Desmet. He ushered the young man inside.

'Come inside Raphael, my dear boy. Have a cognac. There is something I'd like you to have, from me, as a gift. If you would do me the honour.' He went to the cupboard to bring out his treasured Guard uniforms which Raymonde had so carefully brushed and cleaned and repaired for all their married life. He went to fetch them as a breathless Isoline angrily protested. She knew they were valuable and that her mother and sisters could sell them if they had to. They would certainly need all the funds available. Ignoring his daughter, Robert went upstairs to fetch the prized suits.

At this moment Raymonde returned from her first day of skivvying for others. Martine, then fifteen, rushed to embrace her. The daughters reported that 'he' was taking their home apart and was jubilant about leaving them. Exhaustion turned quickly to anger. Raymonde began climbing the stairs two at a time and called to the man she had once loved so much, 'You won't take our home apart, you won't leave. Don't imagine it will be as easy as that. It would be so convenient, wouldn't it?'

Embarrassed, Raphael slipped away. By then Raymonde was weeping and she clung to Robert, trying to hold back his arms from placing the items of their yesterdays, suddenly so important, in the trunk of his tomorrows. With one easy tug, Robert Heldenbergh unhooked this woman, this obstacle to his future. He hit her and kicked her in the stomach, leaving her gasping on the carpet as he walked to his room. His back was turned to the door as Raymonde approached. She took three steps forward and then a little jump. In doing this she swung her scarf in front of his neck.

What happened next was for the court to decide. After she'd called the police, the distraught woman had said that it was after a violent struggle between her husband, herself, and their daughters that she looped the scarf around her husband's neck. Isoline and Martine had each taken an end and pulled because she had no more strength. The girls had also told the police this. There were signs too of a struggle. Furniture was overturned, rugs were crumpled and Raymonde and her daughters each had scratch marks on their arms and faces, signs of a fight.

Then, in the cool light of the next day, it dawned on Raymonde that parricide, the killing of a father, is a heinous crime. Whatever legal punishment the court may have decided was fitting, she knew that her daughters might never be truly forgiven in French society. Whatever the crimes of the parent against the child, the killing of that parent by the child is deemed an unatonable offence. She could bear anything for herself, but it was different for them. Consequently she made a new statement in which she said she committed the crime in self-defence, but entirely on her own. 'I strangled him – the children didn't touch him,' she said. Her daughters also changed their versions of events to calm their mother.

In 1966 the examining magistrate had rejected the plea of self-defence. He was swayed by the evidence of forensic scientists. In a sample of Robert Heldenbergh's blood traces of alcohol were found – which were to be expected –

and also of barbiturates, which were not. The alcohol in his blood was 2.5 grammes per litre, an enormously high amount. There were 30 milligrammes of barbiturate too.

Since the deceased was not in the habit of taking sleeping pills this drug must have been administered by someone else who wished to subdue him. That someone, it seemed likely, was Madame Heldenbergh. But to what purpose? To strangle him when he was semiconscious or unconscious? Raymonde, who admitted everything, denied emphatically that she had any involvement in this aspect of the events of the night. Nothing proved that she was not telling the truth. But the likelihood that it was her work, a sign of a premeditated crime, was enough. Consequently the charge of murder, for which the punishment was the scaffold or life imprisonment, was brought.

On that first day of the Assizes three years later Raymonde and Isoline stood in the dock. Martine, who had been a minor at the time, was to be dealt with in a children's and adolescents' court when the guilt of her older sister had been decided. It was not only the state that demanded to be satisfied by the investigation about to begin. There were also the claims of two other Heldenbergh women, his daughters from his first youthful marriage. They had been wronged by the killing of their father, they said, and they insisted that damages were due. The lawyers, Maître George Myers-Auburtin and Maître Tixier-Vignancour stood ready to defend Raymonde and Isoline. Maître Epinat prepared to speak on behalf of the older daughters.

The judge, the jury, lawyers and spectators were silent as Isoline prepared to speak. Her reddened eyes and 'little girl' voice evoked some sympathy. The women in the court noticed her auburn hair left to fall loosely and beautifully over her shoulders and the elegant red-varnished finger-nails, rare for a mother with three demanding infants. In her favour was the testimony of Dr Martin, the police doctor. 'Yes,' he said, 'one person alone could have strang-led Robert Heldenbergh. Even one not very strong woman.' In her favour also were the words of her mother, 'Isoline was her father's favourite, the only one with whom he had a human relationship'.

Raymonde sought no pity from the court. Her greying hair had received little attention. Her clothes were plain. Her greenish eyes seemed hard and unfeeling. It was as though she dared not allow herself a moment's weakness in the six hours of her ordeal as she took the stand on the second day of the trial. 'Madame Heldenbergh,' neighbours told the police, 'was distant.' As her lawyer coaxed her to tell of years of increasing coldness and brutality from her husband, there was not a tremor in her voice, nor a sign of moisture in her eyes.

She spoke of the nights when Robert would finish his private work at Le Mogador or some other theatre at about midnight but rarely arrived home until four in the morning, drunk, foul-mouthed and ready to set upon her, roughly demanding sex or simply beating her out of irritation.

'Fortunately,' she said with no trace of self-pity, 'when he found a mistress, he came home only once or twice a week.'

'Did this make you suffer?' asked the president of the court. The accused did not answer but the jury recalled that her doctor had given evidence that for two years before the crime she had been taking medication for stress. She always knew of Robert's other women, she said. He liked to tell her, to torment her, to boast that he was still attractive while she was not. After he'd been to the North and met Jeanne Delmotte, Robert Heldenbergh crowed to his wife, 'I've spent three days with her. I want to marry her when we are divorced and that will be just as soon as I can arrange it.'

Raymonde remained cool even when the most self-possessed would have become shaky. 'I am going to ask you to do something painful but necessary,' said the president. 'Please take your handkerchief and carry out, once again on your daughter, for example, exactly the action that you carried out that evening on your husband.' Isoline obediently turned her back on her mother. Without hesitation Raymonde put the handkerchief round the young woman's neck and made a motion of pulling it towards her. She said nothing. She showed nothing, not even when the woman responsible for her greatest unhappiness, Jeanne Delmotte was called to approach the bar. Isoline pierced her with a look of pure hatred. Raymonde merely turned her head away slowly as if to say, 'Madame, I do not know you'.

Jeanne Delmotte did not fit the image of the femme fatale. The fifty-year-old woman with grey hair and the look of a comfortable housewife didn't fit the image of a mistress of any kind. 'Were you Robert Heldenbergh's mistress?' she was asked. 'Not his mistress, an old friend,' she replied. 'Please do not play with words. Did you have a relationship with him, yes or no? Did he credit your account with 6,400F lifted from his savings account, yes or no?' The witness answered in the affirmative twice. 'You seem to have no regrets?'

191

'Regrets? Why should I?'

The president's tone became stinging. 'Thank you, Madame, your answer is enough. You may sit down.'

Next came the medical reports on Raymonde. Psychiatrist Dr Dublineau and psychologist Dr Laton had each examined her. They agreed that her action in killing her husband may not have been a result of self-defence, but she was extremely fearful of him and had acted from that. Dr Laton added that the group effect was important in this instance. People do not behave in the same way when they are alone as when they are in a group. On a broader scale this had been the partial cause of the street demonstrations Parisians had been able to witness. On the evening of 26 September there were three highly emotional women present. The excitement of each was multiplied by three.

Assistant Public Prosecutor Poumeroulis is a lawyer rightly feared by defendants to this day. He almost always achieves his aims and the defendants are sentenced in the manner he demands. He has the wisdom and the skill to demand only what he knows he can get. His speeches are calculated precisely. Nothing is left to chance. So it was in the case of Raymonde Heldenbergh on the third day of her trial.

It seemed then that the general impression of her had changed during those previous two days. A cold and calculating woman was the way she was first perceived. Now she was a woman of some dignity who had been humiliated, battered and ruined. A whiff of acquittal was in the air on that Wednesday morning. Bookmakers would have taken short odds on it. The pleas of her lawyers were likely to whip that faint whiff into a pungent scent and Poumeroulis could feel it coming as he entered the court. He judged that he should not ask for harsh punishment – the death penalty or life imprisonment. The result of that – even though the jury was of twelve men and no women – could be one of indignation. They could bring a verdict of not guilty and an acquittal would be an outrage, a blot on his reputation. He knew he must temper his demands. Skilfully he guessed that the defence would plead that there were mitigating circumstances; he stole their thunder and pleaded exactly that in the first words he spoke:

These two women were victims of a brutal man. But this is not a defence. There is no doubt at all that they are also guilty of the most serious crimes. Gentlemen of the jury you have to choose between two truths or a truth and a lie. The truth was in Madame Heldenbergh's first version of the facts which she gave immediately after the event. 'I strangled my husband helped by my two daughters whom I called to my aid.' The second version, when she took the whole responsibility upon herself is perhaps a fine action for a mother, but it is a lie.

The defence was clearly surprised. The lawyers had to abandon their prepared speeches and respond with simple common sense. Maître Tixier-Vignancour, known for his ranting style in political trials, knew to keep his tone modulated. The drama of the case against Isoline needed no extra flourish anyway.

The prosecutor is right. There is in this affair both a

truth and a lie. It's a pity he mistook one for the other. The truth was in the second version which the accused asserted boldly and have not departed from over three years. If in the first instance the girls claimed to have taken part in this, it was out of sympathy and to show solidarity with their beloved mother, to share in her suffering. A grand gesture of filial affection but a lie. Isoline is innocent. She was her father's favourite. She was horrified that he was leaving but she would not have assisted in killing him. He himself, from his grave, demands that you should acquit his daughter.

Then Maître Myers-Auburtin spoke for Raymonde. It was, naturally, an emotional moment. 'Have pity on this woman, beaten down, run to earth, who trembled with fear every day at the return of this drunkard and who finished up by killing him in a moment of panic,' he said solemnly.

'I agree with Maître Tixier-Vignancour. Isoline must be freed. She must be freed for the sake of her three young children. But the mother, the grandmother of those children, whom she has not seen for three years, should she stay in prison?' And the counsel for the defence ended by begging, 'Do not leave her all alone. She has suffered enough.'

But the jury of twelve men could not feel this woman's pain. Meekly they followed the prosecutor, the man of law. Had he not been mild in his demands? They believed that the women's first statement was the truth. The daughters' hands had pulled on the ends of that scarf as Raymonde sobbed. They gave the star of that court, Monsieur Poumeroulis, what he'd asked for and perhaps what he wanted. Not a fearsome penalty, but not a merciful one either.

In 1969 the French had no great understanding of what drives a woman who has been repeatedly treated like a lesser being by a violent husband to commit acts of violence herself. But perhaps they had appreciated one thing. In a country where a man's blood relatives are always entitled to a portion of his estate on his death, irrespective of the wishes or circumstances of his widow, it was judged that day that the daughters of Robert Heldenbergh from his first marriage, both in their thirties then and well used to life without him, were not justified in depriving his youngest children of the small amount of capital they had to their name. Their life would be hard enough with no father and a mother who admitted killing him. They had demanded 100,000F (£7,520). They were granted 10,000F (£750).

A sentence of five years' imprisonment was passed on Raymonde Heldenbergh. A sentence of three years, to be suspended, (two fewer than were demanded), was passed on Isoline, her father's favourite. The crime of parricide may be terrible, the stigma may be for life, but when the parent is a man like Robert Heldenbergh, when his actions leave no escape possible from the cycle of suffering for the family he once loved, the mark must quickly fade.

Isoline cried for her mother. Raymonde looked lovingly at her, relieved that she was free. Then her jaw set as she was taken down.

A Patio Grave

Jill Devaughn looked around her. She glowed with pride at the sight of her eight-year-old son and three-year-old daughter playing happily. To top it all, she kept thinking to herself how lucky she was to have a smashing new man in her life – Peter Stubbs. It appeared to be a scene of perfect domestic bliss, but behind the smiles Jill hid a terrible secret. For buried under the patio in the garden was the body of her husband, Michael. And it was she who had killed him.

Jill had met Peter, a stock controller with PSM International at Willenhall in the West Midlands, in March 1990. At thirty, she was two years older than him. She told him that she was separated from her second husband Michael Devaughn. What she omitted to mention was that Devaughn's body had lain under the patio slabs of her semi-detached house in Pugh Crescent in the Bentley district of Walsall for the past three months.

At first Peter was a little wary of getting involved with Jill, simply because of Michael Devaughn's awesome reputation. Throughout the pubs and clubs of the industrial area of England to the northwest of Birmingham known as the

Black Country, Devaughn had a reputation as a violent man. The former marine had earned the nickname of 'Mad Mick'. In the circumstances, Peter Stubbs thought it wise to tread carefully for fear of upsetting Devaughn. At that stage, of course, he didn't know that Devaughn was no longer capable of hurting anyone.

Jill and Peter grew steadily closer. He was a kindly man – the complete opposite of her second husband – who not only looked after her but also revelled in the role of surrogate father to Louis and Olivia, her two children by Devaughn. But as their love blossomed, Jill found herself faced with a terrible dilemma. She knew that if she was to have a future with Peter sooner or later she would have to confess to him that she had killed Michael Devaughn.

She kept putting it off, fearing that once he knew her awful secret he would decide to terminate their relationship. But the longer she delayed the revelation, the harder it became. Eventually, some six weeks after they had first met, Jill plucked up the courage to tell him. They were alone when she said quietly, 'There's something I have to tell you'. She proceeded to relate the whole story of her nine-year ordeal at the sadistic hands of Michael Devaughn and how the only way out she could see was to murder him.

Jill had married Michael Devaughn at Walsall Register Office on 20 December 1980. She knew he had a violent past. At Stafford Crown Court in 1977, he had been convicted of beating up Miss Josie Large, the pregnant girlfriend with whom he was living at the time. He broke her nose and cut her shin with a bottle because her shape upset him. He faced two charges of wounding, and also admitted burglary, theft and passing dud cheques. As a result, he was jailed for three years and three months.

If Jill harboured any illusions that he would change, they were shattered on their wedding day when he brutally attacked her during an argument. The situation did not improve. As a builder Devaughn was a powerful man who, even his own mother admitted, would often lash out first and ask questions later. He was basically a bully who liked to throw his weight about and the chief recipient of his anger was his wife Jill.

He subjected her to nine years of terror. The drunken nights were the worst. It reached the stage where she dreaded hearing the key in the front door. He would swagger in and start knocking her about for no reason. Her only crime was that she happened to be there. Even the children were not free from his violence and, in the course of one drunken rage, their son was struck with a domestic iron. To instil absolute obedience into Jill, he often threatened to kill her and the children and she was left in little doubt that these were not idle threats. He meant it. Apart from the fact that she was nowhere near strong enough to compete with Devaughn, Jill dared not retaliate for fear of incurring an even more savage beating.

She tried to leave him several times but he always managed to hunt her down and, on more than one occasion, literally dragged her back through the streets. The humiliation, the physical pain and the resultant threats made Jill realise that leaving him was not that easy. She stayed with him through sheer terror. When the abuse was not physical, it was verbal or sexual. There was no respite. Inevitably, the strain of coping with the beatings plus that of shielding the children from their father's behaviour finally took their toll on Jill's health.

She began suffering from depression. In December 1989,

the years of pent-up misery exploded. 'He came in drunk and started knocking me about,' said Jill. 'You cannot imagine how much he battered me around this room. I was at the sink. He started on at me. He threatened to shoot me and the kids. I thought he would kill me.'

As Devaughn threw himself into yet another manic attack, Jill struck out in desperation with a heavy cast-iron saucepan, rendering him unconscious. She looked at him lying there, strangely silent. She could not believe that, after all the years of punishment, she had suddenly been able to stop him in his tracks. What should she do next? Terrified that if he woke up, he would carry out his threat to kill her and the children, in her confused state of mind she decided the only solution was to finish him off.

She fetched a replica pistol and while he lay unconscious on the floor, tried to shoot him through the eye. When that failed, she set out to strangle him instead. The only handy implement was the washing line. She wound it around his neck and, using the handle of a hammer to tighten the noose, squeezed the life out of her vicious husband.

It was the one thing killing him but another disposing of the body. Frantically trying to keep calm, she reasoned that the safest place was under the patio in the garden. So she taped Devaughn's ankles and wrists and buried him in a shallow grave beneath the paving slabs.

There remained just one matter to be dealt with – the explanation of his sudden disappearance. Given Michael Devaughn's track record over the last dozen or so of his forty years, it was hardly stretching the bounds of credibility that they should have split up and so Jill told anyone who inquired that he had left her.

At Christmas 1989, Jill sent her mother-in-law, who ran a florist's shop in Telford, Shropshire, a card containing a photograph of the children and a message saying that Michael had left. The deception was made simpler by the fact that her in-laws were not particularly close to the family. For the time being at least, no questions were asked. Jill's next move was to file for divorce which she did by forging Devaughn's signature on the necessary papers.

At last, she started to feel that she might be able to put her past torment behind her and to live some sort of life again. That optimism was heightened when she met Peter Stubbs.

When Jill eventually told him her story he listened with a mixture of shock and horror. He could scarcely believe his ears; in fact he found it inconceivable that the woman he had grown so close to was a killer and thought that she was making the whole thing up.

'I just don't believe it,' said Peter. 'It can't be true.'

'It is,' replied Jill. 'I'll even show you where he is buried.' When Jill pointed out the patio, Peter somehow became convinced that she was telling the truth after all.

One day, Peter was looking forward to a happy future, the next his world had come crashing down around him. At first, he didn't know what to do for the best. All he did know was that there was no way he wanted to lose the woman he loved. Jill's relief at having finally been able to share the burden was diluted by her worry about Peter's reaction. In the event, she had no cause for concern.

Whilst many men would have beaten a hasty retreat, Peter Stubbs was made of sterner stuff. He had no intention of deserting her in her hour of need. They would see it through together. The bogus divorce became absolute in November 1990 on the grounds of two years' separation, and the following month, seemingly free at last, Jill married Peter.

In the summer of 1991, she gave birth to their son, Connor. But the spectre of what lay beneath the patio continued to haunt both Jill and Peter. Hard though they tried, they simply could not blot it out of their minds. It was as if Michael Devaughn, even covered in concrete, was still exercising some dreadful hold over Jill. Would she ever be truly free?

Peter was determined to protect her in her darkest moments but, while able to be strong and supportive on her account, he found that the grisly secret was gnawing away at him too. A problem shared may be a problem halved, but it can also be a problem doubled. Meanwhile Peggy Smith, Michael Devaughn's mother, was becoming increasingly concerned that she had not heard anything at all from her son. News had filtered back to her that he and Jill had divorced and that Jill had remarried and subsequently had another child, but in all this time there had been no word from Michael.

In the past, he had often gone away for long periods and had frequently travelled abroad, but he had always contacted his mother from time to time. By the late spring of 1992 it was nearly three-and-a-half years since Mrs Smith had heard from her son. She had a feeling that something was wrong and began to voice her worries to other members of the family. She seriously contemplated reporting her son missing. It seems that news of this got back to Jill and renewed her fears that the grave beneath the patio might soon be uncovered. Every sighting of a police car brought her and Peter out in a cold sweat, every knock on the door made them fear the worst. It was a living nightmare – nowhere near as awful as her life with Michael Devaughn – but extremely unpleasant nonetheless.

At the start of June 1992 Jill learned that she was pregnant again. More than ever, the fear of discovery became unbearable. Another member of the family meant another person who would suffer if Jill were sent to prison.

Peter loved the two older children as his own and with little Connor and now a new baby on the way, he simply couldn't stand the thought of Jill being taken away from them. He knew the misery it would bring to the children and, on a purely selfish basis, he couldn't bear to lose her either. He decided Jill had suffered enough. Something had to be done. The pressure had been building up anyway. For months Peter had been agonising over whether to go to the police. On 14 June, he could take no more.

That Sunday evening, he told Jill he was going out for a drink with friends but at 1am, he walked into nearby Darlaston police station. Apart from the customary trickle of weekend drunks, the station was quiet that night. But if the duty officer was contemplating a peaceful evening of paperwork, his dreams were rudely shattered when Peter Stubbs came to the front desk.

'I want to confess to a murder,' said Peter. The surprised officer fetched reinforcements and Peter calmly related how he had killed Michael Devaughn and buried him under the back garden patio. He was quizzed by detectives for two hours before being arrested and put in a cell for the night. But the police were not wholly convinced by his story. They suspected he could be covering up for someone and when a worried Jill went to a public telephone box the next day to report Peter missing, the police approached her and brought her in for questioning.

She could not let Peter take the blame for a crime he didn't commit and duly confessed. Detectives went to Pugh Crescent and Devaughn's body was exhumed from beneath the patio. It was exactly where Jill Stubbs had said. His wrists were taped behind his back and his ankles were taped together. Cause of death was pinpointed as strangulation. In the meantime, Peter was released and Jill was charged with murder that same day.

The police allowed him to see her. 'Are you cross with me?' he asked. 'No, of course not,' she replied. 'I'm just glad that it's finally out in the open. It's such a relief after carrying it around for all this time.' Unusually for someone facing a murder charge, Jill Stubbs was freed on bail – not only was she pregnant but there was little danger of her absconding or re-offending. Her trial opened at Stafford Crown Court on 12 January 1993. By now heavily pregnant, she denied murdering Michael John Devaughn but admitted manslaughter on the grounds of diminished responsibility. Mr Douglas Draycott QC, prosecuting, recounted Jill Stubbs' sorry nine years with Devaughn.

It was a story which shocked the most hardened onlooker. 'There is no doubt,' said Mr Draycott, 'that she had married a sadistic man who submitted her to verbal, physical and sexual abuse which makes one wonder if there was something mentally wrong with him. She undoubtedly led an appalling life.' And these were the words of the prosecution.

He went on to say that 'severe depression had impaired her responsibility for the killing'. With regard to Peter, Mr Draycott said, 'He found the strain of living a lie too much for him and in June confessed to murder. But when his wife was questioned, she admitted what she had done.'

Defence counsel Mr William Andreae-Jones QC told the court, 'She had put up with violence and abuse for virtually ten years. Before their marriage, he was convicted of a serious assault and they even had a fight on the day of their marriage. And matters continued in that vein.'

The trial lasted only one day. In the light of other cele-brated cases and in view of the acknowledged suffering to which she had been subjected over a long period as well as her current physical condition, Jill Stubbs expected to be placed on probation. But Mr Justice Ebsworth had other ideas.

Pointing out that she had married Devaughn knowing that he was a violent man, the judge told her, 'Matrimonial disorder ought to be resolved by separation and divorce, and not by a spouse taking into his or her hands the law. I take into account the background to this offence and the fact that this man was undoubtedly given to gross violence. But the offence is so serious it can only be dealt with by a term of custody. Therefore I have come to the conclusion that this is a case where it is necessary and right that I impose a prison sentence but I reduce that sentence substantially because of the background.'

He sentenced Jill to two-and-a-half years' imprisonment. Her solicitor, John Walker, said Jill was 'absolutely shat-tered' by the sentence. He added, 'It had been indicated to the court in reports that she was suitable for probation and she was very shocked to get a prison sentence'.

Nine days after being sent to jail, Jill Stubbs gave birth a month prematurely. Her daughter Frances was born in a special unit at Cheshire's Styal Prison. In early February Mr Justice Coleman ruled that Jill could appeal against the sentence, but hopes that she would be able to take the new baby home pending the appeal were dashed when the judge rejected a plea for bail. Although he ordered the case to be brought to court as quickly as possible, it meant that Jill had to remain behind bars, locked away from the family she had sought to protect from Michael Devaughn.

Her appeal was eventually heard in the High Court in London on 29 April 1993. Miss Rachael Brand, presenting the appeal, said that it was a very sad case of a woman driven to the end of her tether who, at the time of the killing, was suffering from severe depressive illness.

The point had been made, she said, that once Mrs Stubbs had felled her husband with a saucepan she showed a determination to finish the job, and that having strangled him and buried him she then kept quiet about her crime for three years. But in fact Mrs Stubbs was terrified that if Michael Devaughn woke up, he might kill her and their children as he had threatened to do many times in the past. After killing him, one of the principal factors in her mind was the safety of her children – and since she had been in prison one of them had been experiencing considerable difficulty coming to terms with the situation.

Ruling, Lord Chief Justice Taylor said, 'We have examined the circumstances of the case with great anxiety'. He went on to say that sentencing had been approached with great care and due regard had been taken of the history of violence. In considering the sentence, the trial judge had to decide whether there remained a degree of responsibility despite the fact that it was diminished by depressive illness.

Lord Taylor said that the circumstances of the killing suggested a degree of deliberation. It had to be remembered, he said that diminished responsibility did not exhaust responsibility; it did not necessarily mean there was no blame deserving of punishment. Jill Stubbs began to fear the worst and her fears were justified. Lord Taylor concluded, 'Thirty months for manslaughter, even with diminished responsibility, might be regarded as very lenient. We do not say this was a lenient sentence, but one which was perfectly proper, and one this court ought not to interfere with.'

As the decision was announced, Jill held her head in her hands in despair. She could not understand why she had failed to have her sentence reduced – it was almost as if she was being penalised for marrying someone whom she knew had a history of violence, as if that were a justification for his terrorising her for the subsequent nine years.

She had tried many times to escape the clutches of the man whom even the prosecution labelled 'sadistic', but to no avail. Ultimately, for Jill Stubbs, killing Michael Devaughn was the only way out. It is to be hoped that by the time this book appears in print, compassion will have prevailed and she will be back where she belongs – with her family.

Saved by a Son

The sun always seemed to shine on James Cooney. Of course, it shines on all the inhabitants of Florida, the Sunshine State, but it shines particularly brightly on those golden boys from ritzy Palm Beach. Sunny good fortune shone on James from the day he was born. His family was made up of wealthy doctors and lawyers. His father was Palm Beach County's first neurosurgeon. James grew up clever, nice looking, well loved and well motivated. Captain of the college swimming team and graduate with honours from Nôtre Dame University, James was now a sought-after tax attorney. He wanted to succeed. Perhaps, like many American men of his generation, he wanted too much.

His pretty, slim, chestnut-haired wife Linda thought so. When she could think about him at all calmly, without wanting to cry, that is. You could say that for a long while Linda could at least cry in comfort. She and their two sons lived in a condominium in Juno Beach, the classy, select resort a few miles up the coast from Palm Beach. It was a house that would make most millionaires a touch envious. But then the thing about domestic violence is that it's not fussy. It hides behind dented doors of ordinary homes and behind the imposing mahogany portals of grand mansions.

The style and the results of such violence vary very little. The relationship is generally volatile, the man is stronger, the woman and her children are more frightened. Everyone suffers. In America in 1991 an average of 1,500 women were killed by their husbands or boyfriends who had been abusing them for some time beforehand. Each year another 400 to 800 women were fighting back and killing them. The numbers have probably gone up by now. But on Thursday 7 February 1991 Linda became one of the women in those statistics. James Cooney, then forty-two, was one of the men killed.

On that very morning James Cooney managed something he'd been trying to achieve for sometime. He persuaded a judge to order a psychiatric examination of his ex-wife. He wanted custody of his sons and he was planning to let his ex-wife know that night that he was going to get it.

The judge never signed the order. Seven hours later the police found Cooney lying in the hallway of the house they used to share, in palm-fringed Olympus Drive, clutching a knife with a seven inch blade. Linda had shot him three times with a .357 calibre revolver. She had called them and the tapes of those 911 emergency calls told in screams of panic the story of their far from golden marriage.

In 1979, the year that Jimmy Carter tried unsuccessfully to talk the Ayatollah Khomeini into releasing American hostages, James and Linda met at a party in Palm Beach. They married that year. She had not wanted to wait – he was too good a catch. She was a legal secretary from Port Washington, a small town twenty-five miles north of Milwaukee. She had been married briefly in her twenties and had been working for her firm for thirteen years.

The newlyweds lived in Palm Beach Gardens among a small cluster of neat homes. Many rising legal stars were neighbours. One was Moira Lasch, prosecutor in the William Kennedy Smith rape trial. James and his family had been close friends of David Bludworth, the Palm Beach Country state attorney for more than twenty years.

The couple did the usual right things. These included producing two sons, two years apart. They gave and attended the right parties with the right people in the right places. Places such as The Breakers, the stunningly elegant hotel designed by Leonard Schulze in the 1920s before he went to work on the Waldorf Astoria in New York. The right cars glistened in their drive. The right clothes hung in their wardrobes. The right jewellery was stashed in their safe.

But the right conversations were not being enjoyed by this couple. According to Linda's friends and some of the neighbours James began knocking her about in 1983. She didn't tell people, of course. Smart women don't blurt out the fact that there's a snag to life with their smart, 'ideal' husbands. But people guessed. Twice Linda went in to hospital. A neighbour said, 'The doctors and nurses asked her why she was so black and blue. She said she had fallen down but she hadn't. He could be a very angry man.'

In 1983 and 1984 police were called four times to the Palm Beach Gardens home when neighbours complained of disturbances and said they knew Cooney was beating his wife. Battering can be mental as well as physical, of course. In a place like Palm Beach, it can also be social. Linda

Cooney was to be a victim of all three, but she tried to retain her dignity.

Twice in 1987 James filed for divorce, but the couple got back together for the sake of the boys. Later that year they made a 'fresh start' in the condo in Juno Beach, about a block from the Intra-Coastal Waterway and near to Juno Park. But the rows and the beatings continued and James moved out for good in November. The divorce was final the following July.

In her divorce papers Linda claimed that the problems began after Cooney started seeing another woman. His stated only that there were irreconcilable differences. But the settlement was by most standards generous, suggesting perhaps that Cooney did feel he was to blame. He gave Linda their 1984 BMW; half their shares in Seaco Inc., a company which makes inflatable rafts; and half his interest in a local property company. She was also awarded custody of the boys and alimony of $900 a month plus $1,200 in child support.

It looked good on paper. In practice Linda and James, backed by his parents and seven brothers and sisters, were now locked in a bitter battle. They claimed that Linda, frozen out of their charmed circles, tried to retaliate by making scenes. James's sister Patricia picked up the telephone when Linda tried to contact James at his father's house. Patricia said later that Linda screamed and swore at her, threatening that they would have to 'pay for this'. She also arrived uninvited with the boys at a Cooney family Christmas party and caused a rumpus, distressing the children.

In early 1988, when James's father had heart surgery,

Linda tried to contact James by ringing the hospital. James's family said later that Linda pretended there was an emergency involving the children. James later told his family that he'd arrived at the house to find it was a false alarm, maliciously false. But what really happened? A violent argument, perhaps? In February the records show that Linda filed a criminal charge against him of abuse. She later dropped it, almost certainly under pressure.

When James's father died in April of that year, Linda arrived at the funeral wearing a white dress and refused to leave. 'She insisted on staging an appearance, mocking his memory and our grief,' Douglas Cooney fumed. What was interesting was that their father had divided $1.5 of his estate into eight shares. James's sister Rosemary got two of those shares; James, the eldest child, got nothing. Could his father have known that James was not the reasonable man he liked to appear? Might he have believed that James was indeed a tyrant, a cheat and a wife beater?

A neighbour told the *Palm Beach Post* that the illustrious Cooney family had always treated Linda with disdain. 'They always included him in invitations but not her,' he said. 'She would tell me how rude they were to her.' Of the allegedly mischievous phonecalls and embarrassing scenes, Linda's friend June Rubner, from Milwaukee, said, 'She was just trying to maintain some sense of relationship with the children and their father'.

But the Cooneys did not agree. In a letter filed with the court, James's brother Douglas alleged that he and his brothers and sisters lived in fear of Linda and her irrational outbursts. 'Her rage included references to handguns, assaults, trespass, vandalism, slander, public profanity and uncontrollable hysteria. Door locks have been changed to protect us from Linda. Telephone numbers have been changed to protect us from Linda. We cannot afford to take her malicious threats lightly.' He added that Linda planted in her sons' minds the idea that James's sisters 'were sluts and his brothers were preoccupied with sex'. Disagreeable if true, but hardly unbearable. Not, surely, to a group of brothers and sisters who included four lawyers and two doctors. Hardly equal to the misery and humiliation being suffered by one divorced wife with no relatives and no money of her own.

In court Linda was to testify that by the time of the killing James was $67,000 behind in child support payments and that he had never paid alimony. 'He uses support payments as a means to have me come to him and beg for money,' she said. He had ruined her credit rating because he had not paid the credit card bills for necessities. In 1990 she had to go to court to force him to pay a bill for $629 for electricity. For Linda the golden life had turned to dross. Shunned, harassed by her husband, worried about mounting debts, she clung to her children then aged eight and ten. At least she had them – until that Thursday in February when she faced the prospect of losing them.

James drove fast from his father's home, where he'd been living, to Juno Beach and arrived at the house early in the evening. He felt triumphant. This time he'd 'got her'. This time there wouldn't be any nonsense. How his blood boiled to remember other times when he'd come to see the boys. The bitch had insisted on calling the police to stand by 'in case'. In case of what? He'd like to know. In case she drove him to argue back? Did she seriously expect him to take all those criticisms, the don't do this and don't do that, trying to dictate how he should spend his time with them, which of his sisters was good enough to be allowed to see the boys, where they were allowed to go and how they should be returned? So what if once or twice he'd sent them back to her by taxi? It was merely to avoid the unpleasantness of seeing her. So what if once or twice he'd left them at the house of one of his relatives? They were perfectly happy. Who the hell did she think she was?

But this time, he needn't listen to any of that. Not a single, lousy word, thank heaven! He was fed up with her crazy moods, her yapping and nagging. He'd been to see Circuit Judge John Hoy that very day and had received a verbal approval to have the stupid, incompetent little typist from Milwaukee seen by a shrink. Not one of her pathetic, pussyfooting therapists either, but someone who knew about kids, knew she was a danger to those boys, knew her behaviour was erratic and getting worse. She was unfit, as he'd told her so many times. Those boys would be out of her house before she could open her mouth.

It was the third time Cooney had tried to get Linda certified in this way. In 1987 a judge had agreed to a psychiatric examination but insisted the report be sealed, which was no use to him. The second time, the judge realised how Cooney was trying to manipulate the court and refused.

Exactly how much of this James Cooney was able to tell his wife before the fighting started, only Linda knows. When the 911 call went out, the police officers speeding to Olympus Drive knew from what the computer immediately told them that the Cooneys had an 'ongoing domestic problem'. They arrived within two minutes and saw that it was ongoing no more. Linda had shot her husband. Was it from across the room, with presence of mind? A calculated step to end their arguments? Or did the fighting escalate wildly so that he was on the verge of attacking her and almost certainly killing her with the knife? Was it then, as her elder son Kevin stood there screaming and terrified, that she did the only thing she could think of doing to save herself and pulled the trigger again and again till Cooney stopped coming at her? Three shots and the predictable efforts of the close Cooney family of well-connected lawyers made the odds that the jury would believe her story very long indeed.

Linda and the boys were in a bedroom as police used yellow tape to cordon off the area where James Cooney lay. She had called for her lawyer Bert Winkler. He arrived half an hour later and told the police that they could not search the house without a warrant. This meant a four hour wait. Juno Beach Police Chief Mitchell Tyre said this was not unusual and that since lawyers were already on the scene they were determined to do everything by the book.

James Cooney's friends in high legal places could do him no favours as it turned out. State Attorney Budworth had to step down from leading the shooting investigation because, he said, his friendship with James and the fact that he had once, in 1981, employed Linda in his office for a few weeks, meant he had a conflict of interests. He asked that two prosecutors from neighbouring Broward County be hired. Even Palm Beach Circuit Judge Marvin Mounts, due to sit at the trial, offered to excuse himself and suggested that it might be better if the trial were held in another county altogether but both counsels, assistant Broward

County prosecutor Pete Magrino and Richard Lubin for the defence, said they preferred to stay in Palm Beach.

In April Linda was jailed after a grand jury indicted her for first-degree murder. She admitted that she had shot Cooney three times when he came to take custody of their two boys. When the trial began in the first week of May, it looked as if the sun was shining again on Linda.

Steven Lord, an investigator from the department of Health and Rehabilitative Services, told Judge Mounts that it would be best for the boys if they could have their mother home. 'The sun and moon rise for these boys on their mother,' he said. He was also able to report that since the shooting his department had not been able to take custody of the boys away from Linda. The judge at that hearing had dismissed evidence that she was an unsound parent. So Linda was set free on bail despite Magrino's description of her as a cold-blooded killer and despite his suggestion that the Cooney family were afraid of her.

But then clouds began to gather. One of the first witnesses was Rod Englert, a crime-scene expert from an Oregon sheriff's department. He testified that James was in a 'defensive posture and retreating' when Linda shot him with her .357 Smith and Wesson revolver. He said the first two shots, to the left shoulder and right underarm, were fired from a few feet away. Cooney then fell to the ground. The third shot, to the back of her ex-husband's head, was fired from just a few inches away. This, the fatal shot, was delivered deliberately to kill, he said. What's more, he believed the knife in Cooney's hand, the sign that Linda needed to shoot to protect herself, was planted.

On the second day Gerald Styers, a ballistics' expert

hired by the defence, disagreed with Englert's findings. He said that James Cooney was standing within two feet of Linda when she shot him. He said that Cooney could not have been lying on the floor when she delivered the fatal shot to the back of his head because the bullet had passed through his head and had ended up in another room. If the victim had been already on the floor when this shot was fired, the bullet would have been found near the body. However, under cross-examination, he agreed that the bullet might have been kicked from near the body into the other room.

Rising to sum up his defence, Lubin told the jury that the prosecution's experts had not done a complete job. Had they test-fired the gun? No. How accurate then could they be in judging how close the victim was to Linda Cooney when she pulled the trigger? And how had this reed-slim woman managed to turn a sixteen stone, six-foot-three inch man from his stomach to his back after shooting him to place a knife in his hand without getting a speck of blood on her clothes?

'It's a horrible tragedy, but not a murder,' he said.

Magrino argued that if Linda had been defending herself against her husband she would have called the emergency services immediately. Instead it was Kevin who rang them and Linda interrupted the call to ring her friend who was also her attorney.

Linda was not called to the stand, but in a surprise move Kevin himself gave evidence and the jury asked to have it read back to them. This took more than thirty minutes of the one-and-a-half hours the jury needed to deliberate.

They found Linda innocent of murder, accepting that she

had acted in self-defence. The words of one of the boys over whom their parents had fought so bitterly, had saved her. The last thing James Cooney did before his death was to finish the paperwork and sign the cheques to pay for his sons' college education. In his grave, of course, he wasn't able to learn that you can't buy love.

After the
Lord Mayor's Show

The streets of London were thronging with spectators, a sea of colour brightening up the drab November day. They had turned out in force for one of the capital's annual showpieces – the day of the Lord Mayor's Show, a splendid display of pomp and pageantry. The onlookers had come from every stratum of society. Poor mothers from East End slums, wrapped in threadbare shawls to protect themselves from the winter chill, rubbed shoulders with West End gentry in their finery, all eager to catch a glimpse of the procession as it wound its way through the City streets en route to the Mansion House.

It was a day for the people. Lombard Street, site of the Bank of England, served as a particularly popular vantage point on that lunchtime of Monday 10 November 1902. Outside the post office, situated at the western end of Lombard Street, near the junction with King William Street, the crowds stood three deep. At the back, jostling for position, an undernourished boy of about eleven or twelve, in a hand-me-down jacket several sizes too large and shoes with gaping holes in the toes, fretted that his younger brother would be unable to see. 'Oi, mister!' he cried, prodding the cloth-capped figure standing immediately in front, and indicating his sibling. 'Will you give him a leg up?' The man nodded, and hoisted the frail specimen firmly onto his shoulders. The boy's face lit up as he was held aloft with a perfect view over the heads of his elders. Such camaraderie was repeated right along the line although the St John's Ambulance Brigade reported that the crush of anticipation brought about a total of sixty-three casualties in the course of the day. Elderly women spoke of not having missed a Lord Mayor's Show for years. Everyone was in high spirits. And at the end of the day as they returned home, the vast majority were blissfully unaware that, at around 2.30pm when the crowds were at their most vociferous, a frenzied murder had taken place in their midst.

Kitty Byron was twenty-three at the time. Her family background is shrouded in mystery. All that is known is that she was christened Emma, but chose to be known as Kitty, and that she sometimes worked as a milliner's assistant. She was a pretty, dark-haired girl whose pale complexion and slender figure meant that she looked considerably younger than her age. Perhaps that was what attracted the attention of a married man more than twenty years her senior, Arthur Reginald Baker.

At forty-five, Baker was a stockbroker in the City of London and, dressed in his silk hat and frock-coat, exuded the respectability normally associated with the Stock Exchange. But, in Baker's case, outward appearances were deceptive. He had long strayed from the straight and narrow path trodden by his colleagues and had acquired a reputation as a drunkard, a brute, a debtor and a philanderer. As a consequence, he had few friends at work. He had a wife and children but, due to his inability to support them financially, they lived with his wife's parents somewhere in the West Country. Having spent Kitty's meagre earnings from her occasional periods of employment, he was now virtually penniless and only survived on money borrowed from his brother. But Kitty Byron adored this wastrel.

In this instance, if love was not exactly blind it was certainly in need of an eye test. On 21 July 1902, Baker took a bed-sitting room at a boarding house at 18 Duke Street, which runs between Oxford Street and Manchester Square in London's West End. As now, it was an affluent neighbourhood and so, when about a week later Baker installed Kitty there as his wife, the landlady, Madame Liard, had no reason to suspect this was not the truth, even allowing for the considerable age difference between the pair. After all, it was not Soho.

Cynics might suggest that Baker and Kitty argued so much they simply had to be married. Few lovers would put up with the constant physical and verbal abuse to which poor Kitty was subjected. The principal cause was Baker's heavy drinking. The more he imbibed, the more violent he became, regularly knocking his young mistress about and on one occasion half strangling her. His drunken rages shook the whole house at night, greatly disturbing Madame Liard's other guests and reducing Kitty to a quivering wreck. Kitty herself did nothing to provoke these outbursts. It appears she did not drink and tried her utmost to persuade Baker to kick the habit or at least cut down his intake to manageable proportions. Her pleas fell on deaf ears and matters came to a head on the evening of Friday 7 November. Baker was drunk again and the row was louder and more violent than usual.

Hearing the commotion, Madame Liard marched upstairs. The sight with which she was greeted on entering the couple's room was every landlady's nightmare. A tornado would have caused less disarray. The bed clothes were strewn about the floor where they were joined by sundry other items. In one corner lay a hat which had been ripped into shreds.

Madame Liard confronted Baker. 'What in God's name has been going on?' she demanded. Before Baker could manage to slur any form of reply, the ever protective Kitty interjected. 'Oh, there's nothing the matter,' she said, 'we've been playing milliner.'

It seems highly unlikely that any landlady (who by nature are a suspicious breed) would believe such an explanation but Madame Liard liked, or at least felt sorry for, Kitty and therefore did not wish to add to her humiliation. So she decided to opt for a policy of discretion, turning a blind eye to the incident in the hope that her obvious disapproval would prevent any further fracas.

Given Baker's state, she was being remarkably optimistic. Not long after her departure, the quarrel started up again. At first, it was relatively low-key, but as evening became night it built to a crescendo. Eventually, at 1.15am, with most of her guests trying to get a decent night's sleep, the remarkably tolerant Madame Liard could take no more.

Setting out to quell the combatants, she found Kitty on the landing, shivering in her nightdress as if seeking refuge.

'What is happening?' asked the landlady. 'You look terrified. What are you doing out here?'

'Really, it's nothing,' insisted Kitty. 'There's nothing the
matter at all.'

Fearful that her house would begin to acquire the wrong
sort of reputation if her rowdy lodgers stayed, Madame
Liard gave Baker notice to quit the following morning.
But the pair made no attempt to leave immediately and,
possibly in a last-ditch effort to stave off his impending
eviction, Baker behaved himself over the weekend. Indeed,
displaying entirely uncharacteristic tenderness, he even
took Kitty a cup of tea on the morning of Monday 10
November before setting off for the Stock Exchange. She
responded by gently kissing him goodbye. Yet within five
hours of this touching domestic scene, Reginald Baker
would be stabbed to death by his lover.

Baker's fatal error was in revealing his true nature to the
landlady just before leaving the house at 10.30am. He asked
for a quiet word with her, out of Kitty's earshot. He said he
had a proposition. 'If I can keep the room,' he suggested, 'I
will guarantee that Kitty will leave.'

Madame Liard was in no mood for bargaining. Apart
from the fact that her sympathies lay very much with Kitty,
she was furious because Baker still owed her rent, having
given her a cheque which bounced all the way from the
West End to the City. So she insisted that they must leave
as arranged. Baker then saw fit to disclose the truth about
his relationship with Kitty – that they were not man and
wife. 'She is the cause of all the trouble,' he sneered. 'She
has no class.'

After Baker's departure, Kitty apologised to Madame

Liard for the rowdy goings-on of the 7th. 'I am very sorry that we have to go,' she added. Madame Liard was also sorry to see Kitty go, but she was not sad to see the back of Baker. Deploring Baker's attitude and realising that he was using Kitty as nothing more than a doormat, she decided to relay some of his comments to her. 'He tells me you are not his wife,' said the landlady.

'That is true,' replied Kitty. 'Next week you will hear of a law suit.'

'What is it?' asked the inquisitive Madame Liard.

'If I tell you, don't tell him, because he will bang me so. He will have a divorce from his wife.'

Madame Liard felt compelled to offer a little maternal advice. 'As you are not his wife, why do you stay? Why do you live with a brute like that? Why don't you leave him?'

'I can't,' sighed Kitty. 'I love him so. Besides, I have lost my character and have no work.' Madame Liard resigned herself to the fact that she would be unable to make Kitty see the error of her ways, but on her way back to her room Kitty was approached by the housemaid, Isabel Kingate, who had overheard the earlier conversation between Baker and the landlady.

'There is something I feel I ought to tell you,' said the maid, 'something that Mr Baker said to my mistress. I think it is in your interest to know.'

'What is it?' queried a puzzled Kitty.

'He said that you had no class – he feels you are beneath him.' She went on to add that Baker had said he was planning to rid himself of Kitty. Hearing this, Kitty's mood changed dramatically. 'Will he?' she fumed. 'I'll kill him before the day is out!'

Kitty's loyalty to Baker was wavering at last. She felt that the man she loved so deeply had betrayed her, and dreaded the prospect that he would send her away to her sister. Bitter and bewildered, her mind was in a turmoil when she left Duke Street at 11.50 that morning.

Stepping out into the cold November air, her hands warmed by a fur muff, she headed for the shop of James Moore, a cutler, in Oxford Street. 'I want a knife with a long and strong blade,' she said on entering the premises. Mr Moore produced a large knife with a spring blade that fitted into the hasp. He thought Kitty seemed too slight a girl to handle it, and suggested looking for a different model. But Kitty was happy with that one – she said she had a strong grip and proved it by operating the spring action several times while the cutler looked on. Having completed the sale for 5s. 6d. Mr Moore prepared to wrap the knife in paper. 'I don't want it wrapped up,' declared Kitty. 'Give it to me. I can take it in my muff.' Acceding to the customer's wishes, the shopkeeper handed Kitty the closed knife and she duly secreted it in her muff.

From there, Kitty made her way through the assembling crowds to the post office in Lombard Street, arriving at 1.15pm. She went to the area of the office provided for members of the public to send telegrams and wrote out a message on a telegraph form. It read: DEAR REG STOP WANT YOU IMMEDIATE IMPORTANTLY, KITTY STOP. She then asked counter clerk Joseph Frayer for a stamped envelope. It cost her 3d. to send the message by express letter.

Having put the message in the envelope, she sealed it and returned to the telegraph desk. Then, after addressing it, she handed it to another clerk, Arthur Chivers. Making polite conversation, Chivers asked, 'Have you seen the Lord Mayor's Show?'

'No,' answered Kitty, rather abruptly, 'and I have no wish to see it.'

Chivers took the express envelope at 1.22pm and handed it to a messenger boy, William Robert Coleman. The envelope was addressed to 'Reginald Baker Esq., Westralian Market, Stock Exchange'.

The Stock Exchange was but a short walk away and Kitty anticipated a swift response. However young Coleman eventually returned with neither Baker nor a reply. He told the waiting Kitty that he had been unable to deliver it as 'the gentleman had not come down'.

By now, Kitty was becoming increasingly excitable. Even the staff had begun to notice her strange behaviour. When she first entered the post office, she seemed perfectly calm but had subsequently started to show distinct signs of impatience and anxiety. Coleman's return did nothing to ease her state of mind.

'Take it back,' she insisted.

If Coleman thought another journey fruitless, it was not his position to say so. Instead he did as he was told. This time, he did manage to locate Baker who, on reading the express letter, fought his way through the masses and returned with Coleman to Lombard Street.

It was 2.25pm when the two reached the post office. Kitty was not in the building at the time but her absence was only momentary. As soon as Kitty and Baker came face to face, they argued. It is an indication of Kitty's fragile temperament at the time and of Baker's inherent meanness that the trivial dispute that followed should have become blown up out of all proportion.

It began when William Dunn, a clerk at the post office, asked Kitty for an excess payment of 2d., chargeable for the additional time incurred by the messenger boy in having to make two journeys to deliver the letter to the Stock Exchange.

Turning to Baker, Kitty said caustically, 'All right, old boy, I am worth 2d.'. Baker showed no signs of taking the hint. Kitty became more emphatic. 'You must pay the 2d.,' she told him firmly. Baker, embarrassed and angry at being called away from his work, flatly refused. 'No, I shan't,' he replied bluntly. Adopting her usual role of conciliator, Kitty produced a florin. She held it up and said to Baker, 'Pay it with this'. Unaccountably, Baker turned down her offer and steadfastly refused to pay. She even tried to put the coin in his pocket but he merely shook his head and retired backwards towards the door.

As Baker made his exit, still relentlessly pursued by Kitty (who was persisting with her attempt to put the coin into his pocket) and still arguing, clerk Arthur Chivers saw a knife flash in the girl's hand. 'She has got a knife,' he called out. Baker did not hear him. Outside, hundreds of people were waiting patiently for the Lord Mayor's procession. Their eyes were trained along Lombard Street rather than on the post office behind them. Thus only a dozen or so saw Kitty Byron standing at the top of the steps leading from the door of the post office clutching an open knife in her hand.

She descended the steps so that she was on a level with Baker and stabbed him. Reeling from the blow, Baker staggered off and reached the wall of the building in front of the post office. But there was to be no escape. Kitty followed him and stabbed him twice more in swift succession. One of the blows was so severe that Baker died almost instantly.

Seeing what had happened, a workman rushed over and grabbed Kitty's hand, causing the knife to clatter to the pavement. By then, Baker was probably already dead. Kitty was seized with the type of immediate remorse so often associated with a crime of passion. She threw herself upon her victim's body, sobbing hysterically. 'Let me go to him. . . . Let me kiss my Reggie. . . . My dear Reggie. . . . Let me kiss my husband.'

The vast majority of the crowd had no idea what had happened just a few yards away. Even those who had seen Kitty actually strike him were amazed to discover that there had been a murder. They saw no blood and some, their view of the knife obscured, merely thought she was hitting him with her muff. To them, it was nothing more than an everyday domestic quarrel, a sight all too familiar in Edwardian London.

The police, whose efficiency remained open to question in the wake of the Jack the Ripper murders, were not taxed to make an arrest in this case. The smartly dressed, waiflike figure of Kitty Byron, looking anything but a murderess, was taken to Cloak Lane Police Station. By a macabre coincidence this building, where she was held for the night, stood on the site of the deceased's boyhood home.

Meanwhile, Reginald Baker was taken to St Bartholomew's Hospital where he was pronounced dead on arrival. From there, his body was removed to Cloak Lane mortuary. A search of his pockets revealed only an empty sovereign purse, a card case and a wallet, empty except for a divorce court citation from Mrs Baker which he had received only that morning and which named Miss K Byron as co-respondent.

Kitty was brought into Cloak Lane at 2.45pm. In the course of the day, she made two vastly different statements to Inspector Fox of the City police, an officer based at that station. Shortly after her arrival she told him, 'I killed him willingly, and he deserved it, and the sooner I am killed the better'. But at 5.40pm, when Inspector Fox visited her in her cell, she apparently said, 'Inspector, I wish to say something to you. I bought the knife to hit him but I did not know I was killing him.' The discrepancy in these statements can lead to two interpretations. Either Kitty was still in a state of shock when she first spoke to Inspector Fox and it was not until later that she was able to compose herself or, of course, she realised that her first statement was highly incriminating and changed it accordingly. After the Lord Mayor's Show, events moved speedily.

On the following day Kitty was, somewhat ironically, brought before the new Lord Mayor, Alderman Sir Marcus Samuel, in the Justice Room of the Mansion House. There she was 'charged with the wilful murder of Arthur Reginald Baker by stabbing him in several parts of his body with a knife'. Public sympathy lay firmly with Kitty. She was seen very much as the victim of her lover's brutal ways and this was illustrated on 25 November when the coroner's jury returned a verdict of manslaughter. The court officials could hardly believe their ears.

The coroner himself felt it necessary to clarify their verdict. 'Do you mean unlawful killing without malice?'

'Yes,' answered the foreman, 'killing on the impulse of

the moment. We do not believe she went there with the intention of killing him.'

The stunned prosecution nevertheless asked the Lord Mayor to commit Kitty on a charge of murder. His Worship duly obliged. Kitty may have thought he was getting his own back after she had marred his glorious day.

When the truth of Baker's treatment of Kitty emerged at the committal proceedings, his own Stock Exchange colleagues were so appalled by his behaviour and so moved by her plight that they actually clubbed together to provide the money for the girl's defence. As a result, she was able to afford the finest counsel, led by Henry Dickens, son of the great Victorian novelist. Her trial began at the Central Criminal Court on 17 December, shortly before old Newgate and the adjacent buildings were demolished.

One observer noted, 'Men and women crowded the inconvenient old court to the point of suffocation. The prisoner looked little more than a child, and was obviously frightened by the proceedings and by the crowds about her.'

Kitty Byron certainly made a pitiful figure in the dock – so young, so delicate, so innocent-looking. She wore a neat blue serge suit and a white shirt with a high collar which gripped her neck like a linen noose. The outfit was completed by a black tie. To those in the gallery, she looked incapable of any act of aggression, let alone the wielding of a heavy knife with murderous intent. Sir Travers Humphreys, then a junior brief for her defence, later recounted how Kitty clung grimly to the wardress who led her into the dock. 'It seemed as if she would break down at the very outset.'

Kitty's dark eyes darted nervously around the courtroom. When asked how she pleaded to the charge of murder, she whispered plaintively, 'Not guilty'. The prosecution case was presented by Mr Charles Matthews and Mr Archibald Bodkin. The former spoke in that familiar thin, high-pitched voice which he so often used to such cutting effect. Here he had no need to summon his full repertoire of invective. He called a total of twenty witnesses.

Dr Gordon Brown, surgeon to the City police, described Baker's injuries. He said there were three stab wounds on the dead man: a three-inch horizontal wound above the left ear; one over the right shoulder; and the fatal wound, which penetrated the breast bone. As the surgeon was indicating on his own body the precise location of her lover's stab wounds, Kitty broke down. The pain of the memory was too much for her to take. A stifled wail was heard from the dock and the gaze of the court was directed at the frantically sobbing defendant.

Dr Brown went on to testify that as Baker had slumped to the ground following the final blow, he had also cut himself above the eye. Eliminating the possibility of an accidental death, Dr Brown said he did not believe that the chest wound could have been caused by the weight of Baker's body falling on the knife. Examination of Kitty's body showed a number of bruises on her legs.

Further witnesses recalled Kitty's state of mind in the post office. One said that the time of the killing, the accused seemed 'dazed and silly'. Counter clerk Joseph Frayer, explaining her declining composure during the hour-long period between sending the express letter and Baker's eventual return added, 'If I was allowed to surmise, I should say that she had gone somewhere and had some brandy'.

Such evidence was not supported by that of Isabel King-ate, Madame Liard's maid who said that while Baker drank every day, Kitty never touched a drop. Madame Liard went on to describe Baker as 'a very great drunkard'. It was not intended as a term of praise. Curiously, the police uncovered a series of affectionate letters written to Kitty by Baker, in one of which he begged her not to drink since it would ruin her health. Perhaps this was just a piece of advice lest she should ever be tempted to follow in his inebriated footsteps.

The defence called no witnesses, not even Kitty herself. Mr Dickens brought forward no plea of insanity – instead, with a flair for fiction of which his father would have been proud, he urged the jury to believe that Kitty had purchased the knife to kill herself, not Baker. He insisted that the purpose of Kitty's express letter was so that she could tell Baker that she was going to kill herself at his feet because she was so upset at the prospect of having to leave him.

'She hoped by saying that,' said Dickens, 'that the old love would come back again and that they would live together as before.'

Unfortunately, this theory of suicide or emotional black-mail was totally at odds with the evidence. Dickens was on safer ground when he sought to win the hearts of the jurors by depicting the sad lifestyle and unblemished character of the defendant.

'Evidence showed that the prisoner was devoted to the deceased man,' he said. It was only another instance of how a woman's love passed all understanding.

There was no evidence whatsoever to support the sugges-tion of the prosecution that she left the house on 10 November with a feeling of resentment against him. On the contrary, her last words on leaving were, 'I love him'. (Mr Dickens clearly preferred to overlook the conversation with the maid.)

> He treated her like a brute but there was never a word of anger from her. In spite of the ill-usage which she received at his hands, she still loved him. When he was sober, he loved her, and it was drink which drove him to the excesses and made him treat her like a brute.

Dickens was determined to bow out with a flourish.

> The Court in which we now sit will soon be demolished and in it there have been many tragic scenes and many terrible sights. But I doubt whether there has ever been so tragic and so piteous a sight as the spectacle of this young girl, on the very threshold of her life, standing there awaiting your verdict as to whether she is to live or die. May Almighty God be with her in this last hour of her trial.

In his summing-up, the judge, Mr Justice Darling, told the jury that it was a mistake to think that it was only the prisoner's advocate who felt the tragedy of a trial of this kind. He was remarkably candid about his own emotions. 'Gentlemen of the jury,' he said, 'if I had consulted my own feelings, I should probably have stopped this case at the outset.'

He was equally honest in dismissing manslaughter as an appropriate verdict, telling the jury that it needed more than their sympathy to justify such a finding. With manslaughter ruled out, there could be only one possible verdict. It took the jury just eight minutes to reach it. They found Kitty Byron guilty of murder, but added the strongest possible recommendation to mercy. Asked by the judge whether she had anything to say before he passed sentence, Kitty said quietly, 'I am not guilty'.

Apart from her plea at the very start, these were the only words she had spoken in court. Just as there was only one possible verdict, a conviction for murder meant only one possible sentence. The black cap was brought forth. Her wan face paled even more as Mr Justice Darling announced that she was to hang by the neck until dead. But he added that he would pass on the jury's recommendation for mercy, the reasons for which he said he could very well understand.

Given the weight of public feeling, there was little danger of Kitty Byron going to the gallows. The offices of her solicitors were overrun by those eager to put their names to a public petition. No fewer than fifteen thousand signatures were obtained in a single morning, three thousand of them from the dead man's fellow clerks at the Stock Exchange.

As it transpired, the petition was not needed for the Home Secretary granted a reprieve before the document could be presented to the authorities. Kitty's sentence was commuted to penal servitude for life and then, in 1907, it was reduced to ten years. In the event, she was released twelve months later, in 1908, having served just six years in prison. Upon gaining her freedom, she changed her name and went to live in the country where she was finally able to put the misery of her time with Reginald Baker behind her.

Cucumber in the Freezer

For five years Janet Gardner lived a double life. There was the normal one in which she was a fifty-one-year-old grandmother who had run her own business and worked part-time for a charity for the homeless. There was also the abnormal life in which she was a sparring partner in a macabre match of strength with a madman called Peter Iles.

'I went out with him for just nine months and I'll pay for that mistake for the rest of my life,' she said when it was all over. By then Peter Iles had already paid. She killed him in her kitchen in Southsea on the night of Friday 7 September 1990 while he was smashing her head against the door frame. He called her a stupid bitch and tried to batter her into submission, but it was to be for the last time. It was an ugly death according to the police. Yet a jury believed this was not murder and three appeal court judges decided that society should seek no further revenge. For an answer to the question of why an intelligent, independent woman who knew the difference between right and wrong should 'get away with it', we must begin at the beginning.

This is not a story of a foolish young woman trapped in marriage to a violent man. This couple never even lived together. This is not a story of love warped into a pattern of pain and remorse. This is a story of a man in late middle age who saw his chance of a colourful and comfortable old age slipping through his hands.

Peter Iles had a dream of owning a bar in the Costa Del Sol, Spain. He had loved it there when he'd been on package holidays; had loved the weather, the pace of life, the chance to wear casual clothes. He relished the prospect of standing behind his own counter, ministering to the constant stream of lonely women who went there on holiday, game for casual sex.

Iles, as you will gather, was a man's man. He knew what worked with women. Oh, yes. A bit of flattery, a bit of humour, a lot of taking the lead both in bed and out. Iles was a gambler who had rarely had money and had certainly never been able to save it. He was married for more than twenty years until his wife could stand no more and their divorce came through in the early 1980s. Their son Ian would later tell the court that his father liked and wanted the benefits of a stable family life but he also wanted his freedom.

In those days he had the freedom, lodgings in 21 Albert Road, Southsea. It wasn't much, but he told himself it wasn't for long – not now that he'd met Janet. But when his plan to hook himself a bright and well set-up divorcee who'd hand over the reins and the bank books to him showed signs of going wrong, he knew he needed to adapt. This called for cunning, a lot more charm and a lot more showing her who was boss. He knew she'd be too ashamed to tell anyone about their fights. Anyway, he thought, she needed a man and she liked the rough stuff really.

Most women on their own can use a little love and friendship and in 1985 Janet Gardner was no exception. She would have been horrified if anyone had suggested then that she might have fallen under the influence of a violent man. She would have said, had she heard this of another woman, 'How could she let this happen? Hasn't she any self respect?' She was sure nothing like that could happen to her.

She was then, and still is, a handsome dark-haired woman of medium height, well groomed and easy to talk to. When she ran a shop selling nearly-new clothes and stylish women brought in their elegant outfits (whose only faults were that too many of their friends had seen them once or twice) she often wished she were taller and slimmer so that she might enjoy wearing them herself. But she was never vain and while she was healthy she was too sensible to care a great deal. She had had bouts of depression and her GP, Dr Young, had prescribed antidepressants, but after a few months she'd felt better.

By that time Janet had been divorced from her husband for twenty years. It had been a civilised divorce as these things go and she had kept custody of the three children, Stephen, Kevin and Louise. She also kept the family's five-bedroom house – 6 Beach Road in the lively seaside resort of Southsea, the prettier part of Portsmouth. They lived quietly and comfortably. She was a trained bookkeeper and money was not a problem in her life. Nor were men.

That changed in October when she took on the job of keeping the accounts for the Granada Bingo and Social Club in Portsmouth. She met the maintenance man there. Peter Iles was a bit of a character. Later, laughingly, she described him as Prince Charming. He was fifty-seven, shorter than her but agile, athletic and he could flatter for Britain in the Olympics. They began to go out and it was fun. But she didn't have to wait long for the first signs of his other nature.

When he discovered that she hadn't bought him a Christmas present he flew into a rage. She was sitting in a car at the time with the seat belt in place across her body. Angrily, Iles pushed her head sideways, squashing it against the frame of the car door and yanked the belt up so that it was taut across her throat. She thought he would strangle her to death. 'I had never known violence before,' she told the police when the full story began to pour out. She certainly knew it after that.

But Janet Gardner must have decided that Iles was genuinely upset that she had not wanted to buy him a token to acknowledge their relationship. She must have thought that perhaps she had made a mistake. After all, although she didn't feel different, she knew she was moving towards the menopause – that age at which women do make mistakes and do forget obvious things. At any rate she didn't tell her children about Iles' assault and she didn't tell her colleagues at work about the arguments they went on to have.

In that year, 1986, Iles brought Janet a ring. He said it should be a wedding ring. She told him she didn't want to marry him, not then at any rate. But he insisted she keep it so that she always knew he was serious. She never doubted he was serious in his intentions, if not his affections. It weighed on her mind all day, everyday. Without realising it, she was slipping slowly back into a depression. It was a triumph at the time that she carried on, got through each day of the 'normal' life. She did not tell her children what was going on. 'She didn't want to worry us,' said Kevin, then thirty. Only when it was all over and she was alone in her cell in Holloway Prison did she realise that for four out of five years she had kept a piece of frozen cucumber in her freezer to soothe her punched and puffy eyes, a bottle of witch hazel to bring out the bruises and an assortment of cosmetic concealing creams to hide the signs of her abuse.

When the marks were too livid to conceal she told colleagues she had been mugged. On the days when she was too upset or shaken to function she simply telephoned, cancelled her meetings and stayed at home. Perhaps she had a drink which dulled some of the pain but added to her weight and made her even more depressed. She told only one woman friend who advised her to tell the police. She didn't do that but she did resolve to finish with Iles and end their abnormal life.

But Iles wasn't having that. By this time he had revealed his plans for their future. All Janet had to do was to agree to live with him, sell her house and invest the money in his Spanish dream. It wasn't her dream but she agreed to consider it and she even went so far as to put her house on the market. In December 1986 they went to Torremolinos to look at businesses. It was there that they had a bitter row. Iles punched her and knocked her head against a bar. It caused a serious cut. It was then that Janet decided that life with him in Spain would be too much of a risk. If he wished to run a bar in Spain, he should finance it himself, she said.

But he had no money. He thought that they should go on seeing each other so that, with a little rough persuasion, he would change her mind. He never did, although the persuasion got rougher and rougher. On one occasion during 1987 he cut her neck with a knife. She still bears the scar.

Janet Gardner tried to forget she'd ever met him. She changed her phone number five times in all. She changed jobs. But he tried harder. He stalked her. He waited for her in the alleyway behind her house and grabbed her. He leapt from his car as she walked along the Southsea streets and once punched her when she refused to get into the passenger seat. He succeeded one time in making her get into the car and, in crazy desperation, tried to kill them both by driving straight into an on-coming coach. Luckily the driver of that swerved and avoided a crash.

On another occasion Iles hid in a neighbour's garden and jumped out at Janet as she braved the night to buy a tin of cat food from a nearby shop. When a neighbour tried to stop him hitting her he yelled, 'She belongs to me, I'll kill her if I want to!'

How did Janet Gardner cope with this? She carried on trying to pretend to herself that he would give up and it would be over soon. Twice she went to hospital to be X-rayed and patched up. Perhaps she reached her lowest ebb in August 1987 when they were on holiday together on his beloved Costa Del Sol. It was supposed to be a new beginning for them but over a meal in a restaurant Iles said that he had been sleeping with another woman. Janet was not surprised as there had been long spells when they had not been together as a couple. She was even a little relieved. Another woman would take the pressure off her.

Another woman could possibly free her for ever. But was it a lie? Three years later the court was to learn that there probably had been another woman, more than one perhaps.

But Janet was the one he wanted and couldn't quite possess. With a couple of drinks under his belt, he became increasingly angry. He'd wanted her to show her jealousy to prove to him that he was the man she wanted. Outside the restaurant he began punching her and she fell to the ground. A police car drew up but Iles gave the policemen money to go away. He told them she was his wife and so it was his right to 'correct' her. In that land of machismo, they understood. Back at their hotel he hit her again. She searched for the packet of strong headache pills in her suitcase, took them into the bathroom with her, swallowed them all and sank into a warm bath to wait for oblivion. Before that happened, Iles had sobered up, noticed her absence, barged in and dragged her out, slapping her into wakefulness.

'I wanted to go home but I couldn't get the plane ticket off him and there weren't any other plane seats,' she remembered later. When they finally returned, her spirit was broken. The other woman seemed her only hope.

By the following St Valentine's Day, that other woman was still a weapon he tried to use against her. He'd taken Janet out but they returned home early because, he said, he was off to see someone else. He pulled out a bunch of flowers from the back of the car and gave it to Janet as a sort of consolation prize. She told him she didn't want the flowers. It was not the response he wanted: he wanted her to show she was hurt, he wanted her to plead. Instead he said she was an ungrateful bitch and hit her around the face, blacking both of her eyes.

Janet decided that she would move to avoid him. She took over her daughter's flat and hoped he would not find her. By this time she had changed her job. But Iles was not easily given the slip. He tracked down her new place of employment and, at the first opportunity, followed her home from work. Alarmed, Janet decided finally that she must tell the police but was told they had better things to do than interfere in private squabbles.

It was then that matters became even worse. During one of their high voltage arguments, Iles hit her hard across the eye. She knew it would mean more shame when she tried to go to work the next day. It was humiliating having to make excuses when people noticed, as they always did. He'd hit her and blacked an eye about a month earlier and she'd told people at the Housing Association that she'd been mugged. She couldn't use that excuse again, nor could she keep changing jobs to hide her shame.

When he next came to her house to see her, an argument flared instantly. She was so angry she picked up a small hammer and hit him with that. Then she was horrified. For the first time she realised that he had turned her into a savage. She had not thought herself capable of striking another person with force and with hatred in her heart. 'I wanted to kill him then,' she told the police later. 'That frightened me.'

So Janet went to her solicitor to seek an injunction restraining Iles from trying to see or contact her. Her solicitor wrote to Iles' solicitor. Iles saw both of them. 'What a fuss about nothing,' he must have sighed, perhaps adding with a worldly smile, 'You have to feel sorry for these neurotic, menopausal women, don't you? Leave it to me. I'll apologise, smooth it over, calm her down and that'll be that. I'll stay away. I had every intention of finishing with her anyway. Just thought she needed a friend during this difficult phase. Know what I mean, old chap?' Both old chaps knew exactly and both agreed not to take the matter any further.

When Iles did see Janet his tone was different. She was to tell the court that he was furious and shouted, 'I had respect for you before. Now you have gone to the authorities, I could kill you.' Repeatedly he said he would kill her after that. But it was she who killed him.

She was charged but allowed bail. Then on Tuesday 19 November 1991 Janet Susan Gardner stood in the dock at Winchester Crown Court accused of the murder of Peter John Iles. She pleaded not guilty to murder and not guilty to manslaughter. She had acted in self-defence. While the prosecuting counsel, Nigel Pascoe QC, intended to prove that she was a violent woman who gave as good as she got, her defending counsel, David Owen-Thomas QC, planned to prove that she was provoked and had not intended to kill.

It was not a long trial and the Honourable Mr Justice Swinton-Thomas was patient and polite to the jury of eight men and four women when he began summing up on the second day. He reminded them that Iles' colleague, Mr Luazoo, the maintenance foreman at the Granada Leisure Group, had testified that Iles was an easy-going, helpful person. He had been surprised, therefore, to notice on two occasions cuts on Iles' face, cuts deep enough to cause blood to drip onto his jacket. Mr Kay, another workmate, recalled having seen Iles with a black eye on one occasion, scratch marks on his face on another and a dressing on his head on another. Two other people from work, both women, had noticed scratches, clearly of nails or claws, on Iles' face at different times. But whose nails were they? Janet Gardner's friends had mentioned that she used to bite her nails to the quick. A sign of nervousness, no doubt. At any rate it would have been impossible for her to scratch someone's face. Could these marks have been made by the other woman?

Janet Gardner denied that she had ever blacked Peter Iles' eyes. She did not cause the gouge marks to his cheek and she did not, could not, scratch his face with her chewed down nails. But the injury to his head may have been her doing. It was probably caused by one of her boots that she sent flying through the air. On this occasion sex had made Iles' fury flare. Janet Gardner had had the audacity to state her terms. Janet told the court that it had happened after she had been free of him for a long time. They had met and she had let him talk her round again. She went to his room and they were at the point of having sexual intercourse. She asked him to wear a condom as she thought he'd been with other women. He refused and became angry. She picked up one of the boots she had just slipped off and threw it, aiming it at his head. Those months away had sharpened her resolve and her eye. She hit the target.

Both the defence and the prosecution wanted to show the jury that the Iles/Gardner relationship was fiery and had been so almost from the first moment. Nigel Pascoe needed to show that Janet, who was an inch taller and a stone heavier than Iles, was no weak woman. She could have injured Iles. There was no shortage of witnesses to their frequent arguments but few had seen her actually strike Iles and none had seen her strike first. Mrs Lee Marsh, daughter of Iles' landlady, who also knew Janet, told how when she visited her mother's house the couple arrived and went to the room above where she was sitting. She heard 'crash, bang, wallop!' she said. Shortly afterwards Iles came down with blood running from his forehead and the back of his head. As he came into their room, he was holding a shoe.

There was also the evidence of the note which had been attached to a bunch of eighteen red roses sent to Janet in July of 1990. The note read: 'To Jan, Sorry about last Saturday night. I love you, Peter.'

The tell-tale marks of those fights that Janet Gardner had tried to hide with concealing cosmetics had been noticed too. Into court had come John Matthews, who was supervisor of the Portsmouth Housing Association who had trained Janet Gardner to work for him in February 1988. He saw a black eye, marks on her neck and the signs that she was limping. Mrs Southall, who knew Janet from the voluntary work she did at the Harbour Community for addicts of drink and drugs, had noticed the marks too. From 1987 onwards Janet had often had bruises on her arms and legs and Mrs Southall had noticed a black eye that had lasted for three weeks, so serious was it.

Valerie Nash, a neighbour in Beach Road, remembered a swollen bruise on one side of Janet Gardner's face in the summer of 1989. Young Susan Blake remembered looking out from a window during Christmas of 1989 from her parents' house in Somerset Road, which lies behind Beach

Road. She saw an argument raging between the pair. Peter Iles hit Janet and pushed her to the ground. Janet got up, but fell a second time. Mrs Powell, a nurse who had known Janet for twenty-five years, described an incident near the pier at Southsea when she saw Iles strike her friend violently. She saw Janet the following day with severe bruises to her chest, arms and shoulder. Subsequently she had seen Janet with similar bruises and she understood that Iles had caused them all. Dr Young, Janet's GP, reported that he had treated her for signs of distress when she saw her in December 1987 and he had prescribed hormone replacement therapy. Just short of a year later, she consulted him when she had a badly bruised face. She told him that a former man friend had punched her. He sent her to the local hospital to be X-rayed for a suspected fractured nose. A month later she attended the surgery again and was found to have bruises to the ribs, shoulder, chin and nose. It appeared that they were from two separate incidents and the patient, he said, was tense and frightened.

Dr Young told the court that during the next year, 1989, he had seen Janet Gardner on several occasions. She had needed stitches to a cut on her head after being knocked over and hit. She also needed stitching on an ear where someone had kicked her after knocking her to the ground. Both injuries, the medical notes showed, had been caused by an ex-boyfriend.

Similar problems came to the attention of Dr Young and Janet Gardner's colleagues during 1990. By August the problems were not only physical but also mental. Gardner was prescribed sleeping pills and anti-depressants. But, according to the notes, by August 1990 Janet Gardner was

Janet Gardner and her children, Louise and Kevin, admire flowers from well-wishers (*Solent News and Picture Agency*)

Since 1988 Brenda Clubine has run the support group Convicted Women Against Abuse in the Californian Institution for Women at Frontera. Her requests for parole have been turned down twice (*Myung J. Chun/Los Angeles Daily News*)

Above Michael Meade – 'an evil man who behaved like an animal' (*Newcastle Chronicle & Journal*)

Above right Danny Boyes, who had agreed to murder Meade for £15,000 (*Newcastle Chronicle & Journal*)

Right Susan Harrison. Ten years with Michael Meade had transformed the 'happy-go-lucky' girl into a disturbed, nervous woman (*Newcastle Chronicle & Journal*)

Pamela Sainsbury (*Richard Lappas*)

Paul Sainsbury running in the annual Sidmouth half marathon (*Richard Lappas*)

Emma Humphries continues to campaign for her murder conviction to be quashed (*Yorkshire Television*)

Kiranjit Ahluwalia and her supporters celebrate her release (*Syndication International*)

feeling more positive. Did this mean she had decided to act, had formed a plan or hatched a plot to take revenge on the man who ran her life? Or was it a brief spell of recovery, a little patch of optimism that somehow she would make him see reason and they would part?

The judge instructed the jury to consider carefully the evidence of the night of the crime and Janet Gardner's words at that time. She had dialled 999. To Mr Barratt, the civilian in the control room at Kingston Crescent Police Station, she had said, 'I stabbed him. He's dead. We had, we had an argument. I put a knife in him and he's, he's almost, he's dead.'

PC Crompton who was on mobile patrol on that balmy September night, told the court how he arrived at the house and went through the open front door and immediately saw in the doorway to the kitchen at the back of the house the body of Peter Iles. Blood was trickling from it and there was already a pool forming.

Janet Gardner had not stabbed Iles only once. The newspaper headlines soon screamed LOVER KNIFED SEVEN TIMES. How many of those seven were stabbings, how many were sharp thrusts and how many were merely superficial cuts was a question over which the experts argued long and hard. Janet's evidence was vague because she had been drinking, taking pills for depression and she had a bump on the head. Eventually it was established that two forceful incisions to Iles' heart and lungs led to the bleeding which caused his death. But had he received those wounds by rushing at her?

PC Crompton told the court that on arrival he noticed that the house was unkempt and untidy. Furniture was overturned. He also noticed that Janet's clothes were smeared with blood and that on the draining board of the sink was a knife with a long blade. There was blood on the blade and on the handle. 'There's no one else, it's just me that did it,' Gardner told him. He thought she was drunk. She was slurring and unsteady on her feet. She added, 'He deserved to die'.

The doctors then went ahead with their different work. Two doctors examined Janet Gardner and found her to be slightly bruised on the right side of the back of her neck and on one arm. She was also hazy. She thought she had taken nine measures of vodka with orange juice in the four hours before Peter Iles had come round the back of the house and surprised her. She had forgotten – perhaps because she was too tipsy – to lock all the doors and windows in what she called her normal routine. There was an empty vodka bottle in the house and a half-full one. The defendant had been taking her anti-depressant pills, but had not taken them for two days before the crime.

In the police station later that night, Janet had been interviewed by Detective Inspector Donovan. She told him that Iles had arrived at about 6pm and they'd had a drink and talked while watching athletics on television.

Then an argument evolved out of that for no reason and he took the ring off me which he had given me and he wanted his suit which he'd left at my house and he just said he was going and an argument evolved out of that. . . . I know I did stab him but I didn't mean to. I was scared of him and I cannot remember at this stage exactly what did happen. It wasn't through drink, it's just an absolute blank. Next thing he was lying on the floor and I thought that he was skylarking around . . . I cannot remember picking up the knife. I know he had his hands at the back of my neck. It's just what he used to do. Just on the pressure point at the back. Just there, just holding it down so I couldn't move, couldn't move.

Days later police searching the Beach Road bathroom found a ring under the towel rail. It jolted Janet's memory and she made a further statement. She said that she had remembered more clearly what had happened during that final argument. She recalled that as they sat on the settee they argued about the ring, which she was wearing and which he had demanded back.

I threw it and it went inwards towards the bathroom . . . and he marched me to the kitchen but on the step before you got to the kitchen, he banged my head against the door frame, the left side of my head and as he did so . . . I put my arm round on the wall and took the knife off the wall and he said that he would get his suit from the front room and I was just poking him . . . never stabbing him . . . just poking in the back and he turned round and went to grab me and as I had the knife down like that, as he grabbed me, come towards me and it was so quick, he more or less came towards the knife. It wasn't a case of me pushing the knife. Then he saw what happened and said 'You stupid bitch!' and went to grab me again.

Next thing I remember I was pushing him away and he fell on the floor.

She went to get his suit, threw it on the couch and told him he could go. It was only when she saw the blood and the yellow colour of his face that she realised that he could not go. She realised what she had done, she said.

In his summing up Mr Justice Swinton-Thomas reminded the jury that in the months before the crime Janet Gardner's health had been poor. She was going through the menopause and she was depressed. She had taken a job in the accounts department at P&O Ferries but had lost it in August because she couldn't concentrate. She had to take a job as a packer in a factory and her depression grew deeper. If she took her antidepressants in the morning, she found she was unable to work, so she often took them only at night. She was also seeing Peter Iles almost daily at that time. He liked to drink but she had been advised not to drink while taking the amitriptyline tablets. On the day before the killing Iles had stayed with her, but there had been no sexual intercourse. He went out on the Friday morning, returning that evening and had watched television with her. She made a curry for them.

'You don't expect me to eat that shit, do you?' he said. They were drinking vodka and orange and he left at 7.30pm to buy a second bottle. He returned and there was a row about her having lost her job with P&O. He said something about having her committed to a mental hospital. That lead on to a row about his suit and his ring. He started grabbing her finger to pull off the ring, which he said she wasn't good enough to wear. Enraged, she threw it into the bathroom. He told her to go and fetch it and, pulling her hair and squeezing her neck, began forcing her in that direction. He banged her head against the door frame. She wanted to get away, to stop him hurting her and she reached behind to grab the pipes to steady herself. In fact her hand went to the rack of knives. He had his back to her and she prodded him, piercing the skin. He turned around and came at her. She could not remember the knife going into him, but she could remember that he said, 'You stupid bitch'. She was then holding the knife level with her waist and she thrust it into him again. He looked, she said, as though he could kill her. At the police station she felt unwell as her period began. This was important, said the judge, in assessing her general state of mind and health.

Nigel Pascoe for the prosecution claimed that her account of the violence was exaggerated and one-sided. His view was not shared by the jury who, after a short discussion, agreed that Janet Gardner was not guilty of murder but of manslaughter. The judge, in passing sentence, said that he had little doubt that she was the subject of provocation and for that reason he would mitigate what must otherwise be a longer sentence. The sentence he did pass was that she should serve five years' imprisonment. The four women on the jury were noticeably shocked by the severity of this.

Janet went numbly to Holloway Prison. Again and again she relived the experience. 'Every night I would wake up after having the same nightmare,' she said in an interview on her release. She became depressed, almost suicidal. For many months she told no one there the details of her offence. She said that Iles had taught her one useful thing:

not to talk back. It served her well inside. The warders liked her and she was made a trustee, allowed out on shopping trips and allowed to meet her lawyers to lodge an appeal. Her suicidal tendencies were checked and a report on her psychiatric state was prepared that stated she was still clinically depressed.

Eleven months later, Lord Justice Leggatt made legal history after hearing her appeal. He said she had been suffering from Battered Woman Syndrome. It was the first time a British court had recognised that battered women may be driven to kill and that the way they are provoked is different from the 'sudden and temporary loss of control' experienced by others who commit manslaughter. Janet Gardner suffered, he said, from 'a depression so hopeless and profound that the will to survive is lost'. She was allowed home on probation. While she'd been away her daughter Louise had got married so she had a new son-in-law to meet. She also had a new purpose in the normal life she could begin to lead. Having met Kiranjit Ahluwalia, whose appeal was heard only weeks before her own (see p. 303), Janet Gardner decided that she would help other women whose lives were being wrecked by brutal men. She determined to make a room in the house that Peter Iles had wanted her to sell so badly into an office for just this work.

The Army Wife

Julius Walzer looked at his watch. The Austrian night porter at the army's families' hostel at Klagenfurt had a horrible feeling it was going to be a long night. Only twenty minutes earlier, one of the British army wives had been carried kicking and screaming to her billet. But for now, at least, all was quiet. He thought he would make the most of it by reading his newspaper when suddenly the same woman came running down the stairs. She was wearing pyjamas and was in a highly agitated state. From the words she blurted out, Herr Walzer only managed to comprehend 'my husband' and 'knife'. Putting two and two together, he raced upstairs to room 54 where he found the body of Sgt Maj. Montague Cyril Williams slumped in an easy chair. The soldier had been fatally stabbed and his killer was the distraught woman – his wife, twenty-one-year-old Margaret Laughlan Williams, a private in the Women's Royal Army Corps.

One of the first on the scene was Sgt Kenneth Rouse. When he was summoned to the room he found Margaret Williams kneeling by the side of the chair, sobbing uncontrollably while holding a piece of bloodstained material over the wound on her husband's chest. Too late to stop the flow, her soothing was in vain. 'Speak to me, Slim, I did not mean to do it,' she wailed to the corpse. Sgt Rouse asked her how she had done it. 'With a knife,' she answered, and made towards the window. She returned clutching a weapon with a four-inch blade and a sharply-honed point. Sgt Rouse looked at it despairingly, horrified to think that this weapon had just taken the life of a colleague. Four days after the stabbing, Margaret Williams was flown back to Britain. She landed at Hendon airfield and was then taken to London's Cannon Row Police Station where, after being questioned by Chief Inspector Digby, she was formally charged with the murder of her husband.

Her statement to the police was barely coherent. She said that her husband had hit her on the chin and the face, as a result of which she decided to sleep on the sofa that night. He then made a less than complimentary reference to her mother which started another row. He slapped her again. 'I saw a knife . . . I picked it up . . . I raised it. . . . He came towards me . . . I hit him with the knife near his shoulder. . . . The second time was further down. . . . He walked to his chair and sat down. He was bleeding and groaning . . . I didn't mean to kill him.'

Army marriages have a reputation for being notoriously stormy, particularly when conducted in a foreign land. With both partners away from home and struggling to come to terms with a different culture, the lifespan of such unions is sometimes barely longer than that of the average mayfly. Margaret and Cyril Williams had been wed for under three months. Their marriage had had even less chance of most than succeeding for, right from the outset, it was blatantly obvious that only one of them was in love.

Margaret Black hailed from Edinburgh and was an attractive fair-haired girl who, although slight of build was deceptively strong and athletic. She opted for a career in the Auxiliary Territorial Service, or ATS as it was usually known. She joined up in 1945 and was posted to the Austrian town of Klagenfurt on 11 June 1949. Soon after her arrival in Austria, she met Sgt Maj. Cyril Williams of the Royal Corps of Signals. A native of Harrow-on-the-Hill in the northwestern suburbs of London, he had been posted to Klagenfurt shortly after the end of the war. He was fourteen years older than Margaret, but was immediately attracted to her vivacious personality.

In truth, they were like chalk and cheese. She was young and fun-loving while he was quiet and studious. When asked to describe the couple at the trial, Private Muriel Jesse Pickering of the WRAC referred to Margaret as a nice, kind-hearted girl, but said that Sgt Maj. Williams tended to be rather sullen. No doubt adhering to the adage that opposites attract, Sgt Maj. Williams pursued his quarry with relentless enthusiasm. On several occasions, he asked her to marry him but she always refused. Margaret knew what she wanted when she was sober – and that was her freedom – but when she was drunk, a state into which she fell all too often, it was another matter entirely.

One night in November, she was incapable of resisting his overtures and finally agreed to become his bride. When she sobered up, she realised the awful truth of what she had done. However she also realised that it would break his heart if she terminated the engagement so, in the foolhardy hope that she might one day grow to love him, she consented to a spring wedding. On 15 April 1949, the sergeant major and his young recruit took leave to get married in the Lothian village of Torphichen, some sixteen miles west of Edinburgh.

If Sgt Maj. Williams thought that marriage would change things between them, he was gravely mistaken. For a month after the wedding, they occupied separate billets at Klagenfurt until in May they were given a room in the married couples' hostel. Not that the new arrangement spiced up their love life because Margaret had insisted from the start that there would be no sex between them until she was sure that she loved him. And as the weeks went by, she became increasingly certain that she did not love him. Thus the marriage was never consummated. There seems little doubt that this decidedly unusual stipulation did nothing to improve the relationship between husband and wife. He desperately wanted to be alone with her, but that was just about the last thing she desired.

She rejected his most modest advances and instead made a habit of staying out drinking late at night, hoping that by the time she returned to the loveless nest, he would be fast asleep. Inevitably, the situation began to affect him. Previously regarded as a model soldier, he too lapsed into bouts of heavy drinking. Maybe he thought it was one way to have something in common with his wife.

On the first weekend in July, they decided to spend a couple of rest days at the Grand Hotel at Anneheim, twenty miles from Klagenfurt. Even by their high standards, a lot of alcohol was consumed. Driving back on the evening of Sunday 3 July, the normally cautious Sgt Maj. Williams was carefree in his control of the wheel to the point of recklessness while Margaret sprawled either on the back seat or on the floor of the car. Her energy suddenly returned when they arrived back at Klagenfurt. Three Austrian soldiers saw the couple arguing in the street and watched as Mrs Williams kicked her husband. To the sergeant major's fury, she then went off with the three men to a local inn. There the quartet drank, danced and drank some more until transportation arrived to take Margaret back to the hostel. But it was no chauffeur-driven limousine, it was an army lorry, containing her irate husband and two burly soldiers.

Acting on the sergeant major's orders, the two hired hands dragged Margaret kicking and screaming from the inn. She said that in the back of the lorry, the soldiers twisted her arms up behind her back and held her face downwards. She added that her husband instructed the men to press her arms up, then slacken, then press them up again, a sequence of actions which, repeated throughout the journey, left her in considerable pain. But it took more than a couple of men to subdue a spirited woman like Margaret Williams and, back at the hostel and momentarily freed from their grip, she wasted no time in landing one a hefty blow with her boot. The men having departed, their evening's work done, Margaret was left alone with her husband in room 54.

Twenty minutes later, he was dead.

After appearing at Bow Street Magistrates' Court, still wearing the khaki uniform in which she had flown over from Austria, Margaret Williams was committed for trial at the Old Bailey on 15 September 1949. Her defence was in the capable hands of Mr Christmas Humphreys who attempted to prove that the accused acted in self-defence.

He also set out to show that Margaret Williams did not mean to kill her husband. There was, of course, no dispute as to the fact that she had delivered the fatal thrust. In a voice scarcely audible, Margaret Williams pleaded not guilty to the charge of murder. Mr Anthony Hawke, prosecuting, outlined the case against her. He said that the victim was sitting in a chair at his billet, already wounded in the shoulder, when a knife-blow to the heart killed him. Mrs Williams's recollections of the fatal night were remarkably (the prosecution would say conveniently) vague.

But in her statement to the police, she did contend that her husband was standing when she stabbed him the second time. It was crucial to the defence argument that the fatal second blow should be seen to have been delivered when Sgt Maj. Williams was still in an upright, threatening pose, having just struck the accused. If it could be proved that the two wounds were administered in rapid succession, the claim of self-defence would be greatly advanced. On the other hand, if it could be proved that the deceased was sitting down when receiving the second stab wound, and that a short period of time had therefore elapsed between the two blows, her case would look considerably weaker. A seated man poses far less of a threat.

Explaining the fact that her husband was wearing neither shirt nor vest when his body was found, Mrs Williams said in her police statement that he had taken them off on his way over to the chair after being stabbed twice. Expert medical witnesses testified that the second wound would have caused more or less instant unconsciousness and collapse. Consequently Mr Hawke found the defendant's version of events hard to accept.

'The dead man's shirt had a slit in the shoulder,' he said. 'It was surrounded by blood and showed that he was wearing the shirt when that first blow was struck.' Referring to the second stabbing he continued, 'It may be that after a wound like that, this man could have staggered across the room and fallen into the chair, but what is quite inconceivable is that after receiving the wound, he should, to use her words, have walked across the room to the chair and taken off his shirt and vest on the way.'

Forensic examination of room 54 showed that Sgt Maj. Williams did walk across the room. A trail of bloodstains led from the window, around the table, finishing at the foot of the chair. There were further stains on the back of the chair. Doctors stated that if Sgt Maj. Williams had been standing when stabbed the second time, they would have expected to find a lot more blood. 'Yet,' said Mr Hawke, reiterating the medical evidence, 'little or no blood came from that wound externally. But if that man was leaning back in the chair at the time of the blow, then the wound would not bleed externally. It would bleed heavily internally. That is what this one did.'

An intriguing item of evidence was a letter found in the defendant's pocket after her arrest. She had written it to her husband a few days before his death, but had never actually given it to him. Its contents revealed that she was on the verge of leaving him. It read:

Dear Slim,
Perhaps on paper I can give you a better idea of just how mean I am. You will probably be writing to me as well. In the first place, Slim, I do not want to hurt you, but I cannot help it. It was from the beginning a

certainty that this would have to come. I thought in time I would get even more fond of you than I was when we married. That, and the fact that I just could not bring myself to shatter all your illusions, was my basis for the marriage. It was not good enough. Now I find that every time we are together and alone in our room, I want to scream, to get away from everything. I know something of what you feel. It is not nice. It makes one want to cry, become dramatic, scream and fling things about, and upsets one in general.

What have I done, what can I do about making it all right? It is much better we should part as friends. Tell the folks I went off with another man or something and that will be that. I only wish I could have done this before it went so far, but while it lasted I think you were happy. That much is always something.

I will get a job somewhere. I won't be going back home after I leave and I am going to leave those that I really love, and know that I cannot come home to them again. That will be punishment enough.'

Private Muriel Jessie Pickering told the court that the murder weapon was a knife used for wood-carving, an activity which Sgt Maj. Williams had encouraged his wife to pursue. By a sad irony, it was he who had sharpened it for her to make it more effective. Cross-examining, Mr Humphreys asked Pickering, 'You were against the marriage and told her that she would be a fool to marry him because she said she was not in love with him?' Pickering said this was true and added that she knew of the no-sex arrangement between the couple. 'Do you think that got on both their nerves?' asked Mr Humphreys. 'Yes,' she replied.

The prosecution hinted that one of the real reasons the marriage was doomed to failure was because Margaret Williams allegedly had lesbian tendencies. They claimed she was unable to have strong feelings for any man. She was said to have told Chief Inspector Digby, 'I have always been attracted to women, more so than men, but I did not know there was anything wrong in it until a girl I fell in love with told me all about it some time ago. I have tried hard to fight against it, and that was another reason why I got married.'

Prosecution witness Sgt Peggy Snow of the WRAC recounted her conversation with the defendant in the early hours of 4 July. Margaret Williams said her husband had struck her adding, 'I saw the knife. I said to myself, "I will do you". I picked it up and stabbed him.' She was also said to have warned her husband after he had hit her, 'If you come nearer, I will knife you'.

Medical examination of Mrs Williams after the incident revealed a superficial bruise on the angle of the lower jaw, two superficial bruises on the back of the right upper arm, another on the buttock and abrasions on the leg. The bruise on the face was described as severe, the remaining injuries were comparatively minor. It tallied with her story of having been assaulted about the face by her husband.

Margaret Williams herself was the solitary defence witness. On the verge of tears, she said she had spent every night for the two months since the murder wondering what had happened, but still had no clear recollection. She did, however, concede that she had been drinking that night. 'I must have been drunk because I do not remember things. I must have been annoyed too.'

Mr Humphreys asked, 'Is it true that he (your husband) started hitting you for the first time?'

'Yes,' she answered. 'When I told my husband I was not going to sleep with him that night, he struck me a heavy blow across the face.'

'It is said you deliberately stabbed him in the heart as he was in the chair,' continued defence counsel.

'No, I did not do that. He was standing. I would not have hit him if he had not hit me first.'

Mr Hawke, prosecuting, wanted some answers. 'Can you tell me why you used a knife at all?' he demanded.

'I do not know,' she whispered.

'You mean that you do not remember using the knife at all?'

'I can remember I hit my husband.'

'What with?'

'It must have been with the thing I picked up off the table which must have been a knife.'

'You hit him with a knife. That is the whole point. Was it in anger or in fright?'

'He had hit me such a blow that I hit him back. I did the natural thing. I think it was an instinctive thing to do – to hit back.'

'Is it just a coincidence,' demanded Mr Hawke, 'that you can remember quite clearly everything your husband did to you, but you cannot remember with any accuracy anything you did to him?'

'I cannot remember anything I did to him.'

'It is a remarkably convenient coincidence?'

'It may be so, but I must have been awful angry. I know when I am drunk and anyone tries to get rough with me, I fight back.'

Mr Hawke was satisfied. In his closing speech, he said the jury might think the story created a picture of a defenceless woman being brutally knocked about by a man very much larger. 'If you think she was defending herself from violence when she used this knife, then acquit her and acquit her gladly.'

He went on to say that if it was a state of resentment brought about by her treatment which caused her to use the knife in the heat of passion, the jury might find her guilty of manslaughter. 'But,' he maintained, 'the proved testimony shows beyond any possible doubt that this woman was the aggressor right the way through. So if you think the wounds were inflicted when Mrs Williams was in a foul temper, and with an appreciable interval between them, you might think that her feeling had ceased to be resentment and had become revenge.'

Sensing that the verdict could still go either way, Christmas Humphreys made an impassioned plea in Margaret Williams's defence. Referring to the incident at the inn, he demanded, 'What right had the husband to lay hands upon her and to send for two British soldiers to use brutal violence on his young girl wife? I suggest this man was in a white heat of temper. Is there anything worse than a man who has so lost control of himself that in silence he is knocking his wife about for the first time?' He half turned to the dock. 'She is not a girl to take that easily. She retaliates and scratches his face – the only weapon she then has got. There is a lull. There was this knife on the table –

fatally enough. There was nothing else. If there had been something else, say a paper weight or a bottle, she would have used that and nothing would have been heard of this case. Then it all happened very quickly – that last fatal blow. It was a very easy blow to give. The appalling tragedy is that the weapon was lying to hand. How easy to slip that knife in. It was pure chance that the knife went between the ribs. But it did.'

He added that they were both half-drunk and she was righteously very angry. It was, he insisted, a case of self-defence against the attack of a man whom she had warned not to go against her again or he would get it. 'Provoked under the stress of terrible emotion and blind fury at this man, is she to pick and choose the weapon to defend herself, or is she entitled to use what there is at hand to stop another blow of the type which had half knocked her out?'

Summing up, Mr Justice Streatfeild described the couple's marriage as a sad, sorry tale. 'What an object lesson the whole story is – he very much in love with her, she not with him, and an agreement was made that the marriage should not be consummated until she felt she loved him.' He referred to the 'rather sordid background of the marriage – a marriage entered into in that way and with her drinking too much. And she had been indulging in the worst form of drinking – drinking solo. It has been said that this young woman was being chastised by her husband. You may think, or may not, that perhaps she deserved it after what had gone before, but a young wife is not obliged to submit calmly to an act of chastisement by her husband even if it is deserved. She is perfectly entitled to defend herself.'

The judge stated that the key to the case was the precise circumstances of the fatal stabbing. 'Although the sergeant major's shirt was found slit, corresponding to a stab wound in the back, what inference can be drawn from the absence of a slit in the shirt and vest corresponding to the chest wound? The man must have removed his shirt and vest. The all-important thing was, what happened after that? Did he receive the wound in the chest which caused almost instant loss of consciousness when he was standing up or sitting in the chair?'

The trial had lasted just three days and now the jury, which contained three women, went away to deliberate. They clearly had many reservations and after two hours returned to ask the judge what the state of mind of a person charged with murder must be to enable the jury to reduce the verdict to manslaughter.

Half an hour later, they filed back into court with their verdict. As they did so, one of the jurywomen was in tears. The foreman announced that they had found Margaret Williams guilty of murder, but wished to add a recommendation for mercy. Mr Justice Streatfeild had no option but to sentence Williams to death. He was visibly distressed as he passed sentence and a number of women in the public gallery wept openly. It was a highly emotional scene.

The *Daily Mirror* reported: 'When Margaret Williams, wearing a simple cream coat and pale blue dress, was asked if she had anything to say, only her bitter sobbing could be heard.'

The young widow was taken to Holloway Prison where her date of execution was fixed for 11 October. Her legal advisers decided there should be no appeal but, as in the

Renee Duffy case six months earlier, such was the depth of public feeling that a petition was sent to the Home Secretary, urging her reprieve. He bowed to their wishes and on 30 September Margaret Williams learned that her death sentence had been commuted to one of life imprisonment.

The tragedy of the case is that, judging by the letter found in her possession, Margaret Williams was about to find a peaceful way out of her unhappy predicament. But in the heat of the moment, fuelled by alcohol and stirred by her husband's uncharacteristic violence, she had chosen a different route. At least she did not have to pay for her decision with her life.

The Fatal Power of Cold Duck

Almost one-and-a-half million people live in the San Fernando Valley on the northeastern corner of Los Angeles. The sprawling 170 miles of hills is an inland copy of Los Angeles itself, a gridwork of characterless homes and shopping malls usually shrouded in smog. The smog does not disturb the former inhabitants whose current home is the spectacular Forest Lawn cemetery found in the grassy hills off South Glendale Avenue. There in splendour are replicas of Michelangelo's 'David' and the John Trumbull painting of the signing of the declaration of independence, signs that culture and justice have not deserted this place where high spending holds hands with high crime rates. For the living, one of the busiest parts of The Valley is Glendale with its mammoth stores, civic centre, teaming restaurants and bars. Brenda Clubine is a Glendale woman, but Glendale does not celebrate that fact. Though the day may come.

Brenda Clubine never planned to become famous. She never dreamed of becoming a movie star or a television personality. That she became well known on television talk shows and in campaigns for changes in the law is not something she would have wanted had she not been judged guilty of second-degree murder in 1983.

She is a small woman, barely five-feet tall and less than six stone in weight. After nearly fourteen years behind bars she seems to have grown smaller, certainly thinner, though her voice is stronger now than it was when she was a nurse, a busy mother and wife to Robert Clubine. He was six-feet-four-inches tall, weighed seventeen stone and worked as a policeman. He was fifty.

When they found him, he had two stab wounds in his back: the one in his shoulder blade was a sixteenth of an inch deep; the one in his shoulder, a quarter of an inch deep. They were, in other words, superficial; little more than scratches. They hardly harmed him.

What killed Robert Clubine was a blow to his head. At the trial the pathologist gave evidence that his skull was the thinnest he had ever encountered. The normal skullbone is five millimetres thick. Robert Clubine's was half this. His head was fractured when it was struck and his brain haemorrhaged. It took him between sixteen and twenty-two hours to die.

His was a long and lonely death. He lay on the floor of a motel room for three days after his and Brenda's last fight and no one knew he was there, bleeding. Brenda telephoned the motel and asked to be put through. She was worried and she was afraid. 'I called trying to see what was happening to him because I kept expecting him to come to my house. I knew he was going to kill me,' she was to say, ten years after that night of 23 January 1983, when she tried, yet again, to have the violence against her taken into account, to be judged as a victim of abuse.

'I wanted to know where he was and what he was doing.

I talked to the motel manager and he said he wasn't there, that he'd just left and no one was answering the phone.' Finally someone did answer the telephone. It was the police. They didn't tell her the bad news then. They never do on the phone in case the relative collapses with shock when all alone. They then went to Brenda's house to notify her formally that her husband was dead. Three days later they called again to arrest her.

Brenda Clubine had never imagined the day when she would be the perpetrator of what lawyers call a 'crime against the person'. She was no stranger to such crimes because apart from those she'd encountered in her work as a nurse, the crimes had been against her. She had been abused in many ways for a good part of her life.

In the account she gives of her childhood and first marriage in *Wednesday's Children*, a collection of first-hand recollections of imperfect childhoods written by adult survivors of abuse, Brenda recalled loveless years. She had become the family maid after being adopted as a baby. When her adoptive mother had a nervous breakdown, the nine-year-old Brenda missed a year of school to look after the cooking and cleaning.

Her mother beat her with a belt, with an extension cord and punished her by making her lie face down on the carpet for up to six hours at a stretch. When the PE teacher spotted Brenda's bruises and made a report to the authorities, her mother became so outraged that the beatings became even more savage and frequent. Her father seemed powerless to stop it.

When she was thirteen she was grabbed by a man one evening in a shopping mall. He dragged her into a car, took her to a motel room and raped her repeatedly at knife point. When he fell asleep she ran naked to the police station. When called, her mother refused to allow Brenda to go to a rape crisis centre or to have a pregnancy test. She gave the child no comfort. Consequently, Brenda left home two weeks later.

She worked as a waitress and a year later met a twenty-eight-year-old helicopter pilot from the Air Force. They dated for a year and at sixteen they were married. But two weeks after the wedding he was sent to Vietnam. By then she was pregnant. He came home on leave when their daughter was just one month old and when he left she was pregnant again. Seven months later he was a casualty of the war. When this young mother recovered she met a man at the hospital where she was working and within the year she had married him. They both realised quickly that it had been a mistake but by then she was expecting another baby. It was during this pregnancy that Brenda met the big teddy bear of a man who made her happy again. He was almost twenty years older than her although, as she would later discover, emotionally he was a child. But at that time Robert Clubine was a protector to her and her children. He made her feel safe and seemed content to go along with whatever she planned. He was also a romantic; he sent flowers to her at work and collected her at lunchtimes. While they lived together on and off for five years, things were grand between them. When they married, Brenda's luck ran out.

Perhaps what did most to break the spell was the tension when they decided that Robert's mother should live with them. But it was not the older woman who caused the trouble. It was the fact that Brenda witnessed her husband slapping his mother across the face. She protested and placed herself between. A red mist seemed to descend in Robert Clubine's mind. He grabbed his wife, lifted her from the floor and flung her against the door shouting that it was none of her business. He began hitting her, she said, but she pulled free and tried to telephone for the police. Robert yanked the phone lead from the wall but the neighbours, hearing the kerfuffle, called them. The patrol car drew up, but Robert Clubine went into the drive to talk to the officers who were colleagues. He told them it was a little misunderstanding and they drove off. That was the beginning.

Why wasn't it also the end? Why didn't Brenda Clubine leave then? She was a resourceful woman who had managed somehow to bring up three young children without a man to tell her what to do next. But Brenda Clubine put up with eleven years of marriage, eleven years of conflict, the details of which meant nothing to the California court after 23 January 1983. During those years, she claimed Robert Clubine sometimes threatened to drop her as he dangled her by her feet from the edge of a third floor balcony. He grabbed her by the throat to show how choking would feel. He hit her. She did leave him. She did find another home. But he drove to the Country Club where she worked, found her car in the car park and smashed the windscreen. Then he yelled that if she didn't come home, the next time it would be her head he'd smash. It cost her the job. When she continued to live apart from him, he gained access to her apartment one day and, after punching her in the face, dragged her round the rooms by her heels.

It tore the skin from one side of her face and broke three ribs. One rib punctured a lung. On another occasion he broke a collarbone and tried to spear her throat with a knife. She tried to take hold of it and the knife went through her hand.

Brenda tried to leave Robert many times but she knew he would hunt her down so she returned to be with him and her children and his mother. His outbursts had become more frequent and more senseless. He was paranoid about what Brenda did. He was suspicious about letters addressed to her or if she seemed to take longer than he thought necessary in the supermarket. He would strip-search her. She didn't act decisively 'because I didn't realise that I could'. When she considered that her adoptive mother had blamed her for everything, that this man blamed her for everything, that a psychologist she was consulting had said she must be doing something to provoke Clubine and her preacher had said 'You've got to work this out', she was sure she must be at fault.

In six months of 1982 she complained more than forty times to the police about Clubine's violent and threatening behaviour and filed for a restraining order. She tried to kill herself with thirty Valiums, thirty Darvons and six Quaaludes and was sorry to wake up in hospital. But when she went home, there was relief: Robert Clubine had left. By now she had a judge's order protecting her and had pressed charges to have Robert arrested for 'felony battery'. She took the intelligent final step and filed for divorce. Sadly six weeks later she did something quite unintelligent. She agreed to meet Clubine to collect the papers he would by then have signed. At least she tried to hold the meeting in a public place. Robert suggested she see him for dinner at Bob's Big Boy. It was 23 January 1983.

Psychologists say that women who have lived with continual beatings learn to sense the moment when their violent partners are ready to injure them seriously or to kill them. They sense a difference in actions, a shift in attitude. This is what Brenda, then a thirty-three-year-old nurse who had almost made it to the other side, to a freedom from battering, believes she sensed on that night. During dinner Clubine told her that he had left the papers in his motel room and when she told him she did not wish to go to the room with him, he told her there was nothing to worry about. He seemed calm, almost the old Robert, the gentle one. She went to the room. 'When we got there, he locked the door behind me, tore up the divorce papers and threw them in my face,' she said. 'He started questioning me about the warrant I'd filed against him for felony battery. He told me he had a copy of it and that I wasn't going to make him look a fool. Then he asked me to give him my wedding rings. I did but asked why. "Because without these they're not going to be able to identify your body," he replied. He snapped his finger,' she went on, ' "I can kill you that fast and nothing will happen to me." I knew that was true. I knew he had friends.'

Brenda says that she was convinced he meant to kill her and when he went to the bathroom, she fled to her car. He rushed out after her and blocked the way. Then he pulled her from her car and carried her back to the motel room. 'He smacked the back of my head onto the table. Then he smacked my face into the table and broke my front teeth.' Brenda says she didn't react violently then. She tried to humour him as he began drinking Cold Duck wine from the bottle. She offered to rub his back as he sat on the bed. While his face was turned away from hers she suddenly saw his right arm go up. 'I didn't know if he was going to hit me or not,' she said. 'But I saw that bottle of Cold Duck on the floor and without thinking I grabbed it and swung.' She missed him then but after they'd both struggled for the bottle she regained control and swung again. 'This time I hit him with it.' He fell across the bed moaning. At that point, she says, she grabbed her car keys and ran from the place in a state of terror. She added that she didn't remember stabbing him, but accepts that she must have done so since no one else was there. She recalls only that she saw a knife on the table.

Brenda went meekly to jail to await her trial. Two years later she stood in front of Judge Lillian M. Stevens at Passadena Superior Court. She admitted clubbing her husband over the head with the wine bottle. There was the evidence of the two wounds made by the pocket-knife. There was also evidence that Brenda had made her husband drowsy by slipping two cold capsules into his wine. There was a further charge that she took money from his wallet before she went. Under oath she was asked, 'After you were done repeatedly hitting him in the head with the wine bottle, you twice stabbed him with a knife, is that true?' She responded, 'Yes, sir'. She was then asked 'After you stabbed him with a knife, you stole what money he had. Isn't that true?' Again she answered 'Yes, sir'.

Her attorney Theo Poloynis-Engen argued that she acted in self-defence because Clubine repeatedly beat her. But the judge would allow no evidence of the beatings; they were deemed irrelevant. She also refused to instruct the jury in self-defence. Without a full picture of the volatile relationship between the Clubines, without the evidence of the complaints to the police, of Brenda's history of injuries and of the order for her husband's arrest, the plea of self-defence probably did sound farfetched.

The jury pronounced her guilty and the sentence was fifteen years to life.

In the Californian Institution For Women at Frontera, Brenda Clubine made two applications for parole. They were unsuccessful. She then began asking her prison programme administrators about counselling. She was first told that there had been an attempt to form a group but few women had turned up. Brenda began reading everything she could find on the subject of domestic violence. By then she had realised that many of her fellow inmates had suffered as she had and were in prison because they had fought back. She asked to be allowed to try to form another group and in November 1988 chaired her first meeting of Convicted Women Against Abuse in the programme administrator's office. Ten women came. Within weeks the numbers had grown to more than forty. Their ages ranged from twenty-six to seventy-six. All say they killed to protect themselves from being killed.

During their meetings they talk of lost love and failed marriages. Many still cannot understand how their belief in the romantic idyll could have left them locked in a cycle of brutal beatings, tears and a deepening hopelessness. One thing none of them asks is why she didn't just leave. Many of them ask, 'Why did he beat me?' or 'Why didn't anyone help me?' They were not to know that by staying, many of them saved their own lives. For the National Clearinghouse Against Domestic Violence, a pressure group, has studied the records. Battered women who attempt to leave are at a 75 per cent greater risk of being killed by their batterer than women who stay. Most of the Frontera women stayed, they say, because they still remembered the early days. As one of Brenda's group poetically said, 'I loved that man with all my heart. I have so much love for him even to this day. I'm sorry he's gone, he was rainbows and dreams. The first couple of years there was such happiness. You want that back so much, you take anything.'

Brenda stayed because no one would listen, she said. 'If all the people had done their part, none of us would be here now.' Police complain that many women make and then drop charges against their violent partners. In Brenda's case, she said, the police dropped her. 'Every time he was in violation of the restraining order, whether it was because he vandalised our house or physically beat me, the police wouldn't do anything,' she said. 'They came to my home, they would meet my husband in the driveway and he would just tell them that I was being emotional. They wouldn't talk to me. In the last severe beating, the district attorney finally filed charges and issued a warrant. They didn't execute the warrant. They said they didn't execute it because I didn't know what I wanted. But I called them every day for six weeks to try to get them to file charges.'

The support of other women and the knowledge that the meetings have helped many understand the roots of their problems for the first time in their lives has kept Brenda Clubine buoyant.

Seven years after her conviction in 1985, there was a

change in thinking in Californian courts. When considering the defence of self-defence in murder trials, judges began to recognise Battered Woman Syndrome, a condition in which women who have been abused over a long period kill their abusers in the face of imminent danger. What about Brenda Clubine and the hundreds of women like her already in jail serving long sentences? Her requests for parole have been turned down twice. A petition for clemency for thirty-four Frontera Prison women including Brenda, renewed publicity about her case and resulted in her picture being widely seen. Also, because such things are possible in America, she has appeared from jail on television. There was a promise that all the cases would be reviewed in time. But there was also a firm refusal from Governor Pete Wilson to accept that Brenda was a victim of Battered Woman Syndrome.

It was almost as if she had wrecked her chances by being too vocal. According to Wilson, Clubine repeatedly lied to the police, the court, the media and the parole board. By this he must have meant that while she admitted at her trial that she had hit her husband repeatedly with the wine bottle, she later claimed to have hit him only once. Similarly while at her trial she admitted that she had taken Robert Clubine's money, she later denied having done so. Furthermore she had not mentioned at her trial that in her struggle with her husband on that night, he had knocked out her front teeth.

Most people would see these discrepancies as minor details. Brenda Clubine never denied killing her husband. She had, however, always been denied the chance to say why. Her prosecutor, Terry Green, now a judge, acknowledges that Clubine was beaten. But he has said that he believed the case as presented at trial lacked the factual underpinnings of self-defence. He says that he does not see grounds for clemency. When the judge at her trial, Lillian M. Stevens, was asked to explain her reasons for disallowing the evidence of battering, she told the *Los Angeles Times*, 'The only thing that really matters is, was there an immediate danger? There can't be an old grievance.' Talking about Brenda's case she said, 'It seemed to be the beatings were some time ago. And there was evidence that a lot of it was mutual.'

Brenda longs to be with her children again. 'All my life I've been in situations where I am out of control. I have a lot of feelings about that. I get very frustrated realising I have put myself in one situation after another where I have no control. Starting my support group has come back to me in many positive ways. Every time I meet with them I see how they've grown and how they feel about themselves. I believe, no matter what's happened, I'm here for a reason. I feel one day I'll be free. At least,' she adds, wryly, 'I survived. It was an awfully high price to pay for survival though.'

A Missing Head

It was a juicy item on the local news and the neighbours were soon talking. Human remains had been dug up by the side of the A3052 road on the outskirts of Sidmouth, South Devon. They were in black dustbin bags. There had been a tip-off and a woman was helping police with their inquiries.

Juicy but surely not real. This wasn't Chicago. It wasn't Birmingham or Glasgow. This was Sidmouth, the sleepiest little coastal town you could expect to find anywhere in Britain. The townsfolk are proud of it, its Regency history and the fact that poet John Betjeman delighted in its unspoilt charm, likening its surroundings to a tropical forest.

People come to Sidmouth each summer to take holidays by the sea often doubling its 12,000 population. Some of them return again and again until they come to see out their days in bungalows or flats, enjoying the bowling green and the golf course while they may. The young of Sidmouth like to watch the pensioners around them and joke that people come there to die. If they do, they come to die of natural causes. The person whose remains were being gingerly examined had not enjoyed that luxury.

That examination took place on 5 June 1991, a day after

the police had knocked on the door of a house in one of Sidmouth's few council estates, Le Locle Close, to talk to a young mother. She was Pamela Sainsbury, shy, old fashioned in her clothes and manners but well liked by neighbours and the other parents who met her when they took their children to primary school down the road. The neighbours had been shocked, of course, when they heard the patrol cars noisily draw up and officers get out and walk down her front path. People in small seaside towns like Sidmouth care about each other and visits from the police are rare.

In Le Locle Close that day the neighbours thought the worst; that some harm must have come to young Mrs Sainsbury and her two kiddies. They knew her husband was trouble – that's why he'd gone away. They thought he must have come back and they waited behind their net curtains to find out.

Few of them made the correct connection. Le Locle Close was three hundred yards or so from the field where the five rotting, half-buried dustbin bags had been found once the police knew where to look. Officers had been to the house, number 15, the month before and found nothing. Nothing except a fairly dreadful smell. At that time the police didn't have a reason to investigate it. They'd had an anonymous letter suggesting they should search the place and ask the whereabouts of the man who'd lived there for five years but was no longer to be seen. They had been slightly suspicious when the woman said at first that her husband did not have a bank account and then contradicted herself by saying she had tried to have the account transferred to her name. But she seemed a gentle, pleasant person. The letter writer must have been some crank, they'd decided, after finding nothing and not wanting to stay because of the smell.

When they returned in June the smell had gone, thank goodness. It wasn't a mystery. Pamela May Elizabeth would later tell them that it had gone because the last part of her husband had gone. His severed head was no longer fouling the air. She had removed the rotting, stinking head, wrapped in another of those black plastic bags, from the corner of the meter cupboard where it had been kept for more than eight months and put it out for the dustmen. She had kept it that long to prove to herself, if ever she needed that proof, that the man who had made her life unbearable for so long, really could not return.

On the afternoon of 6 June, Pamela was wearing a yellow, short-sleeved top, long blue skirt and sandals to appear before the Honiton magistrates at a special sitting of the court. With her long, loosely pinned back blonde hair, she looked younger than her twenty-nine years and seemed composed, some might have said relieved. Her solicitor David Williams asked for legal aid and it was granted. He also asked for bail for his client, which was refused. Momentarily her composure cracked. She realised that someone would have to look after her beloved children, daughter Lindsay, then eight and Terry, five. They could stay in London with her parents who loved them and not miss too much school. And at least the summer holidays were coming up.

The case was adjourned and Williams was to ask again and again over the coming weeks for Pamela to be allowed out on bail. She'd stay with her mother, he said and would cooperate in any way. Neil Lawson, prosecuting, opposed the idea of bail. Pamela Sainsbury must remain in custody while vital information needed by the police had still to be traced. What he meant, but didn't want to say, was that the whereabouts of the head – the only thing that might allow a true identification of the body – remained unknown. It was an annoyance for the police; better if they could wrap it all up, so to speak. Home Office pathologist Dr Bill Hunt was still examining the contents of the bags and police officers were talking to Philip Sainsbury, brother of Paul David William Sainsbury, the self-employed builder aged thirty-five, whom Pamela was charged with having murdered.

Murdered. The word should have cut through her. Instead she felt numb, as she had for so many of the past eight years, doing what she had to do unfeelingly. Before the guilt of it all came to her, long before the police called at her house, she had felt elated, suddenly alive and free. That feeling had begun at 4am on the morning of 29 September the year before, the morning after the night when she and Paul had fought their last fight. She had drawn an asterisk on the calendar hanging on the kitchen wall and written 'This is the first day of the rest of my life'.

The sensation had passed, though, and she had many moments of fear and indecision. It wasn't as though she had never shared her secret. She had half told several people. She told some friends and neighbours that Paul had left after they had had a row and hinted that he was now working somewhere in the North. To others, such as her neighbour Debbie Remnant, she showed the scars and bruises, the evidence of how he hit her that last time. She gave them to understand that he fled when she threatened to go to the police about his assaults. But she had tired of those incomplete stories.

When she began to go out again, to feel like a human being again, she had told Steve Curry, the good-looking young nightclub bouncer she had met around Christmas time, that she had taken far more drastic action to be rid of Paul. Steve had listened, horrified, to the stories she told of her life and stayed silent about her confession. After the trial he poured out his heart. They were no longer close, but his feelings were still strong.

He called her his perfect woman. He added, 'I couldn't tell the police because I've never met a woman like Pam – she's kind, caring and dotes on her children. No woman on this planet ever suffered as much as her. All she ever wanted to do was look after her kids without living in daily fear of that man.'

Pamela had also confided at the start of June to her friend Angela Davey. It was she who a day earlier had gone to the police. She had known both Pam and Paul and believed what she was doing was for the best. Ms Davey was to tell the *Sunday Mirror*: 'She just stared at me and said, "I killed him. I killed Paul." It was a cry for help. I couldn't have slept knowing what happened. I had to go to the police. I think Pam knew it was the right thing.'

Pamela Pressman had grown up knowing clearly what was the right thing. She had grown up in a secure, middle-class home in a comfortable London suburb to become a 'bonnie and clever teenager' as the court was to hear at her trial. She was made a head prefect and had gained ten O-level passes and two A-levels in chemistry and physics. She had planned to go on to work in scientific research. In the event she went into something where her scientific and technical knowledge were important and her pleasing personality and organisational ability were also needed. She was employed in a small handmade-chocolate company and rose to become the manageress.

That was her job in the summer of 1982 when with her parents and thousands of other Londoners, she went on holiday to Sidmouth. In Carina's Nightclub she met a local lad who said little but danced well. He had an attractive mop of dark hair, thick eyebrows and a moustache. His tan from working in the open and from the sports he enjoyed was impressive. His body was muscular and strong and Pamela was smitten.

Paul Sainsbury had grown up on a council estate and had never put much store by school. Perhaps it had never had much success with him. Neighbours with long memories remember that he was often in trouble there. He lost his temper and struck out. When he left school he became a labourer and, beyond wanting to be his own boss, he had no ambition. Women were always important to Paul Sainsbury, too important. As a teenager he had trailed a girl he had fallen for until she lodged an official complaint. Another girl he had wanted rejected him. He raged and caused criminal damage at her home and had been punished for it. Neither of those girls were as special as Pamela would be.

Almost as soon as they met, there seemed no question of their not being together from then on.

To the dismay and anguish of her parents, Pamela travelled south to Devon at weekends to visit her rough-and-ready new boyfriend and soon decided to give up her job and move to the West Country for good to be with him. The couple lived at first in a rented place in Exeter. She used his name, although they never made their partnership legal. Perhaps that's because it was never a partnership, more a relationship of his power and her spellbound subservience. At first, she was to tell the court, she was flattered by his obsessive and jealous treatment of her – the classic early reaction of a battered woman.

Black-eyed Paul was apt to be violent, but the slappings and punchings were bearable, she felt, even if he never showed he was sorry afterwards. She also believed, when she became pregnant in 1983, that with the new baby he would settle down. Paul had plenty of other interests, after all, to occupy him. He fished, he liked pigeons, he was extremely proud of his neat garden and he enjoyed exercising in a gym, cycling and running. At the annual Sidmouth half marathon he was a familiar figure.

But it was only in his running shorts or track suit that Paul Sainsbury was ever seen and then he was usually distracted, never friendly. He didn't socialise, didn't share his life with Pamela with other people. Pamela went out even more rarely. Neighbours who knew the couple at their later home, in the village of Sidford, reported that they were a very private couple. 'She had this severe, pulled-back hairstyle and seemed almost Victorian in her attitudes,' one said. Others noticed that her husband seldom let her out of his sight. 'He would see her to the minibus which picked her up for work and he would be there to meet her when she came home. It was only because he was obsessional about whom she met. He never let her go out with women friends, especially if they were married.'

When the children came along, they were never seen to play with the other kids in the street. This family was different. Quite how different, not even the nosiest neighbour could have guessed.

It's hard to judge at which point Pamela knew she had made a serious error. Certainly when baby Terry was born, his father's need to lash out and brutalise the woman he claimed to love increased. An early sign that Paul Sainsbury was not 'right in the head' was his rage when Pamela used a word he didn't understand. He loathed being reminded of her education and his lack of it. Long words would cause him to flare up so fiercely that she was reduced to speaking in monosyllables. She was almost reduced to making noises, like an animal, the animal Paul, in his perverted way, tried to make her become.

Paul stopped seeing his own friends. Perhaps he didn't want a repetition of what had happened when he met a chap with whom he used to go fishing who remarked casually to Paul that Pam looked nice. The next day Paul visited him with the message that there would be hell to pay if he ever spoke to her again. He accused the friend of being patronising and condescending to her. It was nonsense of course. He must have been trying to express the slights he imagined were aimed at him.

The same friend happened to meet Pamela after September 1990. 'She seemed to be relieved about something. She said Paul had left her having nearly broken her leg before he went. She said she did not care where he had gone and did not want to see him again. I think she was getting it all off her chest.'

The leg injury was only one of Paul Sainsbury's farewell gifts to his wife. A friend who saw it described it later as 'like raw liver'. She'd earned it at Carina's Nightclub. But how different they were from the young people who met and smooched and changed each other's lives eight years before. This time Pamela had gone there – as she went everywhere and did everything – almost like a zombie, doing as she was told. The alternative was by then unthinkable.

In those eight years, defence counsel Helena Kennedy QC told the jury at Plymouth Crown Court in December 1991, Pamela had been treated like a dog, becoming Sainsbury's slave. She continued, 'Few cases could be as bad as this of one human's abuse of another'.

The details which emerged in court must have shamed Pamela and her parents as much as they shocked all those who heard them being coolly listed. This outwardly health-conscious man was inwardly sick. Only the police knew that the real Paul Sainsbury was a man who drank to excess and was given to sadistic cruelty. He had convictions for both. Psychiatrist Dr Patrick Galway described him as a paranoid psychopath with a need to be sadistic and to degrade Pamela.

'She killed her husband in a sudden and impulsive act in which fear and hopelessness appear to have played as much a part as anger,' he said.

When Helena Kennedy began to describe the crimes of the man Pamela Sainsbury was accused of murdering, the court was hushed. Paul Sainsbury believed he owned Pamela. She was his prisoner. He regularly beat her and kicked her. He whipped her with a cane. He forced her to strip naked, wear a dog collar round her neck and eat from a bowl on the floor. He subjected her to perverted sexual acts, often waking her in the middle of the night to repeat the beatings and sexual abuse. He made her pose for degrading nude photographs and threatened her that if she ever tried to leave he would send copies of them to her parents and friends. He also vowed to burn down the home of her parents, those people who did not think he was good enough for their girl.

Ms Kennedy told the court:

Nothing brought an end to this catalogue of violence. Pamela felt as if she were in a shell, her autonomy having been totally sacrificed within the relationship. Her only release was sleep but even that was interrupted at times when the sadistic side of her husband's nature was aroused.

Her children were her salvation and it was for them that she stayed, fearing Paul's threats that if she left they would be hurt. She still has the scarring across her shoulders caused by pencil stabbings and she still bears the imprint of his boot on her leg from the attack on the night of his death.

She was forced to wear a collar as if she was an animal and she found the violence so hard to describe the reports of the psychiatrists say she was psychologically numbed. She could not feel anything within herself. She says she felt like an eggshell. She told one psychiatrist that if she had not killed him, he would have killed her.

That seemed to be what he was trying to do to her after the

night in September at Carina's. Paul had taken her to a number of pubs first where he swigged beer rapidly. They ended up at the nightclub. Paul was by then interested only in the next drink and when a friendly man spoke to Pamela she replied. As they left shortly after 1am, a jealous rage was boiling up inside Sainsbury. He began shouting at her. When they arrived home, he walked their young baby-sitter to her home and then, on returning, he began to give Pamela the worst beating he had ever given her. It was also the longest. He threw her downstairs, knocked her against the walls, trod on her legs.

Two hours later as he fell into a drunken stupor, she thought he had broken one of her legs. He roused himself, went to bed and fell into a deep sleep. To her surprise, she found she could move. To her astonishment, she found she had more physical and mental strength than she had long dared hope.

In court Dr Galway described that moment as her crossing of the Rubicon. As she dealt with him in the hours that followed she told him that she had never been unfaithful, had never deserved his savagery and she asked him why he had treated her in that way.

What she did was due partly to the few sessions she had spent at the gym when he'd allowed her to accompany him. She was not a small woman but she had never thought of herself as strong. On this night, she was invincible. She had spotted her weapon – it was a length of nylon cord Sainsbury used as a plumb line. It was loose in his tool bag. She tied one end of it to the end of the bed, coiled it around his neck and applied all the pressure she could muster, all that she felt for all those punches and kicks and disgusting acts he had made her perform.

He stirred and struggled and fought back. But the drink had slowed him down, the breath was leaving his body too quickly. He gasped his last air as the woman he had wronged finally had her say. At 4am she was sure he was dead and she dragged him across the room and stuffed his body into the wardrobe. The rest of her life was indeed beginning.

When she had told the children that their father had struck her for the last time and she had made him leave, she began to see friends again. They saw her wounds. They also saw over the next weeks, that those wounds, mental and physical were healing. The neighbours too noticed an almost immediate change in the young resident of Le Locle Close. She was no longer isolated. She could lift her head and talk to whomever she pleased.

'It was like she had turned a switch on,' said one. 'She had this severe hairstyle before. Then she started to do her hair properly and wear mini-skirts. It was like she had drawn curtains apart and shut them behind her. She had just shut the past out of her mind, I think.'

Helena Kennedy did not have to argue that Pamela Sainsbury was not guilty of premeditated murder. Despite the lengths to which she went to dispose of her victim's body, the Crown and the court accepted her plea of manslaughter on the grounds of diminished responsibility, self-defence and provocation.

This would not have been possible had not all four psychiatrists agreed that at the time she garrotted her husband she was suffering acute stress reaction. This was brought on by the vicious beatings Sainsbury had just given her. The court accepted that as a woman who had been battered for eight years, she did not have to fight back using the Marquis of Queensberry rules. The judge, Mr Justice Aulds, told her, 'For many years you suffered regular and increasing violence and other forms of extreme sadism and sexual degradation at his hands. His domination of you mentally and physically was such that you lost the nerve to run away. One doctor describes you as being psychologically paralysed by this violent, jealous psychopath.'

On 13 December 1991 the Plymouth jury was guided by Mr Justice Aulds to accept the manslaughter plea. He pointed out that Pamela had no criminal record, was unlikely to re-offend and had spent six months in custody awaiting her trial. The jury also accepted Sainsbury's plea that she was guilty of preventing an inquest by hiding her victim's body. She was sentenced to two years' probation and left the court to build a new life with Lindsay and Terry, helped by her parents.

The news of this sympathetic verdict pleased campaigners for recognition of the special problems of battered women who kill. It did not please one of the West Country's prominent moral campaigners, Dr Adrian Rogers, who was also the chairman of Exeter Conservative Association. He commented to the *Western Morning News*: 'I believe myself that Mrs Sainsbury deserved to hang for what she did to her husband. If women who kill their husbands are going to get two years' probation then very few husbands are going to be safe in their beds.'

Paul Sainsbury's relatives may or may not have agreed with Dr Rogers. What is certain is that they were relieved on that day in December. They had had to wait until then to have the remains in those black sacks removed from the mortuary. Because they had lain for eight months in the fields, DNA testing was inconclusive. Because the head was never recovered no dental records could be checked. Paul Sainsbury was never formally identified but the inquest accepted his killer's word that the remains were those of her husband. The funeral could finally take place.

What few appreciated was the final irony. Not only had Pamela used her builder husband's plumb line to throttle him. She had also found his tools handy when it came to disposing of the body. Working at night on the floor of her bedroom four days after she had strangled him, she used his tenon saw with a foot-long blade to cut up his body.

She sawed off arms, legs and head and hacked the torso in half before shifting the remains into the black plastic bags. She dragged each downstairs to the garden shed. Using a wheelbarrow and making two journeys she took the bags to the cornfields behind the hedgerows on the A3052.

She told the police all this plainly, showing no emotion. Flatly and as if listing the steps by which you repair a garden gate, she concluded by telling them that she kept the head in the meter cupboard in the hall in case she needed to convince herself that it had not all been a dream, in case she ever feared he would walk back into her life and make it hell again.

She need not have kept it. The scars left by the cord which ripped her hands would always be there to remind her. She also told the police that she had wanted to bury Paul Sainsbury in the back garden, but the ground had been too hard to dig.

Come to Grandpa

The police officer sighed as he pulled up outside 40 Adams Lane, Southampton on the south shore of Long Island that bright Sunday in September 1985. The holiday makers had all gone home. The fashion parades had almost finished. Yuppies down from Manhattan for the weekend had stopped looking out for Mick Jagger and Jerry Hall or Alan Alda or any of the other celebrities who often came to kick the white sand and watch the ocean. No need now to pretend not to be impressed. All was quiet.

He'd been relieved to get into the patrol car that day, escaping work his wife had lined up for him in the garden. He hoped for an easy shift, spent largely at the Suffolk County station, watching the Giants' game on the sergeant's television set. He'd had an idle few hours so far, moving papers around, drinking coffee, catching up with the gossip. But there was a job waiting, one that had been sitting in a tray being successfully ignored by his colleagues. A tip-off about some old guy called Robert Caris who hadn't been seen around for a couple of months, had come in days ago. Some pal of his thought something might have happened, something bad. He was probably a screwball.

The case sounded about as urgent and necessary as a door-to-door check on the judge's wife's missing cat.

But now he was there, about to walk up the wooden steps to this respectable house. New paintwork, neat deck, flowers in the pots well tended, clean curtains, two cars gleaming in the opened garage. He checked his belt. The gun was there of course, so was the baton and the badge on his breast pocket glinted in the early autumn midday sun.

A grey-haired, heavy-set woman in stretch slacks, long-sleeved blouse and a woollen cardigan was getting out of one of the cars. It later transpired that she had driven her son-in-law Gerard Campanella to the railway station.

'Mrs Caris?' The woman nodded.

'Has there been a break-in?'

'No ma'am. Is your husband home?' She shook her head. 'Uh, uh.'

She reminded him of his mother: a decent woman who'd worked hard, not had any hand-outs, had a tough life until now. Could have been fifty, sixty.

'May I come in and talk to you, ma'am?'

She was opening the outer door, turning the key of the inner one. He followed, placing a foot firmly in her hallway before the house-proud owner could give her consent.

She looked at his shoes, concerned perhaps about the carpet she'd done double shifts to afford, and led him into the large, well-furnished living room. Through an open door to the kitchen he saw a younger woman, her daughter Rosalind, still in a housecoat although it was almost time for lunch.

She was coaxing a child, a dark-haired little girl of about five, to finish playing with her spoon and eat up some pasta.

Seeing him, she stopped, a flash of something like fear crossed her face; the child fell silent.

'He's away,' Mrs Arlene Caris was saying, as she picked up one of the child's toys from the couch. 'Took a trip. We – we're not together these days. I don't hear from him. Don't want to.'

'When d'you last make contact?' The woman was looking nervous now. 'Friend gave out he was in Saudi Arabia, working. He was there for years. It's more like home to him. I . . . I don't . . . Look. I told you, I don't want to hear from him. He don't live here no more. What's this about, officer? What exactly do you want?'

'Mind if I look around?' the police officer said, moving towards what looked like the bedroom. She was agitated now. 'You got a warrant?'

'Nope. You want me to radio through and get one? You got things you don't want me to see?' his voice was still calm. The younger woman was holding her mother's arm by now. But they said nothing.

A few minutes later he was pushing open the trap door to the attic. Inside, hidden amongst old curtains, behind dusty boxes and a couple of broken chairs was a large plastic-wrapped mattress. There was something on top of it, bound up tightly with it. The officer was immediately on his radio, calling for help. Arlene Caris was staring blankly at her daughter. He'd found the rotting corpse of her third husband, sixty-eight-year-old Robert Caris. You didn't need forensics to tell you he'd been shot in the head.

The next day, Monday 9 September, Arlene Caris was being held without bail in the Suffolk County Jail. Assistant District Attorney Steven Wilutis told the United Press that a Suffolk County Grand Jury would start hearing the case that week. By then fifty-six-year-old Arlene Caris, a nurse, had been arraigned, accused of fatally shooting her husband and then hiding his body for more than five months. Because the body and the mattress had been sealed in plastic so well, and placed in a part of the attic which was relatively remote from the rest of house there had been no noticeable odour.

The accused, he went on, had admitted shooting her husband after they had a heated argument in the house on 29 March.

'She said she went to a closet following the argument, took out a loaded .22 calibre rifle and shot him once in the head as he lay on the bed.' State police had checked on the deceased. He had worked for twenty years in the Persian Gulf area as a radio operator for Aramco, the oil company. Later he worked for more than twelve years as a radio operator in Southampton for ITT World Communications Inc. before retiring in 1984.

What the state police didn't discover was that Robert Caris was a brute to his wife and a molester of small girls. One of these was Arlene's granddaughter, then aged five.

A native of Georgia, Arlene married in her teens and moved to New York in the 1950s with her first husband. He drank heavily and eventually his liver gave up the fight and he died. Arlene, a practical nurse, wasn't too hot at diagnosing alcohol addiction it turned out. Her second husband, an honorary sheriff's deputy in Long Island, also drank and when his brain was sozzled enough he would beat her and their four children. Eventually she summoned the courage to get away. She bundled the kids into the car one night and fled making sure he couldn't find her. When she'd found somewhere to live, she changed her social security number so that he couldn't trace her. In time the divorce came through and she and the children were free.

She met her third husband at a Parents Without Partners meeting. A ship-to-shore radio operator, he was comfortably off, interesting and seemed a mild enough man. He was pleasant to her children, even more so to the grandchildren. They married in 1971. She thought it was third time lucky. She carried on nursing, doing overtime shifts when she could, saving for the secure retirement she hoped they'd both share.

But the statistics show that abusive behaviour often doesn't develop until well into a marriage and Robert Caris eventually began knocking Arlene about. He constantly lost his temper, shouted at her, mocked her for being unworldly and small-minded and for not having travelled as he had.

After he retired from ITT it got worse. He sank into moods of self-pity. He resented her busyness. He raged with jealousy, accused her of imagined affairs, belittled her, insulted her children. When she devoted time to them, he was nastier still. Her son developed cancer but to sneering Robert Caris he was a whingeing mummy's boy. Until the day he died his stepfather accused him of faking it. Arlene had to cope with his bile at her lowest moment.

He smashed her head against the wall until her hearing in one ear had all but disappeared. His punches to her stomach left her with a hiatus hernia and a dropped bladder which made her constantly prone to infections and pain. Arlene was not a brave woman, she didn't fight back. Not then.

Four times the rows became so fevered that Caris

threatened to kill her. He was strong, he had a rifle and he wasn't afraid to use it, he said, as he kicked and punched Arlene. She took to wearing long sleeves to hide the black and blue marks and treated herself for the pain. She carried on driving to work, smiling at the neighbours, telephoning the kids. Why didn't she seek help?

'I was so embarrassed and so ashamed to be in the same situation, constantly humiliated, degraded and made to feel worthless. I kept plunging towards the inevitable – a crisis,' she now says.

The crisis came in March. One of Arlene's daughters and her daughter, just five, a gorgeous child had been staying at the Caris house. Arlene loved all her grandchildren – there are six now and even two great grandchildren – but back then this child was the apple of Arlene's eye. She and Arlene's daughter were frequent visitors. But lately the child had been moody and seemed disturbed. Arlene noticed it first. Then, when she was examined by her doctor, there were the dreadful signs on her body that medical people are taught to look out for. She had been molested sexually and not just once. Grandpa Robert liked to play with her, liked to touch her and he liked her to touch him. He made her promise not to tell. Said it was their secret, said he'd hurt her if she told. Her mother guessed and told Arlene. In that moment her last scrap of hope that the monster she'd married would change back into the decent man he had once seemed was demolished. She determined she would leave him even if that meant losing her home and losing face.

She carried on doing night shifts and banking the money, every penny of which she'd now need. Arriving home at seven one morning she crept into the house hoping to slip into bed without waking the man who frightened her so. But he was waiting. He spewed out insults, accusations, criticisms. On and on the storm went, all day long and into the night, until, exhausted from the blows and from the sleep she never had, she began throwing clothes into a suitcase to leave. Seeing this, he became even angrier, beating her in the stomach and throwing her around the room. When he lay on his bed, exhausted from shouting and punching she sank onto hers. He roused himself, went over to her and threw her off onto the floor. As she lay there the thought of what he had done and would probably try to do again to the child flooded into her mind. She wanted, she said to the police when they came all those months later, 'To put an end to the bickering and hostility'.

She staggered to the cupboard where she knew he kept the loaded gun. To this day she says she doesn't remember the moment well. It's as though she became an automaton. What is certain is that she took it out, pointed it at him and fired. One bullet in his head stopped her torment.

He lay there bleeding on the bed while Arlene sank to the floor unable to believe what she had just done. Hours later she telephoned her daughter Rosalind who drove fast to the house. It was Rosalind, the assistant district attorney claimed, who had helped her mother wrap the hated man in the bed sheets and then in plastic. She had also helped to store him in the attic while they decided what to do.

'I know it was terrible to put him in the attic,' Arlene wrote in her clemency application. 'The next six months until I was arrested was a living hell. I worked every hour I possibly could. I told people who asked that he had gone away for a time.'

At her trial in March 1986 Arlene Caris pleaded guilty on the advice of her lawyers not to murder but to the lesser offence of first-degree manslaughter. She had no criminal record, but Judge Thomas Mallon sentenced her to a term of eight to twenty-five years. The court did not hear evidence of the man who had made her life hell for fourteen years.

After a few years she settled into the routine of prison. At Bedford Hills Correctional Facility she was more than thirty years older than the average woman inmate. She was and probably still is a model prisoner. Towards the end of 1992, the white-haired greatgrandmother in the neat blouse was one of a group of women prisoners who appealed to New York State Governor Mario Cuomo for a commuted sentence. She was not even granted a hearing. There was no clemency for her announced the following January as there was for some of the women.

She said then that at least she had become more self-confident and assertive since she began attending classes in prison. She could not sleep, however.

'With all the words in Webster's dictionary, I still can't find the ones to appropriately describe the trauma of taking life and never being able to give it back,' she said sadly.

A Taste of His
Own Medicine

He pressed her head down on the ironing board and held
the red-hot iron right next to her cheek, scalding her skin.
She shut her eyes tight, praying that he would not go any
further, that she would not have to endure any more of the
excruciating pain. At best, she could be scarred for life; at
worst, he could kill her.

Petite Kiranjit Ahluwalia had faced such a scenario
countless times before during her ten years with husband
Deepak. He had regularly beaten her, raped her and tried
to strangle her. On one occasion, he had threatened to
gouge her eyes out. Twice, in the depths of despair, she had
attempted to take her own life. But this night would be
different. It would be the last night that Deepak would
ever be able to subject her to his own hideous form of
torture.

Finally, his sadistic lust satisfied, Deepak put down the
hot iron. Kiranjit pulled herself free, relieved to be alive
but vowing that she could not take any more.

She went to bed around midnight but was unable to
sleep. She lay there thinking about her years of suffering at
the hands of the man who had once promised to love and

303

cherish her, but who had instead brutalised her in the most intimidating way imaginable.

She went to his room, saw him asleep and thought, 'How can he sleep when he has done this to me?'

Twice she called him. 'I wanted to talk to him. I wanted to tell him, "I can't sleep, I can't eat. You are sleeping, you are talking, you are enjoying your life. Can't you see me, the way I am living now?"

'But he just turned his face and completely ignored me the way he ignored me before.'

The more she brooded, the more determined she became to give him a taste of his own medicine.

Her mind turned to the can of petrol which was kept in a lean-to store outside the kitchen. Certain that Deepak was asleep, she crept downstairs some time after 2.30am and, fortified by a stiff drink of alcohol, poured about three pints of petrol into a nappy bucket. She then lit a candle from the gas cooker, took hold of a little stick and picked up an oven glove to protect herself. Reaching her husband's room, she put down the candle and, her hand trembling, emptied a quantity of the petrol over the duvet under which he was sleeping.

Then she poured some more petrol over his feet. She wanted him to feel pain, to suffer the kind of agony he had repeatedly inflicted on her. And she wanted to hurt his feet to stop him coming after her.

As the petrol slopped over Deepak Ahluwalia's feet, he woke up with a start and leapt from the bed. Knowing that it was then or never, Kiranjit quickly dipped the stick in the petrol, lit it from the candle and threw it back into the room. The petrol vapour ignited in an almighty fireball, consuming Deepak and sending him screaming from the room.

'I'll kill you, I'll kill you,' he shrieked at Kiranjit, his pyjama bottoms blazing as he rushed into the bathroom in search of water to put out the flames. Consumed with pain, he then ran outside, pleading for help. His next-door neighbour heard the frantic screams. She went downstairs and, from the light in the hall, saw his badly burned figure. His skin was hanging off and he was bleeding. Her husband put Deepak's arms in a sink of water but this had an adverse effect and Deepak ran from the house screeching. He collapsed in the front garden, rubbing his arms in the grass. The woman of the house put a coat over him but he threw it off.

'I feel sick, I feel sick,' he cried.

With that, she said, he began retching and 'brought up some black stuff'.

Hearing the commotion, other neighbours rushed to his aid. They found Deepak's house locked and spotted Kiranjit, who herself suffered burnt hands and arms in the fire, standing at a window clutching one of her sons. She appeared to be calm and staring at the flames.

As the heat intensified, Kiranjit fled with her boys and, having seen the flames at the windows, neighbours called the fire brigade and the police. The badly burned Deepak managed to telephone his mother to tell her what had happened, to report his wife's dreadful deed.

None of the family or the local residents were surprised to see the emergency services turn up at the house in Crawley, West Sussex, in the middle of the night. The feeling was that it was bound to happen sooner or later. The only surprise was that it was Deepak, and not Kiranjit, who was being carted off to hospital, his life hanging by a thread.

Kiranjit was arrested and taken to Holloway Prison on a

charge of attempted murder. When six days later, thirty-four-year-old Deepak succumbed to his terrible injuries (burns which covered 40 per cent of his body), the charge became one of murder.

On his death-bed, Deepak told the police that Kiranjit was a wicked woman who had treated him terribly throughout their married life. He said he was terrified of her, that she kept him a virtual prisoner.

Kiranjit was born the youngest of a family of ten (five brothers and four sisters) in Chak, a village near Jullundur in Indian Punjab. Her father died when she was just three months old and her mother when she was sixteen. Consequently, the family moved to Ahmadabad, the Gujarat capital, where Kiranjit studied with the intention of taking up teaching or the law. Having obtained her arts degree, she had her mind set on a professional career but her brothers had more traditional ideas for her. They wanted her to get married. 'You don't need to work,' they told her. 'Take however much you want from us.'

She agreed to join her married sister, Surindra, in Toronto, Canada, and studied to become a solicitor, accepting, albeit reluctantly, that in her absence, her brothers would do their utmost to match her with a suitable boy.

Her family worked hard on her behalf and soon came up with a likely lad, handsome engineering graduate Deepak Ahluwalia who, originally from Kenya, now lived in Crawley, England. He was shown a photograph of her and since he came from a suitable caste and the right culture, a meeting was arranged. In 1979, Deepak went out to Toronto. Kiranjit had just a week to get to know him before arrangements were finalised with a haste which would horrify Western couples.

But although it meant the end of her career at the age of twenty-three, Kiranjit was now perfectly happy at the prospect of the arranged marriage, principally because she considered Deepak to be quite a catch. In many arranged marriages, women are foisted on men with whom they have nothing in common and also whom they find unattractive. But as far as first impressions went, Kiranjit came to the conclusion that Deepak was charming as well as goodlooking, and he also made her laugh. In short, he was everything she had hoped for. Quite how she formed this appraisal is unclear since, on her own admission, she was too shy to talk to him and doubts whether they spoke to each other for more than five minutes before they were married. This is not necessarily the ideal recipe for future happiness.

Given their brief encounter, there was no possibility that they could be in love but the marriage was what her family wanted, and that, in itself, made her happy.

Following a register office ceremony in Canada, they flew to England where, within five days, the marriage was solemnised with a Sikh temple wedding in Southall, West London. She had never wanted a rich husband so Deepak's modest home in Coombe Close in the Langley Green district of Crawley suited her perfectly. Kiranjit thought she could be happy with Deepak but no sooner were they married in England than she began to see a dark, disturbing side to his character. Within two days of the wedding, the 'charming, fun-loving boy' had turned into a vicious brute.

Her first insight into Deepak's evil side came when he deliberately smashed the suitcase and the presents she had brought for him and his family from Canada.

A couple of days later, the object of his violence was Kiranjit herself. He hit her on the stairs, pulled her hair and knocked a pan onto her feet. He started swearing at her.

'I was very frightened,' she says. 'I had never seen a man's anger like that before.'

She tried to run away but he came and stood in front of her.

'You want to run to the police, don't you?' he yelled. He seized a milk bottle. 'I'm going to break this bottle and push it in your stomach now.'

Again, she attempted to escape.

He taunted her. 'Come on, run, you bastard!'

Kiranjit was in a turmoil. She explained later, 'I didn't know whether to run or to stay in the house. If I went back he would beat me badly, if I ran to the police, he would beat me badly or kill me with that bottle. I was so confused.'

Over the next ten years, Kiranjit was put through a systematic catalogue of torture. Deepak had moods when he would insist on cooking his own food and on banning his wife from the room. More alarmingly, she would see him explode into violence. He also believed that he was a reincarnation of Hanuman, the Hindu monkey god from the Indian epic, the *Ramayana*, and consequently he became convinced that he had superhuman powers. The difference was that Hanuman respected women.

Deepak waged his war of attrition on Kiranjit without mercy. She stood only five feet two inches tall and weighed just seven stone, whereas he was seven inches taller and a hefty thirteen stone. It was no contest. He could push her around at will – and he did, almost everyday for ten years.

The onslaught was virtually relentless.

Occasionally, after a particularly savage thrashing, he would appear repentant. He would apologise profusely, begging forgiveness. The next day, the beatings would start all over again.

He smashed her face with shoes, hit her with the buckle end of belts and even the telephone. Basically, he used whatever came to hand as long as it was something which could cause sufficient injury. He cut her, broke her teeth, broke her finger, ripped out handfuls of her hair, threw her down the stairs and tried to run her over with his car at a family wedding. He attempted to strangle her several times, scalded her and threw boiling tea over her. One beating was so severe that she was knocked unconscious.

He once pulled her by the hair into the back of their car, held a screwdriver to her eyes and threatened to gouge them out. 'Pray to your God and father,' he said menacingly.

The most trivial thing would set him off. Once, he complained that his dinner was too hot. 'Eat it, or I will beat you,' he threatened. As always, Kiranjit did as she was told. She started to eat, but suddenly he seized her arm.

'Stop, or I will beat you,' he yelled.

She could not win. Whatever she did, he was going to hit her, just for the fun of it. He seemed to take pleasure in humiliating her, physically and verbally. Sometimes he attacked her simply because she dared to speak without first asking his permission.

All Kiranjit wanted was to be a good wife, to uphold the family values that she had been taught to believe in. She did everything she could to please Deepak. Nobody could have done more. But as her unstinting efforts continued to meet a violent rebuttal, she realised total subservience was not the answer and desperately tried to leave him or seek outside help.

By 1982, her hair started to go prematurely grey as the traumas of life with Deepak made her age way beyond her twenty-six years. She hoped his family, who lived nearby in Crawley, would prove sympathetic. She showed them the cuts, bruises and scars, and begged to be allowed to press for a divorce. They would not hear of it and, according to Kiranjit, invoked the izzat (an Asian code of family honour) which effectively secured her domestic imprisonment. She became trapped in a conspiracy of non-intervention by Deepak's family.

Although accepting that she was being beaten (they once intervened to prise Deepak's fingers from around her neck), they seemed more concerned that she had not yet borne Deepak a child and told her to undergo medical examinations to find a solution to her problem. That, at least, was resolved when she gave birth in 1984 to Sanjay and again, two years later, to Ravi.

Their sex life was a simple affair – whenever Deepak wanted sex, he raped her. Kiranjit had no option. If she so much as thought about physical resistance, she would incur another fearful beating. In the circumstances, it goes without saying that Kiranjit was a reluctant mother. She did not wish to bring children into that world of violence and she also knew that having children would make it harder for her to leave her husband.

When she became pregnant, she prayed that she would have boys because she feared that Deepak might harm girls in the same way he hurt her. Her pregnancies did nothing to stem the torment. Once when she was eight months pregnant, she was reduced to cowering on the floor, protecting her stomach and her unborn baby while her husband mercilessly rained a succession of blows on her back. Another time, she was brutally dragged upstairs while pregnant.

Strangely, despite the fact that he nearly killed both children before they were born, Deepak was very fond of his two sons. He even helped to change their nappies. But his attitude towards Kiranjit did not change one iota.

One of his favourite methods of torture was to hold a knife to her throat, threatening to slit it open. This became such a regular occurrence that she finally summoned the courage to notify the police. In 1983 and 1986, Croydon Crown Court granted injunctions to restrain Deepak from assaulting her. They had little to no effect.

Her next port of refuge was to her family in India. She and Deepak took a rare holiday there although Kiranjit had bought an open ticket since she had no intention of returning to England with him. It was shortly after he had scalded her with boiling tea and she showed the scars to her brothers. She told them about all the other beatings, too.

'You must stop,' they told Deepak.

He was contrition personified. 'I am very sorry. I promise I will never ever do it again.' Then, turning to Kiranjit, he begged, 'Please, please give me one last chance.'

For two days, he was as good as his word. They were the only happy days of Kiranjit's marriage.

Kiranjit remained unsure of his sincerity, but her family put her under substantial pressure to take him back. Divorce meant dishonour in the Sikh culture, not only for her but for the entire family.

'A bad marriage,' they maintained, 'is better than the disgrace of no marriage at all.'

She was told that once a girl married and left home, her life belonged to her husband. There was no divorce. She was made to understand that she would lose the children and finish up on the scrap heap.

'Oh, Kiran,' they argued. 'Deepak has apologised. He says he won't do it again. Give him one more chance.'

Reluctantly, she relented. No sooner were they back in Crawley than the beatings resumed, every bit as bloody as before.

Nobody could accuse Kiranjit of not trying to free herself from her husband's tyranny. She did actually begin divorce proceedings in 1986 before being talked out of it by both families. Besides telling the police, she consulted her doctor on a regular basis from 1981 and once even ran away from home. It was a short-lived taste of liberty, for Deepak tracked her down after a day and hauled her back to the happy family home. With her own family five thousand miles away in India, with no support from her in-laws, few friends in England, and only a limited grasp of the English language, she naturally felt frighteningly isolated. She was a woman alone in a strange land. And Deepak went out of his way to prevent her integration into the Western lifestyle. He insisted that she wear her hair in an Asian style and never took her out to restaurants or the cinema. Her one small act of rebellion was to wear Western clothes instead of the traditional Indian dress.

In line with his isolationist policy, Deepak did not

approve of the prospect of Kiranjit going out to work. Once when she said she wanted to, he held her by the neck and told her that he would not permit it. However, their financial needs eventually dictated that she find employment and so he allowed her to take a job in a caustic soda factory in Crawley.

Kiranjit's plight and loneliness reached the stage where she twice tried to commit suicide by taking overdoses of sleeping tablets. When those failed, she turned to drink – vodka, whisky – whatever happened to be in the house. She said, 'I could not tell anyone. It is against my culture and I was very ashamed. I drank not for pleasure, but to stop the pain.'

But the pain persisted, especially when Deepak, who had risen to the post of supervisor at the Royal Mail sorting office in Gatwick Road, Crawley, began a string of affairs with other women.

He openly flaunted his relationship with a woman at work in front of Kiranjit, another method of humiliating her and making her feel utterly worthless. He used to drive around in a car which he had bought for his lover and tried to pressurise Kiranjit into obtaining money from her family to pay for the debts which he had accumulated through his womanising ways. The children frequently went without so that he could buy presents for his mistress.

Eventually, Kiranjit lost the will to fight. She had tried everything, but felt that everybody had let her down. Her weight plummeted dramatically, she became increasingly nervous and repeatedly burst into tears. She was in a state of severe depression. She resigned herself to her fate and began saving money for her funeral, so convinced was she that Deepak would one day kill her.

Although Kiranjit was by far the major recipient of Deepak's brutality, she was not the only one. He assaulted workmates and complete strangers alike and once went to see a psychiatrist after it was suspected that there was a psychopathic element to his violence.

In April 1989, Kiranjit's life sank to an all-time low. Her face swollen, her arms and legs bruised and battered from her husband's beatings, and her mind in an emotional turmoil, she found herself sitting down to write a letter begging her oppressor not to leave her for his mistress.

In this pitiful letter, she promised Deepak: 'I won't laugh if you don't like it. I won't touch black coffee. I won't ask you for any help. I will eat to get fatter.' It continued in the same desperate vein as she offered to agree to abide by all of Deepak's demands in return for his affection. She promised not to go shopping, not to visit friends, not to dye her hair, not to talk to her neighbour and not to eat green chilli.

A month after Kiranjit wrote this sad, sorry note, Deepak finally pushed her over the edge. A family cousin had been lodging with them over the previous few months and had observed Deepak's cruelty at first hand. He noted how Deepak often lost his temper and began throwing cups and plates around.

The day before the fire, Kiranjit went to see her mother-in-law and told her, 'Either he will die or I will'.

By Deepak Ahluwalia's barbaric standards, his actions on the evening of 8 May were no worse than usual. But this time they cost him his life.

It was around 10.15pm when Deepak returned home. Kiranjit dutifully gave him his dinner.

'Can we talk about our future?' she asked.

'There is nothing to say,' he replied bluntly. 'It is over between us.'

To emphasise his point, he started attacking her and tried to break her legs. He then demanded money to pay the telephone bill, threatening to inflict further physical pain if she did not hand over £200 out of her wages the following morning. His own wages had been spent on keeping his mistress.

He started to iron some clothes and when Kiranjit showed a reluctance to leave him alone, he thrust the hot iron next to her cheek and threatened to burn her unless she left him in peace. For Kiranjit, he committed one atrocity too many that night – and he was to pay for it dearly.

Kiranjit insisted that she never meant to kill Deepak. 'It all became too much that night,' she said. 'He had made me a physical and mental wreck. I lost it. I had told him many, many times that I didn't ever want to lose him. That night, I just wanted to cause him pain, like he caused me. I could see no end from his violence and pain I was getting day by day. I went downstairs and got the petrol and threw it on his feet. I don't know where I got the idea from. I don't know where I got this strength from. But that night I was taking that petrol and that little stick in my hand. It could have burned me alive but I was not thinking about that. I never thought he would die.'

She stood trial at Lewes Crown Court in December 1989, pleading guilty to manslaughter on the grounds of provocation but not guilty to murder. Her case was that she only intended to inflict pain – provocation was her secondary line of defence.

Kiranjit did not go into the witness box to give evidence.

She was too ashamed to admit that she had been drinking, something which would cause acute embarrassment to her family. Nor did she wish to talk in front of relatives about the sexual abuse to which she had been subjected. When the matter was raised as to why Kiranjit had simply not walked out on her husband, she argued through her defence counsel that her attempts to leave him were constrained by his violence and control and by the family's invocation of the izzat.

In his summing-up, Mr Justice Leonard discussed Kiranjit's state of mind and intent. He suggested that because she had been able to walk downstairs to fetch the petrol, the candle and the stick and to bring them back up again, she may have been thinking clearly and have been in control of her actions. Furthermore, he said that taking the time to collect together the equipment needed to kill her husband might be an indication of her malicious intent to commit murder, rather than merely inflict pain. Her plea of provocation was questioned because there had been a three-hour period between the last occasion she was assaulted and the time when she got out of bed to prepare the fatal fire. She had waited until Deepak had fallen asleep.

The jury was unable to reach a unanimous decision and were instructed to agree on a majority verdict. Shortly afterwards, they returned and found Kiranjit guilty of murder by a majority of ten to two. She was sentenced to life imprisonment.

Kiranjit was stunned. 'I always had faith in the British law. I thought, you know, there were two court injunctions which were the biggest proof, the doctor's report and family evidence. But nobody tried to understand – they just ignored all the proofs which they had in front of them. Nobody tried to understand why, in the end, this woman put herself in this situation.'

Although she missed her children desperately, in many respects Kiranjit found prison life a merciful relief after ten years of hell with Deepak. At Bullwood Hall Prison at Hockley, Essex, she was able to improve her English and began taking courses in typing, hairdressing and fashion. She could finally wear her hair in a modern Western style, something Deepak never permitted. She confessed, 'I am happier in prison than I ever was during my marriage. People – the other prisoners, the prison officers – they are all nice to me. I never knew that from my husband.'

From prison, she sent a note to her mother-in-law. Phrased in terms reminiscent of Sikh cleansing rituals, it read: 'Deepak did so many sins, I gave him a fire-bath to wash his sins. I did a prison pilgrimage to wash my sins.'

Everybody who met Kiranjit during her imprisonment became enchanted with her. Lorraine Butler of the *Daily Mirror* wrote: 'She's so slim and frail. So affectionate and open. So polite and eager to please that you cannot help but feel anger towards the man whose beatings crushed any spirit she ever had.'

It may have been Kiranjit who was found guilty but after she had received such a harsh sentence, many members of Deepak's own family came to realise that much of the guilt lay with them. They admitted that they had known about the beatings, but had urged Kiranjit to stay with Deepak for the honour of the family. Now they felt they had let her down and certainly did not believe she deserved to be imprisoned for life. They wrote to the Home Secretary saying that the Asian community was partly to blame for not supporting Kiranjit when she had been crying out for help. They began a campaign to win her release.

The case came to the attention of Crawley Women's Aid who in turn notified Southall Black Sisters, the West London-based women's rights group.

That organisation's Pragna Patel visited Kiranjit in prison and months of counselling, much of it in Hindi, built up her confidence, enabling her to pour out the full horrors of her marriage, details of which she had been too embarrassed to reveal to her lawyers at the trial. On the basis of this fresh evidence, an appeal was organised.

Kiranjit remembers, 'At first I was a bit embarrassed about the campaign. I was a bit ashamed – I thought I did not want more people to know about my case. But then I thought, "Sod this! Family, honour, religion, what have they done for me?" So I told them to go on and do my campaign.'

In 1991 Mr Justice Steyn gave Kiranjit leave to appeal, ruling that the original trial jury had been misdirected on the law of provocation.

The appeal was heard in July 1992, by which time Kiranjit had spent over two-and-a-half years in jail. As public interest in the case intensified, Kiranjit's family wrote an emotional letter to the *Guardian*.

My wife and I, as Kiranjit Ahluwalia's sister- and brother-in-law, are waiting for judgment on her appeal against conviction anxiously and hoping that she will be freed. We have worked hard for the last three years to make sure she is united with her children and we witness their daily suffering. It is the children who suffer most when their mother is locked away for life.

Kiranjit Ahluwalia had a very violent marriage from the very beginning. She approached us for help after being badly beaten and bruised and at times she came to stay with us. Whenever problems occurred in her marriage, we acted in a traditional way.

We advised Kiranjit to make her marriage work in consideration of family honour and cultural values and social pressure.

We always sought to patch up the marriage, which Kiranjit wanted to end. Looking back, it was not the best thing to do. We could have acted in a more progressive and positive manner in order to help Kiranjit to do what she wanted. We failed in the end.

This failure has resulted in a great tragedy for Kiranjit and for all of us.

Locking Kiranjit up for life is not a solution. The longer she stays in prison, the greater the suffering of her children and family. It would be a fair and just act by the Court of Appeal to quash her life sentence and set her free.

Her children miss her and want to be with their mother.

Sukhjit Sing Walia

At the appeal, while Kiranjit's supporters demonstrated outside, her counsel, Geoffrey Robertson QC, argued that the trial judge had misdirected the jury by not asking them to take into account the years of battering which prompted Kiranjit to act as she did. He described her marriage as 'a charter for slavery' and said that the years of beating and humiliation had reduced her to the 'nadir of abasement'. He added that the written pledges to her husband made a month before his death were 'a classic example of a woman who has suffered domestic violence and humiliation, who had entirely lost her self-esteem and who is prepared to sacrifice everything to succumb to the most outrageous demands in order to retain her family honour'. It was stated that some relatives, who knew of her injuries 'bitterly regretted' not intervening, and that their cultural and religious background had also prevented them giving evidence at her trial.

Mr Robertson also entered a plea that at the time of the killing, Kiranjit had been suffering from diminished responsibility, a factor which had not been raised at all at her trial. He said that a report by consultant psychiatrist Malcolm Weller was supported by the evidence of four other psychiatrists, showing that when Kiranjit set light to her husband, her mental state was such that her responsibility was severely diminished. Although her lawyers at the trial were aware of Dr Weller's findings, they apparently did not pursue them or seek another opinion.

Sitting in the dock listening to the evidence, Kiranjit looked pale and drawn. From time to time, tears would trickle down her cheeks.

Lord Taylor, the Lord Chief Justice, began by ruling on provocation. He said that the trial judge had directed the jury in accordance with the classic definition of provocation, as stated in the Renee Duffy case of 1949 (see p. 159), namely as conduct 'which would cause in any reasonable person and actually causes in the accused, a sudden and temporary loss of self-control'.

On Kiranjit's behalf, it was said that the phrase 'sudden and temporary loss of self-control' might have led the jury to think provocation could not arise for consideration unless the defendant's act followed immediately upon the act or words constituting the alleged provocation. It was also suggested that although an interval of time might in many cases be a 'cooling off' period for regaining self-control, in other cases, particularly those of long-abused women, the time lapse might have the opposite effect, marking a 'slow-burn' reaction rather than an immediate loss of self-control.

But Lord Taylor and his colleagues decided that the longer the delay and the stronger the evidence of deliberation on the defendant's part, the more likely it was that provocation would be ruled out. At the trial, despite the lapse of time, the judge left the issue of provocation to the jury. He did not suggest to the jury that they should reject the defence of provocation because the deceased's provocative words or acts were not followed immediately by his wife's fatal acts. That direction, ruled Lord Taylor, was correct and in accordance with the well-established law.

Lord Taylor also rejected the argument that the trial judge should have directed the jury to consider the possibility that Kiranjit was suffering from the characteristic of Battered Woman Syndrome. He said that there had been no medical or other evidence at the trial to suggest that she was suffering from such a syndrome.

However, Lord Taylor said that the appeal was on much stronger ground on the question of diminished responsibility. The fact that this defence had not been raised at the trial, plus the new medical evidence and the accused's strange behaviour after lighting the fire, led the judges to regard the verdict as 'unsafe and unsatisfactory'.

So Kiranjit's murder conviction was quashed and a retrial was ordered, to take place as soon as possible. In the meantime, to the dismay of her supporters who had been hoping that she would be freed immediately, it was decided that she must remain in prison until the fresh trial.

The date was set for 25 September 1992 at the Old Bailey and it was a brief affair. The prosecution accepted Kiranjit's plea of guilty to manslaughter on grounds of diminished responsibility and Mr Justice Hobhouse sentenced her to three years and four months in prison, the exact period which she had already served. He said, 'I consider justice does not require you to be detained in prison any longer'.

Kiranjit Ahluwalia was free at last.

The court erupted into cheers. Kiranjit said later, 'I didn't know what was happening in court. It was fear, nerves, my ears started blocking. I could not hear. The only thing I heard was people clapping and then I realised it must be good news. I couldn't believe it, I just covered my face and put my head down. I wanted to ask the judge, "Can I feel my children? Can I play with my children now that I'm free?" I was not expecting so many people. Everyone was so pleased for me. I could not cry. It took me two days to cry.'

Outside, supporters bearing slogans proclaiming 'Self-defence is no offence' and 'Domestic violence is the crime' released dozens of coloured balloons.

The decision was seen as a great victory for battered

wives everywhere and Kiranjit was quick to urge her followers not to forget other women including Sara Thornton, still in jail for similar crimes. 'They have already suffered enough. I cannot forget them,' said Kiranjit. 'We deserve some happiness in our lives.'

Speaking in a whisper outside the court, Kiranjit said, 'I am very pleased to be out. I don't believe it somehow. It is a big shock for me because I was not expecting anything. I just want to see my children. I am really excited. I want to spend a lot of time with them. I haven't seen them in their school uniforms. I don't want to hide anything from my children – I will tell them the truth when they are old enough to understand.'

Her brother-in-law, Sukhjit Walia, said, 'All her life Kiranjit has tried to please people. She tried to keep her marriage together. What has happened to her is cruel and unfair. She is not and has never been a criminal. To treat her like one was shameful. To punish her life was a miscarriage. It was a torture for us. Now we can start building a new life for her.'

A huge party was thrown to celebrate Kiranjit's release. The woman who, during Deepak's reign of terror, was so shy and nervous that she lacked the confidence to go to the doctor by herself, had regained her self-esteem. The timid mouse was being hailed as a champion of the women's cause.

But her life has remained tinged with sadness. 'I can never forget what happened,' she said at the start of 1993. 'It is with me for ever. It comes into my mind once or twice a day. I remember the beatings, the fear. When I get angry with my husband, I look at my sons and I think their father died because of me, then I regret it. I always will.' But she adds pointedly, 'I was a good wife.'

She Couldn't Even Cut Her Wrists

It was a cold, damp February night and the only people still out in Nottingham's dilapidated district of Bulwell wished they were not. One driver, a chap called Purvie, was just thinking about his bed as he turned on to the St Albans Road and got into fourth gear. Then he saw what he thought was a child standing in the road, no coat, fair hair in her eyes, shouting and waving her thin arms like a mad thing. Was she drunk or out of her mind from drugs? He pulled up and saw that she was not a child but a pale young girl, with eye make-up smudged and lipstick smeared. She might have been his daughter, he thought. She didn't seem to be drunk, but she was deeply distressed. Her jumper sleeves covered her wrists. Had they not, he might have seen that her wrists were cut and bleeding as they had been more than a dozen times before.

'You must come with me, you must come with me,' she said, as she began running into a side road. The thought crossed his mind that he should drive on, forget her. Who would blame him? This could be a set-up for a mugging such as you read about in the papers. But he found himself getting out of the car and following. She went into the open front door of a house in Turnbery Road, a cul de sac no estate agent could call desirable. He was panting as he reached the top of the stairs. Then he saw what he was meant to see. The body of a man wearing only a shirt lay on the floor of the landing. Near it was a radio and cassette tape-player from which a tinny version of Marvin Gaye could still be heard. Also near the body lay a kitchen knife, the sort you'd use to cut carrots. It had a blade about six inches long and the man could see, even in the bad light, that it was sticky with blood. It was 1am. The start of a day that was to be the first of a new, long chapter in the sad life of the girl.

'He's been stabbed. He's dead, I'm sure he is,' she gasped. Then she added, 'I've killed him, haven't I?'

And he knew, without touching the man, without waiting for the police, that the answer was yes.

In the prosperous mid–1980s, before the coalmines were closed and when recession was thought to be a disease suffered only in the North, Nottingham liked to describe itself as the Queen of the East Midlands. Students rated the university as the coolest in the country. Salesmen wangled overnight stays in the city known for its lively night life. Everyone wanted to live there. Even a wandering waif called Emma Humphries.

She wasn't born in the place. Her original home was Dolgellau, Wales, but when she was five her mother split with her father, a car worker, and moved to Nottingham to live with a tailor. It wasn't long before Mrs Humphries met a Canadian offshore driller who seemed to offer more. Within a month they were married and the couple, with Emma and her two sisters, set off to live in his home of Edmonton, Alberta.

It was exciting to begin with, she recalled. But not for long. Then the new life turned sour, for everyone. She and her sisters were mocked at school for their strange accents. Her mother and stepfather began to argue. Far worse, he revealed himself to be a man of violence.

'Me and my sisters used to huddle at the top of the stairs at night. There were three of us and we'd be listening to it all happening downstairs and wondering, when the noise and everything stopped, what state my mum was going to be in when we walked down the stairs, whether she was going to be dead or alive. It was horrible.'

She remembered that her stepfather hit the girls too – he knocked her and her mother's head together at one point.

Not surprisingly Emma was disturbed. She began playing truant from school and, by the time she was thirteen, she'd found a way of getting attention and money. She began working as a prostitute on Edmonton's streets. She was soon scooped up by the police and handed over to social workers who, for the next three years, moved her between foster parents and homes for 'difficult young people'. She moved eleven times. She had also taken to expressing her unhappiness by slashing her wrists.

Finally she was given a choice: to stay in a supervised flat or to return to Nottingham to the father she could hardly remember and a stepmother she had never met. She chose Nottingham. Not surprisingly Robin Hood Street, where her father now lived, didn't seem too welcoming to a troubled teenager. Very soon she was borrowing the money to fly back to Canada in the hope that one of her former foster mothers could give her a home. Sadly, although the woman was willing, the Canadian social services were not willing to pay for her keep. She was soon sleeping in a flat shared by people she'd met on the streets.

When one of the women in the flat stabbed herself to death there, the authorities rumbled that Emma was not under supervision and she was sent on her way again back to England and the city once famous for lace and Robin Hood. Not that Robin Hood would have wanted to be associated with Bulwell in its northwesterly corner, which is where she ended up and was soon working in the only way she knew – as a prostitute.

In 1984 Trevor Armitage was thirty-three but as mixed-up as the girl who was about to change – and end – his life. When he was a little older than she, trying to do a decent job as a solicitor's clerk, living with his decent family in Hamilton Road, on the outskirts of Sherwood Rise and not far from the Goose Fair, he was charged with murder. At Lincoln Assizes in October 1969 the jury heard how a newsagent's scribble of an address – his address – on the paper which wrapped a shotgun, stored in a left luggage office, led to his arrest. Constable Leslie Ward, searching those lockers on another inquiry, found the gun which forensics' experts identified as that used at around 3am on the morning of 21 June on taxi driver Sidney Ockleford. The young man who flagged him down in the city, climbed into the back seat and demanded the ignition keys was Armitage.

Whether he was drunk, whether he needed money desperately or whether he was working with others, will probably never be known. But the driver delivered his passenger and at the end of the ride, near Bulwell in Nuthall, by way of payment plus tip, he received two almost fatal bullets from the gun. Armitage later admitted that he had stolen it from a sports shop. At the trial he pleaded not guilty to attempted murder, but guilty of wounding with intent to do grievous bodily harm. He was sent to borstal for corrective training, but was trained for very little.

He had subsequent convictions too, including two for violence. One in 1973 was for threatening behaviour and possessing an offensive weapon. In 1977 he was convicted of common assault of a prostitute he picked up in Hyson Green, the red-light district of Nottingham.

So he probably had no intention of repeating that crime when he met Emma Humphries in the late summer of 1984. By then he was working as a sales representative and doing quite well. He was engaged to be married and his family had high hopes that he would begin a settled chapter in his life. He also had a son, the same age as Emma, of whom he was fond. He saw him often.

The police knew a different man. To them he was 'a persistent punter', the trial jury was later to learn. So he still had needs which, it suddenly seemed, a pretty blonde girl might fulfil. Emma too had needs, of course, but they were rather more basic ones. By September of that year, her only home was in a slum with dossers. She had tried, briefly, to live with her grandmother but, as with her father and stepmother earlier, this had not worked out.

When she went back to work selling sex, she said to herself that she would throw in her lot with the first man who asked her so long as he was clean, respectful and had a bit of money. There were other offers but, tragically, the man who fitted the bill best and most quickly was bearded, beefy Trevor Armitage. That month she moved into his house in Turnberry Road. For her it was convenience. For him, it was love.

Interviewed in the *Guardian* more than ten years later she said: 'He was so insecure, he would keep telling me that he loved me. I found it hard because I'd never met a man who said "I love you". We were two people who were bad for each other. He was looking for someone to worship and to dominate and I had never had a boyfriend before.'

It wasn't long before she discovered what possessiveness could mean. She was returning to the house by taxi when the driver, who had befriended her earlier and had heard that she had been looking for somewhere to live, offered to help her find a place. As she said in the Yorkshire Television documentary *Women Who Kill*, 'I was quite chuffed in a way and I mentioned it to Trevor when I got home that night and that was the first time he hit me.'

An older, wiser woman might have known better than to blurt out such a thing, likely as it was to fire a jealous row. But Emma, for whom no one had ever cared, chose to believe that the pain of a punch was a way that feelings of affection were shown. 'I thought, this guy cares about me. But I couldn't relate to him once he was hitting me and stuff, I couldn't sleep with him. I couldn't mix the violence with "I love you" so I started to withdraw from him sexually. I didn't want to sleep with him.'

She thought she was better off in his house. She was so wrong. While she wanted him to be her father, she could not accept him as her lover. His round stocky body repelled her. Instead of being able to stop work on the streets, as she'd planned, she now had to do it with the knowledge that there would be an interrogation about it later. Armitage would want to know who had asked for what and for how much. Sometimes he would follow her and, when she was home and refused to do the same with him, he would rape her. Ironically she was not a very good prostitute anyway. In those six months she was twice cautioned and twice charged with soliciting by the police. One night she was gang-raped. She was too shaken and upset by the attack to go home, knowing that Armitage would not offer sympathy and might even assault her again. When she finally returned a few days later, that was exactly what happened. She told the *Guardian*'s Duncan Campbell that going back was 'like I'd walked into my coffin'.

As the difficult months went by, the man who needed to worship and control her made sure he did not easily lose her again. He nailed down the windows and kept the portable phone in his car. If he'd been a disturbed man before she met him, he was more so now. On one occasion after they'd argued and he'd hit her, he drove off naked, she recalled. He would, however, allow her out to work. That was why on the night of 25 February, she took a taxi from Hyson Green to the corner of Turnberry Road, discovering too late that she had no change with which to pay the fare. Her solution was to invite the driver to go with her to a bar where they could have a drink and she'd get change. By a coincidence that now seems inevitable, Trevor Armitage saw her there and knew she was not working. She was spending time with a man she preferred to him.

She went home, knowing she was heading into trouble. Once there, she dithered. She took a bottle of vodka upstairs. She put a Marvin Gaye tape into her cassette player, hoping the soul singer could make her feel sexy. She put lipstick on her mouth and looked at herself in the mirror. Then she decided to hurt herself once more. She didn't even look at the livid mess of scars on her wrists from earlier cuts.

This is how she remembered it when she appeared on *Women Who Kill*:

What I'd done once before was I'd cut my wrists to make him know I can't take no more. At one time when we were going through a very bad patch and it really made him stop and think and it just came into my mind to do that. And so I went downstairs into the knife drawer and took out a knife. The drawer was still open and I thought this was going to be really dramatic for when he walked in. I'm really going to let him know that I've had enough, so I got another knife and I went upstairs. I didn't want to do it but I had to get his attention. So I cut my wrists and I sat down waiting for him to come home and I heard the door go, and he slammed the door shut and I panicked then.

I was on the landing, basically cornered, there was no time to move, no time to do anything. I pulled down my jumper sleeves, just put the knives under my legs, I didn't have time to move anywhere. I just sat there and he came up the stairs, never spoke to me, he came up behind me, went into the bedroom and I could hear him taking off his clothes. I was praying 'please go to bed' and I was waiting to hear, but he didn't he came out of the bedroom and I am sat here and he laid down. He had a shirt on but nothing else on and he just lay there silent beside me and I was just waiting for it to start and once I knew he was stripped I knew it wasn't going to be just 'you slut'.

He wanted to have sex with me and I was sat there knowing that as soon as he and I saw this thing started there was going to be two knives and we were both going to be up on the landing and I don't know if he was going to turn around and say, 'Well if you want to help the guy you go and stick a knife in me'. I just thought I'd got to stop him. But to get that knife from under my leg and stab him was one of the hardest things I've ever done in my life. I just grabbed it and shoved the knife and turned around and I didn't even look. Because his bottom part was down here I knew where he was and I just did it.

Mr Purvie and then the police officers he called saw that indeed she had done it. Questioned at the police station by Detective Superintendent Alan Gash and Detective Chief Inspector Melvin Cross, Emma said that while in the bar with the taxi driver Armitage arrived with his son. She said he was moody and sarcastic, asking her, 'Who's your friend? Why has he left? Are you making a lot of money these days?' She said that she told them that, like her, Armitage had been drinking and seemed in the mood to do what he had done several times before: give her a 'good hiding'.

She went on to tell them that while he was driving his son home, she took the knives and cut her wrists. When he returned he sneered at them, taunting her, telling her she hadn't done a very good job. Asked why she stabbed him, she allegedly said, 'I don't really know. I always told him I was going to kill him.'

The jury of eight women and four men at her trial, which

began on 30 November 1985 at Nottingham High Court, had no chance to hear any of this. All they saw was a thin seventeen-year-old wearing blue jeans and a white woollen sweater who twisted a handkerchief nervously in her hands as she took the stand to answer the charge of murder. Her plea was not guilty.

Scott Baker, prosecuting, pointed out that the fatal blow was so unexpected that Armitage had no time to defend himself. He later pointed out that there could be no question that Emma acted in self-defence or from diminished responsibility. Psychiatric nursing sister Elizabeth Bailey of Standhill Road, Carlton, told the court that she had had a seven-year relationship with Armitage and that he had threatened her only once but had never used violence on her.

Emma hadn't been so lucky. Nicola Whitehead, a West Bridgford housewife with whom she'd talked in Osker J. Spielberg's Music Bar in Mansfield Road only hours before the stabbing, told the jury of Emma's state of terror. 'She seemed very lonely, very depressed and very desolate,' said Mrs Whitehead. 'She said that if she did not go out to work he would get angry if she did not supply him with drink. She seemed very afraid. She intimated that if she did not do certain things or was not there at certain times, he would get very angry.'

Other witnesses told how they had seen Emma with bruises and black eyes. Psychiatrist Michael Tarsh said that Emma had a seriously abnormal personality with a tendency to cut her wrists. 'She partly loved him and partly loathed him,' he said of Armitage. 'He was to some extent a father substitute and to some extent an exploiter. She was torn in her relationship with him. She had exploded under stress when she stabbed him.'

Emma herself did not give evidence. She said later that she could not talk in front of so many strangers and she knew, also, that they would find her guilty. In her defence David Clarke QC said that she had spoken with hindsight when she had told the police that she intended to kill Armitage. 'This did not necessarily represent what was in her mind at the time of the stabbing. Her claim "I was not thinking" may be as close to the truth as we will get. She had indeed lost her self control.'

He asked the jury to look at the evidence with 'compassion, sympathy and understanding'. The judge, Mr Justice Kenneth Jones, went on to instruct the jury to do the opposite. 'Do not be dictated by sympathy or by any emotion,' he said.

The jury duly found her guilty and Mr Justice Jones ordered that eighteen-year-old Emma Humphries be detained during the Queen's pleasure. 'It is a merciful sentence in view of her age. It gives room for her to receive help, which she badly needs,' he said.

Within months a request for an appeal hearing against the murder conviction, on the grounds that the judge should have raised provocation as a possible defence because Armitage's violent behaviour could be seen as long-term provocation, was flatly turned down.

Humphries was sent to Durham's notorious women's wing where she developed anorexia and slashed her wrists again until there was no skin unscarred. As a result of this she was sent in an unrippable gown to a strip cell – a bare cell with only a mattress on the floor for a 'cooling off' period of a couple of days. Her case was twice considered by the parole board and twice she was rejected.

Early in 1993, she wrote to the then Home Secretary Kenneth Clarke saying that she no longer wished to be considered for parole: she wished to fight her conviction itself. At the end of the year she was asked, through the group Justice For Women which had taken up her case, if she would agree to take part in the television documentary. By then the twenty-six-year-old had been transferred to Holloway Prison, where as part of the rehabilitation process she is allowed out on occasional supervised shopping trips. It was during one of these days out that she nervously went before the cameras and told her story along with other women who had been driven to kill.

It was an ordeal for her. 'I just didn't think anybody would understand before,' she said on the programme. 'I thought with being a prostitute and an alcoholic and with my history, people would just look at me . . . And when the jury came back with a guilty verdict, I was expecting it.'

She has served nine years now. That is longer than many 'life' sentences for the most brutal of murders. She wants her conviction quashed because she does not believe she was tried fairly. She was not treated as a woman who killed a violent man to save her own life.

When the authorities at Holloway Prison discovered that Emma Humphries had used her day release to appear on a television film, it was decided she had misused her privilege. The result was that she was punished: her leave to attend hospital to have plastic surgery on her selfmutilated arms was withdrawn. She was also refused permission to see her family during Christmas 1993.

Index

INDEX

INDEX

PASSION

Julie Ellis is the l... other novels, *The Only Sin*, *The Velvet Jungle* and *Far To Go*. She is an avid conservationist and a full-time writer. She lives in Manhattan. *Publishers Weekly* hailed her as 'a master of the genre'.

BY THE SAME AUTHOR

The Only Sin
East Wind
The Velvet Jungle
Glorious Morning
Rich is Best
Maison Jennie
Loyalties
No Greater Love
Trespassing Hearts
Lasting Treasures
Commitment
Far To Go
A Woman for All Seasons

JULIE ELLIS

Passionate Obsession

HarperCollins*Publishers*

This novel is a work of fiction.
The names, characters, and incidents portrayed in it
are the work of the author's imagination.
Any resemblance to actual persons, living or dead,
events or localities, is purely coincidental.

HarperCollins*Publishers*
77–85 Fulham Palace Road,
Hammersmith, London W6 8JB

This paperback edition 1998

1 3 5 7 9 8 6 4 2

First published in Great Britain by
HarperCollins*Publishers* 1997

Copyright © Julie Ellis 1997

The Author asserts the moral right to
be identified as the author of this work

ISBN 0 00 649900 7

Set in Postscript Linotype Sabon by
Rowland Phototypesetting Ltd,
Bury St Edmunds, Suffolk

Printed and bound in Great Britain by
Caledonian International Book Manufacturing Ltd, Glasgow

All rights reserved. No part of this publication may be
reproduced, stored in a retrieval system, or transmitted,
in any form or by any means, electronic, mechanical,
photocopying, recording or otherwise, without the prior
permission of the publishers.

This book is sold subject to the condition that it shall not,
by way of trade or otherwise, be lent, re-sold, hired out or
otherwise circulated without the publisher's prior consent
in any form of binding or cover other than that in which it
is published and without a similar condition including this
condition being imposed on the subsequent purchaser.

In memory of Arthur McBride, Jr,
a fine and talented young man who died tragically young
– and for his parents,
Rae and Arthur McBride, Sr.

Chapter One

On this sharply cold eve of November 9, 1938 – in Berlin, Germany – small, delicately lovely, 13-year-old Vera Mueller walked towards the family flat in the four-storey house at the corner of Wilmersdorfstrasse and Kurfürstendamm with a hand tucked firmly in one of her father's. Her lush blonde hair was tucked beneath a knitted cap of the same dazzling blue as her eyes. She walked with quick small steps to keep pace with her father, who towered above her in the bleak twilight.

Mature beyond her years because of the cataclysmic upheaval in her life these past five years, Vera was conscious of the blanket of doom that seemed to hang over the Jews in Germany these past two days.

On October 28 the Nazis embarked on a brutal action – grabbing thousands of German Jews of Polish extraction from their homes, children from the streets at play, thrust them into trucks and trains and deported them across the Polish border, where they were abandoned in bitter cold to a hostile country. Then two days ago, a 17-year-old in exile in Paris – distraught over this latest atrocity, his parents among those displaced – shot a German official in Paris.

Here in Berlin – as throughout Germany – the tension was agonizing as the official hung between life and death. German Jews feared that even more Nazi rage was about to explode into fresh horror for them. Papa said they must be honest, Vera remembered. '*Vera, my love, not all Germans are Nazis. There are many who live in fear themselves. . . who hate what has fallen upon Germans who happen to be Jews.'*

But not for one minute of a day could Vera brush aside the upheaval in their lives since Hitler had steamrollered into power. Papa had lost his position as professor of languages at the university. He was not allowed to teach except in the classes for Jewish students, which he – along with another teacher – had organized in a meeting room of their synagogue. The books he'd written had been burned – along with the books of other Jewish writers.

The family had lost its beautiful apartment 'to the needs of the German economy.' They lived now in three tiny rooms in one of the few Berlin buildings where Jewish tenants were accepted. Papa said that Frau Schmidt was taking a risk to allow them to live in the building owned by her husband and herself.

'Say nothing to Mama and Ernst about what we've just heard,' Papa cautioned Vera when they arrived at their door. She understood he referred to the news – ricocheting throughout Berlin – that the German official shot by young Herschel Grynszpan had died in a Paris hospital early this afternoon. 'You know how Mama worries.'

Vera nodded. Mama was so scared that Ernst, who would be 17 in a month, might be drafted into the German army.

The family's closest friends had left or were trying to leave Berlin – but how could the Muellers survive when no more than 10 marks could be taken out of the country? They had no family in other countries to receive them. And Vera knew that her father was determined to remain in order to teach the Jewish children forbidden to attend German schools. Mama complained that Papa was obsessed about the importance of education – but she knew her mother was proud of this obsession. Mama was proud that her two children spoke French and English almost as well as their native German.

Encased in prescient foreboding, Vera walked into the small foyer of their apartment house and followed her father up the three flights to their own front apartment. The rear was at the moment without a tenant. The Schmidts occupied the two floors below their own – the ground floor was occupied by an elderly woman who took in boarders. The only child living in the building other than Vera and Ernst was Frau Schmidt's daughter Alice, a few months older than Vera. Since August, Alice had lived with her grandmother in Switzerland because her parents were anxious about conditions in Germany.

'Vera, remember. Not a word to Mama and Ernst,' her father repeated as he reached to unlock the apartment door.

But before he could turn the key, the door was pulled open. White and trembling, Lisl Mueller hovered before them.

'Viktor, you've heard?'

'I've heard.' He nodded with fatalistic calm.

'We can't stay here,' she whispered, reaching to pull Vera into the apartment. 'It's suicidal!'

'Where can we go?' He closed the door behind them. 'Where would we get the emigration taxes? Who is there in another country who would take us in? Only rich Jews with bank accounts in Switzerland leave. But this insanity will run its course,' he soothed. Would it? Vera asked herself fearfully. 'This madness can't continue.'

'Viktor, we still have some money,' her mother tried again. 'Perhaps if you talk to the right persons –'

'What remains will get us nowhere.' His face was grim. 'They tell us to go, but they rob us of the means to do this. Enough of this, Lisl. Give us our supper.'

*

3

Because of the anxiety that permeated the atmosphere, the Muellers retired for the night far earlier than normal: Her parents in the small bedroom, Ernst on his cot in the kitchen, Vera on the sitting room sofa. As though, Vera thought as she huddled beneath the blankets, the darkened apartment provided them with some safety. It would appear that nobody was home.

Even the children at school today had felt the fresh dangers that threatened them, Vera admitted reluctantly, lying awake in the darkness. Everybody knew the terrible Nazi rage. With a German official assassinated by a young Jewish boy, how could they not be afraid of repercussions?

Eventually Vera fell into troubled sleep. She awoke to an urgent pounding on the apartment door.

'Mama,' she called in alarm and leapt from the sofa. Moments later her mother rushed into the sitting room. The pounding continued.

'Don't turn on the lamp,' her mother cautioned and hurried towards the door. 'Who is it?'

'Lisl, open the door,' Frau Schmidt pleaded. 'We must talk!'

While her mother hurried to comply, Vera groped in the darkness for her robe. She was conscious that both her father and Ernst had come into the room – summoned by the middle-of-the-night invasion.

'Lisl, there's terrible trouble!' Frau Schmidt's voice was harsh with alarm. 'My sister just phoned to tell us. For almost an hour – since 2:00 AM – shop windows have been smashed, fires started!' In the distance they could hear the ominous sounds of shattering glass. 'The Gestapo and the SS are breaking into Jewish homes and dragging them away. Let Vera come with us. If anyone asks, we'll say she's our daughter Alice.'

'Mama?' Vera turned to her mother, then her father. Her eyes beseeching. 'I don't want to go –'

4

'You must,' her father ordered, his face taut. Sounds in the street warned them a mob was close at hand.

'Throw some clothes in a bag,' her mother said. 'Take –'

'No!' Frau Schmidt interrupted. 'There's no time. Vera, come with me.' She reached for Vera's hand. 'They mustn't find you here!' Subconsciously Vera remembered that the Gestapo knew about her father's organizing the school and disapproved, knew that they lived here in 'an Aryan building.'

With one last supplicating glance at her parents and her brother, Vera allowed their compassionate landlady to pull her from the apartment and down the stairs to hopeful safety.

Inside the exquisitely furnished Schmidt duplex, Vera clung to the foyer door – discreetly locked now and in total darkness.

'Vera, we must be quiet,' Helene Schmidt warned. 'Say nothing.'

Galvanized by fear Vera listened to the menacing sound of feet climbing the stairs, heard shouting on the floor above. She heard her father's rebellious retorts and shivered. Her heart pounded as she listened to the noisy descent from her family's apartment. She'd heard terrifying stories about what happened to Jews who were dragged off in the night. *What would happen to Mama and Papa and Ernst?*

Now the hallway was quiet. The sounds of shattering glass continued in the night-dark streets. In the distance were sounds of shots. Helene Schmidt pulled Vera into her arms, murmured words of comfort.

Herr Schmidt came into the foyer.

'Helene, make tea,' he ordered. In the streets SS men and the Gestapo rounded up Berlin Jews, and Hitler Youth gangs continued their wanton vandalism. 'Let's go out to the kitchen – the lights can't be seen from there. Let nobody know we're awake.' The SS would hesitate to awaken an important businessman like Herr Schmidt, Vera understood.

Numb with shock, too stunned to be afraid for herself, Vera sipped at the hot cocoa Frau Schmidt placed before her. Traumatizing sounds continued in the distance. Relentless smashing of glass. The sirens of fire trucks howling through the streets. Obscene shouting. Though Helene and Anton Schmidt knew their voices could not be heard, they spoke in muted tones.

'You'll stay with us,' Frau Schmidt told Vera. 'If anyone asks, you're our daughter Alice.'

'Let's try to get some sleep,' Herr Schmidt said at last. *How could she sleep? Vera asked herself – recoiling from the prospect.* 'I must go in to my office in another four hours.' Vera knew he was a very successful exporter. 'But neither of you is to leave the house tomorrow.' His eyes focused first on his wife, then on Vera. 'It won't be safe. But I must go in to the office as though nothing happened tonight. Life must go on as usual.' He flinched in rejection. 'If anybody comes to call, Vera – which is unlikely in these conditions – you will stay in Alice's bedroom with the door shut.'

'Anton, *drive* to the office tomorrow –' She paused. 'Drive this morning,' she corrected herself. 'It could be dangerous to take public transportation.' She sighed. 'I wish you would stay home for the day.'

'That would be unwise,' he objected. 'Also, I need to make arrangements for a business trip to Copenhagen.' Vera sensed a silent conversation between the other two. 'Now,' he reiterated, 'let's try to get some sleep.'

Obediently Vera allowed Frau Schmidt to take her upstairs to Alice's bedroom, accepted one of Alice's lovely nightgowns. But how could she sleep when she didn't know what was happening to her family? Where were Mama and Papa and Ernst? *What was happening to them?*

Twice during the morning and again in the afternoon Helene Schmidt talked with a woman-friend on the phone. The phone was a stranger to Vera these days – Jewish homes were denied phone service. After each call Frau Schmidt reported on the latest news of what was being called *Kristallnacht*. Crystal Night. Not only Berlin was experiencing this carnage. It was happening in every city, town, and village in Germany.

'Gerda says we wouldn't recognize Kurfürstendamm. Plate-glass windows have been smashed from one end to the other, the shops vandalized. You know the wonderful Margraf Jewellery Store on Unter Den Linden? It's in shambles. Even the branch office of Citroën – a *French* company, Vera,' she emphasized, 'has been wrecked.'

Despite the horror still erupting through the city at dusk, Helene Schmidt went about preparing dinner while Vera set the dining room table. Tantalizing aromas emerged from the large, comfortable kitchen – lending a specious air of well-being – as though nothing untoward was happening. On schedule – as on any other business day – Herr Schmidt arrived home.

While Vera listened in muted terror, Frau Schmidt plied her husband with questions.

His face etched with pain, he reported on what he had seen in the course of the day.

'You would not believe the fires that are still raging in the city,' he wound up. 'The broken glass that litters the streets.' He hesitated, his eyes resting compassionately on Vera, yet some compulsion forced him to continue. 'The beautiful Great Synagogue is a burnt-out shell. I suspect not one synagogue in Berlin still stands intact.'

7

'What's happening to the people they took away?' Vera asked in an anguished whisper. She remembered the shots fired in the streets at regular intervals. 'When will we know?'

He sighed before replying. 'Thousands have been taken away to camps. We –'

'Nobody does anything to stop them?' Vera interrupted in a surge of rage. But she knew the answer before he replied.

'People are afraid for their lives,' he said gently. 'To object is to be an enemy of the government. We won't know for a while what will be done with those in the camps. Perhaps they'll be released in a week or two,' he said with an effort at optimism. 'But it isn't safe for you to remain in Berlin. We'll wait another two days, Vera, until the violence simmers down. Then you'll go with me to Copenhagen.' Her eyes widened in disbelief. 'You'll pretend to be Alice. I have a friend in Copenhagen – a high-level government official. You'll live with his family and help with their two small children. You'll be safe there.'

'But I have to be here for Mama and Papa,' she protested, dizzy with shock at the prospect of leaving Berlin. 'And Ernst –'

'They would want you to be away from Germany in these times,' Helene soothed. 'We'll keep in touch with you. When we know where they are, we'll write you.'

Three days later – with no way of learning the whereabouts of her family, still encased in shock – Vera went with Anton Schmidt to the Anhalter Bahnhof, the largest of Berlin's railway stations. She wore clothes that had belonged to Alice and altered to fit her more slender frame. Herr Schmidt carried a forged passport, identifying her as Alice Schmidt.

Vera's eyes swept about the bustling railway station.

Her heart pounded. It was terrifying to be going so far from home – to a foreign country. Alone. She had never spent one night of her life away from Mama. *Would she ever see Mama and Papa and Ernst again?*

'How will I talk to the children?' she asked Herr Schmidt when they were at last seated in their train compartment. She knew that she was to live with a Danish government official and his wife and was to help care for their year-old son and three-year-old daughter. 'I don't speak Danish.' Where would she go if they didn't like her?

'You're fluent in English,' he pointed out. 'The Munches – like many Danes – speak English. And they're eager for their son and daughter to learn the language. You'll have no difficulty,' he promised.

Frightened for her family, suffering an aching loneliness, Vera strove to make herself acceptable to Mr and Mrs Munch and little Nils and Krista. The household included a cook-housekeeper and a part-time nursemaid. Vera would care for the children when she came home from school each day and over the week-ends. She was relieved that she would be allowed to attend school. Papa would be very upset if she didn't continue her education.

She was grateful that the Munches brought English newspapers into their house. They were eager to perfect their knowledge of the language. But she was stricken by what she read there. The British newspapers told of 20,000 Jews being held in three camps: Buchenwald, Dachau and Oranienburg-Sachsenhausen. Where were Mama and Papa and Ernst? Those last moments together would be forever etched on her memory. There had not been even a moment to kiss them goodbye before Frau Schmidt snatched her away.

Helene Schmidt wrote that she was struggling for

9

information about Vera's parents and brother. Thus far she had been able to learn nothing.

'But we keep trying, Vera. When there's word, we'll be in touch immediately,' she promised.

Vera was astonished at the warmth and compassion she felt in the Munches. She was conscious, too, of the sympathy she felt in the Danish people towards the refugees from Germany who came into the country. Nowhere did she see any sign of anti-Semitism.

At the end of her sixth week in Copenhagen, Vera was alarmed when Mrs Munch called her from her room after she had put the children to bed for the night and was engrossed in homework for school. Panic drained her of colour as she joined Mrs Munch in the family sitting room. They were unhappy with her, she thought in terror. *Where would she go? Where would she live?*

'Vera, you must be brave,' Mrs Munch said gently when they were seated. 'We've heard from Herr Schmidt in Berlin –' She hesitated. Vera was all at once ice-cold, knowing what she was about to hear. 'He has finally been able to get word of your family.' Vera was aware of tears in Mrs Munch's eyes. 'Your father was shot to death on *Kristallnacht*. Your mother and brother died in Oranienburg-Sachsenhausen. Through special channels – since he's not a relative – Herr Schmidt was able to collect their ashes for the regular fee.' The dead were cremated, Vera interpreted in a corner of her dazed mind. 'The ashes were buried in synagogue ground and a service conducted for them.' Mrs Munch reached to bring Vera into her arms. 'You'll stay with us,' she said gently. 'You'll be safe here.'

Vera awoke each morning with reluctance – dreading to face a world devoid of parents and brother. She went through each day in an aura of painful unreality. She ordered herself to focus on the wishes of Mr and Mrs Munch. They were her new family, and Copenhagen was her home. But she listened every day to the reports on the radio, read the news in the English newspapers that came regularly into the house, and she was fearful of the relentless onslaught of the Nazis. And with devastating frequency she relived in nightmare dreams that November night in 1938 when all she loved was wrested from her.

On March 15, Nazi troops occupied Czechoslovakia. On August 31 – anticipating war with Germany – the British government evacuated women and children from London. The following day the Nazis invaded Poland. On September 3, Britain and France declared war on Germany. But soon, Vera told herself defiantly, the British and French would put a stop to Hitler's march across Europe.

A few months later – on April 9, 1940 – the Nazis invaded Denmark and Norway. Denmark had declared itself neutral, Vera remembered in shock. Mrs Munch was so proud of that. But on the night of April 9 – in a surprise move – Nazi forces invaded Denmark.

What had happened in Berlin would happen in Copenhagen, Vera thought in rising terror. *Would she be sent to a concentration camp or shot dead on sight?*

The Munches tried to assuage Vera's fears.

'Denmark won't be like Germany,' Mr Munch explained. 'The Danish government realized it was futile to fight. We've made an agreement with Germany. They recognize our sovereignty. We've become a kind of protectorate. We'll negotiate those matters that concern both Denmark and Germany. Vera, it won't matter in Denmark that you're Jewish,' he said forcefully.

But Mr Munch bought a gun to keep in the house – locked up, he pointed out, so that Nils and Krista could never find it. But if Nazi soldiers ever came into the house to take her away – or to hurt the children – she would use the gun, she vowed. She would fight back. Papa would have done that if he'd had a gun in the house.

Chapter Two

On this sunny late May day in 1940, Paul Kahn left his room in the John Jay Dorm at Columbia and strode across the summer-garbed campus towards the West End Bar to meet his roommate for a late lunch. Every corner of the campus exuded an aura of pleased excitement as students prepared to take off for home for the long summer vacation. But Paul was acutely conscious of the news this morning that German armoured columns were arriving at the English Channel – trapping 400,000 British and French troops at Dunkirk.

Slim, handsome – his dark hair rumpled, brown eyes sombre today – Paul wrestled with the decision he must make within the next twenty-four hours. It was a decision his roommate – Chuck Jourdan – had already made. A third-generation of French descent, Chuck carried on a personal vendetta with the Nazis. Paul sighed. Dad would be shocked and upset if he went to Canada with Chuck and enlisted. But he was 19 years old, he thought defiantly. Wasn't it time he called the shots in his own life?

Chuck was waiting for him in their usual booth.

'Hey, you're late,' Chuck scolded good-humouredly. 'I'm starving. I ordered burgers and coffee for two.' His cool grey eyes searched Paul's – but Paul's provided him with no answers. 'Hear this morning's news?'

'Yeah.' Paul nodded sombrely. 'It's grim.'

Like most students their age, Paul and Chuck had been brought up to believe that war was to be avoided at almost any cost. Yet they realized that Hitler was a madman who must be stopped. When a group of Columbia students – like the thousand at Dartmouth – sent a telegram to President Roosevelt to keep the United States out of the war, Paul and Chuck had not been among the signers.

'I can't get over some of the crap that keeps turning up. Like that character who said, "Why doesn't the British government give up the British Isles and just retreat to Canada?"'

'You're dead set on going to Canada to enlist?' Paul asked, knowing the answer.

'Look, we're going to get into this war. Everybody's saying we'll have a military draft within ninety days. Why wait? The sooner we get in and get it over with, the better. We're going to have to fight. I don't know why Roosevelt's not moving ahead. Let's stop that bastard Hitler. Right now,' he wound up. 'I'm leaving for Canada tomorrow. My folks are carrying on like mad. They want me to stay on in college and get my degree. But that's two years away. The war can't wait.'

Half-listening to Chuck's monologue, Paul considered his rebellion at having to settle on his major. He didn't *know* yet what he wanted to do with the rest of his life. He'd chosen engineering because it sounded kind of adventurous – travelling to all parts of the world on assignments. Deep inside he knew he'd chosen engineering because it meant getting away from Eastwood – and his father.

He loved Dad. And he knew how deeply Dad loved him, wanted the best for him. But he could never truly forget that Dad was responsible for Mom's death. He'd only been six – the whole awful tragedy was cloudy in his memory. All that remained clear in his mind was the devastating image of his adored mother falling to the floor dying from a gunshot wound inflicted by his father. A horrendous accident – the whole town had mourned for Mom and felt compassion for Dad. *Why couldn't he forgive Dad?* He loved him so much – but he couldn't forgive him.

Their hamburgers and coffee arrived. For a few minutes they focused on eating. But Paul's mind was racing. Dad expected him to come into the business this summer even though he was an engineering major. *'It's time you got your feet wet in the business. Eventually it'll be yours.'* Four generations of Kahns had been gunsmiths. His great-great-grandfather had set up the Kahn Firearms Company in the tiny upstate New York town on the Vermont border. Dad had gone through tough times, but now – with the Depression over – he was doing well. He'd just hired new workers. The fighting in Europe had opened a new market to him. Dad figured he'd play awhile at engineering, then settle down to learn the family business.

Dad didn't know how he hated guns. Only his sister Doris knew how he dreaded the hunting season each year. He'd grown up in a town where every man and boy hunted and fished. To folks in Eastwood it was strange – *unmanly* – not to hunt and fish. He'd been ribbed plenty about that, he remembered wryly.

It was weird, he mocked himself, that he would even consider running up to Canada with Chuck to enlist in the Canadian Air Force. Still – each time he went home from school – his father talked with such anxiety about the way country after country was falling before the Nazi onslaught. Dad was sure America would be sucked into the war. *'Why is Roosevelt dragging his heels? With France and England under attack, how can we stay out?'* And Dad – who considered himself an American 'who happened to be Jewish' – felt a new, strong awareness of his Jewish heritage and a horror at what was happening to Jews in Hitler's path.

'If we enlist together, we have a real chance of serving together.' Chuck interrupted his introspection. 'Come on, Paul. Let's do this together. Or would you rather go home and learn all about how to manufacture guns?'

Paul hesitated – his mind assaulted by the craziness at Dunkirk.

'I'll go with you,' he agreed. 'But I'll have to stop off at Eastwood for a day so I can break the news to Dad.' He sighed. 'Oh God, he's going to be upset.'

Paul and Chuck were jubilant when they were accepted for training in the RCAF – the Royal Canadian Air Force. Most of those enlisting were eighteen or nineteen or twenty – and proud of the white tabs on their overseas cap that identified them as aircrew students ... all of them anxious to emerge as pilots – a role glamorized by Hollywood movies, fiction, and comic strips.

Paul and Chuck began their training at a manning depot, remaining there for three weeks for intensive physical training, learning to march with the high Air Force swing. Then came a dreary month of walking a post at an RCAF station until they were given places in a five-week class at an Initial Training School – where they were subjected for long hours each day to arduous training, both impatient for actual air experience. Still, both Paul and Chuck felt triumphant when they were advanced to 'flying' in a synthetic plane – the Link trainer.

Paul and Chuck emerged with their wings – to their joy – with commissions, plus the knowledge they were headed for combat training in England. They understood they would be assigned to the RAF, per arrangement with the British government, desperate for aircrews. Landing in England, Paul and Chuck were assigned to the same

Operational Training Unit. In fifty hours they must be prepared for action.

'Hey, we're making it!' Chuck chortled when he and Paul settled down for their first night on British soil.

'Yeah.' Paul patted the coveted double wings pinned above his breast pocket with affection.

The 'O' with a single wing indicated the wearer was a bombardier navigator – in Air Force slang, the 'flying asshole.' The rear gunner was labelled the 'Ass-end.' Yet every pilot knew that the bombardier navigator and the rear gunner were as indispensable as the pilot. They depended upon one another for survival.

Months blended into a year and then it was yet another year. Their lives – night and day – revolved around flying. They flew a seemingly endless stream of missions over northwestern Europe. Then on the same mission – in the early summer of 1943 – both Chuck and Paul were hit with their respective crews. Chuck's plane burst into flames before Paul's eyes. He knew Chuck and his crew could not have survived. And a few minutes later his own plane was crippled – his gunner and himself badly injured. He managed to fly back to their base in England, but he and his gunner spent long weeks in recovery.

At last Paul left the hospital for a recuperation centre, then was released from active duty with appropriate medals for his valour. On the day of his dismissal, he offered his services to the American army. He was welcomed with enthusiasm.

Now his train was pulling into Waterloo Station in London.

He was to report for a special assignment – secret, dangerous, but of utmost importance. He wasn't sure what it involved, other than some intensive non-military training.

He was assaulted by fresh anguish as he strolled from the train, through Waterloo Station, and into the September twilight. He and Chuck had thought themselves invincible – together they'd survived the unbelievable. Until that last mission. What about this special assignment? Paul asked himself with new ambivalence. Was he insane to take this on, when he could be going home? But he wasn't ready to go home, not with the war not yet won. At least for a little while he would sleep in a decent bed, be able to shower at regular intervals, maybe even eat decent meals.

Now he glanced about for a taxi to take him to the small hotel where he was to stay. London taxis – small enough to turn on a dime – had never ceased to operate despite the war. London, he thought in a moment of whimsy, had become his home away from home. He and Chuck had spent many leaves here.

While he signed the register at the hotel desk, Paul was conscious of the clerk's curiosity.

'You in the RAF?' he asked, reaching for a key.

'That's right.' Paul smiled faintly. He still wore his RAF uniform.

'You talk American,' the clerk said.

'That's right, I'm an American. I enlisted in the Canadian Air Force before my country got into the war.'

'Hey, mate, you're all right.' The clerk's smile was broad, approving. 'Together we'll lick those bastards.'

Paul sat across the desk from the colonel who was now his immediate superior and listened intently to what was being said.

'You don't have to accept this assignment,' the colonel stressed. 'God knows, with your record you've gone far beyond the call of duty. We won't think less of you for turning it down.'

'I'm accepting it, sir,' Paul said, almost with detachment. He wasn't ready to go home. His job wasn't finished.

The colonel's smile radiated relief.

'We're pulling all the pieces together for this operation. We're set to move on the groundwork now that you're in place. You're scheduled for eight weeks of rigorous language study. You'll spend eight hours a day learning German. We know you have college French behind you –'

'It's not great,' Paul warned, his smile wry. But Chuck had spoken French as a second language, and some of that had rubbed off on him.

'You'll know enough to get along when you're dropped into French territory. It's what you can pick up with the knowledge of German that's important to us. You don't have to worry about speaking it,' he emphasized. 'We need you to be able to understand what you hear. Give yourself a week off, then report to this department and expect to work your rear off. We've arranged for you to take over a small flat close by. In London today, that's a real accomplishment.'

They talked a few minutes longer, then Paul was dismissed. One week from now – at 7:00 AM sharp – he was to report to a room where a communications instructor would be waiting for him. At 8:00 AM, he'd go to another room to study with a German tutor who must in eight weeks stuff his head with that language. That would be his schedule for eight weeks. Today he'd renew his acquaintance with London. He'd have dinner at one of the great restaurants, then go to the theatre.

With rationing what it was in England, anybody who could afford it ate out, Paul reminded himself. Though the government decreed that no restaurant meal could cost more than five shillings, plus a fancy cover charge for special spots, no ruling existed to prevent restaurant hopping. He'd eat well tonight. It was amazing, he thought humorously, how preoccupied Londoners were with eating.

For a week he'd forget the ghastly war. It was incredible how there were sections of London which showed little of the devastation that affected so much of the city. Trafalgar Square, Bond Street, much of the West End. He'd live in that London for this week, he promised himself with defiant gaiety. Make it a small, luxurious respite from reality.

Chapter Three

Despite the passage of time – and the continued reassurances of Herbert and Margrethe Munch – Vera never felt totally at ease in Copenhagen, though she'd come to love the bright and shining city. How could she not be fearful, she asked herself at painful intervals – when they lived surrounded by Nazi police? Since the German takeover, it was almost impossible to learn what was happening to the Jews in other parts of Europe. Mr Munch no longer received British newspapers – Denmark was now a German 'protectorate.'

But the Danish government permitted no anti-Jewish measures, she conceded. The synagogue remained open. The Jews in Denmark lived normal lives except for the constant awareness of the Nazi presence.

Yet – as with all Danish citizenry – Vera was aware that the situation was deteriorating. The underground Resistance fighters were becoming bolder, their numbers increasing. Though the Danish government called for law and order, acts of sabotage continued, infuriated the Nazis.

In late September 1943 – three afternoons before Rosh Hashanah Eve, the beginning of the Jewish New Year – Vera sat in the family sitting room with Margrethe Munch and watched while her benefactor applied the finishing touches to the dress Vera meant to wear to the synagogue services on that High Holiday eve. The family maid had gone to bring Nils and Krista home from school.

'You chose the perfect material,' Margrethe said with

21

pleasure. 'This blue velvet is lovely, the colour just right for –' She paused at the harsh sound of the front door of the house being opened and slammed shut.

'Vera!' Herbert Munch called out in agitation from the foyer. 'Margrethe!'

'We're in the sitting room.' Margrethe Munch laid aside her sewing and rose to her feet. Her face was drained of colour. Normally her husband was a quietly spoken, reserved man. 'Herbert, what has happened?'

'The Nazis have executed saboteurs. In reprisal, the Danish government has resigned. The king is under house arrest. Martial law is about to be declared.' In the past two weeks sabotage and strikes had brought brutal reprisals that had enraged the Danish people. He drew a long, nervous breath. 'And there's more. A German attaché with a conscience has warned us of a roundup of all the Jews. They're to be deported to camps outside of Denmark. It's to happen on the eve of Rosh Hashanah,' he told Vera, 'when they expect Danish Jews to be at home or in the synagogues.'

'What do we do?' Margrethe demanded, instinctively drawing Vera into her arms.

'We're making sure the word is spread. Vera, you'll go to Sweden and –'

'Herbert, you know how the borders are guarded,' his wife interrupted. 'And the Swedish are protective of their neutrality.'

'That is about to change.' His face was grim. 'Already negotiations are under way to make Sweden understand that it must provide sanctuary. We have to establish escape routes immediately. Over 7,500 Jews must be rescued!'

'But can this be done quickly enough?' Margrethe clung to Vera. Both were trembling, ashen.

'I've already made the first arrangements.' His face was

encouraging as he turned to Vera, yet she was terrified. 'Tonight you'll be admitted to a private sanitorium for a supposed emergency appendix operation. At dawn you'll be driven to a house on the coast – presumably your family's. You'll be told when a fishing vessel is to take you to the Swedish coast.'

'I'll go with you, Vera,' Margrethe said instantly. 'I'll stay until you're on the boat.'

'It's better that you don't,' Herbert told her. 'But we must sit down and work out the plans. I've already talked with a friend in Sweden. He'll be there to receive you when you're across the Sound, Vera. He'll help you get to England. There another friend attached to the British government will see that you have employment as an interpreter. You speak fluent German, English, and French – this is a valuable asset. You'll be all right.'

Margrethe accompanied Vera to the hospital as her 'aunt.' It was clear that the staff understood what was happening but was determined to rescue the Danish Jews who came to them. Then – with a hospital gown over her clothes – Vera was bundled in blankets, placed on a stretcher, and carried to a waiting ambulance. Earlier Margrethe had wrapped a scarf about her waist and whispered that money had been sewn into the folds.

Vera was taken by ambulance to a modest cottage right on the sea. An elderly Danish couple received her with compassion and a determined optimism. Here she would be hidden until fishermen could take her across the Sound to Sweden. She understood now that, with astonishing swiftness, massive Danish rescue efforts had been set in motion.

Two days later – on a cold, cloudy night when the lack of visibility was on their side – a pair of Resistance workers appeared to escort Vera and another escaping Jew to a waiting fishing vessel. Vera was conscious that each man held a gun. Minutes later she froze in terror when a young harbour policeman suddenly approached the fishing vessel when she was about to climb aboard.

'Who goes there?' the policeman demanded brusquely.

'You don't wish to know,' one of the two underground workers responded and pointed his gun at the policeman. 'Talk to your superior,' the other added with a chuckle – but he, too, held his gun ready for action. 'He'll explain.'

Stumbling in her haste, Vera climbed into the fishing boat.

'It's all right,' the other fugitive told her gently. 'The police know to look the other way. This one will learn fast enough.'

From what was said, Vera gathered that Danish fishermen had been involved in shuttling refugees across the Sound for the past two nights and this would continue as long as there were Jews who needed to be rescued.

Still, she understood the danger that lay ahead of them. Would there ever be a time when she lived without terror?

On this – her third morning in London – Vera came awake in her drab, shabby 'bed-sitter' with an instant realization that today she was to begin her first assignment, as arranged by Mr Munch's London contact. She must do well, she told herself anxiously. She was on her own in a strange city. The most expensive city in the world right now, she had read in a London newspaper. She was nervous about money – she'd have to learn to budget, the way Mrs Munch had instructed her.

In a corner of her mind she remembered that she had been told few bombs were falling on London of late. Still, her first sight of London had been unnerving. Copenhagen had not prepared her for what she found here. The shattered buildings, whole blocks reduced to rubble. The FAP – first aid signs – everywhere. The signs for day shelters, night shelters, huge tanks labelled 'static water' for use in fighting fires. The anti-aircraft guns in Hyde Park, brick blast baffles positioned to protect doors and windows, rotting piles of sandbags.

She left her bed – shivering slightly in the morning chill. It didn't matter that she had arrived with only an extra change of clothing beyond what she had worn on the nerve-racking dash from Copenhagen to Sweden, across Sweden and Finland to England. Her British benefactor – who had helped her obtain the necessary ration card as well as her tiny flat – had assured her that in London everyone except for the rich appeared slightly shabby.

'*When you can find what you want, clothes are dread-fully expensive,*' he warned her. '*Plus we have all these restrictions.*'

She put up water for tea, decided to heat up a roll left over from yesterday: No butter in London, she thought wistfully, remembering the rich, creamy butter in Copenhagen. A dab of margarine. That would be quicker than making herself a dish of porridge – unappealing with powdered milk and no sugar.

While she ate, she considered what lay ahead of her this morning. She was to report to the room in an American government building where she would meet the American military man who was to be her pupil. For eight hours a day, six days a week for the next eight weeks she was to try to cram as much German as possible into the mind of this military man.

'*You'll be provided with a textbook, but you may devi-ate as you see fit. Don't concern yourself with the quality of his accent. It's comprehension that is of utmost impor-tance.*' The colonel knew she had learned English and French from Papa – on a one-to-one basis.

It had been explained to her that she was not to discuss the assignment with anyone. It had something to do with

Allied security, she understood. It was like being part of the war effort, she told herself with a flicker of pride. *The Nazis must be defeated.* She knew vaguely of the war being fought in the Pacific – but that seemed too distant to visualize.

At 8:00 AM sharp – in her freshly pressed blue wool dress made for her by Margrethe Munch – Vera presented herself per instructions. The colonel who had interviewed her sat behind a desk. In a chair beside the desk sat a young man in what Vera guessed was an Air Force uniform. He rose quickly to his feet as the colonel made the introductions. Now, she reminded herself, she was Vera Miller – the English interpretation of Mueller.

He was polite, Vera thought, but Paul Kahn was shocked that his instructor was someone so young. She intercepted the colonel's smile of mild amusement.

'I'll leave you two to settle down to work,' the colonel said briskly. 'Take an hour's break for lunch – whenever you decide.'

Vera forced herself to focus on the task ahead, earnest about fulfilling her obligations. If she pleased the colonel, instinct told her she would find other assignments. But she was conscious every moment of the nearness of her handsome young student.

His name was Kahn. That was German or German-Jewish, wasn't it? She remembered Papa saying that Americans were not bi-lingual or multi-lingual like many Europeans. But how strange, she considered in a corner of her mind, that if his family had emigrated from Germany he had made no effort to learn the language.

For most of the morning, Vera and Paul concentrated with mutual determination on his introduction to the German language.

'I'm a little ahead of the game,' he chuckled at one point. 'I know about eight words of Yiddish – which is closely related to German.' *Did that mean he was Jewish?* 'I learned them from my grandfather.' He paused, his eyes bright with curiosity. 'I can't quite figure out what's your native language. Your English is terrific – and you wouldn't be here with me now if your German wasn't great. And the colonel says you're fluent in French –'

'I was born in Berlin,' she told him, all at once self-conscious. 'I managed to get out when I was thirteen. *Good* Germans helped me –' She saw the sudden compassion in his eyes. He was sensitive; he understood that she alone of her family had escaped. 'I was taken in by a family in Copenhagen, where I helped with the children. I'm sure you know what happened there.' She gestured eloquently. 'A wonderful Danish couple got me out of Denmark and to London.' She paused, fighting against recall. 'I've been here just a few days.'

'You've been through the mill,' he said gently and smiled at her blank glance. 'That means you know what the war is all about,' he interpreted. His face was taut now. 'I flew with the RAF on more missions than I want to remember. Then my luck ran out somewhere over Germany.' Her eyes clung to him. 'We managed to limp back to our base, but I spent weeks in the hospital. More weeks in a recuperation centre. I won't be flying again – my right arm isn't as good as it should be to handle a bomber.' He shrugged this off with an air of impatience. 'I was released by the RAF and signed up with the American forces. I'm on a special assignment now. Later I'll join my regular unit.' Vera knew they must not discuss this.

'We'd better get back to work.' All at once she was conscious of a special bond between Paul Kahn and herself. She felt less desperately alone in London. 'We'll be taking – how do you say it?' She fumbled for the right words. 'Taking a break for lunch soon.'

'We can go for lunch now. There's a great pub two

blocks over,' he said impulsively. 'Let me take you to lunch there.' His smile was ingratiating.

'Oh, but – but –' She was startled by his invitation.

'I'm bored to death alone in London. I don't know anybody here anymore. Take pity on me,' he coaxed. 'Colonel Brett won't mind.' He'd read her thoughts.

Vera and Paul left their 'classroom' and walked out into the crowded London street to the nearby pub. It was as though she had suddenly moved into an exciting new world, Vera thought with heady delight. Paul Kahn was so nice. *And he liked her.*

She'd known few young men in her life. None who was so warm and understanding, she decided. None with whom she could laugh as she was doing now. Since she was eight years old and Hitler came to power, a pall had hung over her life. She'd always known a sense of fear that had been elevated at times to terror. Paul had flown planes over Germany. He'd been shot down by Nazi guns. But he knew how to laugh.

The pub was busy, as Paul had warned it would be, but they found a table. He joshed about the red leather and chrome chairs, the chandelier that was reminiscent of another time and another place.

'I know you've only been in London a few days,' he said with a light, conspiratorial smile, 'but that's long enough to know that food in London in these times is limited.' He uttered a mocking sigh. 'The eggs are powdered and so's the milk. Forget about sugar or butter or fresh fruit – and oh those hard, grey rolls! But we survive.'

'In Copenhagen, we survived,' Vera conceded, 'though much food was shipped out of Denmark to Germany.'

'Thank God, bread isn't rationed – but, of course, there's that constant reminder that we should eat potatoes instead of bread. Everybody in London claims to have lost weight in the course of the war – but they all admit that's healthy.'

Vera was relieved when Paul suggested he order for them. '*I know all the pitfalls.*'

In truth, she hardly tasted the food when it was served. She was mesmerized by Paul's ebullient conversation, his high-spirited teasing. Back in the room where they'd worked together, he'd seemed charming but so serious. This new mood was ingratiating, contagious.

'Do you know how long we've been here?' she asked in astonishment as they dawdled over their custard and tea. 'We must get back to work!'

'So I'm dealing with a slavedriver,' he drawled. 'For that, you have to go with me to the theatre tonight.' Her eyes widened in astonishment. 'We'll go straight from the classroom to queue up. Because of the blackout, curtains have to come down by 8:00 PM. Then we'll go out for dinner,' he plotted in high spirits. 'But I promise you'll be home by ten o'clock. London's night life is on a weird schedule these days.'

'But I – I can't let you –' How did she explain that she couldn't permit him to spend so much money on her?

'I've got all that back pay piled up! Somebody has to help me spend it.' *He'd understood her reluctance, she thought tenderly.* 'We've got eight weeks of intensive work together. So let's have a little fun with it, too. It's your patriotic duty,' he said with a flourish. 'Help entertain a member of the Allied forces.'

They returned to the office – both determined not to shun their obligations. Promptly at five, they left to join another of the endless queues that were part of London wartime life. Paul had decided they would see a Shaw play, 'The Doctor's Dilemma.' For an instant Vera was caught up in anguished recall. *Mama's favourite play.*

In Berlin – before Hitler – her family had attended the theatre often. Though she was a little girl, she had gone with them because Papa considered this part of her education. In the Copenhagen years, there had been no such diversion. They'd lived under a constant cloud – presumably safe yet ever humiliated by the Danish defeat. It amazed her that here in London – where the people had suffered so from the bombings – life went on as usual, though with an amended timetable.

In the queue at the theatre, they exchanged lighthearted conversation with the young couple ahead of them.

'Night life in London isn't dead,' Paul pointed out, an arm about her waist as the queue advanced.

Yesterday, Vera recalled, she had gazed into shop windows that displayed elegant jewellery. She'd walked through the aisles of the fine department stores. Here and there a shop-window sign announced some shortage. But life these last months – with few bombs falling now, Paul said, seemed almost normal. Even the children were being brought back to London.

The stage performance was superb, Vera thought, exhilarated by the small adventure. But how strange to be leaving the theatre at 8:00 PM! They found a nearby restaurant – where the waiters knew Paul from earlier leaves – and ate amazingly well in the face of the shortages and restrictions. But best of all about this evening, Vera told herself with awe, was that Paul had brought laughter back into her life.

It was as though in the rush of London they lived in a private world of their own, Vera thought at the end of their first week of daytime study and evening play. Observers of that other world around them – isolated from that world by a kind of magic. For eight hours they were teacher and student – both dedicated to the job at hand. For the next four or five hours Paul showed her London, which he clearly loved. From 7:00 AM to 8:00 AM Vera understood he was receiving technical instruction that had to do with his mission.

They strolled along Piccadilly and through Leicester Square – both populated day and night by young men and women in uniform. Young people in search of romance. They visited Trafalgar Square, remarkably unscathed, with Lord Nelson still atop his column and the National Gallery still open to the public, though its priceless masterpieces were hidden away in bomb-proof safety. They saw the serious damage meted out to Westminster Abbey and the House of Commons, where its members had met for almost a century. Big Ben had been hit in a heavy raid two years earlier but continued to tick.

On their seventh evening together, Paul began to talk about his father and his sister Doris. His mother, Vera understood, had died when he was six.

'Eastwood's a tiny little town in upstate New York. My great-great-grandfather emigrated from Germany in the early 1800s. I know,' he joshed, 'in Europe that's being newcomers.'

'I don't understand.' Vera was apologetic. 'If your family came from Germany, how is it you don't know the language?'

Paul chuckled. 'When immigrants from Europe arrived in the US, they were consumed by a desire to be full Americans. Their first priority was learning to speak English. From toddlers to grandparents, they flooded the classrooms so they could speak like other Americans.'

'Yes.' Vera's eyes glowed. 'This I can understand.'

'My great-great-grandfather looked around for a good place to practise his trade and raise a family. He settled in Eastwood and opened up a gunsmith shop. It's been the family business ever since. It was tough during the

Depression years. Dad had to fight to hang on. But once war broke out, the business took off. Dad's the major employer in Eastwood now.'

'An important business,' Vera said respectfully.

'Doris says he's working sixteen hours a day, always fighting to fill orders. He's so proud of being part of the war effort.' He paused, squinted in thought. 'I think we first became truly conscious that we were Jews after *Kristallnacht.*'

So he was Jewish.

'We knew five years earlier.' Vera was sombre. 'All of a sudden we weren't Germans. We were Jews – the enemy.'

'Everybody back home has always thought of the United States as the great "melting pot." Generations of foreigners poured into the country and became *Americans.* Why should ethnic roots divide us now? But to some people back home, Americans of German descent, of Italian descent, of Japanese descent are suddenly enemies.'

'I don't understand these things,' Vera said. 'My father would have understood. When he could have gotten out of Germany, he stayed – to help provide education for Jewish children who couldn't go to the Berlin schools. To him, education was so very important.'

'Enough of serious talk,' Paul ordered and reached for her hand. 'Let's go for a walk along the Thames Embankment. On a moonlit night like this, the river is magnificent.'

They strolled in silence, enjoying the spectacle of moonlight upon the Thames. And when they paused, it seemed only right that Paul should draw her into his arms and kiss her. A soft delicate touching that sent her heart into chaotic racing. And then his mouth released hers and she felt the warm closeness of him moving away.

'Let's find a place where we can have a cup of tea and a piece of cake, and then I'll walk you home,' he said gently.

Chapter Four

In the days ahead, Vera waited wistfully for Paul to take her into his arms again. Those few moments when he'd held her, kissed her, lingered in her mind in exquisite recall. Her last thoughts before drifting off to sleep each night, the first on awakening each morning.

Was he sorry that he had kissed her? Was there a girl back in that town he called Eastwood whom he loved? *Had she disappointed him?* But she knew she loved Paul Kahn with a love that would be eternal. She hadn't expected it to happen. She wasn't ready for it to happen. But she understood that in a handful of days her whole life had changed yet again.

When they were together now, it was as though those moments in the moonlight along the Thames Embankment had never existed. They shared a warm camaraderie – nothing more. But she longed for so much more.

They spent exhausting hours working on his comprehension of German. They played after hours just as determinedly. On Sundays – supposedly their day away from the improvised classroom – they were together for hours that included her ordered conversations in German.

Italy had declared war on Germany. 'Three years late,' Paul declared. She'd hoped – naively, Paul chided – that this meant the war would soon be over.

'We have far to go yet,' he told her tenderly. 'But now we're on the offensive.'

She had no conception of what Paul's special assignment was about, yet she was convinced it was very dangerous. Once it was over, he'd confided, he would join the Army Air Force unit to which he was now officially attached. Secretly she was relieved that his flying days were over.

At the beginning of their third week of working together, Vera spent a half hour in earnest conversation with Colonel Brett. She was appalled that he was having afterthoughts about her ability to provide Paul with the knowledge of German he required.

'Perhaps we should split the day with someone more trained in rapid instruction,' the colonel said uneasily.

'It would be unproductive to divide Paul's teaching that way,' Vera objected, quoting her father's words in a similar situation. 'Paul doesn't need perfect grammar – he needs comprehension.' Now she quoted the colonel himself. 'We work so well together,' she finished lamely, all at once aware that the colonel suspected some romantic involvement and was disturbed by this.

Vera returned to their improvised classroom and told Paul it was his turn to confer with Colonel Brett.

'He's worried that I can't teach you enough,' she explained, her eyes desolate. 'He talked about your working with me in the mornings and with somebody else in the afternoons.'

'Nobody can do better than you,' he said, his face taut. 'I'll make Colonel Brett understand that.'

He stalked out of the room, returned fifteen minutes later with a complacent grin.

'Nothing's changed,' he reported and reached for her hand. 'We're in this together, baby.'

But something had changed, Vera realized. She felt a soaring protectiveness in him. His eyes told her what he had not put into words. It was difficult to focus on their work. *Paul returned the love she felt for him.*

The morning had been unseasonably cold, depressingly

grey. By the time Vera and Paul left the office for the day and ventured out into the street, an icy rain had begun to fall. Paul reached for her arm.

'We'll never find a taxi at this hour in this weather. And we'll be sopping wet if we wait for a bus.' He hesitated. 'My place is close by,' he reminded. Her heart began to pound. 'We could make dinner there. I keep a few tins for emergencies.' His eyes pleaded for agreement.

She hesitated for a second. 'All right.' Nothing was going to happen.

Paul's smile was dazzling. He reached for her hand as the rain assaulted them. 'Let's make a dash for it.'

Paul's flat was small but larger than hers. A tiny sitting room and another room – his bedroom, she guessed – right off it. In a corner of the sitting room was a makeshift kitchenette.

'Let me take your coat – it's dripping wet,' he said solicitously. 'And your shoes are sopping. Kick them off.'

They made a small ceremony of hanging away her coat and depositing it along with her wet shoes in the bathroom. Paul reached into a closet for a flannel shirt and held it for her.

'Not your size but it'll keep you warm.' He glanced down at her wet stockings. 'Take those off and hang them up to dry.' He prodded her into the bathroom and turned away to remove his own wet socks.

'I hope they dry,' she said with shaky humour. But she was conscious of a delicious exhilaration at being here this way with Paul.

'God, I hate this ruling against central heating!' He grimaced. 'Back home, oil is rationed, I gather, but there's enough to keep the house fairly warm during waking hours.'

He was talking compulsively, she thought, to make her feel at ease.

'It's good to be inside.' In bare feet, Paul's shirt lending welcome warmth, she gazed out the small window that looked out upon the street. 'What a dreary day.'

'I'll put up a pot of tea,' he said, 'then we'll make dinner.' He was at the tiny two-burner gas range, reaching for the kettle. 'Nothing fancy,' he warned. 'Dad and Doris keep me supplied with American salamis and cookies. And everybody in England keeps a supply of potatoes.'

They warmed themselves with strong Earl Grey tea, then began to prepare dinner. Together they peeled potatoes for boiling. When the potatoes were almost ready, Paul decreed, he'd make salami omelets. For now, the potatoes cooked gently on a gas burner.

'The salami is great – it kills the lousy taste of the powdered eggs. And we'll sauté the potatoes with some onion. Because I'm out of margarine,' he conceded humorously.

Despite the chill in the tiny flat, the atmosphere was festive. Paul flipped on what he called the *radio* and which to Vera was the *wireless* and – courtesy of the BBC – the strains of a Brandenburg Concerto filled the room.

'Your feet are like ice,' Paul scolded as he reached down to touch one. 'Let me get you a pair of my socks.'

'Paul, no.' She choked with laughter. She'd look ridiculous wearing a pair of Paul's socks.

'Vera, yes,' he ordered. 'I won't have you catching cold.' All at once the atmosphere was electric. 'You're very precious to me, you know.' He reached for her hand, pulled her close. 'I've never felt this way about anyone. I sit there in that classroom every day, and all I want to do is hold you in my arms. I walk with you in the street, and I want to hold you close.'

'Paul, we shouldn't,' she said unsteadily. *Mama would be shocked.*

37

'Why not?' he challenged. 'All we truly have in this world is today. Vera, I love you so much –'

'I love you,' she whispered. Paul was right. How did they know they'd be alive tomorrow? She'd tried not to think about where Paul would be sent in a few short weeks. She never truly forgot that a bomb could fall from the sky and kill them any night.

His mouth was warm and sweet, then passionate on hers, his hands evoking feelings she'd regarded earlier with alarm. But how could this be wrong when they loved each other so deeply?

The chill in the tiny flat was forgotten as she moved with him. She thought not about tomorrow or next week or next year. Only about *now*.

Each day became doubly precious because once gone it could not be retrieved. She gave up her bed-sitter to move into Paul's flat because he was arranging for her to take it over when he must leave. He worried about her finances. She wasn't sure when she would acquire another tutoring or translation job. And he insisted they be married as soon as possible.

'You'll be the wife of an American soldier,' he explained. 'You'll receive an allotment cheque every month. I'll feel better knowing you have that security.'

They were married on a fog-drenched Sunday morning by an Army Air Force rabbi and spent their first night as husband and wife in a suite at the unscarred Ritz. They knew they might have to cram a lifetime into these short weeks. Vera understood she was not to question Paul about his secret assignment. She was sure he would write when he could. The assignment would be brief, he hoped. Then he would join the unit to which he had been assigned.

With reluctance they left the Ritz the following morning, yearning to prolong the pleasure of the night, and stopped at a Lyons Corner House for breakfast.

'Breakfast in London is always the worst meal of the day,' Paul said with wry humour. Vera was always touched by the way he insisted on carrying their trays himself. So often she saw women performing this chore for themselves and their men.

'I won't notice this morning,' Vera said, her smile dazzling. It was still unreal that she was Paul's wife – but she had the paper attesting to this in her purse. She wouldn't let herself think about how little time they had left together – for now.

'You'll love breakfast back home,' Paul mused as they settled down to eat. 'On weekends it's always pancakes with real maple syrup. And *real* coffee. Nobody in London knows how to make coffee.'

'Will your father and sister be upset that you've married somebody who's not an American?' she asked, anxious now. Paul had said they would wait until the war was over to tell his father and sister.

'They'll love you,' Paul promised. 'Dad's always been afraid I'd marry out of our faith. There are only two other Jewish families in Eastwood – and not a girl anywhere near my age among them. Doris married a few months ago – her husband was born and raised in Palestine, became a parachutist for the British military. He had a bad injury and was sent to New York on some diplomatic mission. He decided to stay there. That's where he met Doris. He's working for Dad now. If you listen to Dad, Wayne's the greatest thing since the invention of the wheel.' *But would Paul's father approve of her?*

The days were rushing past. Paul was convinced that soon there would be an Allied invasion of Europe – what he called 'the beginning of the end.' But Vera tried not to look beyond each day. With Paul she felt reborn. So many times she'd asked herself why she had survived when Mama and Papa and Ernst had died. But now she had a reason to live. She had Paul.

She tried not to show her fears as the last week of Paul's tutoring arrived. At his insistence, she had gone to the British diplomat who had acquired this assignment for her and was told that additional work as a translator would be available shortly. While London seemed safer now than at any time since the beginning of the war, she could never thrust aside the fear that one day the Nazis would invade London.

'I'm going to be so afraid while you're gone,' she confessed to Paul as she lay in his arms in their blacked-out flat on his last night in London. For the past week – in addition to their arduous sessions – Paul had been in conference with Colonel Brett and a team preparing him for other aspects of his assignment. 'I wish I had a gun to keep beneath my pillow,' she said with childish ferocity.

'Vera, you'll be safe. There'll never be a land invasion by the Nazis,' he soothed. 'We've reached the turning point in the war. The Allies will soon be on the attack in Western Europe, everybody's expecting that.'

'When?' she whispered.

'Baby, only the big wheels know when that'll come. But we're moving towards the end of the war.' She knew he was trying to be optimistic for her sake.

'I'm going to miss you so much.'

'I'll miss you, too,' he soothed.

When would she see Paul again? He'd warned her it could be months. '*When you hear that Paris has been liberated, then expect a letter from me soon.*'

They made love with a special urgency tonight – each conscious that there would be a long interval before they could be together this way again. Exhausted, they fell asleep in each other's arms, awoke to feel the stirring of fresh young passion.

The early morning was grey and cold. Paul insisted that Vera remain in bed while he made breakfast for them.

'Damn this lack of central heating,' he swore yet again as he brought scrambled eggs spiked with cheddar cheese to disguise their powdered taste, burnt-at-the-edge toast, and tall cups of tea to the tiny dining table. 'Now you can come,' he decreed.

The atmosphere was heavy with their anguish at imminent separation, though each strove to mask this.

'Now that I'm going to war again, it's sure to be over soon,' Paul drawled. 'And in Paris I'll buy you a giant bottle of perfume and one for Doris.' He hadn't said so in words, but she knew he would be dropped over occupied France. Though he'd never told her, she suspected his early morning training had to do with radio communications. 'And before we go home to Eastwood, I'll show you New York.' She heard the nostalgia in his voice. 'I'll take you up to the Columbia campus and show you where I lived for two years.'

'Paul, be careful,' she whispered. 'Remember, I'll be back here waiting for you –'

Vera didn't leave their flat for the next forty-eight hours – when her new job as translator would begin. She clung to the memory of Paul's presence here. The scent of his shaving cream – his ultimate wartime luxury here in London, he'd joshed – evoked tender memories of her standing by in the minuscule bathroom while he shaved. She was Paul's wife, and he was coming back to her.

On the new job she met a high-spirited London girl married to a Canadian Air Force sergeant. Almost immediately she and Iris were drawn together.

'Hank says his folks back home just can't understand

how we survive in the blackouts. And he's forever writing me to stay at home at night because God knows what can happen to a girl out there alone in a blackout.'

Iris had a brother fighting somewhere in Italy. Her widowed mother and sister-in-law lived in a small town in northern England. Iris had been working in London for three years.

Iris had married her Canadian sergeant early in the year. All she knew of his whereabouts now was that he was part of the aircrews that had been wreaking havoc on Germany. Mail arrived intermittently. Iris refused to allow herself to be afraid. Hank was coming home to her, and that was it.

Vera was grateful for Iris's presence in her life. Iris helped alleviate her towering loneliness. The British were wonderful, she thought recurrently. They'd been through so much, yet accepted it all with such calm.

She was touched when Iris insisted she come to her flat for dinner on the approaching New Year's Eve.

'And you'll sleep over,' Iris said firmly. 'It's taking your life in your hands to walk around in the blackout.' With Paul she'd never worried, Vera remembered wistfully – though most people were uneasy about the freakish accidents that kept occurring on nights when not even a sliver of moonlight lightened the streets.

The two girls were determined to make New Year's Eve a festive occasion. The moment they walked into the flat Iris flipped on the wireless, and music filled the room.

'I have a tin of baked beans to go with the sausage – such as it is.' She grimaced apologetically. 'Mostly flour and what else, let's just don't speculate. And I'll make a quick custard to go with our tea.'

'Let me help,' Vera said and paused to cover a yawn.

'You are the sleepiest one,' Iris scolded good-humouredly. 'Anybody would think you were pregnant –' She stopped dead as Vera gasped in sudden comprehension. 'Oh God, are you?'

'I lost track of time.' Vera was pale, her eyes a mixture of shock and glorious discovery. 'Iris, I may be.'

'That's wonderful!' Iris's smile was dazzling. 'I was dying to get pregnant before Hank's squadron was moved too far for him to get into London even for a day. But he was always so damn careful.'

'Paul was careful, too.' Alarm closed in about her. Would Paul be angry?

'They've got this crazy idea we're delicate little flowers,' Iris said, reading her mind. 'They worry about us, love. But you'll be fine. You see all the prams out on the streets again. The Nazis are too busy trying to save their own hides to drop bombs on us. And you're the wife of a fighting man – you'll get all the medical care you need. Vera, I think it's wonderful,' she repeated.

Later – on Iris's sofa beneath a mound of frayed blankets topped by her winter coat – Vera lay sleepless far into the night, enveloped in wonder that from the love she had shared with Paul had come this child within her. Tears of joy stung her eyes. Oh, she wished Paul could know! Where was he now? And all at once joy was joined by fear.

Please God, let Paul come home to them.

Chapter Five

Vera had known that Paul's absence from her life would be agonizing. It seemed doubly so now that she realized she was carrying their baby – and at the same time she found sweet solace in this new knowledge. Rumours persisted in the weeks and months ahead that the war could not last much longer . . . that there was to be an Allied invasion of Europe.

Vera was in the last weeks of her pregnancy – with not one word yet from Paul – when the news that Allied forces had landed on the coast of Normandy flashed around the world. It was D-Day – June 6, 1944. Early in the morning, Vera – like other London insomniacs – had heard the clamour of endless bombers taking off. Later she was to hear Edward R. Murrow describe this as 'the sound of a giant factory in the sky.' Later still, they were to learn that 11,000 planes had taken part in the first day of the invasion.

It was only a matter of weeks now before Paris would be liberated, Vera told herself with exhilaration. She would hear from Paul. But again – as at recurrent intervals during the past months – she asked herself if Paul were regretting their hasty marriage. Was he sorry he'd married her? Would he be upset about the baby? Would he feel he was too young to be tied down to a wife and child? She was impatient to hear from Paul – yet fearful.

Six days after D-Day, Hitler launched fresh vengeance on London.

'This wasn't supposed to happen!' Iris wailed to Vera. 'We're supposed to be winning the war!'

'Our planes will find their launching pads,' Vera said with a confidence she didn't feel. For the past six weeks she'd been working at home on translations. Iris was her conduit with the office. 'They'll destroy them.'

'I'm moving in with you till the baby's born,' Iris said firmly. 'You're not staying alone with all those things flying over our rooftops.'

The new buzz bombs became a way of life. A hundred a day fell over the city. Many Londoners declared these deadly robots harder to endure than the blitz. All at once, the British reserve seemed to disappear. Total strangers exchanged conversation about 'those pesky things making life miserable for us.' And with typical British calm and humour, they adapted. There were sirens punctuating the air day and night because radar detected their approach over the Channel. Independent warning systems were set up in public places, stores, large offices. The warning systems were geared to go off only when a bomb was almost overhead – to allow life to go on normally as long as possible.

Vera and Iris abandoned the cherished weekly visit to their neighbourhood restaurant because of its skylight and mirrors. Broken glass caused frequent injuries. Queuing up – a necessary part of life these days – was a time of anxiety for Vera, though most Londoners seemed to show a remarkable lack of unease.

'People are too nonchalant about the buzz bombs,' Vera said worriedly.

Only a handful of cinemas and theatres remained open, though the restaurants continued to serve the usual number of patrons.

'People want to eat,' Iris pointed out.

Like most Londoners – those who didn't go to the

45

shelters – Vera and Iris remained at home in the evenings. As the havoc continued, mothers and children were urged to leave the city. Churchill warned that conditions could become worse before they became better. Iris tried to persuade Vera to leave, but she refused.

'I'm not letting the *doodlebugs* drive me away,' Vera insisted, even while she was terrified for the baby's safety. 'I have to be here when Paul writes me.' She was terrified of the prospect of missing contact with him. And – again – she was tormented by nightmares, awakening in a cold sweat. Remembering *Kristallnacht*.

Late in July – with enemy raiders overhead – Vera gave birth after a lengthy labour to a daughter and named her Laurie Anne Kahn. At Iris's urging Lisl – her maternal grandmother's name – had been Americanized to Laurie. Anne had been her paternal grandmother's name.

'Isn't she beautiful?' Vera asked when Iris came into the hospital ward after seeing tiny Laurie, with her incredible mass of burnished gold hair and dainty features. 'Do you think Paul will love her?' Her voice was wistful. She still harboured fearful doubts that Paul might be overwhelmed by the new responsibility of fatherhood.

'He'll adore her,' Iris prophesied. 'I can just imagine his feelings when he gets the word.'

Again early in August Iris tried to persuade Vera to take Laurie and leave London. Most outlying areas were happy to receive evacuees.

'My head tells me to go,' Vera admitted, 'but my heart says *no*. I must be here when Paul writes me.' She refused to consider that he wouldn't – or couldn't.

Now British morale was lifted by rumours of dissension in Germany. On July 29, an attempt was made to assassinate Hitler. Word filtered through that many Germans were prepared to admit defeat. Still, the Nazi forces continued to fight doggedly.

As always, Vera worried about the Schmidts. Berlin had been under such intense bombing. *Were they all right?* And the Munches in Copenhagen? What was happening to them?

Vera and Iris were devoted listeners to the BBC reports of the fighting in France. Then at last – on August 25 – word came through that the suburbs of Paris had been liberated. The following day Allied troops entered the city. Paul had promised, '*You'll hear from me soon after the Nazis are driven out of Paris.*'

'Iris, I can't believe it! Paris is free!' Vera greeted Iris on her return from work on Saturday afternoon. Though Iris kept up her own apartment for the day that Hank would return, she continued to stay with Vera.

'Everybody is so excited!' Iris hugged Vera exuberantly.

But Vera sensed a wariness in Iris. Because she, too, worried about Paul's welfare. *Was he all right?* His special assignment was dangerous. And only after Paris was free was he to assume regular duties.

'How's my precious little love?' Without waiting for a reply, Iris sauntered into the bedroom, where Laurie lay in her crib. 'Oh, I woke her,' Iris reproached herself as a plaintive cry filled the air.

A week after the liberation of Paris – a week of painful waiting – Vera received her first letter from Paul. Her heart pounding, she gazed in wondrous excitement at the small, tight handwriting on the envelope. Paul's handwriting, Paul's APO number. *He was all right.* In tumultuous impatience she ripped open the envelope, began to read. He was fine, he insisted – though he admitted he'd experienced some difficult moments.

'*Everyone is sure the war in Europe will be over soon – but it can't be soon enough for me. I can't wait to hold you in my arms again, and we can begin to live normal lives.*'

Vera read and reread Paul's letter – segments cut out by a censor. He was safe. He still loved her. And now she must write and tell him about his very young daughter. Though it was difficult to come by, Iris had acquired – in anticipation of this moment – a roll of film, along with a borrowed camera. Too impatient to wait for the film to be developed, Vera wrote Paul the day she received his letter and promised that a snapshot of Laurie would follow soon. Yet her pleasure at hearing from him was invaded at intervals with fear of his reaction to fatherhood.

But the swift conclusion to the war in Europe that so many yearned to see eluded the Allied troops. Though American and British bombers were devastating German cities, the Allies still couldn't penetrate German borders by land.

How many more must die before it was over? Vera asked herself in recurrent terror.

Paul was grateful for the small luxury of being billeted in a modest hotel in liberated Paris while he was to pursue a new post with an intelligence unit located in a nearby building. After witnessing the destruction in London, he was astonished by the well-being of Paris – saved by surrender.

He was shocked that Paris showed so few signs of having been a captive city. The woman appeared well-dressed – with none of the rationing limitations imposed on British and American women. The French textile industry had prospered, he learned. The French had devised television sets and transmitters. In an odd fashion, the French experience irked him.

He was distraught over the reports from London about the daily barrage of buzz bombs hitting the city – following a path across Kent, Sussex, and Surrey on their way to London. During the period between June 17 and the end of last month – August – 5,479 people were killed. Another 15,934 were injured, most of them women and children. He had tried – futilely – to have someone check on Vera in London. He admitted it was too much to ask in these chaotic times.

Arriving at his desk this morning, Paul hoped anxiously for word from Vera. So often in these last months he'd asked himself if he had made a terrible mistake in tearing off on a dangerous mission that meant leaving Vera – so young and vulnerable and scared – alone in London. He'd been so optimistic that this mission would be over in a matter of weeks rather than nine frustrating months. But he'd made the commitment before they even met. Now it was hard to realize there was a time she wasn't part of his life.

Paul glanced up with a surge of anticipation when a corporal appeared with a handful of mail.

'Come and get it,' the corporal called out ebulliently, and every man in the sprawling office area rose from his desk with a matching alacrity.

His pulse racing, Paul reached out for the pair of envelopes the corporal extended in his direction. He guessed the V-Mail – which arrived with such speed – would be from his father. The other was unmistakably Vera's handwriting. She was all right, he told himself with a surge of relief. Eagerly he ripped open the envelope, began to read.

'*My darling, it was so wonderful to receive your letter. I have news that will be a shock to you – but I hope a wonderful shock. We have a daughter who is seven weeks old today. Her name is Laurie Anne.*'

'Oh my God!' His head reeling Paul read on. 'Oh my God!'

'What? What?' The young major at the desk across

from his own – philosophical at not receiving mail this morning – swung around to face him.

'I have a kid – a daughter!' *And Vera went through it all alone.* 'When I left London, we didn't even know she was pregnant!' He tried to visualize this tiny miracle that was their daughter. Laurie Anne – Anne for his mother, he thought tenderly.

'Hey, put in for leave,' the major urged. 'With your background, you rate it.'

'I'll never get it.' Paul was sceptical, even while the prospect was exhilarating.

'Try,' the major ordered.

On September 8, 1944 the London blackout was lifted after 1,843 nights of darkness – but not for long. On that same night, the first of a series of blasts hit London. They were reported in official communiques as gas-main explosions, but Londoners quickly understood this was a censorship ploy. Hitler had unleashed a devastating new weapon. The terrifying aspect of this latest Nazi menace – arriving just as the doodlebugs had been eliminated by Allied destruction of their launching pads – was that they landed with no warning. They could be neither seen nor heard – until one hit with the force of a minor earthquake.

Vera emerged from her flat each day with trepidation – never knowing where one of these new rockets had landed since she had last been outdoors, what huge crater would meet her eyes. Knowing what was happening in London, Paul wrote and pleaded with her to leave the city.

'Remember, you have money in the bank to see you through in addition to your allotment cheques. I worry every minute about you and the baby.'

Paul wrote about trying through special channels to have her go to stay with his father in Eastwood, but the prospect of putting an ocean between Paul and herself was too alarming. While she cherished his eagerness to see them safe – and in her mind she knew this would be the prudent measure to take, she couldn't accept it. How could they know, she tried to reason, that the ship wouldn't be bombed on the way to the United States? And she clung to the conviction that since she had survived so much in her brief lifetime, she would survive this, too. Londoners called the new missiles *Bob Hopes* – 'You bob down and hope for the best.'

For weeks Londoners tried to convince themselves that the war was almost over, but the continued assault of what were now labelled V-2 bombs splintered that hope – despite the fact that American troops had crossed the border and entered Germany itself. Then, late in October, Vera opened the door to the flat – expecting to see Iris there with her usual remorseful explanation that she had forgotten her key.

'Baby! Oh, baby, how I've missed you!' Paul hovered in the doorway, his face luminous as he reached for her.

'Paul!' She gazed at him in a mixture of disbelief and wonder. 'You're really here!' She moved back to inspect his face as they swayed together.

'Just for a five-day leave,' he cautioned. 'Then it's back to my unit. Now, introduce me to my daughter –'

Vera stood beside the crib while Paul scooped up Laurie and held her in his arms. Tears blurred her eyes at the infinite tenderness she felt in him as he inspected Laurie's minute features.

'She looks just like you,' he decided, pleased with this discovery. 'The same gorgeous hair, the same blue eyes.'

'All babies have blue eyes until they're about three months,' Vera said, her own eyes lit with laughter. 'Will you disown her if her eyes turn out to be brown or green or grey?'

'Vera, there are no words to tell you how much I love her,' he said softly. 'I wrote Dad and Doris. I'm sure they're out of their minds with excitement.'

'They'll love her, too?' She needed this assurance. They would be Laurie's only family other than herself and Paul.

They started at the sound of the door to the flat opening.

'Vera, you forgot to lock the door,' Iris called out. 'You thought I'd forgot my key again –' She stopped dead at the tableau that met her eyes. 'Welcome home,' she told Paul with infinite warmth. They'd never met, Vera realized, but who else could he be? 'I'll pick up a few things and head for my flat.'

'He'll just be here for five days,' Vera explained, her head on Paul's shoulder, her eyes shining.

'Enjoy every minute of them,' Iris ordered, her smile sympathetic. 'I know when three's a crowd. Four,' she corrected herself. 'And may there be no Bob Hopes for the next five days.'

Chapter Six

Vera fought against despair as the war in Europe refused to come to a halt. In mid-December, Germany launched a savage offensive in the Ardennes Forest, soon labelled the Battle of the Bulge because of the shape of the battle-ground on an army map. The battle took a heavy toll on German forces – almost 100,000 casualties plus another 110,000 taken prisoners.

'This has to end soon, love.' Iris comforted Vera at regular intervals as Vera comforted her in other moments. 'Hank keeps writing that we're just around the corner to peace.'

But it wasn't until May 7, 1945, that Germany surrendered unconditionally to the Allies. The following day, the world learned that formal papers had been signed at General Eisenhower's headquarters at Rheims. Simultaneously – in London, Washington, and Moscow – Churchill, Truman, and Stalin announced on the radio that May 8, 1945, was V-E Day. The end of the war in Europe.

Vera knew nothing until Iris – leaving work in the sudden wild celebration that gripped London – came rushing into the flat. The wireless was off so as not to disturb Laurie, napping in her crib.

'Haven't you heard?' Iris grabbed Vera and spun her about the room. 'The war's over in Europe! It's over!'

'Iris, you're sure?' Vera veered between exultation and scepticism.

'I'm sure, I'm sure!' Iris was euphoric. 'Hank and Paul are coming home!' She released Vera and rushed to open a window. 'Listen to the crowds pouring out into the streets,' she ordered exuberantly.

Vera heard the sound of singing in the streets – groups and individuals, all caught up in the magic of the moment. The sounds of 'Roll Out the Barrel' suddenly erupted in the hallway and awakened Laurie.

Vera darted into the bedroom and scooped her up from the crib. 'Laurie, your Daddy's coming home!'

Caught up in the excitement of the occasion, Vera and Iris left the flat with Laurie – who, without comprehending, seemed to understand that this was a time of supreme celebration. The atmosphere in the crowded streets reflected the joy – the relief – that at last men and women in uniform would be coming home . . . those who had fought in the European theatre of war – the Allies still fought the Japanese in the Pacific, Vera forced herself to recognize. And underneath the joy, Vera was conscious of a poignant sadness, too – because so many were not alive to share in this day. The war had not been officially declared when Mama and Papa and Ernst died, Vera thought in painful recall – but they, too, were war casualties.

Vera waited impatiently for word from Paul. Five days later, he appeared at the door to the flat.

'I'm on a six-week furlough,' he announced ebulliently as he pulled her into his arms, then laughed at her bewildered stare.

'Furlough?' she asked.

'Honey, we'll be shipped out to the Pacific after furloughs back home. I went through all kinds of red tape to have my furlough here in London. I'll travel to the States with another unit.'

'You'll have to go to the Pacific?' She was cold with shock. 'Paul, you've had enough of fighting!'

'It won't last long over there,' he promised. 'A few weeks – maybe a few months.' *But in a few months – even in a day – he could be killed*, she thought in terror. 'Honey, we're almost out of the woods.'

The weeks of Paul's furlough flew past. He was enthralled with Laurie, sent a flood of snapshots home to his father and Doris. Vera revelled in the admiring smiles that Paul – now a major – garnered from passing Londoners when they took Laurie for outings in Kensington Gardens and Regent's Park. He glowed with pride when Vera showed him the white, asbestos-roofed temporary houses that 3,000 US Army soldiers – assigned by General Eisenhower – had built to give shelter to some of the families made homeless by bombs.

'Nobody could believe how fast they went up,' Vera told Paul. 'Each one has two bedrooms, a bath, and a living-dining-kitchenette area.'

'They look like igloos,' Paul said, chuckling. But his eyes showed his pleasure that Americans had made this possible.

Each night Vera and Paul closed the door to the bedroom when Laurie was asleep in her crib and made passionate love. It was as though, Vera thought as she lay in Paul's arms on the small, cramped sofa, they were trying to make up for the long, empty nights of separation. And afterwards they talked in muted tones far into the night.

'Dad's going to be upset that I don't want to go back for my engineering degree,' he confided sombrely. 'He figured I'd work as an engineer for a while, then come in and take over the business later.' He frowned in distaste. 'I don't want any part of dealing with guns.' He smiled wryly. 'I know – that's a weird thing for a soldier to say.

I could handle it because I knew this was a war that had to be fought. But guns kill.'

'Guns don't kill,' Vera objected gently. 'People kill.' Instantly she regretted this remark. She knew how Paul's mother had died. He'd never truly forgiven his father for that awful accident, she remembered compassionately.

'For four generations, the men in my family have been gun-smiths. My great-great-grandfather, great-grandfather, my grandfather, and my father. Dad looks upon guns with such reverence. He knows everything there is to know about them. To him a fine gun is a work of art. I don't share that feeling. To me a gun is an instrument of death.'

'Sssh,' Vera said gently. 'In the hands of our fighting men, they've saved lives.'

'The company did well in the First World War, but this time Dad was able to expand beyond his wildest dreams. In a few years, he's become a rich man. By Eastwood standards,' he amended. '*Because of the war.*'

'Paul, he performed a service for his country,' Vera said. 'You've told me how hard he's worked – and that was part of winning the war.' In a corner of her mind she recalled the traumatic moment in the fishing village near Copenhagen when a harbour policeman had threatened her escape to safety. Except for the guns in the hands of those two Resistance workers, she might be dead.

'Vera, I know now what I want to do with my life. It's not romantic and exciting, but it's what I want to do. I'll go back to college for a teaching degree. Hopefully go on to a PhD in education so I can teach at a college level.'

'If that's what you want, then do it.' She felt a fierce determination to see Paul pursue this new dream.

'We've fought two awful wars already in this century,' he said, a messianic glow in his eyes. 'If this world is to see lasting peace, we're going to have to educate the people. They have to learn to think for themselves . . . to be able to listen to a maniac like Hitler and understand his twisted mind.'

'You talk like my father.' Tears welled in her eyes. Papa had stayed in Berlin because he thought it was so important to be there to teach. Oh yes! She could understand what Paul was telling her.

'I won't make a lot of money,' he warned. 'But we'll be comfortable.'

'You'll be happy,' she said with conviction. '*We'll* be happy.'

'It'll be rough at first.' He squinted in contemplation. 'I'll go back to school under the GI Bill. We won't have much money.'

'I can work, too,' she said eagerly. 'At home. Tutoring or doing translations. I'll work.' Her smile was dazzling. 'We'll manage.'

In late July, Paul joined his assigned unit for the trip back to the States. Vera tried to convince herself that very soon she and Laurie would follow him. The US government was already making plans to transport GI brides and children to the United States to join their husbands when the war in the Pacific was over. Paul wrote that he was stationed in Texas. He expected to be transferred soon to the Pacific. But that was not to be.

On September 2, 1945 Japanese surrender ceremonies took place. The war was over. Impatient to have Vera and Laurie with him, Paul wrote that he was trying to get passage to England to bring his little family home without waiting for government help. Both he and Vera soon realized this was impossible. Every available ship had been commandeered to transport the American fighting men in Europe back to home ground. It would be months before this could be accomplished.

The Red Cross was organizing GI Brides Clubs because

over 66,000 brides of American servicemen were waiting to join their husbands. Vera signed up along with over 300 other young wives – most of them between 18 and 23 – in her area. Iris was preparing to go home to spend some time with her mother, brother, and sister-in-law before joining Hank in Canada.

'Mum thinks I'm out of my blinking mind to have married somebody from Canada.' Iris giggled infectiously. 'Can you imagine what she would be saying if I'd married an American?'

Vera knew that Britishers looked down on girls who married American fighting men. And some, Iris had guessed, were worried about their giving a bad impression of Great Britain to America. The general impression here was that only girls from the slums or 'Piccadilly commandos' were marrying GIs.

'On the other hand,' Iris drawled, 'do you think all those American girls who're looking for husbands are going to be happy about 66,000 British girls walking off with *their* men?'

Conscientiously Vera attended all the meetings held by her GI Brides Club. She listened with eagerness to all they were told about life in the United States. They were even taught to make coffee American style, she wrote Paul.

'Can you imagine?' a pretty 18-year-old whispered to Vera at one meeting. 'In the United States folks keep their houses heated to 70°. It must feel like being in the tropics!'

Vera and Iris talked about the courting between British brides and their servicemen husbands – often, she insisted, longer than that between American girls and servicemen.

'Hank and I didn't just jump into marriage,' Iris said. 'We went out together for five months. Of course, you and Paul jumped,' she kidded. 'But that's all right because you're perfect for each other.'

How would Paul's father and sister feel? Vera asked

herself with recurrent nervousness. Paul said they were pleased – but they wouldn't tell *him* if they weren't. He said his father kept snapshots of Laurie on his office desk and showed them off to everybody. She was glad that Paul was already back in school – though not at Columbia. He said it would be too expensive for them to live in New York. He was going to school in a city called Albany – where he could commute from Eastwood. She was a little uncomfortable at the prospect of their living with Paul's father for now – but as long as Paul was in school, it was the best thing to do.

'You know,' Iris mused, 'I think Canadian men are more like Americans than British. Hank just bowled me over. He was *nice* to me.'

'The girls at my Brides Club talked about that,' Vera remembered. 'They said American fellows made such a fuss over them – bringing them candy and flowers.' She giggled in recall. 'One of the girls was so impressed because her American boyfriend brought her nail polish.' Difficult to acquire in London. 'Paul took me to fancy restaurants – even before we were truly serious.' Yet, in a corner of her mind, she knew that Paul had been serious within days.

'Our boys take us for granted.' Iris nodded with conviction. 'They play the love-'em-and-leave-'em game as long as they can get away with it. American and Canadian men are the marrying kind. That's the way they were brought up,' she said with relish.

'I didn't go out with any men before Paul came along,' Vera said softly, 'but it wasn't long before I knew I wanted to spend the rest of my life with him.'

Vera tried to comfort Paul at the delay – the 'infernal red tape,' he called it – that kept the hordes of GI brides apart from their husbands. Still, both realized the frustrating slowness of transporting servicemen across the

Atlantic, even though every ship was packed beyond capacity. This, of course, took precedence over wives and children.

Finally, word came through early in the new year. Vera and Laurie would be aboard the first ship – the *Argentina* – that would carry GI brides to their husbands. She was eager to be with Paul, yet nervous at the prospect of beginning a new life on a strange continent. But Paul would be with her – so it would be all right. She wasn't running *away* this time – she was running *to* Paul.

Now Vera was caught up in the excitement of imminent departure. She went with Laurie to her assigned camp. Three such camps had been set up by the US government in England – and another in France. Here the GI brides and children were processed, given the necessary shots. Then on the appointed day, 456 brides and 170 babies – destined to be scattered across 45 states – were transported to Southampton to board the 20,600 ton *Argentina*, totally refitted to suit the needs of its passengers.

Standing on the deck in the bleak winter cold as the ship moved slowly out of the harbour, Vera joined the other very young wives in singing 'There'll Always Be An England.' She was conscious of a kind of bravura among them, a forerunner of the homesickness that would surely attack some before the *Argentina* completed its crossing.

'If we'd waited a week, we could have crossed on the *Queen Elizabeth*,' one starry-eyed bride bubbled. 'But I can't wait to be with my Joe!'

'In eight days you'll be with him,' Vera said blithely, yet she felt an unexpected apprehension as she jiggled Laurie in her arms. She was putting an ocean between herself and every place she'd ever known. She remembered stories she'd heard about Americans: 'They're always going on strike – they're noisy – always in a hurry – always drunk.' But Paul wasn't like that.

The unorthodox passengers of the *Argentina* were enthralled by what they found aboard. The crew included two army doctors, five army nurses, eight WACS to help care for the children, and many stewardesses and matrons. The sleeping quarters were admittedly small, 'but 4.6 times what was allotted to each soldier when the *Argentina* carried troops.' Sleeping accommodation – lower or upper bunks – was assigned without reference to the rank of spouses. There were cribs and playpens, special dishes for the babies, an abundance of toys.

'Did you ever see anything like this?' murmured one wide-eyed young mother. 'My little fella will be out of his mind with all of this!'

'And disposable nappies,' another effervesced.

'I know,' the other girl giggled. 'They figure on sixty nappies for each during the crossing. All of them going overboard when they're dirtied. But there's a laundry room for clothes.'

Meals this first day out brought expressions of amazement and delight. They gaped at platters of beef and chicken, bacon and eggs, even bowls piled high with oranges – all so scarce in England. Everyone was eager to shop in the canteen, which offered candy, lipsticks, even cigarette lighters. But by the third day, few passengers came to the dining saloon. Winds blowing up to 65 miles per hour were pounding the ship. The fog horn blared. Warnings to stay below came over the public address system at regular intervals. Vera was relieved that she was among the few who were not attacked by seasickness.

The weather continued unpleasant for much of the trip, though once some of the brides had overcome their seasickness they organized to present a show, dubbed *Argentina Antics*. There was a beauty contest for the babies. In calm weather, Vera joined those who enjoyed walks around the deck. And all the brides appreciated the services of the WACS.

'It's like a holiday,' the bride in the bunk above Vera's declared. 'Let's enjoy it. It won't be for long.'

For Vera, the shipboard days were both euphoric – weather permitting – and frustratingly slow. And rumours were circulating that because of the weather, the trip would probably extend to nine days. At unwary moments, Vera was assaulted by memories of the harried years behind. She wished wistfully that she could have gone to the synagogue in Berlin where her parents' and her brother's ashes had been buried. But they would be happy for her, she comforted herself. How they would have loved Paul and Laurie!

The rumours proved correct. The ship would arrive in New York in nine days rather than the estimated eight.

'My poor Bill will be hanging around the city for an extra day,' one girl mourned. 'He came all the way from Alabama to meet me.'

'You just hope he doesn't pick up some gorgeous chorus girl in New York,' another teased.

Except for their night clothes, Vera packed the night before they were to dock. She was on the deck with others in the raw, cold February dawn when the ship chugged into the iced-over harbour. Her heart pounded as the New York skyline came into view.

'That's the Statue of Liberty!' somebody cried out as the floodlit landmark became visible.

Soon the decks were mobbed with brides, ricocheted with the sound of excited conversations. At last the ship was at anchor. The gangplank was set in place. The Army band waiting at the pier broke into a rendition of 'The Star-Spangled Banner.' The joyous war-brides and their offspring began to disembark, some singing their new national anthem as they made their way down the gangplank. The day was grey and cold, but none paid heed to this. Their children were already American citizens, Vera remembered. In two years, the brides would acquire that status.

After physical examinations, brides and babies were transported across town, and in the cosy warmth of the Red Cross Chapter House they were at last greeted by their husbands.

'I've never seen you out of uniform,' Vera confided with wry amusement when she and Paul had exchanged kisses and Laurie had been tenderly greeted. 'Not ever!'

'You want to turn me in for another model?' he joshed.

'I never want to see you in uniform again,' she declared. 'No more wars! No more separations!'

'God, it's wonderful to have you both here!' His voice was fervent. 'I was too excited to sleep last night.'

'Me, too,' Vera confessed, her eyes clinging to Paul's face as though to reassure herself that she was really here with him. 'And I had this awful fear that we'd get off the ship and not be able to find you.'

'I've been here since yesterday,' he reminded with a chuckle.

'Walk,' Laurie said determinedly, squirming in Paul's arms. 'Wanna walk.'

'Tell me again,' he coaxed. 'Who am I?'

'My Daddy.' Her smile was angelic. 'My Daddy!'

'That's my baby,' Paul crooned and deposited her on her feet.

'Hands,' she ordered, all at once aware of the jostling crowd around them, and held up a hand to Paul and Vera.

'I can't believe we're here.' Joyous tears blurred Vera's vision as they made their way through the festive reunions on every side. 'It's been so long.'

'Dad and Doris are dying to meet you both,' Paul told

her. 'Would you be disappointed if we drove straight up to Eastwood instead of staying here in the city overnight?'

'Whatever you say.' Vera was euphoric. She was here in the United States – with Paul. *It wasn't a dream. It was real.*

'I'll bring you down to New York another time,' he promised. 'Let's go home now.'

Her smile was tremulous as her eyes held his. 'Let's go home.'

Chapter Seven

Paul lifted Laurie into his arms again so they could make better time in reaching the car.

'It's a long haul,' Paul warned Vera apologetically. 'About four hours' driving time. But we'll look for a diner soon and stop off to eat. No rationing, no shortages.' His eyes were teasing. 'Think you can handle fresh eggs, fresh milk, fresh fruit?'

'I'll make an effort.' Vera revelled in Paul's levity.

'You like ice cream, Laurie?' Paul asked gently.

Vera laughed at Laurie's bewildered stare.

'Paul, she's such a little girl. She's never had it.'

'We'll have to fix that.' Paul deposited an exuberant kiss on Laurie's cheek.

They settled themselves in the car – which Paul confided would be theirs as soon as new cars came off the line and his father had received delivery of the one on order. Now Paul drove across town towards the Westside Highway.

'That'll take us northward to the new twin-lane Henry Hudson Parkway,' Paul explained.

On Vera's lap, Laurie stared avidly at the passing landscape.

'I'm out of classes all this week and next,' Paul confided. 'It's the "winter break." The ship docked at the perfect time.'

Vera listened with rapt attention while Paul talked about his classes, about the provisions of the GI Bill to further the education of World War II veterans.

'This will be the best-educated generation in history,'

he predicted, grinning. 'With the government picking up the tab.'

'Papa would have been so impressed,' Vera said. She hesitated. 'Your father won't be upset that we're driving straight up to Eastwood? I mean, he wasn't expecting us until tomorrow.'

'Honey, he can't wait to see you two. But yeah, I should phone him when we stop off at the diner. He'll want to call Doris to be there with him to welcome you. And probably Wayne – that's Doris's husband – will be there, too. If I'd allow it, Dad would have hired a brass band.'

'You said Wayne is from Palestine,' Vera recalled, fighting against a tide of alarm at the prospect of meeting her in-laws. 'He fought with the Haganah.'

'That's right.'

All at once Paul seemed oddly withdrawn, Vera thought. Didn't he like Doris's husband?

'I think you'll be pleased with the house.' Instinct told her Paul was making a point of redirecting their conversation. 'It was built back in 1792 – when the country was just sixteen years old. But it's been enlarged and remodelled several times.' He took one hand from the wheel for a moment to caress one of hers. 'My great-grandfather bought it just before the Civil War. Then there were just two rooms downstairs and two upstairs – with a kitchen connected by a long ell. When Doris and I were little kids – and the house twice the original size, we found a secret panel in a second-floor ceiling. That's when the family discovered the house had been a stop on the Underground Railroad that took Southern slaves to Canada.'

'Tell me about the Civil War,' Vera prodded. She had acquired some knowledge about American history but was eager to know more.

Paul launched into a long monologue about the Civil

War, punctuated at intervals by questions from Vera. He segued into tales of earlier days. It was obvious he enjoyed retelling stories handed down in his family. Vera was mesmerized, too caught up in learning American history to note that they had left New York City behind them and were travelling over the rolling hills of Westchester County, gaunt and bare in midwinter. In contrast, Laurie was intrigued by the passing scenery – chortling at excited moments when she spied a dog or a horse or cow.

'Let's cut off here and look for a diner –' Paul interrupted his history lesson '– before Laurie falls asleep. I'll call Dad from there.'

In the sprawling living room of the charming – almost elegant – two-and-a-half-storey clapboard house that had served the Kahn family since 1859, Joel Kahn waited impatiently for his daughter to respond to his phone call. At 54 he was still a handsome man, his dark hair slightly tinged with grey, his manner quiet and almost courtly.

'Hello,' Doris's voice replied at the other end.

'Doris, I want you and Wayne to come over here.' Pleasurable excitement coloured his voice. 'Paul just called me from the road. He's on his way home from New York with Vera and Laurie. They decided not to stay overnight in the city. I want you to be here to welcome them. He said they should arrive in about two hours.'

'Perhaps I ought to fix dinner for them,' Doris began, her own voice vibrant with anticipation. 'It'll be –'

'No, they were having dinner down below,' Joel told her. 'We'll have cake and coffee ready for them. I'm sure Henrietta left something we can serve.' Henrietta was his long-time housekeeper and familiar with his habit of raiding the kitchen for pre-bedtime coffee and cake.

'It's still unreal to me –' she managed a bewildered laugh. ' – that Paul has a wife and daughter.'

'We'll love them both,' Joel said with a show of conviction. He brushed aside the question that he knew entered the minds of other in-laws of GI brides. *Had Vera married Paul to get to the United States? The golden land.* 'Paul says Vera's very special. And he adores Laurie.' His first grandchild, he thought in a surge of sentiment. He knew that Doris yearned to have a child, but thus far it wasn't happening.

'I'll tear Wayne away from those reports he brought home from the office, and we'll drive right over. See you, Dad.'

Restless – too stimulated to settle down to read, though like Paul he was addicted to reading – Joel headed for the kitchen to make himself a cup of tea. It had been wonderful these last months – having Paul home. He had been proud of Paul's military service during the war years – but God, the nights he couldn't sleep for worrying!

With the same efficiency he used in running the factory, he poured exactly one cup of water into the kettle – to ensure speed. He switched the electric burner on *hi* and reached into an old-fashioned glass candy jar for a tea bag. The candy jar was a bit of whimsy introduced by his wife. All these years later, he still felt Anne's presence in the house – especially tonight. He had never remarried, though there had been women who'd pursued him. It wouldn't have been fair to marry again. His two kids would always take first place in his life.

The water boiled. He poured it over the tea bag, walked with cup and saucer back into the living room. He settled himself in his favourite armchair, glanced about at the eclectic collection of furniture – from comfortable to truly beautiful, acquired by four generations of Kahns. Would Paul's wife want to make changes? he asked himself

68

uneasily. After all, for the next two years it would be her home, too. Until Paul had his degree and was teaching. Once Paul was working, they'd want a house of their own – like Doris and Wayne. He'd see that they got it.

It was strange how Paul always shied away from talk about the war. Wayne was almost compulsive in talking about his own experiences – bloodcurdling years with the Haganah from the time he was fourteen. Then the training by the British to parachute into enemy territory. He'd thought that would be a bond between Paul and Wayne, but Paul had ordered him to say nothing about his intelligence mission. Nor would Paul say any more than he'd already said in his letters about his years with the RAF. He'd come home, Joel comprehended, a confirmed pacifist.

He'd been astonished when Paul enlisted. They never talked about it, but sometimes he was sure Paul was unhappy about the family's involvement in the manufacture of firearms. As though it were somehow slimy. For an unwary moment he felt the sharp pain of recall. Though Paul's memory of his mother's death was clouded, Paul knew how she'd died.

Hell, he wasn't ashamed of the business! The Kahn factory had made a contribution in four wars! As three generations before him had been, he was proud of that. Sometimes he suspected Paul was uncomfortable, too, in the way their finances had escalated. He wasn't the only one who'd made a fortune in the war years, he told himself defensively. Not a colossal fortune like John D. Rockefeller or Henry Ford – but to the average small businessman, he was a huge success. Paul and Doris knew they'd never have to worry about money during their lifetimes.

Joel's face softened. Thank God for Wayne. If he couldn't have his son in the business, at least he had a son-in-law who had great respect for the Kahn Firearms Company, as it had become known in his father's lifetime. Wayne had astonished him by becoming an immediate asset. What he didn't know, he learned quickly – and he was a super salesman. During the war years, this had been an unnecessary talent. In peace time, the competition would be rough again. But that was now Wayne's department, he thought in relief. He himself loathed selling.

The phone rang. Joel put down his cup of tea and went to respond.

'Hello.'

'Dad, is the driveway clear?' Doris asked, faintly breathless. 'There was no snow when Paul went down to meet Vera and the baby.'

'The driveway's clear,' he soothed. 'Remember, I had to get home, too. Cal cleared it, as always.' Cal was their sometime handyman. 'Stop fussing and drive on over. You don't need to walk,' he joshed. 'We don't have to worry about gas rationing anymore.'

'This is a ten o'clock town,' Paul said humorously as they drove through the centre of Eastwood. Few people on the streets, shops closed, only a local tavern showing signs of life.

'It looks so pretty.' Vera gazed out at the one- and two-storey structures, the vintage church on Main Street, a filling station closed for the night – all snow-brushed, along with the ground on which they stood.

'Peaceful,' Paul said, almost with reverence. 'I loved my two years in New York, but I was always glad to come home on the school breaks.'

'How far to the house?' she asked, heart pounding now at the imminent confrontation with Paul's family.

'We make a left at the next corner. It's a mile up the hill. Laurie still asleep?'

'Once she's off, nothing wakes her,' Vera said with tender laughter. 'Nothing except the buzz bombs.'

The moonlight lent an eerie illumination to the snowscape on both sides of the road. There was a quietness that was simultaneously beautiful and ominous. They drove past modest homes set close to the sidewalks; then the houses became far apart, larger and more impressive.

'Here we are.' Paul's voice was electric as he turned off the road into a circular driveway that led up to the brilliantly lit house that sat perhaps a hundred feet ahead. 'There's Doris's car.' He identified an old-model Chevvie that sat at one side. 'She and Wayne must be here.' Again, Vera sensed a hint of dislike in Paul for his brother-in-law.

Before Paul had drawn to a complete stop, Vera saw the front door open. A man and a young woman hurried out despite the icy cold of the night. In moments, Vera and Laurie – angelic though just awakened – were being warmly welcomed, drawn into the comfort of the foyer. The air was electric with the joyous excitement of the occasion. She needn't have worried, Vera told herself in relief and pleasure. Paul's family wanted Laurie and her here.

Vera stood with Paul's arm protectively about her while his father lifted Laurie from her feet and swept her up into the air while she chortled in approval.

'Vera, she's adorable,' Doris said, while Vera admired her tall, slender, dark-haired sister-in-law. So much prettier than the photo Paul had carried in his wallet. 'Dad's so proud of his first grandchild.'

Tears of elation glistened in Vera's eyes as she felt the sincerity of her father-in-law's show of love for Laurie. Paul's family was hers – and Laurie's, too. She felt reborn.

'Wayne's finally off the phone.' Doris's face lit up as a tall young man of about Paul's age – with a burnished tan, sand-coloured hair, and magnetic blue eyes strode down the hall.

Immediately Wayne welcomed Vera with a brotherly kiss, reached to take Laurie from his father-in-law. He would be the focus of attention in any gathering he joined, Vera thought in a corner of her mind. Tall and muscular – in grey slacks and a maroon turtleneck that emphasized his broad shoulders – he exuded an air of good-humoured rebellion. Paul said he'd been a member of the Haganah – the secret Jewish army in Palestine. She could envision him leading a furious counterattack against Arabs intent on a Jewish massacre. Why didn't Paul like him? Probably because he thought no man was good enough for his sister, she thought with indulgent humour.

Exhausted from her hectic day, Laurie began to yawn. Paul pantomimed to Vera to follow him. The room adjoining what was to be their own was now designated 'Laurie's nursery,' he explained. Doris hurried out to the kitchen to put up a bedtime bottle.

'Dad had a door cut through our room to the next one,' Paul indicated, Laurie's head on his shoulder. 'So she'll be practically with us.'

Their bedroom was a large, square room that would be drenched in sunlight in good weather, Vera guessed. The brass-framed bed sat in the centre. The dresser and chest of drawers, the night table, the lounge chair before the marble-faced fireplace were beautiful examples of an earlier period.

'What a beautiful rug!' Vera said, her eyes nostalgic as they rested on the rich, deep-toned Oriental at their feet. Much like the one she remembered from her childhood apartment in Berlin – and which had been sold because food on the table was more important than a fine rug.

Laurie was in her crib, in pyjamas, and already asleep

by the time Doris arrived with the night bottle. Leaving the nursery door open in the rare event that Laurie awoke, Vera went with Paul and Doris to the dining room on the lower floor. Already aromatic aromas were filtering through the house. She smiled, remembering Paul's promise of 'real coffee back home'.

Inevitably – over coffee and warmed cheese Danish – the conversation moved to the late war. Vera saw Paul's air of levity give way to an impatient frown a moment later, banished out of respect for his father and Wayne. He wanted so to put the war years behind him, Vera thought compassionately. She remembered what he'd said in those first hectic weeks together in London, about why he'd re-enlisted after his discharge from the RAF: '*I'm not sure I'm ready to go home yet. Back home, will people understand what we've been through over here? How can they understand? They haven't gone through it.*'

'Wayne was born in this country,' Joel told Vera.

'In Brooklyn,' Wayne filled in, grinning. 'We moved to Palestine when I was six. I was a little kid,' he reminisced while Doris listened, her face rapt. 'I remember when we first moved into the kibbutz. My mother loved it. My father and my sister and I hated it. We felt like celebrating when my mother decided two years later that we should go to live in Tel Aviv.'

'Tel Aviv couldn't have been a picnic, either, in those days,' Joel sympathized. Vera suspected he'd heard this many times.

'Tel Aviv was founded in 1909 with sixty families, but by the time we arrived there must have been 20,000 people there.' Wayne chuckled. 'At first I thought it was noisy and crowded and ungodly hot. Then we realized that parts of town were nice. Rows and rows of little houses, each with a tiny garden. Pepper trees and casuarina lined the streets – paved where we were to live. But there were areas that were a mess – half-finished, haphazardly set up. Not good.'

'But it was more comfortable than living in the kibbutz,' Doris prodded. She was madly in love with Wayne, Vera thought tenderly. Probably many girls were, she guessed and was all at once self-conscious. It wasn't wrong of her to admire Wayne – the way she'd admired American movie stars she and Iris had seen at London cinemas. 'You were glad to be there, weren't you.'

'Oh God, yes! We had our own apartment, our own bathroom – which a lot of apartments even in Tel Aviv didn't have,' he admitted. 'My parents wanted to become American-style capitalists. They opened a tiny shop in Tel Aviv. Even Beth and I helped out. Small as we were, we helped out.' Vera was aware of his intense scrutiny. Was he comparing his life in Palestine to hers in Berlin and Copenhagen? 'I'm glad they believed in their dream of a homeland in Palestine.' Now he was sombre. He turned to Vera. 'My parents and my sister were murdered by Arab terrorists.'

'My parents and my brother were murdered by SS men on *Kristallnacht*,' Vera whispered. For a moment it was as though they were alone in the room – two people sharing memories that the others could only imagine.

'Doris, are there any more of these Danish out in the kitchen?' Paul asked. 'You don't know how often I dreamt about American Danish when I was in Europe.'

Later – despite her exhaustion from the day's activities, the trauma of meeting Paul's family – Vera lay sleepless in Paul's arms, her head on his chest. Paul snored softly, an aura of contentment on his face. She had come home, Vera told herself. She felt reborn – as though nothing but good could ever happen to her again. For now she put aside her painfully learned knowledge that in this life tragedy may lie only seconds away.

Chapter Eight

Vera awoke this first morning in Eastwood with a sense of 'all's right with the world.' Morning sunlight filtered through the drapes, lay a ribbon of gold across the olive-tinted top blanket. Heat rattled in the radiators, lending an aura of comfort. Today, she thought with a flicker of humour, she relished the American habit of overheating houses.

Paul was asleep beside her, his face buried in his pillow. From habit she glanced at the clock on the night table, then remembered there was no need to check on the hour. Paul had no classes this week. The silence from the adjoining nursery told her Laurie, too, was still asleep.

Now she became aware of faint – oddly comforting – sounds on the floor below. That would be Dad, preparing to leave for the factory, she interpreted. She felt a shyness in calling her father-in-law *Dad*, but Paul had told her this was proper. Paul's father was so loving, she thought in a surge of gratitude.

Dad said that Henrietta came in every day at 1:00 PM and stayed until 7:30. She cleaned the house, made the beds, did the grocery shopping, and prepared and served dinner.

'She won't help with Laurie or even baby-sit,' he'd apologized. 'She can be ornery sometimes, but it's tough to get domestic help these days.'

She'd been startled that he could think she'd expect help with Laurie. *In London I took care of Laurie and the apartment and did translations at home.*

Doris had teased her father about not having more help in the house. 'Dad, you're just not comfortable at being rich,' she'd joshed. 'You've worked hard and have been very successful. Why should you have to make your own breakfast and wash breakfast and dinner dishes? You're a big wheel in this town now.'

Hereafter, Vera promised herself, she'd make breakfast each morning for Paul and Dad and herself. Laurie always slept till 8:00. By then Dad would be off to the factory and Paul heading for his first class – once the winter break was over. Dad had insisted – when she'd made a tentative offer to take over some household chores – that Henrietta took care of everything.

'You just worry about looking after Laurie,' he'd said. 'And you'll have to rustle up your own breakfast and lunch and Laurie's.' She'd laughed at his air of apology. 'Anything that isn't there that you'd like, you just tell Henrietta.'

In mid-morning Paul took her and Laurie on a tour of the town. She'd never lived in a small town before. All the buildings were so low, she marvelled. Nothing taller than two storeys. No signs here of war except for a small monument in a tiny park in the centre of town. A memorial to Eastwood residents who had died in the First World War. Paul said another was to be erected in memory of those who'd died in World War II. A marker in front of one of two churches in town indicated it had been founded in 1702. Everything seemed so peaceful. Even during the war it must have been like this.

'Oh, you haven't seen the supermarket,' Paul remembered when they were about to head back for the house. 'It's only been open six months, but people can't imagine how they ever got along without it.'

She was awed by the seemingly endless rows of food on display – such a contrast to London. She allowed

Paul to buy only one box of cookies because Laurie's consumption of sweets was strictly limited.

'I can't believe the way people buy,' she whispered, watching customers wheel shopping carts piled high with groceries to their waiting cars. She remembered the food shortages that were still rampant in Europe.

On Friday evening Doris and Wayne came to the house for dinner. It was the family ritual, Paul explained to Vera. The others gathered in the living room while she took Laurie upstairs and put her to bed. She was nervous that Laurie kept making excuses to keep her in attendance. Henrietta liked to serve at 7:00 PM sharp. By 7:30, she was heading out of the house to her ramshackle car. With Laurie at last making no more demands, Vera hurried downstairs. She smiled, remembering what Dad had said last night: '*The minute those automatic dishwashers they keep talking about come on the market, I'm buying one.*' He had been touched when she insisted she would do the dinner dishes until that time arrived.

Joel and Wayne were heatedly discussing the troubles in Palestine, where Jewish refugees were being denied admittance – and where Arabs were attacking Jewish communities. Paul listened in pain, wishing the other two would change to another subject. For Paul, the fighting was all too fresh.

'Where are the refugees supposed to go?' Wayne demanded. 'After what they've been through – the years in concentration camps – *how can they be turned away*?'

Perhaps Mama and Papa and Ernst had been lucky to have died rather than to have endured the horrors of concentration camps like Auschwitz and Bergen-Belsen.

'I saw what the Nazis did to those they captured!' Wayne's voice was mesmerizing. 'I jumped behind German lines – I saw!'

A pulse hammered at Paul's temple. Why must they

talk so much about the war? Vera fretted. It upset Paul so. Yet she felt herself drawn into Wayne's spell. She could visualize him in action – moving ahead fearlessly, intent on saving lives of Nazi victims.

'I'm puttin' dinner on the table,' Henrietta announced from the doorway in her brusque fashion. 'Eat while it's hot.'

Vera saw Doris's faint sigh of relief at the derailment of talk about the refugees. She suspected Doris worried that, despite his protestations that Eastwood was home now, Wayne might be drawn back into the conflict in Palestine.

Over dinner – as though sensing a need to introduce a lighter mood – Wayne regaled them with stories of his brief time in New York, where he'd lived on the Upper West Side with cousins.

'New York to me was insanity,' he confided ingratiatingly. 'So many people, the noise, that constant feeling of rush, rush, rush.' He chuckled. 'Remember, I was the kid who thought Tel Aviv was big and noisy.'

'You stick with me, Wayne,' Joel encouraged. 'Eastwood is a fine place to live. You learn the business, and one day you'll take over for me. When I retire to sit back and enjoy my grandchildren.' His eyes moved lovingly from Vera to Doris.

After dinner Doris joined Vera in the kitchen to do the dishes.

'Next week Paul's back at school,' Doris reminded. 'I'll give a small luncheon party, and you'll meet some of the girls. During the winter months, we're all inclined to hibernate. I went to school with them, from kindergarten through high school. Only a few of the girls in my class went on to college – and most of them are married now and settled down.' She paused in contemplation. 'Maybe I've changed in the years I was at school in New York.'

Vera recalled Doris had gone to Barnard and – after a year at home – to the Columbia School of Social Work. 'We just seem to have so little in common now.'

'Maybe we're what Paul calls oddballs.' Vera was sombre. 'I remember how it was on the ship coming over. Except that I was married to an ex-serviceman and had a child, I just didn't think like the others I knew on board ship.'

'But we have to try to fit in.' Doris was firm. 'This is our town – where we'll spend the rest of our lives. Maybe once Wayne and I have kids, it'll be different for me. But right now I want to talk about something besides what wax to use on the kitchen floor and who's easier to toilet train – boys or girls.'

'Women did so much during the war years. Not just in Europe – here in the United States, too, Paul said. Why are they satisfied to go back to the way everything was before the war?' Vera probed.

'Not all of them are,' Doris conceded while Vera stacked dishes in the sink. 'The smartest girl in my high school graduating class got married during the war. She couldn't wait for her husband to come home from Italy. Last month she left him – she's filing for a divorce. She spent three years in a responsible government position down in Washington, but he blew his stack when she wanted to open up a business here in town. There're more of us than you think.'

'Have you considered going to work?' Vera asked curiously. She doubted that Paul would be upset if she found some tutoring assignments – though she knew this was improbable here in Eastwood.

'Oh, Wayne would be furious.' Doris grimaced eloquently. 'It would be an affront to his manhood – as though he weren't able to provide for his wife.' She paused. 'I went for a masters in social work because it seemed the thing to do, but I really wanted to be a commercial artist. I don't have a big talent – but enough to make it in the commercial field. But that would mean living in a fair-sized city instead of Eastwood – and Wayne would hate it.'

'Back in London, girls just thought about getting married and having babies as fast as they could,' Vera remembered wryly.

'Damn it, Vera, don't they care what's happening in the world? They never even read a newspaper – or a magazine that deals with something besides "What Can You Do to Help Your Returning Veteran" or "How to Decorate Cupcakes for Halloween."'

'They just want to relax in this wonderful peace,' Vera alibied gently.

Still, there were many in the country who complained loudly – about the way prices were soaring, about the shortage of housing, about the strikes that afflicted the country. But to her, life had never seemed so wonderful. And Paul was happy. He was eager to be teaching. He'd already decided to go to summer school to hasten that time.

But he dreaded all the war talk that erupted when Wayne and his father were together.

As promised, Doris scheduled her luncheon party once Paul's classes resumed.

'You'll bring Laurie,' she told Vera. 'Nobody can get babysitters during school hours.' Doris had explained that – when available – local teenagers baby-sat for twenty-five cents an hour. 'The other girls will bring their kids, too. And don't dress. We'll all be in slacks and sweaters.'

Vera understood that Doris's party was an innovation in Eastwood. On the day of the party she waited with a glow of anticipation for Doris to drive over for Laurie and her. Laurie would be so happy to be with other little ones, she thought tenderly. These first two weeks in Eastwood, Laurie had seen no other children. Their neighbours on either side – each an acre away – were elderly couples. It wasn't like in London, Vera reminded herself, where she took Laurie to the park every day unless the weather was bad. She knew nobody here with children, but that was about to change.

Doris arrived in high spirits, hoisted Laurie into her arms.

'Oh, you're going to have a great time,' she crooned. 'You're going to make some new friends.'

'Let me get her into her snowsuit.' Vera reached for Laurie.

Again, snow threatened. The temperature was on a sharp, downward slide. With Laurie and Vera dressed for the outdoors, the three hurried from the house through the dank cold into the warmth of the car.

'Oh, the heat feels good,' Vera murmured gratefully.

While she drove, Doris explained that there would be four young wives and six little ones at the luncheon.

'I should say six and two-thirds,' Doris said humorously. 'Elaine is going into her seventh month. Two of the husbands work for Dad,' she added with an enigmatic smile.

Doris had shown her the house last week. She loved its spaciousness, its elegant grounds – impressive even in this drab weather. Doris said her father had given her and Wayne the down payment as a wedding present. What had Doris called it? A colonial cape, she remembered. The downstairs was furnished with beautiful antique reproductions, but only one of the four upstairs bedrooms had been furnished. 'But with the way Dad is giving Wayne raises, we should be able to furnish the upstairs real soon.'

'Doggie!' Laurie chirped. 'Doggie!' She leaned forward

in Vera's arms to wave to a wandering Irish setter.

Doris shot a swift glance at her watch as they walked from the car.

'I left the chicken roasting in the oven, and the salad's ready. I picked up dessert at the bakery this morning. The girls won't be here for at least fifteen minutes.'

All four guests arrived almost simultaneously. As Doris had said, everyone was in slacks and sweaters – slightly self-conscious at this unexpected socializing, candid in their curiosity about Doris's house. Vera suspected the others lived in more modest circumstances. None of them seemed intimidating, Vera realized with relief, struggling to absorb the introductions. Two of the girls had babies under a year – and one an infant plus toddler, the fourth a three-year-old plus a toddler who gave her doll to Laurie in an immediate gesture of friendship.

The living room ricocheted with high spirits – the little ones seeming to understand this was a festive occasion. Doris swept a mound of cushions onto the floor as a nesting place for the babies.

'I thought we'd have lunch off trays,' Doris said. 'So we can be comfortable with the kids.'

Everybody seemed to be enjoying the occasion, Vera told herself. She was aware of furtive inspections. She gathered from the candid remark of one of the girls that she was the only war bride in town. But they were friendly, she sensed with relief – no hostility on their part.

'How's Wayne?' the pretty blonde with Betty Grable legs asked at a break in the lively conversation. Her husband, Vera pinpointed, was an inspector at the factory.

'Oh, working like mad,' Doris said.

'Tell your old man to keep them all working hard,' the very pregnant redhead said good-humouredly. 'With another baby coming, Fred needs all the overtime he can get. The way prices keep going up, wow!'

'That is one handsome guy.' The blonde pantomimed her approval. 'If he weren't married to you and I weren't married to Lou, he could park his shoes under my bed anytime.'

Vera tensed. It disturbed her that she, too, felt drawn to Wayne in an unexpected fashion. Nothing had happened in her love for Paul, she told herself defensively. *He was her life.* But sometimes, when Wayne looked at her in that disconcerting way of his, she was conscious of feelings that were unnerving.

The girls talked briefly about their husbands – all of whom had seen active duty. Doris reminded them that Wayne had served under the British.

'He would have enlisted with the American forces after he came back to this country, but with the little vision he has in his right eye after the war injury, they said *no.*'

The conversation quickly settled into discussion of domestic matters. These girls might have grown up with Doris, but they'd moved far apart from her, Vera sensed. Their lives revolved in a tiny circle – around husband, babies, and house. There was a wall between them and Doris, Vera realized.

Vera was relieved when the first of the wives decided it was time to leave.

'David is a hellion if I don't put him down for his nap in time – and his father thinks he's on a starvation diet if I don't have a roast in the oven every night. You know – after all that Spam and army rations.'

'It'll be better once winter is behind us,' Doris consoled Vera when they were alone again. Neither of the toddlers' mothers had suggested getting together for playtime. 'Anyway, by then you'll have your driver's licence.'

'I have my library card now,' Vera said with an effort at lightness. 'Thank God for books.'

*

Early in April, Vera suspected she was pregnant again. Bursting to share this, yet wanting to be sure before she told Paul, she confided first to Doris, who had dropped by for an afternoon visit. The two women sat over coffee in the den while Laurie napped upstairs.

'You mean you haven't told Paul yet?' Doris was intrigued at being the first to know.

'I thought I'd wait another week – I could just be late.' But she was convinced she was pregnant again – and nervous that they were being irresponsible when Paul wasn't yet in a job. Their expenses were low – but so was Paul's allowance under the GI Bill. And he worked so hard, she thought lovingly – that long commute in all kinds of weather and the studying that spilled over into the weekends.

'Paul will be thrilled,' Doris predicted. 'And Dad will be popping the champagne.' She sighed now. 'I don't dare tell him Wayne doesn't want to have kids yet. I wish Wayne weren't always so damn careful.'

'Don't let on to Paul that you know,' Vera cautioned. 'I'll probably tell him tonight. And then we'll tell Dad.' And she'd write Iris, up in Nova Scotia. Iris was expecting in four months.

'We don't have any fancy obstetricians here in town, but Dr Evans – the local GP – is terrific. The hospital is small but decent.'

'Make Wayne change his mind,' Vera urged impulsively, 'so Laurie's brother or sister will have a playmate.'

She was an outsider in this town, Vera forced herself to recognize. Paul laughed and said you had to have lived in Eastwood for forty years before local people figured you belonged. Doris kept saying when the weather really warmed up and people started circulating more, there would be kids for Laurie to play with, she reminded

84

herself – yet instinct warned her that not until *she* was accepted would Laurie have friends.

'I'm running down to New York weekend after next with Wayne.' Doris broke into her introspection. 'He's got some business deal going for Dad, so I figured it was a chance for me to visit with this friend from grad school. She's working for a social service agency down there. We'll drive down Saturday morning. Wayne has a one o'clock luncheon appointment with this man. I'll spend the afternoon with Sally, and we'll meet the two husbands for dinner. Wayne and I will drive back Sunday. I'm hoping to get a chance to see a play while we're there. I'm dying to see the Eugene O'Neill play, but I suspect Wayne will be more interested in a raunchy musical.' Her smile was indulgent.

What Wayne wanted Wayne would get, Vera suspected. Doris adored him. When his name had come up at the luncheon for the girls, they'd all reacted as though he were Clark Gable playing Rhett Butler, she thought self-consciously. But she was coming to dread the Friday-evening dinners at the house. Too often when she and Wayne were apart from the others for a moment or two, he gazed at her in the blatant way of a drunken soldier on leave in London. Wayne shouldn't look at anyone but Doris in that way. Nor should her heart begin to pound at such moments.

Vera revelled in Paul's delight – and his father's – that she was pregnant. But she was upset that Henrietta was showing impatience with Laurie – for no reason, she thought defiantly. Then on the Friday evening before Doris and Wayne were to leave for their New York visit, Henrietta announced while she was serving dinner that she wouldn't be back after tonight.

'I don't like working in a house overrun with kids,' she

said scathingly, her gaze focused on Vera for an instant. 'Mr Kahn, you get somebody else.'

'We love children in this house,' Joel said with deliberate calm, but Vera felt his rage. 'Yes, I think it's best that you leave.' He waited until Henrietta had finished serving, had left the house, and was headed for her car. 'That rotten bitch!' His voice soared in anger. 'I've only kept her on through these years because I figured she needed the job. With her disposition she'd have a rough time keeping one.'

'I can take over,' Vera said with determined confidence. 'I won't be as good a cook as Henrietta, but –'

'We'll hire another housekeeper,' Joel interrupted gently. 'I'll run an ad in the local newspaper and the one in Salem. Don't worry your head about it, Vera.'

'I'll ask around next week,' Doris promised. 'Maybe Betsy will know somebody.' Betsy was Doris's once-a-week cleaning woman.

'Laurie never caused Henrietta any trouble.' Vera was defensive now. 'I don't know why she was so upset.'

'She's a bitter, nasty woman,' Doris said. 'We always tried to close our eyes to that because during the war it was so impossible to get domestic help. They were all running to the war plants – or to the factory,' she teased her father. 'We'll find somebody. Maybe a live-in housekeeper,' she suggested. 'That way, if Paul and Vera want to go out in the evening, they'll have a built-in babysitter.' Joel offered babysitting services, but they all knew how often he was called back to the factory in the course of the evening or was involved with local civic organizations.

'Forget about it for now,' Joel ordered. 'You and Wayne have a great weekend in New York. But before you go, find a babysitter for tomorrow night. I'm taking Vera and Paul out to dinner and to a movie. We'll drive over to Saratoga.'

'Do you think it's all right to leave Laurie with a strange babysitter?' Vera was ambivalent. She'd never left Laurie with a sitter.

'Doris will find somebody who'll be fine,' he reassured her. 'This is Eastwood. We have great kids here.'

'I think it will be fun.' Vera exchanged a warm glance with Paul. This was the American way, she told herself. And she wished so much to be a real American.

Chapter Nine

A red velvet robe over her slip, Doris stood before her closet and debated about what to wear for the trip to New York. The morning was awash with sunlight, with the promise of a balmy spring day. From the bedroom window she saw the golden splash of forsythia that divided their property from their neighbours. Thank God, winter was behind them.

'Doris, you haven't started breakfast?' Wayne emerged from the bathroom – his perennially bronzed, muscular body wrapped in a towel. It was weird, Doris reproached herself, how she could get so aroused just looking at Wayne this way. 'I told you, we have to be on the road by eight.' His voice oozed impatience.

'I'm going right down to the kitchen. By the time you're dressed I'll have breakfast on the table,' she soothed.

'The house is beginning to look like a pigsty.' Scowling, he crossed to the chest of drawers that held his underwear and shirts while Doris gaped at him in shock. The house was immaculate. 'Bring Betsy in another day each week. And if she can't do a decent job, dump her and hire somebody else.'

'All right, Wayne.' Forcing a smile, she hurried from the bedroom, down the hall to the stairs. He didn't mean it, she told herself – about the house looking like a pigsty. He was just over-tired from the job. Even with the war over, he worked late three or four nights a week. It didn't matter that most of the country was back to the 40-hour work-week that went into law back in 1940, she thought with an effort at humour. Still, it unnerved her when Wayne was cranky this way.

By the time Wayne sat down at the breakfast table, Doris was sliding his eggs onto a plate. Toast and coffee were ready and his orange juice squeezed. Wayne was contemptuous of the new frozen orange juice that had just come onto the market.

She served Wayne, poured herself a cup of coffee, and sat down at the table with him, sitting on the edge of her chair.

'I'll just have coffee, then run upstairs and dress,' she placated when she saw his eyes move to the wall clock.

'If this deal goes through today, I'll be in for a big salary raise.' All at once his mood changed – a trait that was sometimes disconcerting. 'We might even be able to afford a housekeeper.'

Doris was startled. They didn't need a housekeeper. Maybe she'd ask Betsy if she could come in a second day during the week.

'Dad's always complained about how he hates selling.' She knew this was Wayne's first selling assignment – one that he had initiated.

'He never had to worry about selling for the past seven years,' Wayne scoffed indulgently. 'Business just poured in. But now the situation is different. We have to go out and push. And I just happen to have some important contacts.' His smile was dazzling. 'Hang out with me, kid, and you'll be rich without Daddy. You'll throw out the muskrat and replace it with mink.' She still occasionally wore the muskrat coat that had been Dad's twenty-first birthday present – mainly because it pleased her father.

'I know you'll do just great.' The earlier hurt vanished. It still amazed her that Wayne had brushed aside all those New York girls who'd chased after him to marry her.

'Move your butt, baby. I want to be in the car in half an hour.'

In twenty minutes Doris was hurrying down the stairs with the valise that held weekend necessities for Wayne and herself. She'd packed the black chiffon nightie that had been part of her trousseau. They'd spend tonight at the Essex House – where they'd spent their brief honeymoon almost two years ago. They'd have breakfast tomorrow in their room – with a view of Central Park, she promised herself in sweet nostalgia.

Wayne had brought out the car, was parked in front of the house.

'Okay, let's get cracking.' He took the valise from her, smacked her on the rump. 'I've got business to conduct.'

Every minute of their stay in the city was scheduled; Doris pinpointed them in her mind as she settled herself in the car. They'd check into the Essex House. Wayne would dash off for his luncheon appointment. She'd phone Sally and arrange to meet her in midtown. Sally was taking a half-day of annual leave. They'd have a long lunch, then grab a taxi up to the Metropolitan to see some exhibit Sally said was sensational. She and Wayne would have dinner with Sally and her husband, then – hopefully – they'd see a Broadway show. Tomorrow Wayne just wanted to lounge in their room, have breakfast sent up from room service, and read the *New York Times*. They'd head back for Eastwood in midafternoon.

'What does Sally's husband do?' Wayne asked.

'He teaches at NYU,' Doris told him. 'This is his second year.'

'Another one of those,' he derided good-humouredly. 'Like Paul. Satisfied to make do with little.'

'He and Sally are doing all right,' Doris said defensively. 'Sally has her social worker job, and Phil teaches. They earn a decent living between them.'

It wouldn't be that easy once Sally got pregnant and had to quit work, Doris acknowledged to herself. Still – despite all the cries about inflation – Sally said they'd manage. She and Phil were both anxious to start a family. *Why was Wayne so against that?* He drew a good salary. They were paying off their mortgage with no problems. Why shouldn't they have a baby?

Doris dozed much of the drive into the city. She awoke as they were heading across town to the Essex House.

'I can't wait to see Sally.' Doris glowed. 'It's been almost a year.'

'I'm meeting a man I haven't seen since 1942 – when I was being trained to parachute behind the German lines. He's come a long way since then.'

'Wayne, is this about selling arms to the Haganah?' Doris asked, simultaneously awed and unnerved by this prospect.

'That's illegal, Doris,' he reminded, an amused glint in his eyes. She'd heard many discussions between her father and Wayne about this ruling – which both abhorred. 'Don't ask questions.'

'Dad knows?' she asked after a moment.

'He knows.' Wayne's smile was enigmatic.

They arrived at the hotel and registered. Doris was exultant that they had been given a room on a high floor overlooking Central Park, where the first indications of spring were on display.

'You unpack for us,' Wayne instructed. 'I'll meet you back here by five.'

'That's going to be a long lunch,' she joshed.

'There's a big order at stake.'

In moments Doris was on the phone with Sally.

'There's a Longchamps right near the hotel. Let's have lunch there,' Sally said ebulliently and gave Doris directions.

In the red, yellow, and gold splendour of the Long-champs close to the Essex House, Doris and Sally talked exuberantly about their lives during the past year.

'I can't believe you're not involved in a job by now,' Sally scolded. 'You were so gung ho about social work at school.'

'There're no jobs in Eastwood,' Doris pointed out. 'Even if there were, Wayne would throw a fit.' She was always candid with Sally. 'I was thinking that maybe I could start a play group for pre-schoolers. Just a part-time deal –'

'Doris, we're living in a whole new world now. Women don't have to sit at home and clean the house and bake cookies.' She bristled at this vision. 'Look what women were doing during the war years! They worked in war plants. They drove trucks and ambulances. Some ferried planes. They served in the military. Now we're supposed to sit back and be second-class citizens? Phil's proud of me for having a career.'

'Wayne was brought up in a different culture.' Doris sought for an alibi. 'He –'

'Bullshit,' Sally interrupted. 'A lot of men don't realize the world's changing.' She sighed. 'A lot of women don't either. They think the war's over, and everything's going back to the way it was. But times are going to have to change. Too many women got a good look at the world outside the home, and they want to be part of it.'

'It'll take a long time,' Doris said wryly.

'Maybe. But we have to work at it.' Sally exuded determination.

'What about your job?' Doris asked. 'You're happy with it?'

'Happy and frustrated at the same time,' Sally conceded. 'Part of the time I feel as though I'm doing something useful. And then I run into a situation where I feel so damn helpless. Like the case that came in just this morning. She's a widow with a little girl just under two. Her husband was killed in service so she has his $10,000 GI insurance. Sure, she's got money to live on for a while. But she'd like to find a job so she can hold on to most of it – to make sure her little girl goes to college.' Sally's voice was rich with compassion. 'The only jobs she's ever held were doing housework – she says she wants better than that for Adele.'

'She's a good mother,' Doris said gently.

'But she can't go out to work because she has nowhere to leave her kid. Her mother has a full-time job. She came to us in the hopes that we might have some day-care programme. I explained that our waiting list was a mile long. It's so sad not to be able to help.'

Doris's mind clicked into action. 'Would she leave the city for a job? A sleep-in job?'

'Honey, I'm sure Fiona would love it. But what about Adele?'

'My sister-in-law has a little girl about the same age. Vera would adore having a playmate for Laurie. Part of the time Vera could watch both kids – and other times, Fiona. It could work out well for both of them. And Dad needs a housekeeper.'

Sally hesitated. 'Fiona is coloured –'

'What difference does that make? Does she have experience as a housekeeper?'

'Fiona's worked since she was fourteen. She earned her high school diploma at night school. She can clean, do laundry, and she's a good cook. And what she doesn't know, she's sharp enough to learn fast.'

'I'll call Dad tonight and talk to him.' This would be good for Dad, for Vera and Laurie – and for Fiona and her little girl. 'The house has gone through several additions through the years. There's a large room off the kitchen that used to be a playroom for Paul and me when we were little. Dad even put in a bathroom for us so we could shower there after we'd gone swimming in the summer. Fiona could have her own apartment.'

Both in high spirits after this plotting, they finished lunch, headed for the Metropolitan Museum for an afternoon of pleasurable browsing. At shortly before five, Doris returned to the Essex House. Wayne wasn't there yet. He'd be pleased that Sally had managed to acquire good seats for 'Annie Get Your Gun', she told herself. Everybody said Ethel Merman was marvellous.

She changed from the grey-wool slacks and matching sweater she'd worn into the city to the simply cut black-velvet cocktail dress that she'd bought at Lord & Taylor three years ago but seldom had occasion to wear. She'd brought along the double strand of good pearls that had been her mother's. She placed them about her throat – remembering with sweet nostalgia how as a little girl she'd been allowed to play 'dress-up' with them.

She glanced up with a welcoming smile at the sound of a key in the door. Wayne strode into the room. His face radiated triumph.

'The meeting went well,' she said in relief.

'Great,' he conceded. 'Your old man ought to be thrilled.'

'We should be leaving in about thirty minutes. Sally got tickets for "Annie Get Your Gun." We'll have an early dinner at Toots Shor's. Nice, hunh?'

'It beats hamburgers at the West End Bar,' Wayne said, then frowned as his eyes focused on her dress. 'Don't you have something a little more exciting than that? Black is for old ladies.'

'It's supposed to be very smart.' Crestfallen, she inspected her reflection in the mirror above the dresser.

'And those pearls,' he derided. 'They look like something from Woolworth's.' *Mom's pearls*? 'Oh well, I don't suppose you brought anything else?'

'No. I thought this was fine.' Her earlier exuberance evaporated. *Was* black for old ladies? Did Mom's pearls need a cleaning?

Her pleasure in the evening's festivities was shaky. Sally loved this dress. She remembered it, and the pearls. When they were back home, she'd drive over to Albany and buy a cocktail dress that didn't look so matronly, she promised herself. She'd take Vera with her. Vera had wonderful taste.

On Sunday evening Paul went directly upstairs after dinner to focus on studying. Vera remained in the living room with Joel to listen to the radio for a while, then joined Paul in their bedroom. Ever conscious of her own lack of a college education – so important to her university-professor father – Vera was making an effort to read everything assigned to Paul in his English Lit course. Now she curled up in the slipper chair beneath a well-placed reading lamp and concentrated on *The Great Gatsby*.

Caught up in the novel, Vera started at the sound of Joel's voice calling from down below.

'Vera, phone call for you,' he yelled from downstairs. 'It's Doris.'

'I'll get it, Dad.' She darted across to the bedroom extension, picked it up. She kept her voice low so as not to distract Paul. 'Hi, Doris, how was New York?'

'Did Dad tell you?' Doris effervesced.

'Tell me what?'

'That, if you approve, he's hiring this woman down in New York to come up as his live-in housekeeper. She has a little girl about Laurie's age, so it'll mean you'll probably be stuck with watching her some time during the course of the day – but I figured she would be a playmate for Laurie.'

'Of course I agree.' How wonderful for Laurie to have another little girl in the house! 'But tell me about it.'

Vera listened avidly to Doris's report, then left the phone to hurry downstairs to discuss this with Joel. She'd been so worried about Laurie's lack of playmates. Ten minutes later, he was on the phone with Doris. The job was Fiona Garrett's. He dismissed the thought of having her come up for an initial interview.

'If your friend Sally recommends her, I'm sure she'll be fine.'

Two days later Doris and Vera, along with Laurie, were at the tiny railroad station – flanked by beds of daffodils – to meet Fiona's train.

'The only thing that worries me a little,' Doris confessed while they waited for the New York train to arrive, 'is that they'll be the only coloured family in this town.'

'There're only three Jewish families in town,' Vera reminded her. 'That hasn't bothered you.'

Doris hesitated. 'There were occasional incidents,' she confessed. 'When I was in third grade and this punk kid yelled *Christ-killer* at me. Dad said it was just that he was ignorant and brought up badly.' She shrugged this away. 'The only time I was ever seriously conscious of any difference between me and the other kids when I was growing up was on Rosh Hashanah and Yom Kippur, when Paul and I stayed out of school and Dad went to Albany for synagogue services.' Unexpectedly she chuckled. 'Wow, was New York an eye-opener for me. There the entire public school system closed down for the High Holidays!'

Then the train was chugging into the station. Vera and Doris waited expectantly. Laurie was enthralled with a friendly calico cat that had appeared.

'Nice kitty. Nice kitty,' she crooned, patting the sleek fur.

Two men stepped down from the train. Then a slender coloured woman in her late twenties appeared. She glanced about, seeming faintly apprehensive, Vera thought in instant sympathy. She deposited her large valise on the ground and reached up for the toddler being handed to her by the conductor.

Doris moved forward with a welcoming smile.

'Fiona?' she asked and the woman nodded shyly. 'I'm Doris Solomon. My father asked me and my sister-in-law to meet you. The car's right over there.'

'Thank you.' Fiona bent to retrieve her valise.

'Let me take Adele,' Doris said, holding out her arms to the dubious little girl.

'Laurie, this is Adele,' Vera said, her smile indicating this was a special event. 'You're going to have a playmate.'

Now the two little girls exchanged warm smiles.

'Did you see the kitty?' Laurie asked ebulliently. 'Look!'

It was going to be fine, Vera told herself. Dad would have a full-time housekeeper, and Laurie would have a friend. She brushed aside incipient anxiety about Fiona's loneliness in a town where there was no other coloured family. That, too, would change, she reassured herself. Paul said towns like Eastwood would surely become integrated. 'It's part of the changing climate of the country.'

Chapter Ten

Vera was grateful for the presence of Fiona and Adele in the Kahn household. Fiona gentle and efficient, Adele a warm, affectionate playmate for Laurie. Only with their arrival did she admit to the depth of her loneliness in Eastwood – though she had denied this when Paul questioned her.

Both Paul and his father were absent from early morning until early evening. Two or three afternoons a week, Doris popped in for a brief visit. On Friday evenings Doris and Wayne came over for dinner. Weekends were a major study time for Paul. At rare intervals his father cajoled Paul into taking her out to the new drive-in movie outside of town. In pyjamas and with a light blanket tucked around her, Laurie slept blissfully on the back seat – oblivious to the film's soundtrack and the rush to the refreshment stands at the designated break. This was the extent of her socializing.

Before Fiona and Adele arrived, Doris had ordered a playpen, crib, and high chair from Sears for Adele. Together Vera and Fiona worked out a comfortable schedule. It was an arrangement devised in heaven, Vera declared. She insisted on preparing breakfast for the family – allowing Fiona time to deal with Adele's waking-up period. After breakfast, Vera settled the two little girls on the living room floor or in the playpen Joel had set up in the den for Laurie. The lower floor ricocheted with their high spirits. Vera contrived to watch Laurie and Adele and to read at the same time. Within weeks, it seemed to her that Fiona and Adele had always been there.

Vera's pregnancy was proceeding comfortably. Joel talked with enthusiasm about the 'little Hanukkah present' Vera and Paul were giving him. Vera was touched, too, by Doris's solicitude for her, sensing a fresh sense of anticipation in her sister-in-law. She waited for word from Doris that she, too, was expecting. It was a time of an exploding birth rate. The world was replenishing itself from the devastating losses during the war years. It was such a happy time, Vera thought in approval.

The one sombre note intruding on this was the period on each Friday evening when Wayne sounded forth with such rage about the happenings in Palestine – a rage that Joel, too, expressed. In June, the British government had rejected a plea by Palestinian Jews for the issuance of 100,000 immigration certificates – for which President Truman had given his approval. When this was denied, the Resistance Movement blew up bridges linking Palestine with neighbouring Arab states. On June 29 – Black Saturday – the British hit back, arresting members of the Jewish Agency, sent soldiers into dozens of Jewish settlements, arresting many. The Haganah was forced into hiding.

'The Haganah is not a terrorist organization,' Wayne explained while the family lingered at a Friday-evening dinner table, enjoying Fiona's superb pecan pie and robust coffee. As always in Wayne's presence, Vera felt uneasy. Didn't the others see the way he looked at her? Didn't they notice that while his kiss in greeting was casual, his hand at her waist was that of a lover? And he *knew* how she reacted to his silent overtures, she tormented herself. *This was crazy.* 'The Haganah is a self-defence force organized to protect Jewish communities from Arab extremists – and now,' he conceded, 'to help victims of the Holocaust to reach Palestine.'

'You told me that during the war the Haganah worked in close cooperation with the British military,' Doris reminded, her face luminous.

'Oh sure.' Wayne's eyes reflected a bittersweet recall. 'We blew up oil refineries in Tripoli to deprive Nazi planes stationed at Syrian bases of the fuel they needed to fly. We were involved in a stream of special missions for the British.'

'Paul flew with the RAF,' Joel said, though Wayne knew this. 'And then he joined up with the American forces. As if he hadn't seen enough.'

'I got turned down flat by the American army.' Wayne's smile was rueful. 'They didn't want a guy who'd lost most of the vision in his right eye.'

The words of the blonde at Doris's luncheon party darted across her mind: 'If he weren't married to you and I weren't married to Lou, he could park his shoes under my bed anytime.' The American army might turn him down. Many women wouldn't. If she weren't married to Paul and he weren't married to Doris, how would she react?

'Hell, you did enough,' Joel said quickly. 'I'm proud of my two boys.'

In early December, Vera gave birth to a second daughter, Tracy Anne. Paul was jubilant at being with Vera for this second birth – shocking the doctor with his insistence on being with her during the delivery. Tears of happiness blurred Vera's vision as she watched Paul hold his new daughter in his arms with an air of love and wonder at the miracle of life. Joel was so elated at having two grandchildren now that he immediately opened a bank account for each. A month later, Fiona shyly admitted she'd opened a bank account in Adele's name.

'I can't put much in it,' she admitted, 'but it'll grow. And she'll have a chunk of her Daddy's insurance money. I want Adele to be a teacher – like Mr Paul. That's a fine profession.'

Paul rejoiced in the knowledge that he would receive his degree in June. At his father's prodding, he'd applied early in the new year for a position at the local high school.

'Paul, so many women teachers are leaving to have babies,' Joel had pointed out. 'Get your application in there fast. And it won't do any harm that you're a Kahn. This family's done a lot for the town.'

Seven weeks before graduation, Paul received word that he would teach history at Eastwood High School in September. During the summer session he would already be working towards his master's.

'When I complete my master's, my salary goes up,' he told his father and Vera while they waited for Doris and Wayne to arrive for the usual Friday-night dinner. 'We won't have to keep sponging off you, Dad.'

'I can afford to pay for keeping up the house,' Joel said gruffly. He gazed from Paul to Vera. She saw the wistful question in his eyes. 'If you have extra money, throw it into the bank.' He cleared his throat in the way that telegraphed his anxiety. 'There's no rush for you to move into your own house. There's plenty of room here. I know you and Vera must look forward to having your own place –'

Vera exchanged a swift glance with Paul.

'Dad, we'll stay here as long as you want us.' Her voice was deep with love. 'You've been so good to us.'

'Then it's settled.' Joel's face was etched with relief. 'This is *our* home. When I go, the house will be yours. Another generation of Kahns will grow up within these walls. Paul, your mother would be so pleased.'

At a special session of the UN General Assembly, an international committee was appointed to go to Palestine to study the situation there. The British Mandate was scheduled to expire on May 14, 1948. The Higher Arab Committee – under the thumb of the Mufti's men – boycotted the study of the UN Special Committee on Palestine. There were ugly hints that the Arab world was considering armed intervention. Vera tried to convince Doris that Wayne would not walk out on his job with the company – growing in importance – to return to Israel to join up with the Haganah again.

'Vera, I'd die if anything happened to Wayne,' Doris told Vera in soaring alarm. 'Hasn't he been through enough for one man?'

'Wayne loves his job. He won't leave,' Vera said firmly.

'If I were pregnant, maybe he wouldn't want to leave me. *But nothing's happening.* At first, he thought we should wait to start a family – but that's all over. Now we both want to have a baby –'

'Wayne's ambitious,' Vera reminded. 'Dad's giving him more and more authority in the company. He won't run off to Palestine,' she insisted. Yet she remembered his fervour at the Friday-evening dinners. To Wayne this might be a challenge he couldn't resist. 'Oh, Dad's planning a surprise dinner party for the five of us after graduation.' She deliberately diverted the conversation. 'Tell Wayne not to let on to Paul, but keep that evening open.'

On schedule Paul began the summer session at the college. He was taking a full load since he was not to start teaching until September.

'Mom would have been so pleased that I'll be teaching history,' Paul said in tender recall on the evening of his first class. He and Vera sat in the pleasant twilight with the pungent scent of roses and honeysuckle permeating the air. The pesky mosquitos had not yet arrived. Laurie and Tracy were asleep in their room; their grandfather was attending one of endless civic meetings. They heard the faint hum of the radio in Fiona's tiny apartment – kept low so as not to awaken Adele. 'She was such a history buff.'

'She'd be proud of you, Paul.' Vera remembered the circumstances of his mother's death. How she and his father had been telling him about early pioneer days in the West. His father had brought down a pistol kept locked in the cabinet so they could act out a wagon trail scene, where pioneers were being attacked by unfriendly Indians. His father hadn't realized the pistol was loaded. One shot had killed his mother. 'And my father,' Vera continued whimsically, 'would be proud of a son-in-law who is a teacher.'

'Eventually I'll teach at university level,' Paul plotted. 'Maybe someday Laurie and Tracy will teach. We'll be a teaching family. Instead of a gunnery family.' Bitterness crept into his voice. Paul saw only the ugliness of guns, Vera thought unhappily. He didn't understand that guns – military weapons – were essential to holding the peace.

'Aren't the flowers coming up gorgeously?' Vera reached for Paul's hand. 'It was all that rain these past two days.'

'We'll sit out here another ten minutes and enjoy the scents,' he decreed. 'Then it's upstairs for me – time to crack the books.'

On this late July afternoon – with the temperature soaring to record heights – Paul was impatient to be in his car and driving away from steamy Albany. Somehow, the heat always seemed less oppressive in Eastwood. But the sooner he acquired his master's, the sooner his teaching salary would rise. He felt a compulsion to show his father that he could acquire financial stability without being part of the family business.

Finally the school day was over. With a sigh of relief, Paul headed for his car. The long commute in this weather would not be pleasant, he acknowledged – but at the house he'd collapse before a fan and swig down a tall glass of lemonade.

'Hey, Paul!' A student from his last class of the day was charging after him.

Paul turned to face him. 'In this weather you don't run,' he joshed. 'We're breaking records today.'

'Tell me about it.' David Meyerberg was grim. 'I can't get my car to move. You go to Eastwood, don't you?' His eyes were hopeful.

'You need a lift?'

'To Schuylerville,' David explained. 'My car's such a heap I want my own garage man to take care of it. Can you drop me off at Schuylerville?'

'Sure thing. I'll be glad for the company,' Paul told him. 'It's a real *schlep* to Eastwood.'

For a few miles they talked about the school programme, then about the way ex-GIs were flooding the campuses.

'We'll be the best-educated generation in history.' Paul repeated the popular platitude.

'It's costing me,' David said, his smile wry. 'I spent the war years in Palestine. No GI benefits for me. But I wasn't sitting on my butt.' All at once he was defensive. 'I fought with the British. I came back home right after the war because my father was in bad health and my mother needed me.'

'I spent almost three years with the RAF,' Paul acknowledged, startled by David's revelation. 'Then I switched over to American intelligence.' Usually he was reluctant to talk about those days, but he felt a special kinship to another American who had fought for a country other than his own. 'My brother-in-law was in Palestine, too. He put in a lot of time with the Haganah. Was that your deal?'

'We operated under a British commander but in close contact with the Haganah. A lot of us were Haganah members.'

'Wayne joined the Haganah when he was sixteen,' Paul recalled. 'He was born in Brooklyn, but his family moved to Palestine when he was six. He jumped behind the German lines to help bring out refugees. I gather they were working in conjunction with the British.' Paul was assaulted by recall of his own months behind the German lines. Wayne could talk about those times. He couldn't – except with Vera.

'Wayne? You're not talking about Wayne Solomon?'

'That's right.' Paul swung his gaze from the road for an instant. 'Do you know Wayne?' How weird, he thought – to meet somebody in Albany, New York, who might know Wayne from Palestine. 'Were you in the same unit?'

'Not exactly.' David seemed suddenly wary. 'But we had encounters at intervals.' He paused. The atmosphere laden now with unspoken recriminations. 'I was familiar with his activities.'

Paul hesitated. 'I get the feeling that you know more about Wayne than we do.'

'Look, I'm not sure you want to know –' David was uneasy.

'He's married to my sister. He works for my father. I want to know,' Paul insisted.

'God, I feel funny telling you this,' David admitted.

'Tell me.' Paul's hands were tense on the wheel. He'd never liked Wayne, never trusted him – but everybody else thought he was a super-hero.

'I gather Wayne was terrific in his early years with the

Haganah. He had nerves of steel – nothing fazed him. He was chosen to be trained for the parachute jumps. Oh, he did a lot of good behind the German lines – but then he went bad. He was making fantastic personal deals, piling up a bankroll for himself. To hell with the Haganah. He was caught in the act.'

'God, the crap he throws around!' Paul's throat tightened in rage. 'To listen to him, he was the hero of the Haganah.'

'He was lucky not to have been shot as a traitor – but we had more urgent problems at that time.' David was grim. 'The last I heard, he'd managed to slip out of Palestine and had headed for South America.'

'He landed in New York,' Paul picked up. 'He lived with cousins there while he took some courses at Columbia. That's where my sister met him.' But there'd been trouble with his cousins, Doris said. They'd expected him to come into their firm – and he'd left to move to Eastwood. Doris said they weren't on speaking terms now.

'Look, I hope I didn't do wrong in telling you.' David was troubled.

'I'm grateful,' Paul said. 'Now we'll know how to deal.'

Paul said nothing about David Meyerberg's revelation when he first arrived home. He played briefly with Laurie and Adele until both little girls were whisked off to be prepared for bed. He listened to the radio news with his father, discussed Truman's chances of winning the presidential election the following year. Since last November's off-year elections had swept so many Republicans into power, the polls were predicting that the tide had turned in their favour. Congresswoman Clare Boothe Luce had cheerfully declared that 'Truman is a gone goose.'

'Don't write off Truman,' Joel insisted. 'He's done much for a lot of people. He was the first to commission

Negro officers. He's gone to bat for the farmers, vetoed bills that were against labour. He tried to put through a major housing programme plus medical care for the elderly. Come election day, a lot of people will remember.'

Paul was relieved when Fiona came to tell them she was about to serve dinner. His father had a meeting with his veterans' group this evening. He'd have a chance to talk with Vera about Wayne. Later, he'd have to face his father with this.

Normally dinner was a relaxed time of day that he enjoyed. Tonight he was impatient for it to be over. He ate Fiona's delicious meal without tasting. *How could everybody be so fooled by Wayne?*

After dinner – with his father off to his meeting – Paul suggested to Vera that they take a stroll in the approaching dusk. The heat had receded. There was a comforting breeze outdoors.

'Tell Fiona. She'll listen out for the kids.'

Not until they were well away from the house – because he felt an obligation to keep this within the family – did he reveal what David Meyerberg had told him on the drive home.

'You believe Wayne's been lying all along?' Vera was visibly shaken.

'There's no reason for David to have dreamt this up. Dad's going to be so upset. And how are we going to tell Doris?'

'I don't think we can. I doubt that she'd even believe it, Paul. She adores him.'

'We must tell Dad. God knows what he could pull in the business.' Paul sighed. 'It seems wrong not to let Doris know the truth.'

'It would crush her,' Vera warned. 'If she believed it.'

'We'll put it up to Dad,' Paul decided after a moment. 'How can she spend the rest of her life in a lie?'

'She'll hate us for telling her – and she won't believe it.'

They returned to the house. Paul focused on studying. Vera made a show of trying to read, but Paul knew she was distraught about what he'd confided. *Was* David lying? What would be the purpose?

Paul and his father sat on the screen porch, and avidly discussed Jackie Robinson's performance as the first Negro baseball player in the National League. Vera rose from the glider, headed into the house for a pitcher of ice tea.

'I'm glad the Brooklyn Dodgers had the good sense to grab him,' Joel said with satisfaction. Vera recalled Paul's explaining to her that club owners were nervous about offending customers by bringing coloured players onto their teams. When Robinson was hired, the Cardinals had threatened a boycott. 'If I were a betting man, I'd put a bundle on Brooklyn's winning the pennant this year.'

From Paul's taut expression, she knew he was about to report his conversation with David to his father. When she returned with a tray laden with a pitcher and glasses, Paul leapt to his feet to take it from her. The atmosphere crackled with tension. Joel was gaping at Paul as though in shock.

'You believe that idiot?' Joel challenged, his face flushed.

'Why would he lie?' Paul countered.

'Wayne parachuted behind the lines to bring out Nazi victims. He put his life on the line time after time. You know about his war injury – he has almost no vision in his right eye. That man resents Wayne,' Joel scoffed. 'It happens all the time. Wayne's a war hero. He's a damn fine-looking man. That creep probably did nothing more than some pencil-pushing. He ought to be horsewhipped for lying like that! Don't say a word about this to Doris,' he ordered. 'It would break her heart.'

Chapter Eleven

Vera knew that Paul must respect his father's wishes regarding Wayne, but she feared it was creating a barrier between them. She felt disloyal to Paul in agreeing mentally with his father. Now she dreaded the Friday-evening dinners, when Wayne and Joel were inclined to dissect the volatile happenings in Palestine. Tonight, she vowed, she and Doris would focus much of the conversation on the opening of school on Monday morning. Paul was simultaneously excited and nervous about taking on his first classes.

Vera had enjoyed these past days. Paul was out of summer school and free to spend much time with her and the children. Out of his father's hearing, Paul acknowledged that he worried about Wayne's real background.

'Maybe I'm overly suspicious,' he conceded to Vera while they prepared to go downstairs on this Friday evening. Laurie and Tracy were asleep in their room. Tantalizing aromas drifted through the house. The heat wave that had imprisoned the town for days had let up. 'Dad could be right. Anyhow, I'll probably never run into David again. He's moving to Florida with his wife. They both hate the rough winters up here.'

'You don't really know this man,' Vera reminded gently. How could it be true, when Wayne was so obsessed by the volatile situation in Palestine? Doris was terrified that he'd run back to rejoin the Haganah, now illegal and underground. She paused at the sound of a car pulling up downstairs. 'That's Doris and Wayne.'

Despite Vera and Doris's efforts to steer the dinner conversation away from the tensions in Palestine, the five at the table were soon engrossed in the situation. On September 1, the UN Special Committee on Palestine had presented a recommendation that Palestine be divided into a Jewish state and an Arab state, with Jerusalem becoming an international city. Now it must be considered by the General Assembly.

'The Palestinian Arabs won't accept it,' Wayne predicted contemptuously. 'Hell, they could have had their own Arab state back in 1937 – and they turned it down flat. Why should we expect anything different today?'

'If the Jews get their own state – and I pray it happens – then half-a-dozen Arab countries will be poised to pounce.' Joel was pessimistic. 'Who's going to fight for them?'

'The Haganah,' Wayne pinpointed, a pulse hammering at his forehead. 'They're waiting for the day to show what they can do.'

'That can't be until the British Mandate goes off,' Doris reminded. 'You said that won't happen until May 1948. Wayne, let's not worry now.' She was struggling for calm.

Wayne's concern was so very real. How could she and Paul believe what David Meyerberg said? Vera taunted herself.

'Are you anxious about the first day of school?' Joel turned to Paul with a joshing smile.

'I'm a little nervous,' Paul admitted. 'And excited. This is what I want to do with my life.' Vera intercepted his fleeting, defensive glance at Wayne. To his father, he was thinking, teaching was pallid beside being a member of the Haganah.

'Doris, have you talked to the people at the church about setting up a nursery school group there?' Vera intervened.

'I have an appointment tomorrow morning.' Doris glowed. 'It'd be very small at first, of course. And just for three hours each morning.'

'Laurie and Adele would love it,' Vera said enthusiastically.

'Wayne doesn't.' All at once Doris's voice was reproachful. 'He thinks I'm out of my mind.'

'It'll work as long as you're willing to contribute your time.' Wayne was casual. 'But the minute they have to pay a salary, it'll fall apart. And how long will you be able to stay with it?'

There was a silent communication between Doris and Wayne that she and Paul and Dad were not supposed to understand, Vera thought. Wayne was saying that Doris would surely be pregnant soon and not available to run the day nursery. Oh, let it happen, Vera prayed. Doris would be so happy.

She was grateful for Doris's friendship, Vera thought, drawing away from the unexpectedly argumentative undertones of the dialogue between Doris and Wayne. More than friendship, she amended. Doris was the sister she'd never had. Now that Fiona was in the house, Doris would coax her out on small excursions. The two of them would drive to Cambridge or Greenwich or Schuylerville for lunch. They would drive to Saratoga or even Albany for a 'change of scenery,' as Doris would laughingly describe these outings.

She sensed that Doris's father, too, was aware of some dissension between Doris and Wayne of late. It seeped through in small ways – such as the faint recrimination on Doris's part that Wayne disparaged her efforts to start up the nursery group with one of the local churches. Doris and Wayne were both unhappy that she wasn't pregnant, of course. Once that happened, everything would be all right between them again. Yet Vera was ever conscious that Wayne – without the others being aware of this – was fighting to draw her into a traitorous situation. She was furious at herself for feeling attracted to him. *This was crazy.*

She forced herself back into the conversation. Paul was talking earnestly about the shortcomings in American education.

'I look at these kids, and I know we have to give them more to prepare them for the future. They're the leaders of tomorrow. If we allow ourselves to be caught up in another war, they're the ones who'll die.'

'Somewhere in this world, there'll always be fighting.' Wayne shrugged. 'It's human nature. That's why you're in the right business, Dad,' he joshed. 'There'll always be a need for guns.'

There was much apprehension in the Kahn household in the ensuing weeks as the General Assembly of the UN at Lake Success, New York, debated the Palestine problem. For Vera, Friday-evening dinners were an emotional battlefield. More than the others at the table, she acknowledged, she and Wayne knew the urgency afflicting Palestinian Jews, realized the impact of the decision on Holocaust victims yearning for a safe home. The crisis situation evoked a bond between them that she struggled to destroy.

On a blustery Saturday afternoon in late November – after putting Tracy down for a nap – Vera headed downstairs with Laurie. This was the one weekend in six when Fiona went with Adele to visit her mother in New York. Always on these occasions, Joel insisted on taking Vera and Paul out for Saturday-evening dinner. Cal's wife would come over to sit with Laurie and Tracy.

Arriving in the foyer, Vera was conscious of the excited voices of Paul and his father talking over the sound of the radio.

'Vera!' Joel greeted her with an air of triumph while Paul reached to scoop up Laurie. 'It's happened! The General Assembly voted this afternoon in favour of partition!'

'Oh, that's wonderful!' But to Vera it was a bittersweet victory. If this had happened in 1937 – when it was first proposed – the Jews in Germany would have fled there. *Mama and Papa and Ernst would still be alive*.

'We'll see a lot of trouble,' Paul warned. 'The Arabs are against it. They're talking already about war.'

'Let me call Wayne,' Joel said. 'He may not have heard the news.'

'Why don't you ask him and Doris to come over for dinner,' Vera suggested impulsively. Wayne could tell them what the Jews in Palestine would be up against. 'I can throw something together easily. I'll drive over to the butcher's for a roast and –'

'Great!' Joel beamed. 'This is a time for the family to be together.'

'It took Hitler to make us realize we were Jews,' Paul said with a touch of humour. He smiled at his father's glare of reproach. 'Oh, we knew in the general sense – and in big cities like New York, Jews were more aware of what was happening in Palestine all these years.' He reached for Vera's hand – knowing, she guessed, that her thoughts were with her parents and her brother today. 'I'll drive over with you to the butcher shop. Dad can practise up on his babysitting.'

'I know,' she jibed. 'You don't trust my driving.'

Three hours later, the three men sat at the dinner table while Vera and Doris brought in platters of food.

'Let's face it,' Wayne said bluntly. 'The Jews in Palestine are not entirely satisfied with the partition. But we'll accept it because it's a chance to live in peace. The Palestinian Arabs are going to riot. We *know* that.' Vera saw

Doris tense – she'd caught the 'we' that Wayne unconsciously used. 'Again, the Arabs have a chance to proclaim their own state and they're rejecting it. So what will happen? The other Arab countries will move in to grab as much of Palestine as they can manage.'

'What will happen to the Palestinian Arabs?' Vera asked.

'Those who've lived in what is to be the Jewish state will run,' he predicted. 'Oh, some will stay – the intelligent, thinking ones who're not eaten up by hatred. Most will run. They could have their own state,' he reminded. 'But they'll get lost now in the other Arabs' grab for land. We're not prepared for war, but we can be sure it's coming. The whole Arab League will be out for Jewish blood.'

It was a disquieting evening, yet Wayne spoke about the fighting spirit of the Palestinian Jews with an eloquence that was magnetic.

'They'll need money,' Joel said at last with fatalistic calm. 'And where better to look for it than from American Jews? If the homeland is to be established, it must be now.'

As usual on Monday morning, Wayne arrived at the factory a few moments past eight – emulating his father-in-law. But this morning he didn't settle himself at his desk to focus on the day's long-distance calls to be made. He went straight to Joel's office.

'Dad, let's talk,' he said, pausing at the entrance. A confident, determined figure in what was his daily uniform – expensive flannel slacks and one of the array of turtlenecks that Doris ordered for him regularly from Brooks Brothers in New York. Attire that established him as a rebel.

'Problems?' Joel glanced up in welcome.

'I see some tremendous business out there if we handle ourselves right.' He walked to a chair across from Joel's oversized desk, sat down. 'It's off beat,' he admitted, 'but it'll earn us a bundle and do a lot of good for the right people. I want to reach out to my contacts with the Haganah.' He chuckled. 'I'll run up a hell of a phone bill.'

'Sell them guns?' Joel was startled. 'Wayne, that's illegal.'

'We won't sell to the Haganah,' Wayne pinpointed. 'We'll find some small principality that we'll sell to. It's not our concern if they resell to somebody else. It won't happen right away. Lots of money will have to be raised before they can buy. You wouldn't believe how little they have! A few thousand rifles, some hand guns, machine guns. They have no tanks, no cannons. Against the heavy arms of the Arab nations. But we can help,' he pursued earnestly. 'We can put guns in the hands of the 45,000 men, women, and teenagers who make up the Haganah. Not right away,' he soothed. 'But it's time to lay the groundwork.'

'Wayne, it's illegal,' Joel repeated.

'It's illegal for Arabs to riot and kill Jews,' Wayne shot back. 'Riots are breaking out all over Palestine today. Jews are being killed for no reason other than that they're Jews. It's Hitler all over again!'

'I've never done anything against the law,' Joel stalled, but Wayne knew he was emotionally involved in the situation in Palestine.

'It was illegal for the American colonists to fight the British – but it was necessary. It's *necessary* for the Jews in Palestine to be armed. Egypt, Syria, Iraq, Saudi Arabia, Lebanon, Transjordan – they'll all be on the attack. We'll only be one supplier – but every one will count.'

'It's dangerous.' Joel was ambivalent.

'We'll be in the clear,' Wayne insisted, leaning forward zealously. 'I know how to handle this deal. Let me start laying the groundwork now.' His mind was rushing ahead. 'The British Mandate will be up on May 14, 1948. They'll withdraw. The Jewish state will be born. Between now and May 14, the Jewish defences have to be set up. We can be sure fundraising – in amounts you won't believe – is already in progress. I'll arrange meetings in London – say, sometime in March.'

'Will you be safe?' Joel was anxious. Wayne felt a rush of relief. The old boy was on his side now.

'Doris and I will fly to London for a second honeymoon,' he improvised. 'We'll go to Switzerland for another three days. Nobody will know that I'm conducting business.'

'I don't want anything to happen to you and Doris.' Joel was torn between the need to help, the realization that this was not a strictly legal transaction, and fear for the safety of Doris and Wayne.

'We're a young couple deprived of a honeymoon because of the war,' he said with deliberate calm. 'The business is doing well. You're giving us this as a belated wedding present. It'll work,' he said with conviction. 'No problems.'

Not until early in the new year – with Golda Meir on a frenzied fundraising tour in the United States and Palestinian Jews under violent attack by Palestinian Arabs and neighbouring Arab cohorts – did Wayne begin his campaign. Doris was enthralled when he announced her father was giving them a 'second honeymoon' in London in the spring. Guiltily she agreed that her nursery group could be postponed until the fall.

'And we'll pop over to Switzerland for three days – since everything is so close by plane,' Wayne told her. He exuded anticipation.

'We're going to fly to London?' She was simultaneously fascinated and alarmed at the prospect.

'Sweetheart, it's the only way to travel now,' he soothed. 'I'll make all the arrangements for transportation and hotels. You go for your passport. Oh, you'll want some new clothes. Drive down to New York for a day to shop. Take Vera with you,' he ordered. 'She has perfect taste. Let her choose.'

Later in January, Joel asked Vera if she would come into the office for an afternoon to serve as translator for correspondence Wayne was sending to Europe.

'Wayne is a real entrepreneur,' he said with pride. 'He sees whole new markets for us.'

'I'd love to help,' Vera said eagerly. 'I can type, too. If you can use me in the office for two or three hours each day, Fiona will look after the children.' This was a welcome adventure.

'You mean, come in on a regular basis?' Joel was startled by her offer.

'I have so much free time, Dad. I like to be busy.'

'Then Wayne will have a part-time, multi-lingual secretary,' Joel gloated. 'He will give you the letters in English. You can translate them into either French or German – whatever Wayne needs – then type them up for us. You'll go on salary,' he insisted and shook his head when she began to protest. 'You work, you're paid. I won't have it any other way.'

Now, each afternoon, Vera went into the factory. She looked forward to these brief excursions. A tiny office was assigned to her. Wayne gave her only two or three letters each day, but often revised them several times. It was clear he was serious about this new campaign.

Vera arrived at her usual time this Friday afternoon – the end of her second week on the job. Wayne was waiting in her office with two handwritten letters – already in the process of being revised.

'Hi,' he greeted her exuberantly. 'I want these two to go out today. No more revisions,' he promised with a chuckle while she slid out of her coat and hung it away. 'This may seem like chasing rainbows, but even one sale sets us up in a whole new arena.'

'I understand that,' Vera said softly.

'Oh, I have a special assignment for you today. I want you to write for reservations for Doris and me at a hotel in Geneva. Here's the address. The Geneva Intercontinental. Ask for a suite with a beautiful view. That's all part of the scene,' Wayne pursued. 'I must make people over there believe that Kahn is an important firm.' He leaned over her shoulder while she slid a letterhead into the typewriter, turned to read the first sales letter.

She was conscious of his hot breath on the back of her neck, the closeness of his firm, muscular body. Today, the door to the office was closed because he had said the noise from the factory floor was destroying his concentration. She was aware, too, that their father-in-law was in Albany on business.

'Wait,' Wayne ordered peremptorily. 'I want to change the second paragraph.' He reached to take the letter with one hand while the other fastened itself at her shoulder. A moment later it slid from her shoulder, under her arm, and to her breast.

'Wayne –' She stiffened in shock. 'Don't do that.'

'Why not?' he challenged, his mouth at her ear now. 'We've been fighting this since you arrived in Eastwood.'

'No!' She reached to remove his hand. Her heart was pounding. 'Wayne, stop it.'

'We were born to be together,' he said urgently and swung about to draw her to her feet. 'I dare you to deny that!'

'We can't do this,' she protested while he nuzzled against her. *What kind of magic did he hold over her?* 'It's wrong.'

'Who's to know?' he challenged, exuding triumph. 'We'll be discreet. Nobody will be hurt, but we'll grab a chunk of heaven for ourselves.'

'No,' she rejected, struggling to draw away. Assaulted by reproachful images of Paul and the children. Of Doris. 'I'm serious, Wayne,' she warned. 'You let me go or I'll scream.' Her eyes dared him to defy her. Wayne was too ambitious to gamble on losing this way of life. He wouldn't take a chance on her creating an ugly scene.

'I thought you were a ball of fire,' he taunted in rage. 'You're a scared little girl.' He bent to retrieve the letter that had fallen to the floor. 'Translate this and get it out airmail to Geneva.'

Vera sat immobile as Wayne stalked out of the office. She'd face no more such encounters with him, she calmed herself. But she didn't want to lose this small job with the company. Not even to Paul would she admit that she was increasingly restless in the pattern of her life. She needed these hours away from the house to use what skills she had to offer. If the company's foreign sales grew, she could move into a full-time job. It was a stimulating prospect. But she must be careful not to allow Wayne to interfere with that.

In the cosy dark warmth of their bedroom, Vera lay awake beside Paul, who was already half-asleep. This afternoon's confrontation with Wayne had left her shaken. It wasn't love that she felt for Wayne. What was the American word for it? She searched her brain, pulled out a sentence she had read in a woman's magazine. She was infatuated with him. *It had nothing to do with love.*

She moved closer to Paul, tossed a slender leg across

his, burrowed her face in the crook of his neck with a need to reassure herself that all was well in her marriage. Iris used to say that American men were faithful to their women – European men considered it their right to play on the side.

'Vera?' A faint surprised arousal in Paul's sleep-muffled voice.

'Oh, Paul, I love you so much,' she whispered.

'I love you, baby,' he murmured, his arms encircling her. Fully awake now. 'There's a poem by a much-loved British woman poet that begins with "How do I love thee? Let me count the ways." I love you, Vera, in every way a man can love –'

Chapter Twelve

Sitting in a corner of the living room sofa, Vera listened absorbedly while Paul and his father discussed the Soviet takeover of Czechoslovakia – just discussed in sombre detail on a radio forum.

'The world grows more insane every day,' Joel sighed. 'Last month Gandhi – a man of peace – dies at the hands of an assassin. Now Stalin has taken over a small, defenceless country. What'll he grab next?'

'Why has the world let the Communists do this?' Vera asked passionately, then paused, her eyes bright with comprehension. 'They're afraid of starting another world war –'

'Something like that,' Paul acknowledged.

'I'm not sure I'm happy that Doris and Wayne are going to London and Geneva in April.' All at once Joel appeared apprehensive.

'Dad, they'll be fine,' Paul soothed. 'We're not on the brink of war again.'

'Tell that to Stalin,' Joel said grimly.

'Doris and I are going into New York Saturday week,' Vera reminded. It was unnerving to think about war again. *No more such talk*. 'To shop for clothes for her trip. You two will be on babysitting duty.'

'We'll survive it.' Paul chuckled.

'Oh, Fiona's going into the city, too,' Vera added.

'Let's live it up, Dad. Call in Cal's wife to stay with the kids while we go out to some fancy place for dinner. Vera and Doris probably won't get home until midnight.'

'Wayne will be on the loose, too,' Joel pointed out. 'We'll bring him along with us.'

Instinctively Vera glanced at Paul. The less he saw of Wayne, the happier he was, she thought ruefully – and was uncomfortable, remembering her ugly encounter with Wayne. He'd made no further physical overtures, yet at intervals she was conscious of his scrutiny. Sometimes mocking, other times amorous. And she was always fearful that others in the family would notice.

This Saturday morning was one of those rare March days when the promise of spring permeated the air, Vera thought with pleasure. Spring was her favourite season. She dressed in the bathroom so as not to awaken Paul. Laurie and Tracy, too, were asleep. They seemed to know, she thought tenderly, that Saturday was Daddy's day to sleep late. Later they'd sit before the television set their grandfather had just bought and watch cartoons. She glanced at her watch. It was a few minutes before seven. Doris would be here soon.

The downstairs quiet was broken only by Adele's effervescent chatter. She and Fiona were driving into New York with them. Fiona would visit her mother in Harlem, then meet them at the 116th Street subway stop at Columbia for the drive home. In a freshly pressed skirt and sweater, beguiling Adele sat at the breakfast table – small legs swinging back and forth in anticipation of a day with her much-loved grandmother.

'I'm just putting up pancakes.' Fiona smiled in high spirits. 'And the coffee's ready. Sit yourself at the table.'

They had just finished breakfast when Doris arrived.

'Fiona, nobody makes coffee like you,' Doris said, dropping into a chair at the table. 'May I have a cup before we leave?'

'You know you can,' Fiona said affectionately and reached for the percolator.

Traffic on the road was light this morning. Earlier than anticipated, Doris was turning off the highway and listening to Fiona's directions. Fiona's mother lived in the Harlem River Houses, the first large-scale Federally funded housing provided for low-income residents of Harlem.

'My mother was real lucky to get into the project,' Fiona said. 'There's room for only 574 families.'

The development was divided into three groups, Fiona explained. Her mother lived in one of the two buildings west of Seventh Avenue – arranged around a large rectangular plaza. The red-brick buildings consisted of four storeys and basement, with glass-enclosed stairshafts. Very simple, but pleasant, Vera decided.

'She's got electric refrigeration and steam heat. And there's a nursery school for working mothers,' Fiona added wistfully. 'But I wasn't allowed to move in with Mama. It would have been too many in that one apartment – her and my two sisters and two brothers and my older brother's wife. Even if I could have got on the list, it'd be five or ten years before I'd be up for an apartment.'

At Fiona's direction, Doris pulled up at the entrance to one of the buildings. Fiona and Adele emerged from the car with smiles of anticipation.

'Be sure to watch the time,' Doris cautioned.

'I know,' Fiona said lightheartedly. 'We'll be at the Columbia subway stop at six o'clock sharp.'

Vera was aware of Doris's odd silence as they drove away from the housing project. She seemed troubled.

'I always had a feeling of guilt the years I was at Barnard, then at Columbia grad school,' she said at last. 'There're maybe a dozen blocks between the campus and

Harlem – but they're worlds apart. I grew up in Eastwood, protected from so much. Even during the Depression years, I don't think I truly knew what it was like outside Eastwood. We read the newspapers and heard the radio – but Paul and I were so coddled by Dad. Then I went away to school – and so did Paul – and our eyes were opened.'

'Fiona's family sound like such good people,' Vera said. 'Her mother's always busy with some church activity.'

'When I was up at Columbia grad school, Sally and I used to go for long walks around Harlem. Once we went with some other students to the Apollo Theatre to see a show. The audiences there were mixed, but the performers and theatre staff were all Negro. And then we discovered the two synagogues for coloured Jews.'

'I didn't know there were coloured Jews.' Vera was astonished.

'The congregation on West 128th Street is mainly Ethiopian. Services are held in English and Hebrew. Oh, these are not the Falashas,' she began and laughed at Vera's bewildered stare. 'A few Falashas – also coloured Jews – live in New York, but they're a different group and don't mix with these. The Falashas claim to be descended from King Solomon and the Queen of Sheba. The Ethiopian Jews at the synagogue here trace their ancestry from Judah and Benjamin. I know,' she joshed. 'You're going to run for books to read up on all this.' Vera's thirst for knowledge was almost an obsession.

'I never knew any coloured people until I met coloured American soldiers in London.' Vera frowned in recall. The British couldn't understand the segregated armies. Paul had told her that after the war the situation was sure to change – and it had. 'I wonder sometimes if Fiona feels as though she's living in exile –'

'She goes to church every Sunday,' Doris reminded. 'I

don't think she socializes with any of the churchgoers, but she's welcomed there.'

'Adele and Laurie start kindergarten next September. I hope the children there don't see Adele as something – exotic. It doesn't mean anything to Laurie that Adele's skin is darker than hers – but I'm uneasy about other children,' Vera confessed.

'They'll see that Adele and Laurie are close friends. It'll be fine,' Doris insisted. 'Let's start our shopping at Altman's,' she effervesced. 'My favourite of all New York stores. And that means we can have lunch first at the Charleston Gardens. I'm famished.'

Vera was caught up in the excitement of Doris and Wayne's trip to Europe. She had briefed Doris on not-to-be-missed points of interest in London. For her, London would always be special. She was anxious to learn first-hand about conditions in London – which were said to be desperate, as in all of Europe.

On April 3, President Truman signed the Foreign Assistance Act of 1948 – already being called the Marshall Plan, for Secretary of State Marshall. Like many Americans, Paul and his father were jubilant.

'It's a wonderful effort on the part of this country,' Paul told Vera with pleasure. 'It'll help Great Britain and Europe get back on their feet. There'll be sufficient food, warm clothes, raw materials to rebuild factories and railroads. It's part of building a peaceful world.'

A few days later, Vera drove Doris and Wayne to the railroad station. From New York, they would fly to London on a TWA Constellation, remain there ten days, then fly to Geneva for another three days. Vera was enthralled at the thought of crossing the Atlantic in a matter of hours. She remembered her nine-day crossing with Laurie on the *Argentina*.

'I wouldn't dare tell Wayne,' Doris confessed as he brought their luggage out of the car, 'but I'm scared to death of flying.'

Doris fell in love with London. Their room at the famous Savoy Hotel was elegant. They dined in only the finest restaurants. Wayne was smug about the dollar exchange, hugely in their favour. They saw the Tower of London, Westminster Abbey, the British Museum, the Changing of the Guard at Buckingham Palace – all the landmarks sought out by tourists. Doris was awed by the magnificent art collections at the National Gallery and at the National Portrait Gallery behind it, though Wayne had little patience for her dalliance there.

At intervals their sightseeing was sidetracked so that Wayne could meet with what he called 'business contacts' that could mean possible orders for the Kahn factory in the future. On three evenings, they went to the theatre.

Because Joel had requested this, Wayne took Doris on a tour of London's East End – the equivalent, Joel had heard, of New York City's Lower East Side. They visited the Great Synagogue at Duke's Place.

The one disconcerting note, Doris admitted, was the feeling she sensed here in London that most Americans were boorish. The British were astounded at a standard of living that allowed so many Americans to travel abroad – too often, noisy Americans with undisciplined children. From a casual conversation with a pair of French tourists, she gathered that many Europeans were balking at the Americanization of their continent. They feared their own culture would be lost to that of America.

At the end of their ten days in London, Doris and Wayne flew to Geneva. On the late-afternoon taxi-ride from the airport, she was impressed by the city's air of immaculateness and serenity. She was delighted with their reservations at the elegant Hotel Richmond.

'Oh, Wayne, look at the view!' She stood awestruck at a window that looked out over dazzling blue Lake Geneva and across the lake to Mont Blanc in the French Alps. 'It makes me wish I had a canvas and paints right here.' For a few wistful moments she was catapulted back to those precious days at the Art Students League.

Wayne chuckled. 'Honey, it takes a master to do justice to something like that.'

'Wayne, not everybody is a master –' Should that relegate them to being only observers? she asked herself in silent defiance.

'Let's unpack and go down for a drink before dinner,' Wayne said. 'It'll be relaxing.'

Over a glass of white wine and later a superb dinner, Doris was conscious of an unfamiliar euphoria. Their coming on this trip was the best thing that could have happened to them, she decided. Wayne was in such a good mood. He'd been working too hard – that was why he'd kept tearing her down the way he had. He hadn't meant to be nasty. And *she* should have been more sympathetic.

As they prepared to retire for the night, Wayne talked ebulliently about the Swiss banking system.

'The Swiss have this terrific respect for money,' Wayne told her. Like himself, she thought involuntarily. 'They have the greatest banking system in the world. You wouldn't believe the amount of Jewish and German money that poured into Switzerland when Hitler started his rampage. And fortunes from royal families who've been thrown out of power.'

'What's so special about Swiss banks?' Doris asked curiously. 'I know they have that reputation –'

'They're the most solid in the world,' Wayne said with

gusto. 'And private. A Swiss bank assigns you an account number. Nobody in the world except you and one director of the bank knows that number – and he can't divulge it to another soul. You bank by number. Your name is never mentioned.'

Doris laughed. 'I don't know enough about business to understand why that's important.'

'You don't have to know.' He reached out to pull her close. 'You're looking beautiful tonight.' He nuzzled his face against hers. 'What's that perfume you're wearing?'

'Chanel No. 5,' she whispered. It had been an anniversary present from him.

'A great perfume but not right for you.' He made it a faint reproach. 'Try something else.'

'All right,' she promised, yearning to please him. 'I'll go shopping tomorrow.'

This would be a night when he was an eager, passionate lover, she told herself, exhilarated by the prospect. It wasn't always like that . . .

Doris awoke in the morning with an instant realization that she was alone in their suite. The slacks and jacket Wayne had dropped across a chair last night were gone. The scent of his after-shave lotion filtered into the bedroom. She pulled herself into a semi-sitting position, reached for the note propped against their travel clock.

'I've gone out for an early business appointment. Have breakfast and go shopping. Everybody will expect us to bring back clocks from Geneva. Use your American Express cheques. I'll be back at the hotel around noon.'

Doris fought down a wave of insecurity. It was ridiculous to feel this way because she would be on her own for a few hours. Many people spoke English here – and her college French was serviceable in a pinch. Not like

Vera's, she conceded – but she could manage to order breakfast, to shop for clocks for gifts back home.

She left the bed and crossed to the window. Lake Geneva lay before her – exquisite and serene. Beyond rose Mont Blanc, its peak wrapped in clouds. Now she noted the telephone book that lay open on the floor. She picked it up, saw the pencilled check mark beside the name of a bank. Why was Wayne going to a bank this morning? They could cash their American Express cheques here at the hotel.

Fiona had prepared a festive dinner to welcome Doris and Wayne home. Vera had decorated the living room and dining room with displays of golden forsythia. Now the family settled in the living room for more of Fiona's superb coffee. Paul was eagerly questioning Doris about London.

'Oh, I went to see the building where you and Vera lived in London,' Doris said conscientiously. 'I said *hello* for both of you.' And Vera glowed.

'Conditions will ease up with the Marshall Plan in effect now,' Paul surmised, and Vera nodded in agreement. 'It's time.'

'The British are so grateful,' Joel picked up. 'I read somewhere that Churchill called it "the most unsordid act in history" and that the London *Economist* wrote that it was "the most straight-forward generous thing that any country has ever done for others." I think most people realize that we're truly one world today.'

'Or should be,' Paul added, all at once sombre.

'How's the teaching?' Doris asked Paul.

'To me it's exciting,' Paul told her, his face brightening. 'I know, it seems mundane to others.' Vera intercepted his subconscious glance at Wayne. *Why must Paul apologize for teaching? It was important.* 'But I see an urgent need for better education in the years ahead. The future of the earth depends on that.' He paused, chuckled. 'Of course, not everybody agrees with my interpretation of how to achieve that. We had a special Parents Night last week. One mother was disturbed that I've set up my classroom in a non-traditional fashion. I like an informal arrangement – with chairs set up around tables. I try for a team effort, with teams competing. She shook her head and said, "Mr Kahn, I think you need a housekeeper here."'

'The kids love Paul,' Vera intervened defensively. She was proud that he was taking night classes towards his master's, would take additional classes during the summer session. 'Next week, he's taking a group to New York by charter bus to see "Kiss Me, Kate".'

'Have you been going into the office while Wayne's been away?' Doris asked. Only Doris knew how she welcomed the opportunity to be involved in activities outside the house. As Doris, too, yearned to be otherwise engaged. Why must women be satisfied being wives and mothers? *Some women wanted that plus more.*

'Dad's letting me take on some of the routine correspondence to relieve Gloria,' Vera told her. Gloria was Joel's longtime secretary. 'I love it.'

'Vera's sharp,' Joel said approvingly. 'She set up form letters that can be used with personalized figures. It saves a lot of work. She may be a kid in years,' he joshed, 'but she sure as hell has an old business head.' Now he glanced about at the others with an air of apology. 'You won't mind if I drag Wayne off to the den for business talk –'

'Did you take a lot of photos?' Vera asked Doris while Joel and Wayne secluded themselves in the den.

'I've got rolls of film to have developed,' Doris effervesced. 'That 35-millimetre camera Dad gave us never stopped working.'

Vera welcomed the arrival of spring. Still, Laurie and

Tracy had no playmate other than Adele. There were no others in their age range in the neighbourhood – but the three were a happy trio. Because of Doris, Vera acknowledged, Laurie had been invited to a birthday party next week. But Adele had not been included. Only to herself would she admit this was because Adele was their housekeeper's daughter – and coloured.

In September, Doris would open her small nursery group. Laurie and Adele would be part of it. And in another year, they'd both be in kindergarten. Their social lives would improve, Vera promised herself.

Because of Paul's role as a teacher, he and Vera were becoming involved in the social circle composed of local teachers. Most, Vera noted quickly, harboured thoughts far more conservative than Paul's. She was aware, too, of the undercurrent of politics that hardly meshed with Paul's own ambitions for the high school. Still, he was doing the work he loved.

In the weeks ahead, the table-talk at the Kahn household zigzagged between the happenings in Israel and in the Soviet Union. This was supposed to be a time of peace, Vera agonized along with Paul. The war was *over*. At the factory, Vera was conscious of the escalation of orders. Joel had scheduled a second shift again – the first since the end of World War II.

On May 14, 1948, the British Mandate in Palestine was lifted. At shortly past 4:00 AM on that afternoon, David Ben-Gurion announced the birth of the state of Israel. It was immediately recognized by the United States and tiny Guatemala. By the morning of May 15, the armies of Lebanon, Iraq, Syria, Transjordan and Egypt – with soldiers from Saudi Arabia fighting beside those of Egypt – had invaded the new state. The Arabs boasted they would crush Israel within ten days. But it soon became apparent that this was not to be.

At a Friday-evening family dinner in early June – after Laurie and Tracy had been put to bed – the three men were in noisy argument about conditions in Israel.

'Enough of this,' Vera interrupted with mock sternness. 'The dining room is becoming a war room in this house.'

'The Arabs won't be satisfied until they wipe Israel off the map,' Wayne shot back. 'Each time the Palestinians are offered their own state, they shriek No! They want all of Palestine to be Arab. They won't be happy as long as one Jew lives in Israel.'

'You said that the Israeli Jews didn't want the Palestinian Arabs to leave,' Vera pinpointed. 'You said Golda Meir pleaded with them to stay. The Haganah urged them not to leave. Why –'

'There was panic,' Wayne interrupted impatiently. 'They ran because they didn't want to appear traitorous to the Arab cause. Not millions left,' he emphasized, 'as the Arabs claimed. A little over a half a million became refugees because of the Arabs' determination to destroy Israel. They could have remained to live side by side with the Israeli Jews. In *peace*.'

'We must never forget that the Arabs invaded Israel.' Joel was grim. 'Nobody can expect Israel not to fight back. It needs help – not an arms embargo.' An embargo imposed even by the United States.

Was she right, Vera asked herself, in suspecting that in a small way the Kahn factory was helping to alleviate Israel's arms shortage? The letters she translated for Wayne were strangely cryptic. Was the company selling guns to Israel through secret channels?

'Everybody ready for dessert?' Fiona's cheery voice punctured the sombre mood about the table. 'I'm bringing in hot deep-dish apple pie and ice cream.'

Chapter Thirteen

A week later – with the Friday-evening dinner to be delayed because Joel and Wayne had a special meeting with clients at the factory – Vera allowed exuberant Laurie and her eager cohort Tracy to postpone bedtime by almost an hour.

'No more stalling,' she told them sternly at last, kissed each good night and headed downstairs to join Doris.

'I'm turning off the TV,' Doris said as Vera strolled into the living room. 'This business with the Soviet Union is too depressing.' Stalin had ordered a halt to rail traffic between Berlin and West Germany, stopped traffic on a highway bridge under the guise of making repairs.

'I'm worrying about all the violence and crime that's creeping into children's programmes.' Vera settled herself in a lounge chair across from Doris. 'I don't let Laurie and Tracy watch unless I'm with them – or Fiona is. I don't want them seeing all that gory junk that's being shown. Of course, there're some awfully good programmes, too.'

'You know what the producers say.' Doris grimaced. ' "The programmes we're producing are no more violent than 'Jack the Giant-Killer'." But when Jackie Owens – all of three and a half – came in with two toy guns, I confiscated them right away. Dad says the number of toy companies making guns has exploded.' She paused. 'Sometimes I wish Dad were making toy guns instead of the real things.'

'I know Paul feels that way,' Vera said gently. Yet if the company were supplying guns to Israel, she could accept that. A tiny little country surrounded by hostile forces should be provided with the means of self-defence.

'I guess it's because of what happened to Mom. It was worse for Paul than for me. He was there.' She sighed. 'I cringe every time Wayne goes out hunting. I know – this is hunting country. The men up here hunt and they fish. But I remember Mom taking Paul and me to a game farm and the way we loved all the animals.'

The sounds in the hall told them Joel and Wayne had arrived.

'I'll tell Fiona she can serve dinner.' Vera rose from her chair. 'And call Paul.' He was in the den – correcting term papers.

Increasingly Vera dreaded these Friday-evening get-togethers. The atmosphere of conviviality seemed fragile, she thought. Everything was supposed to be so right with their world as opposed to what was happening in other areas. Yet there was an undercurrent of desperation when they were together that had nothing to do with the troubles in Israel and the Soviet Union.

Paul could not brush aside the sense that in his father's eyes he was a failure. What had happened to his RAF-hero son that he was content with his present ordinary life? Wayne filled that image now. At unexpected intervals, Doris appeared to be baiting Wayne into a battle, and her father was upset by this. She was ever-uncomfortable in Wayne's presence, Vera conceded – whether at the office or at the house.

At least she'd convinced Wayne she wanted no part of him. He concealed his anger, but she felt his resentment. He could not accept rejection. Thank God, he was unaware of the unsettling feelings he evoked in her at unwary moments – like tonight, when he talked so ferociously about the attacks on Israel. *How could she let herself feel this way?*

On June 24, Stalin imposed a blockade on West Berlin – based on his paranoia about the recovery of Germany. After much debate, the Western Allies voted against retaliation against the Soviet Union. Yet some serious action was required or West Berlin would be isolated. A major airlift to supply food and necessities to the two-and-a-half million people in West Berlin was launched.

'It won't work,' Wayne declared. 'The requirements are too high.'

'It has to work,' Joel reproached him. 'Those people have to be fed.'

Those who worried about the fate of the world watched and applauded the incredible efforts of American, British, and French fliers. Weeks became months and the airlift continued – now called *Operation Vittles*. Even coal was flown into the city to be rationed to its inhabitants. And Vera worried constantly about the Schmidts, who'd saved her from the Nazis. All her efforts to get through to them after the war had been futile. She corresponded three or four times a year with Margrethe and Herbert Munch. They were fine, thank God.

Word filtered back about the activities of a compassionate young lieutenant named Carl Halverson, who was parachuting bags of candy to Berlin youngsters on his route in and out of Tempelhof Airport in the American area – and the idea soon caught on among other fliers. At Christmas they began Operation Santa Claus, dropping thousands of tiny parachutes with toys and candy for the children of West Berlin – everything financed by the crews themselves.

At this same time, the UN was struggling to negotiate an armistice between Israel and the Arab states. Combat had not been continuous in these last months – there had been truces at intervals, which were soon broken. Despite its limited forces – with amazing determination and brilliant strategy – Israel had pushed first one and then another Arab state out of Israeli territory until at this time it was fighting only Egypt.

Vera knew Paul was upset that peace still did not prevail. He worried about the possibility of war in China. The Soviet Union appeared to be a growing threat. Greece was in the midst of civil war. Last year Truman had said, 'I believe that it must be the policy of the United States to support free peoples who are resisting attempted subjugation by armed minorities or outside pressures, and that American assistance should be primarily through economic and financial aid.' Meaning, no armed intervention.

Paul was troubled, too, by the plight of American Negroes – though President Truman was fighting for civil rights. He read William Faulkner's novel *Intruder in the Dust*, which pleaded for more time to bring about integration in the South.

'Doesn't the man understand that changes have to start now?' he said to Vera when she'd finished reading the popular Faulkner novel. 'You know what life would be like for Fiona and Adele if they were living in the South. We have to start making changes now!'

But most Americans, Vera thought, closed their eyes and ears to anything that disturbed their pleasant way of life. *Their* war was over. They were proud of their new houses and new cars – or plotted how to acquire these. They bowled and went to the movies and took endless photos of their little ones with the new Polaroid cameras that had just come out. Paul said they didn't want to know about pain and anguish and death that was outside their small, private worlds.

Would she ever be able to push aside the memory of *Kristallnacht* and live just for the present? Vera asked herself. Not even Paul knew the nightmares that disturbed her sleep at unexpected moments. He didn't know how she awoke cold and trembling, remembering the sounds in the hall on that November night in 1938 in Berlin – when Mama, Papa, and Ernst were dragged away from her forever. Her family. Her precious family.

Wayne flew to England again in February '49. On this second trip he travelled without Doris. It was admittedly a business trip.

'I couldn't go with Wayne this time,' Doris said as she drove with Vera to a Saturday benefit luncheon for the nursery group. 'I mean, I have to be here for the class.' She hesitated. 'I know it's ridiculous, but I hate seeing him go off alone for a whole week. You know how women chase after him. And he's so upset that I don't get pregnant.'

'Doris, why don't you see a doctor?' Vera suggested gently. 'There might be some simple little thing that could change the situation for you.' Wayne always made a fuss over Laurie and Tracy, she remembered – and each time Doris flinched because she felt she was failing him by not giving him a child.

'I'd be afraid of its getting all over town. You know Betty in Dr Evans' office. Dad calls her Eastwood's Walter Winchell.'

'Then go to a doctor down in New York,' Vera urged. 'Ask your friend Sally to recommend someone.'

'I'm scared,' Doris said after a moment. 'If the doctor says I can never have a child, then I'll be afraid that Wayne will leave me. I'd die if he did.'

'It could be his fault,' Vera said bluntly. 'Would you leave him if it were?'

'No.' Doris hesitated. 'All right, I'll talk to Sally.'

Three weeks later, when Wayne and her father were

in Boston for a gun show, Doris drove down to New York – ostensibly to spend the weekend with Sally and to see her seven-month-old son for the first time. Sally had made an appointment for Doris with her obstetrician. Vera waited anxiously for her return from New York.

Early Sunday afternoon Doris called.

'Can you run over for coffee?' Doris asked.

'Sure,' Vera said. 'Paul's playing with the kids.' Sunday was his special time with Laurie and Tracy. 'I'll drive right over.'

Doris was waiting for her in the French provincial living room of which Wayne was so proud.

'Hi.' Vera was breathless with anticipation, her eyes questioning.

'I've made fresh coffee.' Doris's smile seemed forced. 'I'll bring it in.'

'Let's have it in the kitchen.' Vera slipped out of her coat, dropped it on a chair. Don't rush Doris, she cautioned herself. Yet she was suddenly apprehensive.

Vera sat in one of the captain's chairs in the breakfast nook and waited for Doris to bring the percolator to the table.

'How's Sally?' she asked. She and Sally had never met, but Doris spoke often about her Manhattan friend.

'Dying to get back to work. But the baby's adorable.' Doris paused. 'The doctor gave me a thorough checkup. He says there's no reason why I shouldn't get pregnant. He – he suggested that Wayne have a checkup.'

'Will Wayne agree?' Instinct told Vera he would balk.

'I can't tell him.' Doris closed her eyes in anguish for a moment. 'Do you know what that would do to him? To discover it's his fault that I don't get pregnant?'

'Is it better to let him go on waiting for it to happen?' Vera reproached gently. But she knew Doris would say nothing of this to Wayne. 'Doris, you can adopt.'

Doris shook her head in vigorous rejection. 'Wayne would never agree to that. And I can't tell him the truth. If I tell him, I could lose him. I couldn't bear that, Vera. He's my life.'

Vera sighed in frustration. Wayne held Doris in a relentless bondage. That wasn't love – it was something evil. How could *she* have been so drawn to him? Now – at last – she felt free of that insane infatuation. Seeing what he did to Doris – all the sly put-downs – had accomplished this.

At Doris's encouragement – and with Joel's instant approval – Vera gave a small dinner party during the school spring vacation. The guests would consist solely of Paul's fellow teachers. But what began as a party for six mushroomed to twelve – an awesome number to Vera – because she had been fearful of hurt feelings among the uninvited. Now – dressing for the party – she felt the first flurry of nerves. She'd never entertained before.

Savoury aromas drifted through the house. Bless Fiona, Vera thought in gratitude. She'd insisted she would handle everything.

'You just make yourself beautiful for your guests,' Fiona had ordered. An outsider herself, Fiona was conscious of Vera's need to become accepted in Paul's hometown. Iris wrote that in the small town in Canada where she lived with her husband the situation was similar. 'First, I took away a man that belonged to a Canadian girl – and I hadn't lived here for a hundred years.'

'Paul, is this dress all right?' Vera turned to him with a need for reassurance.

'It's great.' His eyes swept over her full-skirted, turquoise silk dress. 'You look so gorgeous I'd insist you get right out of it if we didn't have guests coming.'

'Paul, we didn't forget anybody?' she asked in sudden panic.

'We can't invite everybody.' He reached to pull her close. 'I'm sure Martin Caine wouldn't have accepted if we'd asked him. He's still angry that I was hired when his girlfriend was still on the waiting list. He made cracks about Dad's throwing his weight around.'

'You deserved to be hired. You were a returning veteran.'

'Hey, that's what I love about you,' he joshed. 'You'll always vote for me.' He smacked her lightly on the rump. 'Okay, let's go downstairs and play host and hostess.'

Most of the talk at dinner revolved around the school and local politics. So many people in the country were isolated from what was happening in the world, Vera considered – more concerned with what affected their own lives. After dinner, Vera was astonished when the women gathered on one side of the living room and the men on the other.

The women talked about the latest in household appliances, whether it made sense to buy a television set when there were so few channels – though they were impressed that Truman's inauguration in January had been televised. The men argued about the best new car to buy and what baseball team would win the pennant the coming season. And both sexes were eager to own their own houses. Paul said it was natural in the aftermath of the war years for people to reach out for material things.

Paul was happy, wasn't he? For the moment she could block out the covert tensions between him and Wayne. Paul had a job he loved; he'd soon have his master's, and he adored the kids. He hadn't told his father yet, but he meant to put off going for his PhD for a while. He wanted to continue teaching at the high school level.

'These are formative years, Vera,' he'd said last night.

'And not all students go on to college. Yeah, I know,' he chuckled, reading her mind. 'Never before have so many high school graduates gone on to college – thanks to the GI Bill. But we shouldn't underestimate the value of vocational training. We should have respect for skills that don't require a college degree.'

Paul said that, once he wasn't caught up in the heavy commute to Albany, they'd drive down to New York once every two or three months for a weekend of theatre or ballet or museum-hopping. He was eager to see 'Death of a Salesman' and 'South Pacific'. Though she never admitted it aloud, he sensed she missed some of the advantages of city living. He always laughed and said it was a trade-off. You gave up some pleasures and acquired others. But she'd spent most of her life in exciting cities like Berlin and Copenhagen and London, she reminded herself. There were times when Eastwood seemed a wasteland.

In September, Laurie and Adele entered kindergarten. Each weekday morning, Vera walked the two little girls down to the spot where the school bus picked them up. Both were enthralled at being in kindergarten, were full of talk about what happened each day.

'You were worrying needlessly,' Paul scolded Vera gently at the end of Laurie and Adele's first week of kindergarten classes. 'The other little kids didn't notice that Adele's skin was a little darker than theirs. They haven't learned intolerance yet.'

'In Southern schools they would have noticed.' Vera's smile was rueful. Adele wouldn't have been allowed to attend classes with white children. 'But you're right, of course. Intolerance has to be taught.'

'Changes are coming,' Paul predicted. 'A lot of books about the evils of school segregation in the South are being published. Coloured soldiers who fought in the war want their children to go to school with white kids – and get a decent education.' He paused. 'I want to talk to Mr Kerrigan about setting up some after-school activities. All on a volunteer basis, of course. I'll bet Doris would be glad to contribute one afternoon to an art class. I'd like to work with a group on current events – what's happening in the world today. What do you think, Vera?'

'Paul, it's a wonderful idea!' Vera glowed.

'I may have a battle,' he warned. 'Kerrigan's set in his ways.' He chuckled reminiscently. 'Remember the fight when I wanted to set up my classroom with the cluster of tables? The only reason I got that through was because Dad offered to provide the tables. Kerrigan didn't want to tangle with the town's leading philanthropist.' Vera knew that at intervals the school system benefited from Joel's contributions – 'in memory of Anne Kahn.'

'Go for it, Paul,' Vera urged.

The next three weeks Paul fought to inaugurate a volunteer after-school programme at the high school. When he enlisted the help of the local small paper, Vera knew he'd win despite Kerrigan's opposition. Three dedicated faculty members in addition to himself agreed to serve. Doris was delighted to take on the art class on Wednesday afternoons.

'Mr Kerrigan delicately warned that nudity was not to be a subject,' Paul reported, grinning. 'Doris agreed.'

Every morning after seeing Laurie and Adele off to kindergarten, Vera drove Tracy to Doris's nursery group and often remained to help. The church provided free accommodation. Doris donated her services, and mothers were expected to serve as volunteers. But often the volunteers of the day were caught up in problems at home.

By the approach of the new year, Doris confessed that

she was having serious battles with Wayne about her determination to continue the nursery programme.

'He complains that I'm neglecting the house,' Doris said. 'I'm not. He tells me I'm not getting pregnant because I tire myself out. I tried to talk about our adopting – he screamed at me. Which was about what I'd expected. Most of the time he's so sweet,' she added hastily. 'I can't tell him the truth, Vera. I just can't.'

Vera knew that her father-in-law – like Paul – saw little of the tensions in Doris's marriage. Joel was spending interminable hours each day at the factory. He struggled to schedule the soaring orders that Wayne brought in. And now he was expanding the factory yet again and retooling to supply more sophisticated weaponry – a fact that, she knew, would upset Paul.

By midyear '50, Wayne had become a commuter between the United States and Europe, a fact that puzzled Paul.

'What's all this business Dad's doing in Europe?' he asked Vera on a lazy summer Sunday afternoon when they'd taken Laurie and Tracy on a picnic in the nearby woods. Now both little girls napped on blankets. 'And how did Wayne set it up?'

Vera shrugged. 'Wayne's always boasting about his "contacts."' As his translator and privy to his business correspondence, she continued to harbour suspicions she'd never verbalized.

'Do you think Wayne persuaded Dad to work out some kind of deal to sell guns to Israel?' Paul asked uneasily. Vera tensed. That was her suspicion – that the company was contriving to sell guns to foreign corporations that were reselling to Israel. She'd felt it disloyal to Joel to discuss this even with Paul. 'Vera, that's illegal.'

'I don't know,' Vera said after a moment of debate. She *didn't* know.

'Am I never to get away from instruments of war?' A pulse hammered at Paul's temple. 'Is the world intent on destroying itself? Maybe it was a mistake to come back to Eastwood. Perhaps we should have stayed in New York.'

'Paul, you don't mean that,' she reproached. 'You love the school. And your father would have been so unhappy if you hadn't come home.'

'Would he?' Paul countered. 'He has Wayne now. How can I measure up to that dazzling image?'

Chapter Fourteen

Vera was delighted when Doris invited her and Paul to spend two weeks at the cottage on Cape Cod that Wayne had rented for the month of August. They would go for the last two weeks, when Paul would have finished his stint of summer-school teaching and Wayne would be flying to Europe on a business trip.

'I'd be terribly lonely all by myself in the cottage,' Doris pointed out. 'I need you all there with me.'

'Oh, the girls will love it,' Vera bubbled. 'They've never seen the ocean.' Laurie had, in truth, seen the Atlantic when they'd crossed the ocean on the *Argentina* but had been too young to remember this. And Paul recalled with deep pleasure the times he'd spent with his college buddy at a beach house on Long Island.

'Next summer they'll have their own pool,' Doris reminded. In a burst of pride at his soaring commissions on the job, Wayne had bought an acre plot adjoining their own and was having a swimming pool installed. Now he talked about buying a new foreign car – the first in Eastwood. 'We'll have to teach Laurie and Tracy to swim.'

Vera was touched by Doris's devotion to her only nieces. Doris was resigned to never having children of her own, Vera realized. She'd admitted to one ugly encounter with Wayne when she'd suggested adopting. Now the matter was a closed subject. How tragic, Vera thought. Doris would be a wonderful mother.

Vera and Doris spent two hectic afternoons shopping

in Albany for beachwear. Frugal in memory of the war years, Vera had to be persuaded by Doris and Paul to buy clothes for herself. Doris had studied resort-wear in current issues of *Vogue* and *Harper's Bazaar*, daringly chose a black halter-neck swimsuit with midriff on display but countered this sophistication with the addition of an apricot romper-look suit.

'Black?' Vera protested, gazing at Doris in the halter-neck swimsuit.

'Wayne says today black is so sophisticated,' Doris said. 'I'm sure he'll love it.'

They bought bikini tops, shorts, shirts, slacks, and flat, comfortable beach shoes – aware of the warning that they should wear special all-over makeup to keep them from tanning or burning.

Vera was amused by the seriousness with which Laurie and Tracy tried on their new beachwear. Even at six and four they were very much 'girls,' she told Paul as Laurie and Tracy modelled their new attire for him.

On the first of August, Doris and Wayne left for the Cape. Two weeks later, Vera and Paul and the girls piled into Joel's new Cadillac convertible – which he'd insisted they take for their trip – and headed for Cape Cod. Vera had packed puzzles and other diversions for Laurie and Tracy. She'd gone to the library to research Cape Cod and spouted information to Paul while he drove.

'Did you know it was one of the first sections of this country to be settled?' she effervesced.

'I knew,' he said, grinning. 'But tell me more.'

'It still has houses dating back to the seventeenth century – but that's young to somebody like me,' she joshed. 'Remember when you took me out to St Albans – or was it St Michael's – outside of London and we had tea at a thirteenth-century house?'

Arriving on the Cape – en route to their specific

destination – they were intrigued by the ancient light-houses and windmills, the sand dunes and salt marshes, the stretches of long, sandy beach. Then at last they approached Doris and Wayne's rented cottage – a charming white clapboard, yellow-trimmed, pitch-roofed little house with its own private strip of beach.

Vera was startled to learn – as Doris helped her unpack in the bedroom assigned to her and Paul – that Wayne was not scheduled to leave for another two days.

'He had to change his plans so he could meet with some buyer in New York before his flight to London,' Doris apologized. She was ever-unhappy at the covert hostility between Wayne and Paul and knew Vera and Paul had expected Wayne to have left already for London.

The two women went out on the deck of the beachfront cottage, dropped onto floral-cushioned chaises to watch Paul stroll with Laurie and Tracy to the water's edge – both little girls fascinated by their first glimpse of the ocean, a dazzling blue today. Inside the house, Wayne was involved in a long phone conversation. Why couldn't he have been gone? Vera fretted.

Three hours later – vowing they were not sleepy – Laurie and Tracy were drifting off before Vera had them into their pyjamas. They were exhausted from the long drive, the excitement of the day, she thought tenderly while she pulled a light blanket over each small frame. The night air was cool, the sound of the ocean lapping at the shore a soothing symphony. Vera tiptoed from the room, closed the door behind her.

Doris was bringing food to the dining table. The two men were absorbed in a news programme on television. More unpleasant news about the fighting in Korea, Vera noted. The first US ground troops had landed there the first of last month. Ten days ago, 62,000 reservists had been called up for active duty.

'Turn off the TV and come to the table,' Doris ordered while the programme moved on to the latest antics of Senator Joseph McCarthy. 'I can't bear that man!'

One area in which Paul and Wayne could talk without disagreement was about Senator McCarthy. Both men were too angered by their deep-seated dislike for the senator's politics to notice Doris's grim expression.

'All right, enough of politics tonight,' she intervened after a few minutes. 'Somebody's got to put a stop to that man soon.'

'Not as soon as we'd like,' Paul surmised. 'But what's happening with your nursery school group in the fall?' He knew Doris wanted to enlarge but was encountering financial difficulties.

Doris brightened. 'We're trying to open up a book shop in town, with the profits to go to the nursery school. I was talking to Dad about it last night. I didn't know he owned that little store on the corner of Main that just closed up. He said we can use it rent free.'

'This is not a book-shop town,' Wayne scoffed. 'You'll be wasting your time. You've lived in Eastwood all your life, Doris, and you still don't understand the people.' It seemed such a quiet, staid town, Vera thought, yet she often wondered about life behind the closed doors.

Earlier than she'd anticipated, they all retired for the night. It was the sea air, she thought sleepily, pulling the blanket over herself and Paul. He was already off, she observed with a surge of love and nuzzled close to his warmth. Poor Doris. Wayne was still taking potshots at her. That nasty crack about her black swimsuit – 'Anybody would think you'd just buried me. What possessed you to buy a black suit?'

In the morning Vera came awake slowly. She could hear the waves lapping at the shore. What a beautifully serene sound! Sunlight poured into the bedroom, filling her with a sense of well-being.

She turned on her side, discovered Paul was gone. Now she was conscious of the aroma of fresh coffee brewing in the kitchen. She heard Laurie and Tracy's voices. They were laughing at something Doris had just said. Paul must have gotten them up, she realized, and taken them outdoors so she could sleep. The girls sounded so happy, so delighted with the sight of the long stretch of beach and ocean, she thought with pleasure.

In record time, she showered and dressed, hurried out to the deck. Paul was nowhere to be seen. Doris and Wayne were playing ball on the sand with Laurie and Tracy while a joyous puppy of huge dimensions tried to join in.

'Paul drove to the bakery in town for fresh rolls for breakfast,' Doris called to her. 'We'll eat as soon as he gets back.'

The puppy abandoned his efforts to grab the ball. He was digging vigorously in the sand.

'Damn!' Wayne yelled, holding a hand to his left eye. 'The little bastard flipped sand in my face!'

Doris was instantly solicitous. 'Let's go inside. We have eye drops in the bathroom.'

'Come on, kids,' Vera called to Laurie and Tracy. 'Into the house. We'll have breakfast as soon as Daddy gets back.'

Vera sent Laurie into their bedroom for a puzzle – a favourite diversion – and Tracy trailed behind her. In the bathroom Wayne was cursing the puppy while Doris struggled to provide first aid. Perhaps Wayne ought to go to the hospital emergency room, Vera thought uneasily. He'd had a bad experience with an eye already. She hurried towards the bathroom to suggest this.

'Doris, you idiot!' Wayne yelled, a hand still cupped over his left eye. 'Eye drops aren't going to do it. There, the eye wash on the top shelf,' he said, pointing. 'In the blue bottle. Give that to me.'

Vera froze. Wayne's left eye – his *good* eye – was covered. But he could see the blue bottle of eyewash with his right eye . . . the eye that was supposed to have almost no vision. He'd said that had kept him out of the American army during the war. *He'd lied. Everything that David Meyerberg had told Paul must be true.*

She turned away, headed back for the kitchen. She forced herself to consider the situation with utmost fairness. Was it possible Wayne had known the eyewash was on the top shelf – that he hadn't needed to see it? She doubted that. She'd watch, she told herself with grim determination. Wayne would slip up again. Not until then would she tell Paul. But in her head she was convinced Wayne was a fraud.

With Wayne gone, Vera found the days at the cottage delightful. A teenager from a neighbouring cottage called to offer her services as a babysitter. Laurie and Tracy were enthusiastic about her presence. Vera hired her immediately. Now the three adults were free for sight-seeing around the area. On two evenings they went to the nearby summer theatre.

On the Thursday before the Labor Day weekend, Vera and Paul headed home with the girls. That evening Wayne was scheduled to arrive at the Cape. They left the cottage midmorning, stopped at a roadside diner for lunch. After lunch Laurie and Tracy fell asleep on the back seat of the car. Vera debated with herself, remembering her earlier determination not to tell Paul about the incident with Wayne's eye until she had more substantial information. But her need to share won out. In a rush of words she reported what had happened.

'I've never trusted Wayne since that talk with David,'

Paul admitted. 'But we don't have positive proof. He may have known the eyewash was on the top shelf.'

'I'm sure he saw it, Paul. He's been lying all along! But, yes, we need more proof.' Vera sighed, fighting frustration. 'At least, we're on the alert now. We'll watch.'

'And if we know for sure?' Paul's hand tightened on the wheel. 'What do we tell Doris? That her husband is a fraud? That everything he's told us about his life is probably untrue? She'll never believe it. And you know how Dad feels about him.'

'But Dad isn't blinded with love,' Vera pinpointed. 'If we show him positive proof, he'll believe. David told you Wayne was a step ahead of a charge of treason.'

'Wayne's a winner business-wise.' Paul was troubled. 'Dad's forever boasting about the soaring sales figures at the company – mostly due to Wayne.'

'David said he was thrown out of the Haganah for crooked deals,' Vera shot back. 'How do we know what he's doing to Dad's business?'

'We can't argue with the sales he brings in,' Paul said reluctantly.

'Whom is he selling to?' Vera countered. 'I have this crazy feeling he's selling to Israel.' She saw the glint in Paul's eyes. So, he, too, harboured the same suspicions. 'But would they deal with him, knowing what he is?' At intervals this question haunted her.

'Honey, in Israel's position, they'll buy from anybody who delivers,' Paul surmised. 'I know – it's illegal. And in normal circumstances Dad would be the last person to do anything illegal. But Israel's in a desperate situation. This embargo on arms to them is insane.'

'Then all we can do is watch for proof and build up a case. I worry about Dad's being so deeply involved with somebody whose background is as questionable as Wayne's.'

'I worry about Doris,' Paul said after a moment. 'She's living a life built on lies.'

Vera spent the first few days back in Eastwood in shopping for clothes for Laurie's entrance into first grade – '*Real* school, Mommie!' Fiona accompanied her on two such excursions so that Adele, too, could be properly prepared.

'Fiona's so eager for everything to be right for Adele,' Vera confided affectionately to Paul on a warm evening when they went for a stroll. 'She won't spend on herself, but Adele must have the best she can manage.'

'How's Doris doing with plans for the book shop?' Paul asked.

'She hopes to open by October 1. You're enlisted along with Dad to help with carpentry.'

'Wayne's too busy dreaming up big deals?' Paul drawled.

'Something like that, I gather. You don't mind, do you?' Vera smiled, confident that Paul would be willing to help. 'I promised to work in the shop one afternoon a week.'

'Sure, I'll help. This town needs a book shop – even one that'll be open only afternoons and Saturdays.' He hesitated. 'Ted Mills told me he's having trouble about one of the books he's ordered for his senior English class. The school board told Kerrigan that they want to be sure no Commie authors are included. Censorship hits Eastwood,' he said ruefully, 'but Ted's fighting. The whole damn situation's got out of hand.'

'I remember in Berlin when books written by Jews were burned. I was nine years old, but I understood what a terrible thing it was to burn books.'

'That won't happen here,' Paul said quickly, but Vera knew about the Red-baiting that was infecting the nation and was afraid.

Vera enjoyed Paul's pleasure in setting up his lesson

153

plans for the new term. This was the most impressionable age, he reiterated regularly – when students moved into their teens. But she shared his rage when early in the school year a parent appeared to denounce his bringing his pacifist leanings into his after-school group.

'She lambasted me for being unpatriotic at a time when American boys are being shipped to Korea to fight against Communism,' Paul reported. 'Not that most people seem to realize there's a shooting war going on over there.'

'What are you going to do?' Vera asked.

'I'm not tailoring my group – or my classes – to suit one parent,' Paul told her. 'I think if we're going to have peace in this world, we have to make these kids understand its value. Our civilization is becoming so complex we're going to have to retailor our schools to meet the challenge – but principals like Kerrigan fight change. Anyhow, I haven't had any flak from Kerrigan so far.' But he was worried, Vera suspected.

At the factory, Vera was ever watchful for some move where Wayne would betray himself – and frustrated that this wasn't happening. Doris tried opening the book shop on schedule, but she was running into staffing problems.

'When women offer to help, why do they change their minds two days later?' she wailed. 'All these ego problems that pop up. Linda called up mad as hell because the *Herald* gave Sonia credit for suggesting we give part of the profits for the first month to the library to buy new books. Wayne tells me I'm stupid to think it's ever different. But we can't afford to pay salaries.'

'Paul said he'll give some time on Saturdays,' Vera consoled. 'And once Gloria gets back to the office, I can help.' Joel's secretary was recovering from a broken ankle, and Vera had been drafted for full-time duties at the office until she returned. At intervals she felt guilty that she wasn't there when Laurie and Tracy came home from school and nursery group. But Fiona was wonderful with the children. They loved her.

Everybody thought teaching was such an easy job, Vera mused. Short hours, much vacation time. They forgot about the time for setting up lesson plans, for correcting papers and tests. And Paul was giving after-school time to work with students who were having problems keeping up. Paul said that many people didn't understand the special problems of handling teenage students struggling through the most difficult of all ages. Still, he loved his work. That made it all worthwhile.

Paul was in a job he loved. They loved each other deeply. They both adored the children. Living in the family house and with Fiona taking over much of the household responsibilities, she should be extremely happy, Vera told herself. Why did she so often feel a strange restlessness? As though she ought to be doing more with her life.

In mid-September, Doris ran into complications regarding the projected book shop. Two women who'd pledged financial support withdrew their offer. The husband of one suddenly rejected her participation, and the husband of the other made a counter suggestion. 'My husband says we should open a thrift shop. That way we just collect merchandise without having to pay for it. We won't run up bills.'

Wayne brushed off Doris's hints that he should help the nursery group's effort to raise funds. He was annoyed at her involvement. It was her father who made a substantial donation – 'in memory of your mother.' Now Doris pushed ahead with the opening. In mid-October – only two weeks behind schedule – the small cluster devoted to the nursery triumphantly opened the book shop. The local newspaper – which appeared every Wednesday afternoon

– carried a glowing report of Eastwood's first book shop.

Books became a primary topic of conversation in East-wood three weeks later. A parent descended on the high school principal's office in rage because Ted Mills had included on his senior English class's reading list a title by Theodore Dreiser.

'The man's a Commie!' she shrieked indignantly. 'I read all about it in a newspaper. We don't want our children reading a book by some dirty Red!'

Mr Kerrigan agreed to look into the matter immediately. By nightfall, the word had ricocheted around town – building to the conclusion that Ted Mills himself must be defiled by Communist thinking. Paul was indignant that Kerrigan had approached Ted about the novel.

'The Dreiser book the stupid woman's complaining about is *An American Tragedy*. It's a classic! Dreiser's no Communist. What the hell is going on in this country these days?' he railed. At regular intervals in the past year, one book or another had been banned by a school board or a library. But to see it happen in Eastwood was unnerving to Vera and Paul.

Vera was uneasy when the local paper reported on the incident of the book-banning in the high school without taking a stand one way or the other. With painful frequency, the memory of book-burnings in Berlin jogged across her mind. Another mother explored the shelves of the tiny public library, discovered the Dreiser book – admittedly seldom checked out, and demanded its removal.

'Ted's had to take it off his reading list,' Paul reported to Vera and his father at dinner two nights later. 'It was an order from Kerrigan's office. He could lose his job if he refused. I can't believe we're seeing something like this here in Eastwood!' He grunted in exasperation.

'Can't Ted fight back?' Vera asked.

Paul hesitated. 'We're talking about writing an article under both our names and taking it to the *Eastwood Herald*. He'll be over later to work on it with me.'

'That might be a mistake,' Joel said, visibly disturbed. 'This is a conservative town.'

'This is beyond conservative!' Paul shot back. 'This whole craziness has to be stopped!'

Late that night – both too upset to sleep – Paul and Vera discussed the situation. Paul admitted he wasn't sure that the newspaper would run the article he and Ted had laboured over earlier.

'Why don't we ask Doris to order a dozen titles of the book and show just that in the window of the shop? That'll make a statement.' Vera glowed in anticipation. 'It can be our contribution. We can afford it, can't we?'

'We can afford it,' Paul agreed tenderly, 'and we'll do it. Tell Doris to make it a rush order.'

The following evening – alone with Vera at dinner because it was Joel's night at the Lions Club – Paul reported that the newspaper had refused to run his and Ted's article. 'They complain it's too controversial.'

A week later – because of vigorous efforts on Doris's part – twenty copies of *An American Tragedy* arrived at the bookstore. That evening Doris commandeered Vera and Paul to help change the window display. By the following evening, the whole town was talking about the book shop's window display.

'Doris says she'll have to pull it soon because she's getting too much flak from other members of the nursery group. But she'll hold out as long as she can.'

In midevening Ted Mills arrived at the house.

'You won't believe what's happening,' he chortled when Vera opened the front door. 'Where's Paul?'

'Right here,' Paul called from the entrance to the living room. 'What's up?'

'I just had a phone call from one of my seniors. A half dozen of them are pooling their spending money to go over to the book shop after school tomorrow to buy two copies of *An American Tragedy.*'

'It would be an American tragedy if some of our kids didn't understand what's happening in this country. Ted, as teachers we must be doing something right.'

Minutes later Joel arrived from his Lions Club meeting. Vera went out to the kitchen to prepare coffee for the four of them. When she returned, the men were discussing the jail sentences meted out to The Hollywood Ten and how The Kellogg Company had dropped its sponsorship of Irene Wicker, the 'Singing Lady' – much loved by Laurie and Tracy and millions of other young children. *Red Channels* continued its nefarious name-calling.

'I'm not sure Doris is smart in thumbing her nose at those people who're nervous about that book,' Joel said sombrely.

'Dad, not everybody in town feels that way,' Paul said. 'A few creeps –'

'The display at the book shop was my suggestion,' Vera told her father-in-law. 'How can people in a country like this sanction the name-calling that's going on? People's careers – their lives – are being wrecked by gossip.'

'Vera, you don't understand.' Joel seemed to be searching for words. 'This is a very small town. Sometimes it's wiser to flow with the tide than to try to buck it. This kind of thing won't go on. It'll peter out soon.'

'People have to begin to take a stand.' Paul leaned forward earnestly. 'We have to –'

'Paul, we have to live here! We're part of this town. We don't want to create enemies.' Joel was pale now. He didn't want to lose his place in all his local organizations, Vera thought. He was afraid of becoming an outsider.

'Not everybody feels the way those parents do about

banning the book,' Paul reiterated. 'Some of our high school students are ready to fight it. We have to let them know it's right to fight against what's wrong.'

'The more fuss you make about this, the more important you make it seem,' Joel said impatiently. 'Just let it fade away.'

Vera was shaken. How could something like this be happening in the United States? Not just here in Eastwood, but in towns and cities all over the country. Was there a place in the world that was safe for decent human beings? She'd been frightened in Berlin, in Copenhagen, in London. *It wasn't supposed to be this way in America.*

Chapter Fifteen

Along with Paul, Vera worried that the war in Korea would escalate into World War III. Too often for comfort these evenings, she listened while Paul and his father debated the situation.

'It could be out of control so fast,' Paul argued. 'If Russia or China intervenes, it could become catastrophic.'

Side by side with American troops were soldiers from England, Australia, New Zealand, Thailand, and Turkey. General MacArthur was promising to 'have the boys home by Christmas.' Paul rejected this, refusing to accept his father's conviction that this was a 'tempest in a teapot.' And now there was posturing by Chou En-lai in China. Chou En-lai vowed to drive 'American aggressors' out of Asia and went on to notify the world that the Chinese People's Republic would fight beside the North Koreans if the UN forces crossed the 38th Parallel.

Vera was grateful for Paul's pacifism. If he'd joined the reserve, he could be fighting in yet another war. A pall hung over Hanukkah and Christmas this year. Chinese Communist troops were unofficially fighting on the side of North Korea. No chance now that American troops would be home for Christmas. And casualty figures were appalling.

Paul was concerned, too, that – except for a handful of students – the high school body of Eastwood High seemed disinterested in the fighting in Korea, in any of the problems that racked the world.

'They're more interested in what's new on the jukeboxes and when's the new Doris Day picture coming to town than what's happening in Korea and how do we stop this Joe McCarthy guy.'

By February of the new year, Vera was outraged that people had 'lost interest in the war in Korea.' The newspapers complained that few people bothered to read the news reports.

'Here at home we have a booming economy,' Paul derided. 'Everybody's concerned about making a lot of money, buying a new refrigerator or television or dishwasher. Don't they understand American boys are dying every day in Korea? Is this the way it's going to be forever? *Why can't we learn to live in peace?*'

Vera was astonished when Joel asked her if she'd like to come into the office on a regular basis. Gloria was back; but at the end of each week, he'd asked, '*Are you clear for next week?*'

'You're more than a secretary,' Joel said with candid respect. 'You make a great sounding board for me. You've got a great instinct for business.'

'I'd love to be permanent,' she said instantly.

But once her permanent status was announced, Vera sensed that Wayne was annoyed by this. Was he afraid she'd discover something he didn't want Joel to know? Or was she being paranoid?

She couldn't erase from her mind the encounter at the beach when she'd been convinced Wayne had lied about having no vision in his right eye. And the regular flow of letters she translated into German and French were strangely phrased – almost as though in some secret code. If Paul's friend at school could be trusted – and instinct told her he could – then Wayne had been thrown out of the Haganah for crooked deals. Let her watch to see what she could learn. *If Wayne were cheating Dad, let them know.*

New houses were going up in Eastwood. New shops appeared. New people were taking up residence in town. To the family's astonishment, Wayne invested in a small liquor store.

'It's the way to go. I would have thought by now you'd own half the stores in this town,' he jibed at his father-in-law at a Friday-evening dinner. 'With a little effort, you could be one of the richest men in the state.'

'Wayne, we're doing great at the factory.' Joel chuckled. 'How many Cadillacs can I drive? I don't need a swimming pool – you've got one. I don't need a mansion. Though maybe Vera would like to chuck out the furniture and redo the house.' He shot her another indulgent smile. 'We can afford that right now.'

'I love the house the way it is,' Vera said quietly, loathing Wayne's arrogance. His greed. To many of the girls and women in town he was Eastwood's younger version of Clark Gable, but to her he was an atomic bomb that could explode at any time. Thank God, she could look at Wayne now and see him for what he was.

On a rainy Saturday morning Vera sat reading in her favourite lounge chair in the living room while the three little girls sprawled on the floor and concentrated on the latest puzzles provided by Doris. When the phone rang, she rose to answer.

'I've got it, Fiona,' she called, reaching for the receiver.

The caller was Laurie's classmate, Serena Robinson. Vera knew of the family, though they'd never met. Serena's father was an attorney with an impressive practice in Manchester, Vermont, roughly twenty miles across the state line. Divorced from his wife, he lived in the most luxurious house in Eastwood, with a housekeeper to raise seven-year-old Serena and her four-year-old brother Lance.

'It's for you, Laurie,' Vera said. 'Serena Robinson.'

'For me?' Laurie scrambled to her feet in a flurry of excitement. Phone calls were a rarity in her young life. She darted across the room to take the receiver from her mother. 'Hi, Serena.'

After a few moment's conversation, Laurie put down the phone. 'Mommie, can I go spend the day with Serena at her house?'

'Let me talk to Serena's mother,' Vera stipulated, then rephrased this. 'Let me talk to their housekeeper.'

The housekeeper explained that with the weather expected to be rainy all day she'd offered to let Serena invite a friend over.

'They can watch television and play Serena's records. I'll make them a nice lunch and give them ice cream and cookies in the afternoon,' the housekeeper said good-humouredly. 'And I'll keep an eye on them, of course.'

'Can I go?' Laurie asked eagerly when her mother hung up the phone.

'Oh, I think we can handle that.' Vera was suffused with love. 'Go upstairs and get your raincoat. I'll drive you to the Robinsons.'

All at once Laurie seemed puzzled.

'Mommie, is Adele supposed to come with me?' Adele was in their class, too.

'I don't think so, darling.' Vera contrived a casual air. She suspected that Serena's father – who was considered a blatant snob in local eyes – was not inclined to invite the daughter of a domestic into his home. At school it was accepted that Laurie and Adele were 'best friends,' lived in the same house. But there was a social division that was sure to exclude Adele from occasions where Laurie would be welcomed. How did you explain that to an almost-seven-year-old? 'Adele and Tracy will play together,' she soothed.

'Okay, I'll go get my raincoat.'

On the floor of the Robinsons' spacious living room, Laurie and Serena sat enthralled, listening to a recording of 'Peter and the Wolf,' which included narration along with the music. Serena's little brother listened from the archway that led into the hall, where an electrician laboured to repair a ceiling fixture.

'Let's hear it again,' Serena said when the last words of the narrator and the final strains of the Prokofiev score faded away. She reached to return the needle to the beginning of the LP.

'I gotta go back to the shop for something,' the electrician called to the two little girls. 'You tell Mrs Hall I'll be back in twenty minutes.'

'Sure,' Serena said, 'I'll tell her.'

Lance opened the hall closet door to pull out his latest truck, which Serena said he was allowed to play with in the hall but not in the carpeted living room. Moments later, Mrs Hall looked in on the children.

'Are you ready for chocolate cake and ice cream yet?' she asked, her eyes teasing.

'Yeah!' the three youngsters yelled in unison.

'The man fixing the lights said he'd be back in twenty minutes,' Serena told Mrs Hall. 'He had to go back to his shop for something.'

The two little girls focused again on listening to 'Peter and the Wolf,' though they knew every word of the narration by now. This was the mostest fun she'd ever had, Laurie thought, giddy with the pleasure of Serena's company plus the diversion of 'Peter and the Wolf' and the imminent arrival of chocolate cake and ice cream.

'Lance, what do you think you're doing?' Serena shrieked in sudden outrage. 'Come down from there this minute!' While they'd been listening to the record, Lance had climbed up on the ladder, which he'd pulled to the closet door, and was gingerly descending now. '*What have you got?*'

Lance waited until he was at the bottom rung of the ladder to reply. He swung about with a dazzling grin.

'Let's play cowboys and Indians!' he said exuberantly, holding out a revolver. 'I'll be a cowboy. Bang, bang!'

'You give that to me!' Serena scrambled to her feet and charged towards Lance. 'You know Daddy said we're never, never supposed to go in that closet!'

'I wanna play,' Lance howled. 'I'm Hopalong Cassidy!'

'You're a bad boy!' Serena reached to take the gun from him. He tried to move away without relinquishing it. 'Give me the gun!'

All at once a shot rang out. Laurie gaped in terror as Serena – still clutching the gun – fell to the floor.

'Serena!' Laurie screamed. 'Serena!' She rushed to hover above Serena, lying inert on the floor while blood began to stain the front of her pretty dress. 'Mrs Hall!' she screamed, her eyes fastened to the widening stain of red across Serena's chest. 'Mrs Hall, come quick!' She was vaguely aware that Lance was crying uncontrollably.

'Was that a car backfiring?' Mrs Hall arrived at the archway to the living room – tray of cake and ice cream in her hands. Her eyes took in the tableau. 'Oh, no! No!' The tray fell from her hands. She collapsed unconscious to the floor.

For a moment Laurie froze, then with an intuitive knowledge that action was urgent darted to the phone, dialled. Her heart pounding, she waited anxiously for someone to answer.

'Hello.' Her mother's voice greeted her.

'Mommie, come quick!' Laurie pleaded. 'Serena's been shot and Mrs Hall fainted. I don't know what to do!'

'I'll be right there, darling. Just hold on.' Pale and

shaken, Vera put down the phone. 'Paul,' she called to him in the den. 'Bring the car out of the garage. We have to go to Serena's house. Something awful has happened.' Barely aware of his anxious reply, she rushed into the hall and towards the kitchen. Fiona was there, allowing Tracy and Adele to help with baking cookies – a rainy day diversion for the little girls. 'Fiona, call the hospital,' she gasped. 'Tell them to send an ambulance to the Robinson house. Serena's been shot!'

Vera heard the car emerge from the garage. Without stopping for a coat, she hurried outdoors and moments later joined Paul on the front seat of the car.

'Laurie just said that Serena's been shot and that Mrs Hall had fainted.' Her voice was raspy with alarm. 'Fiona's calling for an ambulance.'

'What the hell happened? Where was the housekeeper?' Paul's concern revealed itself in an air of rage. Vera knew he had plunged into the past, when another such incident had taken his mother's life.

'I didn't take time to ask. My poor baby,' Vera moaned. 'To be alone at a time like this!' Only a few months older than Paul had been when his mother was killed, she thought.

Paul drove with unprecedented speed. In the distance they heard the sound of the ambulance siren. Few such emergencies arose in a small town such as Eastwood, Vera thought. The local ambulance responded quickly.

Before Paul had pulled to a full stop, Vera thrust open the door and hurried to the stairs that led to the Robinsons' Georgian mansion.

'Laurie,' she called out, striding into the foyer.

'In the living room, Mommie.' Laurie's frightened young voice guided her. She could hear someone being violently ill in the rear of the house. Instinctively she knew this was the housekeeper.

In the living room Vera saw Laurie leaning over the prone body of Serena. With a towel already crimson with blood, Laurie was trying to staunch the wound. Without reaching for Serena's wrist, Vera knew she was dead.

'Darling, the ambulance is here.' She heard the shrill siren become a whisper as the ambulance drew up before the house. 'You can let go now.' Gently she pried Laurie's small fingers away from the blood-soaked towel, lifted her to her feet.

'What happened?' Paul demanded. *'Laurie, what happened?'* He ignored Vera's pantomimed plea to avoid questions.

'Lance went up on the ladder and brought down the gun. Serena tried to take it away from him. It went off – and she fell down. Mommie, will she die?' Laurie's eyes begged for reassurance.

'Here comes the doctor now.' How could she tell Laurie that Serena was dead? 'Paul, try to call Serena's father,' she began and froze. Paul had dropped into a chair, his face in his hands.

'Oh, my God,' he said. 'Oh, my God!'

The doctor on ambulance duty rushed into the room, followed by an attendant. For the next few moments Vera was involved in explaining the situation. Then she became aware of a child crying inconsolably. Lance had taken refuge in the hall closet. While Serena was being taken to the ambulance, an unsteady Mrs Hall stumbled down the hall and into the living room. She forced herself to take charge of Lance, drawing him out of the closet and into her arms.

'I'll call Mr Robinson at his office,' Mrs Hall stammered. 'I was only out of the room for a few minutes. I went to bring the children cake and ice cream.'

'Will you be all right?' Vera asked, clutching Laurie's

hand in hers. Paul sat motionless in the chair, his head still in his hands.

'Yes, I'll be all right,' Mrs Hall stammered. 'I can't believe this happened. I was only gone a few minutes. Sssh,' she whispered to Lance, whose arms clung about her neck. 'You're all right now. Nobody's going to blame you.'

Why had Mr Robinson kept a loaded gun in that closet? Vera asked herself in anger. How many children had to die before people realized that was criminal?

'I'd like to take Laurie home now,' she told Mrs Hall. 'If you're sure you're all right.'

'As all right as I can be,' Mrs Hall said in anguish. 'I just fell apart when I saw what happened. Thank God, Laurie knew to call you.'

'Paul, let's go home.' Vera dropped a hand on his shoulder. He was reliving those awful moments when his mother had been shot, she understood. 'Paul –'

He lifted his face – etched with pain – to hers.

'Yes, let's go home.'

Only in the car – in the comfort of her mother's arms – did Laurie begin to cry.

'Serena's going to be all right, isn't she? I didn't know what to do. She didn't open her eyes. She kept on bleeding.'

'We'll talk to the doctor at the hospital later,' she hedged. 'You were wonderful, Laurie. You did everything right.' Oh, yes, for a little girl not quite seven, Laurie had been wonderful.

Paul drove the short distance home in silence. His tense grip on the wheel, his pallor, the set of his jaw told Vera he was caught up in recall of his mother's shooting. Laurie sobbed softly in her arms, exhausted by the harrowing experience at the Robinson house.

How could Serena's father have left a loaded gun on

a closet shelf? Vera asked herself with recurrent fury. There were no guns in their own house – none since Anne Kahn's death. The huge cabinet that contained guns collected by four generations of Kahns had been moved to the factory, were on display there as fine examples of Kahn craftsmanship.

Paul had told her how he had refused to set foot in the living room for months after the shooting. That was when his father had added the den. He loved his father dearly, yet deep in his heart Paul had never forgiven him for his mother's death. Now it was all fresh in his mind again.

Fiona rushed onto the porch as the car drove up before the house. Her face anxious, she watched Paul take Laurie into his arms and walk up the stairs, Vera at his side.

'Tracy and Adele are watching television,' she said, her eyes full of questions. Mutely Vera shook her head. 'Let me put Laurie down for a nap. There's a pot of fresh coffee on the stove.'

While Paul walked trance-like into the living room, Vera headed for the kitchen. Coffee in tow, she joined him there a few minutes later. She sat beside him on the sofa, deposited the coffee tray on the table. What could she say to ease his pain?

'Vera, I walked into that room and my mind exploded.' He began to tremble.

'That was natural,' she said gently.

'Vera, you don't understand.' He closed his eyes, shook his head in a gesture of incredulity. 'All of a sudden I remembered. What I'd shut out of my mind all those years ago leapt into place before my eyes. Dad didn't kill Mom. *I* did.'

'Paul, no,' she rejected. 'Your father told me what happened. It was a tragic accident that –'

'I held the gun.' He was ominously calm. '*I can see it right this minute*. I ran over to the cabinet, took this gun that my grandfather had especially prized, and I pointed it at my mother. I pulled the trigger, and there was this awful noise. Then she fell to the floor. She died instantly.'

'You're fantasizing, Paul,' Vera insisted. 'We know what happened.'

He shook his head – again and again.

'I know what happened. I remember.'

'We'll talk about it when Dad comes home,' Vera soothed. 'You're letting what happened to Serena confuse your memory.'

'Dad won't be able to deny it. I must have been so terrified that I blocked it out all these years. *Dad didn't kill Mom. I did.*'

Two hours later, Joel arrived home from the factory. He was ashen when Paul haltingly told him what had occurred at the Robinson house.

'How awful.' He was shaken. 'To happen again in this town.'

'Dad, I was holding the gun that killed Mom. Not you,' Paul said.

'No,' Joel shot back, unnerved by this accusation. 'I shot your mother.'

'I remember, Dad – as clear as though it were yesterday. Why did you take the blame all these years? And don't deny it. I know.'

'It seemed too much for a six-year-old boy to carry on his shoulders,' Joel said after a moment. 'I never wanted you to have to deal with that. And it wasn't your fault. It was a tragic error. The guns in the cabinet were never loaded. My father – who was so proud of that particular revolver – had taken it out to show to a business associate in town for the day. They went out behind the house for target practice with it. A phone call summoned them inside. Papa put the gun away without removing the bullets. It was a terrible, terrible accident that I'm sure brought on his fatal heart attack a few weeks later. It wasn't your fault, Paul,' he reiterated.

'You loved me enough to take the blame.' Paul's voice was a shaken whisper.

'Of course I love you that much,' Joel said gruffly. 'You're my son.'

Vera felt tears well in her eyes. The barrier between Paul and his father had crumbled. But how would Paul deal with the knowledge that *he* had held the revolver that had killed his mother?

Chapter Sixteen

Vera knew that the Robinson tragedy would evoke recall in Eastwood of the similar tragedy in the Kahn family twenty-four years ago. She worried that Paul would insist on retracting the original story of what had happened. She was relieved that her father-in-law was adamant when Paul brought this up the evening after Serena's funeral.

'It serves no purpose,' he rejected. 'It would only reflect badly on your grandfather – that he could leave a loaded gun where a child could reach it. Enough already about this.'

Later – privately – Joel promised Vera that no reprise of the earlier tragedy would appear in the local newspaper.

'The *Eastwood Herald* knows not to drag it up again. I carry some weight in this town. Now's the time to use it.'

The town was, of course, shocked and horrified by Serena's death. With his small son, Mr Robinson moved immediately from Eastwood. The Robinson house was placed on the real estate market. Visitors to town were shown the site as though, Paul said indignantly, it were a tourist attraction.

Vera worried about both Paul and Laurie in the months ahead. She knew Paul's inner battle to accept his own part in his mother's death – and his guilt at blaming his father all these years. She was anxious about Laurie's recurring nightmares, the blend of shock and rage that had eradicated her young exuberance. Thank God for

Adele's presence in the house, she told herself at grateful intervals. Laurie clung to Adele.

At intervals she'd worried that Fiona would tire of her 'life in exile,' as Paul sympathetically referred to it, and return to New York. It couldn't be easy for her to be the one coloured woman in Eastwood. Far more difficult than being one of three Jewish families in town, she conceded. Most of the time they were assimilated into the Eastwood population. At the turn of the century, Paul's grandfather had been the mayor of the town for several terms.

But she knew that Fiona was concerned that even at her tender years Adele's social life was limited. Yet, she comforted herself, Adele was not conscious of this. Not yet. She'd been so relieved, Vera thought, when Fiona confided after her last visit home that she was happy to be able to keep Adele out of a city housing project.

'I'm not sure why it's happening, but the city projects are becoming awful places. Nothing ever gets repaired. The elevators don't work half the time – and when they do, some people use them for toilets. And kids just roam around – inside and out – with nobody looking after them. That's not the way it was supposed to be. I don't want to bring up Adele in a place like that.'

Three months after Serena's death, when Joel was preparing to leave for a gun show in New York City, Vera came face to face with Laurie's rage. The family was at dinner. Joel was talking with pride about the magnificent workmanship of an antique revolver he'd been invited to display at the show.

'I hate guns!' Laurie shrieked. 'They're bad! They kill people! I hate you for making them!' she told her grandfather while Tracy gaped in disbelief. To Tracy their grandfather was the source of unbounded love, support in parent-daughter battles, and gifts.

'Laurie!' Vera was pale with shock. 'Apologize to

Grandpa this minute.' She turned to him. 'Laurie didn't mean that, Dad.' But Laurie was already running from the dining room.

'She's still hurting,' Paul said gently. 'It'll take time to pass.'

All at once Vera understood the reproachful glances in Laurie's eyes each morning at breakfast. Dad and Paul had breakfast earlier – Dad to be the first at the factory in the morning and Paul to be in his classroom early. Breakfast with Laurie and Tracy was a special time for her – but now she understood Laurie's oddly reproachful glances each morning. Laurie resented her going in to work in an office associated with guns, just as she resented her grandfather's being in the business of manufacturing guns.

'Vera, it'll fade away in time,' Paul comforted when she confided her fears to him. 'Poor baby, she's so young to have been put through such an ordeal.' One he, too, had survived.

'She's still angry with me and Dad because of the factory. In her eyes we make guns – and guns kill. She doesn't understand that guns help to keep peace in the world, that they protect against criminals. It's not guns that kill but the people who use them.' She realized she was quoting Joel. 'Paul, there's this wall between Laurie and me now. I can't get through to her.' She felt so helpless. And Dad was so hurt. What was happening to their beautiful family? And for an agonizing few moments, her mind bolted back through the years to the devastating night when her family in Berlin had been taken from her. And now she felt as though she were losing her precious Laurie.

'We'll be going to the Cape soon with Doris,' Paul intruded on her recall. 'You know how Laurie loves the beach. She'll put all this behind her.' *Would she?*

Over the sultry July 4th weekend Tracy came down with chicken pox, and a few days later both Laurie and Adele were displaying the familiar symptoms. Again, Dr Evans came to the house.

'Now you remember not to scratch,' he told Laurie with mock ferociousness, 'or you'll have to take the most evil-smelling medicine.' He turned to Vera. 'You know the routine,' he said good humouredly. 'Call me if her fever goes up – but it won't, young lady,' he told Laurie, 'because you're going to do whatever Mommie tells you.' He lingered briefly, then left to look in on Adele.

'Mommie, it itches,' Laurie complained when they were alone. 'When will it stop?'

'I'll put the lotion on, and then it'll feel better,' Vera soothed and reached for the bottle and a swab of cotton.

'Mommie, I love you,' Laurie said a few moments later when Vera had applied ample lotion. 'I love you so much.'

'And I love you, darling.' She reached to draw her small daughter into her arms. Was Laurie over her anger about the factory? Maybe Paul was right when he said she was just imagining it now.

Dad was pleased with her latest suggestions for speeding up the work, she thought with satisfaction. For over a month she'd had her own small office – and a title: Assistant to the President. And a salary raise that had impressed Paul. She knew Wayne resented her growing involvement in the business. She ignored his snide remarks – made behind their father-in-law's back. Was Wayne afraid she'd find out something he didn't want her – or Dad – to know?

Moments after Vera heard Dr Evans' car drive away, Fiona came to Laurie's bedroom.

'It's confirmed,' Fiona said, chuckling. 'Adele's got chicken pox.'

'What a surprise!' Vera joshed.

'That Dr Evans is so sweet.' Fiona seemed simultaneously grateful and self-conscious. 'You know, he wouldn't let me pay him? He said he had to come here anyway to see Laurie, so why should he charge me?'

'The town's lucky to have a doctor like him.' Vera nodded in respect.

'Mommie, I'm thirsty,' Laurie said. 'Can I have some orange juice?'

August arrived. Vera looked forward to two weeks on the Cape with Doris – to coincide with Fiona's vacation time. Again, they'd avoid being there with Wayne, who was off on some business jaunt in South America. Paul was philosophical about their not being able to trip up Wayne. She harboured a continuing frustration over this. But then, she rationalized, Paul was wrapped up in his battles at school regarding book censorship. Ted had agreed to withdraw *An American Tragedy* from his reading list on the grounds that it was too 'sophisticated' for high school seniors but won out on the book's remaining on the library shelves. A clique of parents assiduously followed the advice of McCarthyite groups and demanded the removal from reading lists and library shelves of book after book.

'Most people are decent,' Paul said with an optimism Vera found difficult to share. Some were decent, she conceded – remembering the Schmidts in Berlin, the Munches in Copenhagen, and those who had helped her escape from Denmark. 'A small group of nasty, noisy people are always the troublemakers. This can't go on much longer.'

By early in the new year, Vera had convinced herself that Laurie was her effervescent self again. She and Adele were caught up in a good-humoured competition over grades – the two brightest in their class, their teacher had confided. Paul admitted to some trying periods, but he accepted the fact that he had unwittingly held the gun that killed his mother. '*Damn it, Vera, people who own guns have to realize they have a tremendous responsibility. There should be some kind of legislation to establish that.*' Still, at disconcerting moments she felt as though she and her father-in-law were defiled in the eyes of Laurie and Paul by their involvement in the firearms industry.

Did Paul expect his father to throw aside a flourishing, four-generations-old business? she asked herself in defiant moments. His father was proud of the contribution the family had made through four wars and now, in a small way, in the Korean War. She tried to block out of her mind the possible – probable, she conceded – sale of arms to Israel, where the tiny country was ever-battling to strengthen its forces because Egypt vowed to see its extermination and candidly prepared for war.

She respected Paul's dedication to peace. She shared that dream, she told herself. Along with him, she worried about possible Soviet aggression, about the rumoured development of more weapons of destruction. But the Kahn factory made handguns, rifles – only small weaponry. They sold to sporting goods stores, gun clubs, governments. *What was evil about that*?

Wayne was spending much of his time 'on the road,' as he preferred to call it. Joel confided to Vera that he was worried about the state of Doris and Wayne's marriage.

'Do you think he's spending more time away because Doris seems to be picking fights when they're together? Or is she picking fights because he's away so much?' Joel sighed. 'I wish she'd get pregnant – then she'd have a baby to occupy her time.' Vera forced herself not to point out that Doris was not beset by idle time. Sure, she had a housekeeper now because Wayne considered that enhanced his image as a successful businessman, but she spent long hours at the nursery group and the book shop. They constituted a full-time job.

'It's something they'll have to work out for themselves,' Vera said after a tortured moment. Doris was a sweet, wonderful woman. Why couldn't Dad – and Paul – see what Wayne was doing to her? Should *she* bring it out into the open? Yet each time she considered this, she backed away. Dad and Paul didn't understand what Wayne was doing to Doris, and Doris herself would deny it. And she was under oath to say nothing to anyone about Wayne's inability to father a child. 'Doris would love to adopt,' she said – and reached out for help on this. 'Maybe if you could – could kind of hint to Wayne about their adopting, he might agree. Doris tried, but Wayne just gets angry.' *Doris could have a baby. Why couldn't she tell Wayne the truth?*

'I'll try,' Joel said, yet instinct told Vera that he wouldn't. Why did men always think it was the woman's fault if she didn't get pregnant?

It seemed to Vera that time was racing past. Still, the fighting continued in Korea and McCarthyism raged on. In October 1952, the British made their first atomic bomb test in Australia. The following month, the United States exploded a hydrogen bomb – the most destructive weapon in history – at Eniwetok Atoll in the Pacific. Paul agonized over both events. Wayne derided this reaction.

'Look, the only way to guarantee peace in the world is to let the bastards know we've got what it takes to blow them off the face of the earth.'

With a new year rolling in, business at the Kahn factory continued excellent, though Wayne focused mainly on international sales. Then, at Joel's suggestion – and after serious prodding – Vera agreed to take on the task of approaching new American accounts.

'Joel, you're off your rocker!' Vera heard Wayne's

explosion when he discovered this. 'What the hell does Vera know about selling? And in a man's field at that!'

'Wayne, calm down,' Joel soothed. 'You don't have time for that. You're after bigger game. And you know how I hate selling. She's young and enthusiastic and, let's face it, she's got one great advantage over me: She's young and beautiful. The buyers – all men – will like her.'

'Watch it, Joel,' Wayne warned. He'd long ago dropped the more affectionate 'Dad' to use his father-in-law's given name. To him, Vera guessed, that put them on an equal footing. 'Don't let her screw up some big deal for you.'

Joel admitted that her first assignment was a rough one.

'For several years we did business with the three Gregory Winston sporting goods shops. Then, just as they began this tremendous expansion about four years ago, we lost the account. Wayne couldn't get through to them. I understood they were getting impossible discounts from somebody else. Anyway, this is a test run for you,' he said good-humouredly. 'If you don't land an order, don't cry about it. Just go on to the next candidate.'

In an odd fashion, Vera analysed, she enjoyed the challenge of selling. Still, she was a nervous wreck, she confided to Paul as they prepared for bed on the night before her first trip to an account in New York City.

'Honey, you don't have to do this.' Paul was solicitous. 'Dad'll understand –'

'I have to do it,' she insisted. 'I have to prove to myself that I can do it. It's kind of an accomplishment.'

'Hey, you keep this up,' he teased, 'you'll be making more money than me.'

She settled herself in bed and watched while Paul did

his nightly push-ups. 'I hope I don't get lost in the city.'

'You?' Paul chuckled. 'A girl who escaped from Berlin, then from Copenhagen?'

'I've only been in New York three times since I arrived,' she reminded. A year ago – with Fiona and Joel watching over the girls – they'd gone into New York for the weekend. They'd stayed at the St Moritz, gone to the theatre to see Tennessee Williams' latest play, 'The Rose Tattoo'. On Sunday, before they headed back for Eastwood, Paul had taken her to the Columbia campus. They'd gone to the West End Bar across from the campus for an early dinner. And a few weeks ago they'd gone to New York to see Laurence Olivier and Vivien Leigh in 'Anthony and Cleopatra'. 'But I don't have far to go,' she said with a fresh burst of confidence. 'From Grand Central to the Winston Stores office on Madison Avenue. And the weather's fine.'

Early next morning – crisp, cold, but sunlit – Joel drove her to the Albany railroad station. 'We'll make better time in the car than the train from Saratoga to Albany with all the backing up they do.' After her luncheon appointment with Gregory Winston, she would take an afternoon train to Albany, where Paul would pick her up. Paul had given her his copy of the new Hemingway novel, *The Old Man and the Sea*. Settled in her seat on the train, she opened the short novel – which Paul had claimed that she would finish before the train pulled into Grand Central.

The book lay open but unread on her lap as the train chugged southward. Her thoughts dwelt on Doris. Perfectly suited to working with the young children in the nursery group, she was developing such insecurities, Vera fretted. Even at the book shop Doris was doubting her ability to order what was saleable; she constantly questioned the other volunteers. Wayne was doing that to her – with what Dad thought were affectionate witticisms. Paul worried that she seemed depressed so often.

Lately Wayne had taken Doris with him on some of his whirlwind trips to Europe, even to Rio between Christmas and New Year's. He made such a fuss about her shopping in New York – at Saks and Altman's – for a beautiful wardrobe. But that was for his own pride, Vera thought in bitter candour. Wayne Solomon's wife must wear the most expensive clothes – a testament to his success.

Every woman in Eastwood seemed to admire the mink coat Wayne had given Doris on their last anniversary. Didn't they remember – didn't Wayne remember – that Doris had finally come out and admitted she loathed furs? 'They belong on the animals that grew them – not on women.'

Because she'd slept little the night before, Vera began to doze. She woke up when the train passed through the 125th Street station – and recalled what Doris had told her about the poverty of Harlem. Fiona had escaped that, she thought tenderly – so determined to give Adele the best she could manage. Yet at times she suspected Fiona felt that she lived in exile.

Vera was conscious of a flurry of excitement when she walked from the train and up through the splendour of Grand Central Station. She glanced about at the other women, hurrying to their own destinations. Was she dressed smartly? It was important to appear successful when she met Gregory Winston. Her black coat was cut in the new princess line with the belt high at the back, as decreed by Christian Dior. Her grey suit was a copy of a Dior of last year – ultra feminine, the jacket cut on the cross and with raglan sleeves. She'd spent far more on the suit and the coat than she'd ever intended – but

Paul, who had been with her, had insisted on both purchases. Now she was glad he had.

Walking across 42nd Street to Madison Avenue, she felt herself caught up in the electric atmosphere of midtown Manhattan – in such contrast to the streets of Eastwood. Her earlier insecurity evaporated. When the receptionist at the Winston offices inspected her suit with candid admiration, she was conscious of a surge of fresh confidence.

From almost her first few moments with Gregory Winston – a slender, grey-haired man in his late fifties – she sensed he had agreed to see her out of curiosity. Over luncheon in an elegant French restaurant off Madison Avenue, she realized he had revised his initial impression that she meant to use her femininity to snare an order. She talked about Laurie and Tracy, and he brought out snapshots of his young granddaughter.

'I'll be blunt,' he said when she began a low-keyed sales pitch. 'I was annoyed when Kahn sent that arrogant young salesman to call on me. My impression was that he didn't really want our account. Maybe we weren't big enough for him.' His smile was wry. 'That was in '48. We had three stores then. Now we have twenty-three.' He paused. 'And the prices he quoted were exorbitant. Up till then, your prices had been competitive and the service excellent.'

'Mr Kahn would have been furious if he'd known,' Vera apologized. 'That's not the way he operates his company.' *What had been wrong with Wayne?*

Now they settled down to frank dickering. Winston was buying for twenty-three stores. Vera knew he would want special volume discounts. She relished the game, wound up with a large order at prices above Joel's bottom line. She knew her father-in-law would be delighted. But Gregory Winston's last words – spoken in jest – ricocheted in her brain: 'Maybe he just didn't want to sell in the United States. He talked about having no problems with his price list in Europe.'

On the train ride to Albany, she dissected the situation. Winston had been talking about four years ago. Had Wayne been trying to divert most of their production to Israel? Even now, the arms embargo on Israel remained in effect. Did Wayne have some scam going on overseas? Was she being paranoid? Believing what David Meyerberg had told Paul, she doubted that Wayne harboured any loyalty towards Israel – other than what profits it could mean for him.

Paul was waiting at the Albany station for her.

'I could have taken the train up to Saratoga,' she said tenderly when they were settled in the car. 'You wouldn't have had this long *schlep*.'

'This way you'll be home by the time Laurie and Tracy are ready for bed,' he reminded. 'They're eager to hear all about your trip to New York.'

'Oh, Paul, I forgot to pick up presents for them!'

'Presents are in the car,' he soothed. 'I figured you'd be all excited about your lunch meeting and then you'd be rushing for the train. I picked up two puzzles.'

Now she talked about her meeting with Gregory Winston and her suspicions about Wayne.

'You figure Wayne may have dreamt up a way to skim off the top?' Paul asked.

'It's a gut feeling,' she admitted. 'But I don't know how he could do it.'

'If there's a way, Wayne would find it,' Paul said. 'You're there in the office every day. Start watching the correspondence. I mean, all of it – not just the translations you do for Wayne.' The translating was a small part of her duties these days. She managed the small office staff, was the liaison with the warehouse division, sought for ways to increase factory efficiency. And now she would be pursuing new accounts – via phone or personal approach where practical. 'Somewhere in the correspondence we'll find the answers.'

Vera made a point now of checking on all correspondence that dealt with Wayne's activities with the company. His major accounts were out of the country – what he boasted was an untapped market for American small-arms companies. She studied the bills of lading for the destination of shipments. They all appeared routine: sporting goods stores and rifle and pistol clubs. His volume was heavy, she conceded – and he connived on occasion to make sure shipments went out to his accounts ahead of hers when there was an inventory problem. He seethed each time their father-in-law mentioned a new account she'd brought in, she sensed – though he was too canny to allow this to be obvious.

She was impatient that she could make no real deductions about possible clandestine operations on Wayne's part. The European accounts were steady, ordering regularly.

'It's not going to happen overnight,' Paul soothed, 'but one day Wayne will slip up. That is, if he is pulling something crooked on Dad.'

'Paul, we know he is!' Vera sighed in frustration.

Early in the summer Wayne announced at a Friday-evening dinner that he was buying the Robinson house. Doris dropped her eyes to her plate. It was clear she had opposed this.

'It must have cost a bundle,' Joel said in shock while Paul stared in disbelief. It was commonly assumed that the house – Eastwood's showplace – would be sold to an outsider, someone who was unaware of the tragedy it had witnessed. How could Wayne consider living in that house? Vera asked herself – knowing that the others at the table shared her revulsion at his action. *How could he be so insensitive?*

'I got it at a steal,' Wayne boasted. 'And with real estate prices rising the way they are, we'll sell our house at a substantial profit. Oh sure, we'll have to carry a huge mortgage,' he conceded, 'but it's a terrific investment. We'll close in sixty days.'

'Have you approached the bank yet about a mortgage?' Joel seemed uneasy. 'With a house like that, they'll want a big down payment and –'

'Robinson is giving me the mortgage himself,' Wayne broke in. 'No sweat there. He just wants the property off his back.'

On Saturday afternoons, Vera and Paul alternated helping out at the book shop. The following afternoon was Vera's turn. Paul would take Laurie and Tracy – along with Adele – on a trip to a nearby game farm. Vera was anxious for some time alone with Doris – which she hadn't been able to manage last night. Instinctively she knew that Doris wasn't happy about the new house.

'Vera, I didn't know a thing about the Robinson house,' she confessed moments after Vera walked into the shop. 'Wouldn't you think Wayne would have consulted me?'

'And now it's too late.' Vera tried to be calm. That house was full of terrible memories. How could Wayne expect Doris to be happy there? But he didn't care about her happiness. 'Has he signed the contract?'

Doris nodded. 'Oh, he's playing this great scene about how it was his big surprise for my birthday,' she said bitterly. 'I'll hate living there.' Now Doris forced a welcoming smile – their first customer of the day had walked into the shop.

News in Eastwood always circulated with telegraphic speed. Still, Vera was startled when Olivia Ames – a veteran local real estate broker – came into the shop to buy a children's book as a birthday gift and proceeded to scold Doris for ignoring her to buy a house direct from the seller.

'Mr Robinson gave me the listing the day after that poor little girl died,' she rattled on. 'Of course, it wasn't exclusive – Sally Rice and Bill Edmonds have it, too – but to go right over our heads and approach Mr Robinson direct? We were all so hurt.'

'I'm sorry,' Doris stammered. 'I didn't know a thing about it. Wayne bought it as a birthday surprise for me.'

'That huge house for just the two of you?' Olivia clucked sweetly, but Vera saw the malicious glint in her eyes. 'It just cries out for a big family.'

'Do you suppose we'll ever be able to persuade Laurie to come to the house?' Doris asked when she and Vera were alone again.

'It'll be a while,' Vera admitted. 'We won't even drive by if Laurie is with us.'

'I don't know why Wayne lied about the mortgage,' Doris said and Vera stared in surprise. 'I shouldn't be saying this, of course. I told you how Wayne won't let me go into his office at the house. The maid's not even allowed to go in there to clean. But he left the window open when he drove into Albany this morning on some business appointment. Remember that sudden downpour earlier? I had to go in and shut the windows. There was this file on his desk – and I opened it. The contract for the house was in it. Vera, he's paying *cash*.'

Vera's mind was in instant turmoil. Where had Wayne come up with that kind of cash? Was it money he'd sneaked out of Israel? Or was it from some scam he was pulling on Dad?

'He's not earning commissions in that category from the factory.' Vera was blunt. 'He might have smuggled a big bankroll out of Israel and kept it for something special,' she acknowledged.

'Vera, he left Israel ten years ago!' All at once Doris was distraught. 'Everybody in New York thought he was penniless. He was living in a tiny room in his cousin's apartment. Could he have been lying all this time?'

'Maybe he borrowed it from one of his "connections."' Wayne dropped hints at regular intervals about wealthy, important connections. But why would anybody loan him such a huge chunk of money – unless he was providing some urgent service? *Such as illegal arms.*

'Vera, don't say anything about this to anybody,' Doris pleaded. 'Not even to Paul. I just can't believe that Wayne would keep something like this from me. He was making remarks how we'd have to watch our spending because he'd taken on such a big mortgage –'

'I won't say a word,' Vera promised. 'Maybe Wayne will come up with some reasonable explanation.'

'He lied to me. That's what hurt worst of all.'

She mustn't tell Paul, Vera warned herself. She'd made a promise. But it would be so hard not to tell him. Somehow, she must break through this dark, secret cloud that surrounded Wayne. Yet even as she considered it, she felt an overwhelming sadness. Whatever was discovered, instinct told her, would be devastating to Doris. It could present a ghastly legal entanglement for Dad.

Chapter Seventeen

Vera felt an overwhelming sense of relief when late in July the Korean armistice was signed – though President Eisenhower told the country that 'we have won an armistice on a single battleground, not peace in the world.' She knew how the fighting in Korea had troubled Paul. She, too, had worried about the unnecessary deaths caused by the war, but for Paul the Korean War had resurrected his anguish over the deaths his RAF bomber squad had caused in World War II.

'*My mind tells me that the fight against Hitler was necessary – but I'll forever be haunted by the lives we took each time we dropped a bomb over enemy territory. Civilians had to have died in those attacks.*' At regular intervals Vera wondered if the Schmidts had survived the war – if they were all right. Every year at Christmas she heard from the Munches in Copenhagen and Iris in Canada.

Vera's relief that the Korean War was over was short lived because the following month – when again she and Paul and the girls were at the Cape Cod cottage with Doris – news flashed around the world that on August 12, the Soviet Union had exploded a hydrogen bomb. After Laurie and Tracy had been put to bed that evening, the other three sat before the television set and listened to a recap of the news about the bomb. After a few minutes Paul leapt to his feet and strode across to the TV to switch off the news programme.

'God, are we out to destroy ourselves?' He grunted in frustration.

'The Soviets are not about to use the bomb,' Vera soothed. 'It's their way of saying, "Don't mess with us."'

'There'll be peace in this world when not one gun, not one weapon of war can be had,' he warned.

'That'll never happen,' Doris predicted.

Vera intercepted the guarded exchange between Paul and Doris. Meaning, she interpreted, that their father manufactured guns – a source of distress to both.

'We're not involved in the armaments race,' Vera said defensively, for a moment erasing from her mind her conviction that Kahn Firearms was supplying arms to Israel. 'We make handguns and rifles.'

'Vera, who do you think went in to do the final cleanup in the battles in the Pacific?' Paul demanded and she winced at his caustic tone. 'The riflemen!' *But that had been a necessary war.*

'I know Wayne's making a fortune selling handguns and rifles,' Doris said, her face taut with rejection. 'But I live with this awful guilt that what he sells is taking lives.'

Did Laurie still resent her working at the factory? Vera asked herself, ever troubled by this possibility. Laurie hated fireworks because they reminded her of guns. She'd refused to go to the Fourth of July fireworks display in town. Dad had taken Tracy down to see it.

'I hate when hunting season opens,' Paul said sombrely.

'Over and over again, I ask myself how Wayne acquired the money to buy the house outright –' Doris stopped dead, startled by this admission to Paul. 'He paid cash,' she told Paul. 'And I keep asking myself, where did he get the money? Does it have something to do with guns?'

'I didn't know that.' He turned to Vera in shock. 'You're familiar with the business. Could he have earned enough commissions to buy a showplace like the Robinson house? For cash?'

'No way. Unless,' she made an effort to remove the

stricken expression on Doris's face, 'unless he's been secretly saving since the day he went to work for Dad.'

'How could he save the way we live?' Doris countered. 'Buying the Jaguar, taking over the liquor store, making me hire Millicent as soon as we moved into the new house.' Millicent was their full-time housekeeper. 'Spending a fortune on his clothes. Wayne can't buy around here,' she mocked. 'He has to run down to New York to some fancy tailor. He shops in Brooks Brothers on Madison Avenue, orders shirts from London.'

'What did he tell you?' Paul probed.

'He didn't tell me,' Doris flared. 'I found out by accident. He doesn't tell me anything.'

For the first time, Vera thought, Paul was beginning to understand that Doris was unhappy in her marriage, that Wayne might be less than the ideal husband she'd once proclaimed.

'Where's Wayne on this trip?' Paul asked, clearly troubled.

'Somewhere in Central America.' Doris shrugged, turned to Vera. 'You'd know more about that than I.'

'Wayne's gone to line up some huge game and fishing club in El Salvador, and then he's heading for Guatemala,' Vera reported. 'He's –'

'I shouldn't have said what I did,' Doris broke in, distraught now. 'Wayne was brought up in another culture. He doesn't understand American women. He means well. He works so hard.' Her eyes pleaded with Paul, then Vera, to dismiss her earlier confidence. 'Forget it, please.'

'Sure.' Paul managed a smile. 'Is there any more of that strawberry shortcake we had for dinner?'

'I'll get it.' Doris rose to her feet in an aura of relief that the conversation had been diverted. 'And I'll put up a fresh pot of coffee.'

Later, in the privacy of their bedroom, Vera and Paul discussed Doris's revelations in whispers.

'Maybe I'm way off the track,' Paul said, 'but I have this strong suspicion that Wayne may be selling to revolutionary groups.'

'Dad would be furious!' Vera broke in. Dad wouldn't consider Israel a revolutionary group. 'You know he –'

'Dad wouldn't be aware of it,' Paul told her. 'But you said Wayne was headed for El Salvador and Guatemala. Remember the outbreaks in El Salvador and Guatemala in the past few years? As for his European trips,' Paul pursued grimly, 'there's trouble all the way from Lithuania through the Balkans and the Ukraine. The market for illegal arms is huge.'

'How can Wayne manage to sell to those groups?' Vera shook her head in bewilderment.

'They set up phoney rifle clubs or some such deal,' Paul surmised. 'I'm damn sure Wayne's aware of what's happening. He doesn't care as long as he's bringing in heavy sales. But you said yourself, his commissions wouldn't add up to enough cash to buy the Robinson house.'

'Maybe he's collecting something on the side.' Vera was grim. 'A lot on the side – to keep his mouth shut.'

'Dad would keep silent if he thought the guns were going to Israel, because Israel's still fighting so desperately to survive. But he won't be silent if Wayne's selling to guerrilla groups.' Paul sighed. 'Any way you look at it, Doris is going to be hurt.'

Vera and Paul struggled to unearth proof that Wayne was involved in clandestine arms deals, came up with nothing. True, Wayne's letters – and despite her elevated position in the company, Vera still served as his translator – sounded odd, as though they could be coded. But he had been raised in another culture, Vera reasoned. Sometimes his English was stilted. Yet both she and Paul sensed something unsavoury in Wayne's business deals.

'Keep watching,' Paul urged Vera. 'We'll hit pay dirt yet.' Both knew not to approach Joel without concrete proof.

Shortly after the first of the year, Vera returned from lunch at the nearby café – the Blue Lantern – that was her daily destination to overhear Wayne in an argumentative conversation.

'Listen to me,' he said menacingly and Vera froze at attention beyond his line of vision. 'And I'm not going to say it again. This is my last offer for the store. Who in this God-forsaken town is going to buy out the fixtures at that price and pay the outrageous rent you're asking? Who's going to take over a business that couldn't keep Joe Leslie in cigarette money these past two years?' Vera remembered that Joe Leslie – who'd run the only sporting goods store in town for the past twenty-eight years – had recently died of lung cancer. 'You have my price – and it's good only for the next forty-eight hours. After that, I'm out of it.'

Vera hurried to her office. She was disappointed not to have overheard some incriminating revelation. But her mind focused on the efforts of Joe Leslie's landlord to sell the store fixtures and rent the premises. Suddenly decisive, she left her office and strode to that of her father-in-law. He glanced up with a warm smile.

'Got a minute?' she asked.

'For you, anytime,' he said affectionately.

She told Joel in a burst of words that she thought it would be a profitable deal for the company to take over Joe Leslie's business.

'His major sales were handguns and rifles – and we'll show a large profit selling at the retail price. It'll be a simple matter to fill in with sporting goods and attire,' she finished breathlessly. And she'd enjoy beating Wayne to the punch, she admitted to herself without a trace of guilt.

'Aha! The entrepreneur in you comes out,' Joel joshed. 'Okay, run with it.'

'Just like that?' Vera was taken aback by her immediate success.

'Honey, I realized from your first week in the office that you're the smartest woman I know. You make the deal, set it up the way you feel it should be. Hire your staff. You supervise, but I want you here with me,' he pinpointed. 'I need that bright little head of yours.'

As she'd anticipated, Vera was the object of Wayne's rage when he discovered the company was taking over the sporting goods store at her suggestion. He stalked into her office and slammed the door behind him.

'You knew – how I can't figure out – that I was after that store!' he hissed at her. 'You think you're so damn smart. You think you can wind Joel around your little finger.' At the moment Joel was at the monthly Lions Club luncheon.

'You've told Dad half-a-dozen times that he ought to be buying up businesses around town, that he could become one of the richest men in the state.' She refused to be ruffled. 'The store seemed a natural for us.'

'You're a smart-ass,' he snapped, yet she sensed he was oddly aroused by her. 'Pity you've got that stupid puritan streak.' His eyes swept over her for a moment in naked passion. 'Together, we could make it right to the top of the heap. Rich and powerful.' But passion was quickly replaced by fury. 'Don't get in my way again, baby – because you might be sorry.' He spun around and strode from her office.

Vera sat motionless, digesting what he had said. She'd ruffled his feathers, she mocked herself. But she wasn't afraid of his threats. Yet she found it impossible to dismiss the encounter from her mind for the rest of the working day.

At the house she focused her attention on Laurie and Tracy, who were both clamouring to talk about their school day. Why was she letting Wayne upset her? she rebuked herself in a corner of her mind while she managed to appear totally absorbed in what Laurie and Tracy were reporting in their exuberant fashion. There was nothing for her to fear in Wayne's threats. *Was there?*

Now she felt a new urgency in unmasking Wayne's covert activities. She dissected his letters – which she translated into German or French – in a desperate determination to locate clues. She checked the books to confirm her conviction that Wayne's income could not have allowed him to buy the Robinson house. And all the while she focused on setting up the newly formed Kahn Sporting Goods Shop – a diversion she found challenging.

Vera was grateful that the school's spring holidays arrived just as she was preparing to go into New York in her new role as buyer for the shop. Paul decided to accompany her on the two-day trip.

'Live it up for a couple of days,' Joel ordered. 'Fiona and I will take care of the kids – and Doris will love the chance to play surrogate mommie.'

On a deliciously springlike April morning – with promises to Laurie and Tracy to return home bearing gifts – Vera and Paul climbed into the car and headed towards New York. They'd spend the night at the Essex House – in a room facing the park, Paul had reported in high spirits. This afternoon and tomorrow morning Vera would visit manufacturers' showrooms. She and Paul would have a hasty lunch and catch a Broadway matinée.

They'd have an early dinner at Lindy's – close to the theatre – then drive home.

'I feel as though I'm playing truant,' Vera told Paul. 'And it's such fun.'

'Don't say that to any of my kids at school,' he joked. But Vera knew he was proud of the attendance records in his classes. That was a plus, she comforted herself, in Paul's latest battle with Mr Kerrigan. Why couldn't Kerrigan understand that Paul was fighting to bring something fresh and important into the Eastwood school system?

'I wish I'd taken a course somewhere about buying,' Vera confessed. 'I'm going into this whole scene blind.'

'You've got great taste,' Paul insisted. 'And you said yourself that the main thrust of the shop is hunting and fishing equipment – and Dad's taking care of that.'

Vera chuckled reminiscently. 'Wayne's still fuming about the shop. He thought he had the deal all tied up – on his terms.'

'He's doing well with the liquor store, I gather from what Dad says. But Wayne won't be happy until he owns this whole town. His fiefdom,' Paul drawled.

'We're receiving re-orders from both El Salvador and Guatemala.' Vera was serious now. 'I can't believe we're shipping that many handguns and rifles for sporting use.'

'How are they gotten out of the country?' Paul was curious. 'Aren't there governmental rules?'

'There's no federal legislation against shipping what's known as "sporting arms,"' Vera said. 'And the shipments to Israel go by way of other countries.' Because the United States still maintained an embargo on weapons to Israel. 'What Wayne labels a *distribution centre*. I suspect Dad worries about that – he's so very ethical in everything else.'

'I hate our involvement in selling guns even for sporting activities. Yet I understand how he feels about Israel – and that bugs me, Vera. How can I condone being part of war in one instance and reject it in others?' He sighed, his hands clutching the wheel. 'When, Vera – when will the world learn to live without killing?'

In Manhattan, Vera and Paul checked into the hotel, had lunch sent up from room service in deference to Vera's tight schedule. While they ate, Paul gave Vera directions to her afternoon's destination – situated happily in the same area.

'Sure you don't want me to go with you?' he probed.

'Absolutely not,' she assured him. 'I know the streets and avenues I'm heading for – you said yourself, New York cabbies are great.' And she knew he was eager to spend the afternoon at the United Nations.

Driving back to Eastwood the following evening, Vera congratulated herself on a successful business trip. And both she and Paul had enjoyed the non-business hours. The shop was the beginning of a new era, she'd told herself in soaring pleasure.

Early in May, Doris enlisted Vera's help in arranging a rummage sale to benefit her nursery group.

'We can have it in the grounds of the church,' Doris said. 'If it rains, we'll schedule it for the following week. But we do need money for more materials. The group is being so well received, Vera.' She radiated enthusiasm. So often Doris seemed steeped in despair, Vera thought compassionately. At least, she was finding satisfaction in her nursery group.

'I hear great things,' Vera said gently.

'I've got so much stuff stashed away in the basement to dig out for the rummage sale.' Doris sighed. 'I can't get into any of my clothes from last summer.' She tried for a chuckle. 'During the winter it's dismal so much of the time, I head to the refrigerator too often. No, you don't know,' she said before Vera could respond. 'You're one of those people who never gains an ounce.'

'I'll look around, too,' Vera promised. 'I'm sure there're a lot of things Tracy's outgrown that are still good.'

'Neither of us is on duty at the book shop tomorrow,' Doris remembered. Their Saturday off. 'Will you have time to run over and help me sort things out? I don't want to bring over things that are too beat up.'

'Sure.' When they'd first met, she'd admired Doris's self-confidence. Wayne had destroyed that through the years. 'Paul's taking the three girls to see the litter of pups at the MacDonald house in the morning.' Adele was included in most activities involving Laurie and Tracy. 'I'll run over after breakfast.'

'Millicent's off on Saturdays and Wayne's driving over to Manchester for an early golf date with some big wheel over there.' Her smile was ironic. 'You know how Wayne loves to collect "important contacts." Why don't you have breakfast with me? Or at least, coffee,' she amended – aware that Saturday-morning breakfast was a special occasion for Vera and Paul and the kids.

'I'll come over for coffee,' Vera promised.

On Saturday morning, the two women lingered in the charming, sunlit breakfast room over coffee. The scent of the first summer flowers drifted in through the open windows. A deceptive serenity permeated the house. Vera sensed that Doris was upset but determined to mask this. At last Doris confessed to her annoyance. Once again, Wayne had taken the house on the Cape for the month of August.

'He must have booked it weeks ago,' Doris said. 'You know summer rentals are grabbed up early in the year. Sure, it's beautiful up there, but I'm lonely as hell until you and Paul come out with the kids. You will come out again?' she asked, suddenly anxious.

'We love being on the Cape with you,' Vera told her. 'But won't Wayne be there with you the first two weeks?'

'Supposedly he's there.' Doris played with a corner of the tablecloth. 'But I hardly see him. He's either playing golf with someone or heading into New York for two or three days. I don't know anybody there. I don't mix well with strangers.' She gestured apologetically. Doris didn't mix well with strangers since Wayne had destroyed her ego, Vera thought with fresh rage.

'Maybe I can arrange to take three weeks off this summer. Paul will be teaching summer school still, but I could come out with the kids,' she offered on impulse. 'One week alone won't be bad, will it?' But she'd dread that extra week in the house with Wayne, Vera admitted to herself.

'You'd hate it,' Doris said bluntly, 'and Wayne would hate it. But thanks for the try. Now let's go down into the basement and see what I can dig up for the rummage sale.'

In the basement Doris brought out cartons of stored clothing, pulled out garment after garment amid sighs of regret.

'I must have gained twelve or fourteen pounds over the winter. I know I can't get into anything from last summer.' Doris groaned. 'How did I let it happen?'

'You don't look that much heavier,' Vera consoled, yet in a corner of her mind she remembered at one point becoming aware of this. 'You'll take it off during the summer,' she said with conviction. 'Save the best things for next year.'

'I'll start a diet tomorrow,' Doris decided. 'But I won't be wearing any of these this summer.'

'What about those magazines?' Vera pointed to several piles. 'They won't bring much, but it'll add up.'

'Sure, they can all go,' Doris agreed. 'I don't know why I've hung on to them.'

'You have two or three years of *Ladies Home Journals*,' Vera noticed. 'Let me take a few home to Fiona. She collects recipes.'

'Take all you want.' Doris glanced around. 'There're some shopping bags over there. I'll get one for you.'

Vera flipped through the *Ladies Home Journals*, checked the contents of a few for interesting recipes, made her selection.

'They've been lying around for a while. Let me find a dust cloth.' Doris handed her a shopping bag and turned to yet another carton.

Vera glanced curiously at a magazine atop another pile. Nothing familiar. Magazines that Wayne read, she surmised, scanning the title. *Male Adventure. Espionage and Violence.* Oddball publications with small circulations. She skimmed the table of contents of a couple of them. African safaris, daring espionage. Yes, that would appeal to Wayne. Without knowing why, she slid one issue between the copies of *Ladies Home Journal* she was taking home to Fiona.

Vera returned home in time for lunch with Paul and the girls. Fiona – off to some church fair now with Adele – had left a tuna-noodle casserole warming in the oven. Laurie and Tracy were euphoric over their visit with the pups, though they knew they couldn't have a dog of their own because their father was allergic to both cats and dogs.

After lunch Vera and Paul settled on the screen porch at the rear of the house while Laurie and Tracy sprawled on the swing-chair, each involved in the latest book given to them by Doris.

'Wouldn't you say this is the idyllic vision of a small town Saturday afternoon in May?' Paul teased. 'If we can forget the troubles of the world –' Vera knew he was concerned particularly about the fighting in Vietnam. Just three weeks ago, the US Air Force had flown a French battalion there to help Vietnam fight against Communist forces in North Vietnam.

'Let's forget for today,' Vera encouraged lightheartedly. 'Oh, I picked up some weird magazine in Doris's basement. It's on the table here with the magazines I brought home for Fiona.' She leaned forward to ferret out the unfamiliar publication. 'Have you ever heard of it?'

'No,' Paul conceded, flipping through the pages. 'One of those deals designed to appeal to men fascinated by espionage and violence,' he assumed.

Suddenly Paul's eyes seemed riveted to a page. Curious about what had captured his interest, Vera read over his shoulder. Columns of personal ads, she thought.

'Paul, what is it?' She sensed a sudden electric excitement in him.

'You said this came from Doris's basement?'

'That's right. There was a pile of them, going back at least two years, I think. Why?'

'Read this item here.' He pointed to a small listing in the personal column which gave a box number at the magazine's New York office for replies. 'It's carefully worded, of course – but I'd lay odds it's being run to contact revolutionary groups looking to buy arms!'

'You're guessing that Wayne is running ads in *Espionage and Violence* to attract business?' Possibly this ad.

'It's going to be rough to track down,' he warned, 'but yes, I'd swear Wayne is selling arms to illegal organizations – and he's using phoney pistol and rifle clubs as a front. The problem is – how the hell do we prove it?'

Chapter Eighteen

Vera and Paul were impatient to acquire current editions of *Espionage and Violence*. The one Vera had ferreted from the basement was six months old. On Sunday morning, the two of them searched magazine racks in Eastwood and in nearby towns – coming up with nothing.

'Maybe we'll find a store in Saratoga that carries it,' Paul decided. 'Let's give it a whirl.'

A search of every possible outlet in Saratoga was futile. Paul resolved to drive to Albany the following afternoon. But en route to Eastwood they stopped at a soda fountain at the edge of Schuylerville. While they settled themselves at a small marble-topped table for two and waited to be served, Vera glanced about the long, narrow store.

'Paul, they have magazines in the back.'

'I'll look.' He rose to his feet, strode towards the magazine racks. Vera saw his face light up. He held up a magazine in triumph. 'This is it!'

The same ad that they had seen in the earlier issue appeared here. The same ambiguous wording. It probably ran every month, she surmised.

'I think we're in business,' Paul said with quiet satisfaction.

'How do we prove Wayne's running the ad?' If he were. 'The magazine won't tell us.'

'There's this old Columbia buddy of mine who went on to law school,' Paul told her. 'He was brilliant but eccentric, most students thought. He carried on about how he wouldn't be corrupted by large corporations. He cherished his independence. He has a small office in Manhattan – with small billings.' Paul chuckled reminiscently. 'Frank said 85% of lawyers are crooks. Actually he wants to be a mystery writer. Anyhow, he has a collection of offbeat friends – actors and singers and writers on the fringe. He'll hire somebody for us who's hungry for a fast fifty dollars.'

'You mean, once we know Wayne's going to be in New York for the day, Frank will hire somebody to tail him? No,' she corrected herself, 'to be at the magazine's address and watch to see if Wayne goes to their office.' Her mind was on high alert. 'I have some snapshots of Wayne and Doris. I'll have a negative made, then an enlargement. Paul, it could work!'

Paul spoke to Frank, who was sure he could have somebody available. Vera sent an enlargement of the snapshot of Wayne and Doris by special delivery. Now the waiting period began. Ten days later, Vera learned that Wayne was scheduled for a trip to New York at the end of the week. Paul alerted Frank.

'We could be all wrong,' he cautioned Vera, fearful of disappointment.

'Paul, we can't afford not to follow through!'

On the day Wayne drove into Manhattan, Vera jumped every time her office phone rang. Ostensibly Wayne was calling on an old account that was adding two new stores on Long Island. She was convinced the magazine was his major destination.

There were no calls from Frank during the day. When she arrived at the house, Paul indicated by a shake of his head that he had heard nothing. He was sprawled on the floor with Laurie and Tracy while the two little girls concentrated on the 500-piece puzzle they'd been working on for the past two days. Vera sensed his disappointment matched her own.

As usual, Joel arrived home an hour after Vera. Fiona ordered the family to the dinner table. Near the conclusion of dinner the phone rang. Paul rose to his feet.

'I'll get it.'

Joel listened with grandfatherly interest to Laurie's avid report of a class trip to the state capitol at Albany while Vera struggled to conceal her anxiety about the phone call. *Was it Frank?*

Fiona glanced into the room, noted that forks and knives were now idle. Moments later she appeared with dessert.

'Ooh, strawberry shortcake!' Tracy glowed.

'Is it somebody's birthday?' Joel kidded.

'I saw these beautiful strawberries in the store this morning, and I figured everybody here loves strawberry shortcake,' Fiona said good-humouredly. 'But no seconds,' she warned Laurie and Tracy. 'That's a lot of whipped cream.'

Paul hurried into the dining room. He managed a victory signal – unseen by the others – for Vera. They hadn't been wrong, Vera guessed with jubilation. Whatever insanity Wayne had brought upon the company was about to be aired.

After dinner Laurie and Tracy went upstairs to their bedroom to focus on homework. Joel left for one of his endless civic meetings. Vera and Paul settled themselves in a corner of the living room.

'Paul, what happened?' Vera demanded impatiently when Fiona was out of the room.

'Frank's spy nailed him,' Paul said. 'He followed Wayne right up to the magazine's office. He hung around the floor for twenty minutes until Wayne came out. He wanted to make sure he had the right guy. It was Wayne.'

'We have to tell Dad,' Vera said quietly.

'When he comes home from his meeting.'

In the den – the door shut lest Laurie or Tracy should wander downstairs and overhear what was being said – Joel gaped in shock as Paul finished his report on Wayne's covert activities. It was legal – in most instances – to sell to gun clubs in foreign countries. It was a different matter to smuggle guns to illegal organizations.

'Reading between the lines of the ads, we know Wayne's using phoney gun clubs as a front,' Paul wound up.

'I've been used all these years!' Joel's face was drained of colour. 'All that crap about his being an Israeli hero – it was like that friend of yours said! How could this go on right under my eyes?' He turned to Vera. 'You translated his correspondence. Didn't that tell you anything?'

'I translated the letters he wanted us to see,' Vera pointed out. 'But somewhere along the line he must have a secret file.' She hesitated. 'And he had to have worked out some deal where he was paid additional money separately.'

'A lot of money,' Paul said. He turned to his father. 'Wayne paid cash for the Robinson house. No mortgage.'

'This has to be reported to the FBI.' Joel was shaken. 'I won't allow Kahn Firearms to be part of that kind of operation. But oh God, how will Doris take this?'

'Before you do that, Dad, we need more information.' Caution crept into Vera's voice. 'What have we got to tell them? That we suspect Wayne is running an ad in that creepy magazine and using it for illegal arms sales? We've got invoices indicating sales to gun clubs – it appears legitimate. Wayne just might wiggle out of this.'

'We can't let that happen!' Paul's eyes shone with determination. 'We need to make contact through that ad – have concrete evidence of what Wayne's pulling.'

'We can't do that ourselves.' Vera's mind was charging ahead. 'But I may have an angle. Remember I told you about the wonderful family in Copenhagen who helped me escape?' she asked Joel. He nodded. 'Mr Munch is a diplomat with contacts in several countries. Let me write him, explain the situation. He may be in a position to help us track down Wayne's operation, make a direct contact through that box number.'

'It's worth a try,' Joel agreed.

The following day Vera sent an impassioned letter to Herbert Munch. He was at present assigned to an embassy in the Balkans. The three geared themselves to wait for a reply, but with gratifying speed a letter arrived from Munch. He was already making contact through the box number in *Espionage and Violence*.

'Your man will assume an American agent of my so-called guerilla organization put me in touch with his ad. There is much unrest here. He will be confident he's snared a revolutionary group prepared to pay high for weapons.'

Vera was relieved that Wayne was spending little time in the office, that he missed two Friday-night family dinners in a row. His absence lessened the strain of keeping up the pretence that they knew nothing of his covert activities. Then Joel reported that Wayne was fighting with him about their need to produce more sophisticated guns and rifles. He complained the company would lose out to competition.

'Damn him!' Paul blazed. 'He lives on blood money!'

Vera flinched, exchanged a guilty glance with Joel. Both knew that Paul hated their own involvement with weapons of death. But guns were weapons of peace, too, she thought defiantly. Why else had the framers of the Constitution added the Second Amendment – the right to bear arms?

The time was approaching for Wayne and Doris's annual visit to the Cape. Vera was anxious to see the situation with Wayne brought out into the open even though she dreaded Doris's reaction. She knew this was a terrible trial for her father-in-law. And he feared, too, that by exposing Wayne he himself would be found guilty of illegal arms-trading. But it was something he had to do.

Then, with startling swiftness, the proof they sought about Wayne came through from Herbert Munch. The seasoned diplomat had used his contacts to flush out Wayne's operation. A letter had gone out to Wayne's box number at the magazine. He had replied, then negotiated by trans-Atlantic telephone. Munch's letter was explicit.

'He explains how the would-be arms-buyer sets up a dummy pistol-and-rifle club, which orders from Kahn Firearms Company. But before the Kahn company ships, the purchaser makes a substantial deposit into a numbered Swiss bank account. Then the routine shipment goes through. It all appears legitimate. When the orders arrive, they're rerouted to their illicit destinations.'

Through his private sources Munch had discovered that Wayne had sold not only to Israel through the years, but also to Egypt and other enemies of the young nation. He sold wherever revolutionaries were eager to buy.

Simultaneously triumphant and uneasy – not knowing how Joel and the company would fare in this situation, Vera summoned Paul and Joel into the den after dinner and presented them with the communication from Munch.

Joel read and reread Munch's letter plus the incriminating data.

'All right,' he said at last. 'I'm calling Wayne to get over here right now. But first,' he specified, 'let me call my lawyer. And Doris.' The book shop was open one evening a week. Tonight Doris was one of two volunteers on duty there.

Twenty minutes later – while the other three sat in the den with coffee, Fiona went to respond to the doorbell.

'They're in the den, Mr Solomon,' they heard Fiona tell Wayne. 'Would you like me to bring you some coffee?'

'No,' he said tersely.

Vera tensed at the sound of his heavy footsteps striding down the hall. He stalked into the den.

'I hope this is important, Joel,' he said. 'You interrupted me in the middle of my dinner.'

'It's important.' Joel's face telegraphed his rage. 'You have thirty-six hours to get out of the country.' He paused as Wayne stared blankly. 'That's when I'm going to the FBI to tell them I've discovered my international sales manager is selling to illegal organizations.'

'What the hell are you talking about?' Wayne's gaze swept from Joel to Vera, settled on her. 'What kind of craziness did you throw at him?' he challenged. 'You've been after my hide for years!'

'We know about your ads in *Espionage and Violence*.' Vera contrived to sound cool, almost impersonal. 'We know that you've sold to Egypt and other countries hostile to Israel. And to guerrillas in the Balkans and in El Salvador and Guatemala. We –'

'Joel knew about Israel.' Wayne swaggered, feeling himself in safe territory now. He turned to Joel. 'Look, you knew I was selling guns to Israel. What the hell are you bitching about now?'

'To Israel and its enemies,' Joel lashed back. 'And to any group of thugs out to destroy a democratic government supported by its people. We know about the funds paid into your numbered bank account in Geneva. Only because of Doris I'm giving you notice, Wayne. You have thirty-six hours before I go to the FBI.'

'You'll go to jail,' Wayne yelled. 'How do you think Doris will like that?'

'I'll take my chances. But before you leave, you'll sign two papers. My lawyer and a notary are standing by. First, you sign over the house to Doris. Then you sign papers agreeing to a divorce. Then pack your bags and run, Wayne. And be grateful you have a head start.'

'Doris will go with me.' Wayne's eyes exuded confidence. 'She won't believe this shit!'

'She'll believe,' Paul said quietly and walked to the door and pulled it wide. 'Doris, please come in now.'

Wayne stared wildly at Doris. 'Tell them you're going with me,' he ordered. 'We'll live like royalty in Switzerland. We'll –'

'Not Switzerland,' Paul interrupted. 'The Swiss police know now that you're an illicit arms-merchant. You'll be stopped and seized at Customs.'

'We'll go to Israel. Doris, I'm a hero there!' He started at the sound of a car pulling up out front.

'That's my attorney and the notary,' Joel told him. 'You'll sign the papers and leave.'

'Doris, tell him you don't want to divorce me,' Wayne demanded. 'Tell him that –'

'I'm not going with you, Wayne.' Doris was pale but determined. 'I'm free at last.'

The days ahead were tumultuous and nerve-wracking for the family. Vera took over the management of the factory while Joel appeared before committees in Washington DC. Doris accompanied him to supply whatever information she could about Wayne's activities – no doubt in her mind, Vera realized, that Wayne was forever out of her life.

Paul was fearful of punishment that might be meted out to his father.

'Dad's always been so ethical,' he reminded Vera as they sat on the screened porch late on a hot June evening.

'Only where Israel was concerned did he ever do something against regulations. And he was right,' he added defiantly. 'How could he not do whatever he could to help Israel?'

'He brought the whole situation to the FBI,' Vera pointed out. 'From the way Wayne set up the operation – Wayne's Swiss bank account – they must understand that Dad was unaware of the other deals. I'm sure that –' She paused at the shrill intervention of the phone.

'I'll get it!' Paul leapt to his feet and hurried into the house, Vera at his heels. They'd been waiting for a call from Washington all evening.

The caller was Joel. Vera clung to Paul, strained to hear what Joel was saying.

'It's all right,' Joel said jubilantly. 'I've got to pay a stiff fine, but they're letting me off the hook. They know I had nothing to do with what Wayne engineered. Our sales figures will take a steep drop – but we did all right before. We'll do all right again. Thank God, this madness is over.'

But in Paul's eyes the madness wasn't over, Vera thought involuntarily. The madness was the family's being in the business of manufacturing guns. She'd asked herself – over and over again – if Laurie resented her being part of the family business, knowing in her heart that Laurie raged inwardly over this. In prescient moments she envisioned – with soaring anguish – a time when Paul and Laurie would align themselves against her and her father-in-law.

They mustn't become a family divided.

Chapter Nineteen

Vera was anxious about Doris's reaction to Wayne's departure from her life. She knew there would be ups and downs in the course of the next few months. Despite Doris's outside activities, she had considered her main role in life to be that of Wayne's wife. She'd felt guilty that she harboured other ambitions – voiced only in secrecy to Vera. Maybe now, Vera thought, Doris would take up her painting again.

Word ricocheted around Eastwood about Doris's pending divorce – and Wayne's exit from the business. The situation shocked the town, but nobody dared ask questions. Along with Vera and Paul, Joel agonized over the possibility that word of the Washington hearings would leak out.

The former Robinson house now belonged to Doris. Joel had immediately suggested that Doris come home to take up residence in the guest room and list the house with the real estate brokers, but she dismissed this.

'I'll stay in the house,' she told the family a week later. 'I want to divide it into two apartments. One for myself and one to rent out. That'll provide me with a fair income.' It was clear that Doris meant to be independent.

'A great idea.' Joel was eager to be supportive.

'Maybe you'd like to work afternoons in the company shop,' Vera suggested. Doris was accustomed to living well – the extra income would be helpful. Only her mornings were involved in the nursery group. 'Not right away,'

Vera amended hastily, 'but once you've handled all the business of converting the house.' No one doubted that Doris could acquire a loan to cover the construction costs. 'And after you're back from the Cape.'

Doris was startled. 'I hadn't thought about going there.'

'Of course, you'll go.' Paul exchanged a swift glance with Vera. A change of scenery would be good for Doris. 'It's been paid for – why not utilize it?'

'The girls and I will come out with you,' Vera said. 'Paul can come out for the last two weeks. You can manage without me for the month of August, can't you, Dad?' she appealed to Joel.

'Any problems that come up either in the factory or the store you can deal with on the phone.' He nodded in agreement, but Vera saw the concern in his eyes. The three of them – Dad, Paul, and herself – were apprehensive about Doris's emotional state. They knew her control was precarious. 'And I'll come out for the Labor Day weekend,' he resolved.

In the course of the month on the Cape, Vera – on the phone at least once a day with her father-in-law on business – was conscious of Doris's mood swings. There were days when her spirits were high, others when she admitted to Vera that she was unnerved about the future. Despite Vera's efforts to prod her into painting again, Doris resisted. Too early, Vera cautioned herself. But it would be wonderful therapy, she thought impatiently.

Because she knew that Vera limited the sweets Laurie and Tracy were allowed, Doris indulged in her emotionally driven craving for candy bars in the privacy of her room – but her added weight was a giveaway. Still, Doris was determined to get her life back on track, Vera comforted herself.

In September – with most of the work on the house completed and a rental already arranged – Doris went to spend a week with Sally, now living in Westchester County.

'Oh God, I'm glad to see you,' Sally welcomed her with obvious pleasure. 'I think Phil and I must have been out of our minds to move up here.'

'The house is beautiful.' Doris glanced about in admiration while they sat over lunch in the attractive dining area.

'For me, it's a beautiful prison.' Sally's eyes telegraphed her disillusionment. 'I'm dying to get back to work. And Phil has that lousy commute into New York.' She sighed. 'But he's convinced it's great for the children. Conditions in the city have become so bad. The crime rate is unbelievable.'

'It's not just New York.' Doris was sombre, recalling an article she'd read just the previous week. 'The crime in every major city in the country – even in some of the smaller cities – is shocking. And New York isn't the worst.'

But in New York, statistics told its residents, a serious offence was committed in the area every two minutes – and the Police Commissioner predicted the figures were on the rise. She remembered how Fiona worried that there were insufficient patrolmen on duty in her mother's area of East Harlem – where she'd moved last year from her earlier housing project. 'And the way the kids are behaving scares me. They're acting real wild.'

'You don't worry about the crime rate in Eastwood, I'll bet.' Sally's smile was wry.

'The worst crime we see,' Doris admitted, chuckling, 'is when some woman calls up to complain that a teenager is using her bushes for a urinal. Or somebody steals an antique plough from a front yard and then pretends they thought the owner wouldn't mind.'

'You enjoyed your trip,' Vera decided when Doris

returned. 'It was good for you to get away.' They never discussed Wayne, though Vera knew that despite Doris's determination to erase him from her mind she was concerned for his welfare. For ten years Wayne had been the focal point of her life. The last years had been punishing for her, yet Vera suspected there were moments when – remembering the happy periods – Doris wished painfully for his presence. In dividing the house into apartments, she'd made a point of delegating the bedroom she'd shared with Wayne to the rental apartment. She filled the evenings when she was not at the family house with local activities. But it would be a long time, Vera thought compassionately, before she erased Wayne from her heart.

Joel admitted to gratitude that Wayne had vanished. 'The bastard will land on his feet – wherever he is. But thank God, he's out of our lives.' But Vera knew he worried about Doris's future.

Now Joel and Vera were wrestling with the situation at the factory. Sales had taken a deep slump, which both had anticipated with foreign deals no longer coming in to the company. In addition to being apprehensive about the company's financial situation, Joel worried about keeping his employees on the payroll. This was a recurrent topic of discussion. At the approach of Thanksgiving – with Christmas and its attendant expenses not far behind – Joel expressed his anxiety at the dinner table.

'This town expects me to keep our people working. We cut back, they suffer. They *depend* on me.' He seemed drained, Vera thought sympathetically, but she understood his sense of responsibility to the town.

'Shouldn't we consider cutting back on hours?' Vera tried for a calm approach. They could afford to operate in the red for a time – but not indefinitely. 'No layoffs,' she emphasized. 'Put everybody on a four-day week –

and explain why we're doing this. Dad, they realize sales have dropped way off.'

'But with Christmas coming up?' Joel sighed. 'You know how big the Christmas season is here in town.'

'Let it be a little smaller,' Paul said, 'but everybody will have some income.'

'They won't be happy. We haven't cut back on hours since the Depression.' Joel paused in thought. 'But, yes, we'll cut back to a four-day week, stagger the hours – but no layoffs.' He seemed faintly relieved.

Joel cut back on his own salary and Vera's, made this known to the employees. Still, Vera was conscious of a depressing atmosphere in the factory. Now she made a tremendous effort to acquire new accounts – ever aware that the firm was under constant scrutiny by the government because of Wayne's activities.

Though a large number of local residents were feeling the pinch because of the shortened hours at the factory, the town soon wore its usual air of holiday festivity. Immediately after Thanksgiving, red and green lights were strung at intervals across Main Street. Christmas trees appeared before each shop. After dark, most houses were bright with Christmas lights.

The new year brought a burst of prosperity to most of the country – along with an easing of the Cold War due to Eisenhower's proposal that the United States and Russia share aerial inspections and military blueprints. There was a building-boom in cities. Housing construction soared. Sales of big-ticket items such as TVs and major appliances kept cash registers ringing in the stores and factories working. The one troubling note was the situation in the Far East. Hoping to combat Communism there, the United States was giving financial aid to South Vietnam, Cambodia, and Laos.

Paul was at first elated, then wary when Kerrigan announced that he would retire as principal at the end of the school year.

'Kerrigan is terribly behind the times,' Paul said to Vera when the word came through. 'But a couple of the board members are pressing for very progressive education. I can't go along with the super-permissiveness that's growing popular. I mean, this business of no grades – just *satisfactory* or *unsatisfactory*. Maybe it's easier on the kids' egos,' he acknowledged, 'but it does nothing for education.'

'It was dreamt up by lazy teachers,' Vera decided, laughing lightly. 'Think how much easier paper-grading becomes.'

'Progressive education started out fine.' Paul was serious now. 'It was meant to provide an imaginative kid with a chance to develop as an individual. But now, intellectual achievement is taking a back seat to the development of social skills,' he drawled sarcastically. 'What happens when these students go to college? The colleges insist – rightly – on specific courses. They don't want to hear about *progressive education*.'

Fighting for an increase in business, Vera was disturbed when she realized that the orders coming into Kahn Firearms were often from the South. On an unseasonably hot night in early June, she and Paul sat on the screen porch and discussed this situation.

'It's almost unbelievable,' Vera said sombrely, 'but statistics show the sale of small arms all over the South have gone up almost 400%. And the feeling is that it's due to the decision on segregated schools.'

'You're damn right.' Paul was grim. 'All the Washington DC schools were integrated immediately, and some Southern states have seen partial integration – but none in the Deep South. It scares me – the thought of all those handguns on the loose down there. And just anybody can buy a gun.'

'This will blow over.' Vera forced a smile. *Why had she mentioned guns?*

'There'll be hell to pay before we see school integration in the Deep South,' Paul predicted. 'And putting guns into the hands of racist Southerners guarantees explosive situations.'

Vera forced herself to be silent. How would Paul react when he learned – once the mechanics were worked out – that the company was considering going into the mail-order business? Mostly sporting goods, Vera thought defensively – but yes, they'd be selling guns, too ... if Dad went along with her persuasion for the company to move into mail order. In a small way, at first ... selling in a tri-state area. But mail order, she was trying to convince her father-in-law, was the wave of the future.

She remembered what Paul had said just yesterday about de Tocqueville. 'He predicted – maybe a hundred years ago – that the day would come when Negroes would rise up and demand the same rights as whites.' She remembered, too, how Dad had said Jews were especially sympathetic towards the coloured people because they knew what it was to be persecuted.

At uncomfortable intervals she asked herself how to cope with Paul's continuing unhappiness that his father and his wife were involved in the manufacture of guns. She tried so hard not to talk business in the house, but it was inevitable that this happened; and each time, Paul flinched. But that couldn't come between them – ever. Not with the love they shared, even after eleven years of marriage. Could it?

How would she handle it if Paul asked her to leave the company?

*

216

Vera tried to comfort Paul when the school year opened with a new principal – Roland Ames – in place. A man who was the total opposite of Kerrigan.

'Couldn't they have chosen somebody somewhere in the middle?' Paul asked three weeks later as he and Vera settled themselves in bed for the night. 'This guy is so *progressive* he scares the hell out of me. I suggested that I might take a group of our kids to Washington DC next month. And you know what the bastard said? "That's counter-productive, Paul. Take them to the local dairy or perhaps your father's factory. Let them touch reality,"' he mimicked distastefully. 'Can you see me taking a class to a gun factory?'

'Did Tracy tell you she was going to be Cinderella in the class play?' Vera was impatient to divert the conversation. 'I promised to be there, of course.' Her face grew tender. 'She said, "I won't be scared if you'll be there, Mommie."'

'I wish I could come, too.' Paul was apologetic.

'Darling, she understands that you can't take time off from school.'

He paused a moment. 'I didn't meant to yell at Tracy this morning the way I did. But I couldn't believe it when she asked Dad to teach her to shoot.'

'It's because she heard the little Bradley boy bragging about how good he was at target practice with his father,' Vera soothed.

'I don't want her learning to shoot.' Paul was suddenly tense.

'I'll talk to Dad about it,' she promised. This was hunting country. Most little boys learned to shoot. 'He'll make up some excuse.'

She moved her head to Paul's shoulder, thrust a leg across his. She knew the surest way to divert him. It was wonderful, she thought, the way he responded – as though this were still the first year of their marriage. Alone in bed they lived in a special Eden, isolated from the rest of the world.

Nothing must ever come between Paul and her. Doris was learning to survive without Wayne. He'd been a hurtful husband. Paul was so *good*. She could never survive without Paul.

During school vacation in the spring of '56 – when Vera and Paul were taking Laurie and Tracy for a much-anticipated week in Bermuda – Fiona decided to go with Adele to visit her mother in New York for four days.

'Mama just spoils Adele rotten,' Fiona said in high spirits while Vera waited with her for the train to pull into the Saratoga station. 'But she insists that's a grandma's privilege.'

'Adele's so bright and sweet she'll survive the spoiling,' Vera said affectionately. 'Just enjoy your vacation.'

Moments later, the train chugged into view. Fiona and Adele climbed aboard. Vera drove back to Eastwood for her final day at the office before their trip to Bermuda. Paul needed the relaxation, she thought. Pressure at the school was horrendous these days. She knew, too – with recurrent attacks of guilt – that Paul was upset that the company was taking the first move into the mail-order field. With a sporting goods catalogue, they would be selling hunting rifles by mail.

'Don't you realize what this means, Vera?' He'd stared at her in disbelief when she'd briefed him on this new business angle. 'Any lunatic can buy a gun!'

'These are hunting rifles,' she'd pointed out uneasily. 'We'll have a sporting goods catalogue. Rifles are standard items.' While neither she nor Paul wanted any part of hunting, it was a tradition in many parts of the country.

For the first time in their marriage, she felt that Paul

was truly angry with her. As with every couple, they'd had minor tiffs – but this was an unnerving hostility. That evening, she remembered with recurrent anxiety, she had hoped to reconcile in bed. But when she had reached out to Paul, he'd pretended to be asleep. In the morning he had been his normal self, yet she couldn't wash from her mind the memory of those moments when she'd felt a wall rise up between them.

Today, the hours at the office raced past. In the morning they would be en route to Bermuda – Laurie and Tracy enthralled by the prospect of flying. She had been dubious about their taking such an expensive vacation. It was Paul and Dad who had insisted. Would she ever be able to relax totally about money after the fearful years in Berlin?

The week in Bermuda was an oasis of lazy days and relaxing evenings. Their room looked down on the turquoise ocean and pink sand. Too soon they were boarding a plane for the flight to New York. There they collected the car for the drive to Eastwood.

While Laurie and Tracy slept on the rear seat of the car, Paul talked to Vera – her head on his shoulder – about the laws being passed in some Southern states that allowed them to bypass the Supreme Court ruling on school desegregation.

'What they're doing is subsidizing all-white private schools,' Paul said in frustration. 'There's going to be blood shed down there.' He was remembering, Vera thought guiltily, how the sale of handguns in the Deep South had escalated since the Brown vs. Board of Education decision. He knew that some of those guns had been supplied by their company.

'I suspect that a lot of Southerners realize they have a moral responsibility to desegregate in every area,' Vera said softly. 'And this isn't pre-World War II Germany;

Americans are free to speak their minds.' Not every German was a Nazi, but the ones who were out of sympathy were frightened into silence.

'I wish more would speak up,' Paul said bluntly. 'Before more people die. Like that young kid, Emmett Till, in Greenwood, Mississippi.'

When they turned into the driveway – golden with forsythia now, they saw that the entire lower floor of the house was lit. Doris's car was parked far down the circular driveway.

'We've got a welcoming party,' Paul said affectionately. 'I'll bet Fiona's been cooking up a storm.' Fiona and Adele had returned three days ago, Vera remembered. Laurie and Tracy had picked out presents for each.

Before they were out of the car, Joel and Doris appeared on the porch.

'You had a wonderful time,' Joel decided after an exchange of kisses. 'You all look refreshed.'

'It was heavenly,' Vera told him. 'Just what we needed.'

'I can go back to school tomorrow without flinching,' Paul said in high spirits. 'I've got the strength to deal with all the problems.'

'We figured right about when you'd arrive,' Doris said. 'The roast is just ready to come out of the oven.'

'And are we starving! I'll wait until after dinner to bring in our luggage,' Paul decided. 'The kids fell asleep midway, so we didn't bother to stop even for a snack.'

There was something spurious about their conviviality, Vera sensed in a sudden surge of alarm while Doris and Joel plied Laurie and Tracy with questions about Bermuda.

'But Paul said you were all starving,' Doris remembered with an over-bright smile. 'Let me go out to the kitchen and turn off the roast.'

'Where's Adele?' Laurie asked. 'I want to tell her I brought her a present.'

'She's still down in New York,' Doris said, strangely evasive. 'Vera, come out to the kitchen with me.' Her eyes pleaded for compliance.

Her heart pounding, Vera followed Doris down the hall and into the kitchen.

'Doris, what's wrong? Where are Adele and Fiona?'

'Dad and I thought Fiona had decided to stay in New York a couple of days longer. I didn't want to tell you in front of the kids.' Doris's voice broke. 'Fiona was struck by a hit-and-run driver near her mother's apartment building. One of her sisters called this morning. After her funeral.'

Chapter Twenty

Early on Sunday morning – dank and cold with the threat of snow in the air – Vera and Paul headed for New York. Last night they'd talked by phone with Fiona's mother, grieving but resigned. Adele had been asleep.

'It'll be warm in a few minutes,' Paul soothed, switching on the car heater. He paused a moment. 'The kids are awfully upset.'

'Fiona and Adele have been part of their lives ever since they can remember. Adele's like their sister. I just wish Fiona's mother would let her stay with us.' It was as though they'd lost a member of the family, Vera thought disconsolately.

'Her mind's made up,' Paul said gently. 'Let's focus on persuading her to allow Adele to stay with us until the end of the school year.' In a crisis Paul was always practical. 'Changing schools now – upset as she must be – would be traumatic.'

Last night she'd told Fiona's mother – Mary Lou – that they'd be happy to raise Adele, Vera fretted. In a few years Adele would be going off to college – hopefully to Hunter, as Fiona had wished. 'It's real kind of you, Miss Vera.' Born and raised in South Carolina, she was part of the old Southern tradition in many ways. They were Miss Vera and Mr Paul to her. 'But it wouldn't be right for Adele. She needs to grow up among her own folks, to know who she is. I always worried about Fiona and Adele living up there. It was like being in a foreign country.'

'It's good for Adele that Fiona has a large family. All those aunts and uncles.' Paul punctured the leaden silence that engulfed them for painful minutes. 'Three sisters and two brothers?'

'That's right. Two of her sisters still live at home with their kids.' No husbands, she recalled. Five daughters between them, from teenage pregnancies. *Three generations of women*, Fiona had confided in a bitter moment, *And no hope for none of them*. 'Gladys, the youngest, has a civil service job. She's in her own apartment. And the older brother, Henry, and his wife have their own place, too. He has a good job with Con Ed. They haven't seen Tyrone – the other brother – in years.' It had always upset Fiona that two of her sisters were on welfare – with no sign of getting off. She could understand that her mother had been unable to work for the past two years because of her arthritis, but she was ashamed that these two sisters made no effort to find jobs.

'I hope they catch the bastard who ran down Fiona.' Paul exuded fresh rage. 'Why should a fine woman like that have to die?'

On the long drive into Manhattan, Vera and Paul talked in bittersweet recollection of the years that Fiona and Adele had been part of their lives.

'Remember last year when we decided to buy the encyclopedia for the kids?' Tears stung Vera's eyes. 'I told Fiona that Adele could use the books whenever she liked, but Fiona insisted she'd buy a set for Adele. She said, "I always wished I had more time at school. Adele's smart. She'll finish high school. Maybe she'll even get into Hunter College. She wants to be a school teacher like Mr Paul. That's my dream for her."'

'Tracy's upset, yes – but Laurie's desolate,' Vera told Paul when they stopped at a diner for lunch.

She knew the weeks ahead would be difficult. Laurie

was so sure they'd convince Adele's grandmother to allow her to stay with them. Neither she nor Paul felt much hope that this could be accomplished. At least, she prayed in silence, let Adele come back with them to finish out the school year.

'It's always weird for me to come back to the Columbia area,' Paul said wryly an hour later when he turned off the highway and headed for the project where Fiona's mother lived – a dozen blocks north of the Columbia campus. 'That was another lifetime.' One hand left the wheel to reach for hers. 'Before I found you.'

They parked at the project, went in search of Mary Lou's building. Subconsciously Vera reached for Paul's hand. The atmosphere reeked of poverty and decay. Clusters of children and teenagers roamed about the area, noisy in their exchanges. At intervals they spied a neatly dressed family, their attire mute evidence that they were returning from church services. Fiona's mother – like Fiona herself – was very devout, submerged in various church activities. She could hear Fiona's voice now: '*It's the church that gives Mama and me the strength to carry on.*' She and Paul had not even been here for Fiona's funeral, Vera thought in anguish.

The moment she and Paul walked into the neat, modest living room of the apartment, Vera spied Adele slumped in a chair by a living room window – staring out but seeing nothing, she suspected. At the sound of their voices in conversation with her grandmother, Adele straightened up, ran in a desperate race for the comfort of Vera's arms.

'We just found out, Adele,' Vera whispered, tears falling unheeded down her cheeks. 'You have to be brave, darling.'

'Can I go home with you?' Adele pleaded, her dark eyes searching Vera's.

'We're trying to convince your grandmother to let you come with us,' Vera told her.

'Adele, you go out to the kitchen and you tell Edna to make a pot of coffee,' her grandmother instructed. 'Tell her Fiona's folks are here.'

'Yes'm,' Adele said, trained by her mother to be scrupulously polite. But her eyes turned to Vera in supplication before she left the room.

'Adele, you help Edna,' her grandmother added. 'Fix up a plate of cookies real pretty and put out the nice paper napkins.'

Vera understood Mary Lou was providing them a few moments together without Adele's presence.

'We love Adele,' Vera said earnestly. 'We'd be happy to keep her with us until she's ready to go away to college.'

'We talked about that, Miss Vera.' Mary Lou was polite but firm. 'Adele has to know her own folks. It was all right when she was little, but she'll be thirteen next year. Everything changes then. She has to know what her life is going to be like when she grows up. Fiona always talked about how wonderful you were to her and Adele,' Mary Lou said gratefully, 'but she worried a lot about when Adele got a little older and – and began to want to go out with boys.' Her eyes were eloquent. 'I'll raise her the best I know how.'

'Let her come home with us to finish out the school year,' Paul said gently. 'It would be a terrible experience to throw her into a strange school just at this time. It'll be easier for her in familiar surroundings.'

'Please,' Vera pleaded. 'Fiona would have liked that.'

Before they prepared to leave for Eastwood – with Adele – Paul explained to Mary Lou that Adele would receive Social Security cheques from her mother's benefits while she attended school. Mary Lou was bewildered.

'I know most people think it's a joke for employers to pay Social Security for domestic help, but my father realized it was important,' Paul told her. In truth, his father had paid both employer and employee's share.

'I know it's no joke,' Mary Lou told them. 'If the folks I worked for all these years had paid it – and me, too,' she added conscientiously, 'then I'd be getting Social Security instead of being on welfare. But we figured that meant we'd have to be paying taxes, too – and we saw little enough as it was.' She managed a shaky smile. 'But my daughter Gladys works for the government, and one day she'll get a pension – and Henry pays Social Security, and he'll get benefits some day.'

In Eastwood, Adele was welcomed with silent but obvious sympathy. Vera had arranged for Tracy to be promoted to a room of her own – the former guest room. Adele would share with Laurie – as Laurie had wished. It was a sad homecoming for Adele, Vera thought, but at least, she was surrounded by familiar faces.

Vera didn't want to think about the end of the school year – when Adele would have to go to live in the project with her grandmother.

Vera was upset when the junior high school decided to have a prom at the end of the school year. What she had been struggling to face – bearing out that Adele's grandmother was more honest than herself in seeing the problems of early dating – became glaring reality. She overheard a pair of mothers making acid remarks at a PTA meeting about interracial dating.

At the present there were only three coloured students in the entire Eastwood school system. Two were in junior high. Those mothers were fearful their *white* sons might be exposed to Adele on a social basis. How could she allow Adele to face a situation where she might be terribly hurt? Sweet, bright, pretty Adele – so vulnerable at this time.

While Laurie said nothing about a date for the prom, Vera knew she was already anxious about being asked.

'I hate this whole business of junior high school kids going to proms,' Paul said bluntly. 'It's a pressure parents are dumping on them. We don't see it in the cities. It started as a suburban deal. Now they're pushing it in the small towns. "Teach them social skills at an early age,"' he mimicked. 'Is it any wonder we're seeing so many teenage marriages?'

'I heard Tracy ask Laurie why she hadn't tried out for cheerleader.' Vera was sombre. 'Tracy told her that cheerleaders always have dates. But up until now – with the prom coming up – Laurie didn't think about dating. She was happy being with Adele. And thank God, she never brought up the dating question,' Vera said defiantly. 'I don't want to see our twelve-year-old daughter behaving as if she were eighteen.'

'If she gets a date for the prom, she'll take it for granted she can go,' Paul warned. 'Unless –' He hesitated. 'Unless Adele has no date. Then Laurie won't date. And considering the general feelings about interracial dating,' he said ruefully, 'I think we can rest easy.'

But as the prom date grew closer, Vera determined to sidestep the issue. So she was an old-fashioned mother. She didn't want Laurie – or Tracy – going out on dates with boys at their ages. It was absurd.

Vera plotted for a moment to speak alone with Laurie. Together she and Paul had decided to take the two girls, along with Tracy, into New York the night of the junior prom. They'd have a pre-theatre dinner, then go to the theatre to see 'Silk Stockings', the hit musical by Cole Porter. But Laurie was outraged when she talked about going to New York that night.

'You mean, miss the junior prom?' She stared at her mother in disbelief.

'It's a wonderful musical.' Vera struggled to sound persuasive.

'Mom, everybody's going to the prom!' Laurie gazed at her mother with naked hostility.

'Laurie, you love Adele, don't you?' This was a moment when honesty was the only weapon.

'Sure.' Laurie was baffled by the question.

'Well, we – we live in a strange world.' She was groping for words. 'If Adele goes to the prom, I'm afraid she'll be very hurt.' Still, Laurie appeared baffled. 'You know about the trouble with school integration down South.' The grown-ups in this household spoke openly in front of the girls about the Supreme Court ruling and the reaction in the Southern states. They knew about the ugly demonstrations that appeared at regular intervals. It was more important for them to know what was happening in their world, she and Paul had long ago decided, than to 'build social skills.' Laurie and Tracy's school might ignore the integration crisis, thinking families would not. 'It's in the newspapers and on television all the time.'

'We don't have segregated schools here,' Laurie said, growing impatient with this discussion.

'No,' Vera conceded, 'but we have people who don't realize that the colour of somebody's skin shouldn't be important. Laurie, if Adele goes to that prom, she's going to be terribly hurt.' Her eyes pleaded with Laurie to understand what she was trying to say.

All at once comprehension overtook Laurie. She was shaken. She was bright and compassionate, Vera told herself with gratitude. *She understood.*

'Okay,' Laurie said after a moment. 'So we'll go to New York the night of the prom.'

*

Today had been humid and enervating, but now at dusk a breeze brought welcome relief. In the bedroom next to Laurie's Tracy listened to the latest Pat Boone record their grandfather had added to their collection. Both girls were Pat Boone fans. In the bedroom she'd shared with Adele these last weeks, Laurie sat at the edge of her bed while Adele packed. It was going to be terrible without Adele here, she thought in recurrent rebellion. Why hadn't Mom persuaded Adele's grandmother to let her stay with them? She hadn't tried hard enough. All Mom cared about was being at the factory. *Selling guns*.

'Your father said we could put my encyclopedia in two cartons and put them in the trunk of the car,' Adele remembered.

'Sure.' Laurie struggled to sound matter-of-fact. Didn't they understand how awful it would be for Adele? She would have to share a room with her grandmother and a little cousin. A tiny room with bunk beds. Mom should have made Adele's grandmother understand Adele should stay here. 'Mom said I could drive down to New York with you.' Mrs O'Reilly – who came in every morning and stayed until she'd served dinner – would be with Tracy. Grandpa had decided not to have sleep-in help now. Mom and Daddy took turns making breakfast. Mrs O'Reilly came in at eleven.

'You'll write me?' Adele's eyes were wistful.

'You know I will. Every week,' Laurie promised. 'And Mom's going to ask your grandmother to let you come here for two weeks before school opens.' New York was miserable in the summer, she'd heard Daddy say. 'We'll always be best friends,' she said with sudden urgency. 'Forever and ever.'

'Forever and ever,' Adele said solemnly.

Long after they had turned off the lights and settled themselves in their beds, Laurie and Adele talked in whispers. It wasn't fair for Adele's grandmother to make her live in New York, Laurie told herself over and over again. Grown-ups could be so mean.

In the morning Laurie and Adele awoke before the scheduled time, both desolate at the imminent separation. It wasn't fair, Laurie railed yet again, for Adele's mother to be killed that way and for her grandmother to make her go live in New York. Best friends should grow up together. *Why did God let this happen?*

By eight o'clock, Laurie and Adele were settled in the car while Laurie's father brought out Adele's luggage and the cartons with the encyclopedia. Mom gave Adele a box of fancy stationery and a sheet of stamps, Laurie remembered. Adele would write Mom once in a while, Laurie told herself triumphantly, but she'd write *her* every week. She and Adele were *best friends*.

Mom said they'd have breakfast at a diner on the highway. She and Adele could order whatever they wanted. But it would be so awful driving home, she mourned, without Adele.

Early in August – after much persuasion – Vera was able to convince Mary Lou to let Adele come to visit for two weeks. She would be in New York for a business meeting, would remain overnight in the city, pick up Adele the following day. Laurie and Tracy could drive down with her, both thrilled by the prospect of a trip to the city. Midmorning of the second day in the city, Vera checked out of the hotel with the girls, went with them to collect the car, and drove uptown. Her heart ached for Adele when they approached the housing project, so different from what Adele had known most of her life. Fiona had run away from this, wanting better for her bright, sweet child.

In the hot August sunlight children roamed the

grounds, the older screeching orders to the younger. A toddler lay asleep on the ground beside a tree. Inside the building the air was fetid in the oppressive heat. The elevator reeked of urine. Not from pets, Vera guessed; animals were not permitted in the project.

Mary Lou greeted them with warmth. Adele – her face radiant – rushed to exchange exuberant hugs with Laurie, then with Tracy and Vera.

'Edna, you bring out that pitcher of ice tea I just made and some glasses,' Mary Lou ordered her eldest daughter, crouched before the TV set along with her sister, both seemingly mesmerized by the programme.

'Yeah, sure.' Reluctantly, Edna rose to her feet, her eyes following the screen as she ambled towards the kitchen with a perfunctory smile for their visitors.

Vera was touched by the relief she sensed in Adele at the prospect of leaving the project apartment behind her for two weeks. She'd been here only since the close of school, Vera thought, but Adele had matured far beyond her age in that time. But she was a strong little girl, Vera thought tenderly. A survivor.

Driving back to Eastwood – Vera pondered the odd division between Mary Lou's children. Like Fiona, Gladys and Henry were bright and determined to improve their lot in life. Edna and Lottie – and she suspected the same could be said of the long-missing Tyrone – had left school early and were semi-literate, devoid of any ambition. A cross for Mary Lou to bear, Vera thought in sympathy.

She was betting that Adele would pull herself above the project existence, but it would be a long, difficult road. And she was conscious of a lingering suspicion that Laurie held *her* responsible for Adele's having to live in the squalor of the Harlem housing project – just as Laurie had never let go of her anger that her mother and grandfather were involved in the business of manufacturing guns.

How was she to make Laurie understand that she had tried desperately to have Adele remain with them? How did she make Laurie understand that guns were weapons of peace as well as death? Without weapons how would Israel survive? How could the Allies have stopped the madness of Hitler?

Chapter Twenty-one

The blanket of snow that surrounded the house on this New Year's Eve lent a spurious air of serenity. But moving about the spacious kitchen while she prepared dinner – because Mrs O'Reilly was off today and tomorrow – Vera was remembering the crises inflicted on the world during the last twelve months. The riots in Poland, Nasser's seizure of the Suez Canal – with British and French troops bombing Egyptian airfields in retaliation and Israel capturing the whole Gaza Strip and the Sinai Peninsula in less than 100 hours. The Soviet invasion of Hungary, Tunisia's fight for independence from France, Sudan's battle for freedom. Paul couldn't just listen to the TV news and sympathize. He suffered for the killed and the maimed.

She smiled tenderly at the sound of Laurie's voice – in intense telephone conversation with Adele – drifting down the stairs. Because this was New Year's Eve, Laurie had been permitted to phone Adele down in New York. They still wrote each other every week.

In the living room, Tracy and Dad argued high-spiritedly about a chess move. Paul was engrossed in a book. Vera was grateful that Tracy had become so enamoured of chess sessions with her grandfather. There were moments when she feared Tracy felt shut out from the closeness she had shared earlier with Laurie.

'Hi.' Doris strolled into the kitchen, puncturing her introspection. 'I finally found a place that was still open and had vanilla ice cream. You know, Dad, hot apple pie *has* to be topped with vanilla ice cream.'

'Oh, great!'

'I'll have just a smidgeon,' Doris said wistfully. 'I've got to drop twenty pounds.'

'The turkey should be ready in about twenty minutes,' Vera decided, thrusting a fork into one burnished thigh.

They'd had the usual party at the office. Each year they expected to be on the way home by one or two, and always the party dragged on until four. She'd rushed home to put up the turkey – a tradition in the Kahn household at New Year's as well as Thanksgiving. Paul and the girls, of course, had been on school vacation since before Christmas.

Paul was wonderful about spending time with them, but she could never quite brush aside the suspicion that Laurie resented *her* working. She was always there for special events at school, she reminded herself defensively. She went on school outings for both Laurie and Tracy's classes two or three times a year. Yet she knew that to her daughters she wasn't 'like other mothers.' She'd overheard a brief discussion between the two girls once. '*Why can't Mom be like Gail's mother?*' Laurie had complained. Gail's mother was there every afternoon when they came home from school, made fancy cookies, and loved working in her garden. Tracy had said, '*Mom's the nicest mother in the whole world.*'

Vera's mind charged back to the Friday night three weeks ago when she'd come home from a particularly difficult day at the office. After dinner she and Paul and Tracy had settled themselves in the living room. Laurie was away at her first 'pyjama party.' Dad had gone to a Chamber of Commerce meeting. Paul focused on correcting exams, Tracy did homework, and she studied the layout for their spring catalogue. At Tracy's bedtime, she went upstairs with her, ran her bath, and prepared to go downstairs for another hour's work on the catalogue.

And then Tracy had thrust her into troubling self-examination.

'Mom, stay with me while I bathe,' she'd pleaded wistfully.

'Darling, I have this catalogue copy to work on,' she'd begun.

'Can't you do it here?' Tracy asked. 'Put down the toilet lid and sit there. I won't talk. I'd just like us to be here together.'

'The work can wait for later,' Vera had said instantly. How could she put work ahead of her precious baby? 'Tell me what happened at school today.'

She *wasn't* 'the nicest mother in the whole world,' she reproached herself. Tracy and Laurie – *family* – must come before the business. She wasn't some frantic, single mother struggling to survive, who had no choice. If something happened and she couldn't work, the family would manage.

'I hope the dressing is good.' Doris broke into her introspection. This year the dressing had been Doris's project.

'I'm sure it is.'

Together she and Doris brought dinner to the table. She knew that Doris's thoughts on holidays such as this reached out to earlier such occasions when Wayne had been with her. Doris frequently confided her relief that she was a free woman now, yet she also conceded there were still dark moments when she remembered the early *good* years. '*When I loved a man who didn't exist.*'

'Everybody to the table.' Doris summoned the others. 'You'll finish your chess game later,' she told her father and Tracy. 'Paul, yell upstairs to Laurie to come down to dinner.'

Joel sat at the head of the table and concentrated on carving the turkey, amid kibitzing from Paul and Tracy.

'I know,' he drawled good-humouredly, 'every turkey should come equipped with four legs. But this is a big bird – four can share two.'

'How's Adele?' Vera asked Laurie.

'Okay.' Laurie shrugged. 'Except she hates living in that noisy, crowded apartment and hates her new school.' Without meeting her mother's eyes, she extended her plate to her grandfather for a helping of turkey.

Vera tensed. Laurie was still angry with her for not persuading Mary Lou to allow Adele to live with them. But Adele's grandmother was a wise woman. She knew it wouldn't be good for Adele to live up here, one of three coloured children in town.

'How's Adele doing in school?' Vera asked and berated herself for pursuing this. She knew Laurie didn't want to talk about Adele.

'Adele's smart. She's doing fine.' Laurie turned away. 'Aunt Doris, could I have some dressing?'

Vera saw the sympathetic glance Paul beamed in her direction. He didn't want to admit it, but he knew there was friction between Laurie and her.

For a while the table conversation was lighthearted; but as so often happened in this family, a more serious tone soon took over. Paul and Joel began to rehash the events of the past twelve months. She didn't want to think about those things, Vera told herself in simmering impatience. *What was she to do about this wall between Laurie and herself?*

'Look, Nasser grabbed the Suez Canal so that the whole world would recognize him as the supreme Moslem power,' Joel scoffed. 'But the real objective was to destroy Israel. That would clinch it for him. But it still pisses me –' He stopped short, grinned. 'Laurie, Tracy, you didn't hear me say that. It tees me off,' he amended, 'that the UN insisted that Israel withdraw from the Gaza Strip and the

Sinai. It just means more fighting in the years ahead. We'll see –'

'Dad, we're almost at the beginning of the new year,' Doris interrupted. 'No more war talk. Let's feel festive.'

'There wouldn't be war if people didn't make guns,' Laurie said, a defiant glint in her eyes.

'Laurie, don't start up with that again,' her grandfather scolded lightly, but Vera sensed his irritation. 'As long as there's a world, there'll be guns. Without guns there can be no peace.'

'Paul, what's happening with your plans to take a bus-load of kids down to Washington this spring?' Doris asked in an effort, Vera understood, to rechannel the conversation. 'You'll make sure to go during the cherry blossom season?'

'Cherry blossom season, yes,' Paul said. 'But I need another few committed for the trip before I can finalize arrangements. A trip to New York to be in the studio audience for a TV performance by Elvis Presley would generate a lot more excitement.' He gestured his frustration.

'I'd love to see Elvis Presley!' Tracy was enthralled at the prospect.

'What's for dessert?' Joel asked Vera. To him, Elvis Presley was still 'Elvis the Pelvis,' pushed into fame by his hips rather than his voice.

'Hot apple pie and vanilla ice cream,' Vera told him. 'We have to start the new year off right.'

But she was starting the new year with painful anxiety about her relationship with Laurie. Paul kept telling her it was just the beginning of the crazy adolescent period. In a few months they'd be the parents of a teenager. Everybody said that rebellion and protest were part of becoming an adolescent, that this was always a tough period in parents' lives.

Vera's thoughts hurtled back through the years to the time when she had been thirteen – a period when no child, whatever age, questioned a parent's authority. Sometimes she was taken aback when Laurie or Tracy answered a decree with *Why? I don't think that's fair.* Paul said it was the result of the weakening of the educational system. Teenagers were coddled in school – and expected the same at home.

At thirteen, Vera mused in poignant recall, family had been the focus of her life. And then she'd lost her family. The pain had never totally disappeared. And now she was terrified by this breach between Laurie and herself.

Later, as she and Paul prepared for bed, she confessed her fears to him.

'We'll get through this,' he consoled. 'Most parents do.'

'I listen to teenagers today, and I don't believe what I hear sometimes.' Vera turned down the bedclothes and slid beneath. She hadn't been a normal teenager, she conceded. She'd been grateful to be alive, to have a home. 'I heard this sixteen-year-old in line behind me at the supermarket on Saturday. He was complaining because his parents wouldn't let him have his own car. "What's the matter with them? They've got good credit. They can get a car loan." Today's kids – today's people,' she amended, 'have lost all sight of saving for tomorrow. They expect the good times to go on forever.' Even now, with their income so healthy, she saw to it that they saved.

'I work with these kids.' Paul was grim. 'I can't stand what we're doing to them. It's adults who're doing it,' he went on before she could intervene. 'We treat them like royalty, give them every conceivable goodie.'

'So it's natural that they take this for granted – and then demand more.' Vera flinched in comprehension.

'Our whole educational system is going to backfire, Vera.' Paul shook his head. 'We worry so much about

Russia and their grasp at new technology. Hell, Russian kids go to school six hours a day, six days a week. Their kids are *required* to take ten years of math, four years of chemistry, six of biology, five of physics. At Eastwood High, we're not even *offering* physics or chemistry! I'd guess their high school graduates have a stronger background in science and math than a lot of our college grads.'

Vera recalled conversation at the dinner table. 'Laurie says Adele hates her school.'

'Of course she does,' Paul said gently. 'Eastwood schools are full of shortcomings, God knows – but Harlem schools are in far worse shape. But Adele is very bright. She'll dig in her heels and get herself a decent education despite that. She's a determined little girl with her goal always in mind. She'll have to fight for her education, but she'll get it.'

'I worry about Laurie. I worry all the time. She blames me for Adele's not being here. How do I make her understand that we did everything we could to keep Adele with us?'

'You can't.' Paul slid under the covers, reached to draw her into the comfort of his arms. 'It's something she's going to have to arrive at herself.'

'It's so awful,' Vera whispered, 'knowing Laurie thinks badly of me . . . when I love her so much.'

'It's part of being a parent. The rough comes with the good. Laurie's a lot like you, baby.' His voice was gentle. 'You're both so intense about what you think is right and wrong. You're both –'

'Everything I do is wrong in Laurie's eyes,' Vera broke in with painful urgency. 'She hates the business. She hates my working. She hates me for not fighting Adele's grandmother more forcefully.'

'That's for now,' Paul comforted. 'She'll –'

'You hate the business, too.' Vera searched his eyes in the soft light of the night-table lamp. 'You resent my working there.'

'I don't resent it,' he said after a moment. 'I just wish Dad would move into the mail-order business – without selling hunting rifles – and forget the rest. I want our kids to grow up in a peaceful world, a world without guns. Look at England – even their cops don't carry guns.'

'Look at Israel and Switzerland,' Vera countered. 'Almost everybody owns a gun. It makes Israel's survival possible, and Switzerland is the most peaceful nation in the world – and has the least crime.' She paused. 'Sometimes Laurie makes snide remarks to Dad about the business. It hurts him.'

'Dad understands she doesn't mean to do that,' Paul soothed.

'And what's wrong about my working?' she demanded with fresh defiance. 'I don't neglect the girls because I work. What law says I have to stay at home and cook and clean and wax floors? I heard a couple of men at the factory making cracks about *working wives*. To them we're neurotic women with ants in our pants who can't stay home and be real wives and mothers.'

'I don't feel that way,' Paul insisted. 'Dad always says what a major asset you are to the business. I just wish it were another kind of business –'

'For generations your family has made guns and rifles,' Vera said tiredly. 'Dad's proud of his contribution to this country. He feels he's helping to keep the peace.' But Paul was writing letters to the editors of newspapers around the state urging them to promote control of handguns. To a lot of people in town he was an oddball. That was upsetting to Dad, with his obsession to be loved by everyone in Eastwood.

'Baby, relax,' Paul soothed, drawing her face to his.

He knew the best way in the world to make her relax, she thought tenderly, and closed her eyes while his mouth reached for hers and he slid one hand within the neckline of her nightie. Thank God for this, she told herself, already responding to his ardour. Together in bed they could push aside – for a little while – all their doubts and fears. It had been this way when bombs rained over London. It would be this way until death separated them.

She had to believe that.

Chapter Twenty-two

As the months went by, Vera watched for signs that Laurie was forgiving her for Adele's absence in their lives. Only in early spring – when Laurie came down with a bad case of flu – did she feel that Laurie loved her as before. She stayed away from the factory for a whole work-week – something other working mothers might not have the privilege of doing, she admitted to herself – and spent most of her waking hours at Laurie's bedside.

'Mommie, I love you,' Laurie whispered as Vera washed her face and brushed her hair after a bout of nausea.

'I love you, too, darling.' Vera clung to this brief moment. She had not totally lost Laurie. *Mommie, I love you* was sweet solace on those trying occasions when her young daughter seemed to regard her as a mortal enemy – as when she'd refused to allow her to wear lipstick before she was fifteen and insisted on going shopping with her to buy her first bras. Laurie was simultaneously enthralled and embarrassed by the obvious need for this purchase.

'Vera, don't get so upset,' Paul pleaded. 'We've entered a new era. We're parents of a teenager.'

She and Paul socialized mainly with his fellow teachers, some of whom were also dealing with the adolescent phenomenon. At a barbecue at one couple's house at the close of the school year, the subject monopolized the conversation.

'Monica thinks we're millionaires,' their hostess

declared in frustration. 'I tell her that her father is a teacher, not a TV star. I don't want to tell you what she put us through with her senior prom. I know it happens in suburbia, but here in Eastwood?'

'They see television,' a mother of early teenagers picked up. 'They see Hollywood movies. Our world revolves around teenagers. But I told my kids bluntly, if I catch them smoking, they're grounded for a month. I don't care how they carry on.'

'If my kid tells me one more time – when I tell her she can't do something – that Gerry's parents say it's okay, I'll probably wring her neck,' one father contributed grimly. 'They're getting too much too soon.'

By mid-July, Laurie was already impatient for Adele's arrival for two weeks in Eastwood. Adele was fun – she made her laugh. The first two weeks of school vacation had been terrific. She'd slept till noon, spent the afternoon at the pool, listened to her records all evening. Now she was bored. The kids here at home were so *immature* – a word she used frequently these days. Donna and Gail would spend hours just playing around with lipsticks and eye shadow. Or talking about boys. Boys were so silly.

Donna was still moping because she didn't make the drum majorette squad. Her mother had promised her a whole collection of Bobby Darin records if she did. Gail and Donna thought she was a real nerd because she was excited about being on the math team. Dad and Grandpa thought it was terrific. Mom made a big fuss about it – but she didn't really care. She was only interested in sales figures at the factory or how well the shop was doing and how the catalogue mailing list was growing.

She had been the only girl in the after-school Current Events group, then five more had come in because it looked like what Gail called 'a dating zoo.' But none of the boys in the Current Events group were on the football or basketball team, so the other girls dropped out. Was there something wrong with her because she liked math and current events?

On the day Adele was to arrive, Laurie was awake at 7:00 AM even though Adele's train wasn't due for hours. Adele's grandmother worried that nobody would be at the Saratoga train station to meet her. If she and Mom weren't there on time, her grandmother would *never* let Adele come up again.

Laurie felt queasy at the thought that she and Mom might not be there when Adele's train pulled into the station. For the first time since school vacation began, Laurie was at the breakfast table.

'We have to be in Saratoga to pick up Adele,' she reminded her mother anxiously as she sat at the breakfast table.

'We'll be there, Laurie.' Her mother smiled and poured her a glass of orange juice. 'Come over to the factory at eleven and we'll head for Saratoga. We'll stop off somewhere for lunch on the way home.'

'Walk to the factory?' Laurie's eyes widened. 'Daddy won't be here to drive me. He'll be at summer school.' She turned to her father for confirmation.

'It's a ten-minute walk,' he told her and chuckled at her blank stare. 'Laurie, you've got two healthy feet.'

She intercepted the amused exchange between her mother and father. Mom or Daddy always drove her where she needed to go. Was this some kind of strike? Everybody knew parents drove you wherever you had to go. She couldn't wait till she was old enough to get her driver's licence.

Laurie was relieved that they were at the Saratoga station half an hour before Adele's train was to arrive. She'd forgotten, Laurie conceded, that Mom was always early everywhere. They sat down in the all-but-deserted waiting room – hot and sticky today. Her blouse was damp with perspiration, clung to her back. With no real interest, she accepted a segment of the newspaper her mother handed her and scanned the front page.

Mom said Daddy would drive her and Adele out to the Eastwood pool for a swim when he came home from summer school. Adele would like that. She just hoped Daddy wouldn't say something awful about their bathing suits – the way Gail's father had at her church picnic. 'Gail, what's that you're almost wearing?'

Adele's train arrived on schedule. They exchanged exuberant embraces, settled in the car. They discussed the merits of hamburger over pizza, decided on hamburgers and Cokes. 'After lunch, we'll stop for frozen custard,' her mother promised.

The world seemed beautiful as she and Adele sat together after lunch on the back seat of the car and made enthusiastic inroads on cones piled high with chocolate frozen custard. In ecstatic pantomime they discussed the bras each wore now as a symbol of having attained the exalted status of teenager.

Laurie knew it was going to be terrific to spend two weeks with Adele. They laughed a lot, but they could be serious, too. Every night they watched the TV news with Mom and Dad. There was a lot of talk about the trouble breaking out in the Deep South over school integration. Laurie was incensed when Adele remarked that going to school in Harlem was like going to a segregated school.

'But that's not even in the South,' Laurie exploded.

'I know.' Adele shrugged. 'But that's the way it is.'

Laurie listened sombrely while her father – clearly sympathetic – questioned Adele about her school.

'When I grow up and graduate from college, I'll get a

job teaching in my school,' Adele said with calm conviction. 'I want to help make it better.'

Too soon it was time for Adele to return to her grandmother's apartment – *where Edna and Lottie sit and watch soap operas all day*. Laurie watched wistfully while Adele's train pulled out of the station, slowly disappeared from view. It was as if a special part of her life were being snatched away again, she thought. Adele belonged in this family.

'Laurie, we have to go back home now,' her mother said softly.

Along with many Americans, Vera and Paul were upset by the violence that continued to explode in the Deep South over school integration. In September, the family clung to the TV screen every night to see the latest developments in the efforts in Little Rock, Arkansas, to enroll nine brave young Negro students in the Little Rock high school.

'It'll take time, but we'll see integrated schools in the next few years.' Joel was philosophical. On occasion, Vera thought, Dad's determined optimism was trying. 'It'll happen.'

'It's the law!' Laurie blazed. 'Why doesn't it happen now? What's the matter with people?'

Vera watched helplessly while sibling hostility soared between Laurie and Tracy. Tracy felt left out of Laurie's orbit now, she realized in anguish. While Laurie had developed no intense friendship with other girls at school, she made it clear she considered Tracy a 'baby' compared to her newly achieved adolescent status.

'It's normal at her age,' Paul comforted, and Doris backed him up.

On the October night when news spread around the world that the Soviet Union had launched a space satellite called Sputnik 1, Vera made no effort to prod Laurie and Tracy to their bedrooms to start their homework. She and Paul and the girls – along with Joel – were spellbound by the report on TV evening news.

'That's the first step in space travel,' Joel marvelled. 'They've got a space satellite!'

'And we've got egg on our faces,' Paul said bluntly. 'The United States is supposed to be the Great Innovator. How can we be when we're turning out half the number of engineers and scientists than the Russians?'

A month later, the Soviet Union launched its second satellite – Sputnik 2. For once Laurie and Tracy united in their outrage. An Eskimo dog had been sent into space aboard the second satellite.

'That's awful!' Laurie shrieked. 'How can they send up that poor little dog?'

'He'll be scared to death,' Tracy mourned. 'He'll be awful sick!'

Shortly after this Tracy announced to her parents that she intended to be a vet. A few months earlier, she'd vowed to be a rock star, Vera remembered. There would be a dozen other choices, she guessed indulgently, before Tracy found her niche in life. Just let her find some profession that would make her happy, she prayed. She and Paul wouldn't push either of the girls in any direction.

But ten days later, Vera and Paul were shocked when Tracy confided that she honestly didn't know what she wanted to be when she grew up but added one stipulation.

'I just know it has to be something that'll make me rich.'

'Why?' Vera demanded, aghast. What had she and Paul done to make Tracy believe that money was all-important?

'Money buys things. I want to live like a movie star,' Tracy said blissfully. 'Like Natalie Wood and Robert

Wagner. And Tuesday Weld. Did you know that Tuesday Weld owns six cars? One of them is a Mercedes.' *Tracy had never even seen a Mercedes.*

'Where do you find this weird information?' Paul exchanged a bewildered glance with Vera.

'My movie magazines,' Tracy explained. 'They tell you everything. I adore them.'

'And she's not even twelve?' Paul turned accusingly to Vera. '*You let her read movie magazines?*'

'Paul, all the girls do.' Vera was startled by the hostility in his voice.

'And God, do they use that as a force.' Paul was grim. 'Why can't we say, "We don't care what so-and-so's parents let them do. You do what *we* say."?'

'We save it for important matters,' Vera decided after a moment. 'The ones that bring out that wail we all know.' She tried for humour. '"Mom, you, just don't understand!"'

Vera and Paul both worried at the tendency in this decade for girls to marry very young. She had been young, of course, Vera acknowledged – but she and Paul had been living in traumatic times. She couldn't become accustomed to today's high school marriages. Thank God, she thought, Laurie wasn't caught up in the junior high 'going steady' scene. Laurie considered it 'nerdy.' But one of her classmates was already talking about her wedding.

'What's their rush?' Vera wailed. 'Fewer girls are going to college these days than before the war. Wouldn't you think it'd be the other way round?'

With shocking swiftness, it seemed to Vera, they were facing another New Year's Eve. It worried her that Paul felt that he was accomplishing so little at the school. She worried about Doris, who proclaimed herself happy with her new life style but was eating herself into obesity. Dad worried that the country was heading for a serious recession. Was there ever a time when you could just sit back and enjoy being alive?

Dad had been right about a recession, Vera conceded in March of the new year, when unemployment soared to over five million. But he was proud that they were avoiding layoffs at the factory. *We survived the Depression. We can sit this out.* Despite the recession, Vera was expanding their catalogue business. She switched a crew from the factory to the catalogue mailing room.

It was a year of upheavals around the world. After rioting by French settlers in Algeria, France had seized power. King Faisal II of Iraq was assassinated and the country proclaimed a republic. In Hungary, former President Imre Nagy was executed following a secret trial. In Venezuela, Perez Jimenez was overthrown.

Their own lives, Vera mused while she and Doris prepared New Year's Eve dinner, had changed not at all – except that Tracy was almost as tall as she now and Laurie had bypassed her by two inches. Dad was shrugging aside good-humoured taunts of his friends that he could retire. 'So I can apply for Social Security. Then what? Retire to Florida and die of boredom?'

Paul would have loved teaching if he could have instituted some of his ideas for change in the Eastwood school system. While the big city soaring crime rate was not reflected in towns like Eastwood, he warned that the ripple would spread to include them. 'With our slipshod education, what else can we expect? We're losing the education battle!'

As did many Americans, Vera and Paul rejoiced when on the first day of 1959 Fidel Castro and his followers drove the repressive dictator, Batista, out of Cuba. On January 3, Alaska became the 49th state. 'Wow, the flagmakers must be happy!' Tracy chortled. By the end of the month, Paul was agonizing over his approaching birthday.

'Vera, I'll be thirty-eight years old. What have I accomplished in my life?' It wasn't enough, she knew, to remind him that each year he had a core of students who were devoted to him. He wanted to soar, she thought with a rush of compassion, but this happened for only the fortunate few.

At a Friday-evening dinner Vera was ambivalent when Joel announced that for Laurie's fifteenth birthday he was offering a student trip to Paris during school vacation.

'I have to tell you now,' he explained, 'because all reservations must be made by March 15. Do you think you'd like it?'

'Oh, Grandpa, it'd be cool!' She turned warily to her mother. 'I can go, can't I?'

She turned to Paul. He nodded in agreement. 'Of course you can go. It'll be a wonderful experience for you.' She'd be a nervous wreck while Laurie was away, Vera warned herself. Laurie had never been away for longer than overnight. It was scary to envision an ocean between them.

'It doesn't mean Adele can't come here for two weeks?' All at once Laurie was wary.

'Of course Adele will come to us as usual,' Vera reassured her – ever touched by the two girls' devotion to each other.

'It won't all be fun,' Joel teased. 'You'll have French classes every morning. And don't you look so downcast, Tracy. I've got a birthday surprise for you, too. Months early, of course.' Tracy's birthday was in early December. 'What about a student bus tour to the Grand Canyon?'

'Cool,' Tracy echoed and automatically cast an inquiring glance at her mother.

'Dad, you're spoiling them rotten,' Vera scolded good-humouredly. 'They'll have a wonderful time.'

'I didn't tell you and Paul,' he apologized and grinned. 'I was scared you'd spill it before I was sure there were openings. And with both kids away, what are you two planning?'

'We'll think of something,' Vera said, her eyes meeting Paul's. It would be like a second honeymoon – just the two of them. They'd never had a real honeymoon, she corrected herself. The nearest thing to that was Paul's furlough in London at V-E Day – but all the time the spectre of his being shipped to the Pacific had hung over them.

In due time they were seeing Laurie and her group off at Idlewild Airport in New York, and two days later they were down in New York again to see Tracy – struggling to appear confident about the imminent separation – off with her group on a tour bus. She'd be all right, wouldn't she? Vera asked herself in yet another flurry of unease.

She and Paul would spend three nights in New York – seeing as many plays as they could manage – then drive up to an inn at the end of Long Island for ten days. Both had a special fondness for Manhattan, they readily acknowledged – yet they were always happy to be back in the serenity of Eastwood after a trip to the city.

They were triumphant at managing to see three evening performances and one matinee before heading far out on Long Island for a charming inn at Montauk that Doris's friend Sally had recommended. On a brilliantly sunny morning they checked out of their hotel, went to the garage to pick up their car, and drove out of Manhattan en route to Gurney's Inn.

'Do you think the kids are having a good time?' Vera asked, her head on Paul's shoulder.

'They're having a ball,' he surmised. 'No need to worry about Laurie's plane arriving safely,' he reminded. 'You checked with the tour office and the airline office. And

Tracy called from their first stop and told Dad she'd made friends already.'

'I won't think about them again until we're back in Eastwood,' she promised lightly.

'Don't you feel about twenty years younger? Fancy free with no kids around?'

'Let's do this every year,' she said, feeling a rare serenity.

They were charmed by their room at Gurney's Inn, which nestled on a knoll overlooking the Atlantic. The seemingly endless stretch of beach a pristine white, the ocean a dazzling blue beneath a sunlit sky. Without bothering to unpack, they left their room and hurried down to walk at the water's edge.

That evening – lying in Paul's arms – Vera told herself they must learn not to lose themselves entirely in parenthood. They were not just Laurie and Tracy's mother and father, they were Vera and Paul, too. Now they made a point of being two carefree people in love with their surroundings and each other. They explored the quaint little town, visited the lighthouse, walked barefoot along the water's edge. And every night they made passionate love. Even after almost sixteen years of marriage, their feelings for each other hadn't changed.

Only on the night before they were to return to Eastwood did Paul allow himself to become serious. They sprawled on chaises on their deck and held hands while Paul confessed to his anxieties about the coming school year.

'Nobody's coming out and saying it aloud, but everybody's sure Ames is suffering from lung cancer. You know he's always been a chain smoker. Ted says the board is secretly discussing a new principal.'

'You deserve the promotion,' Vera said quickly. But was Paul too innovative, too independent in his thinking to win over the board? There was a clique in town who would want to see him running the high school – but did they have the clout to make it happen? 'Paul, fight for it!'

'Sometimes I think I should have gone on for my PhD, tried for a college post. Here I am, staring at forty and –'

'You're not staring at forty,' she contradicted. Again, with the age! 'You'll be thirty-nine on your next birthday. And that isn't ancient.'

'I want to be principal,' he said with savage intensity. 'I see so much that the school needs to make our students competitive. Too few go on to college as it is. And those few that go are not making it into top schools.'

'What can we do to help your chances?' Her eyes searched his. Oh, he deserved this promotion! She knew that some teachers – and some faculty wives – cultivated members of the Board of Education in hopes of winning favours. In their culture, wives were supposed to help their husbands move up in their chosen fields. Doris's friend Sally had given up her cherished social worker job to become a suburban housewife when her husband moved from teaching to business administration. 'They've moved three times in the past six years. Sally says they're a team, it's her job to entertain couples who can help Phil in his career. She admits she hates it, but that's the scene these days.' She'd done nothing to help Paul's career.

'I guess it's your connections with board members that make a difference.' Paul echoed her thoughts. 'Ted says they may bring in somebody from the outside.'

'Dad has connections,' Vera reminded him. 'He's into everything in town.' Waves of guilt rolled over her. She loved her job. Dad gave her such leeway. Look how he was letting her build up the mail-order catalogue – even though it was a tremendous gamble. But Paul kept running into roadblocks at every turn. 'Talk to Dad,' she urged. 'You know he'll do anything he can to help you.'

'Sure, Dad knows everybody – and everybody likes him.' Paul's smile was ironic. 'But they figure no matter what they do, good-natured Joel Kahn will remain their friend. Don't count on Dad to wield any influence.'

'You deserve to move up to principal. What changes have been brought about at the school in the last twelve years have been because of your efforts. You started the after-school programme,' Vera tallied. 'Without you, it never would have happened. You inaugurated the –'

'Vera, that's not what will propel me into the principal's job.' Paul broke in with rare bitterness. 'And if I don't land it, I know I'm at a dead end. I'll keep on teaching until they put me out to pasture, but I'll never have a chance to make a real contribution to the field. I wanted to make Eastwood High a model school, to demonstrate what public education in this country can and should be. *I wanted to make a difference.*'

She hadn't been the kind of wife that could help make that happen, Vera reproached herself. She'd failed her husband and she'd failed her older daughter. What could she do to make amends at this late date?

It was a terrifying challenge.

Chapter Twenty-three

Vera and Paul waited for official news that Roland Ames would resign as principal. It was clear to everyone that his health was deteriorating. He was irascible when approached with routine school problems, Paul told Vera.

'Not just with me,' Paul pointed out. 'To his camp-followers as well. But the board is being tight-lipped. Not a word is coming through. God knows, Dad has tried to dig up inside information from his cronies. Nothing!' he said in exasperation.

A week before the Christmas holidays, the board of directors announced Ames's retirement. At the same time, his successor – an out-of-towner – was announced.

'The man has a decent background,' Paul reported to Vera and his father at dinner that evening. 'He also happens to be the brother-in-law of a board member.'

'Who?' Joel demanded, a pulse hammering at his temple.

'Steve Jackson,' Paul said wearily.

'The bastard!' Joel exploded. 'I played chess with Steve last week. He knows how much I wanted that spot for you! You deserve it!'

'I'm not traditional enough for some people in this town,' Paul said and shrugged. 'And I'm not the only one disappointed. *C'est la vie.*'

Vera knew the depth of his hurt. She yearned to ease that pain. Perhaps this was the time for him to consider going back to school to work towards a PhD. He'd originally wanted to teach at college level. With a PhD that would be possible. She recoiled from the implications. It would mean moving away from Eastwood – an unnerving prospect. But Paul immediately dismissed her proposal.

'Vera, I'm too old, too set in my ways to go back to school. God, I could be fifty before I pinned down the damn degree. What college would take me on?' he challenged derisively.

'You have such innovative ideas,' she pressed. 'You have something special to offer the educational system. Paul, try writing for some of the educational publications.' She clutched at this new thought. 'Put your ideas into words. Start with one article. Write it. Send it out.' She glowed with enthusiasm.

'I'm not sure I could –' But Vera saw the first inner excitement stirring in him as he spoke.

'Try,' she prodded.

'I'll give it a whirl,' he said after a moment. 'But don't expect miracles.'

At their customary New Year's Eve dinner – to welcome in the new decade – Paul and his father spoke heatedly about the coming presidential election.

'It's time for a change,' Joel predicted, 'but I'll lay any odds it'll be a close race.'

'There's a freshness in the wind,' Paul said with an air of approval. 'I feel something new in the kids going off to college next fall. We've heard a lot about the apathy of this generation, but I don't believe it anymore. These will be the *war-babies*, and they're asking questions. They're not old enough to vote yet, of course –'

'And they're complaining about that,' Vera broke in. 'You hear more and more about 18-year-olds demanding the right to vote.'

'Yeah, why do we have to wait until we're twenty-one?' Laurie demanded. 'We can get married, but we can't vote.'

'This won't be a silent generation.' Paul chuckled. 'I hear questions from some of my seniors that make that clear.'

'You're hearing from your daughters,' Tracy said grimly.

Paul's prediction was borne out in the spring. On February 1, four young Negro students went into a Woolworth store in Greensboro, North Carolina, and sat down at a lunch counter – long off-limits to other than whites – and ordered coffee. In the succeeding days they returned, always with additional Negro students. They were polite, calm, ignoring taunts of angry whites. And then the movement took off. At Yale the following month, 300 divinity students marched through downtown New Haven in support. Three days later, 400 students from Harvard, Brandeis, Boston U, and MIT simultaneously picketed a dozen Woolworth stores in Greater Boston.

Many evenings Vera and Paul – along with Laurie and Tracy – sat glued to the TV screen watching the latest demonstration being televised. Laurie wrote letters almost every other day to Adele about what was happening in the fight for integration, and Adele returned with matching fervour. Adele was graphic about life in a Harlem project – which she loathed. '*It's scary – the gang-fights all the time, the killings* – but when I'm a teacher, I'll come back here and help to make it better.'

Tracy, too, was caught up in the excitement of fighting for integration.

'Mom, do you think it would be making a statement,' Tracy asked while the family watched the latest TV news on student demonstrations, 'if I dated Jeremy Wilkins?' Jeremy was the sole young Negro boy in the Eastwood school system.

'I don't think so,' Vera said, fighting back laughter. 'Darling, Jeremy is nine years old.'

Tracy nodded sagely. 'Yeah. I guess it would be like cradle-snatching.'

Doris launched a Women for Stevenson group as Democrats began to take sides on presidential candidates, though Joel was frank in his conviction that Stevenson wouldn't win the nomination. Paul and Vera, too, were active in support of Stevenson – with Laurie and Tracy delegated to distribute circulars.

'Will he pass a law for gun control?' Laurie asked.

Then all at once family focus zeroed in on Laurie's approaching sixteenth birthday in late July. Vera was relieved when Doris offered to take on the task of arranging for the sweet sixteen party. The party, Vera hoped, would make up for Laurie's disappointment that this summer Adele wouldn't be coming to Eastwood for two weeks as she and Adele had planned. Adele's grandmother had arranged for her to be a mother's helper on Fire Island for the entire summer.

'Don't let the party become a Hollywood spectacular,' Vera warned Doris affectionately.

She had been unnerved, she confided to Doris, when the mother of one of Laurie's classmates told her that arriving at sixteen was the time when Laurie's generation considered it time to 'go all the way.'

'Laurie isn't even going steady,' Vera pointed out in shock. 'And I'll bet anything most of the girls who're bragging about "going all the way" don't. At that age they talk a lot.'

But she knew that another classmate had mysteriously gone to 'live with her grandmother' for a few months – which translated to worried mothers that she was pregnant. And Vera's mind charged back through the years to Berlin, when Frau Schmidt had shipped her daughter Alice to live with her grandmother because she feared for Alice's safety in Hitler's Germany. It was a whole different world today – with new anxieties replacing the old.

Tracy viewed the party preparations with impatience.

'You'd think Laurie was being crowned queen of England,' Tracy said distastefully. 'I'm glad she doesn't want me to come. Anyhow,' she confided, 'I've got a date that night with David.' Tracy had never 'gone out on a date' thus far. There were co-ed parties at one house or another – and David Marcus's name peppered Tracy's conversation. 'We're going for hamburgers and Cokes at The Oasis. Oh, it's all right,' she added. 'David's Mom will drive us there, and then she'll drive us home.'

David and his parents had lived in Eastwood just over a year, Vera recalled. His father was a lawyer with a client list that ranged from Saratoga to Manchester, Vermont. His mother had instantly become involved in local clubs. She made a point, the rumour circulated around town, of entertaining her husband's clients from neighbouring communities at lavish dinner parties.

Vera knew that her father-in-law was pleased that another Jewish family had moved into town, though David's being Jewish had nothing to do with Tracy's liking him. She knew, also, that Joel worried that Laurie – dating now – was seeing boys not of her faith. There were no Jewish boys of Laurie's age in Eastwood, Vera thought uneasily. It was a problem that she and Paul discussed at sombre moments. Her mind shot back to a conversation they'd had just last night with Joel.

'Look, we live in a crazy world,' Joel had said. 'It's better to marry within your own faith. Catholic parents want their children to marry Catholic. Jewish parents live in dread of their kids marrying non-Jews. Protestants feel the same about their faith. It's just one of those things that make life less complicated.'

But Laurie wouldn't be marrying for years, Vera comforted herself. She was so eager to go off to college. She vowed to make either Barnard or NYU. She wanted desperately to live in New York, Vera thought with simmering trepidation. Paul had made it sound so exciting. But New York was a heady place for a girl who had grown up in a tiny town in upstate New York. She didn't want to think about Laurie being away at college. She'd miss her so much. She'd worry every minute.

The plans for Laurie's party escalated to such proportions that Paul was nervous about the costs.

'Vera, we have to have an orchestra?' He lifted an eyebrow in dismay.

'It's just a trio to play for dancing,' Vera explained. 'And Doris is paying for it. It's her birthday gift.'

Vera was relieved when Laurie's sweet sixteen party was over, pleased that it had been such a success. And she was intrigued by a new glow about Doris these days. She suspected it had something to do with Phil Richman, the pianist who'd been part of the group at Laurie's sweet sixteen.

When Phil wasn't playing the piano, he managed a small shop in Manchester – where he'd moved just a few months ago. After the party Doris had drafted him to come in to play for a special Evening with Books at the book shop. He had taken her to a community theatre production in Saratoga. Now she was dieting with frantic determination.

'You think there's something between Doris and that fellow from Manchester?' Joel asked hopefully.

'Don't let on you're even thinking that,' Vera urged. 'But yes, I think they're very attracted to each other.'

During the next month, Vera noted with pleasure, Doris and Phil were seeing much of each other, though Doris admitted to much uncertainty about the situation.

'We're both skittish,' she confessed to Vera. 'Both divorced – you get the picture. But I wish he wouldn't keep on about our going swimming. I look awful in a swimsuit. Why is it so hard to lose weight?'

Paul hurried to the school cafeteria to meet Ted for lunch. He'd asked Ted to go over the article he was submitting – after two rejections – to a third educational publication. One rejection had been tepid. The second admired the article but suggested he was moving too fast. Still, Paul was buoyed by the continuing complaints by leading intellectuals that American education was sadly lacking.

Paul spied Ted at a table for two in the corner of the cafeteria reserved for teachers. He waved, indicated he'd join the line at the food tables. Several minutes later he seated himself opposite Ted.

'I think it's great,' Ted said without preliminaries. 'You don't waste words. You get right down to the heart of the problem.'

'So why am I having such trouble finding an editor who agrees?' Paul challenged.

'Look, it takes time,' Ted soothed. 'Type up a fresh copy. Send it out again.'

'That's what Vera said.' Paul managed a lopsided smile. 'Maybe you two are prejudiced.'

'If you were *Dr* Paul Kahn you'd have less trouble being published.' Ted was unabashedly cynical. 'With a PhD you're a savant.' He hesitated. 'Are you still arguing with our learned principal about setting up special after-school tutoring for students who have borderline chances at a Regents' diploma?' In New York State, to acquire this status diploma it was necessary to pass the Regents' exam.

'He came flat out and said *no dice*.' All at once Paul felt drained. 'It didn't matter that I could round up teachers who were willing to contribute the extra hours. "You're trying to coddle dumb fucks," was his way of putting it.'

Paul regarded Ted with recurrent curiosity. Ted was single, with no romantic attachments, dedicated to teaching, but able to turn off that dedication after hours. He seemed content with his music collection, his books, his pair of Siamese cats. Ted didn't make huge demands of himself, perhaps that was the secret to his contentment.

But Paul wanted to do more than pass through life. He wanted to make some contribution, something that said he'd paid his dues for being in this world. God, he admired those kids at the campuses who were demonstrating for integration in the South. They realized something was terribly wrong in this country, and they were going out to fight for change. Why couldn't he do something to improve education here in his own town? If enough teachers arose and demanded change, it would happen.

At dinner that evening Laurie read a segment of her most recent letter from Adele. Paul listened with recurrent frustration.

'A lot of kids cut classes. You wouldn't believe how many. Still, the classes are so big there's hardly room for the chairs that have to be brought in. A fight broke out in my English class yesterday, and two guys were cut up. There was blood all over the place. If I weren't determined to be a schoolteacher, I'd go to medical school.'

'Adele is sure to teach one day,' Paul told Laurie. 'She'll be a fine teacher.'

'I think maybe I'll go to medical school,' Laurie said, her tone over-casual.

'Hear, hear!' Joel chortled, aglow with approval. 'My granddaughter, the doctor.'

'Of course, medical school is awful expensive,' Laurie conceded. Her eyes reflected sudden doubts.

Before Paul could reply – taunted by guilt that teaching was a low-paying profession, his father rushed to reassure Laurie.

'You want to go to medical school, you'll go,' Joel said with conviction. 'This family can afford it. Just make sure you cram a lot of science into your high school schedule between now and graduation.'

Paul's mind shot back through the years to the traumatic day when he and Vera had arrived at the Robinson house to find tiny Laurie leaning over Serena's body and trying to stop the flow of blood from the bullet wound in her chest with a towel. Perhaps that was the day when the thought of becoming a doctor took root in her mind. Instinct told him this was not a passing fad – like Tracy's catapulting from one avowed career to another.

He knew, too, what was reverberating through Vera's thoughts. Would Laurie come home – after college, medical school, and internship – to practise in Eastwood? He knew Vera's obsession to keep the family together. It was unnerving today, the way so many children found no future in their home towns and ran off to live in a large city, which seemed to offer so much.

Like Americans throughout the country, the Kahn family gathered before the television screen on the eve of the presidential election. Almost everybody expected it would be a very close election. By 10:30 PM Kennedy was projected the winner, but Vera and Paul remained before the TV set until past midnight. By that time, Kennedy's popular-vote margin was dwindling.

'He'll win,' Paul predicted to Vera. 'Let's go to bed.'

Americans awoke in the morning to learn that Kennedy had, indeed, been elected president – by a margin of less than two-thirds of one per cent of the popular vote.

Vera's thoughts focused now on the approaching Thanksgiving holiday. Laurie would still be around for the long weekend. And by Thanksgiving Vera was convinced Doris and Phil were serious about each other.

She'd invited him to Thanksgiving dinner. Joel was euphoric despite Doris's warning that she and Phil merely enjoyed going to the movies together and having dinner. 'His divorce was an awful experience. He just needs a sympathetic ear.'

At Thanksgiving breakfast Vera and Paul were alone. She knew Paul was upset that Tracy and her grandfather had gone off to the nearby quarry for target practice. He hated guns almost as much as Laurie. Tracy had become a crack shot under her grandfather's tutelage. 'She's got a better eye than I do,' Joel bragged. But Tracy never went hunting, Vera reminded herself conscientiously. It was just that she enjoyed 'hitting the bullseye every time.' Laurie would sleep until noon, Vera surmised.

'Dad's all excited because Doris is bringing Phil to dinner,' Paul said when Vera poured him a second cup of coffee. 'He's dying to know more about him but scared to ask questions.'

'Doris said his wife married him because she thought he was going to be rich and famous. When that didn't happen, she was furious. He hung around the music business after college, had a song in an Off-Broadway musical. It was picked up by a record company but never went anywhere. He said he finally realized that he had a small talent – not big enough to make it professionally.'

'The way Doris felt about her art,' Paul said gently. 'But she never really gave herself a chance. I kept telling her that it's not enough to have talent, you have to have the discipline to use that talent. But of course, once she met Wayne, she lost all confidence in herself.'

'She feels very comfortable with Phil. She's even started painting again. And she loves to hear him play. They're good for each other, Paul.'

'You're such a matchmaker,' he teased, but his eyes were tender. He glanced at the wall clock. 'I know you have to cook Thanksgiving dinner and Doris is coming over to help you –' She recognized the ardour in his eyes.

'I won't put the turkey into the oven for another hour and a half, and Doris won't be here for two.' How wonderful, she thought in rising passion, that she and Paul could still feel this way about each other. 'I haven't even made up our bed yet.'

'We'll do it together,' he promised. 'Later . . .'

'It seemed the right thing to do to invite Phil to dinner,' Doris said self-consciously while the family waited for him to arrive. 'I mean, he was going to be alone on Thanksgiving. He has no family except some distant cousins down in Texas.'

'Of course it was,' Joel agreed expansively, with a furtive wink at Vera.

'Let me get back to the kitchen,' Vera decided. 'The turkey may need basting.' She paused. 'Laurie and Tracy, come give me a hand.' Let Phil not be overwhelmed by a huge welcoming committee.

With savoury aromas floating through the house, Vera kept the two girls occupied until she knew from the lively hum of voices in the foyer that Phil was being welcomed. Everything must be right for Doris and Phil today, she told herself.

'All right, everything's under control,' she announced. 'We'll serve dinner in twenty minutes.'

The house reverberated with festive spirits. Joel was reminiscing colourfully about earlier Thanksgivings – when Paul and Doris were little. Then Vera ordered everybody to the table. As always at this time, she thought what a wonderful holiday the early colonists in New England had established for the future country.

After dinner the girls helped clear the table. Everything had gone well, Vera thought with pleasure. This was their first occasion to exchange more than a few words with Phil. He was charming, warm, and gentle, Vera decided. Something Doris needed in a man after the tortuous years with Wayne. He'd won Dad over completely by sitting down at the piano before dinner and playing a medley of Gershwin tunes.

'He's cute,' Tracy told Doris. 'I mean, for somebody that's old.'

When Vera and Doris joined the men in the living room – Laurie and Tracy remaining to stack the dishwasher – they found the other three focused on a special TV news report.

'More trouble down in Peru,' Paul said. 'Revolutionaries killed three Americans.'

'There's been so much trouble down there these past few years,' Vera began. 'First, it was –'

'Ssh,' Joel ordered and leaned forward as a fresh bulletin was handed to the newscaster.

'The names of the three Americans have been released. They're Lloyd Crane of Los Angeles, California; Fred Mitchell of New York City, and Wayne Solomon of New York City and Tel Aviv, Israel.'

'Oh my God!' Doris was ashen. 'Wayne dead? I don't believe it.' Her voice soared in hysteria. 'I don't believe it!'

Chapter Twenty-four

Exhausted from the trauma of the day, Vera settled into one corner of the living room sofa she shared with her father-in-law. Laurie and Tracy – both shaken by the news of Wayne's murder – had retreated to their bedrooms. At last succumbing to the sedative Vera had forced upon her, Doris was asleep in the guest room. Compassionate and yearning to be helpful, Phil had finally gone home. Paul was out in the kitchen preparing a fresh pot of coffee, the family crutch in time of crisis.

'I didn't expect Doris to be so distraught,' Joel admitted. 'Can't she remember what the bastard did to her?'

'She's remembering the first years – when Wayne was her knight in shining armour,' Vera said softly. 'It's wonderful, though, the way Phil's come forward to help.'

It was Phil who'd leapt into action. Already he'd made preliminary arrangements for Wayne's burial, once the body would be released by Peruvian officials. He'd been on long, involved phone calls, first with Washington, DC, then with the American Embassy in Lima – determined to track down the proper parties. Doris had remembered how Wayne had deliberately cut himself off from his only relatives, the cousins in New York. It would be up to his ex-wife to see that his body was laid to final rest. Phil understood, Vera thought with tender gratitude, that if he were to have a place in Doris's life, then he must help her through this period.

'In the early years we all thought Wayne was wonderful.' Joel winced in retrospect. 'How could we have been so stupid?'

'It's over, Dad,' Paul reproached, striding into the living room with a tray laden with tall cups of strong, black coffee. 'It was a shock to Doris, but she'll snap back.'

'How does Phil feel about this?' Joel turned from Paul to Vera.

'Dad, he understands,' Vera soothed.

'He's a good man. I hope Doris realizes that.' Now Joel seemed less tense. 'Ask him over for dinner tomorrow night. Let Doris see how he's handling everything.'

'He's flying down to Washington tomorrow,' she reminded him. He was acting as the family representative.

'I'll blame Wayne if this breaks up the closeness between Doris and Phil,' Joel flared. 'Why did this have to happen just now?'

For the next few days Doris seemed to live in a daze, yet Vera sensed that she was very conscious of Phil's efforts. Phil tracked down Wayne's cousins in New York, persuaded them to follow through on a burial in a Queens cemetery – once they understood all expenses would be borne by Doris.

'I don't want to go to the funeral,' Doris confessed forlornly to Vera.

'You don't have to go,' Vera insisted. 'You've been divorced from Wayne for years.'

'I just can't go,' Doris whispered. 'It'll bring back so much I've tried to forget.'

Early in the new year, Phil coaxed Doris to go away with him for a three-day weekend.

'I didn't tell Dad I'm going with Phil. I know he'd be upset,' Doris confided to Vera in a late-night phone call. 'I said I was going with one of the women from the nursery school.' Her smile was wry. 'Even at my age he'd worry about my reputation.'

Vera broke into laughter.

'Doris, we're living in a new era. College girls go off for weekends with their boyfriends.' But her voice was sympathetic. For their generation it was not routine for an unmarried man and woman to spend a weekend together. Of course, she'd lived with Paul before they were married. But that had been wartime – a special swatch of time.

'I've never come out and told you,' Doris said, colour flooding her face, 'but we've slept together three times. And Vera,' she whispered, 'it was wonderful.'

'It's time,' Vera approved. 'You two are perfect for each other.'

'I've warned him not to rush me. I don't even know how long this'll last –'

'Enjoy,' Vera ordered affectionately. 'Is it a secret? Where you're going?'

'I thought we'd go out to Montauk. You and Paul liked it so much.'

'It'll be off-season,' Vera warned. 'There'll probably be very few people around.'

'Perfect. We'll have the beach to ourselves. We'll dress warmly and walk and walk and walk. I've always had a secret love affair with the ocean.' She paused. 'Remember the Cape?'

'It was beautiful,' Vera recalled. But by then Doris's marriage had been a shambles.

'And now I have a secret lover.' All at once Doris was whimsical. 'Are people talking about us?'

'Of course they are,' Vera joshed. 'You know this town. If you talked three minutes to some man in the supermarket, they'd be gossiping.'

'I'm driving over to Albany tomorrow afternoon and

shop for a gorgeous nightie and negligeé,' Doris said in good-humoured defiance. 'It's crazy! I feel like a kid again.'

On a grey, cold Friday afternoon Doris and Phil drove in his eight-year-old Plymouth into the town of Montauk. They stopped to ask one of the few pedestrians on what they assumed was the main business street for directions to Gurney's Inn.

'We may have picked a bad weekend.' Phil was apprehensive as they turned onto the road flanking the ocean. 'The weather's ghastly.'

'I don't care,' Doris rejoined. 'I have the landlubber's love for the ocean. Vera promised we'll be right on the water, with miles of beach to walk. That's all I ask. Oh, and some good food,' she conceded.

Almost immediately Doris felt herself riding on a cloud of serenity. It was clear that this was off-season. Despite the damp cold, the greyness that enveloped the ocean and beach, she and Phil left their unit without bothering to unpack. Hand in hand they walked along the clean, white sand. Not another human was in sight, only clusters of seagulls here and there.

At last – cold and exhausted, yet exhilarated – they returned to their ocean-facing unit.

'Tomorrow will be nicer,' Phil promised. 'I've put in a special order.'

'This is fine,' she insisted. 'I feel so at peace here.'

'Okay.' He laughed. 'I'll cancel the order.'

Except for them and two solitary diners, the dining room was deserted at this early hour. Dinner was a gourmet feast. They lingered in relaxation, then returned to their unit with an unspoken pact to retire unusually early. This would be the first time they'd spend an entire night together, Doris thought in pleasurable anticipation as she dawdled in a warm tub and Phil watched a TV news programme.

She suppressed a giggle. Would Phil laugh when she emerged from the bathroom in a flannel nightie? She hadn't packed the sheer black nightie and peignoir she'd shopped for this weekend. He'd warned her the nights would be cool with the ocean no more than seventy feet from the door to their unit.

He didn't laugh, she thought exultantly when she walked into the room in her demure, flower-sprigged nightgown.

'You look like a little girl,' he murmured, reaching for her. 'A beautiful, vulnerable little girl – and I can't wait to take advantage of you . . .'

Vera sat frozen at her office phone – the catalogue copy spread across her desk forgotten.

'Paul, what do you mean – Tracy's been suspended from classes for a week! Why?'

'I just got called into Franklin's office,' he repeated tiredly. The new principal whom he had come to loathe. What had appeared to be a decent background had revealed itself as ultra-conservative. 'Tracy was caught smoking in the girls' gym – with two others. Normally Franklin would have expelled them. You know what a tough disciplinarian he is. But one of the other two was Steve Jackson's granddaughter.' Steve Jackson, Vera recalled, was the principal's brother-in-law. 'He's letting them off with a week's suspension.'

'What got into Tracy?' Vera was shaken. She wasn't part of the small, rebellious clique in the high school. She was competitive about grades – that was what was important to her. 'I can't believe she'd want to smoke.'

'Vera, let's play this cool,' Paul said. 'Let's don't get all excited and yell.'

'I don't yell,' she began and paused. 'Not often.' Sometimes – under stress – she could be emotional, she conceded guiltily.

'Maybe this is her reaction to the excitement over Laurie's sweet sixteen party.' But Paul was upset, too, Vera realized.

'That was months ago,' she protested.

'We'll talk to her tonight. We'll make her understand we're disappointed in her.'

'Nobody in the family smokes.' Vera's voice rose in pitch. She remembered the girls' saying 'Mom, don't yell' – but she wasn't yelling, she thought defensively. She couldn't talk on an even level when she felt deeply about something. It wasn't yelling. 'She's heard us talk about how dangerous it is to smoke.'

'This is rebellion.' Paul was blunt. 'And it's hardly uncommon. We'll have to ground her for a week. Then comes the spring break. By the time she gets back to classes, the incident will have cooled down.'

Vera told herself that they'd make Tracy understand she must abide by rules. There was a tacit agreement not to discuss the subject until after dinner, when Dad was scheduled for a town meeting. Vera suspected that Tracy was more upset about her grandfather's learning of her being caught smoking than about her parents' learning of it. There was an endearing special closeness between Tracy and her grandfather.

Not until Laurie had gone up to her room to study and Joel was off to his meeting did Vera and Paul confront her.

'I don't know why they make such a fuss about students' smoking,' Tracy flared. 'Teachers smoke. Lots of them.' She focused on her father. 'Aren't you always complaining how you can't even go into the teachers' lounge because it's so full of smoke?'

'That doesn't mean you should smoke,' Paul said with a calmness Vera knew he didn't feel. 'It's a terrible habit. It –'

'It kills people,' Vera broke in. 'Smoking causes lung cancer, among other things!'

'Nobody really knows that.' Colour touched Tracy's sculptured cheekbones.

'The scientists know,' Vera shot back. 'Smoking kills!'

'And aside from that,' Paul pursued, 'you know it's against the rules for students to smoke.'

'I think it's a kooky rule. If teachers can smoke, why can't students?'

'School rules are made to be observed, Tracy. You'll be grounded for the week of your suspension. We won't talk about it again. Don't let it happen again.' Paul reached for the newspaper on the nearby coffee table. 'Let's see what craziness is happening around the world now.'

Tracy hesitated, turned to her mother.

'Can I call David? Grounding doesn't mean I can't make calls, does it?'

'You may call David,' Vera agreed. 'But don't tie up the phone all night.'

'David has his own phone.' Tracy was faintly defiant. But she leapt to her feet in an aura of relief. The dreaded confrontation was over.

'I think we handled that okay,' Paul said when he and Vera were alone again.

'I'll bet Tracy doesn't even like to smoke.' Vera shook her head in bewilderment. 'What makes it a magic deal to teenagers?'

'It's *cool*,' Paul said ruefully, borrowing Tracy's current favourite bit of slang. 'It makes them feel sophisticated. From what I hear, more than half the kids at the high school smoke. It's a definite problem. Tracy just happened to get caught. Some parents are making rules – their kids can't smoke until they're sixteen. And the fourteen-year-old wants to know, what difference does two years make?'

'I can see why they rebel – when teachers and parents smoke,' Vera admitted.

'We've had a couple of parents come in and ask why we can't set up a special area and a special time for students to smoke,' Paul said. 'For once I agreed with Franklin. No smoking on school grounds. When will people face up to the fact that tobacco is a killer?'

'When we were teenagers, we didn't behave like today's kids.' Exasperation blended with frustration in Vera's voice. 'Why are these kids so different?'

'Because they live in a totally different world from our generation,' Paul said slowly. 'We grew up in the Depression and moved into World War II. They don't know such things. Sure, they've heard us talk about them – *but they don't know*. They don't understand what it is to do without. Except for ghetto kids and the rural poor,' Paul amended. 'But I'm talking average middle-class kids. Parents – and we're no different – want to give their kids everything they possibly can. And the kids assume it's coming to them. Every now and then Dad gets pissed and says that kids today have no respect for their elders. We haven't taught them to have respect. But basically, Vera, they're good kids. They think. They ask questions. I have respect for the students who're fighting for civil rights. Who want to make things better. It's the young who make changes in the world – and God knows, there are changes that need to be made.'

Stifling a series of yawns as she unlocked the door, Doris wished that this was not her Saturday to volunteer at the book shop. She was so sleepy today. And tonight she was having dinner with Phil and going to the movies. Afterwards he'd take her home – and they'd make love. Why was it accepted that Saturday night was the night to have sex? she asked herself querulously. It was as though 90% of couples – married or otherwise – put a mental note on their calendars that Saturday night was sex night.

Phil was being so good, she acknowledged with a rush of tenderness, after that last scene when she'd threatened not to see him again if he persisted in all that talk about their getting married. She loved him, she told herself – yet she shied away from making a permanent commitment. The years with Wayne had left a mark on her. *She was afraid to make the marriage commitment again.*

It was really silly for them to open the shop at 10:00 AM on Saturdays, she thought. Nobody showed up before noon. She hung away her coat and settled down to read the new Steinbeck, *The Winter of Our Discontent*.

She was so involved with the novel that she started when Vera walked into the shop.

'You're early,' Doris said.

'Go on and read your book,' Vera urged. 'I left the house early. Everybody was asleep except me, and I was suddenly restless. I figured you'd be in the mood for company. Shall I put up the tea kettle?'

'Yeah, maybe that'll wake me up.' Doris laid aside her book. 'Anyhow, we're getting off early today. Stella and Rae are coming in at one o'clock to relieve us. I said, loud and clear, that the two of us are being put upon.'

'In any volunteer group, there're the ones who do most of the work and the ones who talk about doing it.' Vera chuckled. 'Dad's forever bitching about that.'

'And I suppose Paul is still moaning and groaning about being so close to his fortieth birthday.' Doris chuckled.

'I remember his holding my hand in sympathy when I got there two years ago.'

'Why is forty supposed to be such a landmark?' Vera challenged. 'Did you feel any different when you hit forty?'

'No.' She reconsidered. 'Just a little pre-menopausal. Another landmark I won't appreciate.'

'I think it's how you face it,' Vera decided after a moment.

'I may be facing it early.' Doris sighed. 'Some women do, you know. It doesn't have to happen between forty-five and fifty. I think I may be hitting it already. I haven't had a period in six weeks. Isn't that the first indication? When you start missing periods?'

'Either that – or you're pregnant.' Vera's matter-of-factness startled Doris.

'Vera, that's ridiculous!'

'Is it? You and Phil aren't just holding hands these days.'

'But at my age?' *Could she be pregnant*? Her mind was assaulted by a medley of emotions. 'No, you're way off base, Vera.' But her heart was pounding. After all those years of marriage? But it was Wayne who hadn't been able to have children.

'You're sleepy all the time, I gather,' Vera picked up. She'd been complaining about sleepiness for the last two weeks, Doris remembered. 'You're late. And I'll bet you and Phil haven't always been careful.'

'At our age it didn't seem important.' Phil said his wife had refused to have children – it would ruin her figure.

'Go see Dr Evans,' Vera ordered.

'Vera, I couldn't!' She recoiled from the situation. 'He'd be shocked.'

'Darling, this is 1961,' Vera reproached. 'But all right, make an appointment with that new woman obstetrician who just opened offices in Albany if you feel self-conscious about this. I'll go with you.'

'I'm not pregnant,' Doris said with fresh insistence. 'But yes, I'll make an appointment with her, and you are going with me. Oh, I feel so silly,' she wailed. 'So I'm a little late and a little sleepy. She'll laugh like hell at me.'

How weird! Wayne was dead – and she might be pregnant. It would be like getting another chance at life . . .

Chapter Twenty-five

Vera sat in a lounge chair in Dr Langdon's reception room and flipped through the pages of *Newsweek* without seeing. Two early-twenties women in advanced pregnancy sprawled awkwardly on the sofa across the room and discussed their weight gains in the past month. Doris had been in the doctor's examining room for what seemed an interminable period, Vera thought. Doris *was* pregnant, wasn't she? During the last couple of days – nervous at waiting for her appointment – Doris had become morbid.

'Maybe I'm not pregnant. Maybe there's something terribly wrong with me in that area. Or maybe –' she'd reached for a less melodramatic note '– maybe it's just early menopause.'

The door to the inner office opened. Vera sat upright. Doris was emerging. She seemed in a trance. Vera's heart began to pound. She watched while Doris paused at the receptionist's desk.

'I'd like an appointment a month from now,' Doris told the receptionist.

Doris was pregnant. Vera felt herself encased in tenderness, her mind darting back through the years to her own two pregnancies. What a cherished period in a woman's life, she thought poignantly.

Doris accepted a card from the receptionist, slid it into her purse. She turned to Vera, her smile simultaneously euphoric and fearful. She didn't speak until they were out of Dr Langdon's office.

'Either I get married or leave town,' she said with an

effort at humour that was overshadowed by a sense of awe. 'Vera, after all these years I'm pregnant!'

'Dad will be out of his mind,' Vera said softly.

'What about Phil?' Doris countered. 'He wanted to marry me when I was a divorcée – an unpregnant divorcée.'

'He'll be thrilled,' Vera predicted. 'Remember, he was married to a woman who refused to have children.'

'Maybe he thinks we're too old to have kids.' Her anxiety lent harshness to her voice. 'We've never discussed it.'

'Tell him tonight,' Vera ordered. 'And apply for your marriage licence tomorrow. So you'll have a slightly premature baby,' she joshed. 'Nobody will care.'

'I'm a little scared,' Doris admitted when they'd settled themselves into the car. 'Having a baby at forty-two isn't the best time.'

'Millions of women have children in their forties. You're a normal, healthy woman.' Unexpectedly Vera chuckled. 'Oh God, we're going to have three very startled males on our hands: Phil, Dad, and Paul.'

Doris was relieved that the restaurant was lightly populated this early in the dinner hour. She'd chosen their favourite place, had asked for a secluded table. Phil had sounded excited when she'd called and said she'd like to have dinner with him this evening – not their customary evening. *We need to talk about something.* She suspected he thought she was ready to talk about marriage. At the same time, she'd detected an undercurrent of alarm in his voice. Could she be telling him it was time to end their affair?

She wouldn't want to think he was marrying her because she was pregnant, she told herself defensively. She had to be sure Phil wanted this baby. If not, she thought defiantly, she'd move away from Eastwood, have the baby anyhow.

Tenderness surged through her. She'd waited so long for this to happen – sure it never would. Involuntarily a hand moved to rest on her pelvis. Their baby was growing within her. Already she envisioned herself holding her newborn in her arms. A small miracle had entered her life.

She glanced up with an incandescent smile when Phil approached their table. His eyes were questioning. Hopeful. Would he be pleased when he heard her news – or would he feel the timing was all wrong? Her smile evaporated. Her throat tightened in fresh alarm.

He seated himself across the table from her, managed small talk as their waiter approached. They made their usual gay production of ordering – as though each such meeting were very special.

'You're looking beautiful tonight,' he said, his eyes making love to her. 'As always.'

'Phil, I'm pregnant,' she said and glanced hastily about in fear she might have been overheard.

'Did I hear you right?' His voice was hushed. 'Say it again.'

'I'm pregnant,' she whispered, simultaneously exhilarated and defiant and awed.

'Then you'll have to marry me.' His face radiated joy. 'You have to make an honest man of me.'

'You're not upset?' She reached out for reassurance.

'Doris, I feel so humble. What have I done to be given such happiness? I've always wanted a family. I won't only be acquiring a wife – I'm getting a son or daughter in the bargain.'

'You're not upset?' she pressed.

'This is the happiest moment of my life.' His hand reached out for hers. 'Tomorrow we go to the courthouse for our marriage licence. I was afraid this day would never happen,' he confessed. 'But I kept hoping.'

A week later, Doris and Phil were married by a rabbi under an improvised *chuppah* according to Jewish tradition in the living room of the Kahn house. It was already understood that Phil would leave his job in Manchester and take over management of the company shop in Eastwood. With his sixty-ninth birthday approaching, Joel hinted at possible retirement – though the family knew not to take him seriously. Still, he made it clear that he felt a certain security in having a son-in-law with a business background, someone who could join Vera in running the family business when he did retire.

Joel was ecstatic at the marriage and the prospect of becoming a grandfather for the third time. 'With a little luck, a grandson. Not that I won't love a third granddaughter just as much.'

In the ensuing months, the whole family became wrapped up in Doris's pregnancy. Laurie and Tracy had already established themselves as future babysitters. Joel revelled in having Phil sit down at the piano – his late wife's joy and the piano where Doris had practised as a very young music student – to play the show tunes of years past that were his favourites.

This was such a happy period in their lives, Vera thought in a tidal wave of sentiment as the family gathered in the comfortably air-conditioned living room on an August evening to hear Phil play the score from *Gypsy*. At intervals she sensed a wistfulness in him that he'd never fulfilled his dream, yet most of the time he seemed to be philosophical about the limitations of his talents.

Phil's dreams, she suspected, would be transferred to his child. Wasn't that a familiar pattern? And Doris was painting again – not with the thought of a professional career but with a need to express herself in the medium closest to her heart. After selling two articles – admittedly to obscure publications – Paul was running into rejections with his latest effort.

Paul was ahead of his time, Vera thought tenderly, and the Eastwood high school was in the grip of an ultra-conservative group. He was in a constant state of frustration. Despite that, Paul was the favourite teacher in the high school. Both Tracy and Laurie – going into her senior year now – attested to that with pride.

'Laurie, what do you hear these days from Adele?' Doris's voice brought her back to the moment.

'She expects to go to Hunter,' Laurie said. 'Her grades are great.'

'Adele knows we'll help her through college if she needs it,' Vera began. 'We'll –'

'She's okay,' Laurie interrupted. 'She wants to handle it on her own – the way her mother would have liked it.' She sighed blissfully. 'It'll be terrific – both of us in New York. Adele will be at Hunter, and I'll be at Barnard.' She held up crossed fingers. 'Freshmen at Barnard have to live in the dorms, I think – but after that, we figure on taking an apartment together. It won't cost any more than a dorm,' she added defensively. 'Adele says we can get a studio on the Upper West Side real cheap.'

'God, it makes me feel old,' Paul said wryly. 'I remember my days at Columbia and roaming about the Upper West Side. It's probably changed a lot.'

Laurie couldn't wait to get away from Eastwood, Vera thought with anguish. They were all so impatient to be on their own. Laurie had grown up so *protected*. Would she be homesick? Would she be lonely in a huge city like New York? But she was determined to go to a college in Manhattan. She wanted to get away from the sight of the family business, Vera tormented herself. She never gave up hating their manufacturing guns.

Paul said that kids today were spoiled. They were the centre of the universe. Her mind hurtled back to her own young years. But you wanted better for your children than what you'd had. An easier, more satisfying life. And Paul admitted, too, that this generation of teenagers were a new breed. They cared about what was happening to others. They were willing to fight for what they believed was right.

Next year this time, Laurie would be preparing to go away to school – and two years later, Tracy would be a freshman. How strange – how frightening – it would seem to come home from the office each day and know that Laurie wouldn't be there. And two years later, neither she nor Tracy would be at home except on holidays and summer vacations. The house would seem so empty.

A sense of panic invaded her. She'd be losing her family – first Laurie, then Tracy. Her mind shot back to *Kristallnacht* in Berlin. She'd lost Mama, Papa, and Ernst. A family belonged together – but her daughters were moving away from her. Not just physically, she taunted herself. To Laurie she was the enemy. And sometimes she suspected Tracy felt that way, too.

On the last Saturday in August, Doris went into labour. Just past midnight, she gave birth to a son, Frederick Neal. The family was euphoric. At last, Vera thought, Doris had come into her own. What she had believed would be forever denied her had come to pass. At odd moments in the years ahead she would be sad that her dreams of becoming a serious artist had never developed, but she would have Phil and her son to fill her life. Dreams came true for a chosen few.

The new school year brought frustrating problems for Paul. At a time when he was fighting for programme enrichments, the school board had to deal with budget cuts. Laurie had taken her college boards and – like millions of high school seniors across the nation – was alternately optimistic and depressed about the outcome, which would not be known for months.

Already Tracy, ever-anxious to be in step with Laurie, was caught up in plans for college. She and David vowed to attend the same school. 'A co-ed school,' Tracy had announced. 'Of course, Laurie will have all of those Columbia boys when she goes to Barnard – but it's not the same as having them in classes.'

Vera had long disapproved of the 'going steady' scene for early teenagers, yet she acknowledged that David brought something special into Tracy's life. *She* had a boyfriend, whereas Laurie avoided any commitments. It was as though she and Paul had acquired a foster son, Vera thought with gentle amusement at intervals. David was constantly underfoot.

She felt a blend of compassion and affection for David. He seemed hungry for approval, love. His father was becoming involved in state politics. Many evenings and weekends, David would have been alone or under the eye of the sleep-in housekeeper, except for Tracy's family. On occasion he and Tracy baby-sat for tiny Neal – who, Vera knew, would never lack for love.

'David's parents are so busy campaigning, they have no time for their son,' Vera fumed to Paul at the end of a weekend when David had spent most of his waking hours at the Kahn house. 'What's the matter with them?'

'Ambition,' Paul said distastefully. 'Ambition and greed.'

Night after night Vera listened sombrely while Paul and his father argued about crises around the world – civil rights demonstrations here at home, the Berlin Wall erected by the East Germans, the handful of American soldiers training the South Vietnamese in guerrilla warfare, instability in Latin America. She'd been so convinced that after World War II the world would learn to live in peace. Would that day ever happen?

At the approach of Christmas, Laurie received a letter from Adele. Her grandmother was in precarious health now but vowing to be at Adele's high school graduation. Reading between the lines, Laurie suspected that Adele would be allowed to visit during the Christmas school vacation if an invitation were extended.

'Mom, let me invite Adele to come up to us for the holidays,' Laurie pleaded.

'Will she want to leave her grandmother at Christmas?' Vera questioned. She sensed that this might be the last Christmas Adele would spend with her grandmother.

'Read her letter,' Laurie ordered. 'I think her grandmother wants her to come to us.'

'Phone and ask her,' Vera said when she'd scanned the letter. 'Adele is always welcome here.' Perhaps, Vera thought, her grandmother wanted Adele to be close to this family when she was gone rather than her own dysfunctional family. She'd always been loving and wise.

'They don't have a phone anymore,' Laurie reported. 'Adele said the money for the phone came out of her bank account, but the others were running up the bill so high her grandmother had it taken out.'

'Write Adele and take the letter over to the post office,' Vera instructed. How much of the money Fiona had saved for Adele still remained? she asked herself anxiously. Tuition at Hunter was free, but Adele would need money to live on while she was in college.

Adele arrived two days before Christmas. Vera was touched by her gratitude that blended with a philosophical sadness. She knew her grandmother was dying but was dealing with this imminent loss. How mature for seventeen, Vera thought.

She was outraged when Adele confessed that much of her funds had been diverted to the needs of her welfare-raised cousins.

'Grandma had to do it,' Adele explained without censure. But a glint in her eyes told Vera that the cousins would not intrude on her life in the future. 'She was trying to keep Tyrone out of jail. He showed up after being away for years. It worked for a while.' Adele shrugged. 'But he was just no good.'

Adele was determined to earn her degree and go on to teach in a ghetto school.

'Nothing's going to change for those kids until they get a decent education,' she said with conviction, and Paul nodded in agreement.

'That and family support,' Vera stipulated. Education was fine, she conceded. But along with that, ghetto kids – and all others – needed parents who were concerned about them, took responsibility for them. She was ever-upset by the flagrant lack of responsibility on the part of David's mother and father. You brought a child into the world, you had obligations to that child.

On New Year's Day, Vera stood with Paul on the porch and watched while Laurie and Adele joined Joel in his car for the drive to the Saratoga railroad station.

'There go two kids with their heads on straight,' Paul said with satisfaction. 'They know where they're headed in this world.'

Unexpected tears filled Vera's eyes. She was remembering her brother. Ernst, too, had hoped to become a doctor. Instead, he'd died in a concentration camp in Hitler's Germany. She was sure that could never happen to Laurie – yet she still grew anxious when she heard about the activities of the Ku Klux Klan and the newly organized ultra-conservative John Birch Society, which labelled FDR, Truman, and Eisenhower Communists.

'You're getting chilled out here.' Paul dropped an arm about her shoulders. 'Let's go inside and have a tall mug of hot apple cider.'

Waiting while Paul did his magic with two mugs of apple cider – cinnamon sticks plus a dollop of rum – Vera worried yet again about Laurie's going to school in New York. It would be a culture shock after growing up in a tiny town like Eastwood. Would Laurie be able to cope?

Paul said she was obsessive about keeping the girls close. Of course, children must have lives of their own – but they mustn't grow away from family. Nothing in this world was as precious . . .

Chapter Twenty-six

Vera frowned at her inability to hear the heated conversation in the living room as she rinsed the dinner dishes and handed them piece by piece to Tracy to stack in the dishwasher. The kitchen was cosy, windows steamed over on this bitterly cold February evening. Doris had gone upstairs to check on Neal, asleep in the crib set up for him in the guest room.

Vera suspected that Paul was arguing with his father and Phil about the presence of American troops in South Vietnam. He dreaded the possibility that once again – only nine years after the end of the war in Korea – Americans might die in battle. He was unnerved by President Kennedy's statement a few days ago that American troops in South Vietnam were to fire if fired upon, 'to protect themselves.'

'I don't know why Laurie always gets off without helping with the dishes,' Tracy complained with an air of martyrdom.

'We only do dishes ourselves on Friday and Saturday evenings,' Vera reminded her. Five nights a week the chore was handled by Irene, the latest in a line of housekeepers. 'And loading them in the dishwasher isn't exactly doing the dishes.' It was growing increasingly difficult to keep domestic help, Vera thought with recurrent frustration, and recalled the pleasant era when Fiona had filled this spot in their lives. 'When I was your age, we didn't have automatic dishwashers.'

'But why does Laurie run off every Friday night and I get stuck?' Tracy challenged.

'Laurie has to go to her debating group four Friday evenings – that's not every Friday night,' Vera pointed out. When did kids outgrow sibling rivalry – or did they ever? 'All right.' She capitulated at Tracy's melodramatic sigh. 'Leave the others and go on over to David's.' David's parents had recently built a showplace of a house just across the road, where they entertained at frequent intervals. The Kahns were not part of their social circle. Few local residents were.

'David and I just have a study date,' Tracy said virtuously, but her smile was dazzling.

'His parents are home?' Vera asked with obvious expectation of a positive reply.

'If they're not, the housekeeper is.' Tracy was already charging towards the door. 'I know. Be home by eleven,' she tossed over her shoulder before the familiar warning was voiced. 'The other kids stay out till midnight on weekends.' But it was a routine gripe that Vera ignored.

A few moments later Doris joined her in the kitchen, pitched in to help.

'Neal asleep?' Vera asked.

'All curled up like a puppy.' Doris exuded maternal love. 'Sometimes when he's asleep, I have to reach out and touch him to make sure he's breathing. I'm so happy sometimes I'm scared.'

'Enjoy him,' Vera said, remembering her own feelings when Laurie was born. 'This is such a precious time.' In a few months Laurie would graduate from high school and in September go off to college. It was absurd to feel she was losing her little girl. They grew up, and you had to learn to let go.

'Sometimes I walk into the nursery in the evening – you know, to make sure he hasn't thrown off the covers or to see if he's dry – and there's Phil, just standing by the crib looking down at him.'

'Ask the guys if they want more coffee,' Vera said.

'When do they not want a second cup after dinner?' Doris chuckled. 'But I warned Phil – no second helpings of dessert. He has to watch his waistline, in a few years he'll have to play catch with his son.'

When Vera and Doris joined the men in the living room with a tray of coffee, they found them arguing loudly – ignoring the TV newscast. Exchanging a glance of mock dismay with Doris, Vera walked to flip off the set.

'I don't care what Kennedy says.' Paul's face was flushed. 'When he tells American soldiers in South Vietnam – supposedly there as advisors – that they're to fire back if they're fired upon, that makes them combat troops.'

'Paul, we have 200 men in Vietnam,' Joel scolded. 'You're making a *tzimmes* out of nothing.'

'Better we should worry about the recession,' Phil said wryly. Vera knew Phil was uncomfortable at talk of war – self-conscious that a punctured eardrum had exempted him from the draft during World War II. 'We thought the unemployment problem was over late last year; now we have a relapse. That's –'

'Things will improve soon,' Joel interrupted defensively. 'We're keeping our heads above water.'

'You're keeping people working whom you don't need,' Phil said gently. 'You can handle that, but a lot of businesses can't or won't.'

'Do they expect us to move into another war to bring on prosperity?' Paul challenged.

'We're not going to see another war,' Joel soothed. 'Communism isn't the wave of the future.'

'What do you think about the Philadelphia Warriors moving to San Francisco?' Phil intervened.

'When will Laurie know if she's accepted at Barnard?' Joel grinned, knowing Phil was sidetracking them from sombre discussion.

'April, I believe,' Vera said.

With Laurie away from home, the gap between them could only widen, she agonized. Why couldn't she come out and talk to Laurie about this? God knows, she'd tried – but Laurie always cut her off.

'Mom, aren't you dressed yet?' In a white evening gown – chosen by the girl graduates of Eastwood High as official attire – Laurie hovered in the doorway of the master bedroom. Her stare was reproachful. 'I have to be in the auditorium in twenty minutes!'

'I'll be downstairs in five minutes,' Vera soothed, reaching for the flowered-print dress that lay across the bed. 'You look lovely, darling.'

'I hope I remember my speech.' Laurie was class valedictorian. 'I don't know why I'm so excited. It's only high school graduation.'

'It's an important occasion, Laurie.' Vera's voice was muffled as she pulled the folds of her dress over her head.

'I'll get my flowers out of the refrigerator and wait in the car,' Laurie decided. 'I don't know why we couldn't have carried red roses instead of mixed flowers. They're so much more sophisticated.' Laurie's favourite new word.

Paul came into the room, beaming as Laurie darted past him. 'Dad said I should ask you if this tie is okay,' he told Vera. 'He's as nervous as a bridegroom. His granddaughter, the class valedictorian.'

'The tie's fine. Where's Tracy?' She reached for a brush to smooth her tousled hair.

'On the phone with David. Where else?' But his eyes were sombre.

'You don't look very festive for the father of the sweet

girl-graduate,' Vera teased, reaching for a quick hug.

'I worry about these kids.' Paul sighed. 'So few of the graduating class are going on to college. Three of the boys are going into the army because it's that or work part-time at the supermarket – if they're lucky.'

'Dad said several have applied for jobs with us, but with the recession we're not hiring.' Vera, too, was sombre now. It was disturbing that there was so little future for the young people in Eastwood. 'People are laying off – not hiring.'

'I hope Laurie realizes how lucky she is – Dad coming across with that student tour of London as a graduation present.' His eyes were nostalgic. 'You and I never saw a London that wasn't wracked by bombs. Our kids have so much, Vera,' he said with sudden intensity. 'I wish we could make them understand how fortunate they are. Not to take things for granted.'

'Mom! Dad!' Laurie's voice called from below. 'I'll get killed if I'm late!'

Vera knew it was absurd, but she sat in her seat in the auditorium and fought back tears while they listened to Laurie make her speech. She wasn't the sentimental sort, she scolded herself – but she glanced across the row of seats and saw that Doris, too, was misty-eyed. Dad was bursting with pride. As though conscious of the emotions that tugged at her, Paul reached for her hand.

In such a little while, Laurie would be going off to college. Vera closed her eyes, envisioning Laurie boarding the train at the Saratoga railroad station. Laurie would turn around to wave goodbye to them – and then she would be lost to their view.

All at once Vera was assaulted by devastating memories. She was hovering in the darkened foyer of the Schmidt house in Berlin, her heart pounding in terror. She heard the noisy clamour as Nazi storm troopers herded Mama and Papa and Ernst down the stairs from their apartment. *She never saw Mama or Papa or Ernst again.*

Vera fought against panic. Laurie was just going to college. She wasn't being dragged to a concentration camp. Laurie would be home for Thanksgiving. What was this madness that attacked her?

Laurie put aside her textbook, reached for her purse, and hurried from the dorm. She was meeting Adele at the West End Bar for a hamburger, then they were heading down to the Village and that coffeehouse her roommate had been bragging about being so cool. She had had to learn her way around the subway system on her own. After four weeks at Barnard she was still nervous about taking subways. But she was here in New York – on her own. Only now and then did it seem scary. College wasn't like high school at all. She wished Adele were her roommate instead of Dodie – but next year, with any luck, she and Adele would have their own pad off-campus.

Her skirt wasn't too short, was it? Dodie said hemlines were going up, up, up. Dodie really wanted to be a fashion designer, but her parents insisted she focus on something more practical, so she was an English major. 'Something to do with publishing' was the vague way Dodie put it.

She waited outside the West End in the final heat wave of the year. Then she saw Adele striding towards her with an air of agitation.

'Hi,' Adele said breathlessly. 'I'm starving. Also, I'm pissed.' Adele's language had become more colourful in her years away from Eastwood. 'Courtesy of the project,' she attributed this. She prodded Laurie towards the entrance. 'Let's get inside and cool off.'

Adele wasn't living in the project anymore. When her

grandmother died in July, she'd moved right out of the overcrowded apartment – where Edna's 14-year-old daughter and Lottie's 15-year-old had added to that state by giving birth to daughters of their own. Now she lived in a furnished studio on West 88th Street. She'd explained to Laurie that she had to watch her money to make sure she'd be able to go full-time to school, but her new part-time job at a bookstore across from the Columbia campus would help.

'What are you pissed about?' Laurie probed when they were seated in the restaurant. 'The job is lousy?'

'No, it's okay,' Adele said. 'It's what happened out on the campus at Mississippi U,' Adele said tensely.

The efforts to enrol Air Force veteran James Meredith at Ole Miss had been viewed by most Americans with horror. Rioting had erupted. A bulldozer had been seized and used to push past the line of state marshals there to protect Meredith and see him registered. Molotov cocktails made from soda bottles had been hurled, bricks and broken benches thrown. Then the 82nd Airborne had been brought on campus to quell the rioting – in the course of which two men had been killed, one a French journalist and the other a spectator. Injuries were high before Meredith was at last registered at the university.

Laurie grimaced in pain. 'I think it's awful.'

'My instinct is to forget about school and get involved in civil rights. But I'm not going to do it,' she added swiftly as Laurie gasped in shock. 'Mom meant for me to go to college – and I mean for me to become a teacher. I won't let anything get in the way of that. I look at Mom's two sisters – and their bunch of kids – and it's scary. The last week before their welfare cheques come in, they're looking at an almost-empty refrigerator. And they don't see anything better in the future. That's the worst of it.'

'But you said your mother's other sister and one brother are doing great,' Laurie reminded.

'They had the strength to fight their way out.' Adele's face was luminous. 'Like me. But I want to go back in there and fight to help the kids who don't have the strength on their own. They don't have a chance without a real education, Laurie.'

'I think maybe we have to be realistic, too,' Laurie said slowly. But Adele mustn't take this the wrong way. 'Not everybody can be a schoolteacher or a business executive or a doctor. You said your mother's sister has a civil-service job and your younger uncle is a supervisor for Con Ed. Maybe the others aren't capable of that. Maybe they should focus on jobs they can handle. Dad says this country desperately needs good vocational high schools to train workers in the crafts. And we need to show respect for craftsmen, Dad says. They're an important part of our daily lives.'

'But all those people in the projects look at television,' Adele said impatiently. 'They see people living so well, and they can't understand why *they* can't live like that. Why do you think Edna and Lottie sit there and watch TV all day long and half the evening? They're living vicariously. They turn off the TV, and they're smacked in the face by reality.' Adele's smile blended compassion with exasperation. 'They'd go without food on the table if they needed money to have their TV repaired. That's their drug, Laurie.'

Now Adele told Laurie about the storefront that a group of young doctors were trying to set up as a free clinic in Harlem.

'They can just be open for four hours a day in the beginning, but it'll be a help,' Adele said with an air of exhilaration. 'I said I'd come in as a volunteer if they need me.'

'Me, too,' Laurie said, churning with enthusiasm. 'I'll do whatever I can. It'll be terrific experience for me.'

'Let's finish eating and run downtown,' Adele said. 'I want to see this coffeehouse you keep yakking about.'

In the weeks ahead, Laurie found herself absorbed in her new life style. She'd been intimidated by the city in her first days at school, but she was soon caught up in its electric excitement. And going to college wasn't like high school. Here she mingled with students who all had high SAT scores, came from comfortable homes, all anticipated fine futures.

As generations before her, she sat up till dawn in heated conversation with other students, exchanging a variety of ideas. *New* ideas, she thought with pleasure. About a new kind of world where people cared about one another, tried to make things right. There was something new in the air these days – and she was part of it.

Then, with surprising suddenness, the Thanksgiving holidays approached. Laurie had expected Adele to go home with her to Eastwood for the long weekend.

'I'll be working over the holidays,' Adele explained. 'Filling in for someone who's taking time off. I can use the extra money.' She hesitated. 'I know – I make a lot of nasty cracks about my family and the project; but if Grandma were alive, I'd be there for Thanksgiving. Gladys and Henry and his wife and kids will be there. I'm pissed at my aunts and uncles and cousins in the project – I hate the way they live. But I *understand* what's happened to them. I think I should be with them for Thanksgiving – even though they figure they don't have much to be thankful for.'

'Okay,' Laurie said softly. 'But we'll miss you.'

Chapter Twenty-seven

The first weeks of the new year – 1963 – brought mixed responses from Americans. Republicans lamented that President Kennedy had sent a budget to Congress that was the largest in history, with a deficit of $11.9 billion forecast. Democrats applauded his programme of federal aid to combat mental illness and mental retardation. And older Americans – including Joel – applauded his proposed Medicare bill, which would provide medical-hospital insurance for those over 65. Laurie spoke enthusiastically about his programme for a Youth Conservation Corps and a domestic Peace Corps.

The situation between the United States and Russia remained difficult. On January 31, the Soviets broke off informal nuclear-test-ban talks with the United States. On February 12, at a 17-nation UN Disarmament Committee in Geneva, the Soviets called for elimination of foreign missile and nuclear submarine bases – but nine days later, Cuban-based Russian jets fired rockets at a disabled American shrimp boat adrift in international waters, roughly 60 nautical miles north of Cuba. Then on March 16, the US made a formal protest to the Soviets when two Soviet reconnaissance planes were seen flying over Alaska.

Each bellicose incident sent chills through Vera. Her frightening childhood in Nazi Germany, the uneasy time in Copenhagen, and living in London under Nazi attack were ever-close to the surface of her consciousness. But the expanding business occupied much of her thinking – and always she focused on the activities of Laurie and Tracy.

She had enjoyed every moment of Laurie's presence at home during the spring break from Barnard. But now – sitting with Laurie and Paul in the living room on this last evening before Laurie's return to the campus – she listened in shock to her older daughter's report on summer plans.

'You're not coming home for the summer?' Disbelieving, she repeated Laurie's pronouncement, familiar fears welling in her. 'What on earth will you be doing? Summer school?' She clutched at this possibility.

'I'll be home for a few days,' Laurie amended. 'Then Adele and I will join this group that's going down to Alabama and Georgia to work on voter registration.' She smiled determinedly. 'You know, to make blacks realize that it's urgent that they vote. We want to make sure they go to the polls in the fall elections.'

'The Democratic party will approve,' Paul joshed. Vera caught the silent message he was sending her: *Don't make a fuss about this*. 'Kennedy needed the black vote to win in 1960, and he'll need it again in 1964 to hang on to the White House.'

'I'll come home for a week before school opens.' Laurie's voice was conciliatory. 'I won't be going into the dorm next year,' she added with the super-casualness that said she hoped not to make waves with this announcement. 'I'll share Adele's studio as we've always planned for my sophomore year. With luck we might even find a one-bedroom apartment at the same rent. Living with Adele won't cost any more than my room and board on campus.'

'I'm sure we can handle that.' Vera exchanged a swift glance with Paul. She mustn't make a big deal of this –

though the prospect of Laurie's living off-campus was strangely unnerving.

Tracy burst into the room with an exuberant grin. 'Hey, guess what? David's mother just came back from London – and she brought him these sensational records by the Beatles. It's a group that all the kids in London think is just sensational,' she explained at their blank stares. 'David's loaning them to me for a whole week!'

'There won't be any peace and quiet in the house for a week,' Laurie predicted. She was relieved, Vera suspected, for this diversion. 'Is David still running around with his hair as long as yours?'

'What's wrong with that?' Tracy challenged. 'College guys are letting their hair grow, too. Carla's brother Robert was home from Boston U. His hair is just as long as David's.'

'You're taking an early train tomorrow,' Vera reminded Laurie. 'Let's get to bed at a decent hour.' Already she felt a sense of loss. Each time Laurie returned to school, she fought against panic. It was as though *Kristallnacht* hovered over her again. It was absurd, she tried to convince herself, to feel this way. Laurie wasn't going to the gas chambers. She was going to a fine school.

'I'll go to bed as soon as Grandpa gets home from his meeting,' Laurie promised. 'So I can say goodbye to him.'

'He'll be up to see you off,' Paul told her. In the last year, Joel had begun to shorten his hours at the factory. He didn't go into the office until ten. 'At 70, I'm becoming a union man – a forty-hour week and just occasionally some overtime.'

'I'm hungry,' Tracy announced. 'Is there any more of that turkey from dinner?'

'Don't you ever stop eating?' Laurie grunted in distaste.

'Hey, I'm a growing girl.' Tracy giggled. 'But I can still fit into that Mary Quant dress that's so-so short on you.'

'I was considering leaving it for you,' Laurie acknowledged. At this point she was two inches taller than Tracy and her mother. 'But what have you got to trade?'

'My newest Peter, Paul and Mary?' Tracy bargained.

'Deal,' Laurie agreed.

'Mercenary characters, aren't they?' Paul drawled to Vera. 'But I'm hungry, too. Let's see what's in the fridge.'

A pall hung over the Kahn living room on this early May evening. Paul and Joel sat hunched on the sofa before the television set, mesmerized by the latest reports on the grim situation in Birmingham. Vera walked into the room, gave a mug of coffee to each of the men, and settled in a lounge chair with a mug for herself.

'What's happening?' she asked when Paul moved forward to mute the commercial, struggling to conceal her inner turmoil. It was so illogical, she taunted herself, to feel threatened because of something that was happening hundreds of miles away. 'Any new developments?'

'He's been summing up what's occurred these past days,' Paul told her. The black children of Birmingham had been enlisted in the crusade for desegregation. Minister-led children – boys in immaculate white shirts and girls in neatly ironed dresses – had marched from the Sixteenth Street Baptist Church to downtown Birmingham singing 'We Shall Overcome.' Almost a thousand of them had been arrested on the orders of the avowed segregationist police chief, Bull Connors.

The next morning other black children and teenagers had marched, and Bull Connors ordered fire hoses turned on them. Day after day, the marches continued – but Connors had grown desperate. Today – at the height of his fury – he had added a new terror and ordered snarling German Shepherds unleashed to attack the marchers, all of this visible to horrified TV viewers.

The events of these past days catapulted Vera into the past – into *Kristallnacht* and her final fear-laden days in Copenhagen. What happened there couldn't happen here, her mind told her – but she saw the terror in the faces of those innocent black children, and she remembered her terror.

'I can't believe what we saw on TV!' Joel's voice reflected the recrimination of millions of Americans. 'Where did he get the nerve to let loose his snarling dogs on those kids? That finishes him!'

'And Laurie talks about going down to Alabama this summer to help with voter registration?' Vera was shaken. 'How can we let her do this?'

'Vera, we can't stop her,' Paul cautioned, but she felt his compassion. And she knew that he, too, missed Laurie. 'She's not a child anymore.'

'We have to let them go,' Joel said gently. *But these weren't normal times. Terrible things were happening.* 'I remember how I felt when Doris went off to school, then Paul. At first I hated to come home to the empty house – but then I adjusted. It was a new phase of my life.' His smile was reminiscent. 'That's when I became so busy with my evening groups. You and Paul have each other,' he reminded her. 'I was alone. You two will be fine. You'll even learn to enjoy the new freedom. It's only natural, Vera,' he added at her stare of shock.

The sharp ring of the phone was jarring. Paul reached for the receiver.

'Hello.' His face lighted. He turned to Vera. 'It's Laurie. She's watching the TV news.' He returned to Laurie. 'Sure, we're watching. It's unbelievable.'

Bringing Adele with her, Laurie came home for four days at the close of school. Again, Vera was conscious of Adele's maturity beyond her years. She felt some relief about the projected voter-registration effort. There would be seven in their group – in addition to Laurie and Adele, two students from Columbia, two from NYU, and one from Fordham.

Their first evening in Eastwood, Laurie and Adele talked with exhilarating enthusiasm about the work that lay ahead.

'We're just one small group that's going out,' Adele explained. 'But it's a movement that's going to grow. Blacks have to learn the importance of political power – and how to use it.'

The term *blacks* seemed harsh to Vera's ears – but it was part of the changing times, she told herself. You didn't say *coloured* or *Negro* these days. Fiona would have been proud of Adele. But in herself, pride threatened to be overcome by fear.

Later – while Vera and Paul prepared for bed – they discussed Laurie's summer project.

'Some of these kids today surprise me,' Paul said quietly. 'I know, the general opinion is that college students are all involved with their personal lives, their hopes for success and security. But if you look around, you see something new. You see those who understand the world must change – and are determined to do something about it.'

'I'm afraid for them.' Vera was sombre. 'I don't want our kids to be part of the violence we knew.' She as a Jew fleeing Nazi persecution, Paul fighting in World War II.

'It won't be like that,' Paul comforted. 'This isn't wartime.'

'But Laurie's going down to Alabama – and I remember what just happened in Birmingham.' She reached out a hand to Paul as he slid into bed beside her. 'I can't help but be afraid.' And each time Laurie left home, she fought against panic – an insidious fear that she was losing a child. That her family was disintegrating.

Vera was grateful that Laurie phoned home every Sunday night. She was anxious because of the violence that was erupting again. White extremists had bombed the Gaston Motel in Birmingham where Martin Luther King had proclaimed a 'great victory' on the part of the black movement. The home of King's brother had been bombed. There was rioting not only in Birmingham but in dozens of other cities and towns.

Laurie remained enthusiastic about their project, talked already about how next summer's effort must be larger and stronger. Tracy – along with David – was on a student tour of Canada for the month of July. These little *vacations from parenthood* – as Paul labelled them – were always oddly refreshing, Vera realized with a flicker of guilt.

She was startled when in mid-August Doris talked about going down to Washington, DC, to be part of the March on Washington that was being planned by black leaders.

'Didn't you read that article in the special July 29 issue of *Newsweek*?' Doris probed. 'This is a time of peaceful revolution.' *Peaceful, when every time you picked up a newspaper or watched the TV news there was fresh violence?* 'Phil feels we should be part of it. Anyhow, he's taking his vacation that week – and maybe Neal will be too young to remember, but I'd like to think he was part of such an important march. Why don't you and Paul come with us?'

'I don't think so,' Vera hedged. From what the newspapers said, there would be a huge crowd from all over the country. Probably a hundred thousand people. The prospect of a crowd of that dimension repelled her. 'It must be an eight-hour drive, Doris –'

'I know.' Doris refused to be disturbed. 'And Washington in August is hot as hell, I hear. But Phil says that thirty years from now we'll be proud that we were part of the march.'

At the usual Friday-evening dinner at the Kahn house – on the night when Tracy returned from her student tour of Canada – Doris brought up the question of the planned March on Washington.

'You're going, Doris?' Tracy – who along with Laurie had dropped the more formal 'Aunt Doris' years earlier – was enthralled.

'I wouldn't miss it. And when I talked with Laurie last night, I promised to fill her in on every detail.' Doris hesitated, turned to Vera with an apology. 'I forgot to mention that Laurie called me last night. She was mourning that she and Adele wouldn't be able to be part of the march. But she's glad family will be there.' *Why hadn't she discussed it with her mother?* Vera tormented herself. *Always that wrenching gap between them.*

'I don't think it's a great idea,' Joel said bluntly. 'It could turn into something ugly. You'll have thousands of angry black radicals chomping at the bit. But I know you're stubborn. At least, leave Neal with me. Don't expose him to what could become an ugly scene.'

'It's not going to be ugly,' Paul soothed. 'The leaders won't let it be. The whole purpose is to make Congress conscious of the need for a major civil rights bill.'

'I want to go, too,' Tracy pleaded. Vera was startled. Since when was Tracy involved in civil rights? 'Can David and I go with you?' Her eyes moved from Doris to Phil. 'David's parents are away in the Greek Islands. His housekeeper won't mind.'

'If your mother and father say it's okay,' Doris stipulated.

'Say it's okay, Mom!' Tracy's smile was electric. 'I know Dad won't mind.'

Vera was unnerved. Did the girls think *she* was less understanding than Paul? It was a disconcerting supposition.

Paul turned to Vera. 'Why don't we go, too? It should be an inspiring experience.'

'How can I leave the office?' she stammered.

'You can take a day off,' Paul insisted.

She didn't want to go! Had he forgotten how she hated crowds?

'Washington is going to be a madhouse,' Joel protested. 'Watch the march on television. Don't go looking for trouble!'

For a moment Doris seemed torn.

'We'll leave Neal with you, Dad.' She rejected her father's anxiety. 'There won't be any trouble. This will be a peaceful demonstration.'

'How many times have we heard that this summer?' Joel retaliated apprehensively. 'There've been over 700 riots in 186 towns and cities. And you're talking about a hundred thousand people showing up for this march!' A vein pounded in his forehead. 'You'll be exposing yourself to all kinds of cranks and crackpots!'

'We'll be all right, Dad.' Paul was firm. *He meant for them to go, too!* Vera thought with astonishment. *Couldn't he consider her feelings on this?* 'And we won't try to drive back the same night.' He turned to Doris and Phil for agreement. 'We'll stay over at a motel somewhere between Washington and New York, then drive home the following morning.'

'Good deal,' Phil approved.

Long after Paul had fallen asleep, Vera lay awake and restless. Life was moving too fast for her. She worried so about Laurie being down in Alabama in such troubled times. She understood – as did most Americans – that blacks must have the rights of whites. She'd recognized that when she met the first coloured soldiers in London. But she was terrified of the violence that was part of the change. These days, the past was too much with her.

Paul and Phil took charge of the plans for the Washington trip – with Joel continuing to be vocal in his opposition. Vera forced herself to remain silent about her own apprehension. Busloads of people – black and white – would be coming in from all parts of the country. It would be a *peaceful* demonstration, she kept reassuring herself – even while she recoiled from being part of such a huge gathering.

Doris had never been away from Neal overnight, but reiterated constantly that he would be asleep when they left on Tuesday evening and would be fine with his grandfather. 'He won't miss me a bit. We'll be back before lunch on Thursday.'

After a very early dinner on Tuesday evening – with Neal happy to remain with his grandfather – the six of them settled themselves in Doris's station wagon for the first segment of the trip to Washington. They'd stop at a motel in New Jersey tonight, leave early in the morning for their ultimate destination. Ceremonies were scheduled to begin at 11:00 AM.

As Tracy had predicted, David's housekeeper had given permission for him to join them. He was almost a family member now, Vera thought with wry amusement. Then amusement was replaced by troubling questions that she usually managed to dismiss. David and Tracy were almost seventeen. How close was that relationship? *How could a parent know?*

Some of the stories that circulated about teenagers

today were unnerving – especially their casualness about sex. All right, she had slept with Paul when she was only eighteen – before they were married – but they'd lived in such a traumatic world. In some ways today's kids seemed so much more immature than they had been, so much more protected.

She'd been upset – was it two or three years ago? – when Tracy had been caught smoking in school. Now Paul said the staff was unnerved to discover marijuana being smoked in the high school. 'You think it's just happening in big cities, but the kids here are getting it, too. They don't want to believe it can damage their health. They just want to get high.'

'What are you reading, Tracy?' Doris asked, puncturing Vera's introspection. Sometimes, Vera thought, Tracy and David acted like a long-married couple. Tracy was reading a magazine and David had his face buried in a book.

'*Playboy*,' Tracy said calmly. 'Do you know they pay a fortune to the girls who pose naked for the magazine?'

'You're not posing naked for anybody,' Paul said bluntly.

'My boobs are too small,' Tracy said and giggled because David glared at her candour. 'Well, they are.'

Vera remembered hearing a pair of mothers complaining that it was ridiculous the way the makers of Barbie dolls were giving Barbie realistic breasts. But in real life, the kids were growing up so fast, she fretted, and wondered yet again about Laurie's social life at college and down in Alabama. How did you know what they were doing? She recalled a remark of Fiona's not long before she died. '*We got a good idea what goes on in the minds of the kids in the ghetto – with fourteen and fifteen-year-olds getting themselves pregnant and thinking nothing of it.*'

'Phil, take a look at that list of motels,' Paul instructed. 'We never did decide just where we're going to stop. Maybe we should call ahead for reservations.'

Not until they were deep into New Jersey and Tracy and David both fast asleep did they pull into a Howard Johnson, where they divided by sex into two units. Early in the morning – with another three hours of driving ahead of them – they headed south. Already the weather was steamy. Approaching Washington, DC, they were frustrated by the tremendous traffic jam. Cars, trucks, passenger-loaded buses were pouring into the city.

With much difficulty, they found a parking area, then began the long trek to the Mall. On the car radio they'd heard that only a small number of people were turning out for the march. '*Around twenty-five thousand are assembling at this hour,*' a radio newscaster had reported at eight-thirty. '*A hundred thousand had been expected.*'

'Wow, this is a mob!' Tracy chortled as they moved along with the hordes around them, everyone in high spirits.

'That newscaster was way off,' Phil said. 'What will you bet they'll hit the 100,000 mark by the time the ceremonies start?'

When they arrived at the Mall, they encountered wall-to-wall people. Wherever their eyes could reach, there were people. Perhaps a fourth of them were whites, Vera surmised. All ages and from every state of the Union, she judged, listening to the accents around her. In truth, she realized, the black leaders would not lead the march. The crowd that had been waiting since early morning had fallen into place, filling the Mall from the Washington Monument to the Lincoln Memorial. Despite the oppressive heat, the blazing sun, the delay in the ceremonies, the mood was upbeat.

'Laurie and Adele should be here,' Doris said sentimentally as they waited for the ceremonies to begin.

'They couldn't take the time off,' Vera commented. Despite her phobia about crowds, she was glad she had come here today. 'They have a job to do, Doris.'

Then at one o'clock Camellia William began to sing 'The Star-Spangled Banner.'

'Marian Anderson was supposed to sing,' Paul whispered in Vera's ear, an arm protectively about her waist. 'But I heard somebody say her plane still hasn't arrived.'

Even before the first speech, Vera knew she would forever remember this spectacle. She forgot her exhaustion as she listened to the speakers – though by three o'clock some of the crowd had begun to drift away because of the excruciating heat. Then Mahalia Jackson rose to sing, and the drifters returned as her magnificent voice soared with 'I've Been 'Buked and I've Been Scorned.' After this, A. Philip Randolph came forward to introduce the final speaker of the evening, Dr Martin Luther King, Jr.

The assemblage listened as though mesmerized to Dr King's speech – and when he concluded with his *I have a dream* sequence, Vera could no longer see him because tears blurred her vision. After he spoke, there was a long moment of awed silence – and then the thunderous response of 250,000 people.

At Vera's suggestion, her small group didn't rush from the Mall. They allowed the crowd around them to disperse. She was too caught up in the events of the afternoon to want to hurry from the scene. It was an afternoon she would forever remember.

'Glad we came?' Paul asked gently.

'Oh yes,' she conceded.

But she suspected that all would not be as peaceful as today in the weeks and months and years ahead. And she worried still about Laurie and Adele, down in what they called 'enemy territory,' fighting to encourage blacks to go to the polls and vote.

Please God, she prayed, let them be safe.

Chapter Twenty-eight

Laurie and Adele arrived for a four-day stay in Eastwood before heading for New York and their respective schools – and to track down a one-bedroom apartment they would share. Eager to see as much of Laurie as possible, Vera took time off from the factory – though she was always within telephone reach if problems arose. Joel was candid in admitting that the bulk of responsibility for running the business rested in her capable hands.

Exhausted from their summer activities – but exhilarated by the results, Laurie and Adele slept till noon each day, lounged around the house in candid delight at this inactivity.

'It was a terrific summer, Mom,' Laurie confided while she and Adele relaxed with Vera over tall glasses of ice tea in the torpid heat of the late afternoon. 'We felt we were doing something useful.'

'There'll be a lot more of us going down next season,' Adele predicted, and Laurie nodded vigorously.

Vera understood now why Laurie had rejected Doris's impulsive offer to throw a 'welcome home' party for her. In the course of a year, Laurie had moved far away from the others in her graduating class. They existed now in different worlds. Two of the girls were studying to be nurses, one had completed a year-long business course and worked as a secretary in Saratoga. Several had married – two of whom were pregnant. Two worked part-time at the local supermarket.

Of the boys, only one had gone on to college. One had

joined the Peace Corps. Two had enlisted in the army – one was among the 16,000 Americans JFK had sent to Vietnam.

Vietnam was becoming what Joel called 'a dirty word' among a small number of draft-age young men, though most Americans considered it the right thing to do, to fight for 'the free peoples of Vietnam.' Weren't the North Vietnamese Communists trying to take over democratic South Vietnam? Joel was upset when he overheard David make a disparaging remark about this country's presence in that tiny strip of land that before 1954 had been part of French Indochina.

Tracy was exuberant in her status as a high school senior, though in constant doubt about where to attend college.

'Talk to Laurie when she comes home for Thanksgiving,' Vera urged.

'I don't want to go to the same school as Laurie,' Tracy said instantly.

'I know that,' Vera soothed. Tracy had hated having teachers recognize her as *Laurie's little sister*. They were both top students, though Tracy never seemed to realize that. 'But Laurie might have some inside information on other colleges. From talking with other students. Discuss it with her.'

'David is acting like such a jerk.' Tracy sighed. 'He keeps telling his parents he wants to take a year off before he goes to college because he doesn't know yet what he wants to do with his life.' Vera tensed in alarm. 'I keep telling him that's crazy. For once his parents are right.'

'He doesn't have to make a decision just yet,' Vera pointed out gently. 'He doesn't have to declare his major until the end of his sophomore year.'

'But his parents have their minds all made up.' Tracy's

tone was scathing. 'He'll be either a pre-law or pre-med student, they keep telling him. Maybe David doesn't know yet what he wants to be – but he knows he *doesn't* want to be a doctor or a lawyer.'

'He doesn't have to make his decision yet,' Vera reiterated. 'Nor do you.' Her voice softened. 'Just make up your mind where you want to go, and take it from there.'

'I think I'd like to go to a state college. Maybe Albany.' She was struggling to sound casual. 'You know – where I can come home for a lot of weekends. David's grades may not be the greatest – not that he isn't smart, he just doesn't study unless it's something that interests him – but they're high enough to get him into SUNY.' The State University of New York.

'You'll go wherever you like – provided, of course, you're accepted.' But Vera was happy that Tracy preferred a school close enough for some weekends at home.

'I'll work on David. I've already told him there's no chance we're going to join the Peace Corps. What good would we be? We don't have any skills. Besides,' Tracy said realistically, 'we're underage.'

Vera was ever-conscious of the tiny but increasingly vocal peace movement. Voracious newspaper and magazine reader that he was, Paul kept her up to date on what was happening. Like Paul, she yearned to see a world at peace – but the peace movement, she feared, would only enhance Laurie's hostility towards the family business. Laurie couldn't understand that keeping the peace was one of the responsibilities of guns. She remembered Joel's oft-repeated observation: 'Switzerland is the most peaceful country in the world – but every home is armed. Israel remains in existence only because every household owns a gun.'

Now – just a week before Laurie was due home from

313

college for the Thanksgiving weekend – Joel was fascinated by the reports coming through on the new M-16 Colt rifle. To Joel, it was a work of art.

'Some army guy has said it's one of the reasons the Viet Cong are being wiped out so easily,' Joel said with satisfaction. 'The M-16 is lighter and smaller than the M-14. It's perfect for guerrilla warfare.'

'Don't talk about that when Laurie comes home next week,' Paul warned his father. 'When I spoke with her on the phone last Sunday night, she sounded so upset about the situation in Vietnam.' He paused. 'Not without reason.'

Vera remembered that last month the White House had issued a statement that American aid to South Vietnam would continue, that the administration anticipated the war might be won by the end of 1965. But how many Americans – as well as Vietnamese – would die by then?

Thanksgiving was the American holiday she most loved, Vera thought. It was a time of families coming together. This year there would be eight at the dinner table. Though she rarely indulged herself by taking time off from the factory during the work-week, this pre-Thanksgiving Friday she plotted a long lunch hour. She would drive to Saratoga to buy a new tablecloth for the occasion. The local shop was limited in choice.

On impulse she phoned Doris at the nursery group, explained her errand.

'Come with me,' she coaxed. 'I'll pick you up about ten past twelve, when the kids have been dismissed.'

'Sounds great,' Doris effervesced. 'I'll leave Neal with Mrs Ambrose. She's always glad for extra hours.' Mrs Ambrose was her part-time housekeeper/babysitter. 'But let's stop off somewhere along the road for a hamburger and coffee. This gorgeous, crisp weather makes me famished by noon.'

On schedule Vera picked up Doris. They decided to stop at a popular eatery several miles out of Eastwood on the road to Saratoga.

'I feel like I'm playing hookey,' Doris confessed in high spirits when they'd settled down at a table with their hamburgers and tall mugs of steaming coffee. 'For once everything's going well with the nursery group and the book shop volunteers. Do you know how wild I get when somebody calls up at 7:40 AM to say, "Doris, I'm so sorry, but something's come up and I just can't make it this morning."?'

'I've heard about it a few times.' But Vera was sympathetic.

All at once Doris was sombre. 'Sometimes I wonder if Phil resents my running off five mornings a week at eight o'clock when he doesn't have to leave for the shop until nine-thirty. I stack the breakfast dishes and tell him to leave them for me – but he always rinses them and throws them into the dishwasher. And he's been so good about helping with Neal.'

'Neal's his kid, too.' Vera frowned remembering her secretary's battles with a husband who resented her going out to work – even when it was his wife's job that was paying the mortgage on their new house. 'Men today help out with the kids and the house. At least, some of them,' she amended.

'I'm not neglecting Phil or Neal by running the nursery group,' Doris said defensively. 'I'd be climbing the walls if I didn't have something besides the house to occupy my time.'

'Is Phil complaining?' Vera challenged, knowing this was unlikely.

'No.' Doris's smile was wry. 'But I hear about other husbands who *do* complain.' She paused. 'I remember Wayne.'

'That was another life,' Vera said gently. 'Phil is the most adoring husband I know. You can't do anything wrong in his eyes.'

'He's so sweet. I just wish he could have done something with his music. I always feel this underlying sadness in him because he could never make it in the music field. Most of the time it's under wraps, but I know it's there.'

'Paul's upset about our school-budget situation. He says it's insane to cut back at a time when school registration is increasing, but everybody balks at raising school taxes.'

'As long as we're going to be in the department stores, I'll look for a sweater for Phil. I'm so glad he insisted I keep a separate checking account for myself – you know, from the rental income for the apartment. This way I can spend as much as I like on a present for him without feeling guilty about wrecking the family budget.'

They shopped with an eye on their watches, left Saratoga on schedule. At a few minutes before three, Vera dropped off Doris at her house and headed for the factory. Walking through the entrance, she realized instantly that something momentous had occurred. The receptionist was not at her desk. There was a strange quiet in the normally noisy building.

Vera rushed down the narrow hall that led to the cluster of offices. All were deserted. Now she became aware of the sound of a radio on the silent factory floor. She opened the door that led to what Joel called the *heart* of the business. Four deep, the workers encircled the supervisor's desk.

'Vera, you haven't heard –' Joel's shaken voice greeted her. 'President Kennedy has been shot!'

From Friday through Monday, when JFK was laid to rest in Arlington National Cemetery, the country gave itself over to grief. Americans clung to their television sets, following every step in this national tragedy. It was an unreal period, Vera thought as the family sat down to dinner on Monday evening.

'What has happened to this country?' Joel asked – half in rage, half in sorrow. 'What – who – was behind this assassination?'

'All it takes is one madman,' Paul said tensely. 'I doubt that we'll ever know if it was more than that.'

'It's a warning that this country has gone off track.' Vera closed her eyes for an instant, remembering Nazi Germany. Remembering her terror on *Kristallnacht*.

'This has been such an awful year. All the riots, the murder of Medger Evers, this business in Vietnam –' Paul's voice intruded on her ugly reverie.

'It wasn't all awful.' Tracy's light young voice was earnest. 'What happened in Washington in August was beautiful. Mom, you said you'd remember it for the rest of your life.'

'Let's pray that we've reached rock-bottom,' Joel said. 'What in our lifetime can ever hit us the way this has?'

Laurie and Adele left their recently acquired one-bedroom apartment in the West 80s early on Thanksgiving morning.

'I wish you were going home with me,' Laurie said wistfully.

'Yeah, it would be fun. But I know Grandma would want me to be with the family on Thanksgiving. She was always big on Thanksgiving and Christmas. I'm not taking any money with me, though,' she said with mild defiance. 'Last time, one of the kids took off with my wallet. They all swore they didn't, but I had it when I went into the apartment and it was gone when I got ready to leave. Why can't they understand that's not the way to live?' Her voice soared in a blend of anger and frustration.

'It'll take more than you and me to figure that one out.' Laurie checked her watch. 'I'd better grab a cab to Grand Central. I don't want to miss the train, and it'll probably be mobbed today.'

'Don't eat too much turkey,' Adele teased. 'I know it beats our tuna-noodle casserole or hamburgers.'

'I'll try to get some studying in –' Laurie abandoned herself to an extravagant yawn. 'We sat up yakking so late last night.'

'Don't sleep past your station,' Adele warned. 'Your father will be there waiting for you.'

'Yeah, Mom's probably been up since six to start on the pumpkin pie – and Doris will bring the homemade cranberry sauce and a pecan pie because that's what Grandpa prefers to pumpkin. But it's kind of hard to think about celebrating Thanksgiving Day when President Kennedy has just been assassinated.'

Fighting off sleepiness, Laurie utilized the travelling time for study. She was pleasantly surprised when she at last put aside her book to realize the train was pulling into the Saratoga station. Peering through her window, she spied her grandfather's car in the parking area. Then she saw her father and grandfather, waiting with eager smiles. Her initial sense of pleasure at seeing them was almost obliterated by a sudden involuntary surge of anger.

JFK had been assassinated by a mail order rifle. Had it been made by Grandpa's company? How could he and Mom be so proud that the company was thriving? *They were selling instruments of death. Dad never said so*, she thought rebelliously as she headed down the aisle with her valise, *but he must hate having his father and his wife selling guns and rifles. He was a pacifist, for God's sake.*

'Let me take your valise.' Her grandfather reached to relieve her of this, then extended a hand to help her down.

'Oh, you look beautiful, baby.' He kissed her with tender pride.

'It seems so long since we've seen you, Laurie.' Her father kissed her warmly. 'Welcome home.'

At the house Vera inspected the turkey. Another forty minutes and it would be ready to come out of the oven. Doris had taken Neal upstairs to change him into fresh clothes because he'd spilled his 'taste' of cranberry sauce over his shirt. In her bedroom Tracy was listening to her new Beatles record. Rock 'n' roll filtered through the house. *Were all teenagers hard of hearing?* Vera asked herself in mild frustration. *Why must Tracy play her records so loud?*

She heard the car coming up the driveway. Her face luminous with anticipation, she hurried from the kitchen down the hall to the front door. Oh, it was good to have her precious baby home!

It seemed to Vera that Laurie had barely arrived when she was driving her to the railroad station to catch a train back to New York. But in roughly four weeks, Laurie would be home again, she consoled herself.

With the arrival of the new year, the family was caught up in Tracy's college plans. She'd finally decided that, yes, she would go to State at Albany. With obvious reluctance, David had agreed to go there, also.

'His parents were livid when he kept talking about taking a year off,' Tracy reported. 'They still think he's going to be pre-law or pre-med, but he's only going to school to make sure he's got draft-deferment. He's not afraid of fighting. It's that the war seems so pointless.'

Vera and Paul knew David's parents only well enough to exchange greetings when they met on the street. Vera was outraged by their lack of interest in their son's activities except where this reflected on themselves. But she was admittedly shaken when word leaked out that his parents had grounded him for a month when they caught the unmistakable scent of marijuana seeping from beneath his bedroom door. Tracy was immediately grilled.

'He was just testing.' Tracy was nonchalant. *Was Tracy, too, smoking marijuana?* Vera asked herself in alarm. 'You know, experimenting. It was no big deal.'

'It is a big deal.' Vera fought for calm. Paul had warned her to be *cool* about this. 'We have no way of knowing yet what damage it causes. We –'

'Mom, it's no different from smoking a cigarette or guzzling Scotch or taking tranquillizers.' Tracy's tone was that of one talking to someone considerably younger. 'It just provides a *lift*. You know.'

'I don't know.' Vera was grim. 'Nobody in this house smokes.' She remembered Tracy's one experiment in that area. 'We don't drink except for an occasional glass of wine.'

'David's parents serve cocktails before every dinner party. His father always has a drink with his dinner. More than *a* drink,' she emphasized. 'So he smoked a joint.' Her ire was becoming obvious. 'It was rotten of them to ground him for a month. He wasn't doing anything different from what they were doing!'

'It isn't a good thing for him to smoke marijuana – or anything else.' Vera was struggling to sound matter-of-fact.

'Some of the kids at school smoke every chance they get.' Tracy sounded simultaneously defensive and rebellious. *Kids needed to know they faced limits*, Vera told herself. *Was the school aware they had this problem with marijuana – and God only knows what else?*

Later – in the privacy of their bedroom – Vera and Paul discussed the situation while they prepared for bed.

'We know there's a small group of kids – very small –

involved in smoking pot,' Paul acknowledged, rinsing his toothbrush, sliding it into place beside Vera's. 'But it's not widespread,' he insisted, walking back into the bedroom. 'I just hope to God none of the kids are into hard drugs.'

'Is the school doing anything about this?' Vera turned down the bedcovers, settled herself on her side of the bed.

'Not much,' he admitted, pausing at his night table to wind up the clock. 'I've read somewhere that back in 1900, statistics showed that 1% of our population was addicted to morphine, opium, cocaine, or heroin. By the early 1940s, marijuana was the fashionable drug. But what the kids are picking up,' Paul continued with a fresh intensity, 'is that the law is moving in on the use of marijuana, but Congress does nothing to stop the sale and advertising of cigarettes – which we *know* cause cancer. There are no figures on death from smoking marijuana. How do we rationalize that to them?'

'I was listening to that song Tracy likes so much,' Vera said reflectively. 'You know – the Bob Dylan song – "Blowin' in the Wind." It tells us what a lot of kids are thinking these days. They're impatient and disillusioned and angry because we're not delivering the kind of world they expect.'

'I love that song,' Paul said. 'I love the kids for what they want to see happen in this world.' In a familiar pattern he began to pace about the room. 'Not smoking pot. The good things. A civil rights bill with teeth. The kind of freedom the Founding Fathers visualized for this country. A world at peace.'

'We can't solve those problems tonight,' Vera said softly. 'Stop pacing and come to bed.' Her smile was a loving invitation.

One thing in their life never changed – and for that Vera was grateful. The world might fall apart, but for a little while they could forget the horrors around them in each other's arms. Tomorrow, she told herself, she would worry about drugs in their high school. But even as Paul reached for her in the cosy comfort beneath the blankets, she was remembering Tracy's reaction to smoking pot.

'*Mom, it's no different from smoking a cigarette or guzzling Scotch or taking tranquillizers.*'

One question plagued her in the weeks and months ahead. Was Tracy smoking pot?

Chapter Twenty-nine

The family was caught up now in Tracy's imminent graduation from high school. Vera was uneasy when her father-in-law announced that he was giving Tracy her own car as a graduation present.

'It'll be easier for her to drive home on weekends if she has a car.' *Laurie wouldn't feel slighted, would she?* Vera asked herself uneasily. *No*, she told herself almost immediately – *Dad had given her that trip to London.* Paul scolded her for being phobic about the girls being treated equally.

Perhaps it was a hangover from her own youth – when every possession was hard-earned, Vera mused – that she worried that material things came so easily to her own children.

'Hey, it's a whole new generation,' Doris said when Vera expressed her fears. 'The middle class and up never had it so good. The poor still have to fight for even the tiniest luxuries. And I don't mean just the inner-city poor. We have it right here in Eastwood. Don't think of the poor as just those on welfare. Phil says that both the Democrats and the Republicans will probably make poverty a big issue in this year's presidential campaign.'

Vera was pleased that Laurie would be home for three weeks before heading down to Georgia and Alabama again on a voter-registration drive. Adele would be going south with her – first coming to Eastwood for a week in June. Tracy pretended to be casual about it, but Vera knew she was delighted that Laurie and Adele would be in Eastwood for her graduation exercises. Following in Laurie's tracks, Tracy was class valedictorian. '*Thank God*,' Vera told Doris. '*There'd be no living with her if she hadn't been chosen.*'

This summer Tracy and David were both signed up to go on a student tour of Israel. Vera had chosen their destination out of a sense of guilt that her daughters were being raised with little religious teaching. They knew all the major holidays, observed by the family. They knew the history of the Jewish people. They knew about her own escape from the Nazis and about their father's war experiences. But there was no synagogue closer than Albany, so this was a good time for Tracy to get in closer touch with her heritage. David was allowed to go along with the group, Vera surmised scornfully, because he would be out of his parents' hair for a month.

Late in June, Laurie left for New York to join her dedicated group for the drive down to Georgia. She was convinced that at this point voter-registration was more urgent than antisegregation demonstrations. Political power was out there for the black *and* the white poor – *if they'd just learn how to use it.*

A week later Vera and Paul drove Tracy and David to JFK for their flight to Israel. In December of last year, Idlewild had been renamed in honour of the assassinated president.

'I feel like such a traitor,' Tracy mourned for a moment, 'leaving my car all alone for a whole month.'

'I'll talk to it every day,' Paul joked.

'Ten days after we get back, I have to register for the draft,' David said grimly. He would be eighteen. 'That's the pits.'

'You kids eat decently while you're in Israel,' Vera ordered. 'Don't try to live on junk food.'

'You're talking to the snack-food generation,' Paul

warned her and turned to the other two. 'Eat something beside hamburgers, peanut butter with marshmallow stuff, and popsicles.'

Finally the group's flight was announced ready for boarding. In a burst of exuberance, the cluster of high-spirited teenagers joined the other waiting passengers. Vera and Paul made their way out of the airport terminal and sought out their car.

'It feels so strange, knowing the kids are heading across the ocean.' Vera reached for Paul's hand. 'And Laurie's already down in south Georgia.'

'I want to see a big smile,' Paul ordered, squeezing her hand. 'We're about to begin our latest honeymoon.'

They would spend tonight at a motel close to the airport, then drive west on Long Island to the oceanfront cottage at Montauk that they'd rented for a week. A glorious week of lying on the cottage deck and gazing at the ocean, Vera thought in pleasurable anticipation. For one week the world would seem to stop. *They both needed that*, Vera told herself.

Paul was exhausted from internecine battles at the school. He was so conscientious, so dedicated to improving the quality of his school – and encountering little success. And she, too, was tired. Not just from the demands of the business, she analysed. They lived in such tumultuous times. Just to turn on the television each night and watch the news was traumatic.

Let this be a calm summer, she prayed – remembering last summer, when George Wallace's defiant behaviour in Alabama had brought federal troops onto the campus of the University of Alabama. Remembering the riots in Harlem, Chicago, Birmingham, Atlanta. *Let everything work out peacefully with Laurie's voter-registration group down in Georgia.*

*

Laurie emerged from the discouragingly inadequate shower in the bathroom of the shabby frame house that was housing their group this summer. The sash of her short, terrycloth robe tight about her waist, clutching perspiration-soaked clothes and wet towel in her arms, she walked down the hall to the minuscule bedroom she shared with Adele and Marian, the Bennington junior who'd come down with the group this summer and was fast losing her starry-eyed attitude about their mission.

'Feel better?' Stretched on one of the cots that occupied most of the room, Adele glanced up from the magazine she was reading. Laurie noted that Marian had already left for her date with Chet, the senior from Howard University.

'I did for about five minutes. God, this heat is unbelievable!' Laurie collapsed on the cot that sat about ten inches from Adele's.

'It was just as bad last summer,' Adele recalled, 'but we were a year younger – and so wide-eyed about what we were doing.'

'I get the feeling this year that some of the group resent some of the others –' She paused, suddenly awkward. How could she express what she was thinking to Adele without sounding racist?

'Sugar, I know what you're thinking.' Adele's smile was rueful. 'I'm okay – up to a point – because I'm black. But some of the blacks look on these white college kids – like you – with something that smells of contempt.' Her voice was calm, but her eyes were furious. 'I want to knock their heads together. But then I realize what it is with them. They know all these white college kids – and they group me along with you – are going back to comfortable lives at the end of the summer.'

'I work as hard as anybody here,' Laurie said defensively, 'but Jock keeps picking on me any chance he gets.'

'Laurie, you know why,' Adele clucked. 'He's pissed because you won't sleep with him.'

Laurie stared at her in shock. 'I don't like him that way.' She'd never slept with anybody – but when she did, she'd have to love the guy.

'I heard him talking the other night.' Adele dropped her voice to a semblance of bass. ' "That Laurie is such a phoney! Pretending she's so liberal and all – but she won't go to bed with me because I'm not lily-white." And why do you think Marian's flat on her back somewhere now with Chet? Because she's proving to herself – and to Chet – that she's not prejudiced. And that's nuts. Before the summer's over,' she predicted, 'there's going to be a real battle between Chet and Joe – because Joe was Marian's boyfriend back home and he figures he's being dumped because he's white. Which is true,' she summed up.

'What's all that got to do with voter-registration?' Laurie challenged impatiently.

'Something happened to the whole scene during the past school year. We were out of it. We didn't get a whiff. Last year white college kids were welcomed; now they're resented. The black workers feel they ought to control this fight – and here they have uppity white college students showing them up.'

'They ought to be grateful,' Laurie flared. 'We've done a lot to help.' She thought about the three workers in Mississippi – black James Chaney and white Michael Schwerner and Andrew Goodman – both New Yorkers – who just yesterday had been discovered murdered. An unnerving situation to their own group.

'The difference between black students and white students is that we don't have the white belief in the system,' Adele said with candour, identifying herself with the black workers. 'I hang in there, hoping it *will* work.'

Laurie was startled. She'd heard Frank – who'd been out with them last summer and now again this year – make cracks about how all his wealthy white parents cared about was making money. *They don't give a shit about segregation or poverty or urban crises.*

Dad worried that the draft was unfair to low-income families because they couldn't keep their sons in college and thereby earn draft-deferment. But she'd always been wrapped up in the belief that the American system was the best in the world. They'd been raised to believe that. Was it working just for middle and upper class families like her own? It was a disturbing thought.

At the beginning of orientation week at SUNY-Albany, sitting in her car – bursting with luggage, record albums, books, and Tracy's recently acquired guitar, Vera yelled to Tracy and David to join her.

'We're coming, we're coming,' Tracy called back breathlessly. 'Mom, you're compulsive about time.'

'I don't like to be late.' Vera was calm but defensive. 'Let's get moving.' *It had never occurred to either of David's parents to take on this chore, of course*, she thought in annoyance.

Her arms clutching a batch of LPs, Tracy was shoving herself across the front seat to allow room for David. The trunk and rear seat were loaded. Tracy's own car – *my precious treasure* – remained in the Kahn garage. There was a question as to whether she would be allowed to keep a car on campus during her freshman year.

'Tracy, why don't you put those in the back?'

'Trust my new Beatles album and the new Bob Dylan back there by themselves?' Tracy uttered a vocal rejection.

'Mrs Kahn, don't you sometimes think Tracy's kind of infantile for almost eighteen?' David said with a mixture of derision and deep affection.

Sometimes, Vera thought, she wasn't sure whether they behaved like brother and sister or an old married couple. And all too frequently she asked herself how far they'd gone together. She couldn't come out and say, 'Tracy, are you sleeping with David?' But the stories that circulated about some of their peers were unnerving.

She reminded herself yet again that she'd been only a few months older than Tracy when she'd first slept with Paul. But those were different times, chaotic times. And she'd seemed so much older than Tracy.

Vera deposited David first at his dorm, then drove Tracy to hers. She made a point of leaving as soon as Tracy's belongings were transferred from car to dorm room. She remembered Doris's admonition about this. 'When I went off to Barnard, I was embarrassed to death at the way Dad was so reluctant to leave. He kept hanging around as though I were about eight and he was terrified of leaving me alone.'

Driving back home – wistfully aware of the absence of Tracy and David – she tried to deal with the knowledge that for much of the year ahead both Tracy and Laurie would be away from home. *But it didn't mean the family was breaking up*, she derided her sense of loss. *They'd be home at intervals – on all the important holidays*. Still, driving back into town she fought against a wave of desolation.

Vera was enthralled on the October afternoon when Paul – home from his after-school group – phoned her at her office to tell her he'd just heard a TV news bulletin reporting that Martin Luther King, Jr was to receive the Nobel Peace Award.

'Paul, how wonderful! I wonder if Laurie knows yet?' Her immediate impulse was to phone Laurie in New York.

'I imagine the whole country will know by dinner time,' Paul said with a chuckle. 'But I can also imagine Laurie's response.' Paul's voice held a hint of warning. 'She'll be thrilled, of course – and then she'll point out that Alfred Nobel established the Nobel Peace Prize out of guilt for having unleashed all those deadly weapons on the world.'

'She'll simmer down, I hope, by the time she comes home for Thanksgiving.' Vera was uncharacteristically sarcastic. The wall between her and Laurie remained in place.

'I hope the radical blacks will be impressed by King's Nobel prize,' Paul said slowly. 'I hope they'll think in terms of non-violence.'

Vera knew he was troubled by the rising militant voices of black Muslims and what was being descried by white columnists as their black racism. And along with Paul, she was disturbed by Laurie's outspoken cynicism about what could and did happen in these United States. Everybody in this country was supposed to have the right to vote, but Laurie was discovering what a rough battle it was to make this come true.

This past summer Laurie had spent twenty-four hours in jail because of her determination to help blacks register to vote – but the man who murdered highly respected black leader Medger Evers roamed the streets a free man. She talked with blazing eloquence about being reviled by whites for her efforts to help blacks to register to vote. *Their legal right.* On two occasions she had personally experienced physical violence.

And Laurie was so upset about the American presence in Vietnam, Vera remembered. Slowing down in an unexpected burst of traffic, she could hear Laurie's voice in exasperated protest on her last evening home before returning to school:

'The government keeps sending troops to Vietnam to

protect it from the Viet Cong, but they do nothing to protect students who're fighting for the civil rights guaranteed by our Constitution!'

A few miles out of Eastwood – after a glance at her watch – she stopped at a gas station to phone Paul at the school. He had a free period now and his lunch period was coming up. She'd pick him up and take him off for lunch. Dad wasn't expecting her to come into the office until early afternoon.

Paul was waiting in the parking lot when she arrived.

'You're feeling like the mother bird who's seen her last little one fly out of the nest,' he jibed as he slid onto the seat beside her.

'Yeah.' Leave it to Paul to know her feelings at this moment, she thought with a surge of love.

'Let's have lunch at that place you discovered last month – the one sitting at the edge of the pond with the pair of swans. Let's be decadent and have a glass of wine with lunch.'

'You've persuaded me.' She followed his light mood with a sense of relief.

But over lunch, the conversation ultimately became serious. Paul, too, was distressed at seeing American soldiers going to Vietnam in increasing numbers.

'It's hard to swallow – this story that we're sending over only advisors. By the end of the year we're expecting to have over 23,000 Americans in Vietnam. Damn it, Vera, how can we pretend they're only advisors?'

'In the face of what happened last month at the Gulf of Tonkin, how can we say we're not fighting a war?' On August 4, Vera remembered – following reports that a North Vietnamese torpedo craft had attacked two US destroyers in the Gulf of Tonkin – US planes were ordered to bomb North Vietnam.

'And according to the polls, 85% of Americans

approved that,' Paul said disgustedly. 'We ought to get the hell out of Vietnam.'

'Don't let Dad hear you say that,' Vera warned. 'He's convinced that by sending troops to Vietnam we're saving the world from Communism.'

'Enough of this,' Paul ordered. 'What are we having for dessert?'

Later – after driving Paul back to the school and heading for her office – Vera felt enmeshed in depression. Where was the country heading? What was happening to so many of their college generation? So bright – so compassionate – and becoming so disillusioned.

Chapter Thirty

The day was cold and depressingly grey. Weather fore-casters were predicting heavy snow by late evening. Paul was relieved when the bell rang at the end of the last period of the day. His mind wasn't on teaching today. He was upset over the battle with Vera last night. She admitted she was furious at the way he'd defended the student who'd burnt his draft card at a public demon-stration last week. 'Paul, that's showing contempt for this country!'

Laurie would be home for the winter break sometime this afternoon. And Tracy was due in tomorrow evening, he comforted himself. He anticipated their arrival with deep pleasure. The house came alive when the girls were home.

A hand moved involuntarily to the pocket of his jacket, and his mood plunged into morbid apprehension. He pulled out the note that had been in his mailbox in the teachers' room. What the hell did Franklin want to see him about now? Another parent objecting to his bringing up the subject of drugs in the high school – so sure they had no such problem. How could they close their eyes to what was happening to their own kids?

All at once tense, he strode down the stairs to the floor below. He'd never liked the principal, but he had to keep up a facade of accepting his school policies – or resign. He wasn't ready to do that, he admitted. If he weren't teaching, what would he do with his life? If he resigned here, he'd have a rough time finding another spot in a commuting-area school. Franklin would make sure of that.

Masking his inner conflicts, he walked to the principal's office, decorated to reflect the Christmas season. He exchanged a few words with the school secretary, then was ushered inside.

'Sit down, Paul.' Franklin was brusque. He waited until Paul was seated, then continued. 'I've kept quiet about your after-school peace group, but in the current conditions I have to insist you drop it. It could have terrible repercussions.'

'There're a total of five in the group.' Paul struggled to appear calm. 'Four boys and one girl. That hardly presents a threat to anyone.'

'Drop it! I won't have my school being part of this insanity we see around us!' The other man's voice was shrill. 'These crazy kids fighting the draft! These stupid demonstrations! It's un-American.'

'It's freedom of speech.' Paul appeared almost detached. Inside he fumed. Now that LBJ had been elected for a full term of his own, what was he going to do about Vietnam? He'd campaigned as the peace candidate. But he remembered a November article in the *Wall Street Journal* that Laurie had sent him. The article suggested that the government was preparing an escalation of the war in Southeast Asia, and that was frightening. 'Clark, let's be glad that our young people are relating to what's happening in the world. We don't have the apathy we saw in students in the '50s. That's –'

'Bullshit,' Clark Franklin interrupted. 'Cancel the group. This school is not catering to those half-baked kids. That's not freedom of speech,' he scoffed. 'They're traitors to this country. I won't allow the school premises to be used for such purposes.'

Paul left the office. Of course, he could meet with the

kids in his own home, he thought in defiance. No, he couldn't. He rejected this immediately. Dad called the anti-Vietnam kids 'young hoodlums who've had it too good.' He'd have to disband the small group. To Dad the war in Vietnam was another battle against Communism.

Most Americans, he thought with recurrent apprehension, were proud that this country was rushing to the aid of the South Vietnamese government. On the surface it appeared a fine gesture. A Harris poll showed 85% approved. Even such liberals as Eugene McCarthy, Albert Gore, and George McGovern approved. After the trouble in the Gulf of Tonkin, the *Washington Post* had written: 'President Johnson has earned the gratitude of the free world.' But South Vietnam was not a democracy, he thought in repetitious rage. It had been ruled by a series of in-and-out unpopular dictators.

Paul drove home, impatient to talk with Vera about Franklin's insistence he disband his peace group. It hadn't begun as an anti-Vietnam movement, but now it would be considered just that. And damn it, why not? He *was* opposed to the war in Vietnam.

He glanced at his watch. It would be another two hours before Vera left the office. On impulse he decided to drop by and visit with Doris. If Doris weren't there, he could at least spend a little time with Neal. It had been a long time since his own kids were three years old, he thought nostalgically. He enjoyed his young nephew.

He saw Doris's car turn into the driveway as he approached the house. Thank God that Doris's life had taken this new path. It was as though she had been reborn when she met Phil.

'Hi!' Emerging from her car, Doris spied him. 'I didn't see you behind me.'

'I thought I'd pop in and yak for a while,' he called, drawing to a stop. 'Remember, you and Phil are coming over for dinner tomorrow night.' He left the car to join her on the stairs. 'But you'd better bring Neal or the girls will send you right home.'

'I wouldn't dare not bring him,' she said, chuckling. 'We saw them at Thanksgiving, but it seems so long ago.'

From inside the house came Neal's sweet, light voice. 'Mommie, Mommie!'

For a few moments they were caught up in greeting Neal. Then Mrs Ambrose coaxed him to join her in the kitchen for a treat.

'You look uptight,' Doris said when they were alone in her cosy den. 'Problems at school?'

'Same old story.' Paul dropped into a chair. 'I don't fit in with Clark Franklin's vision of what he refers to as *my school*. He ordered me to drop my peace group.'

'Because of the Vietnam business,' Doris assumed. Paul nodded. 'So you'll drop it for now,' she advised. 'How long can this craziness go on?'

'Too damn long.' Paul was grim.

'Tracy and I talked about it when she was home for Thanksgiving,' Doris told him and he stared at her in surprise. She hadn't said a word to him – but then, because of Dad, they tried to avoid the subject of the war in Vietnam. 'David was just registering for the draft. As long as he's in school, of course, he'll be deferred; but he keeps talking of dropping out of school, and she worries about that.'

'The deferment rules are a real problem,' Paul acknowledged. 'Laurie told me that Adele is close to some young student from NYU who's going to leave at the end of the school year to work for a while to save up for his senior year. Adele worries that he could be drafted.' His eyes reflected sympathy. 'It seems so rotten that families who can afford to keep their sons in school can be sure they won't be grabbed.'

'Watch the enrolment at the graduate schools surge,' Doris predicted. 'The poor will see their sons drafted. Not the middle class or the rich. Thank God Neal is so young.'

'I thank God both my kids are girls,' Paul confessed. He hesitated. 'I wish Vera understood how you and I feel about this war. Sometimes I'm sure she regards me as a traitor. Damn it, Doris, Vera and I have been through so much together. It scares me that something like this can put such distance between us. Sometimes she looks at me as though she's seeing a stranger. We've always been so close –'

'You'll be close again.' She managed a confident smile, yet Paul realized he'd startled her. 'You and Vera have always had something very special. Nothing can disturb that for long.'

'By the end of this year we'll have 23,000 troops in Vietnam. And there's gossip about a heavy escalation. How many of our kids will die over there? And I think of all the money going into the war that could be used to cut down poverty, improve our educational system. It's such a waste!'

'Let's go out to the kitchen. I'll put up coffee.'

'The universal consolation prize.' Paul laughed, but rose to his feet. 'What did people do before there was coffee?'

'They had tea,' Doris surmised. 'But where else in Eastwood can you get freshly ground, freshly perked coffee?'

Tracy glanced up at the night-dark sky – though it was barely five o'clock – while David stowed their valises in the back of his recently acquired Dodge.

'We should have left earlier,' she scolded. 'The snow's coming down like it's never going to stop.' Weathermen had predicted six to eight inches, she recalled.

'We'll be okay,' David soothed. 'We've got snow tyres – and they'll have the ploughs out on the roads by the time we hit the highway. Hey, this is a great car. I don't know what kind of pills my mother's on this month, but they sure make her happy. I never thought she'd give me my own wheels.' The Dodge – the family's second car – was being replaced by an expensive foreign sports car. 'We're only an hour and a half from home.'

'With the way the snow's coming down, it could be five hours,' she warned, climbing into the front seat.

'Warm enough?' David asked solicitously ten minutes later. The road ahead was one expanse of white, the trees on either side already edged with snow.

'I'm fine. You okay?'

'Yeah.' He was squinting now. 'The visibility is lousy. Turn on the radio, hunh?'

Tracy flipped the selector across the dial from station to station until she located a disc jockey offering a Beatles medley. Now she leaned back in pleasure. It was kind of nice, driving in heavy snow this way – warm inside, David close, the music great.

'We're not going to make any time this way,' David complained. Traffic was creeping over the treacherous road. 'You hungry?'

'Getting there,' Tracy admitted.

'Watch for a diner. We're running into home-bound people. If we start out thirty minutes later, we'll run into less traffic.'

Within fifteen minutes they were in a booth at a roadside diner, devouring mammoth hamburgers. The windows were steamed over. Bob Dylan's voice drifted from a nearby jukebox. A pair of truck drivers straddled stools at the counter. A couple with two small children occupied one booth. No other patrons were in the diner.

Tracy and David lingered over mugs of strong black

coffee, discussed plans for the days ahead. He was excited by the prospect of several days of skiing. New to skiing, she was ambivalent. In the privacy of their booth – at a far end of the diner – David's foot slid beneath the table to contact hers.

'You shouldn't be wearing that red sweater on a night like this,' he reproached. 'You make me so horny.'

Tracy giggled. 'You mean you're not complaining anymore that my boobs are so small?'

'I never complained.'

In his mind he had her sweater off, she guessed, his hands all over her. He knew just what excited her. He knew, also, the limits they'd decided on long ago – everything but . . .

'It's such a rotten night,' he said tentatively, his eyes sending an erotic message. 'We could stop at a motel, call your folks and mine and say we'll be home tomorrow.'

'I don't know –' But all at once her heart was pounding. Lots of the kids were sleeping together – no demarcation lines.

'No,' he contradicted himself. 'We've talked this through a hundred times. We're not ready for that yet.'

'There's the back seat of the car,' she reminded. 'We can play house within our limits.'

'Let's.' His face exuded anticipation. 'By our rules.'

Vera revelled in the presence of Laurie and Tracy in the house, though she was ever-conscious that the war in Vietnam – and this country's participation – only exacerbated Laurie's resentment that her own family manufactured guns. Ever since the tragic death of little Serena Robinson, Laurie had refused to go to the company's Christmas office party – where Joel loved to show off his grandchildren. This year, Tracy had concocted an excuse not to put in an appearance – because of the war, Vera surmised – and Joel was hurt. He loved his three grand-children, but Tracy he adored.

At regular intervals David was on hand, good-humouredly accepting Joel's taunts about his long hair. *What's the matter with young guys these days? They all want to look like girls?* Laurie spent an amazing amount of time each day poring over textbooks. *Look, I know I have to make top grades or I'll never make it into med school.*

On a night when her parents and grandfather were absent from the house for the evening and David had left early to nurse a bad cold, Tracy prodded herself to invade Laurie's room to ask a question that had been invading her mind for weeks – ever since her roommate Claire said she'd gotten sick on morning glory seeds. Sure, she'd been reading the articles in the student newspapers about drugs – but whom did you *believe*?

'Laurie, I have to talk,' she said with a familiar flare of drama. 'It's important.'

'It's important for me to study,' Laurie said, but she laid aside her textbook. 'But what's your problem?' Exasperation gave way to resignation.

'You go to a big-city school. What about drugs on campus?'

Laurie thought for a moment. 'Sure, there're drugs on campus. Not as much at an all-girl campus as at co-ed schools. But it's a bad scene. Tracy, are you messing around with drugs?'

'No.' Tracy was startled at the accusation. 'Well, not really. I mean, everybody smokes pot now and then – but I'm scared of LSD and all the pills.'

'Everybody doesn't smoke pot,' Laurie refuted. 'Some, sure, but –'

'Haven't *you*?' Tracy challenged.

'At parties now and then,' Laurie conceded. 'You

know, when somebody starts passing around joints. But not on a regular basis.'

'David says it's cheaper than liquor and never makes you sick. He said his parents pass around joints at dinner parties.'

'Students are being suspended at some schools if they're caught with marijuana. I know a boy at Columbia who was turned over to the cops by somebody in his dorm for selling pills. He said he was working his way through school by dealing. Tracy, a lot of students brag about taking drugs – but they're faking. It makes them feel they're gaining status. When Dad was in college, he said students would brag about how much bourbon they could drink before they got sick. The ones who're heavy into the drug scene – and they're stupid – don't talk about it.'

'David and I talk about it a lot,' Tracy admitted. 'David got a copy of that summer edition of Harvard Review – about drugs and the mind – and the La Guardia Report on Marijuana that's been reprinted by some group that wants to see marijuana legalized. It claims pot is no worse than smoking a cigarette. But actually we're scared of most of the stuff that's floating around. Except for pot.'

'Who knows what that will do later on?' Laurie challenged. 'I don't think much is happening on a lot of campuses out of big cities. I think a lot of it's talk.' Laurie paused in seeming debate. 'Okay, so I hear a lot about drugs down at NYU – because it's so close to Greenwich Village. There's supposed to be a lot at Berkeley – and some at Columbia,' she conceded with a show of reluctance. 'I haven't got time for that crap,' she wound up bluntly. 'Nobody's going to tell me that a nickel bag is going to see me through a rough exam. Only cramming will do that.'

A week before Laurie was to return to school, Adele came up to visit. As always, Vera was delighted to see her. She listened with pleasure to the earnest discussions between Paul and Adele about the sad state of American education. Listening to them, she could brush aside her unease at Paul's attitude about the war in Vietnam. She couldn't understand this. He'd fought against the Nazis. He'd seen what happened to people deprived of democratic rights. How could he not support the fight to control the spread of Communism? *It wasn't like Paul.*

It unnerved her to feel this division between herself and Paul. The wall between Laurie and her had never been completely obliterated – and now there was this new wall shooting up between Paul and her. Sometimes Doris teased her – lovingly – about her passionate obsession for family. But family, she told herself defensively, was her most cherished possession.

Too quickly, Vera thought, the winter college break was over. Laurie and Tracy returned to school. She knew it was absurd – but each time the girls left Eastwood she was assaulted by panic – a fear that she would never see them again. Always she remembered those terrible minutes on *Kristallnacht* when she'd hidden in the Schmidts' apartment while Mama and Papa and Ernst were dragged away by the SS men.

'I should have taken time off from the office while the girls were home,' Vera reproached herself while she and Doris sat over coffee in the Kahn kitchen while the three men – Paul, Joel, and Phil – watched a basketball game on television.

'Don't feel guilty because you're working,' Doris ordered. 'Laurie and Tracy understand that you're important to the business. Even Dad admits that without you it would be a piddling operation.' Once shorn of Wayne's covert – illegal – sales, business had plummeted. Through Vera's efforts, the company had regained its earlier status.

'I've gotten all wrapped up in expanding the catalogue,'

Vera paused. 'Sometimes I wonder if Paul resents that.'

'Enough of this guilt shit,' Doris clucked. 'You're making a big contribution to the family finances. You've taken a load of responsibility off Dad's shoulders. You've –'

'Phil's doing great with the shop,' Vera broke in. 'And your helping with the buying has been a major asset.' Instinct had told her to enlarge in the women's-wear area – and it was paying off. 'Sometimes I think I get carried away with the potential of the catalogue market, but we're doing so well with it.'

'And you're a damn good mother,' Doris picked up. 'Laurie and Tracy weren't lying around the house expecting to be waited on hand and foot. Those days are gone forever.'

'Laurie seemed so tired when she first arrived,' Vera said lovingly. 'But pre-meds are all so worried about their grades. She said there are about forty or fifty thousand pre-med students applying each year for maybe twelve thousand places in medical schools. She lives in terror of being rejected.'

'She's bright. She'll make it.' Doris nodded with conviction.

'She frets that so much time is spent on studying subjects that she says have nothing to do with becoming a doctor. Why are the young always in such a rush?'

Doris chuckled. 'Honey, we were no different.'

'At eighteen I was worried about survival.' Vera was blunt. She paused for a moment. 'That's what David said,' she recalled uneasily. 'If he gets drafted, how does he know he'll make it home again?'

'WWII was a war that had to be fought.' Doris was suddenly serious. 'If anyone knows that, you do. This is a whole different ball game. It's –'

343

'You sound like Paul,' Vera reproached. Remembering Paul's passionate accusations to his father and herself last night while they were listening to the news. *Let's face facts. The Vietnam war is being fought because of economics. The United States wants to have a stake in Vietnam's rubber plantations, its rice fields, its timber. And the people over there are happy to work for almost nothing. They make designer jeans, TV parts – a long list of things. This war is being fought to make a few Americans richer. It's not going to help the poor or the middle class.*

'Paul and Phil are both sure we're going to see the draft numbers soar in the months ahead,' Doris said. 'The word is that we'll be shipping out a lot of troops.'

'Adele is upset that so many of the kids being drafted are poor blacks.' More and more these last weeks – though she admitted this to no one – Vera was torn between support of the fight to stop the spread of Communism in Southeast Asia and trepidation about the possible loss of American lives in the months ahead. 'And Tracy, of course, is nervous that David will drop out of school and lose his deferment.'

'I'm just grateful that Phil is too old and Neal is too young to be drafted.' But now Doris's face exuded distaste. 'If Wayne were alive, he'd be debating about which side – North or South Vietnam – to try to sell arms to. He'd have been in his glory.'

Vera was unnerved when – in February – President Johnson announced a major escalation of American participation in the Vietnam war. With Paul and Joel she listened to the news on television. The implication was that there would be sustained bombing of North Vietnam.

'We can't let the Communists take over all of Asia,'

Joel said with conviction. 'That's a major threat to the world.'

'Dad, we have no business in Vietnam,' Paul objected. 'We –'

'Paul, we must be concerned about the rest of the world,' Vera broke in urgently. 'If someone had intervened in Germany when Hitler began his rampage, think how many lives would have been saved.' *Papa and Mama and Ernst*, she thought in fresh anguish.

'It's not the Communists who're infiltrating South Vietnam that are causing the problems,' Paul said. 'The workers and the peasants want to rid themselves of vile dictators who rule their lives. It's a civil war – with the South Vietnamese wanting peace and self-determination. We're supporting the wrong people. Remember when Laurie wrote us about Mademoiselle Nhu's visit to Columbia – and how 300 students booed her?' Vera recalled that Mademoiselle Nhu was the wife of the head of the South Vietnamese secret police and sister-in-law of President Diem. 'This is the woman who made a joke of the Buddhist monks and their self-immolation in protest of religious persecution. She referred to these protests as barbecues!'

'Yesterday two of the workers at the factory told me their sons were being drafted,' Vera said softly. 'One's nineteen, the other twenty. It's awful to realize they could die in Vietnam.'

'Don't be so pessimistic,' Joel ordered. 'We send in our forces, this stupid war will be over in six months. Johnson's absolutely right in what he's doing.'

But Vera was beginning to question the validity of this war. Why were we supporting dictators? The reasons to fight in World War II had been so clear-cut. So necessary. It was a war that had to be fought. Why were they supporting unpopular dictators?

Each month 17,000 Americans were being drafted. Where would it end? She thought of David, whom Tracy loved. *Would he become a Vietnam casualty?*

Chapter Thirty-one

Vera struggled to avoid discussion of Vietnam in Joel's presence. She exhorted Paul to refrain from wrangling with his father when Joel praised LBJ's decision to ship 3500 marines to Vietnam early in March.

'We have to prevent the spread of Communism,' Joel repeated endlessly. 'We're the only major power other than Russia. It's our responsibility to keep the world free from dictatorships like Russia's. That's what Communism is – a dictatorship!'

Johnson's escalation of US participation in the Vietnam war accelerated protest demonstrations on campuses around the country. With Laurie and Tracy home for spring vacation, Vera lived in constant tension – ever watchful for volatile outbreaks between Joel and his granddaughters. David – often underfoot – was put on warning, also. But Joel was unexpectedly subdued when the news media told the world that a US spokesman in Saigon had confirmed an ugly rumour. Yes, South Vietnamese forces were using tear gas.

'That's unconscionable!' he raged after watching the evening news on television. 'You'll see – Congress will censure them for that. When something is wrong, I'll be the first to admit it. But these demonstrations on college campuses –' He clucked in disapproval, gazed grimly from Laurie to Tracy. 'They're just a handful of students.'

'But they have the *right* to speak,' Laurie picked up. 'Out at some college in Ohio, the campus police just stood by doing nothing when about 150 right-wing students

347

ploughed into a handful of demonstrators, grabbed and burned their signs, then kicked them.'

'That was at Kent State,' Tracy nodded indignantly. 'David said, "What else can you expect in a conservative town?"'

Most people in this country, Vera surmised, were confused about the war. Like herself. *Was the government behaving immorally*? Or was it determined to assume its responsibilities – not only to its own people but the rest of the world as well?

She watched her father-in-law's bewilderment and pain with compassion. He saw his son and his grandchildren rebelling against what he considered cherished values – the belief that their country could do no wrong. Doris and Phil were careful to conceal their own fears that US involvement in the Vietnam war was wrong, she thought gratefully. Dad was seventy-three years old – and suddenly his deep-rooted beliefs of a lifetime were being challenged.

The uproar from Congressmen in reaction to the report of the use of tear gas by the South Vietnamese forces blended with the rage of many Americans over what was happening right at home – in Alabama. What had been planned as a four-day peaceful civil rights march from Selma, Alabama, to Montgomery – fifty miles away – erupted in violence when, on Sunday, March 6, Governor Wallace ordered the highway patrol to stop the marchers. State trooper cars lined the roadside. When the marchers did not agree to disperse within two minutes, troopers ploughed into the group with bullwhips and rubber tubing wrapped in barbed wire. Tear gas filled the air.

Vera and Paul witnessed the happening when the Sunday-evening movie they were watching – *Judgement at Nuremberg* – was interrupted so that ABC Television could provide a shocking film clip of what was happening in Selma. On Monday morning, the front pages of the newspapers across the country carried the story and graphic photographs of Selma's 'bloody Sunday.' Protest demonstrations took place from coast to coast. In Toronto, Canada, 2,000 people demonstrated.

'Johnson will come forward and submit a strong new voting-rights bill,' Paul predicted. 'Wait and see.'

Laurie reported that she would not be going down South this summer. She wanted to go to summer school in order to carry a light load in her senior year. 'I need to keep my grades up.' As always, she was anxious about being accepted at medical school.

'I don't know why she worries all the time,' Vera confided to Doris – trying to ignore her own anxieties. 'We know how bright she is.'

'Let's face it, Vera – there're a limited number of places in the medical schools.' Doris was realistic. 'And being a woman won't be an asset.'

'I'll feel better knowing that she's in school rather than chasing around down South with that voter-registration team,' Vera admitted. 'I don't think the summer classes will erupt into the *teach-ins* we're seeing everywhere now.'

Across the country, faculty members – usually the younger ones – were joining with students to protest the American intervention in Vietnam. The word had spread from campus to campus. The teach-ins – in the hundreds and held at night so as not to interfere with regular classes – often ran from 8:00 PM to 8:00 AM. It was a crusade to spread the word that the United States was fighting a war they were convinced was immoral.

'We have to spread the truth about why we're there!' Laurie said defensively when her grandfather made a pithy remark about 'these crazy students acting up on the campuses.' Later, she reported with triumph that the 'teach-in' at Columbia – Barnard was its sister college – had brought out over 2,500 students.

Paul said it was always at the elite schools that these rebellions began, Vera thought on this spring morning that seemed reluctant to discard winter cold. They'd listened to the radio news at breakfast about the latest incident. In a surge of restlessness – her mind reluctant to focus on business – she decided to go out for an early lunch. She reached for her black coat, fake fur-trimmed knitted hat, and purse. Checked that her gloves were in her coat pocket. Now she headed out of her office and down the hall to the front door.

'How's your grandson down in New York doing?' She paused to chat for a moment with their janitor. Elijah had come to work for the company almost twenty years ago after being stranded in town when his car broke down. Widowed, he had three daughters and several granddaughters living in Harlem – and one grandson, who was his pride and joy.

'Oh, he's gonna be fine, Miss Vera.' Elijah radiated pride. 'He's joined the army. He ain't waitin' to be drafted.' All at once his face was solemn. 'Best thing in the world for that boy to go into the army, gettin' away from bad friends in that project where he lives. The army'll make a man out of him.'

Not much was said in this town about the war in Vietnam, Vera reflected. People watched the television news, of course; but it was as though here in Eastwood they lived in another world. They were observers, Vera determined, watching the world go round. Only a handful extended their personal involvement beyond Eastwood.

Now and then you heard about a boy being drafted. Then it became personal. In her mind she heard Laurie's frequently repeated taunt: *Not college students. They don't worry about the draft*!

The chill outdoors was reminiscent of dead winter rather than spring, Vera thought, tugging at the collar of her coat. Then, drawing her knitted hat more closely about her head, she walked swiftly to the pleasant small café where she lunched regularly.

'You're early today.' Mary O'Brien's plain face lit up with a bright smile as Vera slid into a chair at her usual table. 'I'll get your cup of tea while you decide.' For Vera the Blue Lantern stocked Earl Grey teabags. Since the years in London, Vera had been addicted to Earl Grey.

She debated about the 'specials' with Mary, chose the split-pea soup and a small salad. Now she relaxed, sipped her tea, and waited for her luncheon to be served.

'I love that hat.' Breaking into her introspection, Mary placed a bowl of steaming split-pea soup before Vera.

'Thank you.' Vera smiled at her long-time waitress. Mary had been here for over fourteen years, she thought. Ever since her little boy – her only child – was old enough to be in school full-time. That was when her husband had walked out on her for a teenage sexpot. But Mary had rallied, found this job, devoted herself to raising her son.

'I got a hat almost like it over in Saratoga.' Mary's eyes were wistful as she gazed at Vera's near-perfect features, highlighted by the hat. 'I hope it looks as good on me as it does on you.'

'I'm sure it does,' Vera encouraged. A tiny white lie.

'I used to think that if I were pretty, my life would be wonderful. Then I understood that even beautiful movie stars weren't always happy. Oh, I didn't tell you my news.' Mary glowed. 'My boy Jimmy is going into the service this week. I'll miss him something awful, but he promises he'll write every chance he gets. I don't have to tell you how proud I am of him.'

Elijah's grandson had enlisted. Mary was sending her

son Jimmy – who'd gone to school with Tracy – off to Vietnam. Both so proud of them. Would *she* feel that way if she had a son? She'd thought she'd seen the end of war when she came to live in Eastwood, Vera remembered with an odd ache. Would the world ever exist in total peace? Paul's dream. Was that all it was ever to be? A dream?

It seemed to Vera that the teach-ins – and Tracy and David were enthusiastic about these – had brought a new closeness between Laurie and Tracy.

'Of course, they've always been close,' Vera said to Doris on a steamy July Sunday afternoon while the two women relaxed in the Kahns' air-conditioned den. Paul and Phil, along with little Neal, had gone off to watch a local baseball game. Joel was at a committee meeting of the Eastwood Chamber of Commerce. 'But there's something new there now.' Why did she feel that that new closeness made her an outsider? Ridiculous, she reproached herself.

'This is a generation like none other,' Doris mused. 'But I'm proud of them.'

'I can't believe that next year this time Laurie'll have her degree – and be on her way to med school.' Vera held up crossed fingers. 'I'm so happy that she knows what she wants to do with her life – but I wish she'd feel less harried all the time.'

'You wish she'd find time for a social life,' Doris said. 'Give her time, Vera. She's so young.'

Laurie came home from summer school for two weeks before returning to campus for the new school year. Adele – who'd spent the summer working in New York with a Harlem youth group – came with her. Much of the talk revolved around the recent riots in Watts, a low-income black community in Los Angeles. Lasting from August

11–16 the riots resulted in 35 deaths – all black – and hundreds of injuries, plus $200,000,000 in damages. It was carnage that had been watched around the world on TV.

'Watts is only the beginning,' Adele warned. 'Not just in Watts, but wherever blacks live in ghetto conditions. I look around Harlem and I'm scared of what's to come. I look at my own family – what exists of family,' she added caustically. 'Maybe in the South there are jobs for blacks, but not in big-city ghettos. And without jobs, there're no families. Mom was smart – and lucky. She got the two of us out of the inner city.'

'Your mom was a wonderful woman,' Laurie said with love.

'But look at my cousins – and their kids.' Adele pantomimed despair. 'For two generations now – all illegitimate. No fathers at home. They have no hope. Without hope, people have nothing.'

'The situation must change,' Vera said with determined optimism. 'Johnson vows to make changes.'

'This is a terrible time for the civil rights movement.' Adele's eyes reflected her inner desolation. 'When Martin Luther King went out to Watts to help calm things, the people there told him to go home – they didn't want his dreams. They want decent housing, jobs. The people in power out in California don't understand! And it's not much different in New York.'

'I think the whole world was shocked by what happened at Watts.' Vera flinched, recalling the nights of watching via television as a chunk of Los Angeles became a panorama of burning, looting, beatings, and killings. And each night her mind rushed back to the horror of *Kristallnacht* in Berlin, almost twenty-seven years ago. But this wasn't fanatical Nazis out for genocide. These were desperate people pushed beyond their limits.

Then once again Laurie and Tracy were off to school. Early in the new school year Paul reported that – as in suburban schools – students in the local schools were voicing dissatisfaction. A new, unexpected experience in the Eastwood school system.

'These kids are demanding more of some of the teachers – and by God, they have every right to,' Paul told Vera in the privacy of their bedroom. His father considered such talk disloyal to the town. 'Sherman and Logan give their students nothing – and the kids know it. But Franklin won't hear a word against them!'

'If they'd raise teacher salaries, they'd get more competent people,' Vera said bluntly.

'But nobody wants to raise taxes,' Paul countered. 'And it's not just the money. I was talking with Ted about it last night.' He grinned. 'The girls aren't tying up the phone for hours now – it's me. There's a lot of rebellion in high schools around the country from what I'm reading. Our standards are dropping so low, a lot of us are ashamed to be teaching. In our high school, Vera! The quality goes from excellent to disgustingly low. We've expanded our school population by twenty per cent in the last ten years, but we haven't added another classroom. And this is happening all over the country.'

'It would be helpful if Franklin weren't such an ass,' Vera sympathized.

'The bastard takes policy-making upon himself.' Paul grunted in frustration. 'That's not his job. The school board is supposed to make policy; the superintendent is supposed to administer. We don't have a superintendent of schools, so principals are supposedly administering. But damn it, they're not supposed to make policy.'

'Paul, why doesn't a group of teachers approach the school board and demand changes?'

'Because our principals have the school board in their

back pockets!' Paul exploded. *Why couldn't he talk with this fervour to the board?* 'Several PTA members tried to talk to Franklin. They got nowhere. All he cares about is that the teaching staff follow the lesson plans he approves. He doesn't give a shit how much the kids learn.'

'With this much foment, there has to be some action soon,' Vera said. If the girls were still in the Eastwood schools, she'd get out there and fight, she told herself impatiently. Once Neal was in school, Doris would fight. Doris's voice might have some value, she thought cynically. Doris *was* old family. Vera had just married into old family. After almost twenty years in Eastwood, she was still an outsider.

'The old-timers don't realize that a new breed of teachers is coming into the system. One that recognizes the problems and is ready to take them on. But dissenting voices have to grow louder.' Paul's anger seemed to have dissipated. 'We can't stay in a rut. We have to move ahead. Our time is coming, Vera.' A fresh hope welled in his eyes. 'It's destined.'

In the weeks ahead, Vera fought to break down the wall of gloom that threatened to enclose her. In her phone conversations with Laurie, she was ever-conscious of Laurie's anxiety about keeping up her grades this last year at college – and about medical school. Phone calls with Tracy revealed Tracy's anxieties about David's dropping out of school – exposing himself to the draft.

This was such a troubled time, she thought tiredly. The country was being torn apart by the battles over civil rights and by the anti-war movement. She was drained by constantly striving to avoid conflicts between Paul and his father over the escalating Vietnam war. And next week, the girls would be home for the long Thanksgiving weekend. She'd have to tell them not to bait their grand-father about Vietnam.

In a need to pull herself out of this mood of depression, Vera forced herself to focus on business. Here was a challenge she always welcomed. She'd thought much in the past months about expanding their mail-order business from a regional to national orientation. It was a major step – and Dad would balk at first, she warned herself. Yet he did trust her instincts.

They wouldn't be trying to compete with Sears Roebuck or Montgomery Ward, she rationalized. They'd sell sporting goods and sportswear, just as with their regional catalogue. They'd stress the service angle – every customer must be satisfied or the merchandise could be returned. And part of the deal, she decided with growing enthusiasm, would be to make the Eastwood shop the centrepiece of the mail-order business.

On a crisp, sunny morning she approached Joel on this expansion. As anticipated, he was uneasy.

'Vera, on a national basis? That'll cost a fortune!'

'We're standing still now,' she pointed out. 'It's time to move ahead. We can –'

'We can lose our shirts,' he broke in and Vera sensed he was unnerved.

'We offer smart merchandise at a sensible price,' she continued. 'With Doris and Phil handling the buying.' There, *that* pleased Dad. They'd be involving Doris as a buyer. Family. 'They have a knack for knowing what sells in the shop.'

'That's Eastwood,' he said warily.

'That's Middle America,' she corrected. 'Attractive but conservative styles. Merchandise that'll be good two years from now as well as today. If I had a crystal ball, I'd see mail-order catalogues growing into a tremendous business – and I don't mean just Sears Roebuck.'

'Let's think about it,' Joel hedged. 'That's big bucks. We'll talk more tonight.'

Joel was humming when he left her office, Vera noted. An unfailing sign that he was pleased by her latest direction for the business. He'd go along with the expansion.

On this Wednesday before Thanksgiving – with Laurie and Tracy due home late in the evening for the long weekend – Vera and Doris conferred in the den about the holiday dinner, determining what items on the menu Doris would bring, what Vera would prepare here at the house.

'David'll be having Thanksgiving dinner here with us,' Vera told Doris.

'So what else is new?' But Doris's chuckle was warm with affection.

'He'll leave around seven to meet his parents. They're going out to some swanky restaurant in Saratoga for the big dinner.' Vera's voice reeked with contempt.

'It always surprises me that restaurants are open on Thanksgiving Day.' Doris squinted in contemplation. 'It always seemed to me a holiday to celebrate at home.'

Both women tensed in alertness at the sound of a car driving up before the house. Paul had driven over to the Saratoga railroad station to pick up Laurie. *They couldn't be home yet*, Vera thought. And Tracy and David weren't due until late in the evening.

'It could be Phil.' Doris rose to her feet. 'I called the shop to tell him I was coming over here before dinner – and that we'd be eating a little late tonight.'

They heard the front door open and close.

'Vera?' Joel's voice was agitated. 'You home yet?'

'In the den, Dad.' Vera exchanged an anxious glance with Doris.

A moment later Joel appeared in the door. His face was drained of colour.

'Dad, what's happened?' Doris demanded.

He took a deep breath. 'You know Mary O'Brien, the waitress at the Blue Lantern?' *Everybody in Eastwood knew Mary.*

'What about Mary?' Vera's voice was sharp with anxiety.

'She just received word from the War Department. Her son Jim was killed in Vietnam.'

Vera stood immobile, frozen in shock. She remembered Jimmy as a shy, towheaded five-year-old, then an awkward, scrupulously polite teenager. She remembered him at high school graduation – self-conscious in his first real suit. He and Tracy had graduated the same year. He'd been in Paul's class. Dad had swung a job for Jimmy at the supermarket after graduation.

The Vietnam war had come home to them, she thought in anguish. All at once it was a personal war. An Eastwood boy had given his life.

This wasn't as it had been in World War II, she thought in sudden, dizzying comprehension. Mary O'Brien's only child had died in a war they barely understood. Why were American boys fighting in Vietnam? For whom? *How many more Americans would die before the war was over?*

Chapter Thirty-two

By late spring, Vera was caught up in Laurie's imminent graduation from Barnard. *How pleased Papa would have been*, she thought nostalgically. *And Mama*. Laurie would enter medical school in September – as Ernst had yearned to do.

Laurie's future monopolized her grandfather's conversation to the point where longtime friends were beginning to tease him about 'your granddaughter the doctor.' He'd never ceased being disappointed that Paul would not follow him in the business, Vera realized – though he found pleasure in Doris and Phil's activity in the expanding mail-order catalogue division, which was attracting national admiration.

With growing frequency Vera mused, *it was the business that saved her sanity*. She could escape problems at home by throwing herself into work. Kahn's Country Store – which Joel heralded as her creation – was becoming an institution, she acknowledged. Even a tourist attraction. Emphasizing women's wear had brought about major success.

She hadn't discussed it yet with Dad, but the next step was to open half-a-dozen stores around the country – all replicas of the one here. Phil was smart about building a recognizable image. He pointed out the importance of advertising, promotion. 'Hey, the shop's great – but you have to let the world know it's here.'

Though she was delighted when the girls came home for their spring break, this year Vera was oddly relieved when the vacation was over. Not because she didn't adore having Laurie and Tracy home, she acknowledged, but because she was upset over the soaring friction arising between her father-in-law and David, who was constantly underfoot when Tracy was home.

Tracy worried that David would be drafted. Especially now when he was letting his grades slide. In February, General Hershey told the local draft boards they could call up college students who fell in the lower-grades group. Also, a national exam would check on grades and general intelligence – and this, too, would be given over to the draft boards.

'Young people are going nuts these days,' Joel grumbled, settling himself in the den to watch TV with Vera and Paul on this first evening after the girls' return to school. 'And that David!' He grunted in disgust. 'All this crap about maybe burning his draft card. Kids like that ought to be thrown in jail! I don't know why Tracy lets him hang around her.'

'David makes a lot of noise,' Paul said evasively. 'So many of the kids do.' He didn't want to start up again with Dad, Vera understood.

'Not a lot of the kids,' Joel rejected grimly. 'It's always the same ones. A few rotten eggs make a lot of noise –' he pounced on Paul's choice of words. ' – and suddenly they're the majority. I read the newspapers. The Gallup polls say that 72% of all students don't get involved in those crazy demonstrations.'

'But they're sympathetic. And every week more students are becoming involved. Look back in history, Dad,' Paul pleaded. 'How many colonists were crying out for independence in 1776? But the word spread and it became a mass outcry.'

'What would have happened in World War II?' Joel challenged, 'if our boys had reacted like these screwballs?

This country would have been overrun by the Nazis! We would have died in concentration camps.'

'Even in the late '30s college students were rejecting the draft,' Paul countered. 'That went out the window when they saw what the world was up against, but this war makes no sense!'

'Dad, why don't you go down to New York with Doris next week when she has that shooting for the Christmas catalogue?' Vera intervened, anxious to redirect the conversation. 'Maybe take her and Laurie out for dinner and to a play.'

Joel shook his head, grimaced in distaste.

'I don't like the city anymore. It was different years ago, when Paul was in college.' He exchanged a nostalgic smile with Paul. 'I'd be in New York on a business trip, and he'd come down from Columbia and we'd go for an Italian dinner in Greenwich Village and maybe see a play at that little Provincetown Playhouse. It wasn't exactly Broadway –'

'It was fun, Dad,' Paul agreed gently.

'But now, what I hear about Greenwich Village – it's a different world. Kids smoking marijuana, tripping, freaking out,' Joel said scornfully. 'LSD takes them to heaven.'

'Dad, where did you pick up that lingo?' Paul joshed.

'I read the *New York Times Magazine*, the national magazines,' Joel said with contempt. 'The whole world's going berserk.'

'We're all going down to New York for Laurie's graduation,' Vera declared. 'The three of us and Doris and Phil. Tracy'll be out of classes by then. She'll take care of Neal. You know Neal adores her.'

'And David will be there with Tracy,' Joel guessed. 'He's bad for her. He fills her head with nutty ideas. And that hair!' He snorted. 'Don't these kids ever go to a barber?'

'It's a phase,' Paul began cautiously. 'Every generation rebels.'

'My generation didn't run around with our hair hanging down our backs and dressed like slobs,' Joel shot back. 'We didn't talk about refusing to fight for our country. Your generation didn't do that.'

'Dad, I'm going to make reservations for us all at the Plaza,' Vera said, desperate to avoid another scene about David. 'We'll –'

'The Plaza?' Joel lifted an eyebrow. 'You're talking fancy money.' Then all at once he was grinning. 'But we can afford it. Sometimes I forget how well we're doing. Maybe you walked out on the business, Paul, but you brought the family the best thing that ever happened to it. Vera, you've got the business head I expected from Paul.'

On the sunny Thursday afternoon of June 2, the Kahn clan was part of the 12,000 spectators in the outdoor amphitheatre created by Low Memorial Library and adjacent structures at Columbia. Paul reached for Vera's hand while they watched the huge procession of blue-robed figures file to their seats. The music was 'March of the Earl of Oxford' by the sixteenth-century English composer, William Byrd.

'I'm so impressed,' Vera whispered, tears blurring her vision as 6,832 students prepared to receive a variety of degrees. 'I wish Papa and Mama could be here today! They'd be so proud.' For Papa, education had been supremely important. He'd given his life to continue teaching in Berlin. *Paul was so like him*, she thought, washed in tenderness.

Vera heard little of the speeches that followed. Her mind hurtled back in time to her last days in Berlin. The constant humiliations, the deprivations, the foreboding fears that became a reality. Papa would be sad that she had not gone on to college – but his granddaughters would have the degrees she wasn't able to acquire. She remembered the catty remarks of one of the faculty wives at a dinner party last week. 'Vera, I think it's amazing that you've gone so far without a college education.'

She was the only faculty wife in their group without a degree. This inescapable fact was constantly tossed at her. And she was the only one who held down a full-time job. The other faculty wives took care of their houses and children, did volunteer work. Only one – Dolores Aiken – complained about being bored with her existence. 'Damn it, Vera – that Friedan woman is so right. Women live in bondage.'

Many of these young women here, she told herself with satisfaction, would not settle for being housewives and mothers. They looked forward to careers. In Eastwood – in their small-town, middle-class world – she was an oddity. But times were changing. Women, too, were rebelling.

Paul didn't resent her working. Did he resent her earning a salary so much larger than his own? Their pay cheques went into a joint checking or savings account, along with the substantial bonuses that Dad insisted on giving her each year. The money question – who earned how much – never bothered Paul. *Or did it*?

Dolores complained regularly about being strapped for money, but she said Lance would be upset if she tried for a career. 'I might be able to do it in a large city, but not here in Eastwood. His precious masculinity would sag to the floor. His professional pride would suffer. But I can't refurnish my living room with his professional pride.'

'It's getting cloudy,' Paul whispered, banishing her introspection. 'I hope it doesn't start to rain before the exercises are over.'

As the exercises drew to a close at four-thirty, the sky became an ominous grey. As the blue-robed figures began the recessional, the first droplets of rain began to fall. Despite this, the crowd seemed to enjoy these final moments.

They'd go back to the Plaza and relax awhile, Vera planned. Then they'd drive down to Ratner's on Second Avenue for dinner. Dad had unexpectedly expressed an interest in a 'real Jewish meal.'

When I was a little boy, my father would sometimes take my mother and me to New York with him on buying trips – and we'd always go down to Ratner's on Second Avenue for dinner.

But the segment of Second Avenue to which Dad referred was no longer the Lower East Side. It had been reborn as the East Village, a special haven of the young. Laurie wrote about going down to the East Village to see Off-Broadway plays. Not in the grand, elegant playhouses where Dad as a small boy had seen the Yiddish stars of the early years of the century, but in tiny playhouses with primitive stages or simply a small 'playing area.'

Vera felt wrapped in warmth this evening as the family lingered over a sumptuous dinner that Doris warned would collectively add twenty pounds to their group. *Dad was in such high spirits*, she thought with pleasure. So often these days he seemed simultaneously bewildered, hurt, and distraught by the changes that coloured this decade.

Through the years, she'd nurtured a passionate obsession to hold the family together. She watched as so many of the young in Eastwood moved away from their families to distant places to come together perhaps once or twice a year. Of course, Laurie and Tracy were away at school now, but that was a temporary situation. She couldn't bear to envision a future where they lived in distant cities.

Unrealistic, yes, her mind rebuked – but this was her *family*, her *life*.

Thus far Dad had been able to block out – most of the time – the knowledge that Paul was an outspoken pacifist. *Pacifist*, he would partially accept, Vera interpreted. The anti-war movement, he abhorred. What had happened to patriotism, loyalty to one's country?

She worried about the hostility that broke out at disturbing moments between her father-in-law and Tracy – which had its roots in Tracy's closeness to David. Sometimes she feared that he would ban David from the house. How would she cope with that situation?

She worried, too, that Paul would – in an unwary moment – admit to his father that he was helping to organize a small, Albany-based We Won't Go group similar to several others being formed around the country. She didn't want to think how Dad would react to that.

Doris and Phil were smart. They didn't let on to Dad that they were harbouring doubts about the country's involvement in Vietnam. But what was most upsetting to her was that *she didn't honestly know how she felt about the war*.

Why did she keep vacillating? She listened to Paul and began to ask herself why American boys were fighting – and dying – in a tiny country halfway around the world. But then she remembered Hitler in Germany. How many lives would have been saved if this country had come in earlier to help stop his mad rampage?

She was haunted by the fear that what was happening in Vietnam would tear her family apart before it was over.

After two weeks at home, Laurie left to work with Adele for the summer on a Harlem youth programme. In September, Adele would teach at a private, experimental school in Harlem. She and Laurie would continue to share an apartment. Vera tried to close her mind to suspicions that the two girls would also be working in the New York City anti-war movement.

As usual, Paul would teach in summer school, but two nights a week he'd drive to Albany for meetings with the grassroots We Won't Go group. She was ever-fearful that his father would learn of this activity. Nor would it set well, she surmised, with Clark Franklin. Tracy had prodded David into joining her for a light summer session at school – her intent, to raise his grades and keep him out of the draft.

Paul carried around in his wallet an article Adele had given him from the *New York Times* that pleaded for public schooling for four-year-olds. '*It doesn't mean trying to push teaching ahead, it's to prepare all those kids who're not ready for the first grade,*' Adele wrote. Paul was enthusiastic about this, though realistically he saw little chance of its occurring on any impressive scale. Now Doris was running into serious financial problems in keeping her long-established three-to-four-year-old morning group in operation.

Vera struggled to bury herself in work. She was unnerved by reports from Vietnam, film footage shown on TV where US marines were torching peasant huts. She was uneasy when, late in the summer, Tracy and David drove up to Canada – presumably for a visit.

'What do you mean, Tracy's driving with David for a vacation in Quebec City?' Joel demanded in outrage. 'Are they married and we don't know about it?'

'Dad, you know how casual young people are today,' Vera soothed. 'They're going with a group,' she improvised. She didn't want to remember that Canada was becoming an escape hatch for draft-evaders. *But David hadn't been called up.*

In New York, Laurie rejoiced in her first year of med school. At last she was involved in subjects that were relevant to her future as a doctor. She knew even before her first class that anatomy would be rugged. 'You won't believe the memorization that's required,' she confessed to Adele at the end of her first month. But still, she revelled in being there.

Banished was her involvement in the Harlem youth group, the anti-war movement. School and study devoured every waking moment. Even when she went home for the long Thanksgiving weekend, she spent much of the time holed up in her room with textbooks.

'The first two years are all pre-clinical stuff,' she explained to Tracy on this weekend. 'Everything's in lecture halls and the labs. Just once in a while – the way I hear it – will we actually get into the hospital and make contact with doctors and patients.'

'I don't know what I want to do with my life.' Tracy sighed. 'I settled for an English major because that's what David chose. His parents are still screaming that he has to go to law school. They'd better be happy if he just stays in college long enough to get his BA.' She squinted inquisitively at Laurie. 'What about your social life?'

'Who has time for a social life?' Laurie countered. 'We're in class eight hours a day, five days a week. We're swamped with learning.'

To Tracy's astonishment, David said he wouldn't be able to have Thanksgiving dinner with her family.

'My folks got this crazy idea we should have Thanksgiving dinner together this year. At a restaurant, of course,' he drawled sarcastically. 'But I'll come over in the evening for pecan pie.'

The moment David walked into the house Tracy knew he was upset. She fretted while he exchanged small talk with her mother in the kitchen – over a huge slab of pie.

'I ate like a pig,' she announced impatiently. 'Let's go for a walk.'

'Let him finish his pie,' her mother scolded.

'What's bugging you?' she demanded as the front door to the house closed behind them.

'You won't believe what my parents have cooked up,' he warned.

'I'll believe it. Tell me.'

'They've worked some deal where I'll be like an exchange student – going to school in London for the next semester. *London, England,*' he emphasized grimly.

'David, that's so exciting!' Tracy's mind was conjuring up fascinating images.

'The school over there is on the trimester system. I have to leave right after Christmas and stay there until some time in July! I'll be earning two semesters under their system – and the school here will give me full credit. It took some manoeuvring, but my old man managed it.' He sighed. 'How do I get out of it?'

'You don't want to get out of it!' Tracy churned with anticipation. 'We have to fix it for me to go, too!'

'How?' David was intrigued by this prospect.

'I'll work on my folks,' she plotted.

'How?' David asked again, uneasy about the outcome.

'You know Mom and Dad – they're softies. I'll cry about how the two of them and Laurie have all been out of the country but I've never been anywhere except Canada – and Bermuda – and that's right here. It'll work.' She nodded confidently. 'You find out everything you can about how it was set up. The junior year is not exactly the time to be an exchange student,' she conceded, 'but I'd love it. My mother lived in London for a while. That's where she met my father. Laurie was born in London. Oh, David, it would be so cool!'

Tracy had expected it would be her father – always sentimental about London – who would help push through the arrangements for her to go to the college at the edge of London – where David, too, would be a student. But it was her mother who went all out to ensure that she could go, even though the new semester was so close at hand. Mom worried about the way Grandpa hit on David all the time, she surmised. Mom figured it would be helpful to have David out of sight for a while.

On schedule – two days before New Year's Day, 1967 – Tracy and David flew to London. Tracy was rapturous at the prospect of spending almost seven months in London. Mom was scared to death she'd get homesick, but that wouldn't happen. Besides, she'd take any bet that Mom would be over in London to visit before three months had passed.

'Call home once or twice a month,' her mother had ordered in the last moment of farewells. 'Collect.'

'Is there any other way?' Tracy'd bubbled.

On the overnight flight Tracy dozed, her head on David's shoulder. In these last couple of weeks, it seemed to her, David had grown up. All of a sudden it was David who was making decisions. During the spring break, they'd travel around Europe. Students travelled cheap, he insisted. They'd save their allowances, maybe even find jobs that didn't require work permits.

They'd send reports to the student newspaper about what was happening on campuses in Europe, David had decided. She'd sensed a new respect for David in her father's long conversations with him about the months ahead. Dad was so concerned about the quality of education – not only here at home but around the world. While the plane – wrapped in darkness – made its way across the Atlantic, she replayed in her mind scraps of talk with him about student rebellions.

'So many people here at home seem to consider it an American experience. It's happening all over the world. Italy, Germany, Sweden, Russia, Spain, Belgium, Japan, Formosa, Poland, Hungary, Czechoslovakia. I read somewhere that students have demonstrated even in Tanzania.'

Because David was with her, Tracy acknowledged to herself, she felt no fear about attending a school in a strange country, where she knew no one, living in a dorm where everybody knew one another except for herself. She felt an unexpected surge of sentiment at being here where her mother had lived in such trying times. Mom had been younger than she, had had to work to support herself.

Hand in hand with David she explored London. It wasn't the war-desecrated London Mom had known, she told herself while she and David stood before landmarks that she'd heard her parents describe in nostalgic detail. She wrote home with enthusiasm about how at London colleges students didn't encounter the heavy studying – except for exams – that American college students knew.

'Oh sure, we put in a lot of time studying and working – but it's not the classroom scene like at home. We go to some lectures but mainly tutorials with professors, one on one. David is just blossoming here.'

Late in February, Tracy received a letter from her mother.

'What did I tell you, David? Mom's coming here!' Presumably on business. *Just for a few days but it gives me a chance to see you.*

'Why didn't Dad come with you?' Tracy demanded when she and David met her mother at Heathrow. 'Doesn't he want to see London again? I mean, it was so important to your lives.' Belatedly, she remembered that Dad said Mom had a thing about going to London. But she'd gotten over the hang-up to come to see her, Tracy thought affectionately.

'I wanted him to come.' Vera's eyes were oddly wary. *This was traumatic for Mom – coming back to London,* Tracy thought compassionately. *Dad should be with her.* 'But he said he'd feel guilty if he took eight days off from his counselling group.'

It seemed to Tracy that her mother had barely arrived when they headed with her for Heathrow. She hadn't expected to feel this awful loneliness when Mom went home, she realized in astonishment.

'Have fun during your spring vacation,' her mother said tenderly. 'You can cover a lot of territory in three weeks.' Earlier she'd handed over a wad of cash to be transformed into traveller's cheques.

'I'll phone the Munches when we're in Copenhagen,' Tracy promised. It was so sweet, she thought, the way Mom exchanged letters two or three times a year with the family that had taken her in when she had had to run from Berlin. 'You'll write and tell them I'll call?'

'I'll write,' her mother promised.

But Tracy and David found their anticipation of travel in Europe eclipsed now by the escalation of the student movement at the London School of Economics. They knew that for months there had been dissension between students and administration at LSE. Students – some of the brightest in Great Britain – had been demanding a more democratic and free university.

Tracy and David had observed some earlier – milder – skirmishes where LSE students had paraded with banners that read: Berkeley, 1966; LSE, 1967 – We'll Bring This School to a Halt, Too. Some, Tracy recalled, had even gone on a hunger strike. Dad had told them that student rebellion was not an American phenomenon, Tracy remembered – but seeing this made his words real. They heard that one of the leaders of the student movement was an American graduate student from Denver named Marshall Bloom. There were 324 Americans at LSE.

On Monday, March 13, Tracy and David met her roommate – an ebullient student-activist named Audrey Sims – at a Lyons cafeteria for a cheap dinner before going to a Students' Union meeting.

'It's true!' Audrey told the other two when they'd settled themselves at a corner table. 'Students at LSE are sitting-in! It's a round-the-clock deal. In the main entrance hall – with a banner that says: Beware the Pedagogic Gerontocracy.'

'I thought LSE was supposed to be such a liberal school.' David was sombre. 'Why did they suspend Bloom and Adelstein for the rest of the school year just because they wanted to discuss university appointments?' Adelstein was president of the Students' Union.

Now their lives revolved around the sit-in at LSE. By Wednesday evening, 104 students had been suspended. The demonstrators were, in fact, in control of the university – though this was not their goal. They wanted a more democratic university.

At other schools sentiment ran high for a show of support. On Friday, March 17, 3,000 students marched through the City of London and the West End – Tracy and David among them. Students from Manchester, Leeds, Cambridge, and other schools joined forces – wearing yellow daffodils, the new symbol of their rebellion.

The Times called the demonstrations 'unprecedented in British university history.' Tracy revelled in being part of this. And in the course of this student rebellion, she arrived at a decision about her future – vague thus far despite her selection of a major.

'David, I know what I want to do with my life now. I want to teach – at the university level. I want to see

372

changes made in our own education system.' She paused to giggle. 'I suppose you'll say I'm doing this because of my exposure to Dad and Adele.'

'I can settle for that, too,' David said seriously. 'We'll both teach at the same university. The academic life has a lot going for it.' He chuckled. 'By the time we're there, the situation will be cooler. Of course, my parents will be furious. They can't exactly bitch – because college professors are considered respectable – but they'll make ugly noises about the low salaries. In their eyes, that is.'

'We don't care about them,' Tracy shot back defiantly.

'No.' He surprised her with this admission. 'All of a sudden I realize I *don't* much care what my parents think. I used to – I wanted so badly to please them. But it doesn't matter anymore. Maybe you can say I've grown up.'

'Dad and Mom will be pleased,' Tracy said, her face luminous. 'Teaching is becoming a family tradition.' Instead of making guns. 'Oh wow, I can just imagine Dad's relief. I know he was scared to death I'd settle on something wildly unconventional.'

'Do you suppose this is the time to announce we're officially engaged?'

'No.' Tracy shook her head. 'That's *too* conventional!'

Early in the new year Laurie found herself reaching out for relaxation. Small groups began to form, with intermittent parties at a student's apartment – usually after a major exam. Through the college years she'd avoided any romantic attachments, but now she was flattered by the pursuit of male medical students.

'This guy Marty Stevens is really coming on strong,' she confided to Adele over a Sunday-morning breakfast in early April after a noisy party that had wound up in a maudlin singfest silenced by an irate neighbour. 'Look, how many women are there in my class? Ten in a class of well over a hundred. I'm convenient,' she rationalized, yet she felt a surge of excitement when she remembered how Marty had stopped dancing to kiss her in the shadowy corner of the living room. Every woman in their group – even the two wives of med students – was attracted to Marty. Sandy-haired, blue-eyed, with moviestar features, a lean, hard body, and a charismatic charm, Marty dominated any gathering, she thought in delicious abandonment to emotion.

'You like him?' Adele probed, shifting a piece of Nova from plate to bagel.

'I could if I let myself,' Laurie admitted. 'But of course, it might have been the tequila we were drinking last night. Yeah, I know,' she said, her chuckle self-mocking. 'I nurse one drink through the whole evening.' She'd sworn off drinking in her freshman year after witnessing the wholesale throwing up of first-year college students after drinking blasts.

'Let yourself,' Adele encouraged. 'But don't get pregnant.' All at once she was sombre. 'I was thinking – if Terry and I got married and right away I was pregnant, he'd be safe from the draft. Lots of guys are taking that route,' she reflected. 'But we sat down and talked about it and it wouldn't work for us. If Terry had a wife and kid, he'd never get his degree. I don't want to stop working. If we can keep this school running, we'll be helping some kids that would otherwise be lost.'

'Med students don't have much time for play,' Laurie pointed out. 'So if we have a little fun together, why not?'

Laurie told herself at the end of her first date with Marty Stevens that her life would forever be entangled with his. His father was a tax lawyer, his mother a psychologist. His parents had what Grandpa would call a mixed marriage: Marty's mother was Jewish; his father,

Protestant. Marty called himself an agnostic. Grandpa would be upset that she was going with someone who was only half-Jewish, she thought. Mom and Dad would understand.

Now she was with Marty every moment they could manage. At parties with their small group, at his comfortable one-bedroom apartment near the medical school, or occasionally at her apartment when Adele gave notice she would be with Terry in his tiny West Seventies studio. Marty couldn't understand why she was stalling on sleeping with him. It was no big deal these days.

'Look, if you're not ready, you keep saying *no*,' Adele advised. 'Of course, I stopped saying *no* to Terry a long time ago.'

'You don't like Marty.' Involuntarily Laurie gave voice to the suspicion that had been haunting her for weeks.

'Laurie, I've never seen the guy for more than three minutes,' Adele scolded. 'All I know is what you tell me.' She paused. 'I think he's hooked on becoming the richest doctor in Manhattan. You know me – that's a real turn-off.'

'He's ambitious,' Laurie corrected. But she felt a tinge of guilt as she remembered what he'd said when they'd first met. 'My old man's a tax lawyer. He said, "To hell with going to law school. I'm a tax lawyer, I know what sharp doctors make. *That's* the gravy train."'

'If he makes you happy, go for it.' Adele's smile was warm and loving, but her eyes – Laurie thought – were troubled.

On the last evening before leaving for home, Laurie went to a party at Marty's apartment. She remained after the others had left to help him clean up. She'd told Adele she might stay over at Marty's apartment – though he didn't know it.

'Let's leave the dishes in the sink,' he said, reaching for

375

her. 'I want to sublet this joint and get something with a dishwasher. My old man can afford it.'

'We've got one year behind us, three to go.' Her voice was unsteady because he was sliding one hand down the low neckline of her dress. He knew what that did to her, she thought, closing her eyes while the hand fondled the lush spill of a breast.

'I don't know if I could survive them without you.' His mouth was at her ear now. 'Honey, when are you going to grow up and show me you're a woman?'

'How about tonight?' she whispered. It was awful to think that she wouldn't see Marty until next fall. She was going home for the summer and just collapse. Adele understood she had to give everything of herself to med school now. No time for anything else. Marty was leaving for eight weeks in Europe with a college buddy.

'Fireworks are going off in my head.' His free hand closed in about her rump, prodding her body against his. 'No more stop lights,' he crooned. 'An express to paradise.'

They'd made passionate love so many times, she thought in soaring anticipation as he lifted her from her feet and carried her into the tiny bedroom, but tonight would be the ultimate moment. They undressed with impatient speed, swayed together in the triumphant knowledge there'd be no denial of themselves tonight. And then the gentle thrust of his hands on her shoulders in the darkened bedroom, and she felt herself falling upon the mattress. Hands reaching for the other, bodies moving with sudden urgency. And – almost too soon – it was over, the sounds of her own passion poignant in the silence.

'Relax, Laurie,' he soothed with smug reassurance. 'The night's just beginning.'

She'd known almost from their first meeting that she'd spend her life with Marty. Together they'd survive the next three years of med school, Laurie told herself – resting in his embrace. They'd intern at the same hospital. They'd set up practice together. Adele would see she was wrong about Marty. He wasn't 'a greedy bastard.' He was ambitious.

Chapter Thirty-three

Vera sprawled on a chaise on the screen porch of the Kahn house on this late August night that was breaking heat records. Since morning the air conditioning had provided only warm air. On Sundays in Eastwood nobody worked. Hopefully, the air conditioning would be repaired tomorrow. Amazing, she mused, how they became dependent on new creations of technology. Fifteen years ago, people took it for granted they'd swelter in summer – though, in truth, she'd been shocked at the discomfort of American summers after the years in London and Copenhagen.

From inside the house came the hum of a fan in Laurie's bedroom. She'd been on the phone for almost an hour with that friend from med school who was visiting Paris. What a phone bill that would be – but not theirs. Tracy and David were at his parents' summer house at Lake George. Dad didn't know his parents were somewhere in Europe.

She heard the muted tones of the TV in the den. Paul was watching the news. This was a summer of such extremes, she considered, tugging at the perspiration-soaked back of her blouse with one hand and smacking an errant mosquito on her sun-tanned leg with the other. The newspapers and magazines were full of articles about the Haight-Ashbury section of San Francisco, where young hippies were spreading the word that love was *in*. And the word was the same in New York City's East Village and in other major cities around the country.

But the *summer of love* was turning into a nightmare, she reflected, remembering the hordes of teenage runaways intent on joining the psychedelic paradise they thought existed in the East Village and the Haight-Ashbury.

This summer the country had seen the worst race-riots in its history – in more than 100 cities. The most devastating had been in Detroit and Newark. In five days of rioting, 45 people had been killed in Detroit. In Newark – also in a devastating five-day spell of violence – 26 people had died. Many more had been injured.

Laurie's accusation last night was seared into Vera's memory.

'When people can stop buying guns whenever they like – when guns are outlawed – we'll stop seeing kids shot down in the streets of urban ghettos!'

Thank God, Dad hadn't been home when she'd said that. He was already upset over all the talk in Washington about another gun-control bill. To him it was an infringement on the individual rights of every American.

She couldn't come out and say to Dad, 'Laurie's right. All those crying out for gun-control laws are right.' But she and Dad weren't villains because they manufactured guns, she told herself defensively – though in Laurie's mind they were tainted by this. Guns were necessary for keeping the peace. Without arms last month, Israel would have been annihilated – instead of winning the Six-Day War that had threatened its existence. If there had not been guns in the hands of good people, she would have been captured in that fishing village in Denmark and sent to a concentration camp. Those terrified moments, too, were seared into her memory.

Paul strolled onto the porch with a pitcher and a pair of glasses in tow.

'Try a glass of lemonade,' he coaxed, settling himself

on a chair beside her. 'It'll cool you off for a little while.'

'We've gotten so dependent on air conditioning.' Her smile was wry. 'But think of all the people who've never had it.'

'Laurie must be roasting up in her room.' He poured lemonade into two tall glasses. 'You think there's something serious between her and that med student who keeps calling?'

'These days how can you tell? They're all so casual.' Vera sighed. Instinct warned her not to ask questions. In her daughter's eyes she was the enemy, the enemy who manufactured small arms. 'And how serious can she get with all that schooling ahead of her?' She worried constantly about this. 'By the time she's in private practice she'll be close to thirty.'

'Women medical students do marry,' Paul pointed out after a moment. He knew exactly what she was thinking, Vera told herself in gratitude. He knew her anxiety about Laurie's future.

'It's tougher for a woman than a man,' Vera said, half expecting a challenge from Paul. 'A man can be a medical student, marry, have children. A woman medical student can marry – and pray not to get pregnant. There's no room in her life for a family. Med school's rough enough – but we've heard more than we'd like to know about the insane hours during the internship years.'

'Ah, you're worried about having to wait to become a grandmother,' Paul chided good-humouredly. 'You're forty-two years old and look thirty. Who'd ever believe anytime soon that you were a grandmother?'

'There's Tracy and David,' she reminded. 'We still have hopes.'

'When do you think Tracy and David'll get married?' He lifted one foot to rest on the chaise. Her sigh was eloquent. 'Don't they realize it would improve his draft status?'

'David says it's a miracle he hasn't been called up so far.'

'He won't go if he is called,' Paul predicted sombrely. 'And you know, I won't blame him.' His smile was quizzical. 'Honey, I'm still trying to figure you out. I know you hate this war. You realize we've gotten into something that never should have happened in the first place. But when Dad shoots off his mouth about draft-dodgers being the worst kind of traitors, you don't say a word.'

'Neither do you,' she said quietly. She didn't want to consider what would happen if Dad discovered Paul was counselling would-be draft-evaders in Albany. 'I don't think Dad will ever understand what's happening in South Vietnam. He sees this country as a defender of democracy, sworn to keep Communism from spreading around the world.'

'There's no democracy in South Vietnam!' A nerve quivered in his right eyelid. 'People here at home have to realize that.'

They both started guiltily at the sound of a car pulling into the driveway. Dad was coming home from one of his interminable meetings.

'I hated to leave my meeting,' Joel called to them. 'The air conditioning was great.'

Drained by the heat wave, he climbed the stairs to the porch with deliberate slowness. He had been over-conscious of his age since his longtime pharmacist friend fell and broke his hip four months ago, Vera thought. She and Doris had debated about giving him a surprise seventy-fifth birthday party, then decided against it. He didn't need to be reminded of the passing years. She'd scolded him when he'd bought himself a new car early in the year and talked about its 'seeing him through.' It was time he stopped looking at the calendar.

'Anything momentous at your civic meeting, Dad?' Paul joshed.

'Only five people showed up.' Joel lowered himself into a chair, reached for Paul's half-filled glass of lemonade. 'Nobody wants to stir in this weather.' He paused, listened to the sound of a typewriter in use in an upstairs bedroom. 'I thought Laurie came home for a rest. She's either on the phone, typing, or with her nose in a book.'

'You know Laurie – the perpetual worrier.' Vera smiled. 'She wants to start the new school-year ahead of the game. She'll be leaving day after tomorrow.' Already she felt a sense of loss. 'And Tracy comes home in the morning and leaves the next day, also.'

'I still have Neal to spoil.' Joel's face softened. Now he took Neal with him for target practice – as he had once taken Tracy. 'I waited a long time for a grandson, but it was worth it.'

Vera knew he was already envisioning the day when Neal would come into the business, to take over eventually what had begun six generations earlier. His big fear, she realized, was that he wouldn't live to see it. She wished there were some way she could make him understand that he should take each day at a time. Enjoy each day. It was from Dad, Vera mused, that Laurie had inherited her tendency to worry.

Laurie waited restlessly for a call from the airport. Marty had promised to phone the moment he was through Customs. She felt guilty about having left home two days earlier than she had to – lying to Mom and Dad. But she hadn't see Marty in ten weeks. *Ten weeks*. They needed these two days together before they were caught up in the old grind.

Adele had made a point of saying she'd sleep over at Terry's tonight and tomorrow night. Adele knew she felt more comfortable staying here than going to Marty's pad. It was kooky to feel that way. Why did it matter where they slept together? Marty didn't say anything about their getting married, but she understood he felt he had to get through med school before taking such a step.

Some of the students were married, she considered – staring out into the night. Some were just living together. Oddly, *she* wasn't ready for that. Anyhow, being together this way – whenever they could fit it into their schedules – was more practical. Med school and marriage could be a killer.

There were moments when the whole med school scene infuriated her, she admitted to herself in a rare moment of candour. They were constantly treated as though they were ten-year-olds. *We're just bodies there*, she railed inwardly, *for them to pour facts over. We're memorization machines, and then come the tests and we have to pour it back out to them. We're not supposed to think – or to have opinions. It's humiliating.* She accused in silence, knowing that other med students shared these feelings with her.

Her introspection was punctured when her eyes focused on the kerb below. A cab had pulled to a stop. The door was thrust open. Marty emerged. He hadn't stopped to phone. With a rush of excitement she darted to open the apartment door. He had a key. He didn't need to be buzzed in. She listened for the sound of the elevator rising to her floor. Then she spied Marty, charging up the stairs.

'Hey, baby! You look wonderful!' He rushed towards her, swept her into his arms.

'You said you'd call,' she scolded, laughter mingling with tears of pleasure.

'I got a lift into the city with this guy who had a limo

waiting,' he explained. 'No standing in a taxi line –'

'Are you hungry?' she asked while they moved arm-in-arm into the apartment.

'Just for you.' Marty stopped dead to kiss her with a passion that matched her own.

They made love, lay together in a torrent of conversation about his summer in Europe, her summer at home.

'Yeah, we've got to get real serious this year,' he said with pleased anticipation. 'No more fooling about whether to specialize – or in what to specialize.'

'No problem with us,' Laurie said, in love with life at this moment. 'We're both specializing.' She'd given this a lot of thought through the years. 'You in surgery, me in pediatrics.'

'Maybe you ought to give that some thought,' Marty suggested. 'Pediatrics is a nice, reliable field. Hell, there're always kids being born. But there's a hell of a lot more money in other areas. Take obstetrics. You know what you can bill a C-section for these days?' He whistled eloquently.

'Marty, I don't want to be an obstetrician.' All at once Laurie was uneasy. 'I want to be a pediatrician.'

'Consider orthopedic surgery,' he pursued, squinting in thought.

'No!' Laurie sat upright in bed. 'I know what I want to do with my life. I want to be a pediatrician.'

'Cool it,' he purred. 'Save all that energy for something important. We've got a lot of making up to do.'

With brutal suddenness she and Marty were caught up in the school rat race again. They quickly realized that their second year would be rougher than the first. Exams were coming along more heavily. Every waking moment was given over to studying. Bedtime was postponed to allow more time with the books. Their private lives were on hold. The only exceptions were the nights after an exam, when groups gathered at a student's apartment for what Marty labelled 'one hysterical blast.'

Now their small clique was expanding to include a woman student – Ava Benson – whose husband was divorcing her. 'He said I wasn't a wife anymore. I was a med school machine.' Ava encouraged Jeffrey Green – probably the brightest in their class, Laurie thought with respect – to join them on a snowy, early December night after a particularly rough exam.

'I'm not sure I can stay awake,' he warned, stifling a yawn. 'I haven't had a decent night's sleep in a month.'

'Sleep? What's that?' Laurie drawled. But she understood his feelings.

'Hey, we have to unwind now and then.' Marty dropped an arm possessively about Laurie's shoulders. 'Have a few beers, dance a little, sing.'

'Make love,' Ava added. 'Hey, what's that?'

'I'll show you, I'll show you,' their class clown offered quickly.

Normally at these parties they focused on grabbing as much fun as possible. Tonight – perhaps because the exam had been such a bitch and they all felt like such klutzes, Laurie mused – they were into talking. As usual, Marty dominated the group.

'Next year we'll be third-year students. That means we'll be spending most of our time in the hospital and clinics. We –'

'You just can't wait to parade around in a white coat with a stethoscope hanging around your neck,' Ava jibed. ' "Calling Dr Kildare, calling Dr Kildare!" '

'Knock it off,' Marty ordered good-humouredly. 'But the time has come to zero in on where we're heading. The big deal on the scene now is subspecializing. That's where the loot's going to be! I'm settling on cardiac surgery. I'll have a house in Westchester and an in-ground pool in five years,' he boasted. 'From there on the sky's the limit.'

'Now that's a callous attitude,' Jeff drawled. 'What happened to public service?' He made a joke of it, yet Laurie sensed an undercurrent of seriousness in him.

'That's for the sucker brigade.' Marty shrugged. 'The missionary division. Look, I'm working my butt off – and there's worse to come. You know about those thirty-six-hour shifts when we're interning. The back-to-back shifts that keep popping up. We have to collect for all that shit! That's our reward, boys and girls.'

'What about Medicare and Medicaid?' Ava demanded. 'Doesn't that come under the heading of doctors' bonanza?'

'That's a whole social revolution,' Marty crowed. 'And with the shortage of doctors, we're in the driver's seat.'

'As soon as Congress started showing serious intent to pass Medicare and Medicaid, a lot of doctors began to double their fees,' Jeff said distastefully. 'Because they knew Medicare and Medicaid fees would be based on what doctors charged in the quarter or so before the bill went through.'

'That's smart,' Ava said, yet Laurie sensed an undertone of guilt in her voice.

'That's fraud,' Jeff retorted. 'And the hospitals are no better. Everybody knew a year ago there was a crisis in health care. Back in March there was a special Report to the President on Medical Care Prices – and it shows that hospital charges that had been rising between 6% and 8% for years went up 16.5% in 1963. And it's kept going up. And that same report said that the jump in doctors' fees last year was the largest in forty years.'

'Back home, folks are talking about awful doctor bills,' a student from Dallas admitted. 'They worry.'

'That's some doctors.' Laurie tried for an optimistic

note. 'We have this wonderful Dr Evans in Eastwood. I don't think he's raised his fees more than five dollars in the last ten years. Everybody in town loves that man.'

'Love doesn't put money in the bank,' Marty drawled. 'We've got special skills. Let people pay for them.'

She wished Marty wouldn't make it seem as though all they cared about was making a lot of money. Sure, there were some in their class who were outspoken about that – but there were others who came to medicine with other motives. Jeff Green, she suspected, would always regard medicine as a public service – and immediately she felt guilty at this thought. She wasn't putting down Marty, she told herself defensively. Marty talked a lot. He'd be a terrific surgeon once they survived their training.

Laurie was sprawled on the living room sofa, listening to the TV news about the 1,000 anti-war protesters who'd tried to close down the New York induction centre – among them Dr Spock and Allen Ginsberg – when Adele unlocked the door and came into the apartment with an expression that screamed *crisis*.

Laurie sat upright. 'Adele, what's happened?'

'Terry's been drafted. Yeah, I know –' She closed her eyes, dropped onto the sofa. 'We knew it could happen. This is his year to work instead of going to school.'

'What's he going to do?' Laurie felt her throat tighten in alarm.

'He's going into the service. You know Terry. He feels it's his responsibility to show he's a patriotic black.'

'But he's against the war,' Laurie protested.

'He thinks it's an immoral war,' Adele corrected tiredly. 'But it would be more immoral for him not to show himself a loyal American citizen. So we're going for blood tests tomorrow. We'll get married at City Hall on

Monday. I don't suppose you can get out of class?' Her smile was wistful.

'If you're getting married, I'll cut a class,' Laurie told her.

If Terry had been able to stay in school this year, he would have been deferred. He wouldn't be going to Vietnam.

Churning after yet another battle with Marty – one that hadn't been resolved in bed because there had been no time, Laurie hurried through the blustery night cold to the Tip Toe Inn. She was fifteen minutes late, she noted with impatience as she approached the entrance to the restaurant. Adele and Terry would be waiting for her. Because the three of them had such tight schedules later in the week, they'd chosen tonight for their wedding dinner. Over the weekend Adele and Terry were making a quick trip to North Carolina – so his mother and sisters could meet Adele and to give him a chance to see his family before his induction.

Inside the cosy warmth of the Tip Toe Inn, Laurie spied Adele and Terry at a corner table.

'My friends are over there,' she told the smiling hostess and made her way to their table. The dinner crowd was just beginning to appear.

'We had our blood tests,' Adele told Laurie and pulled up her sleeve to indicate a Band-Aid. 'We're on our way.'

Their waitress approached. For a few minutes they focused on ordering. Laurie made her decision quickly. Adele and Terry were in good-humoured debate.

This was all so unreal, Laurie thought – Adele and Terry getting married, Terry going into the service. And she felt drained from the row with Marty. He'd been bragging about how Medicare was such a gravy train for doctors.

'Laurie, stop being Alice in Wonderland. This is the real world. Take this guy in the apartment across from mine – fresh out of his residency. He's waiting for a penthouse pad to become available. He tells me how he can run up a scratch on a mild diabetic to *multiple lesions* and a three-hundred-dollar bill. He dabs on ointment, slaps on a Band-Aid, and *voilà*, a bill to Medicare for three hundred bucks.'

In contrast, she remembered Jeff's outrage when an aunt who went on Medicare suddenly found her ophthalmologist's bill for a routine annual checkup billowing to three times its normal size by listing her as a new patient.

'She's afraid to report him,' Jeff had said in frustration. 'He's been her doctor for almost thirty years. She's terrified of going to somebody new.'

Why couldn't she admit to herself that what she'd felt for Marty was dead? They couldn't keep fighting, then making up in bed. What kind of future did that hold for them? She couldn't make Marty over into an image she could accept – and she would never let herself become the kind of woman Marty wanted her to be.

In truth, she told herself bluntly, there was no place in a woman med student's life for emotional attachments. That was the price a woman paid for wanting to become a doctor. It didn't mean she had to live like a nun. Just no lasting relationships. What she wanted most in her life was to become a doctor. *A doctor like Dr Evans up in Eastwood*. He wasn't a vanishing breed, as Dad sometimes mourned. A whole new generation like herself and Jeff were coming along.

'What do you think, Laurie?' Terry's voice – blending cynicism with humour – brought her back to the present. 'Am I crazy to feel it's my obligation as a young black man to serve in Vietnam?'

'You know how I feel about Vietnam,' Laurie reminded.

'He's so tied up in civil rights he can't think of anything else,' Adele taunted, struggling to sound amused.

'I had a weird experience last night.' Terry squinted as he called up the memory. 'I met these two guys – both black, both just back from Vietnam. Two totally different reactions to the war. Both twenty-two, with a tour of duty behind them. One guy cursed Johnson for not letting them atom-bomb Hanoi . . . so sure he was there to save the world from Communism. He said he came back home and was going crazy. He landed a job, but got into a brawl with his boss, who said we didn't belong in Vietnam. He's signing up for another tour – going back to 'Nam.'

'He's one of those guys who thinks if he has a gun in his hand he has power.' Adele grunted in impatience. 'When will they realize that education – *learning* – is power? Not guns.'

'My mother brought up my sisters and me to feel that we owed all our allegiance to God and country. She'll be proud of me for going to Vietnam.' Terry's smile was gentle. 'She'll hurt because she'll be scared for me. But she taught us that things like serving in the military were part of our responsibility as Americans. She said that blacks – she still calls us *coloureds* – have to work hard to "show we can be as good as whites."'

'She's a dear, sweet woman, Terry – but too many of her generation accept that we aren't as good. Our generation *doesn't*.' Adele reached out to cover his hand with hers. 'But it kills me that if you'd have had the means to stay in school, you wouldn't be on your way to Vietnam.'

'This other vet – he came right out and said that the Vietnamese people want us out of there – they're just scared to come out and say it. He said what pisses him off most is that our government was lying to him. All that American propaganda about how democratic and honest the Vietnamese government is! He said his old man went all the way from North Africa, through Sicily, and into Italy in World War II – but they knew why they were there. And his own father –' Terry paused, his smile twisted in compassion '– can't understand why *he* wasn't happy serving his country.'

'At least, you'll be able to finish college under the GI Bill.' Adele was making a desperate effort to hide her own fears, Laurie interpreted. 'And there're some middle-class white kids with college backgrounds showing up at the induction centres now. It's no longer a mostly black, blue-collar army.'

Vera was shaken when she heard on the television news on January 5, that Dr Benjamin Spock – whose book on child care both she and Doris, along with millions of other mothers, considered a national treasure – had been indicted by the Federal government along with four others for counselling American young men in resisting the draft. This could happen to Paul.

'Vera, we've known this was a possibility,' he chided gently while they sat together in the den before a blazing fire in the grate.

'I don't want it to happen to you!' Her voice was uncharacteristically shrill.

'I'm not important enough to be dragged in,' Paul soothed. 'They're going after big names.'

'Do you think Dr Spock and the others will go to jail?' The prospect of Paul being jailed unnerved her.

'These are weird times,' he said after a moment. 'This all goes back to that letter published last October in the *New York Review of Books* and the *New Republic*, which pleaded for faculty support for draft-evaders. Dr Spock signed – with a long list of other people. Including,' he added wryly, 'two Nobel prize-winners, Linus Pauling and Albert Szent-Gyorgi, who contend that since the Vietnam war was never declared by Congress, it's unconstitutional.'

'Tracy doesn't say anything, but I know she's terrified that David will be drafted.' The latest figures showed 485,000 Americans in Vietnam. 'He graduates in June. He'll be losing his college deferment.' And graduate-school attendance wouldn't help. On February 23, that deferment had been abolished.

'He won't go,' Paul said gently.

'If he doesn't, he could go to jail,' Vera reminded. 'Either way – if he goes or he doesn't go – Tracy will be a wreck.' She hesitated. 'Paul, have you been talking to him?'

Paul seemed startled. 'Of course, I've been talking to him – every time he's in the house.'

'You know what I mean,' Vera pushed. 'Have you been advising him?'

'When the time comes, it's a decision he has to make himself. But I've pointed out his prerogatives. If he decides to resist, he can face the possibility of being jailed. It's happening. Or he can go to Canada.'

'Tracy would go with him.' Vera's face was drained of colour as she dwelt on this. Tracy and David in exile – that's what it would amount to, she thought in anguish. *When would they be able to return?*

'Paul!' Joel's voice vibrated through the house. 'Where the hell are you?'

'In the den,' Paul called, exchanging an anxious glance with Vera. 'He sounds terribly upset.'

'Paul, I can't believe what I've just heard.' Joel's voice preceded him into the den. Then he hovered in the doorway, his eyes brilliant with a blend of rage and disbelief.

'What did you just hear?' Vera strove for calm. *Something to do with Paul's draft-counselling?* 'Oh, you've heard about Dr Spock's being indicted,' she guessed with an effort at optimism.

'I heard about my own son heading a counselling group for draft-dodgers in Albany!' A vein pounded in Joel's forehead. 'Paul, tell me it isn't true!'

'I can't do that, Dad.' Paul managed an aura of calm.

It seemed to Vera that her father-in-law aged before her eyes. He stared at Paul as though he'd never seen him before . . . as though he were a contemptible stranger.

'You're disgracing the family.' Joel's voice trembled. 'I'll never be able to hold up my head in this town again! You're a traitor to our country!'

'There're a lot of Americans who don't feel that way. The climate's changing.' Paul strived to sound almost detached. 'This is something I have to do. I'm sorry that you're upset.'

'Kahns fought in the Civil War, in the Spanish American War, in World War I. They must be crying out in their graves for the dishonour you're bringing on them!'

Paul seemed to reel before this attack for an instant. 'Dad, try to understand.'

'How can I understand? I was so proud of you when you enlisted. I was afraid, yes – I admit that. There wasn't a day or night that I didn't pray you would come home to us. I didn't expect this of my son. We've always been loyal Americans. *We believed in our country.*'

'Our country is making a major mistake.' Paul hesitated, inhaled with an air of pain. 'I know how you feel about the antiwar movement. I respect that.' For a moment his eyes strayed to Vera. 'Vera and I will go to a motel tonight. We'll be out of your house as soon as possible.' He took a deep breath, exhaled as though with pain. 'I'm sorry, Dad.'

Chapter Thirty-four

Joel turned to Vera in shock and agonized bewilderment as Paul strode from the room. 'Vera, what have I done? I love you and Paul. My family's my life. I don't know what's happening in this world. Do you believe our country's doing a terrible thing to fight in Vietnam?' His eyes pleaded for understanding.

'For a long time I believed we were doing the right thing,' she said, groping for words. 'Most Americans believed that way. But a lot of us have come to believe – like Paul – that the war is not being fought for freedom in Vietnam. We're propping up tyrannical South Vietnamese dictators whom the people don't want to rule them. Millions of dollars that're being spent in Vietnam every week should be spent here at home – to alleviate poverty, improve our education system, fight crime.'

'President Kennedy thought we ought to fight in Vietnam. President Johnson keeps telling us that –'

'You know how deeply Paul feels about this,' Vera said gently. 'You know how bright and persevering he is. He said that way back in 1954 – when Kennedy was a senator from Massachusetts – he was against our involvement in Vietnam. In 1961 – when Johnson was Vice-President – he went to Vietnam and reported that "American combat troop involvement is not only not required, it is not desirable." In 1964, Paul said, liberal senators like Eugene McCarthy and George McGovern and Albert Gore approved of our sending Americans troops to Vietnam. But not now, Dad.' She churned with a need to make him understand. 'Those same senators are involved in the fight to get our troops out of Vietnam. We made a mistake. The important thing is to recognize that.'

'I can't worry about what's happening in Vietnam,' Joel said exhaustedly. 'I can worry only about what's happening with my family. Talk to Paul. I can't bear to see the two of you move out of this house. What would it be without you?' He spread his hands in a gesture of helplessness. 'Vera, talk to him.'

'I'll talk to him,' she promised. She, too, was shaken at the prospect of moving out of the house that had been home for over twenty-one years. 'We'll work this out.'

Vera went upstairs to their bedroom. Paul stood at a window – the drapes not yet drawn – and stared out into the blackness of the night.

'Paul, Dad's terribly upset,' she began.

'What can I do?' he challenged without turning away from the window. 'Deny everything I believe in?'

'He needs time. He doesn't want us to move out.'

'He's ashamed of me. He said I'm disgracing the family. How can I stay here?' He swung about to face her, his eyes reflecting his inner agony. 'Tell me. How can I stay here?'

'He's your father, and he loves you. You know how deeply he loves you.' She saw Paul flinch and knew he was remembering how his father had taken the blame for the accidental shooting of his mother. 'He's spent all his life with the conviction that his country can do no wrong. We have to be here for him.'

'How?'

'By staying here in the house. That's what he wants. It won't be easy. We'll have to take each day at a time. But he is your father, and we love him.'

'If Dad has heard about the group in Albany, it must be all over town now.' Paul crossed from the window to sit on the edge of the bed. 'I'll have to resign from the faculty.' His smile was lopsided. 'Before I'm fired.'

'That would be best,' Vera agreed.

'What will I do with my life?' Paul tried for cynical humour. 'I've been a teacher for twenty-one years.'

'You could go back to school, work for your doctorate,' Vera suggested.

'It's too late for that.' His smile was wry. 'And with all the rumpus on college campuses these days, I wouldn't be the type to appeal to the administrations. I'd never get hired.'

'I try so hard to understand what's happening in the minds of students these days.' Vera sighed. 'If my father were alive, he'd be so bewildered, so upset.'

'This generation of students is living with a situation no others faced,' Paul pointed out. 'The Cold War. But there's always been student rebellion. I remember back in the late '30s when Doris was in college and she went down to Manhattan to picket in the garment district with a bunch of girl students from fine old families. And there were American students who went off to fight with the Abraham Lincoln Brigade in the Spanish Civil War. Then came World War II – and all we thought about was war. That was our rebellion. Kids today worry about such tough problems – civil rights, Vietnam, all the changes that are occurring in the world. They feel a frightening insecurity and frustration. And remember, there's been a student population explosion since the end of World War II.'

'Young people today see college as their right – not a privilege for the well-fixed. And we need them college-educated,' Vera said with conviction. 'There's been a knowledge explosion, too. So much has been learned – and so fast. It's as though the world of science fiction has become a reality.'

'Kids in middle-class families have been raised to ask questions. And they're asking questions on campuses all over the world. I think,' Paul said humorously, 'that if I were teaching at the college level today I'd be in constant hot water.'

'Paul, you have so much to say – and you say it so well. Get back to writing. That's what you'll do with your life.'

'It'll mean a serious drop in income,' he warned. 'Not that we're suffering – considering your weekly pay cheque.'

'Focus on writing,' she reiterated. 'Run down to New York and talk with that group Adele is working with – you were so excited about what they're doing.' Adele had come up with Laurie this past Thanksgiving. 'And you do what you think is right about the draft-counselling. We just won't talk about it around Dad.'

'Vera, how would I survive without you?' Paul reached to pull her down beside him.

'We survive together,' she said softly. 'We're a family.'

Vera knew that in this pro-war town life was not easy these days for either Paul or his father. The news that Paul was heading a We Won't Go group had raced about town. To many local residents he was a pariah. Their current housekeeper – who had a nephew in Vietnam – quit. Her replacement – another Irene – cared only about her three cats. 'I don't think they'll be drafted,' Paul said with an effort at levity.

Paul and his father had made a silent pact. They could discuss any matter in this house except the war in Vietnam. Vera had heard her father-in-law in terse conversation on the phone with a friend. 'What Paul does is his business. I don't want to talk about it.'

She watched anxiously for repercussions when Tracy

came home for a weekend and announced that she and David would not be here for the spring break. They would join hordes of other young college students who were going to campaign for Eugene McCarthy, who'd announced formally at a press conference last November 30 that he would seek the Democratic nomination.

'He's the peace candidate,' Tracy electioneered earnestly. 'This is my first chance to vote for a president. I want my first vote to help put Gene in the White House!'

Alone in their room Vera and Paul discussed the coming primaries.

'There's the smell of change in the air,' Paul observed. 'You can almost hear people's minds ticking. A lot of those who wanted to keep us in Vietnam are switching sides. The Tet offensive was brutal. It was demoralizing to American forces. For the first time ever, we have to consider that we could lose a war. We can't fight a guerrilla enemy and win.'

'It's weird how little things can switch individual thinking,' Vera said slowly. 'I can't get out of my mind that item in the newspapers. You know –' She couldn't bring herself to give it voice.

Paul nodded. 'You mean the Associated Press report on what that American artillery officer said – after we shelled the hell out of Ben Tre in the Mekong Delta. *We had to destroy it in order to save it.*' Paul grimaced in revulsion, contemplating the additional half-million Vietnamese who became refugees after this action that reduced their homes to rubble.

'What will forever remain in my memory,' Vera said, tensing, 'is that film we saw on television where a Viet Cong officer was captured and beaten, then brought to the head of the South Vietnamese national police – and this executioner reaches for his pistol and shoots him in the head. It was horrible.' She shivered.

'Millions of Americans saw that film. I think it helped to change a lot of minds. I think a lot of people are changing from hawks to doves.'

The next two months, Vera thought in retrospect, were the most harrowing in all the years she'd been in this country. In the March 12 primary in New Hampshire, LBJ led Eugene McCarthy by less than one full percentage point. Four days later, Robert Kennedy announced that he, too, was a candidate for the Democratic nomination. On March 31, President Johnson told the American people that he would not seek another term.

On April 4, Martin Luther King was assassinated in Memphis, Tennessee. Riots erupted in over one hundred cities. Twelve people were killed in Washington, DC, another twenty-five in other cities. In Washington, DC, fires were set in the downtown shopping area as well as in the ghettoes. In New York City, a courageous Mayor Lindsay kept the cool by walking through Harlem streets to plead for calm.

On Tuesday evening, April 23, Vera was shocked when she switched on the TV news to discover that pandemonium existed on the Columbia campus. Columbia and Barnard students had taken over Hamilton Hall and had now moved into Low Library.

Joel was outraged. 'It's a damn Communist plot!' he railed. 'All these college demonstrations around the country! Better they should be fighting in Vietnam!'

Vera motioned for silence from Paul. 'Let me call Laurie and see what she has to say about all this.'

'The medical school is way uptown,' Paul reminded. 'This is all happening on the main campus.'

Laurie was full of sympathy for the demonstrators.

'It has been building up for a long time,' she told her mother. 'Back in February there was a demonstration about recruiters from Dow Chemical – you know – the napalm-makers – being on campus. The students are upset about Vietnam and about the draft and now this business about building a new gym on *public land*. The community – meaning Harlem blacks – will be able to use it only at certain times. This after Columbia – the Great Landlord – is responsible for evicting maybe ten thousand poor blacks in Harlem. It was the final straw.'

Assiduously following the TV news about the trouble on the Columbia campus, Vera learned – along with the rest of the country – that the following night students from the school of architecture took over Avery Hall. After midnight on Thursday, the police were brought onto campus.

The Columbia rioting continued late into May, when most students planned to leave for home. The evening before Laurie was to leave, she met Marty for dinner. She argued with him in soaring heat at their favourite Italian restaurant, just around the corner from his apartment. But tonight she felt no inclination to go up to his apartment, though after tomorrow they wouldn't see each other for weeks. She was increasingly unnerved about the way they fought.

'Marty, how can you be so callous?' Since the first day of the riots on campus he'd been contemptuous and arrogant about the students – and faculty – who were part of the action.

'They're a bunch of shitheads to carry on this way,' Marty said scornfully. 'What'll it gain them? They'll come back to school next semester to find the main campus loaded with security cops, but nothing will change.'

'You're so wrapped up in yourself, Marty.' She was forcing herself to face realizations she'd dodged for months. 'You don't give a damn about the rest of the world.'

'The rest of the world doesn't give a damn about me. We have to look out for what's good for *us*. Like you,

Laurie. Why can't you admit it's smart to prepare yourself for subspecialization? That's going to be the big deal tomorrow. Honey –' His voice softened. His knee sought under the table for hers. 'You're such a sentimental slob. But you're *my* sentimental slob, and I can't bear sitting here and not being able to hold you close. What do you say we forget about coffee and make a wild dash for the apartment?' His eyes dwelt on the lush rise of her breasts with a hunger that all at once was replicated in her.

'Marty, we need to talk –' But already she wavered.

'Later we'll talk,' he promised and lifted a hand to signal their waiter.

Vera was wistful that Tracy and David had not bothered to hang around for graduation. She'd been there for Laurie's graduation, and she'd hoped to be there for Tracy's. Sentimental occasions were – to her – a reinforcement of the togetherness of family. Tracy had been home for just one night, and then yesterday morning she and David had left to join other young volunteers who yearned to see Gene McCarthy win the presidential election in November.

The early June evening was fragrant with the scent of grass mowed late in the afternoon drifting into the den as Vera talked with Laurie in New York. Laurie would be home for a week, bringing Adele with her, and then go back to work with the group of dedicated young doctors who manned a storefront clinic in Harlem.

'What does Adele hear from her husband?' Vera asked sympathetically.

'Terry tries to be cheerful, but she says his bitterness shows through. Oh, she'll just stay in Eastwood for a couple of days, Mom. She wants to be here in case mail comes from Terry.'

'We'll be glad to have her as long as she feels comfortable.' Vera remembered her own anguished wait for letters from Paul during World War II. Her whole life had revolved around those letters.

Off the phone she checked her watch. It was just nine-forty – another twenty minutes before the ten o'clock news would be on TV. She settled herself on the sofa, reached for the current issue of *Newsweek*. Paul was at a counselling session with a local high school graduate who expected to be drafted any day. For counselling sessions here in Eastwood Paul utilized the den in Doris and Phil's house.

Dad had driven over to Cambridge to visit a friend who'd just bought an antique revolver. He'd probably come home with cake from King's, she thought indulgently. And Paul would be home soon, too. She'd put up a pot of coffee.

With coffee on the range, Vera returned to the den. Almost simultaneously she heard two cars pull into the driveway. Dad and Paul, she decided and went out to the foyer to greet them. She was glad Dad had gone over to Cambridge to see his friend. He was avoiding some of his usual evening meetings because of the caustic remarks about Paul that came his way.

'You stopped by King's,' she accused as Joel – with Paul right behind him – walked into the house with the familiar bakery box in tow. 'And I just happen to have put up a fresh pot of coffee.'

Joel launched into a rapt description of the Colt revolver that his friend had acquired.

'Where did he find this?' Vera asked. To Dad antique guns were precious jewels.

'You two go on into the den,' Paul ordered – relieved, Vera knew, that Dad hadn't asked where he'd been. 'I'll rustle up the coffee.' He reached for the box from King's and headed for the kitchen.

'Frank bought it from a private owner,' Joel said in high spirits. 'Somebody his brother down in New York was acquainted with.'

'Is Frank still giving his wife a hard time about his diabetes?' Vera asked with a flicker of humour. The doctor repeatedly told Frank his diabetes was so mild that he required no medication, just an abstinence from sugar. He put her through a three-degree at each meal about its contents, though he was known to ignore the presence of sugar when dining out at his favourite restaurants.

'You know Frank.' Joel chuckled. 'Now that he has Medicare, he's very careful about his health.' Joel seemed all at once grim as he settled himself on the sofa. 'I'm pissed,' he said in an occasional moment of vulgarity. 'He had this little scratch on his ankle – from a playful kitten they've just acquired. So he goes to his family doctor – a young guy who just took over from the old one. He looks at the scratch. "It's nothing," he says, puts on a bit of ointment and a Band-Aid – and when Frank sees the bill, it reads $300 for multiple lacerations. Now tell me, how is something like Medicare going to work with bastards like that on the loose?'

'Not all doctors are like that.' But Vera was shocked. 'You know Laurie won't ever be that way.'

'He's heard other stories.' Joel was grim. 'What's happened to ethics in this country?'

Vera reported on her conversation with Laurie. Paul returned with a tray bearing coffee mugs and a plate of King's locally famous apple fritters.

'Turn on the TV,' he told Vera. 'It's time for the news.'

Vera complied, then returned to the sofa. As she'd expected, primary election returns were of top interest on this Tuesday evening, June 4.

'Tracy's going to be so disappointed,' Paul said

sympathetically. 'Bobby Kennedy's beat McCarthy in a third primary.'

'There're still about nine weeks before the Democratic Convention.' Vera refused to abandon hope. 'Gene might just make it.'

After watching the late news, Vera and Paul went up to their bedroom. Joel remained before the TV set in search of a '40s movie, his latest addiction. They were about to retire for the night when Joel called up in obvious agitation.

'Get down here,' he yelled. 'It's happening again!'

Just past midnight Los Angeles time – fresh from the triumph of winning the important California primary – Robert Kennedy had been shot in a corridor of the Ambassador Hotel's Empire Room.

Vera and Paul sat with Joel in numbed silence while a TV newscaster reported the happenings. At 1:44 AM Robert Kennedy was pronounced dead. He had been assassinated by a snub-nosed Iver-Johnson revolver.

With anguish – listening to the morning news on the radio – Vera remembered that Kahn Firearms manufactured a revolver similar to the one that had killed Robert Kennedy. Lyndon Johnson had just condemned the nation's 'insane traffic in guns'. How would she ever make Laurie – and possibly now Tracy – understand that they were not in an evil business?

Laurie waited for Tracy at the entrance to the Charleston Gardens in B. Altman's in New York. What was so urgent that Tracy had come all the way down here to talk about with her? But then Tracy was always so dramatic, she coddled her unease. She wished the pair of women sitting beside her on the seating circle – both wearing the new 'midi' length that looked so dowdy beside the popular 'mini' and was sure to disappear shortly – would shut up. All this endless talk of the SAT grades of their sons, who'd be leaving for college in two or three days. So smug that college would keep them out of what David called the *Vietnam Annihilation Factory*.

She'd worked all summer with the storefront clinic in Harlem because she considered that a part of her medical education. Sometimes she felt guilty at the way she allowed that to dominate her life. Tracy and David had campaigned for Gene McCarthy right up to the Democratic Convention in Chicago over the last weekend. Like everybody she knew, they'd been shocked and horrified by the assassination of Robert Kennedy. But they hadn't even hung around for their college degrees. They'd gone from their final classes to the campaign trail.

God, what a massacre the Chicago Convention had been! Over 700 hurt – not just college kids but convention delegates, clergymen, middle-aged professional people fighting for what they believed in, even newsmen there to report on the convention. Over 200 cops, too, had been injured. But this time Mayor Daly's police had demonstrated their brutality – well-known to black residents of the city's West Side and South Side – before the world. They couldn't hide from the TV cameras.

Marty was due back from France tonight. He'd gone there to take some special classes meant to glamorize his training background. She suspected he'd been more interested in the partying – though he'd written that students in France clamoured for news about what was happening on American college campuses. He should have spent the summer working at one of the storefront clinics with her. This year he hadn't burnt up the trans-Atlantic phone wires with calls to her. She'd been too busy to notice until he mentioned it. '*I can't believe I'm breaking my butt this way during vacation. But hey, it adds glamour to the degree when I get it.*'

She had been startled when she'd walked into the clinic that first morning to find Jeff Green there – but later, she told herself she should have known he'd be involved in something in public service. They'd been warned they'd work long, exhausting hours – and that was the way it'd been throughout the summer. She was pleased at the warm friendship that had developed between Jeff and herself.

Most nights they ended up in the Broadway cafeteria near her apartment. His own was in the low '90s, a few blocks above hers. Mostly they talked shop – both exhilarated by the hands-on experience they were acquiring at the clinic. But she'd learned that his mother had taken a flier as a Red Cross worker during World War II, met his father, got pregnant, got married – and four years later divorced his father.

His mother had re-married twice since then. He'd seen her once in the past five years. He'd been shipped off to boarding school at ten when she was on her second divorce. His father and grandparents had fought futilely for custody. His father was a writer who'd won critical acclaim – but little money – with his first novel.

'He was on his way to becoming an alcoholic when he died in a car smash-up. I was thirteen. But my grandparents were always there for me. I went to them during most school vacations. They died within six months of each other during my senior year in high school.'

He was proud that he was getting through medical school with no financial help from his mother, though it was clear she was in an upper income bracket. He talked about his grandparents, and she talked about her grandfather – even confessing to the barrier between them because of his business. Jeff had understood. She remembered that first evening when they'd sat for two hours at a corner table in the brightly lighted cafeteria and exchanged confidences.

'My mother comes from an old Boston family. Once my father was out of his Air Force uniform and scrounging for a job to support us, she decided the romance had gone out of their marriage. He was a warm, compassionate man – but always frustrated that he couldn't keep his family together. My mother – and her family – were ashamed that my father's parents were immigrants from Russia. They ran a mom-and-pop grocery store on the Lower East Side. To my mother I was her Big Mistake. To my grandparents I was their treasure – but she would never give them custody. But they had so much love. It's their money that's seeing me through med school.'

At different times during the summer she'd brought Jeff up to the apartment for dinner with Adele and herself. Adele had liked him immediately. In a way, Laurie thought, the three of them had common goals. Last night they'd had dinner at the apartment and talked about Terry in Vietnam and Adele's problems with the mother of a teenager in her summer group.

'I'm furious at the militant welfare-mothers who pop out one kid after another – six, seven, eight. Why don't they stop having babies? With three or four – or more – fathers involved. And then I'm ashamed of my rage because I know what they've come from. We've failed them in our system.'

'You did well for yourself,' Jeff had said gently.

'I was lucky. Mom got us out of the ghetto and into another world. But not everybody is strong like Mom was.'

'Look, this is the generation that has to work to change the system,' Jeff had said.

'Hi!' Tracy's voice intruded on her thoughts . . . faintly breathless because Tracy never walked – she always ran. 'I'm not late, am I?'

'I'm early.' Laurie rose to her feet. There were only

two people ahead of them in the line at the entrance to the Charleston Gardens, she noted. The lunch crowd had eased off. 'So what's up?'

'The shit is about to hit the fan,' Tracy said with a flippancy her eyes belied ... using one of her grandfather's favourite expressions in moments of crisis. 'David just got his draft notice.'

Chapter Thirty-five

'Ooh –' Laurie froze in place.

'We're next,' Tracy said, shoving her towards the entrance to the Charleston Gardens. She anticipated the hostess's question. 'Non-smoking, please.'

They followed the hostess through the maze of tables in the huge, high-ceilinged restaurant with its faded, massive murals that were designed to lend a flavour of antebellum Charleston gardens. She led them to a table for two that flanked the wall.

'What's David going to do?' Laurie asked when they were seated, ignoring the menu.

'Wait,' Tracy ordered, her eyes betraying her tension. 'I'm having the chunky chicken salad on a roll. What about you?'

'I'll have the same,' Laurie said, annoyed by this derailment. 'Tell me about David.'

Laurie frowned as a genial waitress approached, entailing another delay. Then they were alone again.

'Well?' Laurie prodded.

'David talked a long time with Dad last night.' Tracy's eyes were eloquent. 'Then *we* talked on the phone till after midnight. *David got his draft notice.*'

'Oh, Tracy –'

'He wanted to rip it up and mail it to his draft board. He said they can't arrest everybody that does that.' She paused. 'Sometimes I think he wants to be arrested – that it'll be making a statement.'

'Dad says the number of indictments for draft-evasion

are going up,' Laurie recalled uneasily. 'Of course, they'd have to catch David first.'

'I don't want David to go to jail!' Tracy's voice was a ferocious whisper. 'I've heard too much about what goes on in prisons. The fights between the inmates, the gang-rapes. He could get up to five years!'

'There's Canada,' Laurie pointed out. Of course, David knew that. 'A lot of draftees are running up there.'

'I convinced David he mustn't take a chance on going to jail.' She took a deep, laboured breath. 'So we're going to Canada.'

'*We?*' Laurie was startled.

'I wouldn't let him go alone.' Tracy stared at her in reproof. 'I told you – we've gone over the options. Canada's the only way out.'

'You don't know when you'll be able to come back home.' Laurie felt a coldness invade her. *Would David ever be able to come home without facing a prison term?*

'I want to be with David. I guess that's all I've ever wanted. We've talked to Dad about the way to handle this. He's a good counsellor, Laurie.' Her face was luminous with love. 'It's a breeze to get into Canada. We just cross over as tourists. All we need is ID. We have our drivers' licences and passports – either one is enough. Under Canadian law, draft-evaders can't be extradited. We'll go in as tourists and later switch to *landed immigrant* status.'

'Give up your American citizenship?' Laurie gaped in disbelief. 'Tracy, you can't do that!'

'We won't be giving up our American citizenship. Being admitted as a *landed immigrant* just means we have a legal right to be there on a permanent basis. Living there for five years gives us the right to apply for Canadian citizenship.' Tracy paused, squinting in thought. 'We can ask for *student entry certificates*, but they have to be renewed every year. Anyhow, for now we're just driving up as visitors – and we'll apply for whatever we decide after we're there. It's okay to do that,' she insisted because Laurie seemed distraught. 'Anyhow, I told David to meet us at the Madison Avenue entrance at two o'clock. He'll explain everything to you.'

'What do Mom and Dad say about this?' Laurie demanded.

'They don't know. We want you to tell them tonight – once we've crossed into Canada. David thinks Montreal is the best bet for us, and –'

'How're you going to live?' Laurie broke in. *They were two babes in the woods – so bloody impractical! They'd never had to take responsibility for their own lives*, she thought impatiently. 'Do you and David have money to last awhile?'

'We're driving up in my car. David's out at a used-car dealer in Queens now to sell his. That'll last us for two or three months.'

'It's an old car.' Laurie was grim. Mom and Dad were going to hit the ceiling!

'We'll have no trouble finding jobs.' Tracy was determinedly cheerful. 'With a college degree, it's a snap. We've checked it out. There are all those groups up there waiting to help draft evaders. The Canadian Friends Service, the Central Committee for Conscientious Objectors, the Fellowship of Reconciliation of Canada – several church groups.' A wisp of a smile brightened her face. 'The biggest magazine in Canada – *MacLeans*, I think it's called – ran an editorial headed "Draft Dodgers are Refugees Not Criminals."'

'Can't you understand? Our government doesn't feel that way! David might never be able to come back here!' But Laurie knew there was no stopping Tracy and David. 'You could be exiles for the rest of your lives. You'll –'

'We'll play it by ear,' Tracy interrupted. 'And it's not so far from Eastwood that you can't come up and see us. Tell Mom and Dad – and Grandpa – not to worry.' She managed a wry smile. 'Somewhere along the road, David and I will get married.'

Laurie dreaded the call she must make home on Tracy's behalf, yet in a corner of her mind she suspected the family would not be totally surprised. Upset, yes – but not surprised. Certainly not Dad. But David's response when she'd asked him if he'd told his parents still ricocheted in her mind.

'You know my parents, Laurie. They flipped out, washed me out of their lives. They don't want to hear from me anymore. Dad said, "If I were a religious Jew, I'd say *Kaddish* for you."'

Now Laurie paced restlessly about the small living room of her Manhattan apartment. Shouldn't Marty's flight have arrived by now? Why didn't he call?

They were halfway through med school, she thought with momentary satisfaction. But everybody said the third year of med school was when you realized how little you really knew. This was the year you started your clinical rotations, started doing presentations. You learned to call each patient by his or her first name.

It would be weird to call a patient in Grandpa's age bracket by his or her first name, she thought in a whimsical moment. And this was the year you had to learn to deal with your emotions. It wasn't easy to know a patient you were seeing had no chance of survival.

Marty kept saying you had to learn to keep a distance from patients. *Hell, you have no time for compassion!* Her mind travelled to Dr Evans – that most compassionate of doctors. Dad said he was a vanishing breed. She hoped that wasn't so.

She started at the sound of the elevator drawing to a stop at their floor. She heard the elevator door slide open with its peculiar hissing sound and darted to open the apartment door. Last year he hadn't bothered to call – he'd come straight here from the airport.

'Hey, baby, I brought a bottle of bubbly with me,' Marty effervesced, charging towards her. 'Where'll it be tonight – your place or mine?'

'Adele's always obliging,' she reminded, running into his arms. 'She's staying over at a friend's house.'

'Oh baby, I can't wait.'

They moved into the apartment, locked the door behind them, clung together in a passionate embrace. In a corner of her mind she was startled to sense that something was missing in their relationship tonight. Was it the scent of perfume that clung to his jacket? Definitely a woman's perfume ... that must have been overpowering in its intensity eight or nine hours ago when he'd said farewell in Paris.

'I'll get some glasses,' she said, forcing an air of conviviality. Was it a surprise to her that Marty had played around in Paris? No!

'It has to chill first,' he reproached. 'Like me. All the way back on the plane I kept thinking about our reunion. It's been a long time, baby.'

'You chose it,' she said involuntarily.

'Are you pissed at me for going to Paris?' He clucked in reproach. 'Honey, it's going to pay off when we set up offices.' He was full of talk about a group practice now. 'You know, the glamour touch.'

'I've never thought of medicine as being a glamorous field.' Why wasn't she responding to Marty as she had before he went away? He was doing all the provocative little things that used to arouse her to such heights.

'Enough of conversation.' He pulled his mouth away

413

from her ear, his hand from within the neckline of her blouse. 'Let's go into the bedroom and make ourselves comfortable. I've got such a hunger for you.' A huskiness in his voice that should be setting her teeth on edge.

She was conscious of a strange sense of guilt that she wasn't responding to his efforts; then, all at once, she felt a tidal wave of excitement. It was going to be all right.

'Oh wow, you know how to give a guy a real welcome,' he crooned. 'How could I have stayed away so long?'

But it wasn't the way it used to be, Laurie tormented herself.

'Let me get the champagne,' she said suddenly and reached for the shortie nightie that lay across the foot of the bed.

'Okay, so we'll take a break,' he drawled. 'Do you have today's *New York Times* around?' he called after her as she walked to the door.

'Yeah. You want to read the news *now*?' She turned around curiously.

'I was driving a Citroën in Paris. It was great. I want to see if the New York City dealer advertises.'

'You're going to try to buy a Citroën? Your folks will spring for that?'

'I might push them into a little action. They know the kind of money I'll be making once we're out of training.' His smile was dazzling.

'Marty, is that all you think of?' She'd said that a lot of times in the past, but all at once she was revolted by his attitude. Fragments of conversation with Jeff darted across her mind. *A lot of people think doctors are money-grubbers. Why must we be in the top one-half of one per cent of earners in this country?*

'You pick up some strange ideas from that roommate of yours,' he drawled. 'In her field she can't do any better.

We can. We're going to break our butts till we're out there practising – but I mean to make up for every lousy, rotten minute. We've got skills people need – and they have to pay for them.' *How many times must she listen to him say that?*

'I don't think we're on the same wavelength, Marty.' She stared coldly at him. 'I want something more than a Citroën or a co-op on Park Avenue. I want the feeling I'm making a contribution on this earth.'

'You sound like a road company Mother Theresa,' he mocked, all at once hostile. He reached for the clump of clothes that lay on the floor beside the bed and began to dress. 'When you get your mind straightened out, call me.'

Laurie told herself she'd be so caught up in her first hospital rotation – with the traumatic responsibilities this involved – that she'd have little time to think about her break with Marty. She knew it was permanent. *How could she have been so blind?* No, she hadn't been blind, she taunted herself. She'd known what Marty was, but had been too infatuated to admit it. She'd scolded him over and over again about his attitude towards medicine as though he were a naughty little boy. But this summer – working with Jeff – she'd been pushed into blunt recognition.

She could live without Marty. She didn't need a man in her life. A woman in the medical profession was better off alone. There was no room in your life to be a *woman*. Even now, she worried about how she dressed when she was on the wards. If a woman dressed smartly, she didn't look *serious*.

A woman in medicine had to make a choice, she told herself. An occasional woman doctor could have it all – a career plus family. But the odds were against it. More than anything else in the world, she wanted to be a terrific pediatrician. She didn't need Marty. *She didn't need any man in her life.*

Tracy was sombre as they headed for Westchester to pick up the north-bound New York State Thruway – with David at the wheel of her car. They'd both expected more money from the sale of his car. Still, they'd manage, she reassured herself for the hundredth time.

'How long will it take us to reach Montreal?' she asked.

'About eight hours. Don't worry that it'll be so late when we arrive,' he added quickly. 'There're plenty of motels around.'

'But Expo 67 is open again this year,' she reminded him. 'There'll still be a lot of tourists up there.'

'If there're any problems, I have phone numbers to call. We won't have to sleep in the car.' He took a hand from the wheel to grope for hers. 'We've got lots of people on our side up there.'

David said McGill in Montreal was a great school – and they might get fellowships. Later, they'd figure out how to handle going back to school. But right now, they had to pull their lives together and get into a holding pattern.

With the Customs barrier into Canada still a hundred miles distant, Tracy on impulse suggested they spend the night on US soil, then drive up into Canada in the morning.

'Okay.' An unfamiliar wariness that seemed to mask alarm infiltrated his voice. 'You want to think some more before we become exiles?' Humour was meant to hide his unease.

'David, no!' She was shocked that he could suspect this. 'It's just that I want us to sleep together the whole way – without our rules – on home territory. It's kind of

416

like our wedding night.' She dropped her head onto his shoulder. 'So the ceremony will come later.'

'As soon as we can arrange it,' he said firmly. 'You make your mother and dad understand that.'

'So we'll stop at the first classy diner we see,' she ordered. 'We'll have burgers and coffee – no steaks,' she teased. 'Not on our budgets. Then we'll ask about the nearest Howard Johnson's.'

'Maybe we could skip the diner.' A sudden urgency in his voice now.

'No,' she insisted. 'You're going to need your strength.' She reached with one hand to stroke his thigh. 'And keep your eyes on the road!'

Vera struggled to hold on to her shaky semblance of acceptance. The three of them – she and Paul and Dad – had been waiting for the late-night TV news to come on when Laurie phoned and dropped her bomb.

'What are you going to do about it?' Joel demanded. 'Vera, go up to Montreal and find Tracy! Make her understand she can't ruin her life this way!'

'We can't do that, Dad,' Vera said gently. 'We have to respect her decisions.' But she was unnerved at the thought of Tracy in Canada. It wasn't like when she was at school – when she'd be coming home at intervals. 'She's not a child anymore.'

'She's behaving like a child,' Joel shot back. 'Paul, you have to do something. She can't stay up there in Montreal with that hippy!'

'David's not a hippy,' Paul said. 'That's a different breed. Along with a lot of others his age, he's grown up believing in values that he doesn't see his family – or much of our society – recognizing. He's insecure and rebellious.'

'God, Paul, how can you make excuses for them?' Joel shook his head in bewilderment. 'Your daughter runs off to Canada to live with a draft-dodger – and you make excuses for both of them? When will we see Tracy again?' A plaintive note of fear pushed through his belligerence.

'We've always known Tracy and David would be married.' Vera struggled for calm. 'They'll be married up in Montreal. We'll go up to see them regularly; it's only a four-hour drive from here. We have to let them work out their lives as they see fit.' *But why couldn't Tracy have called and told her what was happening? Why had she had to hear it from Laurie?*

'*You'll* go to Montreal to see them,' Joel told Vera and Paul. 'If my granddaughter wants to see me, she'll have to come to Eastwood.'

Tracy sat with a street map of Montreal spread across her lap while David drove at a slow pace along sun-splashed Dorchester Street in search of a tourist home for their first nights in Montreal – until they could locate permanently. She studied the paperback tourist guide they'd picked up in New York.

'What about this place?' she asked David. The past three houses they'd tried were at capacity, but the area offered a feast of tourist homes. It was close to 11:00 AM – probably check-out time.

'Is it listed?' David asked.

What he meant was, is it cheap? *He was so uptight about money*, she worried. 'Doubles are $8.00 a night. Of course, the book was published two years ago, and with Expo 67 the rates could be jumping.'

David pulled up before the rambling white house of indeterminate age. The sign out front indicated they could expect free parking, large rooms – either with private baths or hand basins – and there were TV sets for rent.

'It's not the Waldorf,' Tracy flipped, 'but it could be home for a few nights.'

418

They left the car and walked hand in hand towards the entrance. Mom and Dad must know by now, Tracy told herself. She'd said they were going out to visit a friend from school whose family had a beach house at Wainscott at the far end of Long Island. That they needed to unwind after the awfulness of the Chicago Convention. By now Laurie had called them.

The landlady was friendly but businesslike. She showed them the one double room still available. David winced at the $12.00 a night rental – but with people still coming in on vacation to see Expo 67, what else could they expect? Tracy reasoned.

They paid up front for two nights, then went out to park the car per instructions and brought their light gear to the house. Later, she'd ask Mom to ship more of her clothes and books and records up here, Tracy comforted herself. There was no way of knowing how long they'd have to stay. People back home were already talking about amnesty for draft-evaders, yet instinct warned her they could be here for a long haul.

'Let's go check with the group that'll help us find an apartment,' David said with an air of bravado. 'We have to get this show on the road.'

They left the house and returned to the car. It was so weird, Tracy thought, knowing they were in a foreign country and they *had* to stay here. It wasn't like those months at school in London. Then they'd known that come late July they'd be at Heathrow and waiting for their flight home.

'Let's play today.' Her smile managed to appear dazzling. 'It's our honeymoon. Didn't you register us as David and Tracy Marcus? So the ceremony comes later.'

'Okay.' He followed her lead. 'We'll go out to Expo 67. It's not a fair,' he reminded her, quoting the tour book. 'It's an exhibition. The city of Montreal literally created a new island to house it. We park and take the Metro out there,' he recalled. 'I hear it's real cool.'

Today they'd play. Tomorrow they'd get down to the business of being residents of Montreal. Tracy ordered herself to dismiss the truant doubts that tiptoed across her mind. How would they feel – six months or a year from now – about not being able to go home even for a weekend?

When would they be able to go home?

Chapter Thirty-six

Despite his efforts to conceal this, Vera knew Paul was as anxious as she about Tracy's future. Then, late in September, Tracy phoned to say that she and David were applying for admission to the graduate school at McGill University.

'We'll be able to start in the January term,' she said with clear enthusiasm. 'Would you believe it? After all David's swearing he wouldn't go to law school, that's what he's hoping to do. And I want a master's – at least – in education. How's that for a shocker?'

'Darling, it sounds wonderful,' Vera said with relief. 'But you'll need money. You and David will need money,' she amended. 'Dad and I will –'

'We'll be able to save some between now and January,' Tracy interrupted. 'And if we change from student visas to landed immigrant, then we'll be eligible for financial aid.'

'You keep your student visas,' Vera insisted. 'Dad and I will provide whatever financial aid you and David need.' Hadn't Tracy said she and David would be married 'somewhere along the way'? David was family.

'Hold on, Mom.' Tracy was in consultation with David. Vera waited impatiently. She knew it was absurd, but she didn't want them to be landed immigrants. That seemed so final. 'Mom?' Tracy returned to the phone.

'Yes, darling?' Vera's heart was pounding.

'I talked to David. He says you and Dad are wonderful – and he promises he'll pay you back some day. Thanks,

Mom,' she whispered. 'And let me thank Dad, too.'

A week later Tracy phoned to say that she and David had been married.

'By the rabbi of the oldest synagogue in Canada,' Tracy told her. Paul joined in on an extension in their bedroom. 'It was founded in Montreal in 1768. We thought about a civil ceremony, but we knew you and Dad – and Grandpa – would want us to have a religious ceremony. Don't bother telling David's family.' Hurt mingled with cynicism in her voice. 'His mother hung up on him the first time he tried to call from up here.'

'Neither of you need David's parents.' Paul joined the conversation. 'It's their loss – not yours.'

'Tell Grandpa we had our wedding dinner at Ben's Delicatessen. It's kind of a landmark here in Montreal. Great smoked beef sandwiches on rye, borscht, cheesecake, and tea. Tell him we went there because we knew it was a place he'd love – and we kind of felt as though he were sitting there with us.'

'I'll tell him,' Vera promised. She knew Tracy missed the special closeness she'd shared with her grandfather before he became so hostile to David.

'Tell him David's had a real haircut. He looks gorgeous.' Tracy suppressed an incipient giggle. 'I think he feels naked.'

A letter from Tracy early in November enlightened her parents on a most unusual situation in London – a city she knew they both loved.

'I just received this wild letter from Audrey.' Her roommate when she was at school in London, Vera recognized. 'I can't imagine something like this happening in London, but there was this really super long-planned Vietnam peace demonstration on Sunday, October 27. They were expecting 200,000 to show up. There had been two earlier ones, but nothing like this! Before it even happened, the newspapers were calling it the *October Revolution*. They said the National Gallery, the National Portrait Gallery, and the Tate Gallery would be closed that whole weekend. All the entrances to the Houses of Parliament would be sealed. The British transport police had cancelled weekend leaves and put everybody on standby. American troops in Great Britain – all twenty-six thousand – have orders to stay out of London.'

Vera paused, shook her head in dismay. 'It goes on and on. Can you believe this is happening in our London?'

'The whole world's changing,' Paul replied.

'The police in London aren't even armed,' Vera recalled. 'But perhaps that's good.' *Laurie would say that*, she thought involuntarily.

'What does Tracy say about the actual demonstration?' Paul prodded, and Vera returned to scan Tracy's long letter.

'Despite all the fears and preparations, I gather it was comparatively peaceful. Only about forty demonstrators and six policemen were injured – and nobody was seriously hurt. Forty-three people were arrested – eight of them students.'

'Vera, we ought to take a month off and visit London together. It was so important in our lives.' Paul's face was nostalgic. 'Maybe next summer?'

'I'd love to see London again. Just to walk the streets and know there'd be no bombs. To see all its beauty without the old fears.' Vera, too, was caught up in remembrance. 'When life is on a more even keel, we'll go back to London,' she promised. Yet in a corner of her mind she knew she couldn't go back to London with Paul. Going to see Tracy and David had been different. Going with Paul would be a walk into the past. It would shove her back into years she couldn't bear to face – the years in Copenhagen, the horror of *Kristallnacht*.

Vera was especially conscious of Tracy's absence with the approach of Thanksgiving. While *she* was free to come home, Vera knew she'd never leave David alone on Thanksgiving. Holidays must be poignant occasions for the kids who'd run from the draft to live in Canada, she thought compassionately. She brushed from her mind Mary O'Brien's bitter accusation a few days ago. *How can folks talk about amnesty for those draft-dodgers – when boys like my son lie dead in Vietnam?* Though the bitter-cold weather was on its way, she and Paul should fly up to Montreal to spend a weekend with Tracy and David. Maybe next month, she thought with a flurry of anticipation.

On Thanksgiving morning, Doris came over immediately after breakfast to help with the dinner preparations – always prepared by family now. Paul was upstairs, finishing up an article for the small magazine that was publishing him regularly. His father had gone to help a local group deliver Thanksgiving baskets to several elderly shut-ins. Later Phil and Neal would arrive. There was a soothing quietness about the house on occasions like this, Vera thought sentimentally.

'Who's this fellow Laurie's bringing home?' Doris questioned, settling down to a cup of coffee with Vera, a provocative glint in her eyes.

'Doris, I warned you,' Vera reminded good-humouredly. 'Laurie wanted it understood Jeff is a good *friend*. No romance,' she emphasized. 'He's a fellow med student who was going to be alone on Thanksgiving – and you know Laurie. Right away she ordered him to come home with her.'

'What about the other fellow – the one you said used to call her from Paris?'

'Laurie never let on there was anything serious – and I never dared pry.' Always Vera felt herself on thin ice with Laurie – loved but not *liked*. 'But that was summer before last. This past summer – the little while she was home – there were no calls. But don't you make any bright remarks.'

'I won't. I promise.'

'I've been getting all that garbage from her about how there's no room in a woman med student's life for romance. All she thinks about is finishing med school and going on into her residency.' Vera sighed. 'I know, women are pushing off marriage these days. I know that plenty of women lead happy, successful lives without a man.' She managed a wry smile. 'I've read all those feminist articles you shove at me.'

'But you want grandchildren,' Doris joshed. 'Hey, look how long I'm going to have to wait – and I'm almost eight years older than you.'

'Of course, Jeff's name creeps into the conversation a lot,' Vera conceded. 'But then, these days, women can have close men friends without a physical attraction being involved. She keeps saying he thinks a lot the way she does.'

'Un-hunh.' Doris nodded knowingly.

'Doris, knock it off.' But truant hope welled in Vera. To her, happiness meant *family*. She yearned to see her daughters with husbands and children. At least, Tracy was halfway there. Though Dad was unhappy about Tracy's marriage, she and Paul were pleased.

By late morning Phil had arrived with Neal, Paul had come downstairs, and Joel had returned from delivering the baskets. They gathered in the den to watch the Macy's Thanksgiving Day Parade because this had become a ritual for Neal, who had to be constantly urged to sit an acceptable distance from the screen. 'Why do all kids think they have to climb into the set?' Joel had complained good-humouredly through the years – first with Laurie and Tracy, now with Neal.

Neal was such a darling boy, Vera thought. They were all inclined to spoil him, though Doris warned against this. Phil was enthralled that Neal had asked for piano lessons and was already showing promise.

Just past noon, Paul left the house to drive to the Saratoga railroad station to meet Laurie and Jeff. Almost on sight, Vera decided she liked Jeff Green. He was warm, bright, compassionate. And he was fascinated when Paul talked about Dr Evans and the reverence with which the ageing doctor was held in Eastwood.

'Dr Evans is a holdover from another era,' Joel told him with obvious affection. 'He's been in this town for forty-eight years. Other doctors came and went – Dr Evans belonged to us.'

In a flurry of high spirits, the three women brought the traditional Thanksgiving dinner to the table. Yet Vera was pointedly aware of Tracy's absence. Laurie knew not to ask about Tracy and David in her grandfather's presence. That would just bring on a tirade of recrimination. Yet Vera suspected that her father-in-law was having fresh doubts about the Vietnam war – and that he was troubled by this. It was not in what he said – it was the way he looked when they watched TV news programmes.

Nixon – who'd won the election by the slimmest margin since 1912, narrower even than his loss to JFK in 1960 – talked about carrying out his campaign promise to end the war in Vietnam. It was now the longest war in American history, and Americans were increasingly disenchanted. Once the war was over, Vera thought with shaky optimism, the president would offer amnesty to the thousands of draft-evaders who'd sought sanctuary in Canada and Sweden and other countries. *Wouldn't he?*

The conversation at the dinner table was peppered with reminiscences of other Thanksgivings. Jeff talked poignantly about the Thanksgivings that he'd been allowed to spend with his grandparents. Paul remembered Thanks-givings in Europe during World War II. *Hell, there was no way we could eat Spam and pretend it was turkey.* Vera and Paul recalled a Thanksgiving they'd shared in war-torn, ration-racked London.

While the three women served pecan pie and coffee, the men discussed the need in this country for a national health insurance programme.

'We're the only industrialized country on this planet – except for South Africa – that doesn't provide its people with guaranteed health care. And what we offer people without money is so damned demeaning,' Jeff said urgently. 'Decent health care should be the right of every person in this country.'

'There's too much waste,' Phil said. 'Too much inef-ficiency.'

'But when people talk about changing the system, they don't mean better treatment,' Jeff pointed out, his voice deepening with contempt. 'They're only talking about saving money.'

'When I was a kid,' Phil reminisced, 'people thought about hospitals as being institutions of mercy. They've become big business.'

'Truman fought for national health insurance – to be funded by payroll deductions. But the plan got nowhere, though he kept trying for years,' Joel recalled. 'But at least Johnson pushed Medicare through. Senior citizens are grateful for that.'

'But what about the rest of the population?' Jeff asked with impatience. 'Don't they –'

'Enough shop talk,' Doris interrupted, sitting down at the table again. 'If anybody wants seconds of pie, there's a whole pecan we haven't even started.'

Involuntarily Vera remembered that Tracy always took seconds of pecan pie. Where were Tracy and David right now? *They must be homesick*, she thought in anguish – *so far away from home and family on this special holiday.* All those kids who couldn't bring themselves to fight an immoral war. *She and Paul would go up to Montreal to see Tracy and David late next month*, she resolved. Maybe between Christmas and New Year's – when everything was slow with the business.

On Friday morning Vera came awake slowly, conscious of the comforting sounds of heat coming up in the radiators. She felt a surge of contentment. Laurie was home. She and Jeff would be returning to school on Sunday evening, but for now she was here. Her mind hurtled back through the years to that day in October 1944 when Paul had arrived at their London apartment on a five-day leave. It was the first time he saw Laurie. Oh yes, a few days could be very precious when they brought loved ones together.

She heard the sound of water running in the bathroom. Paul was showering. Through the years of teaching, he'd acquired the habit of rising early. Another few minutes here under the blankets, she promised herself, then she'd get up.

When she and Paul arrived at the breakfast table, they found her father-in-law and Jeff already there – in lively conversation over steaming cups of coffee. Laurie would be sleeping late, she surmised indulgently.

'I'm taking Jeff over to meet Dr Evans,' Joel announced in rare high spirits. Sometimes Vera worried that Paul and Doris had encouraged him to withdraw from the business the way he had. He kept up all his civic activities, but often she felt he was enduring a rudderless existence. 'You know how Doc is always moaning about the new crop of doctors . . . how they're all after fancy, big city or rich suburban practices, when small towns and rural areas are crying for new doctors.'

'You'll like Dr Evans,' Vera assured Jeff. But in a corner of her mind she questioned Joel's motive for taking Jeff to meet Dr Evans. He was harbouring some sweet hope that – once Jeff finished medical school and his residency – he would come to Eastwood to share Dr Evans' practice. Dr Evans was a good doctor and a wonderful man. Nobody here in town wanted to consider that one day – only a few years hence – the years would catch up with him.

Arriving at the house from the office at the end of the working day, Vera heard voices in the den. She found the three men and Laurie – as she'd expected – watching the six o'clock news on television. She sat down to join them. At the commercial break, Joel switched the volume to a murmur and turned to her.

'Guess what we fixed up,' he said jubilantly. 'For the school's intercession Jeff's coming to stay with us. He's going to spend those weeks working with Dr Evans. What Doc calls real *hands-on* experience. These two guys were made for each other.'

Involuntarily Vera turned to Laurie. Her throat tightened in alarm. Laurie was upset that Jeff would be here in the house for almost a month. All at once she understood – as Laurie did. *Dad was trying to play matchmaker between Laurie and Jeff.* If there could have been anything – and deep in her heart she'd harboured a wistful hope – he'd just destroyed that chance.

Vera and Paul decided to drive to Montreal – as she had planned – in the interim between Christmas and New Year's. It was a perfect time, they agreed. Laurie and Jeff would be at the house with Dad. Though his health was good, they worried about his frequent depressions.

Doris had tried to talk to him about seeing a therapist, but he'd erupted in rage. Still, Dad was enjoying Jeff's presence at the house, Vera told herself – the little time he was there. Jeff spent most of his daytime hours and even some evenings with Dr Evans.

Dad warned them they might be caught in a heavy Canadian snowstorm this time of year.

'The highways are kept in great shape,' Paul said optimistically. 'We can drive up in five hours.'

They were in the car by eight o'clock on departure morning, anticipated arriving in Montreal in time for a late lunch. Expecting harsh winter winds and biting cold, they dressed accordingly, though they knew that much of Montreal's population found it possible to live an almost subterranean life in the months when the temperature plummeted to staggering lowness. Tracy had written with awe about Underground Montreal, which roamed for two-and-a-half miles and offered a dazzling array of boutiques, grocery stores, restaurants, a church, a discotheque, and a Metro station.

They arrived in Montreal to feel only a mild breeze that carried a hint of rain.

'Can you believe it?' Paul marvelled while they listened to a local weather report on the car radio. 'It's 38 degrees!'

'Let's find the hotel,' Vera said, impatient to see Tracy. 'The kids will be waiting for us there.' She'd rejected their offer to relinquish their bedroom to spend three nights in sleeping bags.

Astonished by the lack of traffic congestion – because Montreal separated pedestrians, cars, and electric trains – they followed Tracy's instructions and arrived at the elegant Queen Elizabeth on Dorchester Boulevard. With the car in parking facilities, they sought out the palatial black-marble-pillared lobby of the *Queen E* – as Tracy had referred to it.

'Oh God, Paul, will we ever find them here?' Vera said in sudden panic as she viewed the busy area.

'Mom!' Tracy's voice reached her and she spied a waving hand.

'There they are!' Clutching their over-sized valise in one hand, Paul reached for Vera's arm with the other.

'Mom, you're really here!' Vera saw the relief in her younger daughter's eyes as they clung together. 'It seems like forever!'

Tracy turned to embrace her father while David and her mother exchanged a warm hug.

'Let me take your luggage.' Almost shy in this first encounter as a son-in-law, David reached for Paul's valise.

'You're probably starving,' Tracy effervesced. 'Get registered, send up your luggage, and let's go somewhere for lunch.'

'Somewhere very special,' Vera decreed, rejoicing in this reunion. Yet already she had concluded that Tracy was lonely – not happy – in this self-imposed exile. She remembered her own first months in Copenhagen. She'd loved the Munches, was so grateful for their kindness – but had felt such desolation at living in a strange country.

After a brief consultation with David, Tracy decided that they would lunch at Le Café – one of eleven restaurants within the huge hotel complex.

'From there we can go straight to the Place Ville Marie,' she explained with an almost hysterical gaiety. 'That's the Underground Montreal that I wrote you about. We don't have to go out into the street – there's a direct indoor passageway.'

Tracy and David had managed to take the day off from their respective jobs – though they'd be leaving shortly to begin graduate studies at McGill. They were determined to show Vera and Paul as much as was humanly possible today. They visited the Place Ville Marie – where Vera was awed by the network of escalators. In the

Underground – all of which had been completed only within the past four years – they boarded a Metro for their next destination. Vera and Paul were impressed by the blue-and-white Metro cars, which rolled along in awesome quietness and were devoid of the graffiti so familiar in the New York City subway system.

In the light, late-afternoon drizzle they admired the Montreal skyline, pierced in recent years by a series of high-rises.

'The Stock Exchange wanted to build a fifty-seven-storey skyscraper, but the city planning department would only allow forty-seven,' David told them. 'And they only allow construction on 40% of the land, so they'll never have those huge clusters of tall towers like in New York.'

Vera was touched by Tracy and David's insistence that they have dinner *at home*. It was as though, she thought lovingly, they wanted to convince Paul and her that they had a real home here in Montreal. The apartment was tiny but cheerful. The four carried on lively conversation while together Tracy and David prepared a substantial, tasty meal.

'Where did you two learn to cook like this?' Paul asked in genuine admiration.

Tracy giggled. 'We used something called a cookbook. It's real easy if you pay attention.'

The three days in Montreal sped past. Vera and Paul took photographs of the ancient synagogue where Tracy and David had been married. They drove to the top of Mount Royal to gaze down at the winding St Lawrence and to visit historic St Joseph's Oratory. They saw both Old Montreal and the exciting modern Montreal. They visited McGill University – austere structures of brick and Quebec grey stone, campus elms stark and forbidding. Yet the sprawling university grounds – surrounded by the

432

city – seemed an oasis of quiet in the midst of urban bustle.

Vera constantly was conscious of American young men – some with wives and babies – who'd come here in flight from the draft. They were lonely, she thought compassionately. They missed family and home. And Canadian culture was slightly different – more formal, more conservative.

On their fourth morning in Montreal – overcast and with a serious drop in temperature – Vera and Paul headed back for Eastwood. They'd shared a bittersweet breakfast with Tracy and David before retrieving their car. Tracy's last words lingered in Vera's mind. *Mom, come up again soon. Montreal's not really that far from Eastwood.*

Tracy had contrived a few moments of whispered conference with her before breakfast. Paul's fiftieth birthday was approaching, and Tracy wished advice about an appropriate birthday present. *At this point*, Vera thought grimly, *it would probably be wisest just to forget the birthday.*

Paul had made rueful remarks in the last weeks about reaching fifty with few accomplishments to show for those years. So he wasn't earning much money from his writing – he was building up a following, gaining respect in the educational community. That should count for a lot. And even his counselling draft-evaders had lost its sting with so many Americans convinced that the action in Vietnam was a tremendous error.

'It looks as though the sun's going to break through.' Paul intruded on her introspection. 'That's a good omen.'

'The good omen,' Vera said with unfamiliar brusqueness, 'is when President Nixon keeps his promise to pull our troops out of Vietnam.' She paused, took a laboured breath. 'And when he announces amnesty for the kids who ran to Canada and Sweden.'

'Tracy and David are going back to school,' he pointed out gently. 'That's a good omen for the future.'

'But when will they be allowed to come back home?' Her voice was taut with anguish. 'Tracy's so lonely up there.'

Paul hesitated. 'It was a choice she made, Vera.'

'Because she's so loyal to David. But she's miserable.'

'Did she say that?' Paul challenged.

'Couldn't you feel it?' Of course he could. His eyes told her so. 'It broke my heart to say goodbye. Leaving her up there in a strange country when she wants so much to come home.'

'Nothing in life comes without a price tag. Tracy made a decision. All those American kids up in Canada knew what they were doing.'

'I know what it's like to live in exile.' A bitterness that had long lain buried in Vera's subconscious pushed through the surface. 'I remember.'

'Tracy's not living in exile.'

'What else can you call it?' Vera shot back, attacked by memories of Copenhagen, of the loneliness of a London without Paul.

Paul's hands tightened on the wheel. 'She went up there of her own volition. She's with David. She hasn't lost her family. This isn't a rehash of *Kristallnacht*. For God's sake, Vera, when are you going to learn to let go of the past?'

Vera sat very still and silent. As with all husbands and wives, she and Paul had argued on occasions through the years. They'd been through heated battles. But she had never heard that undertone of resentment directed at her before.

Paul was upset, she tried to comfort herself. He didn't

mean to be nasty. He worried about the flood of draft-age boys he'd counselled. Many of them had gone to Canada. He was asking himself if he had done the right thing.

She wasn't living in the past, she told herself defensively. Yet her mind taunted her with the knowledge that each time Laurie or Tracy went off to school, she felt a terrifying sense of loss. She dreaded the day when Laurie or Tracy would settle permanently in a town or city away from Eastwood. It would be as though she were losing her family for a second time.

Every day of her existence on this planet, she lived with the agonizing memory of hovering behind the closed door of the Schmidts' flat while she listened to the shouting on the floor above, heard her father's rebellious retorts to the SS troopers as he and Mama and Ernst were being dragged down the stairs and off into the night. To their deaths.

Without being aware of it, was she being blind to Paul's needs? *Was she in danger of losing him, too? Was it to come to pass as in her nightmares? Was she once again meant to lose those nearest and dearest to her?*

Chapter Thirty-seven

By spring Laurie was already worrying about where she would spend her internship and residency. She meant to heed Jeff's advice to try for a big-city hospital – *where you experience every kind of medical emergency*. An inner-city hospital, she'd narrowed this down, where interns and residents were desperately needed.

Along with Jeff, she was experiencing all the frustrations of a third-year medical student. This was the year of unpredictability. The year when both admitted to a guilt that they were, in truth, using patients to further their own knowledge. And always they were conscious of a feeling of inadequacy.

On this early April morning, Laurie awoke with an instant realization that this was Adele's twenty-fifth birthday. They went through their usual 'happy birthday' routine, then hurried off in their separate directions. Laurie had already plotted with Jeff – providing no emergency arose in conflict – to bring home Chinese take-out and a small birthday cake as a surprise party for Adele.

She was on medical rotation. This was the rotation that filled her with the most insecurity. Here the patients in her care were mostly elderly and she was struggling to cope with putting IVs into fragile and delicate skin. She felt a stab of remorse each time a patient winced in pain.

Early on her rounds she was grateful that today seemed less horrendous than yesterday. And then she went into the room of a woman who had been admitted three days earlier. A vital, vivacious woman about her grandfather's age and with whom she'd felt an instant rapport. Right away she understood that something sombre had occurred. Her doctor and a resident were involved in a work-up. She appeared close to tears. Laurie crossed to take her hand, smiled reassuringly. That was expected of a third-year medical student. But while the doctor and resident continued their work-up, the woman lifted her face to Laurie's.

'It's cancer, they told me.' Her voice choked. 'They can't operate.'

Laurie's hand tightened on the patient's. Tears spilled over and poured down her cheeks. *A doctor was not supposed to cry.*

At the end of the relentlessly long day, Laurie hurried to meet Jeff as pre-arranged.

'Okay, you made it,' he said exuberantly, then paused. 'Rough day?'

'I did the unforgivable,' she told him in a tortured whisper. 'I cried when a patient told me she was going to die.'

'Let's get out of here,' he said gently.

Walking through the balmy early evening, they talked about the special problems ahead of them.

'I couldn't stand the callous attitude of that doctor,' Laurie admitted. 'And I know he's a good doctor. I've seen him be so kind with patients. But he just walked away and left this woman with the resident and me.'

'He knew he couldn't do any more for her,' Jeff pointed out. 'He went on to his next patient. And residents –' Jeff's smile was rueful. 'Residents don't have time to be compassionate.'

'If I can't be compassionate, I don't want to be a doctor,' Laurie said angrily, tears welling in her eyes again.

'Knock it off,' Jeff ordered. 'We have to learn to take the bad with the good. Right now we have a birthday party to organize.'

The phone was ringing in the apartment when Laurie unlocked the door. Jeff balanced the bags from the Chinese take-out restaurant with the minuscule birthday cake they'd bought at Cake Master's. With the door open, Laurie rushed to pick up the phone. The caller was Adele.

'Hi.' Adele's voice came to her in that special tone that said she'd run up against problems at school. 'I called to warn you not to expect me home for dinner. I'll grab a hamburger and coffee here at school. We're having a meeting that'll probably go on until ten or eleven – with some irate politicians.'

'Oh, Adele. On your birthday?' Laurie was exasperated.

'If you brought home Chinese, save some for me. I'll need resuscitation.'

Laurie and Jeff dug into dinner with an effort at enthusiasm. The leftovers went into the refrigerator.

'We'll light the birthday candles, eat a chunk of cake, and toast Adele with coffee,' Jeff ordered. 'We'll save a piece of cake for Adele, of course.'

Jeff knew she felt miserable, Laurie thought. And she'd seen him cut up over a lost patient, she remembered. But he hadn't cried with his patient.

'If Adele is going to put in all the crazy hours plus the headaches she has with teaching, she might as well have gone to medical school,' he joked. 'At least, she'd be seeing decent money at the end of the trail.'

'Adele isn't in teaching for the money,' Laurie shot back.

'And I'm not in medicine for the money,' Jeff retorted.

'I didn't mean it like that,' Laurie apologized. 'I'm just so damn tired. I feel so helpless. Like today with that sweet woman at the hospital. She came in so perky and in love with life.' Her voice dropped to a whisper. 'And I felt so helpless.'

'Doctors can help only up to a point,' Jeff began and stopped short as tears spilled onto her cheeks. 'Honey, you can't make the whole world well and happy.'

All at once she was in Jeff's arms, and he was murmuring endearments. He lifted her face to his, brought his mouth down to hers. Almost in a trance she responded.

'What are we doing?' she asked breathlessly when his mouth left hers, his arms still holding her close.

'What I've wanted to do for such a long time.'

'This is crazy, you know.' But she wanted him to hold her. She wanted him to make love to her.

'So let's be crazy,' he whispered.

Laurie brushed away reality, abandoned herself to emotion. She uttered a faint chuckle of amused derision when he lifted her in his arms, then almost tripped over the coffee table in his impatience to carry her into the bedroom.

'Jeff, what about the door?' she asked in sudden alarm minutes later – after they'd explored each other's nakedness with sensuous pleasure.

'You always lock and put on the chain the minute you come in,' he reminded. 'And Adele's at a meeting.'

'I wouldn't want Margie next door to barge in to borrow coffee,' she said huskily.

'This is our own private world,' he promised, moving with her in passionate rhythm. 'Forget about Margie, forget about Adele, forget about the hospital . . .'

At last they lay motionless, legs entangled, his face against hers.

'I knew it would be great. But not this great,' he said with an air of exultant exhaustion.

'It was crazy.' *How had it happened?* But Laurie was conscious of a feeling of total relaxation.

'Crazy,' he acknowledged.

'There's no future in this,' she warned. 'Nothing permanent.'

'I know,' he agreed. 'We've got our futures plotted for years ahead. Another year of med school, four years of residency. I head for a small-town practice, you to a ghetto hospital. We'll be worlds apart. But for now,' he said quietly, 'we can have something we both need to help us through the training period. No ties. No obligations.'

'And we can still be friends?' Laurie persisted. 'You and Adele are my very best friends in this world.'

'We can still be friends,' he promised and pulled himself above her again. 'But for now, will you please shut up?' he pleaded lovingly. 'More action and less words.'

On a mid-April Friday – with the first signs of spring on display in Eastwood – Vera and Paul headed for Montreal for a three-day weekend with Tracy and David. Vera had tried futilely to persuade Joel to go up with them.

'If Tracy wants to see me, let her come to Eastwood,' he said. '*She* can come home if she likes,' he emphasized.

But he'd self-consciously prepared a *care package* for her: A collection of edible goodies he knew Tracy adored. And they took with them, also, the news that Doris and Phil would be going up with Neal for a week as soon as school closed.

'Let's don't mention that we're working with a group that's petitioning Congress for an amnesty bill,' Paul warned when they stopped in a diner for coffee. 'We mustn't give them false hopes.'

'That's all you think it is – false hopes?' *She hadn't meant to sound hostile*, she thought guiltily. *Why were she and Paul bickering so much these days*?

'Not false,' he corrected himself. 'Just that it could be a long time in coming.'

'Tracy's not going to admit it, but I *know* she's homesick. I hear it in her voice every time we speak on the phone. I feel so helpless.'

'Vera, you can't fix everything.' She was conscious of a hint of impatience in his voice. *Because he was uptight – about Vietnam, about the state of education in this country,* she told herself. *When would he learn to unwind?* 'Right now, Tracy and David are focused on their schooling,' he went on determinedly. 'That's important.'

'I wish we could persuade her to come home for a week or two this summer.' Vera sighed. 'There's no real reason why she can't. And Dad would be so pleased.'

'She's not going to leave David. And there's nothing you can do to make Dad approve of her running off to Canada.'

She shouldn't have mentioned the barrier between Dad and Tracy, Vera reproached herself. It had made him remember his own tenuous situation with Dad. All his life Paul had been so eager to please his father. How could she make Paul understand he *wasn't* a failure?

By the time they approached Canadian Customs, the weather had turned blustery and cold. Ominous clumps of clouds hovered in the sky.

'Snow by nightfall,' Paul predicted while they waited for the always-swift clearance at Customs.

'This late in April?' Vera lifted an eyebrow in doubt.

'In Canada, yes,' he reminded. 'But the roads will be cleared by the time we leave.'

On their arrival in Montreal, they went directly to the hotel, registered, then headed for Tracy and David's apartment. They let themselves in with the key Tracy had mailed and prepared to wait for the other two to arrive from their respective classes.

'Why don't I run down to the deli near here?' Paul suggested. 'I'll pick up dinner makings. We'll eat in the

441

apartment. No need to run around in this weather.'
Already snow was beginning to fall.

Moments after Paul left, Vera was startled by the ringing of the phone. She hesitated a moment, then reached
for the receiver.

'Hello.'

'Vera, I couldn't wait to tell you!' Doris's voice was
electric. 'Dad was just talking with one of his buddies
who follows everything in Congress – and he said that
Congressman Koch from New York City has introduced
a bill that'll offer amnesty for draft-evaders. All criminal
prosecutions will be wiped off the slate. If it goes through,
David and Tracy can come home!'

'I don't understand.' Vera forced herself to be realistic.
'They're still drafting men.'

'The way Dad understands it, there'll be a new
interpretation of CO status. If a draftee can prove he's
opposed to a particular war on moral or philosophical
grounds, then he'll be classified as a CO and will do
noncombatant or civilian service for two years.
Even those in jail or pending criminal prosecution will
be eligible for this. Of course, it hasn't been passed
yet.'

'What are its chances?' Vera asked. *Dad had told Doris
about the bill,* her mind computed. *Dad was so anxious
for Tracy to come home.*

'Who can tell?' Doris admitted and paused. 'Phil
doesn't think it'll be passed. But at least, people are thinking in that direction. Not just little groups like yours, but
those right up there in Congress.'

'I'll tell the kids,' Vera said after a moment. 'But they'll
understand it's just the first efforts.' *Amnesty. What a
beautiful word.*

Over huge pastrami sandwiches and mounds of cole-
slaw and potato salad, Vera and Paul discussed the Koch

bill with Tracy and David. Only now did they drop their masks and admit to yearnings to go home.

'Sure, some of the guys – and their wives – say they don't want to go back until the whole society in the United States changes,' David said seriously. 'But most of those we know – like ourselves – are dying to go home.'

As Paul had feared, the Koch bill did not go through, though Koch made it clear this was not the end of his efforts. Vera and Paul felt encouraged when on June 8, President Nixon announced that, by the end of August, 25,000 US troops would be withdrawn from Vietnam.

'That's the beginning of the end,' Paul said enthusiastically.

'From your mouth to God's ear,' Vera whispered, borrowing a phrase learned years ago from Fiona.

Vera was in high spirits when Laurie came home for a week at the end of school and brought Jeff and Adele with her. Now she learned that Jeff would remain in Eastwood for the summer – living at the Kahn house at Joel's insistence – while Laurie returned to work at the Harlem clinic again. Adele would be involved in a Harlem project for inner-city children. For a breathtaking few hours – on their first arrival – she'd convinced herself that the relationship between Laurie and Jeff had deepened beyond friendship.

'I tell you, Jeff's sure to come back here to go into practice with Doc Evans,' Joel confided with satisfaction. 'Now why can't Laurie see the light and team up with him?' A glint in his eyes said he meant more than a professional arrangement. *But Laurie and Jeff were pulled in opposite directions.*

Vera focused on making this week a warm and loving occasion. Even Dad, she thought with relief, seemed to be emerging from his constant depression. He'd watched

Adele grow up; she was like family. He took pleasure in listening to the earnest discussions between Adele and Paul about the future of American education.

'Paul, you think you know what it's like teaching in a ghetto school,' Adele told him on the evening before she and Laurie were to return to New York. Earlier there had been a family dinner. Doris and Phil had left with Neal because it was now past his bedtime. Jeff had gone on a house-call with Dr Evans. Laurie was in the kitchen preparing a late round of coffee. The others gathered in the den for more conversation. 'You have to be there to know. We spend almost 70% of our time just trying to keep order in the classroom. We're constantly on the watch to defuse violence. And the traffic in drugs is not getting better – it's getting worse. Oh, sure,' she drawled, faintly teasing. 'You're having problems even here. Doris told me how the kids are fighting against the new dress codes.'

'That's not what worries me in our schools, Adele. It's the quality of the education. This is not a rich suburban community. We're dealing here with serious budget cuts. We have a few dedicated teachers in the system; they go out and buy supplies with their own money because they can't bear to see the kids cheated.'

'The kids in Eastwood come to school prepared to learn,' Adele said with quiet intensity. 'Ghetto kids arrive with few of the skills they need to make it in the school world. God knows, some of us try – but it's not enough.'

'I think that the unsung heroes of this country are our school-teachers,' Vera said softly. 'Teachers like you two.' She turned from Adele to Paul. 'Because you care and you're trying to make the system better. You're making a contribution.' She paused. 'Sometimes I envy you.'

Joel seemed startled. Dismayed. 'Vera, you're a successful woman. You're head of a major business. You should envy no one.'

'I think that I've always felt guilty that I'm alive.' Vera spoke compulsively – from the heart. 'I stood by while my mother and father and brother were marched off to their deaths – and I did nothing.'

'Vera, you were thirteen years old. What could you have done?' Paul challenged.

'You've been a fine wife and mother. You've been the centre of this family,' Joel declared. 'You've made the business successful beyond my fondest dreams.'

'I didn't mean to sound maudlin,' Vera apologized, all at once self-conscious. *Why had she said that?* 'It's just that today is my parents' wedding anniversary. Every year I remember. It was always such a joyous celebration in our house.'

Paul reached for her hand. 'As *our* anniversary is in *this* house.' Walking into the den with a tray of coffee-filled mugs, Laurie smiled at this show of affection.

'You talk about making a contribution, Vera.' Joel reached for a mug of coffee, rose to his feet as though propelled by a need for action. 'You're doing that. Kahns have been in business in this town for five generations. We've been there to serve when our country needed us – going back to the Civil War. We –'

'Grandpa, if there were no guns, there could be no wars,' Laurie broke in passionately. 'There'd be less crime. There'd –'

'Laurie, grow up!' Joel bristled. 'Guns help keep the peace. They –'

'Like now, with half-a-million Americans fighting in Vietnam?' she demanded. 'With more than 33,000 dead and many more wounded? With no guns, Tracy wouldn't be hiding away with David in Canada!'

'Stop it, you two!' Vera was pale, her voice strident.

445

She was aware of Paul's supplicating glance in her direction, but she couldn't let Dad and Laurie stand here and tear each other apart. 'We don't have to agree on everything.' She was struggling for calm. 'Dad's entitled to his opinions, Laurie. And Dad, we have to respect Laurie's opinions. Now no more talk about guns.'

But her family was divided, she told herself in anguish. *How could she ever bring them back together again?*

Chapter Thirty-eight

Vera was touched by Joel's pleasure at having Jeff in the house for the summer, though in truth most of his waking hours were spent in Dr Evans' company. Then, over the Fourth of July weekend, Joel confided that he was launching a secret campaign.

'Next June, Doc Evans will have been serving this town fifty years. Let's have a surprise banquet in his honour. Isn't it time we told him how much he's loved and appreciated in this town?'

'Dad, I think it's a wonderful idea.' Tears filled her eyes. Almost everybody in Eastwood had a special story to tell about Dr Evans. 'But I don't know how long you'll be able to keep it a secret.'

'I'm setting up a committee. You and Doris will be on it. Another eight or ten people from different walks of life.' Joel radiated excitement. 'I know it's a long way off, but this has to be something spectacular. Maybe we can have it in the school gym. What do you think?'

Now Vera and Joel debated the initial steps in arranging for the banquet. When Paul arrived home from delivering a talk to a parent/teacher organization in a nearby community, he joined enthusiastically in the discussion. *This would be so good for Dad*, Vera told herself. The family had worried about his depression in these last months. This would pull him out of it.

Again this summer Paul talked to Vera about their going to London for two or three weeks in the early fall. *When the tourist hordes will be gone.* But – fighting guilt that she was keeping him from something he yearned to do – she pointed out that she couldn't take off more than three or four days from the business. Besides, going to London with Paul was an unnerving prospect – a journey into the past that she was afraid to face.

'We'll be going up to Montreal at the end of the month,' she hedged. 'We promised the kids that we'd see Expo 67 with them.' For the third year, Expo 67 was open to the public.

Doris and Phil would be driving up next month. Tracy was hurt and disappointed that her grandfather refused to visit, though he often talked with her on the telephone. He never asked about David. It was as though she were away at school and alone. He was proud that she was at McGill. Impatient to earn graduate degrees, both Tracy and David were taking summer classes.

On a steamy night in late August, Vera came home after a late conference at the office to find Paul and Joel in the den, sitting on the edge of their chairs while they watched a news bulletin on TV.

'Vera, you won't believe what happened!' Joel's face was flushed, his shoulders hunched in shock. 'A United States infantry company in the Rice Bowl –' Vietnam, she understood, '– just refused direct orders to advance! For hours,' he stressed, 'until some veteran with his head on straight convinced them they had to fight!'

'They'd been fighting a hellish battle for five days,' Paul reproached. 'And now they were expected to go into a labyrinth of North Vietnamese bunkers to bring out the bodies of Americans killed in a helicopter crash?'

'But whoever heard of an American soldier refusing to obey an order?' Joel blustered. 'Would *you* have done it? No!'

'In World War II, we knew we were fighting against horrible evil. The whole world saw Hitler as a menace to

448

humanity. Those kids in Vietnam – and most of them are kids,' Paul interjected, '– they *know* the crap we've fed them about fighting for democracy in Vietnam was a crock of shit. They're angry that American leaders have been lying to them. Sure, in the beginning a lot of them felt they were fighting to save the world from Communism, but that didn't last long.'

'How do you know all this?' Joel challenged defensively.

'It's like we've talked about before.' Vera contrived an aura of calm. 'Six years ago even liberals like Al Gore and George McGovern and Gene McCarthy were in favour of our going into Vietnam, but then they realized there is no democracy in Vietnam.'

'Dad, the world agrees that the North Vietnamese were responsible for the terrorism and guerrilla war in South Vietnam,' Paul continued. 'But Ngo Dinh Diem became an oppressive dictator. The US government urged him to change his policies. He refused. Then –'

'I know all this,' Joel interrupted impatiently, yet Vera sensed a new defensiveness in him. 'He and his brother were assassinated by the military *junta*. The new government abolished martial law, promised free elections later.'

'Dad, the South Vietnamese government has gone through a series of changes, but it remains a dictatorship. Innocent civilians – children, women, old men – are being butchered for no reason. *We don't belong there.*'

'I don't want to talk about it anymore.' Joel was brusque. 'Enough already.'

Yet Vera took hope in her suspicion that her father-in-law was at last feeling doubts about the American presence in Vietnam.

Vera looked forward to Laurie's coming home for a few days before the beginning of the new school-year, her final

449

year in med school. She was disappointed when Laurie cut her stay short by two days with vague talk about needing to get reoriented in the school routine.

Would the wall between Laurie and herself – and Laurie and Dad – ever be abolished? she asked herself in recurrent anguish. She knew what would make the difference. All she had to tell Laurie was that she and Dad had decided to close down Kahn Firearms Company – that henceforth, they'd operate only the mail-order catalogue and the chain of shops. *No guns on sale in the shops.* But to lay Kahn Firearms to rest would destroy Dad.

With a sense of loss Vera watched from the porch as Laurie and Jeff settled themselves in the old-model but still reliable Dodge that Dr Evans had insisted on giving Jeff as a reward for his summer work. Already she was impatient for the Thanksgiving weekend, when they'd be home. Already, she admonished herself, she was thinking of Jeff as a son-in-law when both Laurie and Jeff were frank about scheduling their futures in opposite directions.

In the vintage Dodge, Laurie rested her head against Jeff's shoulder as they travelled south on Route 22.

'Hey, I missed you,' Jeff said softly. 'Busy as hell, but I missed you.'

'I missed you, too,' Laurie admitted. 'Whom else can I gripe to? It was a long, hot summer.' She paused. 'That's the phrase journalists use to describe ghetto rioting. This summer was fairly calm in that respect. Oh, we dealt with a lot of heroin overdoses and stab wounds and gunshot wounds, but not on the scale of what's happened in earlier years.'

'This is the year – again – of the anti-war movement,' he speculated. 'I think of guys like Terry – fighting in Vietnam – and I feel a kind of guilt that as a med student

I'm exempt from the draft.' His smile was wry. 'A lot of grad students were caught in the new ruling this year. Since most grad students are over 21, they're right near the top of the draft boards' lists.' Laurie understood that the draft boards were obligated to take the oldest men on the available lists.

'This year's going to be wild,' Laurie predicted. 'All of a sudden we're *almost there* – heading for playing at being real doctors when we feel so damned inadequate.'

'It's a long drive into Manhattan,' Jeff said with a studied casualness that got her instant attention. 'What do you say we find a cosy but inexpensive little motel and have ourselves a real reunion?'

'Are you propositioning me, doctor?' Laurie drawled. Sometimes she worried that Jeff was playing a game, that he was hoping this would be for the long haul. She'd learned that the one thing in life she could count on was her work. Nothing could come before career.

'Don't play coy, doctor,' he admonished. 'Do we stop or don't we?'

'We stop,' Laurie told him.

She was all turned on because they hadn't made love in such a long time, she told herself – conscious of an impatience to be in his arms, to be filled with him. It wasn't *Jeff*, she forced herself to rationalize. She was young, healthy, female – she had needs.

Fleetingly, she dwelt on the knowledge that Jeff was going into his last year of med school. After that, he would be eligible for the draft. Interns and residents were serving in Vietnam. But she didn't want to think about that.

On October 11, the presidents of five Ivy League colleges called on Nixon to accelerate plans to bring American troops home from Vietnam – warning of the imminent

Moratorium. Four days later, millions of Americans across the country – in hundreds of towns and cities – took off from jobs and schools to take part in the first Vietnam Moratorium Day. Laurie phoned from New York to report that, along with college absenteeism, 90% of the city's high school students were cutting classes.

There were mass meetings, candlelight processions, prayer meetings. Church bells rang out through the land. Many demonstrators wore black armbands in memory of Americans who had died in Vietnam. This was unlike other demonstrations in that it was not held over a weekend, nor only in a handful of major cities. Advance advertisements in the *New York Times* listed Republican Senators Mark Hatfield and Charles Goodell along with the expected Democratic names.

At the scheduled time, Vera left the office to join Paul at the small local gathering.

'I have to do it, Dad,' she told her father-in-law, who watched sombrely while three employees in the plant withdrew along with her to demonstrate.

'I know,' he said. With resignation or approval? Vera asked herself.

At dinner that evening, Vera observed that her father-in-law was abnormally silent. Even when they went into the den to watch the evening news, he made no comment.

'I think it's shitty the way TV provided no prime-time live coverage,' Paul groused. 'Just this late-night wrap-up. And don't tell me it isn't because of pressure from the White House.'

'Dad, would you like some hot chocolate?' Vera asked solicitously. He'd been complaining about insomnia, she remembered.

'That would be good.' He managed a wisp of a smile.

Dad was trying to deal with the anti-war movement, Vera interpreted. It was so difficult for him to admit the country had made a bad mistake – possibly an immoral mistake – in sending Americans to fight in Vietnam. A fragment of a letter from Terry that Adele had read to her lingered in her mind. 'This is a bloody civil war. We don't belong here. Is our government so afraid to admit they've lost a war that they'll keep us here till we're all dead?'

On November 3, Nixon addressed the nation on TV to report that the North Vietnamese had rejected the secret peace proposals the government had been offering them. Now he asked for support for his plans to *Vietnamese* the war.

'Meaning what?' Vera asked without stopping to think.

'Meaning, let the Vietnamese fight their war. Let Americans come home,' Paul supplied.

'Maybe then Tracy'll come home.' Vera felt a surge of optimism.

'That doesn't mean amnesty for draft-dodgers,' Joel warned. 'But Tracy's not a draft-dodger.' A glaze seemed to cover his eyes, Vera thought. 'I don't know why she can't come home for a visit.'

'Go up with us the next time,' Vera urged. Dad refused to recognize that Tracy was showing support for David by not coming home for a brief visit. Tracy had always been tenaciously loyal. 'She wants so much to see you.'

'If Tracy wants to see her grandfather, let her come home.' His brusqueness was to mask his yearning to see his adored grandchild. He loved Laurie and Neal, Vera reassured herself, but his relationship with Tracy was special. Joel paused. 'We won't stop her from going back. She knows that.'

The following evening Tracy phoned from Montreal. Vera heard an electric excitement in her voice.

'Laurie called a little while ago,' Tracy bubbled. 'She said she and Adele are going down to Washington for the second Vietnam Moratorium. It's not going to be just another demonstration. This will be a three-day deal – on November 13, 14, and 15 – focusing on Washington DC. I've talked with David about it and he understands. I'm flying down to New York to meet them and –'

'What about school?' Vera interrupted, all at once anxious. A three-day demonstration could involve violence.

'I have no classes on Thursday – that's the thirteenth. I can handle missing one day.'

'Tracy, it sounds dangerous.' Vera was assaulted by images of police in riot gear using tear gas to break up the crowds.

'It's a demonstration for peace,' Tracy reminded. 'The New Mobilization Committee – they're coordinating the whole deal – won't let any radical group take over. Mom, I have to go.'

'Be careful, darling.' Vera's throat tightened.

'We'll be fine,' Tracy insisted. 'Oh, I'll leave Washington late Saturday afternoon by train. I'll let you know when I'll arrive in Saratoga.' *Tracy was coming home*, Vera realized with sudden joy. 'I can get a late-evening plane out of Albany on Sunday night, so I'll be home for a little bit,' she wound up breathlessly.

'Tracy, that's wonderful! Be sure and call to give us your arrival time. It'll be so good to have you home even for a little while.'

Vera counted the days until Tracy would arrive in Eastwood. Paul – and Doris and Phil – kept assuring her there'd be no violence at the three-day demonstration. Newspapers predicted it would be the largest that had ever taken place in Washington DC.

'I don't know why they have to demonstrate,' Joel grumbled, though Vera knew he was elated at the prospect of seeing Tracy. 'Nixon's made it clear he means to bring an end to the war.'

'These young people want it to end now,' Paul said bluntly.

On November 11, Veterans Day was observed throughout the nation. Nixon's *Silent Majority* – those who approved of his handling of the Vietnam War – used the occasion for their own demonstrations. Thousands displayed flags, turned on their car headlights, lighted the porches of their homes. It wasn't the war they were supporting, Paul pointed out to Vera. It was Nixon's way of trying to end the war: 'Peace – but peace with honour.' *But how many more people must die for that peace with honour*, Vera asked herself.

For Vera and Paul, Veterans Day was always an occasion for reminiscing. They'd been actively part of World War II. They'd experienced firsthand the devastation and loss of life that are always part of war. Vera's thoughts focused on *Kristallnacht* and the deaths of her parents and her brother – and on neighbours in London who had died under Nazi attack. Paul remembered the mission when Chuck – his Columbia buddy – had crashed in flames. He and Chuck had thought themselves invincible.

On Wednesday evening November 12, David drove Tracy to the airport at Dorval.

'Look,' he said tensely while they waited for her flight to be announced, 'if you decide to stay in Eastwood, I'll understand.'

'How can you even think of that?' she scolded. 'You know I'm coming back. Home is wherever you are.'

Laurie and Jeff met her flight in New York. They were full of reports about the three-day demonstration. At least 250,000 – most of them young people – were expected to participate.

'And leave it to Jeff,' she said with tender mockery. 'Always so efficient. Everybody's so edgy about where

455

they'll stay in Washington, but weeks ago he reserved rooms for us at the Statler Hilton. *At student rates,*' she wound up triumphantly. 'We're paying thirteen bucks a night rather than the usual $24 to $26.'

At Laurie and Adele's apartment, the four of them talked till past midnight, when Jeff broke up the discussion.

'We want to be in the car tomorrow by 7:00 AM,' he reminded. 'Traffic is going to be hellish.'

The next morning – right on schedule – they headed south, ebullient yet solemn about the purpose of the occasion. The day was cold and grey with the threat of rain. By the time they arrived in Washington, the traffic jams were horrendous. At the hotel they were able to make arrangements for parking, settled in their two rooms – Adele and Tracy in one, Laurie and Jeff in the adjoining room. Then they headed out to join the crowds of young people – in the familiar uniforms of jeans, heavy sweaters, school jackets, and ponchos – that milled about the streets. An endless parade of cars drove at a five-mile-an-hour pace though the streets.

'A lot of guys will be in sleeping bags tonight,' Jeff prophesied, eyeing the equipment carried by many. He chuckled. 'We're getting too old for that.'

'Mom worried about violence here,' Tracy said as they strolled near the White House, where five students were handing out candy corn and gum. Someone else told them that St Mark's Episcopal Church had become a reception centre for demonstrators. 'They're giving out free sandwiches and coffee there. It's real groovy.'

Others told them that 35,000 troops were standing by 'to keep the peace.'

'Don't they know peace is what this is all about?' Tracy demanded.

At twilight – while seven drummers beat a funereal roll

– the opening event of the demonstration began: The March against Death, an event that was predicted to continue through the night and far into Friday. Thousands of demonstrators would march – in single file – the four miles from Arlington National Cemetery to the foot of Capitol Hill. Each would wear a placard about the neck that bore the name of someone who had died in Vietnam or the name of a community that had been destroyed.

In her room at the Statler Hilton, Adele prepared with Tracy's help the placards which each of the four of them was to wear. Her placard would carry the name of Terry's high school buddy who had died in the Tet Offensive. Laurie's remembered the brother of a Barnard friend. Jeff's bore the name of a remote village – where only civilians had remained – that had been wiped out. Tracy's placard remembered Mary O'Brien's son Jimmy, with whom she'd gone to school.

Jeff appeared in the doorway. 'I brought candles.' He held out four in his hand. 'It's dark already. We'll need them.'

Half an hour later, the four of them joined the candle-lit line at Arlington. Rumours told them that the march would probably last right into Saturday morning. Slowly the line moved forward in single file. In the course of the four-mile walk, Tracy was conscious of the crowds of onlookers – many of them in tears. She was here for all those who had died, she told herself, fighting not to cry. *For the soldiers and the civilians.*

At last their group approached the foot of Capitol Hill. There, each name was read aloud and its placard placed in a huge, flag-draped coffin. Tracy wished David could be here with her. In his heart he was.

On Friday the crowds swelled. Reports were that students across the nation were cutting classes in high schools and colleges. Those who could were arriving here to share in the main event tomorrow. By midafternoon a thunderstorm had hit the area, but this did nothing to lessen the enthusiasm of the crowds. Word circulated triumphantly about the hordes of celebrities who were present.

In the evening – with the March of Death continuing – an hour-long service called Liturgy for Peace was held at the 3,000 seat National Cathedral, where there was standing room only. By midnight, reports indicated that more than 40,000 were participating in the march from Arlington to Capitol Hill. And circulars were making the rounds to report that Senate Democratic Leader Mike Mansfield had only praise for the demonstrators. *I applaud the order, dignity and decorum of the demonstrators. These youngsters are our children, our neighbours, our friends. The only sorrow is they can't vote – they can only protest.*

Saturday activities began with a nine o'clock memorial service on the Mall. Then in the sharp morning chill the demonstrators – the police estimated a crowd of 250,000; the Mobilization Committee put the figure close to 800,000 – began the one-mile march down Pennsylvania Avenue to the Washington Monument. The marchers were led by Eugene McCarthy, Coretta King, Arlo Guthrie, and Dr Benjamin Spock. The atmosphere was festive, in contrast to the poignant March of Death that had begun on Thursday evening and had continued for almost forty hours.

The rally began at the monument at noon. In addition to the array of eloquent anti-war speakers, there was much music on the programme – mostly folk and rock, plus a brilliant monologue by Dick Gregory. Pete Seeger brought the crowd to its feet as he sang 'Bring Them Home.' And the crowd responded with 'Give Peace a Chance.' At close to 4:00 PM, Jeff nudged the other three in his group to begin to seek a path through the crowds.

'Let's get on the road before the mass exodus begins,' he ordered. 'Otherwise it'll take us till midnight to get back to New York!'

Exhilarated at having been part of an historic event, they settled themselves in the car for the ride back to New York.

'Turn on the radio,' Tracy ordered Jeff. 'Let's hear what's happening in other places!'

She hid her anxiety as they hit pockets of sluggish traffic. If she missed her train, there wouldn't be another until tomorrow. She wanted so much to be home – even for only twenty-four hours. She didn't want to miss one precious hour.

Kids like themselves whom they'd met in Montreal said it got easier after the first year – but that wasn't true. Would she and David ever be able to go home again? How would they survive – living in exile forever?

Chapter Thirty-nine

Vera was conscious of the Sunday morning quiet as she sat across the breakfast table from Tracy. A cosy warmth pervaded the room, fragrant with the aroma of freshly brewed coffee. The windows were steamed over, providing an aura of strangely pleasant isolation from the rest of the world. Last evening – with the whole family together except for Laurie – had filled her with such contentment.

This early breakfast was an oasis of time she would treasure, she thought while Tracy talked effervescently – despite barely five hours sleep – about the past three days in Washington, DC.

'It was one of the most exciting times in my life,' Tracy declared, only now smothering a yawn. 'You and Dad should have come down, too.' She paused. 'You didn't because of Grandpa,' she guessed.

'We talked about it,' Vera confessed. 'Do you remember when you and David went with Dad and me and Doris and Phil to the civil rights march and we heard Martin Luther King give his I-have-a-dream speech? You were only sixteen,' she reflected.

'Sure I remember. David and I kept talking about it for months. We were so proud to have been there.' All at once Tracy was sombre. 'Grandpa was glad to see me, but he didn't even ask about David.'

'This is a bad time for him.' Vera's eyes pleaded for compassion. 'But I see him coming around to our view about Vietnam.' Polls showed that most Americans were now against the war. 'And he's been upset about the 1968

460

Gun Control Law. To him it's a denial of freedom.'

'Can't he understand that it'll save lives?' Tracy asked passionately. 'Mom, what do we have to do to make him realize that the violence in this country is going to get worse if we don't get tougher on gun ownership? Adele said that –'

'Darling, please,' Vera broke in. 'Don't talk about guns around Grandpa.' *Here it was again*, she thought painfully. Tracy and Laurie's resentment that she and Dad were part of the firearms business. But couldn't they understand that even if she were able to persuade Dad to close up that part of the company – and he would *never* accept that – then others would increase their own production to meet the demand? 'He's so thrilled to have you here.'

'As long as I don't talk about David or about guns.' For a moment Tracy radiated open hostility. 'Okay, I'll be good,' she relented.

'I'll tell Mary O'Brien that you memorialized Jimmy at the march,' Vera said. 'She'll be pleased.'

'Maybe I should go over to the Blue Lantern later and tell her myself,' Tracy said on impulse. 'Does she work on Sundays?'

'In the morning. For the early-breakfast people and the after-church crowd. Shall we go over now? Grandpa and Dad will sleep late.' They had stayed up long past the time when Doris and Phil left with Neal. Oh, it had been wonderful to have them all together! If Laurie had been there, too, it would have been perfect. 'There won't be many people at the Blue Lantern this early on a Sunday morning.'

'Let's go,' Tracy said enthusiastically.

At this early hour it seemed as though all of Eastwood were asleep. The streets were almost deserted, shops closed. At the Blue Lantern, a trio of men occupied stools at the counter. The tables were deserted. Vera saw Mary O'Brien's face light up as she and Tracy walked into the small, modest restaurant. People in Eastwood knew that Tracy was studying at McGill. The fact that she had gone to Canada with David and that they were married was never mentioned. Again, because of Dad, Vera conceded. This was still a Republican town; most residents followed Nixon's lead on Vietnam with unquestioning devotion.

'We've had breakfast,' Vera told Mary apologetically, 'but your coffee's always so good we thought we'd drop in for another cup. And –' she hesitated a moment, knowing that pleasure would blend with pain at the mention of Jimmy '– Tracy was down in Washington, DC, along with Laurie, for the second Vietnam Moratorium demonstration.' She saw Mary's face tighten. 'She was telling me about the very touching march that lasted for forty hours – people marching with placards about their necks honouring someone who had died in Vietnam – or a devastated South Vietnam community.'

'I wore a placard with Jimmy's name on it, and –' Tracy stopped short, startled by Mary's glare of rage.

'That was a terrible thing to do!' Mary spoke through clenched teeth. 'Using my son's name for something that's disgracing this country! Jimmy wouldn't have liked that one bit!' Pale and distraught, Mary stalked away from their table.

'I thought she'd be pleased,' Tracy whispered, shaken by Mary's reaction. 'It was meant to honour Jimmy's memory.'

'I guess we just didn't realize that some people would take it in a different way.' Vera tried for a conciliatory smile.

'Jeff said there would be people who'd feel that way,' Tracy said after a moment. 'He heard somebody in our hotel lobby say that we were making a mockery of all those who'd died in the Vietnam war. That we were saying they'd all died for nothing. I can't see it that way.'

Vera and Tracy sat sipping their coffee in silence – each caught up in private reverie. Mary approached their table again, without a word refilled their cups, and returned the carafe to its customary place behind the counter.

'What can I say to her?' Tracy was desolate.

'Just let it be,' Vera whispered. 'And don't let it spoil your memory of those three days. You were making an important statement.'

'David and I don't socialize with other Americans up there,' Tracy said. 'We don't have time for the meetings and all.' She gestured vaguely. 'Between school and our part-time jobs. And we've signed up for six hours a week of volunteer work at a literacy centre.'

'There's a lot of talk already about amnesty,' Vera began encouragingly.

'Mom, that's a long way off,' Tracy interrupted. 'I was talking with Dad about it last night. But we'll have to wait. I won't let David come home and face a prison sentence.'

Vera glanced up to see Mary approaching their table again. She braced herself for ugly words.

'I'm sorry I talked that way,' Mary said softly. 'It hurts me to think that Jimmy died for nothing. He wrote me just weeks before – before it happened. He said he couldn't stand what they were doing to the people over there. He said we should get out of Vietnam before more died.' Her voice broke. 'It was nothing. Jimmy died for nothing.'

'Mary, no,' Vera insisted, searching for words of comfort. 'His country called, and he answered. He was a hero. You can be proud of him.'

'My baby died for nothing,' Mary repeated. 'Unless this teaches us not to let it happen again this way.'

Within twenty-four hours, a shocking account of American activities in Vietnam burst forth on TV screens and on the front pages of newspapers throughout the country. A newspaper journalist had broken the story of an early-morning massacre at My Lai. A company of 60 to 70 US infantrymen – acting under orders – had moved into the village of My Lai and in a twenty minute massacre burnt down the wooden huts, dynamited the brick one, and shot down the inhabitants – women, children, old men – as they tried to escape.

'I don't believe this,' Joel gasped as they watched the evening newscast. 'I don't believe this!'

'It's inhuman,' Vera whispered, her mind hurtling back to the memory of Hitler's concentration camps revealed to a shocked world after V-E Day.

Now they learned that the massacre had occurred in March of the previous year and would have remained secret except that a conscience-stricken Vietnam veteran – now a college student – had felt compelled to report what he'd heard from men who had been at My Lai. He wrote a stream of impassioned letters to Congressmen, even to the President. A probe had led to formal charges – and now the world learned about what *Time Magazine* labelled 'My Lai: An American Tragedy.'

Television and radio news, newspapers and magazines pursued this American atrocity in the days ahead. Vera was astonished by her father-in-law's obsessive pursuit of every item about My Lai.

'Dad can't believe American soldiers could behave that way,' Paul reminded her. 'He's looking for a way to accept what happened at My Lai.'

Then Joel came to them with a self-conscious, agonized admission.

'We made a terrible mistake in going into Vietnam. It took the kids to understand,' he said sombrely. 'They saw

464

what diehards like me refused to see. I didn't want to believe our country could make a mistake. But we did – and the sooner we get the hell out of Vietnam, the better I'll feel.'

'Amen,' Vera said softly.

Joel paused in thought. 'The weather's on the rough side right now. But next time you talk with Tracy, you tell her I'll be up to visit sometime in the spring. And I expect her and David to take me to Ben's for one of those smoked beef sandwiches she keeps raving about. And tell David to make sure he has a haircut before I get there.'

Vera and Paul anxiously watched for Nixon's announcements about the withdrawal of troops from Vietnam. Paul was realistic, she told herself – he knew there could be no amnesty until every American serviceman was back home. On December 15, Nixon announced that another 50,000 troops would be withdrawn from Vietnam early in the coming year.

'It's slow, but it's coming.' Paul tried to be optimistic. 'We're getting out of Vietnam.'

'But how many more will die before it happens?' Vera countered.

The mood of the country was tainted by bitterness and disillusionment. A new decade was approaching. *Let it be better than the present one*, Vera prayed. *What did she want of this new year*? she asked herself a few days before its arrival – when the house held a spurious serenity for her because Laurie was home and had brought Adele and Jeff with her for ten days. The three of them would return to New York on New Year's Day.

What did she want? she asked herself again. To see Tracy and David back in Eastwood. When their nightmare exile was over, they wanted to live somewhere in the area, for which she was grateful. And she yearned to see Laurie happy in her profession. In June she'd have her medical degree. In July she'd begin her internship – along with Jeff – at Bellevue. Then she planned to practise in a ghetto area. Not here in Eastwood. Was this to be a nation of scattered families?

As always when Adele was in the house, education dominated much of the evening conversation. *Paul enjoyed verbal-wrestling with Adele,* Vera thought indulgently. And Adele was ecstatic that he had mentioned her work at the small Harlem school in his recent article. He was encouraging her to write an article about her current project.

Paul was frustrated that those in power were doing nothing to improve the educational system in Eastwood. He'd tried so hard through his years of teaching. Still, he relished his small success in writing about education, Vera comforted herself. The occasional lecturing. *Not much money, but I feel I'm reaching people.*

Vera sensed, too, that Paul was astonished and pleased by his father's glow of pride each time another article appeared with his byline. She'd seen her father-in-law pull the current article from his jacket pocket to show off to friends. It was important to Paul to feel he had not disappointed his father.

Now – two hours before the arrival of 1970 – Vera sat in her favourite lounge chair in the living room and listened while Paul and Adele talked shop. Phil sat at the piano, playing in muted volume the medley of George Gershwin music that had become part of their New Year's Eve celebrations. At moments in the course of the chess game he was playing with Neal, Joel hummed snatches of Gershwin. Laurie was sprawled in a lounge chair, absorbed in another Steinbeck novel.

Doris appeared in the entrance with a tray of hot apple cider. Vera rose to her feet and crossed the room to help

466

her distribute the cinnamon-spiked beverage. *What were Tracy and David doing at this moment?* she wondered wistfully. All the American kids forced into exile.

'All right, I do sound like Nixon,' Paul conceded to Adele. 'I *don't* think we're getting as much as we should for the bucks we're spending on education.'

'We're not getting enough bucks,' Adele shot back.

'More money means higher taxes and everybody gets upset.' Paul was sombre. 'We need a school system here that understands the needs of today's kids. Here in Eastwood schools haven't changed in fifty years. Too many of our schools haven't changed in fifty years.'

'When are you going to sit down and write that book you talked about?' Adele asked zealously. *What book?* Vera asked herself. Paul had never talked to her about a book. 'You have such insight into educational problems. Put aside the articles, focus on bringing it all together in a book. Education is at a crisis point in this country.'

'I can't waste all that time on a book. On a gamble,' Paul hedged.

'Yes, you can!' Vera's voice was electric. Paul was worried about the loss of income from his articles and the lecturing. Had they drifted so far apart that he couldn't talk to her about this? In earlier years there had been nothing they couldn't sit down and work out together. He had confided in Adele about writing a book – *not in her*.

'It'll take a lot of discipline.' Doris joined in, making this sound more of a challenge than a warning.

'Your brother has discipline,' Joel said, and Vera saw Paul's glow of amazement. 'If he wants to do something, he does it.'

'Paul, it's an obligation,' Vera said softly. 'Take the time off and write the book.'

Paul hesitated. 'I'm not sure I can.'

'You can,' Vera insisted. All at once it was as though she and Paul were alone in the room. 'Remember what you said to me all those years ago in London, when you came to me after V-E Day?' Her eyes searched his. 'You said, "If this world is to see lasting peace, we're going to have to educate the people." That's been your whole goal in life. And now you have a chance – a *responsibility* – to do your share in that monumental job.'

'So it's settled.' Joel broke into the poignant moment between Paul and Vera, startling her. She hadn't been aware that he was listening. 'Put yourself on a work schedule. Set up the guest room as your office. You've got a book to write.'

'Somewhere along the line,' Adele said, 'spend time at my school – which God knows, isn't perfect. But see the difference between it and most other ghetto schools. We still have to watch for drugs,' she granted, 'and we've got kids with major problems. But our kids don't have to ask for passes to go to the bathroom. Or to the library. We don't have teachers and students on patrol duty.'

Now Vera screened out the lively conversation erupting around her. She had not been the best of wives these last few years, she rebuked herself. She'd allowed herself to become too wrapped up in the business – because that had been the way to fight her own demons.

This summer she and Paul would go to London together for two or three weeks, she decided. But already road blocks were zooming into place in her mind. To go to London was to remember what she needed to put behind her. To remember *Kristallnacht*.

Chapter Forty

Vera was astonished at the efforts required to organize the banquet in Dr Evans' honour. Joel and Doris took on increasing responsibility in their determination to make this a memorable event.

'I doubt it's a secret any longer,' Phil said at a family dinner late in March, 'but Doc's cool about it. He's not letting on he knows a thing.'

'How's the song coming?' Joel asked. Phil was writing a song for the occasion.

'It's coming. Not quite the way I want it yet, but I'll get there. Hey, didn't I have a song that made it into an Off-Broadway musical?' he demanded with a wink.

At the end of March, Joel flew to Montreal to spend four days with Tracy and David.

'Canada's been good for David,' Joel commented on his return. 'Got himself a decent haircut. He'd never make it as a hippie now.'

Vera kept remembering how Congressman Koch from New York had gone to Canada at the end of December to talk with draft-evaders in Montreal, Toronto, and Ottawa. He wanted very much to see an amnesty bill passed by Congress. But Paul kept warning her it wouldn't be soon.

In New York Laurie was ever-conscious that she was on the verge of graduating from medical school, that in July she was to start her internship. Though there were four years of internship and residency ahead of them, she could not forget that at the end of those years she and Jeff would head off in opposite directions.

She'd allowed herself to become too dependent on Jeff, she admonished herself. A bad move! They'd been great for each other through med school – and it would be the same for the next four years. But the time would come when she would have to stand on her own two feet and carry on alone.

Mom said that Dr Evans talked about bringing in a second doctor in addition to Jeff – probably a pediatrician – because Eastwood was growing. More young people were staying in Eastwood these days. Most of that was due to the extra jobs the family was creating these days. Grandpa was proud that the company had been written up in a leading trade journal because of the good working conditions and benefits it provided its employees. She was, as ever, astonished at the way Mom kept expanding the business. *But Mom and Grandpa still sold guns,* she thought in distaste.

During the spring break at school, she and Jeff drove up to Eastwood for a brief visit. She was oddly uncomfortable at the way Jeff seemed to have joined the family, she confessed to Adele on their return.

'They're losing a daughter but gaining a son,' Adele flipped, but her eyes were sympathetic.

'They're not losing me,' Laurie contradicted. 'So I won't be practising in Eastwood. I'm still in the family. And I made it clear long ago that Mom and Dad were not to regard Jeff as a son-in-law. I know what I want to do with my life. Almost as far back as I can remember, I knew I wanted to be a doctor.'

'I think you're nuts to let Jeff get away. Hey, it's late and we both have to be up at six,' Adele said abruptly. 'Let's cut the crap and go to sleep.'

As usual on Monday afternoon, Laurie checked the

mailbox before heading up to their apartment. It was stuffed – meaning Adele hadn't come home yet. She unlocked the box, pulled out the usual assortment of ads, bills, and catalogues. She smiled when she saw the letter for Adele from Terry. Adele would be in a great mood tonight.

She was sprawled in the living room lounge chair with a mug of peppermint tea at her elbow when Adele arrived twenty minutes later.

'Don't sit down,' she told her, smiling. 'You have a letter from Terry on the table.'

'Oh, I need that today!' Adele crossed to the table for the envelope. 'It's been a real bitch. We've acquired a new kid who thinks it's groovy to pack a gun along with his school books. He's pissed because we told him that was a no-no.'

'Tea?' Laurie asked as Adele dropped onto the corner of the sofa and ripped open the envelope. 'I've a pot of water boiling.'

'The real thing,' Adele ordered. 'None of the herb stuff.'

'Coming right up.'

'Oh, God!' Laurie froze in her tracks at Adele's sudden exclamation. 'Oh, Laurie, I don't believe it's really happening!' Adele's face was incandescent. 'Terry says he'll be coming home – on rotation or something – in June!'

To celebrate, Laurie and Adele went out to dinner at the new Chinese restaurant a few blocks from their apartment.

'Chinese fits right into my budget,' Adele said as they walked through the sharp April chill to Broadway. 'I thought I'd be able to save money on this job – but no way.'

'Not if you keep spending half your salary on supplies for your class,' Laurie pointed out.

'I keep meaning to put money in the bank every month,'

Adele said. 'You know, to have a nest egg to fall back on when I get pregnant and have to be out of work for a while. Terry says as soon as he's out of the service and into a decent job, he wants us to have a kid.' She paused, squinted in thought. 'You know, for the first year that Terry was in Vietnam, I was scared to death he'd be killed.' Involuntarily Laurie tensed. In a few weeks Jeff would be eligible for the draft. The word was that they needed doctors like crazy. She didn't want to think about Jeff in Vietnam. 'But Terry says that the guys who last through the first three or four months are the ones that are likely to survive. He says that after that you develop a sixth sense. At first you're not cool – you do stupid things. Oh Laurie, I can't wait to see him.' Her face crinkled in laughter. 'He's going to be one tired old boy when I get hold of him!'

Each day Adele came home with a fresh idea about redecorating the apartment. It was taken for granted that Laurie would move in with Jeff while Terry was home.

'I don't understand this rotation bit,' Laurie said on a late April Friday while she and Adele helped Jeff prepare a spaghetti dinner for the three of them at his tiny apartment. 'They can't send him back to Vietnam, can they? Nixon says he's winding down the war in Vietnam. Troops are being brought home.'

'Probably he'll remain in the service but here at home until the whole deal's over,' Jeff suggested brightly. 'It's not going as fast as a lot of us would like.'

'Oh, I had a letter from Mom today,' Laurie told Jeff. 'Nobody's making a pretence anymore about the banquet for Dr Evans being a secret. He said he wants you there, Jeff. He wants to introduce you to the community.'

'I won't be practising for four more years,' Jeff protested, but he appeared pleased. 'I think it's great that the town's giving him that banquet. It must be wonderful to know you've spent fifty years tending to a community and that your service is truly appreciated.'

'In fifty years we'll be attending a banquet for you,' Adele declared.

'Right,' Laurie picked up. 'Adele and Terry will be there – maybe with a grandchild or two.' *Why was Jeff looking at her that way?* 'And I'll take time off from my practice in Harlem or Bed-Stuy to join them.' No time in a woman doctor's life for children or grandchildren. She'd realized that long ago.

'I forgot to pick up wine.' Jeff clucked in disgust. 'Which one of you volunteers to run down to the liquor store? I'm buying. I can't leave my sauce,' he pointed out, stirring the spaghetti sauce for which he'd become famous among money-short med students. 'Flip for it.'

The day had been long and hectic. God, she'd be glad to be out of this nine-to-five school-grind, Laurie thought as she reached for the keys for her apartment door. She closed her mind to the knowledge that starting in July with her internship, her hours would often be longer and even more gruelling. While she dealt with the second lock – because Manhattan had become a city requiring double and even triple locks – she heard the sharp ring of the phone inside.

She pushed the door wide, rushed inside to pick up the phone.

'Hello.'

'Is this Laurie Kahn?' a crisp voice at the other end inquired.

'Yes, it is.'

'This is Detective Rogers,' he identified himself. 'I'm sorry to report that there's been a shooting at the Lancester Special School. The victim – Adele Garrett – carried ID which listed you as next of kin.'

'How is she?' Laurie's heart was pounding. 'Where is she?'

Disbelieving, Laurie listened to the detective's report, wrote down directions.

'Thank you. I'll be at the hospital in twenty minutes!' White with shock, trembling, she disconnected the caller and dialled Jeff's number. She waited impatiently for him to respond. *Where the hell was he?*

'Hello.'

'Jeff, something awful's happened! I can't believe –'

'Calm down, Laurie,' he ordered. 'Now tell me.'

Her words tumbling over one another, she told him what little she knew. Of course, they were aware of violence in the schools – but, somehow, they had never expected it to happen at Adele's school. Hadn't Adele bragged about how they were keeping their kids under control?

'I'll pick you up in a cab in front of your house in five minutes,' Jeff told her. 'She's going to be all right.'

At the hospital, Laurie saw the nurse's start of astonishment when she presented herself at the emergency room.

'Adele considers me next of kin,' Laurie explained shakily. 'We're close friends. Like sisters.'

'She's in surgery,' the nurse told them.

'Where shall we wait?' Jeff asked.

The nurse gave them directions and they sought the bank of elevators. On the surgical floor – too anxious to sit – they paced about the waiting area, talking in muted tones about the shooting, until at last they sat in mutual exhaustion. Moments later, Laurie saw a door swing open, and a surgically garbed man emerged.

'There's the doctor!' She leapt to her feet along with Jeff. Her heart was pounding.

'We're waiting for word about Adele Garrett,' Jeff told him. 'The shooting victim.'

'I'm sorry,' the surgeon said with perfunctory compassion. If he were surprised that they were white, he concealed it. 'She never regained consciousness. She died on the operating table.'

'Oh, my God!' This was insane. Shock merged with rage in her. Terry was coming home – but Adele was dead?

In a daze, Laurie heard Jeff identify themselves as fourth-year medical students. She heard him ask the necessary – practical – questions. Holding her hand tightly in his, he led her outside and hailed a cab for them.

'We'll call Mom,' Laurie whispered. 'We'll need money for Adele's funeral.' Her voice broke. 'Jeff, how could it have happened?'

But she knew how it had happened. The police had told them. Adele had tried to take a gun away from a student who was threatening a 15-year-old girl who had rejected him. The new kid she'd said was a big problem, Laurie guessed. He and Adele had struggled. The gun went off. Adele was shot in the head.

Too numb to cry yet, Vera put down the phone, walked to the sofa, sat at the edge of one corner. *Adele was dead.* This was unreal. Last night Adele and Paul had talked on the phone for almost an hour about a new experiment in her school. He was to drive down to New York to discuss it further with her principal. Now they must rush to New York to arrange for her funeral.

Vera's mind catapulted back through the years – twenty-four years ago – to the morning she and Doris had gone to the railroad station to pick up Fiona and Adele. She'd been so happy that Laurie would have a friend right in the house – and the two little girls had been so pleased with each other. She remembered the

475

childhood illnesses – which had naturally passed from one to the other of the three little girls in the household. She remembered the terrible day when they'd learned that Fiona had been killed by a hit-and-run driver in New York – and her futile efforts to persuade Fiona's mother to let Adele stay with them.

'Vera?' She was startled from her painful reverie by Paul's voice.

'In the den, Paul.'

In a daze – trying to accept ugly reality – Vera told him what had happened, aware of his shock, knowing the memories this would evoke in him. He'd been six years old when he saw his mother crumple to the floor and die of a gunshot wound.

'We'll have to go right down there,' he said, his eyes reflecting his pain. 'I can't believe it, Vera.'

'I know.' She lost her perilous hold on composure. 'Paul, she was twenty-six years old. Terry's scheduled to come home in June. She's been so happy with her teaching.' *Guns again. Guns spreading tragedy among the innocent.*

Paul reached to pull her close. 'We knew there's violence in the schools – but I'd thought Adele's school was free of it. It's something we read about or see on TV news reports.'

'Can you imagine what Laurie's going through?' Vera's mind charged back through the years – to the moment she and Paul had rushed into the Robinson house to find Laurie hovering over seven-year-old Serena Robinson, killed by a gun fired by her small brother. '*How can it be happening this way again?*'

'Laurie'll need us.' Paul glanced at his watch. 'We should be in the car in an hour.'

'I told her we'd be there tonight. She wants us to stay in her apartment – she'll sleep on the sofa. Jeff's with her,' she added. *Thank God for Jeff.*

'Tell Irene to get dinner on the table as fast as she can,' Paul said. 'I'll have to make a couple of calls. We'll probably be down there three or four days.'

'I'll phone Eve at home.' Eve was her long-time administrative assistant. 'She'll make calls, reschedule some appointments.'

'You talk to Irene. I'll go upstairs and start to pack.' He drew her close. 'It's rough,' he said gently. 'Adele was like a member of the family.'

Joel returned to the house minutes before Irene prepared to serve dinner. Paul brought him into the den, reported the tragic news. Joel stood frozen in shock for a moment, his face ashen.

'Those kids are animals!' he blazed. 'She never should have taught in a ghetto school. She knew the crime statistics there!' He turned to Vera. 'How's Laurie taking it?'

'She's devastated.' Vera flinched. 'All those years ago, Serena – and now Adele.'

She knew that Joel was remembering his wife's death. Was this a terrible retribution for the family's manufacturing guns?

'Laurie's going to say we're responsible for this.' Joel was all at once defensive. 'We built the gun that creep used to kill Adele?' he blustered. 'That's bullshit!'

'We'll never change the way Laurie feels about guns. I know it, and you know it.' Vera was fighting for calm. She'd lost one family on *Kristallnacht*. She mustn't spend the rest of her life fearing to lose again. 'I suspect Tracy, too, isn't comfortable that her family is in the business of –'

'Vera, what do the kids want from me?' Joel's voice was strident. He turned accusingly to Paul. 'It's not just Laurie and Tracy. You and Doris have always been ashamed of what your father does for a living. But for generations, Kahns have built guns. *For sportsmen*. And when our country needed arms, we helped supply them. We considered it our duty. We –'

'Dad, nobody has a right to tell you to close your business,' Vera broke in. 'If you did, that wouldn't stop the flow of guns into cities and towns across the country. And you've been an honourable man,' she said gently. 'But the gun situation is going berserk these days. Guns are falling into the hands of dangerous people. Where did a fifteen-year-old boy get hold of a gun?'

'You're talking gun control?' Joel sputtered. 'Guns are necessary to keep peace in the world. To –'

'Dad, you're talking about another era. Do you know how many lives are lost each year because of guns in the wrong hands? Adele would be alive today if that crazy kid hadn't been able to buy a gun!' Her voice was harsh with grief. 'Our crime rate wouldn't be escalating like mad.'

'Vera, Irene wants to serve dinner,' Paul interrupted. 'Let's eat and get in the car.'

'Dad, I'm not telling you to give up the business,' Vera reiterated. 'Guns are important.' In a corner of her mind she remembered the little fishing village in Copenhagen and how guns had saved her life. She remembered how she'd told Paul – when he'd left her in London – that she wished she had a gun to keep under her pillow. Guns had meant protection to her then. And in a corner of her mind she heard Paul's recrimination only two years ago: *For God's sake, Vera, when are you going to learn to let go of the past*? 'But today, guns must be regulated,' she insisted, moving into uncharted areas. 'I think there's a road we can take that will let us keep the business in operation and yet bring the family together again. I think we can do it, Dad.'

'What road?' Joel was wary, yet Vera felt a humility in him, a yearning to mend fences. He loathed this under-the-surface conflict with every member of the family except her. 'What can we do?'

'We'll talk about it when Paul and I get back from New York,' she said gently, feeling his anguish. 'It'll take some negotiations.'

'I'll come down to New York for Adele's funeral,' Joel told her. 'You let me know when to come.'

In the next four days, Laurie was grateful that Jeff never left her side. Along with her mother and father, he took over the myriad details of laying Adele to rest. He notified her estranged family. He wrote Terry. Her grandfather and Doris came down for the funeral. Tracy and David wired flowers. And always Jeff was there beside her.

Walking into the church for Adele's funeral service, Laurie told herself she must make Jeff understand she wanted him to be part of her life forever. He'd played the game according to the rules she'd drawn, accepted what she allowed herself to offer him. But in her heart she'd felt Jeff loved her for the long haul – even while she denied permanence to her own love.

Was she right? Would Jeff always be there for her? All at once it was terribly important to know. Adele would be pleased, she thought with a fresh surge of grief that Adele could never know. She could hear Adele's voice scolding her. *Laurie, you and Jeff are made for each other. Like Terry and me.*

The pews of the church were quickly filled. Others gathered together at the rear. The church that had been so dear to Adele's mother and grandmother, Laurie remembered. She saw clusters of Adele's students – their feelings of loss etched on their young faces – clinging together at the rear of the church. The girls in tears, the boys shamefacedly wet-eyed. Oh yes, Adele had been much loved, would be missed.

With Adele laid to rest beside her mother in a Queens cemetery, her adopted family headed back to their car. Caught up in memories of Adele, Laurie said little on the long drive into Manhattan. She was vaguely conscious of the quiet conversation among the others. Then the car was emerging from the Queens Midtown Tunnel.

'We'll go downtown to Ratner's on Second Avenue for an early dinner,' her father said, circling around the FDR Drive. 'Okay, Dad?'

'That'll be nice, Paul.'

When they left the car at the parking lot on East 5th Street, Laurie fell into step with Jeff behind the others.

'Jeff, I could never have survived this without you,' she whispered. 'I don't think I can survive life without you.'

She lifted her eyes to his, saw his face light up as he comprehended her message.

'Ever since those first weeks in med school, I knew I wanted to spend the rest of my life with you.' He reached for her hand. 'But I was always afraid to push.'

'It won't bother you to share your practice with your wife?' She asked coyly.

'You can call yourself *Dr Kahn*,' he replied lovingly, 'but we'll know you're *Laurie Green*, also.'

'We've got three weeks between graduation and beginning our internship.' Her smile was shaky. 'I know a June wedding is awfully traditional –'

'Let's be traditional.' He squeezed her hand. 'Your family will like that.'

'Will it be wrong?' All at once doubts invaded her. 'I mean, so soon after Adele –'

'Adele would approve. She knew we belong together.'

'You're sure?'

'I'm sure.'

*

Several days after their graduation from the Columbia College of Physicians and Surgeons, Laurie and Jeff were married in the summer-flower-bedecked living room of the Kahn house. A glorious fragrance permeated the air. Phil sat at the piano now and played Mendelssohn's Wedding March as Laurie – flanked by her mother and father – walked to the improvised *chuppah*, where Jeff waited for her.

In a semi-circle of chairs arranged for the occasion, Joel sat between Doris and Tracy. With a sweetly solemn expression Neal sat next to his mother.

While Laurie and Jeff stood before the rabbi, Vera and Paul joined the others in the semi-circle of chairs. The rabbi began the service. Vera reached out for Paul's hand. Her eyes strayed to Tracy. How sad that David could not be here with them today. Jeff's mother wasn't here. He had pointed out that he had no knowledge of her whereabouts. 'I doubt that she would have bothered to come, anyway,' he'd said.

Earlier Terry had phoned to give Laurie and Jeff his congratulations and good wishes. They understood he couldn't bring himself to attend the wedding, just two-and-a-half years after his own City Hall marriage to Adele – where they had been in attendance.

The day would arrive, Vera promised herself, when Tracy and David could come home again. And today she allowed herself hope for a true reconciliation with Laurie and Tracy – a bringing together of the family. She and Dad had worked so hard for this. Please God, let Laurie and Tracy understand that they *could* be a whole family.

And then the rabbi was saying the magic words. 'I now pronounce you husband and wife.'

There was a flurry of embraces, an air of festivity that was marked, too, by sadness because Adele was not there to share the occasion with them.

'All right,' Joel said jovially at last, exchanging a meaningful glance with Vera. 'Let's go into the dining room and this wonderful dinner that's been prepared for us.'

They took their places at the dining table – extended to holiday length. Under the table Vera's foot reached for comforting contact with Paul's. Her eyes met Doris's across the table. Paul and Doris – along with Phil – knew of the extended conferences she and Dad had had with their lawyers. Was she being overly optimistic to believe that at long last family differences would be erased? As much as she, Dad wanted this. Would Laurie and Tracy accept what they had to offer? *Was it too late?*

When the wedding cake had been cut and served, Joel tapped on his champagne goblet for silence, cleared his throat self-consciously, and announced, 'We have a special announcement to make. A momentous decision that is, in part, a tribute to Adele's memory. Adele's death made us understand what had to be done. Vera,' he said gently, 'tell them.'

'We've been working with our lawyers to make some changes in the business,' Vera said, speaking to Laurie and Tracy. 'We've broken it up. Your grandfather and I feel this is something we must do. Kahn Firearms is now one company. The catalogue division and the chain of stores are another.' She paused, took a deep breath. The girls didn't understand yet. 'As of this date, all the profits from Kahn Firearms will go into a fund to support a gun-control group.' She paused again, watching her daughters' astonishment as they assimilated what she had said. 'Paul, you explain it to Laurie and Tracy.'

'To close the gun division would throw a lot of people here in town out of work,' Paul began. 'You know how your grandfather would feel about that. And it wouldn't stop some other firm from picking up the business we'd be turning down. It would be of no real value. Then your mother and grandfather decided to take the gun-division profits and funnel them into a special fund to fight for gun control. The Kahn family will be fighting in a small way against crime on the streets and for a peaceful world.'

'Mom! Oh, Mom!' Radiant, Laurie left her seat to rush to her mother while Tracy turned to embrace her grandfather.

'That's a double wedding present,' Tracy said exuberantly, reaching now to kiss her mother while Laurie moved to hug her grandfather. 'It's for David and me, too. Oh, thank you! Thank you!'

She didn't have to be afraid anymore. Vera felt herself wrapped in a precious serenity. Her family was together again. They would always be together. *At last she could put Kristallnacht behind her.*

Epilogue

The weather – this late January of 1977 – was approaching blizzard proportions in upstate New York. The Kahn house was surrounded by a blanket of snow. The towering trees – edged in white – swayed with a spurious air of fragility. Approaching dusk lent an aura of drama to the winter landscape.

In the living room Paul crouched before a blazing fire in the grate, added additional logs out of exuberance rather than necessity.

'Paul, when will the man with the snowplough be here?' Vera hovered in the doorway. Her eyes – her whole demeanour – exuded a joy that seemed to infiltrate the whole house. 'The driveway should be cleared by the time Dad and Phil return from Albany with Tracy and David.'

'He'll be here any minute,' Paul soothed, rising to his feet. 'Anyhow, the kids' plane came in twenty-five minutes late because of the storm. It'll be at least an hour before they arrive.'

'Vera –' Doris's voice filtered down the hall from the kitchen '– I'm putting the yams into the oven now.' For this festive reunion-dinner, Irene had been given the day off.

'Great,' Vera called back. 'And put up some cider – Laurie and Jeff should be here any minute with Cathy. They'll appreciate a warm-up.'

'I hope Cathy likes the little panda bear I picked up for her.' Paul reached into a breakfront drawer to bring

484

out the latest stuffed animal he'd bought for his three-year-old granddaughter.

'She'll love it. And I hope Laurie and Jeff can get through one evening without a house call,' Vera said with mock reproach. In truth, she was happy that Eastwood's new pair of doctors – with Dr Evans finally accepting retirement – belonged to that vanishing breed of doctors who still made house calls.

'Shall I turn on the news?' Paul asked tentatively.

'Not now,' Vera vetoed. 'I want just to glory in the news we had last week.'

On January 21 – the day after his inauguration – President Carter had made it his first official business to issue an unconditional pardon to almost all men who had peacefully resisted the draft during the Vietnam war. Meant to ease the divisiveness of the war, the announcement had brought about vociferous controversy – though Vera blocked this from her mind. It was enough to know that Tracy and David were coming home.

Various veterans' organizations were upset about the pardon. Senator Barry Goldwater called it 'the most disgraceful thing a President has ever done,' but the parents and wives of those pardoned offered a heartfelt thanks. Some pro-amnesty groups admitted to disappointment that the pardons didn't extend to military deserters – of which there were about 100,000. In addition to the thousands who'd fled to Canada, Sweden, and other countries, the pardon included 250,000 men who'd never registered for the draft.

Tracy and David would be here for this long-awaited reunion but must return to Montreal to wind up their affairs. In six weeks they would be home on a permanent basis. The knowledge was a glorious chorus that sang in Vera's mind.

Tracy and David's child would be born on American

soil, Vera reminded herself with recurrent joy. They didn't know yet, but Dad was buying them a house as a belated wedding gift. A house they would choose. Only to Paul had Vera confessed that she was grateful that David's parents had deserted Eastwood – *too provincial for words* – to move to Albany. But Tracy and David's child – to be named Ernest if a boy, Ernestine if a girl – would not lack for love, she told herself with pride.

'Aunt Vera, where do you want the logs?' His face ruddy from the cold, Neal stood in the doorway, his arms loaded with birch logs.

'Here, let me help you.' Paul crossed to take a share of his logs. 'You look like you're studying to play Santa Claus,' he joshed. 'Or the town drunk.'

'Hey, Uncle Paul, did I tell you what happened in current events class yesterday?' Neal's newly baritone voice echoed with pride. 'We have to do a report on your new book!' Paul's second book had just been published.

'Great,' Paul approved, exchanging a warm glance with Vera.

In time Tracy would teach in the Eastwood school system, Vera told herself. David would be active with Paul in managing the Kahn Fund for Gun Control, utilizing his law training on an in-person basis rather than the long-distance efforts necessary until now. Already Joel was nudging him to become active in local politics once he and Tracy were legal residents – reminding him that his great-grandfather-in-law had been a much-loved mayor of Eastwood.

Then Laurie and Jeff arrived with effervescent little Cathy. The atmosphere crackled with high spirits as Vera and Doris handed out cinnamon-stick spiked mugs of hot apple cider. Hearing the sounds of the snowplough clearing the driveway, Vera smiled. Sooner than they'd expected, Joel and Phil arrived with Tracy and David.

'Darling, you're enormous,' Vera laughed through tears of pleasure, patting Tracy's extended stomach. 'Are you sure you have four months to go?'

'You'll have to be patient, Grandma,' David kidded, clutching Vera in a warm embrace.

'You're probably starving,' Doris said. 'Vera, let's get this show on the road.'

The family gathered about the newly acquired dinner table, large enough to seat a dozen. *They'd be twelve when Tracy's child was born*, Vera thought tenderly. Her family. Her *wonderful* family.

'Paul,' Vera whispered while the others listened absorbedly to a story David was relating about their lives in Montreal. 'I've just decided that we'll expand our trip to London this year.' Each year now, she and Paul spent three weeks in London. 'I want to go to Berlin.' She saw his start of astonishment. 'To see where Mama and Papa and Ernst are buried.'

All these years later she could hear Mrs Munch's voice telling her what had happened to her family in Berlin. *Your father was shot to death on Kristallnacht. Your mother and brother died in Oranienburg-Sachsenhausen. Through special channels Herr Schmidt was able to collect their ashes. The ashes were buried in synagogue ground.*

'We'll visit the synagogue where Mama and Papa and Ernst are buried,' she said softly. 'We'll say a prayer for them.'

But there was a new serenity about her, a new peace in her heart. At last, she told herself, she could truly put *Kristallnacht* into the past.

SP
WORLD
CREATURE OF FIRE

BRUCE COVILLE

DISCARDED

h
Hodder
Children's
Books

a division of Hodder Headline plc

For Diane and Paul

Copyright © 1985, 1996 Bruce Coville

First published in the USA in 1996 as an Archway Paperback
entitled *Chamber of Horrors: Amulet of Doom*,
published by Pocket Books, a division of Simon & Schuster Inc.

First published in Great Britain in 1998
by Hodder Children's Books

The right of Bruce Coville to be identified as the Author of
the Work has been asserted by him in accordance with the
Copyright, Designs and Patents Act 1988.

10 9 8 7 6 5 4 3 2 1

All rights reserved. No part of this publication may be
reproduced, stored in a retrieval system or transmitted,
in any form or by any means without the prior written
permission of the publisher, nor be otherwise circulated
in any form of binding or cover other than that in which
it is published and without a similar condition being
imposed on the subsequent purchaser.

All characters in this publication are fictitious and any
resemblance to real persons, living or dead, is purely coincidental.

A Catalogue record for this book is
available from the British Library

ISBN 0 340 71461 1

Typeset by Hewer Text Ltd, Edinburgh
Printed and bound in Great Britain by
Mackays of Chatham, Kent

Hodder Children's Books
a division of Hodder Headline plc
338 Euston Road
London NW1 3BH

BBRA		BCRO	11 7
BASH		BGRE	4/03
BBIN		BHAR	11/98
BBIR	4/02	BSAN	
BCON		BWHI	

ABOUT THE AUTHOR

Bruce Coville has been scaring people ever since he was born and the doctor screamed, 'Oh, my God! What's *that*?'

His parents were nearly as terrified.

His teachers are still nervous wrecks.

All that took place back in the totally terrifying decade of the 1950s, in and around Syracuse, New York.

When Bruce became a teenager, his grandfather put him to work digging graves in the local cemetery.

His high school's official colours were orange and black.

He spent as much time as possible watching monster movies, reading Famous Monsters of Filmland magazine, and scaring himself by imagining what might be underneath his bed.

Given all that, we have to ask you: Is it any surprise he writes this kind of book?

Mr Coville now lives with his wife, his youngest child, and their three weird cats in a rather old brick house on a hill in Syracuse.

He hasn't dug a grave in years.

Or so he says.

PROLOGUE

The castle stood high on a mountain. Its tall windows—arched at the top and so wide an eagle could fly through them without brushing its wingtips—looked out on billowing clouds and valleys that ran deeper than thought.

Inside, Guptas the demon groveled at the feet of the king. Terror twisted the demon's already hideous face into a mask of despair.

"Don't do this to me," he pleaded in a voice that sounded like rough rocks being rubbed together. "I'm not like the others! You know that!"

The king stared at the scaly creature cowering at his feet. "That much is true," he said at last. Contempt and sorrow mingled in his voice. "You are not like the others." He looked away from Guptas. Anger deepened his lonely eyes, and he bent his head in sorrow.

The king was silent for a moment, as if remembering something. A darkness crept across his face, and his features became like stone. "No, Guptas, you are not like the others." He turned back to the demon, and the weariness in his voice seemed as heavy as the mountains surrounding them. "You are far, far worse."

Guptas howled and grasped the king's sandaled foot, cradling it in his scaly claws. Tears hissed from his eyes. Rolling off the king's flesh without effect, they burned into the polished alabaster floor, leaving black pits where they landed.

"It wasn't my fault! *They* made me do it!" The demon's anguished words echoed off the walls of the great chamber. He began to howl, a cry of fear and despair that would have broken the heart of a lesser man.

The king, unmoved, made a noise of contempt in his throat. "You allowed them to 'make' you do it, Guptas. You were weak, and in your weakness you betrayed me. So now you must be punished."

"Don't do this to me!" cried the creature. "Please! I will never betray you again, I swear it!"

"What good is your word?" asked the king wearily. "You are forsworn already. If I had not been alert, I would be dead."

Guptas rolled over and spread his arms and legs, leaving his vulnerable, scaleless belly open to attack. "Kill me!" he screeched. "Kill me now. But don't do this other thing. I beseech you. Have mercy on Guptas who loves you!"

The king turned his face again so that the creature could not see the tear that had formed at the corner of his eye.

Guptas, lost in his own grief, rolled on the floor and jabbered in terror. Suddenly he rose to his knees and flung his arms around the king's legs.

"Remember your son!" he howled, his gravelly voice desperate. "Remember your son!"

The king sighed, and in his voice was the sorrow of a thousand years of loss and pain. "I had *two* sons."

He looked down at Guptas and allowed the mask of his anger to slip for just a moment. "Yes, Guptas. I remember my son. And I remember how you saved his life, though in the long run it did no good. Are you calling on that debt now?"

"Yes!" cried the creature. "Remember how I risked my own life that day! Remember, and be merciful."

"I remember *everything,*" said the king. He turned and walked to his throne. Guptas followed at his heels, sometimes walking, sometimes crawling. His claws scrabbled on the polished stone.

"My judgment is unchanged," said the king.

Guptas raked his claws against his forehead, howling in terror.

"My judgment stands. But this much I will add. When the time is right, I will come for you. I will come, and I will search your heart. And if I feel that I can trust you—"

Guptas threw himself at the king's feet. "You will see!" he cried joyfully. "I can be—"

His words were cut off by a blinding flash of lightning.

Guptas was gone. A jagged scorch mark scarred the

floor where he had stood. A cloud of acrid smoke hung in the air above it.

And the king, the last king in a long line of great kings, and the last man of his race, sat alone in a hall that was large enough to hold a forest and wept.

Day passed into night. At last the king rose from his throne and wandered out of the great hall, into corridors that wound for miles through the empty palace of his fathers.

In his hand he clutched an amulet.

In the center of the amulet was a scarlet stone, still blazing with a fierce heat.

1

ZENOBIA

"**W**ell, I want to tell you, I never smelled anything so awful in my life. The scent of death was just *clinging* to the thing."

Marilyn Sparks paused, a forkful of broccoli halfway to her mouth, and stared at her aunt Zenobia in a combination of awe and astonishment. It was hard to believe any one person could have had so many adventures—and even harder to believe she would dare to tell them at this table.

Marilyn glanced at her father. He was scowling at Zenobia—the same disapproving scowl he used on his English students when they got out of line.

Zenobia ignored him. A fiercely independent woman who had somehow cropped up in a family full of people pleasers, she was long used to scandalizing her relatives. It was almost a tradition, one that had begun way back when she refused to get married and settle down, at a time when living as a single woman was far from fashionable.

That had seemed funny to Marilyn when she first heard it; Zenobia seemed too young to have had such a problem. But then, Marilyn had a hard time remembering that Zenobia Calkins was really her great-aunt and had already seen her seventieth birthday. Marilyn didn't think about age when she thought about Zenobia. She just adored her.

"Anyway," continued Zenobia, "Baron de Courvis drew out his machete and started to hack away at the dead flesh. Of course, in that climate the thing had become a breeding ground for maggots, and—"

Marilyn's mother cut Zenobia off with a sound that was just short of a shriek. "Really, Aunt Zenobia! Couldn't you tell this some other time?"

Marilyn sighed. She should have known she could count on her mother to stop Zenobia right at the most interesting moment. A story about recovering a giant diamond from the intestines of a five-day-dead rogue elephant, no matter how fascinating, simply did not fall within Helen Sparks's definition of table talk. Not even if it came from her father's sister.

Zenobia looked at Mrs. Sparks with something that seemed like pity. "Of course, my dear," she said sweetly. "I don't know what came over me."

Marilyn put the limp broccoli in her mouth and chewed it morosely. Her family was so stodgy!

"You will finish the story later, won't you, Ms. Calkins?" Kyle Patterson, gangly but good-looking, a year older than Marilyn and unfortunately her brother's

6

best friend, had hardly taken a bite since they had sat down to supper. He was much too excited about being at the same table with a great author to eat. It was the first time Marilyn had ever seen Kyle ignore food—and she had known him since he was three.

"I don't know," said Zenobia, with a touch of petulance. "One has to be in the mood for these things to do them properly."

Kyle looked stricken.

"Of course she'll tell us," said Geoff jovially. "Aunt Zenobia never let a good story go untold, did you?"

Marilyn glared at her brother. He was clearly unaware of how deeply their mother had offended Aunt Zenobia.

"Not if the audience is appreciative," agreed Zenobia, deftly skewering a piece of chicken with her fork. "This bird is a trifle bland, by the by," she said sweetly, turning to Marilyn's mother. "You might want to try using a bit of lemon, Helen. They do it that way in Tangiers. It works quite well."

Silence descended on the table.

It is bland, thought Marilyn, hacking a piece from her own serving of PTA-cookbook chicken—a little more savagely than was necessary—and wishing it were some fierce raptor she had somehow managed to kill with her bare hands. *This whole family is bland. Mr. and Mrs. Normal Q. Boring and their children, that's us. I don't know why Kyle bothers with us.*

She looked across the table to where Kyle was sitting, generally oblivious to her presence—as he had been for most of the last fourteen years—and smiled. He had given up on waiting for Zenobia to resume her story and finally started to eat.

7

That's more like it, she thought fondly. *You could use it.*

It wasn't that Kyle was skinny. But he had topped six feet his year, and his body was still filling out to match the growing he had been doing. He had a thatch of tousled blond hair (which Marilyn was itching to brush away from his forehead) and shocking blue eyes that seemed to bore right through her—whenever he bothered to look her way at all. He was at once more silly and more serious than any person she had ever known, and she had no idea why he bothered with her brother, Geoff.

But she was awfully glad he did.

When they gathered together on the porch after supper, Marilyn thought, for a moment, that Kyle had finally noticed her, too. She was leaning against the railing, and he took a place right next to her. She was thrilled, until she realized his reason: It placed him directly across from Zenobia, who was leaning against the opposite railing, next to Geoff. Her parents, of course, were inside—talking about how awful Zenobia was, probably.

Marilyn looked at her aunt and wondered for an instant if Kyle actually found her attractive. She was, after all, a striking woman. Her hair was pure white, really dazzling, so unlike the yellowy gray she saw on other old people. It curled around her face like a billowing cloud, accentuating the depth of her tan. Marilyn knew the time her aunt had spent in the tropical sun had added to her wrinkles. But like everything else about her, the wrinkles were attractive. Every one of them seemed to speak of experience, wisdom, even

8

adventure. They were part of Zenobia. Zenobia was beautiful. So, by definition, the wrinkles were, too.

She was dressed in white cotton—a crisp skirt and a stylish blouse. A sturdy gold chain circled her neck, holding an amulet that—uncharacteristically, and even unstylishly—she kept tucked mysteriously inside her blouse, so that only its upper edge was visible. Marilyn wondered what it looked like. She had a vague recollection that at some time earlier in the evening Zenobia had mentioned that everything she was wearing had come from Egypt.

"So what happened with the diamond, Ms. Calkins?" asked Kyle eagerly.

Zenobia waved her hand. "Oh, the baron cut open the elephant and there it was. We sold it on the coast for a handsome profit."

Kyle looked like someone had pulled his plug. "Is that all?"

"Well, that leaves out the details. But that's how it all came out."

"But it's the details that make it interesting."

"I know that, young man. I have managed to learn a few things in thirty years of writing best-sellers. But it's a little difficult to leap into the middle of a story with both feet. You have to build your momentum. Mine is still in the dining room, under the cake plate."

"I'm sorry about Mom," said Marilyn. "She's pretty set in her ways."

Zenobia dismissed the topic with another wave of her hand. "I've been dealing with the fogeys in this family since I was six years old and shocked them all by announcing I was going to run away with the minister of the Presbyterian church." She paused to reflect

9

for a moment, then added, "Actually, I think I said I was going to *seduce* him, though where I learned that word, I can't remember."

She took out a cigar and bit off the end of it. "That was the beginning of the end, as far as the family was concerned." She struck a wooden match on the porch railing and lit her cigar. She smoked in silence for a moment. The three teenagers waited for her to speak again.

"Maybe I should have stayed in Egypt," she said with a sigh, flicking her ash over the railing. "I got along quite well there. Felt right at home. I always wondered if maybe I had lived there in a previous life."

"Is Cairo as awful as it looks in the movies?" asked Kyle eagerly. He was an old film buff and tended to view the world in terms of what he saw on late-night television.

"Awful? It's wonderful! Did I ever tell you about the time I got caught in a riot there with that fool Eldred Cooley?"

Without waiting for an answer, she launched into a bizarre story involving Egyptian politics, Chinese jewelry, three dancing girls, and a monkey. Kyle settled back contentedly. Marilyn let herself lean ever so slightly in his direction.

It was very pleasant. The evening had an early summer sweetness to it, cool and filled with the scent of fading lilacs and blooming roses. The moon was nearly full, the sky cloudless and smeared with stars. In the background the spring peepers were in full chorus. And Zenobia was at the peak of her form with the bloodcurdling story she was unfolding.

Until the very end, when something strange happened.

"And that was the last I saw of Eldred Cooley!" she said triumphantly. Then her eyes, which had been blazing, seemed to go all cloudy. "The last time but one," she murmured, placing her hand at her throat. Marilyn could hear a troubled note in her voice, and when she looked more closely, she noticed that Zenobia's fingers seemed to tremble as they clasped the golden chain she wore around her neck. Suddenly she tightened her grip. For a moment Marilyn thought she was going to pull off the amulet. "The last time but one," she repeated.

They waited respectfully. But it was almost as if Zenobia had left the porch. Her body was there—her white hair moving lightly in the breeze, her right hand clutching the last inch of her cigar. But she herself seemed to have vanished.

Finally Marilyn could stand the silence no longer. "Aunt Zenobia, are you all right?"

Zenobia blinked. "Of course," she said hurriedly. "I was just thinking about Egypt. Egypt, and Eldred Cooley, and Suleiman."

"You mean Solomon?" asked Kyle eagerly. "Like in *King Solomon's Mines?*"

"No," said Zenobia sharply. "Suleiman, like in Suleiman. A lot of people get them confused. Remind me and I'll tell you about them sometime."

With that she tossed her cigar butt over the porch railing and stalked into the house.

2

THE AMULET

Marilyn, Kyle, and Geoff stood in shocked silence.

"What did I say?" asked Kyle finally.

"Nothing," said Geoff. "Aunt Zenobia's a few strawberries shy of a shortcake is all. You have to expect this kind of thing from her."

"She's not crazy!" snapped Marilyn. "She's brilliant!"

Geoff shrugged. "I didn't say she was stupid. She may have more I.Q. points than all of New Jersey put together. That doesn't mean she could pass the state sanity test. Come on, Kyle—let's go over to your place and shoot a few baskets before we have to turn in."

The two of them banged down the steps, leaving Marilyn alone on the porch. She twisted a lock of her red hair in tight circles around her finger. She would never admit it to Geoff, but there *was* something strange going on with Aunt Zenobia. She had been oddly distracted ever since she arrived—sometimes seeming like her old self, other times drifting off into a kind of trance, as she had just now. A couple of times Marilyn had caught her fingering the chain of that amulet and staring blankly into space.

Marilyn had mentioned it to her mother last night, but Mrs. Sparks claimed it was just prepublication jitters. "After all, Aunt Zenobia's new book is scheduled to be released in two weeks. It's natural for her to be a bit nervous about what the critics will say. Especially," she had added maliciously, "if it's as weird as the last one. Honestly, I don't know where that woman gets her ideas."

At least Aunt Zenobia has *ideas,* Marilyn had thought unkindly.

She began to dawdle her way down the porch steps. Moving dreamily, she trailed her fingers along the railing, still thinking about Zenobia. When she reached the flagstone walk that led to the street, Brick came wandering up to rub against her legs.

Brick was the Sparkses' cat, a black-and-white stray they had taken in a few years ago. After three weeks of trying to name him, they had settled on Brick, because her father claimed that was exactly what the cat was as dumb as.

Now Brick was meowing for attention. So Marilyn scooped him up. Then she turned to look at the house.

It was an old place, built sometime around the turn of the century. She was glad of that. Occasionally she thought she might like to live in one of the more modern houses that had sprung up lately on the outskirts of town. But every time she spent the night with one of her girlfriends, she realized how much she would miss the creaky old place she had called home for so long. There was something different about a house that had been lived in—a sense of ongoing life, a kind of old-shoe comfort that she never felt in a newer place.

"Isn't that right, Brick?" she asked the cat, as if he could read her mind.

Brick looked at her as if he couldn't believe his ears. Then he reached out a paw and batted her on the side of the face.

"Be that way," she said, dropping him unceremoniously to the ground. He meowed in protest and began rubbing about her legs to be picked back up.

She ignored him and turned her thoughts back to the house. The fact that the place really belonged to Zenobia, that she had lived here as a girl herself, made it even more special. Her ownership was also the reason that Marilyn's parents, even though they paid a respectable rent, could hardly refuse Zenobia whenever she decided to visit. Marilyn was glad of that. Given their own way, they would probably have tried to find some excuse to make the old woman stay at the Kennituck Falls Motel.

She tried to imagine life without Zenobia. The prospect was so dull it made her shudder.

She heard the thump of a basketball on asphalt coming from Kyle's driveway, and the excited shouts of her brother and his friend. The sounds made her feel lonely. Rubbing her arms against the cool of the breeze, which was starting to pick up strength, she hurried back to the house.

Brick, still feeling affectionate, followed at her heels.

In her room she stripped off her jeans and blouse and burrowed into an old flannel nightgown. The pink plaid fabric was far from glamorous, but it did have the virtues of being warm, soft, and exceedingly comfortable.

Marilyn popped the cast album from *Carousel*, her favorite Broadway show, into the CD player, then flopped across her bed and tried to figure out her aunt's curious behavior on the porch. Brick curled up on her back and began to rumble his deep, familiar purr.

After a round of intense but unproductive thought Marilyn decided to chalk Zenobia's mood up to the peculiarities that accompany genius, forget it, and go to sleep.

Hours later she was still wide awake. She tossed and turned, practiced deep breathing, and even tried counting sheep. It was no use. Sleep would not come.

She was not used to being awake at this time of night. Usually she dropped right off.

She sat up in bed. The silence was driving her out of her mind.

Heaving a sigh, she went to her dresser and picked up her brush. She looked in the mirror and grimaced as she began to work the brush through her tangles. Anyone named Sparks should be spared the burden of having such bright red hair.

Well, she thought as she began the vigorous brushing, *at least I was spared the freckles.*

Somewhere after the thirtieth stroke she heard a knock at her door.

Marilyn paused, the brush still in her hair. She glanced at the clock on her nightstand.

It was after two.

"Who is it?" she asked softly.

The door opened a crack; Zenobia peered into the room. A smile creased her face. "Thank goodness you're still awake. I have to talk to you!"

Marilyn put down her brush and crossed to the door. "Come in," she said, swinging it open. She was delighted to see her aunt. But she was also very confused—and a little frightened. Because in Zenobia's eye she had caught a glimpse, brief but unmistakable, of something she had never expected to see there.

She had caught a glimpse of fear.

And the idea of something that could make Zenobia Calkins afraid sent shivers trembling up and down Marilyn's spine.

A moment later Zenobia was sitting cross-legged on Marilyn's bed. She wore a loose-fitting cotton gown and a white linen robe. Except for her white hair, now hanging loose and long over her shoulders, from behind she would have looked like any of a dozen of Marilyn's friends who had sat in the same position while they held forth on life, religion, and the meaning of boys.

Marilyn sat quietly, waiting for her aunt to tell her what was on her mind.

"Egypt is very old," said Zenobia at last.

Marilyn nodded, uncertain of how to respond to such a comment.

"It is filled with strange things," added Zenobia after a another long silence. "Ancient things. Things that perhaps should not be disturbed."

Marilyn remained silent.

"I'm boring you," said Zenobia.

"No!" exclaimed Marilyn. "I just don't know what to say."

"How could you," muttered Zenobia. "I'm rambling like ... like an old woman!" She laughed—a dry, harsh sound. "I'm sorry I bothered you. I had a nightmare, and I wanted to talk to someone."

Marilyn nodded. She knew what it was like to wake up in the middle of the night with terror ripping at your heart. She supposed even the bravest people in the world had nightmares. "Tell me about it."

Zenobia shook her head. "I don't think I want to."

"Then tell me about Egypt. Tell me about Solomon and Suleiman, like you said you would."

Zenobia looked at her suspiciously. "Why do you want to know about that?"

"Because I love your stories," replied Marilyn truthfully.

Zenobia nodded. "Solomon and Suleiman," she said. "History and myth. Reality and magic."

She had a faraway look in her eyes, the same look Marilyn had seen when they were on the porch.

"The thing is, people get them confused," said Zenobia. "Solomon and Suleiman, that is. They're not the same person, as a lot of people seem to believe."

Marilyn, who had never heard of Suleiman, and only remembered Solomon vaguely from some long-forgotten sermon, nodded wisely.

"Solomon came later," said Zenobia. "He's the one

you'll find in the Bible—Solomon's Temple, Solomon and Sheba, and so on. The Koran says he had power over the winds; he would put his throne on a huge carpet made of green silk, and he and his army could fly all over the world that way. The jinn were supposed to be at his command."

"Jinn?"

"Genies," explained Zenobia. "At least, that's how you've probably heard of them. I suppose all that might have been so. But I doubt it. Magic was well on the way out by that time anyway."

"You talk as if magic was real once."

Zenobia shrugged. "Who's to say? When you've traveled in as many places as I have, wild places, primitive places, you see things that can't really be explained. Is it magic? I don't know. It might be. But not great magic. The great magic is all gone."

"Why did you want to tell me about Solomon?" asked Marilyn.

"I didn't. You asked."

"But you mentioned him on the porch," persisted Marilyn. "Egypt, and Eldred Cooley, and Solomon. Or was it Suleiman?" She shook her head in frustration. "Now I'm totally confused!"

"It was Suleiman," said Zenobia at last. "Egypt, and Eldred Cooley, and Suleiman. Egypt is the most important place in the world, at least to me. Eldred Cooley was a friend. Not a particularly good friend, but the most interesting one I ever had. He died late last year."

She shivered, and Marilyn sensed a story, another story hidden behind the one she was being told. She wanted to interrupt, but Zenobia had started again.

"Suleiman made this amulet, which Eldred gave me shortly before his death. It has nothing to do with Egypt, other than the fact that Eldred found it there. How it got to Egypt I have no idea."

As she was talking, Zenobia pulled the amulet from her nightgown.

Marilyn caught her breath. It was unbelievably beautiful.

Zenobia stared down at it for a long time. "Take it," she said at last. "I want you to keep it for me." As she spoke she began to draw the golden chain over her head.

"I can't do that. It's too precious! Besides, it's yours. Your friend gave it to you."

Zenobia snorted. "What sort of a friend do you suppose he was, giving me this?" Suddenly she reached forward and grabbed Marilyn by the wrists, her grip so hard it was almost painful. "I'm *not* giving it to you," she added fiercely. "That's important for you to know. I just want you to guard it for me."

"Aunt Zenobia, you're hurting me," whispered Marilyn.

Zenobia looked startled and released her hold on Marilyn's wrists. Marilyn shivered. It wasn't the strength of her aunt's grip that frightened her so much as it was the look in her eyes—the same look they had held when Zenobia first entered her room; the look of fear.

"I'm sorry," said Zenobia hoarsely. "Please—take the amulet and keep it safe until I can figure out what to do about it."

Though her voice was neutral, her eyes were filled

with desperation. They pleaded with Marilyn, and there was no way she could refuse her aunt's request.

"All right," she said, her voice reluctant. "I'll take care of it for you."

"Thank you," whispered Zenobia. "Thank you, Marilyn. I'll pay you back, somehow. I promise."

Then she rose from the bed and hurried out of the room before Marilyn had a chance to ask any of the dozen questions vying with one another in her mind.

"Wait!" she called, reaching out anxiously. It was too late. The door swung shut, and Zenobia was gone.

Marilyn sat for a long time, staring at the amulet. It was made of a polished blue stone she couldn't identify. Set in its center was a blood-red gem.

She cupped the amulet in her hand, staring at it curiously. It was wonderful to hold something so beautiful, and she felt a surge of possessiveness rising in her, a feeling that she never wanted to give it back.

But when she extended her finger to touch the sparkling scarlet jewel, she cried out and drew back her finger in surprise. The jewel was hot, so hot that it hurt to touch it.

Even stranger, it sent a tingle like electricity racing up her arm.

3

NIGHTMARE

"**M**arilyn! Hey, Marilyn, wake up. Class is over!"

Seeing that the words failed to rouse Marilyn from her trancelike state, Alicia Graves, a short girl with spiky blond hair, gave her a jab on her upper arm and shouted, "Hey, Sparks! Red alert! The aliens have landed and we need every able-bodied woman to keep them from carrying off our men!"

Marilyn came out of her trance with a jolt, knocking three pens and a pencil to the floor.

"Nice work, Airhead," said Alicia sardonically. At the same time she bent to pick up the items Marilyn had knocked over.

Marilyn rubbed her hands over her face. "Sorry, Licorice. I'm kind of out of it today."

Marilyn had been dubbed "Airhead" and Alicia "Licorice" eight years ago, on the first day of third grade, which was when the two girls had first met. The names had been given during a playground squabble. They had patched it up the next morning and been best friends ever since.

"It's all right," said Alicia, depositing the pens on Marilyn's desk. "I suppose it's not easy being a dip. I'll keep the pencil, though. I could use one."

"Spoken like a true dwarf," said Marilyn, tucking the pens out of Alicia's reach, in case she should decide she also needed one of those.

"Hey, short people got rights," said Alicia, drawing herself up to her full five feet one and three-quarter inches.

"That's true," said Marilyn. "They got rights, and they got lefts. They also got tops and bottoms. What they don't got is much in the middle."

"You die, flame-brain," said Alicia, who had (much to Marilyn's astonishment) long envied Marilyn's bright red hair. "But not until you tell me why you're doing such a good imitation of the walking dead today."

Marilyn shrugged. "I didn't get much sleep last night." That was true, as far as it went, though it didn't say much about why.

Alicia knew her friend well enough to make a good guess anyway. "Whassa matter? That crazy aunt of yours keep you up all night telling stories?"

"She's not crazy!"

"Well, she ain't normal."

"Who is? Come on, we'll be late for gym."

* * *

As it turned out, they were late for gym anyway. Marilyn, half-undressed in front of her locker, fell into a trance and was still standing there when Alicia came back from delivering a note her doctor had sent to the instructor.

"Oh, give me a break," she sputtered when she saw Marilyn staring into space. "What is it with you today, Sparks?"

Marilyn looked down at her half-dressed body and shook her head. "Just showing off, I guess," she said, forcing a laugh.

"Save it for someone who can appreciate it. Me, I'd rather go stare at the wrestling team. Finish getting ready before we both get in trouble."

Marilyn changed in silence. But her mind was racing. Her aunt's strange behavior, and the mysterious amulet, had been dominating her thoughts all day, making it impossible to concentrate on anything else. Her thoughts kept drifting back to the conversation in her bedroom, and the fear in Zenobia's eyes.

Part of her wanted to tell Alicia about the conversation—and the amulet. But she knew her friend would merely claim it was her famous imagination at work and tell her to wise up. Another part resisted telling her anyway. Especially about the amulet. That just felt like a wonderful secret that she wanted to keep to herself.

But if she couldn't start concentrating on something else, she was going to end up in big trouble before the day was over. Teachers at Burton-Speake High were not partial to daydreamers.

"I know what it is!" shouted Alicia, interrupting her thoughts. "You're cooking up some lamebrained scheme to go off with your aunt when she leaves on her next trip. Well, cool your imagination, Airhead. Let's head for the gym before we get in more trouble than we're in already."

Marilyn closed her locker and followed her friend's stocky form out of the room. *Cool your imagination!* indeed. Alicia must be really fed up with her daydreaming today or she would never have said that. She knew very well how tired Marilyn was of people telling her not to let her imagination run away with her.

Despite her indignation, Marilyn did try to concentrate on gym class. She wasn't very successful, though, and ended up being hit twice with the volleyball because she was too absorbed in her own thoughts to pay attention to the game.

"You ought to go out for the Olympics," said Alicia as they left the locker room after class.

Marilyn was working on a suitable retort when the lanky figure of Kyle Patterson ambled around the corner. His shirt, as usual, was only half tucked in. "Hey," he said cheerfully. "It's Sparky Junior!"

Marilyn considered punching him. Her brother, not surprisingly, was known as Sparky to all his friends. Equally unsurprising was the fact that about half of them referred to her as Sparky Junior. Even so, the words always activated a primitive instinct deep inside her: namely, the urge to kill.

Even when it came from Kyle.

"What do you want, Lurch?" snarled Alicia. Unlike Marilyn, she was not very fond of Kyle.

"Bug off, fireplug. I'm talking to your friend."

Alicia grumbled something about biting him on the

knee. Marilyn, doing her best to forget "Sparky Junior," smiled sweetly and asked Kyle what he wanted.

"I was just wondering if your aunt told you any more about King Solomon last night." He leaned against a locker. "You're really lucky, you know. Having someone like that for an aunt. She's fantastic."

"I know," said Marilyn. She hesitated for a moment, then said, "Why don't you have supper with us again tonight? I'm sure my mother wouldn't mind. Then you can ask Aunt Zenobia about Solomon yourself."

"Do you think that would be okay?"

Alicia snorted. "Are you kidding? You eat over there so often now her father could claim you as a dependent on his taxes."

"Yeah, but he'd probably rather have you," retorted Kyle. "Then he could use the short form." Turning to Marilyn, he said, "Thanks for the invite. I'll see you tonight."

He walked away too quickly for Alicia to think of a comeback to his short joke. Marilyn watched him go, a dreamy expression on her face.

"I don't know what you see in that jerk," growled Alicia.

Marilyn laughed. "He's adorable!"

"So are teddy bears . . . and *they* keep their mouths shut!"

Supper was a disaster. Instead of being fascinating and witty, Zenobia was cranky and out of sorts. Marilyn had never seen her aunt this way before, and she wondered if she was ill.

Kyle, sitting next to Zenobia, tried desperately to draw her into telling a story until finally she snapped at him. He withdrew like a whipped puppy for the rest of the meal, and Marilyn wanted nothing so much as to reach out and cuddle him and make him feel better.

As soon as they could politely manage it, Kyle and Geoff excused themselves and went off to shoot baskets, leaving Marilyn alone with Zenobia and her parents. After a while Marilyn headed for her room, preferring isolation to the tension that hung over the living room.

She sat on her bed, staring at the amulet, which she had taken from her dresser drawer. It had occupied her thoughts all day anyway. The funny thing was, now that she could really examine it, she didn't know what she was looking for.

Brick sprawled on her lap, purring loudly. Every once in a while he would bat lazily at the amulet, making it twist on the end of the golden chain. The first time he struck at it, Marilyn feared he would get a shock, as she had the night before. When he didn't seem to feel anything, she gathered her courage and touched the jewel again. She was almost disappointed to find that it felt completely normal.

She heard voices downstairs and wondered what was going on. In her usual imaginative fashion she pictured a dreadful fight between Zenobia and her parents. The talking stopped. She was still trying to imagine her aunt's triumphant final remark—her imagination was wild, but not wild enough to conceive

26

of her parents winning an encounter with Zenobia—
when someone tapped on her door.

Brick sprang up and bounded off her lap.

"Idiot," said Marilyn fondly. Then she called,
"Come in!"

It was Zenobia. When she saw the amulet in Marilyn's fingers, she smiled in relief.

"I just wanted to make sure nothing had happened
to it," she said. Crossing to the bed, she sat down and
took the amulet from Marilyn, letting it dangle from
her fingers. The soft burnish of the gold chain gleamed
dully in the lamplight. The red jewel winked and spar-
kled. "Pretty, isn't it?" she whispered.

Marilyn reached for the amulet, and Zenobia
dropped it into her hand. She held it up, letting it
dangle between them like an unanswered question.
"It's beautiful," she agreed. "But it makes me
nervous."

Zenobia raised an eyebrow.

"It's that stone in the center," said Marilyn, feeling
silly. "It's almost like an eye." She shrugged. "I'm
being foolish, I suppose."

"Not really," said Zenobia.

Marilyn started to tell her aunt about the amulet
shocking her the night before, but couldn't bring herself to say the words. It just seemed too ridiculous. In
fact, she was beginning to wonder if she had imagined it.

"Why do you want me to keep it, anyway?" she
asked. "What could possibly happen to it here in Kennituck Falls?"

Zenobia pushed at Marilyn's hand. "It's just safer
with you right now, that's all." She turned to the cor-

ner where Brick was lurking and made a little noise with her tongue.

Marilyn was astonished to see the cat, who usually hated strangers, come bounding over to her.

"Cats are very important," said Zenobia, scratching Brick behind his ears. "Take good care of him."

"I do. But you didn't really answer my question."

Zenobia sighed. "You make me feel like a hypocrite."

Marilyn blinked in surprise.

"Listen," said the old woman. "I've never been one to believe that ignorance is bliss. And I'm certainly the last who can advise against curiosity. But in this case—well, I think the less you know the better."

"Thanks a lot!"

Zenobia laughed. "You're too much like me for your own good. I'll tell you what. Once I solve this mess, I'll tell you the whole story. Will that be a fair trade for my silence now?"

"I guess so," said Marilyn reluctantly.

"Good. Now, why don't you put the thing away. You look like you could use a decent night's sleep."

She rose from the bed and left the room as quickly as she had entered.

Brick yowled as Zenobia closed the door behind her, sounding as though he had just lost his best friend.

Marilyn sighed and tucked the amulet under her pillow.

A few minutes later she was asleep.

* * *

The dream started innocently enough. She and Kyle were bicycling down a country lane, with a picnic lunch stowed in their backpacks.

She was wearing the amulet around her neck.

They found a beautiful tree-shaded spot beside a little stream and settled down to have lunch. The day was warm and sunny, the air sweet and clean. But suddenly everything went dark.

"Give me the amulet!" said a hoarse voice.

"I can't!" Marilyn cried. "It's not mine. It belongs to my aunt!"

"No, it doesn't," said the voice. "It belongs to *me.*"

The sun had disappeared completely. The air was cold and smelled of something terrible and unclean. She leaned against Kyle, but he felt funny. She turned to look at him, and his face began to change, change into something horrible.

"The amulet!" he said, and his voice was the same voice that had come out of nowhere a moment earlier. "Give me the amulet!"

"No!' she screamed. "I can't!"

She tried to draw away from him, but his arms were tight about her, hot and scaly and smelling of death. She beat at his chest and her hands sank right into it.

They burned.

"The amulet," he said again. His eyes were pits of fire now, his nose an upturned horror with ragged nostrils in the middle of his scaly face. He opened his mouth and a forked tongue flickered between yellow fangs. "Give me the amulet!"

When she refused, he lowered his head toward her

neck. She could feel hot breath, and the drip of burning saliva....

Marilyn sat up, her body covered with a cold sweat. Brick stood hissing at the end of the bed, back arched and fur raised as though he had just spotted a dog.

Marilyn fought back tears. "It was only a dream," she whispered. "Only a dream."

Then, prompted by a suspicion she couldn't explain, she thrust her hand under the pillow.

The amulet was gone.

4

THE TOUCH OF
DEATH

Marilyn sat in the small pool of light cast by her
bed lamp, body rigid with fright.

Zenobia, she thought, when the fear released its grip
on her brain enough for her to think at all. *I've got
to get Aunt Zenobia.*

Yet for a moment she was unable to climb out of
bed. The nightmare was too fresh in her memory, the
fear too strong. The bed itself seemed like the only
island of safety in a dark world of hidden horrors.

Brick jumped to the floor. The thump of his landing
sent her heart leaping into her throat, and she let out
a gasp of fear. The cat looked up at her. She could
have sworn he was afraid, too. She cursed herself for
being overimaginative.

Overimaginative or not, the amulet was gone. She
had been trusted with it, and now it was missing.

Taking a deep breath, she climbed out of her bed. But when she reached the door, she stopped. Before she went to get Zenobia, she should make sure the thing was really missing. She'd look like a real jerk rousing her aunt and then finding that the amulet had only slipped to the floor while she was sleeping.

She shook herself and smiled. Of course that was what had happened! The amulet was still under her pillow, just in a slightly different place. That nightmare must have really rattled her brains, for her to panic this way.

Though it was a wonderful solution, unfortunately it turned out to be wrong. When Marilyn returned to her bed and pulled aside her pillow, she found nothing but an expanse of white linen.

Frantic again, she dropped to the floor and reached under her bed, hoping perhaps the amulet had slid over the top of the mattress and landed among the dust kitties.

As she groped in the darkness she felt something grab her hand. Her heart, already in her throat and with no place left to go, seemed to stop for a moment. Then she felt the familiar jab of a sharp little tooth and crumpled against the bed in relief.

"Brick! Get out of there, you idiot!"

She dragged the cat, who went limp in protest, from under the bed. Then she lifted the edge of the sheet and looked into the darkness where he had been lurking.

The bed lamp wasn't bright enough. She needed more light.

Sliding open the drawer in her nightstand, she fumbled around for the little flashlight she kept there. It was a habit she had developed more than ten years ago, to help her through her occasional bouts of fear of the dark. They didn't come often, but when they did they were overwhelming.

Right now she was too worried about the missing amulet to be afraid. She simply needed the flashlight to see better.

Lying flat on her stomach, she cast its beam under her bed and looked anxiously for the dull gleam of gold.

She saw three socks and a great deal of dust, but no amulet.

Cursing to herself, she got back to her knees. She looked at the bed. Maybe the amulet had gotten caught in the sheets, or between the top of the mattress and the headboard.

Five minutes later the bed had been stripped to the mattress pad, and the mattress itself pulled a half foot back from the headboard.

The amulet was nowhere to be found.

Which left her right back where she had started. She had to get Zenobia.

Marilyn hesitated. How could she tell her aunt she had lost the amulet?

"But I didn't lose it," she protested out loud, causing Brick, who had been playing in the pile of sheets, to skittle under a chair. "I *couldn't* have lost it. It was there when I went to sleep."

That was when she realized that the alternative was just as bad: If she hadn't lost it, someone must have taken it. Someone had come into her room while she slept, reached under her pillow, and stolen the amulet.

She shivered, thinking of what else the unknown thief could have done.

But who was it? Who besides Zenobia even knew she had the thing?

She had to get her aunt.

Marilyn took a moment to brace herself. She was not looking forward to breaking the news to Zenobia. Finally she took a deep breath and headed into the hallway. She had her flashlight in one hand, and Brick tucked under her arm. She was taking the cat along for comfort. She would have preferred to have taken him for *protection,* but she was well aware he would be useless in any kind of emergency.

The floor was cold. She wished she had thought to put on slippers.

The silence seemed to beat at her. It was the silence of an old house, filled with memories, filled with the days and nights of the people who had lived here, a silence that was not quite silence, and not quite safe. At least, that was how it seemed to Marilyn in her overwrought condition.

She reached Zenobia's door and knocked softly, then waited, shifting nervously from one foot to the other.

No answer.

She knocked again.

Still no answer.

"Aunt Zenobia?"

She knocked a third time, more loudly still, then dropped Brick to the floor and gently turned the knob.

The cat let out a bloodcurdling yowl and disappeared down the hallway. Marilyn jumped, almost dropping the flashlight, and cursed under her breath.

"Aunt Zenobia!" she hissed. "It's me—Marilyn. I have to talk to you."

Still no answer. She pushed the door open a little farther and shone her light into the room. The feeble beam fell on something that gleamed a dull yellow— a golden chain. Shifting the flashlight just slightly, she felt relief surge through her. The amulet was dangling from Zenobia's fingers, its great central jewel sparkling in the beam of the flashlight. Zenobia must have come into her room while she slept and retrieved the thing.

But why?

"Aunt Zenobia?"

She stepped into the room, overcome with curiosity. Her aunt had been willing to wake her the night before. Surely she would not complain if Marilyn did the same thing now.

"Aunt Zenobia!" she said more loudly. At the same time she moved the beam of her flashlight up the bed.

It clattered to the floor, and she clasped her hands over her mouth as a wave of cold horror flooded her body. She felt herself sway. Afraid she was going to faint, she dropped to her knees and leaned forward, resting her forehead against the floor.

For a long time she could not force herself to move.

That Zenobia was dead there was no question. But Marilyn had seen dead people before. The sight, while unpleasant, was not enough to drive her to her knees.

Part of what was hitting her so hard right now was shock, of course. But beyond that, and far more appalling than death itself, was the rictus of fear that had contorted Zenobia's face in her last moments. It was her open, staring eyes and what could only be a scream of horror frozen on her face that made Marilyn's insides churn.

How long she stayed that way, her body quaking, her head pressed against the floor, she could not have said.

What finally forced her to move was the tiniest bit of doubt. What if her aunt was not dead? What if she had had a heart attack and was still alive, just barely, needing help, needing someone . . .

Marilyn forced herself to raise her head from the floor. Zenobia's arm, dangling over the edge of the bed, the golden chain of the amulet tangled in her fingers, was close enough to touch.

Slowly she reached forward.

The flesh of the wrist was still warm.

But there was not the slightest sign of a pulse.

Marilyn was silent for a moment, grief engulfing her. She couldn't bear to look at her aunt. But the image of that contorted face, glimpsed during one brief instant of horror, still burned in her mind.

She leaned her face against Zenobia's hand and wept.

Her tears fell on the amulet. When they touched it, a rough voice, seeming to come from nowhere, growled, "Give that amulet to me!"

Then, even more terrifying, Marilyn felt her aunt's fingers tighten around the mysterious ornament. At the same time she sensed power in the room, a crackle that was almost electric.

As suddenly as it had come, it vanished. For a moment Zenobia's hand, soft and smelling of spice, rested itself against her cheek.

And then Zenobia's voice, kind and calm, spoke in

her mind: *Be brave, Marilyn. Be brave, because I am going to need your help.*

The joy Marilyn felt at hearing her aunt's voice vanished with her next words, for even after death Zenobia's voice quivered with horror when she spoke them.

Be careful, Marilyn. Be careful ... and beware of Guptas!

The hand went limp. Zenobia's presence vanished.

As if a spell had been broken, Marilyn's voice returned, and she began to scream.

5

A LETTER FROM
ZENOBIA

Marilyn sat in the kitchen, drinking a cup of hot chocolate. She had a dark blue blanket wrapped around her shoulders. Her mother stood behind her, rubbing her neck.

Upstairs they could hear the men from the ambulance service poking around in Zenobia's room.

"Why were you in there, anyway?" asked Mrs. Sparks softly.

Marilyn sighed. She had already answered the question twice. Wearily she told about the missing amulet for the third time. "I was worried about it, because I figured it was very valuable. And I thought Aunt Zenobia might still be awake. Sometimes she writes ..." she stopped, corrected herself. "She used to write in the middle of the night, sometimes."

"I know," said Mrs. Sparks. Her voice carried the old note of disapproval. "She used to keep me awake."

Let it rest! thought Marilyn. *The woman is dead. Can't you finally stop resenting her?*

Her father appeared at the doorway. "Well, they're gone," he said. He walked to the table and dropped heavily into one of the creaky chairs.

Geoff came in after him, looking glum. He had not been nearly as fond of Zenobia as Marilyn was. Even so, her death had struck him deeply.

"What happens now?" asked Marilyn. Her voice had a tiny quaver in it.

"They'll take her to Flannigan's," said Mr. Sparks wearily, as if he knew the routine all too well. "She'll be embalmed. Tomorrow we'll go and pick out a coffin. There'll be viewing hours. Relatives we haven't seen in years will show up, expecting to be fed and sheltered."

"Don't be cynical, Harvey," said Mrs. Sparks. "There'll be plenty of people *bringing* food."

"Don't forget the reporters," said Geoff.

Mrs. Sparks looked startled. "What?"

"Reporters," repeated Geoff. "Aunt Zenobia was famous. Plus she had that new book coming out next month. Her publisher was pushing it as her best ever. This is going to be big news."

"Oh, God," moaned his mother. "I hadn't thought of that."

"Will they be able to fix her face?" asked Marilyn suddenly.

"What?"

"Her face," she repeated impatiently. "It looked awful. Will they be able to fix it?"

Mr. Sparks actually chuckled. "Of course they will, sweetheart. It's not that unusual to have facial contortions with a heart attack. They'll just—"

"I don't want to know how!" said Marilyn vehemently. "I just wanted to make sure they could do it. Aunt Zenobia was beautiful and people should remember her that way."

They sat for another hour, talking quietly in the way that people do when the presence of death has been brought to their minds. The night was still dark when they made their way back to their separate rooms, their separate fears.

It's funny how death enters a house, Marilyn thought, lying in her bed. *It comes to steal the most precious thing of all, and it doesn't make any difference how many locks you have on the doors. When it wants to come in, it comes in.*

She had often wondered if death was accidental or planned. Was there a time when you were destined to die, a time that nothing could change, one way or the other? Or was death just something that happened, willy-nilly, with no rhyme or reason?

She sighed in annoyance, then turned and fluffed her pillow. Those kinds of thoughts confused her. She dropped her head back onto the pillow and drew the covers up around her.

Brick jumped onto the bed and began kneading his paws against the comforter.

Marilyn was glad to have his company. After all that had happened, she didn't want to be alone. Lulled by the low rumble of the cat's purr, she began to drift toward sleep. But as she did, her rebellious mind began to replay the horror of finding Zenobia's corpse, and all the strange things that had happened in her aunt's room.

After several minutes of tossing and turning, Marilyn sat up and looked around her familiar room. Every shadow seemed filled with danger. She pulled Brick to her chest and held him close.

What am I going to do? she wondered. *Aunt Zenobia wants me to be brave. But right now I'm scared out of my mind.*

She thought, briefly, about telling her mother about the things she had heard in Aunt Zenobia's room. But she had been chastised too many times for her "wild imaginings" to think she would get any sympathy for this story.

No, for now she was on her own.

Unless you counted Aunt Zenobia.

To Marilyn's enormous relief her parents didn't force her to go to school. Unfond as they had been of Zenobia themselves, they recognized their daughter's grief and allowed her to stay home to deal with it.

She spent the morning helping her mother make a list of relatives who had to be called. Later they went through Zenobia's clothing and picked out the outfit she would be buried in. The idea startled Marilyn; it had never before occurred to her that someone actually had to do these things.

After lunch she accompanied her father to Flannigan's and helped him choose an elaborate mahogany coffin. That had pleased Marilyn. She thought the coffin was beautiful, and that Zenobia would have liked it.

Somewhere in her mind she was vaguely aware of her father's concern about Zenobia's will. The house they lived in had been hers, after all, and now it would belong to someone else. Possibly them, possibly not. Even Marilyn had to admit that her beloved aunt had been eccentric enough that she might have left the place to anyone. It could well turn out that they had to move.

She shoved the thought to the back of her mind. It was too much to deal with right now.

So the day was sad, but bearable. Things didn't turn terrifying until the middle of that night, when Marilyn woke to find Brick lying on her chest.

When she stirred, the big cat opened his eyes. They were blazing red.

Then he spoke.

"Get the amulet!"

His voice sounded like two rough stones rubbing together.

Marilyn screamed and flung the cat from the bed. He yowled once, a sharp, horrifying sound. Then, looking oddly empty, he crouched by the baseboard, staring pathetically up at her.

Marilyn buried her face in her pillow and began to cry.

What was going on here?

An hour later, when the light began to creep over the edge of her window, she wondered if the incident with Brick had been a dream.

The last twenty-four hours had been like a dream

anyway, a period she had moved through like a mario-
nette, walking, talking, but all the time feeling as
though someone else were pulling her strings. The
feeling came not because she felt she was being forced
to do things she didn't want to, but simply because
she felt too weak to do anything on her own.

She heard Geoff singing in the shower and heaved
herself out of bed. Knowing her parents, it was unlikely she would be allowed another day off from
school.

She looked around. Brick was nowhere to be seen.

She shivered. Had he really talked to her?

Or was she just losing her mind?

She threw on her robe and went to pound on the
bathroom door. Geoff would stay wet and off-key forever if she didn't.

"Be out in a minute!" he yelled, which meant she
could expect him in ten.

Walking back toward her room, she stopped, almost
against her will, beside Zenobia's door.

A thrill of horror tingled through her. In the morning light the rational part of her mind dismissed what
had happened in Zenobia's room two nights ago as a
figment of her overwrought imagination. Common
sense told her there had been no voices, no touch
from the dead woman's hand.

Another part of her, more daring, clung to the
memory and insisted it was reality.

"I'm going to need your help," the voice had
whispered.

The words had been repeating in her mind ever
since. What kind of help could a dead person need?

Marilyn blinked. She had stepped into Zenobia's room without realizing what she was doing.

She looked around. Her mother had had no time to come in here and clean things out. Other than a change of sheets, the place looked pretty much as it had the night of Zenobia's death.

For a moment Marilyn felt like an intruder. Then she decided she was glad to be here, because it made her feel closer to Zenobia.

She had crossed to the dresser and was examining her aunt's bottles of perfume (several) and her selection of cosmetics (minimal) when she spotted an envelope sticking out from under the dresser scarf. Pulling it out, she felt a little tingle run down her spine.

It was addressed to her.

Fingers trembling, she opened it.

Dear Marilyn,

I have just left your room, and I suddenly find myself doubting whether I should have asked you to guard the amulet for me after all. I am feeling very guilty about it.

The rational part of my mind says I am just being foolish. But another part says I may have done a terrible thing.

If I have, I hope Heaven, and you, will forgive me.

I'm afraid, Marilyn. I think I am in great danger. It may seem silly, but if anything should happen to me, there are some things you should know about the amulet.

I had the thing, as you may remember, from my "friend" Eldred Cooley, who was a second-

44

rate archaeologist with first-rate ambitions. Eldred found it in the Egyptian desert several years ago. He showed it to me then, with the declaration that there was something "special" about it that he was going to figure out.

It seems perhaps he did. Last year I ran into Eldred again in Cairo and we went to dinner. After he had a little too much to drink, he began to talk more freely than he should have.

He told me he had discovered the secret of the amulet and that within a month he would be rich beyond his wildest dreams.

When I expressed my skepticism he rattled on with a wild story about an ancient race of giants who had created a great civilization while mankind was still grubbing for subsistence in primitive villages. He called them the Suleimans and claimed they were the basis for any number of myths and religious beliefs throughout the East. He said the amulet was an artifact of their culture.

He must have seen the disbelief in my face, because he got angry and said he would prove it to me. I ignored his comments as the ravings of a drunk—until later that night when he showed up at the door of my hotel room.

He was holding an exquisite metal box engraved with strange markings.

And he was dying.

I took one look at him and dragged him through the door. He was gasping for breath. His skin was mottled with blotches of black and purple, and his hands were horribly swollen.

"Look at this, Zenobia," he whispered, holding

out the box. "Then tell me if you still think I'm crazy."

Ignoring the box, I threw him onto the couch and tore open his shirt collar. It did no good. His neck was so swollen his air pipes were being crushed.

I ran to the phone to call a doctor.

"Don't!" he whispered. "It's too late. And I have to talk to you. I have to tell you something."

I knelt by his side and cradled his head in my arms. I had to struggle to keep from vomiting; a terrible stench rose from his body. My nausea grew when he reached for my hand with his swollen, discolored fingers.

"The amulet," he whispered, holding it out to me with his other hand. "I want you to have the amulet." He smiled. It was pathetic. "I always wanted to give you something special, Zenobia. Here it is."

He began to cough, only his throat was so swollen the air could not get out, and he shook with agony.

"Great power here," he whispered. "But you must be careful. Be careful, Zenobia." He tried to cough again. His fingers tightened on mine. "Be careful. And don't trust Guptas!"

"What do you mean?" I asked.

It was too late. He was dead.

The details of what happened next—the police, the government, the doctors—aren't important, though you should know about the box.

Marilyn, that box was an unbelievable find. I know some archaeology, and the condition, the workmanship, the age of this piece made it the kind of discovery an archaeologist would kill for.

The Egyptian government has it now, and they're not talking about it.

As for myself, I have not spent a peaceful night since then. I have been tormented by the most horrible nightmares, and ...

Well, I think I made a foolish mistake. I don't want to go into the details—if you are as much like me as I think you are, it would only tempt you to try the same experiment yourself.

Right now I just need to separate myself from the amulet for a little while.

I'm tired. Maybe with you tending the thing, I can finally rest.

I'll talk to you in the morning. In fact, with any luck, you will never have to read this letter. I will simply reclaim the amulet and dispose of it in some other way. (I did try to destroy it once. It was impossible!)

One other thing, in case you do read this: Don't let them get you down. You can be anything you want. Just believe in yourself.

Your loving aunt,
Zenobia

PS: Whatever you do, don't try to use the amulet!

6

DEATH DREAM

Other than the fact that she was totally unable to concentrate, returning to school was not as bad as Marilyn had feared. Her friends were sympathetic, and they spoke to her with a kindness that was often hidden in their day-to-day banter. Her teachers were willing to overlook her lack of attentiveness. And best of all, Kyle Patterson caught up with her on the way home, putting his baseball cap on her head and pulling the visor over her eyes.

"Wouldn't you rather be with Geoff?" she asked.

"I was thinking about your aunt. Geoff didn't understand Zenobia. You do." He blushed, and corrected himself. "Did."

Marilyn nodded. "I loved her." She heard her voice start to crack and turned away. She wasn't going to cry. Not now. Maybe not ever.

Kyle put an arm around her shoulder. "I know," he said. "I did, too."

She looked at him in surprise.

His blush deepened. "That may sound stupid. But I read all her books. I felt as if I knew her. And I wanted to be like her. I never admired anyone so much in my life."

Marilyn hesitated. For a moment she wondered if she should show him the letter, which had occupied center stage in her thoughts for the entire day.

She decided against it.

He'll just think Aunt Zenobia was losing her mind and end up feeling disillusioned. And that won't do anyone any good.

"What do you mean, you wanted to be like her?" she asked at last.

He tightened his mouth for a moment, and she was afraid he wasn't going to answer. Finally he said, "I don't usually talk about it, because I'm afraid people will laugh. But I'm thinking of becoming a writer. It's not the kind of thing you can just study and then go into, like carpentry or engineering. People seem to think you have to be weird to do it. But it's what I've always wanted. And knowing Zenobia ... well, she just made me feel like I could do it."

Marilyn was silent for a moment. She knew Kyle had just trusted her with a secret he wouldn't tell his best friends, not even Geoff.

"I know what you mean," she said at last. "At least, I think I do," she added quickly. She glanced up at him. He seemed to be waiting for her to go on. "I want to be a singer. Not just with a rock group. I want ... I want to be on Broadway."

There. It was out. A confidence for a confidence. He had trusted her, and she was responding in the only way she could think of—by trusting him, too.

But something inside her was waiting for him to laugh.

"I think you can do it," he said solemnly.

She looked at him in surprise.

"I've listened to you." He smiled at the blank look that crept into her features. "It was hard not to. You're always practicing in your room while Geoff and I are playing chess."

"You heard me?" she cried in horror. Blushing, but also smiling, she turned her head away. "I can't believe you could hear me."

"I *liked* hearing you," insisted Kyle. "I wouldn't just say that, because I know how hard it is to get the truth. But I like the way you sing. And I know a little about show music, because my old man is crazy for it and plays it all the time. So I think you can do it. And I want you to read a story I wrote," he continued breathlessly, "because maybe you'll tell me if you *don't* like it, which is something almost no one will do, and it would be great to have someone I could trust to tell me when something I do stinks. And . . ." And here he paused, taking a break in the flow of words that had been carrying him away.

She waited patiently.

"And I've been meaning to tell you," he said at last. "I really like you."

Marilyn's first surge of delight was replaced almost instantly by a flood of panic and the desperate thought, *What do I do now?*

Kyle reached for her hand. His own was warm and strong, and it made her feel safe.

She stopped worrying about what to do next. They walked home in a comfortable silence, feeling safe with each other's secrets. They lingered for a while on the front porch, then Kyle headed for home, and Marilyn slipped into the house.

Her sense of safety ended as soon as she entered and crossed the threshold.

Something was wrong.

She had no idea what it was ... or even why she was so sure of it, other than a prickling at the back of her scalp that made her want to turn and run.

She stood in the front hallway and listened. She could hear her mother singing to herself in the kitchen while she prepared dinner. It was a nice, homey sound that should have made her feel better.

It didn't.

The feeling persisted. Something was wrong.

Marilyn remembered a time when she was little and there had been a fire in the house's wiring. She had had the same vague sensation of fear then. As her parents had put it together later, she had smelled the smoke but hadn't known she was smelling it, because the odor was too weak to register at a conscious level. She had only known that something was wrong and had wandered around the house acting nervous and distracted for hours, complaining to her parents that she was frightened.

They had tried to calm her for a while, then finally they grew angry and told her to stop being foolish.

Ten minutes later the fire broke out in earnest.

She had the same kind of feeling now, an unmistakable sense that something was really wrong. She couldn't put her finger on what it was, because it was registering somewhere below the level of consciousness.

But it was there.

And she was frightened.

She went into the kitchen. Her mother was standing at the counter, peeling onions. "Grab a knife!" she said, tears streaming down her face. "It'll give you a good excuse to cry."

Mrs. Sparks believed that crying was good for the soul. Marilyn tended to think so, too, although she had not been able to cry over Zenobia—not since she had heard her voice. She was sure her mother was worried that she was "repressing her emotions," which had become one of her favorite phrases since she had heard a talk show about it a few months earlier.

Marilyn rummaged in a drawer by the sink and pulled out a paring knife. She picked up an onion.

"I don't know how your father does it," said her mother. "He's wonderful about sharing the work, but somehow he always manages to arrange the cooking schedule so that I do all the onions."

Marilyn smiled. But the vague feeling of uneasiness persisted.

When supper was in the oven, she headed for her room. As she reached the top of the stairs she could feel her apprehension increasing.

She was beginning to feel seriously frightened. What was causing this? Was it like the fire in the wiring? Was there something real, registering in her subconscious, warning her that something was wrong? Or was the feeling merely a reaction to everything that had happened in the last few days?

She stepped into her room. A little cry of fear broke from her lips and a thrill of horror shuddered down her spine. Every inch of her skin rose in goose bumps.

Someone had left her a message—scrawled it in dripping, blood-red letters on the mirror over her dresser:

GIVE IT BACK!

Marilyn lifted the back of her hand to her mouth and bit back a scream. For a moment she stood as if frozen.

Suddenly a welcome thought eased her tension. "It's a joke," she said out loud. "Stupid. But a joke."

She could see it now. Somehow Geoff had found out about the amulet and decided to give her a little scare. "He's the one Mom should be worrying about," she said to herself. "I don't know if he's 'repressing his emotions,' but I think he's getting a little too weird for normal people to deal with."

She walked toward the mirror, to see what Geoff had used to put the letters on with, wondering how much trouble it was going to be to clean them off.

She felt a little chill. Not only did they not smear when she ran her fingers over them, *she couldn't feel them at all!* The smooth surface of the glass was unmarked.

So how had Geoff put the message on? Suddenly Marilyn gave a cry of surprise and pulled her hand back as if she had been burned.

Watching in amazement, she saw the jagged, drip-

53

ping letters fade from view. Within a few seconds the words were gone, the mirror as clear as if they had never been there.

All she saw when she looked into it now was her own face, staring back at her with eyes that were pools of fear.

A light rain pattered against the windshield of the car as the Sparks family drove to Flannigan's Funeral Parlor. Marilyn sat huddled in the backseat, still shaken by the incident with the mirror, uncertain whether the message had really been there or if she was simply losing her mind—and wondering which was more frightening.

They arrived in advance of the regular calling hours, and Mr. Flannigan ushered them into a long room. At one end of the room was Zenobia's coffin, surrounded by a startling number of floral arrangements. The bright profusion of gladiolus, roses, carnations, daisies, and lilies (not to mention at least a dozen varieties that Marilyn couldn't name) seemed an odd contrast to the solemn purpose of their visit.

Marilyn and her mother approached the coffin together. Marilyn was astonished when she saw Zenobia's body. Her aunt didn't look natural, or peaceful, or any of the other things her mother had told her people would say. She just looked infinitely better than she had the night she died. Marilyn wondered how the Flannigans had done that, then decided she didn't want to know.

She was surprised at how little she actually felt. Was it because she was numb, emotionally exhausted? Or was it because someplace deep inside of her she did not yet really believe that Zenobia was truly dead? That might explain the weird things that had happened in the last few days, including this afternoon's crazy experience with the mirror. Her mind was refusing to accept Zenobia's death; rather than deal with reality, it was playing tricks on her.

She felt an urge to reach out and touch her aunt in order to make the fact of her death more real, more understandable. She held back, more out of fear of what her mother might say than fear of actually touching the body.

Marilyn was so focused on trying to comprehend the fact of her aunt's death that it took her a moment to realize Zenobia was wearing the amulet. Several thoughts raced through her mind at once: How had it gotten here? Should she try to get it back? What would her mother say if she asked about it?

She settled them all with the thought that, given what Aunt Zenobia had said in her letter, perhaps the best thing to do with the amulet was bury it with her. At least then it would be in a place where it couldn't cause any more trouble.

She followed her mother back to the seats. Soon after, Mr. Flannigan opened the door and the visitors began to arrive, armed with condolences and curiosity.

Marilyn had already been introduced to a seemingly endless stream of cousins, aunts, uncles, and assorted shirttail relations when Kyle came in, looking very adult in his sport coat and tie. Marilyn was impressed; she had rarely seen him wear anything but T-shirts and jeans.

She watched him go to the coffin and stare morosely into it. When he came over to say hello to the family,

Marilyn caught a nod from her mother that temporarily excused her from the receiving line. Enormously grateful, she went to sit with Kyle.

Back at home, alone in her room, Marilyn slipped the cast recording of *Carousel* into her CD player. She flopped onto her bed and said, to no one in particular, "I never knew saying hello to long-lost relatives would be so tiring."

She kicked off her shoes and rolled onto her back. Brick jumped onto the bed and stared at her. Terrified that he was about to speak to her again, she moved to push him to the floor. She stopped herself, turning what was going to be a shove into a caress.

Don't punish the cat because you're *a nervous wreck,* she told herself severely.

As if to prove she had nothing to fear, Brick snuggled up next to her and began to purr.

On the disc the characters Julie Jordan and Billy Bigelow were singing her favorite romantic ballad: "If I Loved You." It was about two people trying hard to pretend not to be in love, and it always made her think of how she acted around Kyle.

She wondered if he ever felt that way, too.

She sighed.

The rest of the house was quiet.

Finally she began to drift toward sleep.

The dream began simply enough: She was in her bedroom. But she was outside herself, in the way you can be in dreams, watching herself sleep.

The dream-Marilyn tossed and turned fitfully, as if something were bothering her. Her hair was plastered

56

to her forehead by an unhealthy sweat. She muttered constantly, words and thoughts that had no connection to one another.

Suddenly she knew, without knowing *how* she knew, that she was seeing the night of Zenobia's death.

What she saw next made her want to wake up.

Only when she tried, she found she couldn't. She was trapped in the dream, which was rapidly turning into a nightmare, and there was no way to get out of it.

"No," she murmured. *"No!"*

Her protest did no good. The dream continued. A helpless observer, she saw her dream-self roll onto its side, kicking at the covers. Then, her stomach knotting in fear, she watched one corner of her pillow lift itself up, moving as if pulled by an invisible hand.

Zenobia's amulet came sliding out from under the pillow.

The dream-Marilyn thrashed about on her bed, her sleep growing more restless.

The amulet floated across the room. Then the door opened, and the amulet was gone.

The scene of the dream changed abruptly, and she found herself in Zenobia's room.

Not merely in Zenobia's room. She was *in* Zenobia, seeing through Zenobia's eyes.

Her heart—Zenobia's heart—was pounding with terror.

It was the same night. The night of Zenobia's death.

Zenobia, and Marilyn with her, sat in bed, waiting. Somehow she knew something dreadful was approaching.

Before long, it arrived.

As Marilyn/Zenobia watched, body rigid, hands clamped like vises against her thighs, the door swung slowly open. And now, looking through Zenobia's eyes, Marilyn saw what she could not have seen with her eyes alone.

She saw the creature that had taken the amulet.

Skin crawling, she recoiled in horror from the monstrosity that approached the bed. It walked with a shuffling crouch, now like an ape, now like a man. Oddly, the claws of its feet made no sound on the hardwood floor.

The amulet dangled from its scaly fingers.

"Take it!" rasped the creature.

He extended a scaly, four-clawed hand. The amulet, catching a fragment of light from a nearby streetlamp, glittered in the darkness of the room.

"Take it!" he repeated. "You tried to thwart me, to hide it. It won't work. Take the amulet—so you can give it to *me!*"

Zenobia's hand reached forward and snatched the amulet from the creature.

"Now give it back!"

Marilyn would never have believed her aunt could be so frightened. But then, she would never have believed the world contained anything this frightful.

Zenobia's body trembled like a leaf in the wind. The creature leaned over her, its eyes blazing.

"Give me the amulet. *Give it to me!*"

In her dream Marilyn could feel Zenobia's heart—or was it her own?—pounding like a long-distance runner's.

The creature leaned closer. Its eyes were yellow and red, flickering like the fires of hell. Scaly skin, a dark red tinged with black, covered a body rippling with powerful muscles. Where its nose should have been were two pointed slits, a fringe of membrane rustling at their edges. Its snout jutted forward, curved fangs thrusting up from the lower jaw.

Leaning over the bed, the creature placed a powerful arm on either side of Zenobia's frail body, then said once more, "Give ... me ... the ... amulet!"

And if Marilyn had been amazed at how frightened her aunt had been, she was even more astonished now at her bravery. With terror coursing through her veins, with a living nightmare leaning over her demanding the amulet, she tightened her grip on the golden chain and said, simply but firmly: "No."

Fire leaped in the creature's eyes. A look of rage contorted its hideous face.

"The amulet!" it roared. Its slash of a mouth drew open, and it lowered its face as though it were about to bite into Zenobia's neck.

Marilyn wanted to die.

Zenobia *did* die. The terror was finally too much, and her heart simply stopped beating.

7

GRAVE
CONVERSATIONS

With a cry of horror Marilyn wrenched herself out of the dream. She sat up in bed, her heart pounding. If that raging monster—jaws open, ready to bite—was the last thing Zenobia ever saw, then it was no wonder her face had been so twisted with fear.

"Now you know what happened that night," said a soft, familiar voice.

Marilyn gasped as Zenobia shimmered into sight at the foot of her bed.

"Please!" said Zenobia, her voice desperate. "Please, Marilyn, don't be frightened. I need your help. You have to get that amulet out of my coffin!"

This bizarre request did nothing to ease Marilyn's fear. But the need in Zenobia's voice was so real that she felt compelled to at least respond. Before she could think of what to say, Mrs. Sparks came running into the room. Her bathrobe dangled from one shoulder, and she fumbled with the other arm, trying to pull it on.

"Marilyn!" she cried. "Marilyn, what is it?"

Zenobia faded from view.

Marilyn shook her head. "I had a nightmare," she whispered, pressing her face into her hands.

Her mother sat on the bed next to her. "I'm sorry, honey," she whispered, slipping an arm around her shoulders.

They sat for a long time, neither of them speaking. Her mother held her close and rocked her gently.

"Of course, given all you've been through in the last few days, it's not surprising," said Mrs. Sparks at last. "To tell you the truth, I don't think I could have handled it as well as you did. That's part of what's helped me get through this, you know—thinking how brave you were that night when you found Aunt Zenobia. I keep telling myself that if you can hold up, I can, too."

Marilyn, leaning against her mother, turned and looked at her in surprise. That her mother was old-fashioned, even prudish, she had accepted long ago. That she would be bothered by Zenobia's death was a surprise to her.

"I thought you didn't like Aunt Zenobia."

Her mother seemed genuinely startled. "Whatever gave you that idea?" Before Marilyn could answer, Mrs. Sparks made a sad little noise in her throat. "Never mind. I *know* what gave you that idea. I didn't *act* much like I cared for her, did I?"

Marilyn shook her head. But she didn't say anything. She just wanted to feel her mother's presence right now, the way she had when she was little and something had frightened her. She was still trembling from the dream—and from what had happened after she woke up. For now it felt good to press against her mother. It helped her mind block out what she had seen. At the moment, that was the only way she could think of to deal with it: pretend it hadn't happened.

Part of her hoped if she pretended hard enough she could forget all about it.

Another part of her knew that was impossible.

"I *did* like her, you know," continued Mrs. Sparks, her voice defensive. "It's just that she was so ... I don't know. So *different*. Rowdy, almost. As if being a woman wasn't enough for her."

The defensive note had dropped away. Now her voice held only a trace of wistfulness. "I do know how you feel, Marilyn," she whispered. "Oh, yes, I do. Because when I was your age, there was nothing in the world I wanted more than to be like Aunt Zenobia."

Marilyn looked at her mother in astonishment.

"Don't be so surprised!" The tone in her voice was almost angry. "I'm human. I had dreams, too. But I grew up. That was something Zenobia never managed."

Any other time Marilyn would have argued with her mother. She didn't believe that growing up had to mean giving up. If becoming an adult meant letting go of your dreams, what good was it?

But right now she didn't want to argue. She just wanted to be held.

After a little while her mother began to hum

"Toora Lura Lura," a little lullaby she used to sing to Marilyn when she was very small. Marilyn hadn't heard it in years. She felt herself begin to relax.

After a while, she slept.

Mrs. Sparks continued to sit beside her for a long time, humming softly, tears rolling down her cheeks. Finally she sighed, wiped her eyes, and left the room.

When she was gone, Zenobia reappeared in the corner, and sat watching Marilyn sleep.

Friday was just like Thursday, a day to be passed through, endured.

Marilyn was vaguely aware of teachers talking. She knew she should be paying attention: final exams were coming up soon, and her grades were only so-so as it was. But somehow she couldn't bring anything into focus—any more than she could really relate to the friends who spoke to her, gently, kindly, throughout the day. All she could think of was Zenobia, and the amulet, and the horrible creature that had stalked through her dreams last night.

She was having a hard time sorting through everything. The dream about Zenobia she could understand. It made sense for her to be dreaming about her aunt right now. But where had that ... that *thing* come from?

It was worse—far worse—than any nightmare her mind had ever conjured up before. Even so, it was easy in the reassuring light of day to dismiss the creature as an invention of her overheated imagination.

What was not so easy was Zenobia. Not only was there the matter of her appearance *after* Marilyn had woken last night—an appearance Marilyn could not convince herself was just part of her nightmare, no matter how hard she tried—there was the fact that she had sensed Zenobia near her all through the day.

It was insane. But she couldn't shake the idea that her aunt was trying desperately to contact her.

"What do you want from me?" she wanted to scream.

But in her heart she already knew.

Zenobia wanted her to get the amulet.

But why? It must have something to do with the creature.

Again, her mind rebelled. Stretched to the limit, she was willing to admit the possibility of a ghost. The idea that someone who had "passed over" (to use a phrase she had heard almost endlessly during the last three days) could actually require something of someone still living was within her comprehension.

But that other thing? That creature? No. That had to be a figment of her imagination.

"You know, of course, my dear Airhead, that you've gone out of your miniature mind," said Alicia as they were walking home together.

Marilyn's heart sank. She had thought her old friend would be the one person she could confide in without ridicule.

"Oh, not because you think you've seen a ghost," said Alicia quickly. "I just meant you're out of your mind if you're starting to get serious about that dork Kyle Patterson. This problem with your aunt Zenobia, on the other hand, requires some serious consideration."

Marilyn smiled. She should have known Alicia wouldn't let her down.

"Now let me get this straight," continued her friend. "You think Zenobia's spirit is still hanging around."

"I've seen it."

Alice shrugged. "You see something worthwhile in that blond beanpole, too. Your eyesight is not the best."

"Lay off, will you?"

"Well, my credulity only goes so far. You can ask me to believe in a ghost, or you can ask me to believe that Kyle Patterson has redeeming features. I can't do both at once."

"Then I'll believe in Kyle all by myself," said Marilyn. "It's Aunt Zenobia who has me going in circles."

"Ah," said Alicia. "We return to the nub of the question. What do you suppose it is the old girl wants?"

"Her amulet," said Marilyn. "The one she asked me to take care of."

"Well, that makes sense. She asked you to take care of it, and now she wants it back. Why don't you just give it to her?"

"Because she already has it."

"I beg your pardon?"

"It's on her body, in the funeral home."

Alicia looked at her strangely. "Marilyn, what is this all about? What's the whole story?"

Marilyn looked away.

"Hey, Airhead—what is it?"

"You'll think I'm crazy."

Alicia snorted. "I *know* you're crazy. I figured that out sometime in third grade. That doesn't have anything to do with the current problem. Why does Zenobia want the amulet if she already has it?" She paused, then asked cautiously, "Is there more to this than just a ghost?"

Marilyn didn't answer for a long time. After they had walked three blocks in silence, she said, "Promise you won't laugh?"

Her face solemn, Alicia drew a cross over her heart, then placed her fingertip against her lips. It was a ritual they had developed years ago to ensure judgment-free listening.

Marilyn searched her friend's face. Alicia stared back at her with clear blue eyes.

"All right," said Marilyn at last. "I'll tell you everything that's happened. And if you ever tell anyone else, I'll kill you."

Alicia pointed to her mouth and moved her jaw as if she were trying to speak. Her lips remained sealed shut.

Marilyn smiled. But she remained silent for another moment. Overhead a cloud moved across the sun, blocking out the light. Marilyn shivered and began to speak, this time telling Alicia not merely that she had seen Zenobia's ghost, but all the details of the story, starting with the night that Zenobia had asked her to care for the amulet.

She went on to tell the story of the nightmare that had woken her the night of Zenobia's death—and of her horror at discovering the amulet she had been entrusted with was missing from her room. As she spoke, she realized for the first time that the creature she had seen in that first dream was the same one she had seen with the amulet last night. The knowledge had been there all along. She had been avoiding it, because she didn't want to deal with it.

She continued, telling Alicia about finding Zenobia's body, her hand still clutching the mysterious amulet, and the two voices she had heard at Zenobia's bedside.

Finally she told her about Zenobia's visit the night before.

Then she handed her Zenobia's letter.

Alicia read it, making little noises of astonishment as she went along. When she was done, she looked at Marilyn and said two things.

The first was: "I believe you."

The second was: "Boy, are you in trouble."

She was going to say more, but the cloud that had covered the sun was joined by several others. The sky opened and a slashing rain began to pour down on them.

Forgetting about the ghost, they ran for shelter.

They were in Alicia's bedroom, wearing bathrobes and toweling off their hair. Their clothes were down cellar in the dryer.

"The funeral is tomorrow," said Alicia. "That doesn't give you much time. Before you know it, Zenobia and the amulet will both be six feet under, and that'll be the end of the problem. Of course, her ghost might still hang around and kind of bug you. But she'll really have to stop harping on the amulet. I mean, gone is gone, and—"

"Alicia!"

"Sorry. I thought a little humor might be appreciated about now."

"It probably would have been," said Marilyn. "If you had managed to come up with any."

"So shoot me! I tend to talk when I get nervous."

"Also when you're calm. Besides, it's four, not six."

"Four what?"

"Four feet. That's how deep they dig graves around here. Five at the most. And they have this big concrete thing called a vault they put the coffin in to keep the wood from rotting."

"You amaze me. Whence comes this great knowledge of the funeral business?"

"My aunt just died, remember?"

"My uncle died last year, but I'm not ready to open a funeral parlor."

"Well, I've been paying close attention to the conversations my parents had with Mr. Flannigan. And I asked a few questions."

"Morbid curiosity," said Alicia. "A bad sign. All right, since you're such an expert, can you tell me why anyone should care if the wood rots once the coffin is planted?"

"I think it's in case they ever have to move the body—like if the state decided to put a highway through the cemetery or something. Maybe it's just to protect the family's investment in fine furniture. Anyway, by the time you get the top on the vault, there's less than three feet of dirt covering the thing. So it wouldn't be that hard to dig one up. Getting the top off the vault would be a problem, but—"

"Marilyn!"

"What?"

"Start over. Scratch that very bad, exceedingly stupid idea out of your mind. You sound like a clip from

68

Monster Movie Matinee. And I have no intention of playing Igor to some scatterbrained gravedigger on a midnight mission to the cemetery."

"Some henchperson you make. You'd better study your dwarf manual again."

"Look, Airhead, you start with the short jokes and you can face the unknown alone. Which is maybe not a bad idea. I don't know why I'm having this conversation with you at all."

"Because you're incredibly loyal. Anyway, I was just thinking out loud. Give me credit for a little common sense."

"I always did, until you started getting dopey about Kyle. A person who could take him seriously might do anything!"

"You want another short joke?"

"All right, all right! I'll lay off about Kyle. But what are you gonna do?"

"Do you suppose I could get the amulet off Zenobia's body during viewing hours tonight?"

"Possible, but not likely. How about if you just tell your mother you want it?"

"I tried. It was embarrassing. Not only did she think I was greedy, she thought I was 'excessively morbid.' "

"You could try telling her about the ghost."

Marilyn looked at Alicia.

"Yeah, I see what you mean," said Alicia. "Your mother already thinks your imagination is out of control. Hit her with this story and she's likely to decide the strain has been too much and you're ready for the funny farm. I mean, I only believe you because I have to."

"Thanks. I think."

"Anyway, to continue digressing, how did the amulet get on Zenobia to begin with?"

"Mr. Flannigan called Mom and asked her for something to 'finish the look.' She thought Zenobia was fond of the amulet, since she was clutching it when she died, and decided it would be a nice thing to have it buried with her. Sort of Egyptian, according to Mom."

Alicia raised an eyebrow. "That was nice of your mom, in a weird kind of way. But the whole thing still doesn't make sense. If your aunt was so fond of the amulet, why does she want you to get it off her?"

"Who knows why dead people do stuff?" said Marilyn, starting to feel exasperated.

Alicia shuddered, then whispered, "I've been pretty jokey about this. But the truth is, that's because you've got me scared. What do you think this is really all about?"

"I don't know."

"What are you gonna do?"

"I don't know," repeated Marilyn. "Nothing, if I'm lucky."

Alicia sighed. "Well, you know what to do if you need me."

Marilyn nodded. "I may take you up on that."

Alicia shuddered and sank back into her chair.

Outside, the rain fell in a slow, steady drizzle.

8

THE HAUNTED
GHOST

Kyle showed up at the funeral parlor again that night, as did a number of writers and editors who had worked with Zenobia at one time or another. They had flown in that day in order to be present at the funeral Saturday morning.

Surrounded by what seemed like mountains of flowers, their odor almost overwhelming her, Marilyn stood at Zenobia's coffin and looked down at her aunt. The amulet rested on her chest, partially covered by a small bouquet of roses and baby's breath. As she looked at it now, the smooth, blue edge peeking out from under a curling petal, she had an almost irresistible urge to reach down and snatch it.

She glanced around. No one was watching.

She shook herself. Craziness! All it would take

would be one person turning in her direction, and there would be an uproar, followed by embarrassment and humiliation, and the rest of her natural life in therapy.

She looked down at Zenobia again. Her sharp features were waxy with the pall of death. *Why are you doing this to me?* thought Marilyn fiercely. *What is this all about?*

To her horror, Zenobia answered her. The words came as a whisper in the back of her mind: *Be patient, Marilyn. Be patient, and brave. I need you.*

The combination of staring at her aunt's dead body and hearing her voice at the same time was too much for Marilyn. She gripped the edge of the coffin as her knees started to buckle. For a horrible instant the coffin wobbled. Marilyn gasped. She thought it was going to tip over, and her mind conjured up a gruesome picture of Zenobia's body falling out and pinning her to the floor.

Her mind continuing to run wild, she wondered if she could snatch the amulet if that happened.

All at once Kyle was at her side. Slipping his arm around her shoulders, he led her back to her chair, supporting her as he did. A small circle of concerned people quickly formed around them.

Suddenly she saw her father come pushing through the crowd, shouldering aside assorted cousins. To her enormous relief he shooed the entire group away, bellowing, "Give her some room to breathe, for Pete's sake!"

He used the fierce voice he generally reserved for his high school students, which caused the murmuring relatives to pull back in astonishment. Standing at a respectful distance, they watched her from the corners of their eyes.

"Hot night," said her father gruffly. "Too much going on. You okay, Marilyn?"

She nodded weakly.

"Good." He took out his handkerchief and wiped his brow. "Take her outside for a while, would you, Kyle?"

"Yes sir," said Kyle. Putting his hand on Marilyn's elbow, he led her through the crowd to the front porch. The air was indeed warm, and still muggy from the afternoon rain. But a gentle breeze offered some relief, and as it lifted the damp strands of coppery hair from her shoulders, Marilyn realized for the first time how stuffy the big room had actually been.

Kyle let go of her elbow. Then he took her hand and led her to the large oak tree at the corner of Flannigan's lawn.

"Okay," he said. "Spill."

"Spill?" asked Marilyn nervously, though she knew perfectly well what he meant.

"Something is really messing you up. And it's not just your aunt's death, though Lord knows that would be enough. But I've been watching you. You are seriously spooked. I've known you too long not to see it. So just spill it, will you? We'll both feel better."

Oh, Kyle, she thought desperately. *How I wish I could. But I don't dare. It's too crazy. You could never believe me.*

Out loud she said, "You're wrong. It *is* Aunt Zenobia. It was all so sudden, and I really miss her, and being the one to find her was just so weird."

Which is pretty much the truth, she told herself, trying to salve the way her conscience was complaining about the lie.

Kyle looked at her suspiciously. "That's all?"

She nodded. "You know how I felt about her. The loss is hard to take."

His eyes, fringed with golden lashes and bluer than a summer sky, peered into hers, searching for something.

"Will you call me if I can help you?" he asked at last.

"Yes," she said simply. "If I think you can help, I'll call."

But I don't think you can. I don't think anyone can help me now. Because either I'm being haunted or I'm losing my mind. And those are both things you do alone.

Of course, she wasn't really alone, Marilyn thought later, sitting in her room. She had Alicia. But she wasn't sure how much of this Alicia believed. She had a feeling her friend was merely humoring her.

She looked around her room. It was familiar, comfortable. She had slept in it all her life.

But she no longer felt safe here, which was why she was awake now, even though she needed sleep so desperately that her eyes were stinging. She was too afraid to sleep. When she stretched out on her bed, her body was as rigid as a board. Her eyes, as if they were out of her control, refused to close. The book she had been trying to read lay on the floor beside her chair. She had been totally unable to concentrate on it.

Brick jumped up and sat in her lap. She reached

down and stroked his head. But she could feel the tension that had formed in her shoulders at his approach. She was still afraid of the cat, and that made her sad. Brick began to purr, pushing his head insistently against her hand to demand more attention.

The clock in the downstairs hall chimed three.

A moment later Zenobia walked through the door.

Brick yowled in protest as Marilyn's hands clutched his body. She felt a cold sweat pop out on her brow. She wasn't dreaming, or just waking up, or just drifting off. All the reasons she might use to explain things away were worthless here. She was wide awake, and the woman who was lying in a coffin at Flannigan's Funeral Home had just walked through her door—which was still closed, now that she glanced at it.

She tried to say something, but her throat seemed sealed shut, her mouth as dry as a day old doughnut.

Zenobia spoke instead. "Don't be afraid."

Though it was clearly her voice, the words didn't seem to come from Zenobia's lips. Instead, they whispered inside Marilyn's head.

Marilyn remained rigid, fear winning out over desire. For part of her wanted to rush to her aunt and fling her arms around her. Another part, stronger, wanted this awful thing to disappear forever and leave her alone.

"It's difficult," said the voice in her mind. "I know you don't understand. But I need your help."

Marilyn nodded.

"You know what you have to do?" asked Zenobia.

She nodded again, then said, "What I don't understand is *why.*"

Zenobia sighed. "Because if I am buried with that

amulet, I will never be allowed to rest. Guptas will see to that. He'll haunt me and harass me through all eternity."

"Who is Guptas?"

"The prisoner of the amulet. Listen quickly. I would come with you, if I could. But this appearing act takes a lot out of me, and I can't keep it up very long. I'm hoping I'll get better at it as times goes on."

Zenobia was already beginning to fade. But Marilyn had one last question, the most important one of all as far as she was concerned. "Are you real?" she whispered desperately.

Dumb! she thought as soon as she had asked it. *Do you expect a hallucination to tell you it's imaginary?*

"As real as tomorrow," replied the voice in her mind.

Marilyn relaxed a little. That was the kind of thing Zenobia would say. And not the kind of thing she, Marilyn, would think of on her own.

So maybe this really was Zenobia's ghost.

With a start Marilyn realized she was glad the ghost was real. She had been half convinced she was losing her mind . . . a prospect she found far more frightening than a mere ghost.

"I have to go now," said Zenobia. "I'll come back as soon as I can." Her figure wavering in the air, growing mistier by the second, she took a step toward Marilyn. Holding her hands out beseechingly, she added, "Don't let me down."

Then she was gone.

But one last thought hung in Marilyn's mind, one last message from Zenobia's spirit. The words had formed even as her image disappeared. And, it seemed to Marilyn, they left her no choice.

"I'm counting on you," she had said.

Marilyn looked around at the empty room. Brick was still on her lap, but he had risen to his feet, and his back was arched like a cat in a Halloween picture. Suddenly she realized he had sunk his claws into her leg. She cried out in pain and swatted at him. He turned and hissed at her, then jumped off her lap and ran under the bed.

She rubbed her leg, wondering how she had ignored the pain until now.

Forget it, she ordered herself. *You've got work to do.*

She slipped into her jeans and a sweatshirt, dug her sneakers from under the bed, then went to her nightstand and took out her flashlight.

This was going to be dark work. She hoped she wouldn't have an attack of her nightfrights.

Glancing nervously around her room, she tried to convince herself to give up the whole crazy idea. But she had promised her aunt. And if she wanted to grow up to be the kind of person Zenobia had been, she couldn't wimp out now.

With a sigh, she stepped through the door.

Save for the distant rumble of her father's snoring, the house was quiet. She turned on her flashlight and walked carefully down the hallway, moving as silently as possible.

A few moments later she stood on the front porch. She felt a twinge of sorrow as she remembered Zenobia standing there, smoking her cigar and telling outrageous stories.

She started down the steps and almost tripped over Brick, who had slipped out the door with her.

"Watch out, stupid," she hissed as the cat wound himself between her feet. He bared his little teeth at her and bounded down the steps.

The night was cooler now, and very still, except for the breeze, which continued to blow gently through the town, carrying the fragrance of a dozen different kinds of flowers that had come into bloom that week.

The sky was clear, moonless but filled with glittering stars.

It was almost too perfect and Marilyn felt a sudden surge of affection for this little corner of the world that she had so often found unbearably boring. After the last few days she was beginning to think that boring wasn't such a bad thing.

Looking around now at the simple, familiar surroundings, it was hard to believe she was on her way to a funeral home to steal an amulet from the chest of a corpse.

Panic gripped her. She wanted to turn back.

"I'm counting on you," echoed a voice in her memory.

She squared her shoulders and started down the walk.

When she reached the corner, a figure glided from the shadows beneath one of the street's old oak trees.

Making no sound, it followed her into the night.

9

MIDNIGHT MOVES

Flannigan's Funeral Home was some fifteen blocks from Marilyn's house. Streetlamps stood at most of the corners, but there were patches of darkness in between. Marilyn focused on the pools of light and set them as goals while she walked through the dark areas. Her old fear of the dark kept trying to rise within, and her heart fluttered against her breastbone like a trapped bird.

Just as she was beginning to think the trip would take forever, she reached the last block before Flannigan's—at which point she realized she was actually going to arrive much too quickly for her taste. She suddenly wished the funeral home were still miles away.

She glanced around and noticed a car traveling

slowly in her direction. As she had twice before during the trip, Marilyn stepped back from the sidewalk. The people who roamed the streets at night frightened her.

Hypocrite, she thought. *You're out roaming the streets, too.* She smiled in spite of herself. *Geez, given what I'm up to, whoever's in that car is probably more normal than I am!*

She began to catalog the possibilities: a tired mother on her way home from her second shift job; some crazed party animal who lived by night; or (getting romantic) some heartbroken lover whose tragedy denied him (or her!) the solace of sleep.

How weird is that, compared to someone who's out to rob a corpse? she demanded of herself.

After the car passed her, she counted to twenty. Moving carefully, checking to be sure it really was gone, she stepped back onto the sidewalk.

When she reached the funeral home a moment later Marilyn tucked her flashlight into the back pocket of her jeans. Terrified or not, this had to be done in darkness. That also meant she didn't dare risk trying the front door, since a bright light burned in the porch ceiling.

Moving quietly, she went around to the back of the building, hoping she wouldn't have to break a window, or anything stupid like that.

She also hoped there was no one here. She knew Mr. Flannigan sometimes worked late. That would be all she needed—to run into the undertaker while she was trying to rob one of his corpses!

At least the Flannigans didn't actually *live* here anymore. The youngest Flannigan boy, Richie, was in her class, and she still remembered coming to his eighth birthday party, back when the family had been living on the upper floor of the big old house. For years afterward she had wondered what it was like to live in a place like this.

She had wanted to ask Richie, but had been too shy to do it, partly because he was such a nice, normal kid and she didn't want to embarrass him. But looking at the house now, the questions came back to her again.

Do the spirits of the newly dead wait here until they're buried? How many ghosts would a funeral parlor attract, anyway?

She shivered and pushed the thoughts from her mind.

The backyard was dark. Too dark. A wave of panic seized her, and she stood for a moment as if frozen. She reached for the flashlight, thinking, *If I get caught, I get caught. I can't go any farther without some light!*

The grass, which had not been mowed back here, was wet with dew. She could feel it beginning to soak through her sneakers. Moving the beam of the flashlight, she picked out the back porch.

Cautiously she climbed the steps.

The door was locked. She rattled the handle hopelessly, then stopped because she realized it was making a loud noise.

She turned and caught her breath. She could have sworn she saw a movement in the row of lilacs separating Flannigan's lawn from the next house.

Holding her breath, she swept her flashlight back and forth across the bushes. When she couldn't see a thing, she cursed the flashlight for being too weak and tried to convince herself it was just nerves.

Don't be foolish, she chided herself. *No one else would be dumb enough to be out here at this time of night anyway!*

But the seed had been planted. She couldn't shake the suspicion that something was watching her.

Her nervousness doubled, she turned back to the house.

How on earth do I get in?

Playing the beam along the wall, she noticed a row of windows leading into the basement.

Maybe one of them would be unlatched.

She went to the corner of the house and started working her way along the wall.

She couldn't believe her luck. Not only was the third window unlatched—it was broken right out. The hole was covered by a sheet of thick plastic, the kind people put over their windows in winter to try to keep the heat in. It was held on by strips of thin wood tacked to the frame with small nails.

She put her fingers at the edge and tried to pull the wood away.

It wouldn't budge.

She put her fingernails against the plastic and tried to rip through it.

Nothing. Made to stand up against fierce winter winds, the stuff was impervious to her efforts. For the first time, she envied those girls who took pride in long pointed nails.

"Here," said a voice behind her. "Try this knife."

Marilyn screamed. The flashlight flew out of her hand and bounced off the wall. She spun about and put her back to the house, as if it could somehow protect her.

"You!"

Kyle Patterson smiled. "None other. What in blazes are you up to?"

"Go away," said Marilyn.

The smile faded from Kyle's face. "Not a chance. You're in some kind of trouble—or you're going to be, if you get caught. I'm not leaving you alone here. So you may as well let me help."

"You can't. And I can't explain. You'll think I'm crazy."

"Marilyn!" He took a deep breath and lowered his voice. "I *know* you're crazy. That's not the point. I'm on your side. Whatever it is you've gotten yourself mixed up in, I want to help." He looked at her, and his eyes were almost fierce. "I mean it!"

She leaned against the wall and let out her breath with a heavy sigh. "You don't know what you're saying."

"I don't care what it is!" Dropping the knife he had offered her, he reached forward and took her by the shoulders. For a moment she thought he was going to shake her. "I don't care what it is," he repeated, drawing her closer.

She collapsed against his chest and, to her own astonishment, began to cry.

He put his arms around her and held her close. "You don't even have to tell me," he whispered, his voice gentle. "Just let me help."

She nodded and pressed against him.

"All right, I will. You don't know how scared I've been, Kyle. You don't know how awful these last days have been. I should make you go, now, before it's too late ... before you're tangled up in this, too. But I can't. I'm too scared."

He tightened his arms around her. "It'll be all right," he whispered. "Whatever it is, it'll be all right."

She drew back from him and wiped her eyes. "What are you doing here, anyway?"

"I couldn't sleep."

She looked at him suspiciously.

He sighed. "All right, if you want the truth, I talked to Alicia. She told me you might be doing something crazy."

Marilyn scowled.

"Don't be angry with her. It just about killed her to call me. But she didn't know what else to do. And even then she wouldn't tell me what this is all about. She just told me you might need help." He took a deep breath. "Which is why I'm here."

She stared at him for a long time.

"All right," she said at last. "If you mean it, let's get busy. We don't have much time."

"What are we going to do?"

She took a deep breath, then said, "I'm here to rob a corpse."

Before he could reply, she bent and picked up the pocketknife he had dropped. Turning back to the window, she opened the long, sharp blade, hesitated, then closed it again. Using the short blade, which was blunt, she was able to pry the wood framing loose from the sill without tearing the plastic.

"Here, let me finish that," said Kyle. Reaching past her, he tucked his fingertips over the top of the wood and pulled. His arm was close to her face and she couldn't help noticing the play of his muscles and the faint scent of sweat on his skin.

"There!"

The strip of wood ripped away from the wall, bringing the plastic with it. He made a few more quick tugs, and the window was clear.

Marilyn looked at the opening and shuddered. It was like a black mouth leading into emptiness.

Kyle put his hand on her shoulder. "I'll go first."

She shook her head. "This is my problem. I go first."

"Suit yourself." She could sense the shrug of his shoulders.

She looked at the hole again and wished he had been willing to fight her for the point. *Too late now, Sparks. Get moving!*

She picked up her flashlight from where it had fallen in the wet grass and played the beam through the window. The light revealed a small room walled in by planks of aged wood. The walls were covered with shelves, the shelves filled with bottles of different kinds—the tools of Mr. Flannigan's trade.

"Here goes nothing," she whispered, slipping her feet through the window.

A moment later she was inside, and a moment after that Kyle was standing beside her, his arm around her shoulders again. "Now what?" he whispered.

"We go upstairs," she answered. "Where they keep the bodies."

10

ROBBING THE DEAD

It was a gruesome passage. Mr. Flannigan had his working space here in the cellar, and they had to pass through it as they made their way to the first floor.

Marilyn clung tightly to Kyle's arm as he swung the beam of her flashlight back and forth, trying to find the stairway. Two tables with white sheets spread over them had distinctive outlines that made her shudder. She tried to think of who had died lately, then tried to push the question out of her mind. She didn't want to know who was lying cold, naked, and dead beneath those sheets.

The whole place had the air of death about it. She found herself afraid to touch things, plagued by the feeling that the essence of death would rub off on her, and that she might never be able to wash it away.

Suddenly Kyle stopped. "What was that?" he hissed.

"What was what?" she replied, feeling a little like a second-rate comic in a horror-film spoof.

"I thought I heard something behind us."

They stood motionless, holding their breath while they waited for another sound.

They heard nothing.

"Probably just my nerves," said Kyle.

"You're nervous?" asked Marilyn, a little incredulously. It had never occurred to her that anything would frighten Kyle.

"I'm scared silly!" he snapped. "If I wasn't so worried about you, I wouldn't be anywhere near here!"

She pulled a little closer to him. "Thanks," she whispered.

"Don't mention it. Let's get this over—"

His words were cut off by a loud crash. Marilyn let out a shriek and clutched Kyle's arm as if it were a life preserver. He, in turn, threw his other arm around her and pulled her close to him. They stood for a moment in absolute silence, straining their ears for whatever had caused the noise.

Suddenly Marilyn began to giggle.

"What's so funny?" demanded Kyle.

"That," she said, pointing to their left.

Kyle swung the flashlight in the direction she indicated. The beam was reflected by a pair of greenish eyes.

"Brick!" he said in disgust. "The world's clumsiest cat."

"He must have followed me," said Marilyn. "I wonder what he broke. I hope it wasn't important." Gesturing to the cat, she called, "Come here, Brick. Come here, kitty."

Brick padded over and rubbed against her legs. She reached down and scooped him up. "You're coming with us," she said. "The last thing I need is to leave here tonight with you still inside for Mr. Flannigan to find in the morning."

Brick purred and snuggled up against her.

"Come on," she said to Kyle. "Let's get this over with before anyone else shows up. For a solo expedition, this has gotten pretty crowded."

"You want me to leave?"

"Don't you dare! Just find that stairway."

As it turned out, he had already located it while she was fooling with the cat. Taking her by the elbow again, he led her to a set of solid wooden steps.

"They're sturdier than you would think, considering the house," said Marilyn.

"Not when you consider what they're used for," replied Kyle grimly.

Marilyn glanced back at the tables and shuddered. They climbed the rest of the stairs in silence.

The first floor of Flannigan's was divided into three major areas. Each was currently in use.

"Which way from here?" asked Kyle, shining his beam along the faded carpet in the hallway.

"I don't know," said Marilyn. "I'm confused."

"You've spent the last two evenings here!"

"I know, but I never got back to this part!"

They went through a door on their left.

Kyle played the flashlight slowly over the room. A ring of floral arrangements surrounded a small white casket at the far end. "Billy Johnson," he said, his voice husky,

Marilyn turned away. Billy Johnson was a third

grader who lived a few blocks from her. He had been killed the previous afternoon in a car crash. "Let's get out of here," she said.

They went back into the hall. "That's it!" said Marilyn, spotting a familiar doorway.

Kyle pushed it open. Marilyn felt a tingle of anticipation.

The room, empty now, seemed strange to her. For two nights she had seen it alive with people; friends, relatives—even strangers who cared, for one reason or another, about Zenobia.

Now there was no one here but Zenobia herself.

Marilyn hesitated for a moment. Suddenly she had an awful fear that everything—all the crazy events of the last few days—had been nothing but a product of her overactive imagination, stimulated by her sorrow over Zenobia's death.

What am I doing here? she thought in panic. The answer that she was here because Zenobia had asked her to be suddenly seemed wildly inadequate. She was here to rob a corpse, and that was that.

"Are you all right?" asked Kyle.

"No."

"Can I help?"

"No."

He let his hand rest against the small of her back and was quiet.

Marilyn was weighing the alternatives. Part of her was terrified that she would go home with Zenobia's amulet in her hand and find that everything had been hallucinations after all. She might never get caught with it. Even if she did she could make the point that Zenobia had given her the amulet.

But whether or not she got in trouble wasn't the point. The point was, in her heart she would know what she had done. In her heart she would remember robbing the dead for as long as she lived.

In fact, she could think of only one thing worse: going home without the amulet and finding it had all been real, and she had let Zenobia down.

In the end there was no choice: She had to do it.

"Stay here," she whispered to Kyle. Taking the flashlight from his hand, she walked toward the coffin. The scent of the flowers was overwhelming, almost sickening in its sweetness.

She hesitated, remembering the moment earlier that evening when she had heard Zenobia's voice. Would it happen again?

She braced herself and stepped forward. Her light hit Zenobia's face, etching her still, cold features against the coffin's satin lining.

She took another step.

There it was! The beam of her light had caught the edge of the amulet.

Now there was nothing to it. All she had to do was reach down and take it.

She couldn't.

She remembered her aunt pleading with her earlier in the evening.

She couldn't let her down now.

Slowly she forced herself to reach out and move aside the spray of flowers that covered the amulet. The red jewel in the center caught her light and sprang to life, as if it were filled with a fire of its own.

When nothing else happened, she began to relax a

bit. She had almost expected a clap of thunder and a heavenly voice chastising her for robbing the dead.

She took a breath and reached down to lift the amulet from Zenobia's chest.

Something was wrong. It took her a moment to figure it out. Then she realized—Zenobia was dead, and being dead was cold. Yet the amulet was warm, warmer, even, than if it had been resting on the chest of a living person.

Marilyn shivered. What was this thing, anyway?

Then a worse question occurred to her. How was she going to get it off Zenobia's corpse? The chain, she now remembered, had no clasp. It was a solid piece of work.

You've come this far, Sparks, she told herself firmly. *No sense in being squeamish now.*

She set the flashlight in the coffin. The beam, playing around the amulet, cast eerie shadows on Zenobia's waxy-looking face, and the wall of flowers behind her.

Marilyn reached down and slipped her hand under the corpse's head. She tried to tip the neck forward.

It wouldn't bend.

She remembered what she had heard about rigor mortis and the stiffness of death. Pulling harder, she was able to raise Zenobia's entire body just enough to free the chain. She was amazed at how light, even frail, her tough old aunt seemed now.

Bracing her left elbow against the side of the coffin, Marilyn held Zenobia's body at a slight angle. Then she took the amulet in her right hand and guided the loop of the chain under the back of Zenobia's head. She moved slowly, trying not to disturb the carefully arranged white hair. Once the chain was free, she continued to slide it along her own arm, until it reached the crook of her elbow. Then she let it dangle against the outside of the casket while she put her hand back under Zenobia's head and gently lowered the body to a resting position.

She had done it!

She grabbed the flashlight and turned triumphantly to Kyle, holding up the amulet. "I've got it!" she whispered. "I've got . . ."

Her words faltered, trailed to a whisper. Kyle was staring at her in horror.

No. He wasn't staring at her. It was something behind her.

She heard a soft noise and whirled around.

Zenobia had placed one hand on each side of the coffin and was drawing herself to a sitting position.

Marilyn's throat closed with fear. She was trying desperately to scream, but nothing would come out.

Zenobia was sitting straight up now. Still moving stiffly, her torso twisted in their direction.

The corpse opened its eyes and looked at Marilyn. A hideous smile twisted its face. Reaching out with its cold, white hands, it said, "Give me the amulet."

Marilyn dropped the flashlight.

It clattered to the floor and went out. Except for a faint glow coming from the amulet itself, the room was pitch black.

But she could hear the sound of fabric rustling, and there was no question in her mind what it meant.

Zenobia was climbing out of her coffin.

11

THE EYE OF
THE AMULET

The darkness was driving Marilyn out of her mind. She couldn't see a thing. Not a thing!

But the sound of the slow, deliberate movements of whatever had climbed out of Zenobia's casket fueled her imagination, and she could almost see the dead eyes looking into hers, feel the cold hands closing on her neck.

Unable to think of anything else to do, she started to sing.

Later, she could never understand exactly why she reacted that way. At the moment she didn't even think about it. It just happened. She opened her mouth to scream, some instinct took over, and the words to "When You Walk Through a Storm"—the anthem of hope in the midst of darkness from *Carousel*—started pouring out instead.

The funny thing was, it worked. She actually felt better, at least for the first few notes.

Better yet, the noise in front of her stopped.

Unfortunately, the moment of relief was short-lived. She had just reached the line "And don't be afraid of the dark" when a harsh voice grated, "Silence, wench! Hand me that amulet!"

At that moment the terror she had been fighting to stave off all night finally came crashing in on her. Her old fear of the dark was multiplied a thousandfold by all the genuine horrors she had had to face, and she began to scream, hopelessly and uncontrollably. Somewhere in the background she could hear Kyle. She thought he was screaming, too, but she couldn't be certain.

"Silence!" ordered the voice again.

The scream died in Marilyn's throat. She was too frightened to force it out.

The amulet was burning in her hand.

Suddenly it blazed into life. A red glow burst from the jewel in its center. By its fiery light she could see Zenobia's corpse standing in front of the coffin.

"Give me the amulet!" repeated the voice. The corpse began lurching toward her, its pale white fingers twitching with anticipation.

"Marilyn, let's get out of here!"

It was Kyle. His wits had finally returned, and he was beside her, his hands on her shoulders, trying to turn her around.

It did no good. She was rooted to the spot, mesmerized by the horror moving step by step in her direction.

"Marilyn!"

"Give ... me ... the amulet!"

The corpse was almost upon them now. They could see, by the amulet's glow, a look of something close to madness in its eyes.

Kyle put his arm around Marilyn's waist and pulled her back. He tried to run, but got no help from her. He turned and linked both hands around her stomach, then began backing toward the door.

"There is no use in fleeing. There is nowhere to run! Give me the amulet!"

Suddenly Marilyn began to struggle with Kyle. "Let go of me!" she cried, twisting in his arms.

Zenobia's corpse, moving slowly, was almost upon them.

The glare from the amulet was brighter than ever.

Kyle tightened his grip; spurred by terror, he lurched backward. As he did, he stepped on Brick, who had been lurking behind him. The cat emitted a piercing yowl of pain and shot away to hide under one of the chairs. But the damage had been done; Kyle's footing had been destroyed. He struggled wildly to keep his balance, but finally failed and fell backward, still holding Marilyn.

Her feet thrust out and tangled in Zenobia's legs, causing the corpse to fall on top of them.

When her aunt's body landed on her, Marilyn screamed, convinced she was going to die of fright if nothing else.

The corpse reared back and opened its mouth. With a fresh jolt of horror Marilyn realized it was going to bite her. She thrust upward with her palm, catching Aunt Zenobia's body under the chin, slamming her head back. "Oh! I'm so sorry!" she gasped.

The corpse howled with rage and began to scrabble at her hand, trying to rip the amulet from her fingers. Marilyn beat at it with her fists, trying to push it away. She was still screaming and crying.

Kyle, pinned beneath both of them, struggled to free himself so he could help Marilyn.

The whole scene was illuminated by the bloody red light still pulsing from the amulet.

"Guptas, let go of that body!"

The voice was Zenobia's, but it did not come from her body. Looking in the direction from which it had come, Marilyn was astonished to see another version of her aunt standing next to them. She had her hands on hips. A furious expression contorted her face. And her body, rather than solid and heavy like the corpse with which Marilyn was now wrestling, was clearly that of a ghost.

"Guptas, let go!" repeated Zenobia.

A howl of despair ripped through the night. Suddenly Zenobia's corpse went limp, trapping Kyle and Marilyn under its dead weight. The light in the amulet died, so that the only illumination in the room came from the pale figure of Zenobia, who was still scowling.

"I hate to see that body treated that way," she said bitterly. "It served me very well for quite a number of years. And you be careful there, young man!" This last was addressed to Kyle, who was trying to roll the corpse away so that he and Marilyn could sit up.

Zenobia's ghost turned and walked toward the coffin, which had shifted when the corpse climbed out of it. Reaching out, she tried to move it back into place.

Nothing happened, and she made a little noise of frustration.

"Well, at least we have the amulet back," she said, turning her back to the coffin.

"Will you help us get out from under this?" asked Kyle, his voice testy.

"I can't!" snapped Zenobia. "I haven't learned how to move things yet. It's all I can do to materialize."

Marilyn, still in a daze, began to come to her senses. Gently she helped Kyle push Zenobia's now empty body away from them. Then she shoved the amulet into her pocket, got to her feet, and reached down to help him up.

When he was standing beside her, she turned to her aunt. "Don't you vanish on me this time," she said. Though she was trembling, her voice had an angry tone, and her jaw was set in a firm line that made it look remarkably like Zenobia's. "I think it's about time you filled me in on a few things!"

"You're right," said Zenobia, looking a little shamefaced. "I should have before. Only I didn't know much. I only had guesses. I still don't understand all of it, but I'm beginning to make sense of things."

She looked around nervously. "We'll have to hurry. We won't have much time before it starts again."

Kyle and Marilyn glanced at each other. "Before *what* starts again?" asked Marilyn.

"Sit down," said Zenobia. "I want to tell you a story."

Kyle went to the row of chairs that had been set up for calling hours. He picked up two, then turned back to Zenobia and asked, uncertainly, "Do you want one?"

Zenobia shrugged. "I have no need to take the weight off my feet," she said with the ghost of a smile. "I'll stand."

Kyle returned with chairs for himself and Marilyn. He placed them side by side, then took Marilyn's hand. The two of them sat down together.

"Damn!" said Zenobia. "This isn't going to be easy. I wish I had a cigar."

"We can do without the smell," said Marilyn impatiently. "Let's get on with this."

"Aren't we touchy?" said Zenobia.

"Considering that I'm sitting in a funeral parlor, which I broke into, in the middle of the night, and having a conversation with a ghost whose body just tried to kill me, I think I'm doing pretty well! Tell me you had an experience that topped this one in all your famous travels."

She was holding Kyle's hand with a crushing grip and pressing herself against him to keep the violence of her trembling from being too visible.

Zenobia shook her head. "Nope. You've got me on that one. I've been almost everywhere and never had an experience to top this one. Nothing like your own hometown for a good time."

Marilyn made a sound of exasperation.

"All right, all right," said Zenobia. "I'll get on with it. But this isn't easy, because a lot of it's my own fault, and I'm going to have to admit to screwing up in a way that I'm not used to."

She looked wistfully down to where her body lay on the floor. "If I'd handled things a little better, I might still be inside that, instead of struggling with all my might just to stay visible for you." She shrugged. "But that's neither here nor there. What you want to know is, what's going on."

Marilyn nodded.

"Well, I don't know," said Zenobia flatly. "At least, not entirely. But I can tell you this much: That amulet is haunted by a demon named Guptas, who was bound to it by the great Suleiman himself.

"What Guptas wants most of all is to be free. But he is subject to whoever owns the amulet. If you know how to use it, you can command incredible power.

"But that's the problem: knowing how to use it. If you try to summon Guptas without knowing the proper procedures, you can end up in big trouble."

"Which is what happened to you?" asked Marilyn.

Zenobia nodded sheepishly. "I really should have known better. Even though I'd never seen anything like that in action, I've spent enough time in the ancient parts of the world to know what can happen. There are strange stories—things *we* would call primitive nonsense—that crop up over and over, linger in the mind, have touches that just don't want to let you explain them away. I should have known better than to fool around with this thing after Eldred died."

"Eldred Cooley?" asked Kyle.

"Yes," said Zenobia with a scowl. "If I ever catch up with him, I swear . . ."

Marilyn caught her breath as a second form shimmered into sight beside Zenobia. "Don't!" it said sharply. "Don't swear to anything, Zenobia. You have no idea how binding an oath is for someone in our condition."

Marilyn had seen Zenobia angry before. She had seen her, in the last week, frightened. But she had never seen her quite this surprised.

"Eldred Cooley!"

The figure standing before them was a small, dapper-looking man. He was slightly overweight, slightly balding, and somewhere, Marilyn guessed, slightly over the age of fifty. Or at least, he had been when he died.

"What is going on here?" asked Kyle. Marilyn squeezed his hand. He sounded like a little kid who had lost his mother in a department store.

Nobody answered him. The two ghosts were looking at each other with an expression Marilyn could not decipher, though it seemed to contain elements of respect, anger, and longing in equal measure.

"Well, what are *you* doing here, Eldred?" asked Zenobia at last.

"The same thing you are," answered Cooley. "Trying to make up for past mistakes."

Marilyn felt Brick rubbing about her legs. She reached down to pick him up and suddenly felt the hair on the back of her neck begin to rise. She sat up straight, the cat still in her hands, and said, "Danger!"

Even as the word left her lips, a searing heat burst against her leg. The amulet had blazed into life again.

Eldred Cooley shouted something in a language that sounded unlike any she had ever heard before. It was too late. Whatever had been started was in motion. There was no stopping it now.

Marilyn leaped to her feet, dumping Brick to the floor. She fumbled desperately for the amulet and finally drew it from her pocket by its chain. Holding it before her, she looked at it and cried out in horror.

The amulet was looking back at her. A single eye, round and red, seemed to be staring into her very soul.

12

"HELP ME!"

Despite the horror of it, Marilyn couldn't tear her own eyes from the gaze of the eye in the amulet. She had a feeling that the amulet had become a bridge of some kind, between her world and this other place, the place from which the eye was looking at her.

This other place filled her with dread. Something spoke to her through the fiery gaze, spoke without words, lashing into her soul with a message that told of thousands of years of waiting, of sorrow, and of anger.

Dimly she could hear the others calling her name. She tried to answer, but could not force her lips to form the words. Frustration began to boil within her, causing her chest to feel painfully full, as if there were a.balloon swelling inside.

Once, when she was five or six, Kyle and Geoff had tied her up while they were playing some stupid game. Being unable to move her arms or legs terrified her, and after only a few seconds she had begun to scream.

She had the same sensation now, only it was worse because there was nothing binding her—nothing but the blazing eye of the amulet. She wanted to scream. She wanted to throw the amulet as far from her as possible. She wanted to grab Kyle by the hand and run from this place, fleeing the terror they had found here.

But she couldn't. She couldn't even move her lips to ask for help. Her breathing had become short and shallow, and her throat felt as though there were a Coke bottle wedged in it.

Then she heard the voice—the same rough voice she had heard before, first speaking through Brick, and then through Zenobia's corpse.

Only now it was whispering.

And it was saying what *she* longed to say.

Help!

The word blossomed in her mind, where none of the others could hear it, and she thought her heart would break, for it sounded like nothing so much as the cry of a lost child.

A teardrop trickled down the amulet.

Help me, whispered the voice in her mind. *Please, help me.*

Marilyn had never heard such sorrow, such longing. It made her think of a warm night the previous summer, when she had been lying in the grass behind her house, staring at the stars, and had suddenly started to weep because she wanted so desperately to reach out and touch them. She had actually raised her hands toward the sky, stretching toward the stars. But they were too far, hopelessly far away. She had felt very small then—small, and trapped, and infinitely sad.

She had felt the way this voice sounded.

Help me, it pleaded again.

And for Marilyn, who was so softhearted she had been known to walk out of her way to avoid stepping on bugs, there was only one possible answer:

"Yes," she whispered. "I'll help you."

A flood of elation seemed to envelop her body. A pleasant warmth surrounded her.

But somewhere in the distance she heard a horrible sound. After a moment she realized it was Kyle, screaming.

"She's on fire! Help her, she's on fire!"

As the words pierced her consciousness, she became more aware of the heat around her.

"Marilyn!"

Zenobia's voice was the final jolt. She tore her gaze from the amulet. Immediately all the screams that had been pent up in her from the time she first saw the eye came tearing out of her, propelled by a new horror.

Her body was surrounded by leaping, crackling flames.

Don't be afraid, whispered the voice in her mind. *I will keep you safe.*

The reassurance did no good. She buried her face in her hands and screamed over and over—until suddenly she realized that, despite the flame, she felt no pain at all.

She was being held in arms of fire, arms that were enclosing her, taking her someplace she had never been before. Someplace where she was desperately needed.

Are you ready? asked the voice.

"Yes," she whispered, before she could even think of what she might be doing.

The sense of heat increased.

Now! cried the voice.

Marilyn felt herself begin to fade.

"Grab her!" cried Zenobia at the same instant.

Marilyn whirled away from the others, saw them spin into the darkness. She felt a hand clutch at her heel. Then everything went black, and it seemed to stay that way for a long, long time.

When Marilyn came to, she found herself lying on a cold, smooth floor. She brought herself to her knees and shook her head, trying to remember what had happened, how she had gotten here.

She looked up. In the distance she could see windows—huge windows, so wide an eagle could fly through them without brushing its wings on either side.

The amulet was still in her hand.

She rolled over and whimpered, pulling her knees against her chest to make herself into a small ball.

Where was she?

She looked up again. How could the windows be so far away? How big was this place?

And *where* was it?

She noticed something and put her hand on the floor, next to her face. The smooth stone beneath her fingers was pitted and scorched, as if something incredibly caustic had fallen upon it.

A cold wind blew over her. She shivered, huddling into herself for warmth.

We're here!

She didn't know if she was glad the voice was still with her or not.

The thought was interrupted by a low moan from somewhere nearby.

She turned in the direction of the sound.

"Kyle!"

He lay sprawled on the floor about ten feet to her left. At the sound of her voice he shook his head and pushed himself to his elbows. A bump the size of a small egg protruded from his forehead.

Raising his fingers, he gingerly touched the lump. "Ouch!" he whispered, making a face. As he did, he seemed to become aware of the room around him. A look of shock crossed his face as he took in the monumental size of the place.

"Where are we?" he asked in a very small voice.

In the Hall of the Kings, replied the voice.

When Kyle made no response, Marilyn realized that the voice was speaking only in her mind. So she repeated the words aloud.

Kyle looked at her. "What's the Hall of the Kings? And how do you know that's what this place is called?"

Marilyn smiled nervously. "A voice in my head told me."

Kyle was still probing at the lump on his forehead. "Are you all right?" he asked, his voice filled with concern.

"No, I'm not all right! I've been attacked by a corpse, swallowed by fire, kidnapped to who knows where by who knows what, and I've got a voice in my head. How can you say 'Are you all right?' I'm going out of my mind!"

"Calm down," said Kyle and the voice in her mind simultaneously.

"I can't stand it!" she screamed. "You! Whatever you are, get out of my head!"

I'm not in your head, answered the voice. *I'm just talking to you that way.*

"Well, why can't I see you?"

I don't think you want to.

"Why not?"

I'm not very pretty.

"I'm not feeling very pretty myself right now," said Marilyn, somewhat irrelevantly.

She received no words in response, only a sense of puzzlement from whatever was talking to her.

"Listen, I don't care *what* you look like. I'd still rather see you if I have to talk to you."

For a moment the voice stayed silent. Marilyn glanced over at Kyle, who was staring at her in astonishment.

"Well?" she cried at last.

I'm afraid, said the voice.

"Of what?" she asked impatiently.

Of frightening you. I need your help, and—

"Look, if you want my help, let me see you!"

You'll scream.

"In about ten seconds I'm going to scream anyway!"

Kyle had crawled over and was sitting beside her. He pressed his hand against the inside of her elbow.

The creature materialized in front of them.

107

Marilyn began to scream. Kyle shouted in terror. The creature vanished abruptly.

I knew you would scream, said the voice petulantly.

"You killed my aunt Zenobia!" cried Marilyn. "I saw you. I saw you in my dreams! You killed her!"

She could feel his chagrin. *That was an accident. I didn't want her to die. I just wanted her to give the amulet back!*

"You killed her!"

Kyle's arms folded around her.

She felt a stony silence in her mind.

"What was *that?*" asked Kyle at last, his voice a mere whisper. She turned to him. His face was etched with lines of fear, and his eyes were deeply troubled. "What's going on?" he asked, sounding so much like a frightened little boy that she could have wept.

"I don't know. I told the voice in my head I wanted to see it."

Kyle shuddered. "You mean that ... *thing* is what you've been talking to?"

"I guess so. The worst part is, I've seen it before."

"Where?"

"In a dream."

"What did you mean when you said it had killed Zenobia? I thought she died of a heart attack."

"She did. But what *caused* the heart attack was that thing we just saw. It scared her to death." Marilyn paused. "Actually, that's just what I saw in my dream. But it seemed so real, I assumed it was what happened." She gave him a weak smile. "Considering what's going on, I guess it makes as much sense to believe in dreams as anything."

"Yeah, I guess so," said Kyle numbly. He stood to

look around and gave a low whistle. "Where are we, anyway? Yeah, I know—we're in the Hall of the Kings. But what does that mean? And how did we get here?"

"I know how *I* got here," said Marilyn. "That creature brought me." She couldn't suppress a shudder when she thought of it. "What I don't understand is how *you* got here."

"I came with you. When you started to disappear, Zenobia screamed for me to grab you. I lunged for you and just managed to catch your heel before you disappeared completely. The next thing I knew, I was lying on this floor, nursing a goose egg." He shook his head and touched the discolored lump. "I can't believe I used to think you were boring."

"I'm beginning to think boring's not so bad," replied Marilyn.

Kyle stretched out his hand to help her to her feet. Once up, she linked her arm through his and pulled herself close.

Why does this make me feel better? she wondered. *I know there's nothing he could do if that monster decides to attack us.*

She looked up at Kyle, who was studying the room—looking for a way out, she assumed. Almost reluctantly she turned her face from his and followed his gaze. For the first time the full extent of the place sank in on her.

It was enormous.

Kyle gave another low whistle. "I was in the Astrodome once. That was like a family rumpus room compared to this."

They turned in a slow circle. On three sides the

polished stone floor swept away for hundreds of feet before coming to a wall. The walls themselves appeared to be carved with some sort of pictures, though Marilyn couldn't make them out from where she stood. The carvings were separated by high, peaked windows. The only thing Marilyn could see through them was clouds.

The walls soared up some forty or fifty feet before the roof took over and continued the upward swing. Kyle guessed out loud that the arch of the ceiling peaked at about a hundred feet above the center of the hall.

The fourth wall was not far from them. Centered against it was a huge throne, mounted on a platform.

Marilyn swallowed uneasily. "Do you think anyone actually sat in that?" she whispered.

"I don't know. If he did, I sure hope he's not around now."

Taking her hand, he led her up the steps of the platform. The seat of the throne—covered with a plush, scarlet material somewhat like velvet, yet different than anything Marilyn had ever seen, or felt—was about shoulder height.

She shivered. "I wonder where the creature went," she said, glancing behind her. "He said he needed help."

"So do we," replied Kyle. "Come on."

He led her across the hall to one of the windows.

Looking out was dizzying, because the ground was nowhere in sight. Pulling themselves up to lean out over the sill (which was nearly as high as Marilyn's chin) they could discern the outlines of the building they were in. It seemed to be a great fortress or castle of some sort, built on the side of a mountain and situated so high that there were clouds *below* them, obscuring the view.

"If I wasn't so scared, I would think it was beautiful," whispered Marilyn. She slid back to the floor. Resting her arms on the wide sill, she gazed worriedly out at the clouds.

"If I wasn't so scared, I would think I was dead," replied Kyle. "This doesn't look real to me. But I don't think your stomach can have this many knots in it once you've actually kicked the bucket."

A cool breeze riffled through his butter-colored hair. Marilyn shifted against him, and he put his arm around her shoulder. She set the amulet on the sill so they could both look at it. The red jewel in the center was flashing angrily.

"What is this thing?" she asked. "Why has it caused me so much trouble?"

Kyle shrugged. "I don't have the slightest idea what's going on. You haven't been willing to tell me anything about it."

She leaned her head against him. "I just didn't want to drag you into this."

"If we ever get out alive, it will have been worth it."

"Right now, that seems like a big *if*." She sighed and began to poke at the amulet's chain, spreading it into a golden circle that glittered on the stone sill. Finally she said, "I'll tell you what's happened so far." Speaking quickly, she filled him in on her experiences since the night Zenobia had first come to her with the amulet.

He listened with growing astonishment. When she was done he said, "If you had told me all that before

111

tonight, I would have said you were losing your mind."

"That's one reason I didn't tell you."

He nodded. His eyes were troubled, and he was silent for some time. Finally he said, "So what do we do now?"

"Look for a way out, I guess."

There is no way out! roared the voice in her mind. The suddenness of it caused Marilyn to shriek and jump. As she did, her hand caught against the amulet, shoving it outward so that it slipped over the edge of the sill.

The chain went slithering after it.

With a little scream Marilyn lunged for it.

She was too late. Her fingers closed on thin air. As she watched in horror, the amulet disappeared into the clouds below.

13

ENTER THE DEMON

Marilyn leaned over the sill, staring down at the billowing clouds.

"Now what do we do?" she whispered, half expecting the voice to answer her. But it was gone again.

"I don't know," said Kyle. "I have a terrible feeling that amulet was connected to our chances of getting out of this place." He had his arm around her waist and was leaning over the sill with her. Suddenly he cried, "Look!"

Marilyn saw it, too: a glint of gold in the air below them. Suddenly they could see as well a flash of red through the clouds, like a stray beam of light at sunset.

"It's the amulet!" cried Marilyn.

With the chain dangling behind it, the amulet floated

back to the windowsill. She snatched it almost before it landed.

Now be more careful! said the voice angrily.

"He's back," Marilyn whispered to Kyle. Looking around cautiously, she said out loud, "Who are you?"

My name is Guptas.

"I figured as much. Why did you bring me here?"

I need your help.

"What's he saying?" asked Kyle impatiently.

"He says he needs our help." Turning to address the air in front of her, she said impatiently, "Isn't there any way you can talk to both of us?"

Not unless you can see me. And you can't bear that.

"I can, too," said Marilyn defensively. "I just wasn't expecting you to be . . ."

So ugly? asked the voice bitterly.

She hesitated. That was it, of course, although *ugly* was a rather mild word to describe this creature as far as she was concerned. But there was such a sense of sadness in the question, she hated to answer it honestly.

Don't worry, said the voice. *I'm used to it. Do you really think you are strong enough now?*

"Maybe if you answer a few questions first."

All right.

"Ask it what it is," suggested Kyle.

The voice didn't wait for her to repeat the question. *I'm a demon.*

"He says he's a demon," she whispered to Kyle. She could feel him shudder. Turning her attention back to the voice, she asked, "So you're evil, right?"

Let's say that I am. If so, would you expect me to answer that question honestly?

Marilyn paused for a moment, puzzled by the response. "How can I trust you?" she asked at last.

A howl of rage ricocheted through her head, and a sorrow beyond anything she had ever known pierced her heart.

You can't trust me! screamed the demon. *I am beyond trust. I am Guptas the Betrayer!*

Kyle looked around uneasily, as if he could sense the power of the emotions swirling around him.

Marilyn acted on instinct. Holding the amulet firmly in her hand, she said, "Let me see you!"

At once Guptas shimmered into being in front of them. He looked at Marilyn warily, waiting for her to begin screaming again.

Despite the fact that this time she knew what to expect, Marilyn still drew back in shock. Cringing against Kyle, she could feel him tremble again, which only increased her own fear. Despite that, she was able to hold in the scream that seemed to be beating at the back of her throat.

The creature confronting her was half again as tall as Kyle and more fearful than any nightmare she had ever known. *Any nightmare but one,* she thought, remembering the dream of Zenobia's death.

Thick muscles rippled over a powerful body covered with rough, dark-red scales. A stiff, scaly crest ran down the creature's spine, then on along the fierce-looking tail that lashed restlessly behind it. The tail ended in a spiked point, which looked as though it could skewer a man's chest with very little trouble.

Its hands and feet were armed with four fierce-looking claws. Thick, sharp, and black, they looked like they could slice through thick leather as if it were butter.

But it was the demon's face that made the whole picture at once so frightening yet at the same time strangely bearable. It had a bullet-shaped head, with two horns curving out in a deadly arc over its brow, which beetled forward like a shelf. At the brow's edges perched the beast's ears, which were absurdly tiny—almost cute, thought Marilyn, if you ignored everything else. Nose and mouth thrust outward almost like an ape's; curving fangs thrust up from the lower jaw. The nose itself was nothing more than two slits, ringed with a fringe of rustling membrane.

All that was horrifying enough. But it was the creature's eyes that held Marilyn's attention. They were as she remembered them from her dream: a flickering red and yellow that made you think when you looked into them you were seeing the fires of hell.

But now she saw one more thing when she looked into them: the private hell of Guptas the demon.

They stood staring at one another until the silence seemed to become a living thing between them—the two teenagers locked together at the window, hardly daring to breathe; the demon leaning forward, resting on his knuckles. Guptas shifted his eyes from Kyle to Marilyn and back again, over and over.

Clearly he was looking for something. But for the life of her, Marilyn couldn't figure out what.

When the silence finally became unbearable she asked, "What do you want of me?"

At least, that was what she tried to say. Her throat had become dry, almost sealed on itself, and the words would not come out.

Kyle squeezed her hand, and she tried again.

"What do you want of me?"

"My freedom," replied the creature, speaking aloud now.

There was a tentativeness about the answer, as if there were more he wanted to ask for.

"What else?" she whispered.

Guptas shook his head. "Nothing," he said sadly. "There is nothing else I need that you can give me."

"What do I have to do with your freedom?" she asked, though the answer was already beginning to take form in the back of her mind.

The demon hesitated, and a wary look came into its eyes.

"And why *should* she free you, anyway?" asked Kyle indignantly. "You killed her aunt."

A look of rage crossed Guptas's face. "Silence, you!" he roared as he slashed toward Kyle's face with his ferocious claws.

"Stop!" cried Marilyn, thrusting the amulet out before her.

The demon stopped as if frozen, then relaxed back into its former posture. It glared at Kyle as if it would like to tear his heart out.

"I didn't mean to kill the old woman," it snarled. "She died all on her own. She wasn't supposed to do that."

"It's the amulet," said Marilyn, as if she hadn't heard him. "You want me to free you from the amulet."

Guptas nodded.

"But Kyle's question still makes sense," she continued. "Why should I free you?"

A sly look crossed the demon's face. "Because if you don't, I'll kill you."

"I think you'll kill me if I do," said Marilyn.

Guptas looked taken aback. A strange expression, half anger, half grief, crossed his face. "I have no hope," he said hollowly.

Marilyn thought her heart would break. It was not only the creature's words, or even his tone of voice. Some kind of connection had been forged between them now, and she could sense his emotional state. She felt a sorrow greater than any she had ever known, deeper and more profound, even, than she had felt at Zenobia's death.

"What happened to you?" she whispered. "Where did you come from?"

Suddenly she cried out. The amulet, clutched firmly in her hand, grew blazing hot. Her body arched once, then went rigid in Kyle's arms.

"Marilyn!" he cried. He took her by the shoulders and shook her. "Marilyn, what is it?"

Her eyes were wide open, but they seemed blank and distant. He shook her again.

She didn't respond.

She couldn't.

Guptas was answering her question.

14

GUPTAS THE
BETRAYER

She hadn't moved a step, but everything was different.

She still stood by the window.

She still looked across that vast chamber.

But now the place was alive with color and activity. Banners of scarlet and gold fluttered from the ceiling. Exquisite tapestries covered the walls. Musicians wandered here and there, playing lively songs on instruments she had never seen before.

She reached instinctively for Kyle, but her fingers touched only the cold stone of the sill. He was gone.

A shudder of horror racked her body. She was alone in a room filled with beings unlike any she had ever seen—they were enormous, for one thing—and creatures unlike any she had ever imagined. Some resembled Guptas. Others were as different from him as he was from her.

The room bustled with activity.

Almost everyone seemed happy.

She pressed against the sill, waiting in terror for the moment when they would discover her. She felt a throb of pain and realized she was beating her hands against the stone wall.

"Don't be so frightened," whispered a gravelly voice. "They don't know you're here."

The words came from Guptas, who crouched beside her, tail lashing, eyes blazing.

"Watch," he said bitterly. "Watch, and I will show you the downfall of Guptas the Betrayer."

Suddenly she felt a blast of intense heat. She cried out in pain, then lost consciousness.

When she opened her eyes again, the room seemed exactly the same as before. The great bustle of activity continued. The pleasant babble of voices was the same—though underneath it all she now sensed a deep current of joy and contentment.

But that, she understood, had been there all along. Then she realized the one thing that really was different. Now she was seeing all this *through* the eyes of Guptas.

The sense of heat remained. Not impossible to bear, it hovered on the edge of pain, like a dull toothache never quite out of mind.

"Relax," whispered Guptas.

Mere words could never have convinced her to do so. But she had become linked with Guptas at an even deeper level, and she could sense what was in his mind. Examining it, she could read no ill will toward herself—only a simmering anger directed elsewhere, and a deep, enduring sorrow.

In relation to herself, she could sense only one thought: Guptas was terribly anxious for her to know something.

She relaxed.

A corona of fire blazed before her eyes.

The final barriers vanished, and in a matter of moments, she knew the story of Guptas's life.

Because she was living it.

Marilyn stood next to the king. His hand was resting lightly on her head; together they looked out at the great hall.

Her tail lashed back and forth in amusement. All this belonged to Suleiman.

And she was Suleiman's favorite.

Hundreds of people filled the hall, all of them tall, all of them beautiful.

Beneath their feet, hardly noticed, scampered the demons. Once even a single demon would have been cause for alarm here. But it had been a thousand years since the king had tamed them, a thousand years since the war between the demons and the people of Suleiman had ended.

The race of the Suleimans had triumphed, and peace ruled the castle.

Life was good.

Or it should have been.

She paused. Something was nagging at the back of her mind, some thought that stood in the way of her happiness.

She tried to find it, but could not. It was locked away more securely than Suleiman's books of wisdom.

She looked back out over the throng and tried to regain the sense of pleasure she had felt. It was gone. Her tail continued to lash, but it was in anger now, not contentment. She wanted to drive the spike at its tip through someone's heart. Maybe then she would feel better.

She recoiled from the thought, and suddenly she understood at least part of what drove Guptas. He was a being at war with himself.

A sudden flourish of trumpets caught her attention. The great doors at the end of the hall swung open and the king's son entered, standing astride a great carpet that floated through the air. A shout went up. The hero had returned.

Marilyn felt her heart leap. The prince was her best friend.

She loved him.

She hated him.

Why? she wondered.

The answer formed as quickly as she asked for it: She hated him because he had Suleiman's love, and she wanted that all to herself.

A murmur rose among the demons. The one closest to the throne caught her eye and snickered.

A fist of ice clutched her heart. She was on the verge of doing something terrible.

She didn't want to do it.

And she knew she would not be able to stop herself.

Again the world seemed to spin around her, and again she was somewhere else—seeing, *living* a different scene.

This time it was a cave, dark and foul smelling. A dozen demons crouched around her, urging her to lead them. Not one of them was more than half her size. She was the greatest demon in the court. And she was Suleiman's favorite.

"Help us, Guptas," wheedled a voice next to her. "You owe it to us."

Again she had that sensation of being torn between two loyalties. The demons were her people. The king was her master. Her heart belonged to both. And it was breaking.

"You're waiting for something that will never happen," hissed a voice to her right.

Still she hesitated.

One more voice, sharp and bitter: "Remember what the Suleimans did to our people."

The speaker was a very old demon. He sat directly across from her, crouching between two stalactites that thrust down from the roof of the cave like fangs. Somewhere behind him flickered an evil-looking fire that caused his shadow to stretch toward her like a dark hand.

He rose and walked in her direction, the shadow moving before him. Marilyn cringed, aching to cry out in terror, to run not only from these creatures but also from the horrible thing they were asking her to do.

She reminded herself that she was only an observer, lodged temporarily in Guptas's body to learn the secrets of his past.

The ancient demon was standing directly in front of her now. He took her chin—Guptas's chin—in his withered claws and held it steady. His eyes seemed to be boring into Guptas's head.

For a wild, terrifying moment Marilyn wondered if the old demon knew she was in there.

His face was shriveled and evil, and she felt she was in the presence of a force as old as time, as wicked as hate.

In a low, gravelly whisper, he hissed, "Remember what Suleiman did to your mother!"

Guptas erupted in rage, and Marilyn felt as if her brain was on fire.

What? she cried out in Guptas's mind. *What did he do to her?*

She felt as if a door had slammed in her face as Guptas's mind sealed the answer away from her.

Suddenly the world spun again, and they left the cave behind. Marilyn seethed with frustration. Guptas wanted her to know something, but he wouldn't show her all of it.

Why the sudden shyness? she wondered. *Fear? Sorrow? Shame? What is it that he won't let me see?*

They were back in the Hall of the Kings; Suleiman's son was still riding his flying carpet up the center of the hall in his triumphal parade. The throng that filled the court was shouting joyfully at his entrance.

Suddenly Marilyn was aware of the old demon who had spoken to her in the cave. Though he was standing on the other side of the hall, he was staring into their eyes—her eyes, Guptas's eyes—and speaking directly into their mind.

Remember, he growled. *Remember, and repay!*

The crowd was shouting the prince's name. For a year he had been traveling the land, doing his father's business. He had extended the rule of the Suleimans. He had brought peace to the borders of the kingdom, burnishing the golden age that had begun with the defeat of the demons.

The magic carpet paused before Suleiman's throne, hovering a foot or two above the ground.

The king rose to greet his son.

Slowly, silently, unnoticed in the joyous throng, a dozen demons crept to the edges of the crowd. They positioned themselves near the prince, waiting.

Guptas stood beside the king. From across the hall the ancient demon was burning a message into his brain: *Now, Guptas. The time is right. But they have to move together.*

Guptas didn't move.

The words rang in her head, and Marilyn wanted to cry out for them to stop.

Now! demanded the demon. *All we need is the signal. All we need is your word, Guptas, to begin our revenge for a thousand years of slavery!*

Still Guptas hesitated.

Suddenly a picture flashed in and out of his mind like a streak of lightning. Marilyn was left with only an impression of a woman, a woman vastly beautiful yet somehow evil, at once more and less than human.

Remember!

Guptas looked down at the carpet. Everything was in place.

Remember!

A red haze seemed to float through his mind. Marilyn caught his rage, felt herself aching with anger, longing for revenge.

"Now!" screamed the demon.

"Now!" screamed the girl.

It came out as a single word.

At their signal the demons leaped. Grabbing the front edge of the floating carpet, they rolled it under itself, peeling it back so that the prince was suddenly standing on nothing. When he stumbled and fell to the floor, his body was instantly covered with a mass of writhing demons.

A roar of anger erupted from the king.

The crowd began to scream.

The prince was battling the hordes of demons.

And he was calling Guptas's name, calling to him for help.

Again, Marilyn felt the world whirl sickeningly around her. When she could focus again, she found herself sitting in the shade of an enormous tree. The prince, younger now, almost a child, was sitting next to her and saying, "They don't understand you, Guptas. They think you're like all the others." His voice was sad, burdened by the injustice his friend suffered.

Marilyn felt a sudden warmth. The prince trusted her. Even if no one else did, the prince trusted her. He would speak to Suleiman for her. He would tell the king she could be trusted.

"I will fight for you, Guptas," continued the prince. "Because I believe in you."

The prince was calling her name.

"Guptas! Guptas, fight for me!"

She was back in the castle. The throne room was in chaos; demons were attacking everywhere. The king himself was battling a dozen or more, trying to fight past them so he could help his son.

He could never do it in time. There were too many of them.

The prince's cries were growing weaker.

"Guptas, help me!"

He had trusted her! Again that red haze seemed to settle over her eyes. The heat she had sensed from the time she had been joined with Guptas began to blaze around her. She was on fire, and she didn't care. Death filled the air, but she didn't care.

They had to save the prince!

With a cry of rage she threw herself into the battle. She was Guptas, greatest of the demons. With every slash of her claws some other demon's scales fell to the floor, scattering like handfuls of dropped coins. With every sweep of her tail its deadly spike ripped into some soft underbelly, spilling dark demon blood that hissed and steamed like the rivers of hell.

The demons threw themselves on her, their weight bearing her to the floor. Untrained in battle, Marilyn shrieked in horror. But Guptas knew what to do. Arching his body, he sent the demons flying in all directions, and once more began ripping the creatures away from the prince, away from his friend.

In the end they managed to save the prince.

But it really made no difference.

A thousand years of peace had ended with the signal given by Guptas.

The Demon Wars had begun anew.

Three days later the prince was ambushed and slain by demons who waited outside his sleeping chamber.

Guptas went into hiding.

He had betrayed the Suleimans, betrayed his only friend, by signaling the attack. Then, unable to live with that betrayal, he had turned back to the Suleimans he still loved, betraying his own people in turn.

The demons would curse him throughout eternity. Now his friend was dead, but the war raged on.

Guptas wanted the demons to win.

He wanted the Suleimans to win.

He wanted to die.

As it turned out, that would be the one punishment denied to him.

Five days later the war was over, and the disaster he had initiated was complete.

Guptas was stunned. The last war between the Suleimans and the demons had gone on for a thousand years. How could it be over in two weeks this time?

The answer was simple. The demons had never been inside the castle before. Now, after a thousand years of serving here, they knew its ins and outs as well as they had known their own winding caves. They fought a war of ambush and sudden death. There were no great clashes of armies after that morning in the Hall of the Kings. There was only lurking, hiding, and ambush.

And death.

Now the demons and the Suleimans were gone, all destroyed in this final cataclysm, which had been unleashed by a single word that should never have been spoken.

A word that had come from his lips.

Guptas wandered the halls, sighing and moaning to himself. The castle was littered with bodies, both Suleiman and demon.

And it was all his fault.

He sat alone in empty rooms, beating his breast

with his claws, pounding the floor in his anger and sorrow and guilt.

Was there no one left alive?

"Yes."

Guptas looked up and cried out in terror.

The king was standing before him.

Suleiman didn't say a word, merely motioned for Guptas to follow him. Meekly the demon walked at his master's heels, back to the Hall of the Kings.

The bodies were all gone, and he wondered vaguely what great magic Suleiman had worked to get rid of them.

The king collapsed onto his throne. Guptas sat with his face averted, ashamed to look at his master. But out of the corner of his eye he could see that the king was pale and exhausted, and that his body had many wounds.

After a while the king began to speak. He told of the war, and how it had been fought. He spoke of the death of his son. And then, in a whisper, he spoke of the final great battle, deep in the bowels of the castle, when he had fought alone, against the remaining demons, finally imprisoning them with a spell so powerful it nearly killed him to cast it.

And at last he spoke of betrayal, and the necessary punishment.

Then, despite Guptas's tears, despite his cries of terror, his pleading, his apologies, his groveling, Suleiman worked his last magic.

With his powers he imprisoned Guptas in an amulet the prince had worn from the day of his birth—cursing him to stay inside it until the day someone trusted him enough to release him.

Carrying the amulet, Suleiman wandered out of his castle and down the mountainside. Then he worked his last great act of magic, shoving the castle and the mountain on which it stood out of the world we know, into another place altogether.

For a time the great king traveled this world, seeking a balm for the pain in his heart—until one day, wandering weak and weary through the deserts of Egypt, he simply toppled forward, crushing the amulet into the sand beneath him. He lay in the blazing sun, sweat pouring from his brow, sand clinging to his skin.

There he died.

And there Guptas stayed, for a time longer than anyone could imagine—stayed until the day Eldred Cooley found the amulet.

15

GUPTAS'S SECRET

Kyle was shaking her.

"Marilyn! Marilyn, are you all right?"

She opened her eyes and looked around. She was back in the Hall of the Kings. Guptas stood nearby, looking at her anxiously.

"Are you all right?" asked Kyle again.

She nodded. "I think so. How long was I out?"

"Only a few seconds. But you had me scared."

"A few seconds! But . . ."

The protest died on her lips. She turned to the demon.

"What do you want from me?"

"Let me go."

"I don't understand."

"Let me go. Free me from the amulet."

"But you're free of it right now."

Guptas shook his head.

"I don't understand," she said. "I mean, there you are—"

While she was speaking, Guptas had raised his arm. Before she could finish her sentence, he lashed out at her with his deadly claws.

"Watch out!" cried Kyle. At the same time he threw himself at Guptas, trying to stop the attack. Marilyn screamed and threw up an arm to protect herself.

Kyle slammed into the demon just as the slashing claws made contact with Marilyn's face.

They passed through her cheek and came out the other side without leaving a scratch. At the same moment Kyle hurtled though the demon's body and ended up sprawling on the floor several feet past him.

"You're a ghost!" cried Marilyn.

Guptas actually smiled, though the effect was more that of a hideous leer. "No, I am not a ghost. But I'm not really here. I'm in the amulet, just as I have been for ten thousand years."

Kyle pushed himself to his knees and shook his head. He had another, smaller lump sprouting next to the first one. "So you're a hologram," he said. Gently he fingered the new protuberance. "Did you really have to give such a convincing demonstration?"

"It's important that you believe me," said Guptas solemnly.

Marilyn crossed to Kyle and helped him to his feet. "I believe you. I just don't understand what I'm supposed to *do* for you. Let's take it step by step."

"I want you to let me out of the amulet."

"You've got to be kidding!" cried Kyle. "You think

she's going to let something like you loose when you're good and safe where you are?"

"She will if either of you ever wants to see your home again," snarled Guptas.

"Don't threaten me!" snapped Marilyn. Holding up the amulet, she added, "I don't want to see you anymore."

Guptas vanished instantly.

"How'd you do that?" asked Kyle in astonishment.

"It's the amulet. I'm pretty sure it controls him. Didn't you notice the other time, when he slashed at you with his claws and I told him to stop? I was holding the amulet then, and he obeyed me instantly."

"He couldn't have hurt me anyway," pointed out Kyle, "since he was only a—what? A mirage? An illusion? What do you call something like that?"

Marilyn shrugged. "I don't have the foggiest. Anyway, the point right now is not what we call him. It's how do we deal with him?"

"I'd say the first thing to do is make him take us home."

She held up the amulet. "Guptas! I want to see you!"

She was expecting his image to materialize in front of them again. Instead, the jewel in the center of the amulet flashed.

She looked at it curiously and found herself looking *into* it.

Red. And walls. Wall after wall of smooth, hard crimson, all at odd angles to one another, all too close together, cramping, crowding, holding ...

She shuddered. This was Guptas's world. This was

the place where he had been imprisoned for ten thousand years.

And now he wanted to get out.

Suddenly one eye appeared in the center of the jewel, as it had in the funeral home. It glared at her sullenly.

"Don't play games with me," said Marilyn fiercely. "I said, 'Let me see you!'"

The jewel flashed again, and instead of an eye, she saw Guptas, impossibly small, crouched and crowded between the facets of the crimson prison.

"Out here!" she snapped.

At once Guptas stood before them. Glaring at her, he said sullenly, "You'll never rest again."

She blinked nervously. "What do you mean?"

"I mean you can control me with that amulet, but only when you're awake. I will be free at night—not free of the amulet. Oh, no, I'm never free of that. But free to haunt you. You'll see me in your dreams. I'll shape myself out of air and stalk your room. When you open your eyes, I'll be there, crouching at the end of your bed, waiting to pounce.

"You may know I'm not solid.

"You may know I can never hurt you.

"But will you sleep? Night after night with me prowling your room, screaming at you in a voice no one else can hear, cursing you with the anger I've built up over a hundred centuries—will you sleep then?"

He smiled fiendishly. "Or will you lie awake night after night, quivering in your bed, trembling at the wrath of Guptas? Will you grow pale and weary—"

"Oh, shut up!"

Guptas fell silent.

Kyle walked over to where the demon stood and thrust out his hand. It went right through the scaly hide.

"Cool," he muttered.

Guptas glanced at him with contempt. Suddenly he threw himself at Marilyn's feet and clasped his arms around her legs. "I want to be real again!" he cried desperately. "Make me real!"

"Talk about co-dependent," said Kyle.

Even though the demon wasn't actually there, the illusion was so powerful Marilyn found herself trying to keep her balance in his grip.

"Please!" he cried. "Please let me out! I won't be bad. You know I won't! You know why I'm there. I've suffered long enough. Let me out!"

"So you can kill us like you killed her aunt?" sneered Kyle.

"I never did!" shrieked Guptas. "I told you, she died all by herself. She wasn't supposed to do that!" His voice grew sly. "Besides, I did that while I was bound to the amulet. I can do it again, whether she frees me or not. I just send a picture, as I'm doing now. As I'll continue to do."

One look at Marilyn's face and he changed tactics again. "But not to you!" he cried, banging his head on the floor at her feet. "You know my story! You know the truth! Let me out! Let me out! Let me out!"

Marilyn hesitated. Finally she said, "I don't think I could, even if I wanted to."

The demon arched his back and spread his arms and screamed. Marilyn covered her ears. But even with her hands pressed against her skull she could hear his anguished pleas.

"What do you mean? Why can't you free me?"

"Because of the curse the king put on you!"

Instantly he stopped screaming and rose to his knees. "What do you mean?"

"Well, what he said when he put you in there. You're bound there until someone trusts you. I can't just say, 'Oh, come on out, it's okay now!' If I don't *trust* you, it won't work."

"You can trust me!" cried Guptas eagerly. "You know that. You can trust me. I'll even be your servant. I'll fetch and carry for you and always do what you ask and ..."

Marilyn actually broke out laughing. "What would I do with you if I had you?"

"I'm a very good servant," said Guptas sullenly.

"No, you are not," replied Marilyn sternly. "You betrayed your master before. You would do it again."

"Not if my master was true!" cried Guptas. "What about that? What about that, eh? What about what Suleiman did?"

"What did Suleiman do?" asked Marilyn. "You wouldn't show me. You kept it hidden."

Guptas turned away. "He was cruel."

"That means nothing," said Marilyn. "What did he do? You want me to trust you, but you won't trust me. You won't even tell me the whole story."

Guptas turned back to her.

"If I tell you, will you let me go?"

"If you don't, I won't."

"That's not the same thing!"

"I know that. But it's the best you're going to get. Never mind. I'm getting tired of you anyway. Get ready, Kyle. I'm going to make him take us back now."

"Wait ... wait ... wait ... wait ... wait!" howled Guptas. He was rocking back and forth, clutching his knees.

"Well?"

"All right, I'll tell you."

Marilyn tightened her grip on the amulet and waited expectantly.

Guptas hesitated. He glanced at Kyle, then turned again to Marilyn.

"Suleiman was my father," he said at last.

16

THE LAMIA

The three of them—Marilyn, Kyle, and Guptas the demon—sat in a circle on the floor, their legs crossed Indian fashion, trying to make sense of the story the demon had just told them.

At one point in his tale Marilyn had interrupted to fill in Kyle on her earlier experience of seeming to live part of Guptas's life.

"How did you do that, anyway?" she had asked the demon.

He shrugged. "You asked me a question while you were holding the amulet. That gave me permission to answer it."

"But how did you answer it? Did you just send a picture from your head to mine, or—"

. Guptas broke in. "No, you were *there*. I took you

back in time to the reign of the Suleimans. And then I let you merge with me, so you could see my story."

"You mean I was really there—really in the past?"

He smiled and nodded. "Fun, wasn't it?"

She shivered a little.

"Let's get back to the point," said Kyle. "How do we find out if you're telling the truth about your father and this ... what did you call her? A lamia?"

Guptas did a backward somersault and stood on his head. "You can't. You'll just have to take my word for it."

"Can't you show us, like you did before?" asked Marilyn.

"I can't take you back to before my birth. How can I show you things that happened before I was born?"

Taking a guess, Marilyn whispered, "Then show us her death."

Guptas tumbled to the floor. He actually seemed to go pale for a moment. Looking up at her, his eyes filled with misery, he hissed, "No."

"It would make things easier."

"No."

"I could command you."

The demon shrugged. "I won't be responsible for the consequences."

"Which would be ..."

He looked directly into her eyes. She flinched, but did not turn her gaze away. Once again she had the sensation of looking into the fires of hell.

"A memory," he said at last. "A memory you will

139

carry with you the rest of your life. A nightmare you'll have to live with."

"You've already threatened me with that if I don't free you. I'm stuck in the middle."

"I shouldn't have threatened you before," said Guptas. "I'm sorry."

She looked at him in astonishment. His voice sounded genuinely apologetic.

He read her eyes. "Don't be so surprised! I know right from wrong. You've seen part of my life. You know I'm different from the others. Look at me! I am not a demon! I am Guptas—half Suleiman, half demon, and different from anything or anyone you've ever heard of. Don't judge me by what you think or what you fear or what you've heard! Judge me by what I am!"

"Right now you're hysterical," said Marilyn softly.

Guptas began to laugh—a harsh, coughing sound that was two steps on the far side of pleasant.

"Do you really want the story?"

She nodded.

"Him, too?"

She looked at Kyle. His face was grim. But he nodded.

She held up the amulet. "Tell us both. No tricks."

Guptas looked hurt. "I had no tricks in mind. How do I make you trust me?"

"You don't," said Kyle softly. "You just make it *possible*—by being trustworthy."

Guptas shot him an angry look. "Put your hand on the amulet," he said. "Both of you hold it. And remember ... you asked for this."

Kyle slid around next to Marilyn and closed his hand over hers.

And they were gone.

Guptas stood cowering behind his father. Suleiman laid a hand on his head to comfort him.

Marilyn relaxed at the touch. The king had the hands of a healer.

Only he wasn't king yet. Guptas aimed some thoughts in her direction, and she understood that what they were about to see predated her last experience in the past. The king she had seen that time was still a prince now. His father was on the throne.

His name was Suleiman, too—as was that of every king who had reigned before him.

Guptas's father wore a short tunic made of black and scarlet cloth embroidered with gold. A band of silk circled his forehead, binding his long jet-black hair. He had a strong nose, olive skin, enormous dark eyes. He was incredibly handsome.

Marilyn felt a surge of emotion. It was coming from Kyle. With a start, she realized it was jealousy.

"Where are we?" he asked.

"In the Hall of the Kings," replied Guptas.

"I know that," he said sharply. "But where in the hall? Where are Marilyn and I?"

"Inside me," said Guptas simply. "Just watch. Both of you."

She watched. The hall was filled, as before. And there was an air of expectancy. But this time it was not joyful. There was fear in it, and horror.

Two guards brought in a woman. A murmur of disgust rippled through the court.

Marilyn cried out at the surge of emotion that ran through Guptas. She felt Suleiman's hand slide down his neck and onto his shoulder, drawing him close. Guptas clung to his leg, which was like a young oak. Suddenly she realized that at the time of this scene Guptas was little more than a babe.

"Twelve hundred years," said Guptas, in answer to her unspoken question. "This is twelve hundred years before the last scene I showed you. The Demon Wars are still raging in their full fury. Suleiman-the-king, he who sits on the throne, has reigned for over eight hundred years. In all that time he has never been able to defeat the demons."

He paused, then added: "Now his son has fathered one."

The woman struggled wildly, until she looked over at Guptas. Then she stopped. Marilyn read a terrible longing in her face.

Whatever else she was, she was beautiful.

It was a wild, terrible beauty—untamed, fascinating, almost frightening.

She was dressed in gossamer rags. Marilyn had the feeling they were the remnant of some once beautiful gown she had destroyed in her fury.

Her hair was fire red, redder even than Marilyn's, something she would never have thought possible.

And her eyes . . .

Her eyes were locked on Guptas now, looking right into him—and at the same time, it seemed, into Marilyn. As in the demon cave, she had the uneasy sensation that perhaps her presence here was not a secret after all.

They were wild eyes, wild and filled with anger. But

there was a softness in them when they gazed on Guptas.

The demon tightened his grip on his father's leg, digging his claws into the flesh.

Prince Suleiman seemed not to notice. His eyes were riveted on his wife. Marilyn felt a tremor run through his body.

The king rose from the throne. He was tall, taller even than the prince, with a great gray beard that flowed over his chest. He wore a thin circle of gold on his brow. His face was deeply troubled.

He went to the woman.

"Behold!" he cried to the court. "Behold, the lamia!"

Reaching out, he grasped her hand.

Marilyn recoiled in horror as the woman dropped her human shape and revealed herself for what she really was.

Her skin blistered over, turning red and scaly. Great peaked wings shot out behind her. Dark claws curved out from her fingertips.

Prince Suleiman flinched. This was the woman he had loved, the mother of his child.

Two guards held her, but it was the power of the king that kept her in check. She writhed in their hands, cursing the king, cursing the race of the Suleimans. Her eyes were like fire. Her tongue, flickering out between blackened lips, was like a cleft snake.

"Will anyone speak in her defense?" asked the king.

The court was silent, a silence that seemed to fill the great hall with a heavy sense of doom.

The lamia wrenched herself around to face the

prince. Her demon shape faded and she was a woman again, soft and desirable. Her eyes pleaded with him.

Prince Suleiman shuddered, but remained silent. Blood trickled down his thigh where his half-demon son was sinking childish claws into the flesh. The prince tightened his grip on the demon child's shoulder.

"Father?" whispered Guptas.

The prince said nothing.

The woman faded, and the lamia reappeared.

They brought in the ice, and she began to scream.

They were back in their own bodies, in the echoingly empty Hall of the Kings.

"What happened?" cried Marilyn. "Why did you bring us back?"

Guptas turned on her in fury.

"Wasn't that enough?" he cried. "Must I watch my own mother be executed a second time just to satisfy your curiosity?"

He strode away from her. "Ice," he whispered. He spun back, and his voice rose to a shout. "They did it with ice! She was a creature of fire, and ice was fatal to her. They brought in a great jagged block of it and slowly pushed her into it. The first bits of it that touched her hissed and melted against her flesh."

He shuddered.

"Her skin began to peel off. She screamed and cried to my father for help. I turned his leg to ribbons with my claws.

"But there was no help for her. No compassion from anyone in that hall—because she was a lamia, a mother of demons, and had tricked the prince into loving her. So they stood in silence as the king's murdering guards pushed her into the ice and her skin sizzled away from her body."

The demon's image walked back and stood before Marilyn. "Do you still wonder," he whispered, his voice intense, harsh with pain, "why I had mixed feelings about my father?"

He paused, then stretched his claws upward and screamed, "Or about myself? Look at me. Look at what they made me! I was the firstborn child of the firstborn child! I have royal blood coursing through my veins! I should have been king. I should have been Suleiman!

"But my father loved a lamia, and then let her die."

He turned away and sat huddled into himself.

"That was the beginning of the end of the Demon Wars," he said after a while. "My father fought as no Suleiman ever had before. He led the people into battle, and they were invincible. But I know that with every slash of his sword he was slashing at his own heart. I know his guilt. I know his fury at himself for remaining silent.

"I even understand it! That's the hardest part of all! I can't even condemn him totally. She should never have come to him. She was wrong. He was wrong. Everybody suffered. And in the end I destroyed their world. And my own."

"I'll let you go now," said Marilyn.

Guptas turned to her in astonishment.

"What?"

"I'll let you go now. You've suffered long enough."

He threw himself at her feet. "Thank you!" he cried. "Thank you. Oh, thank you!"

"Stop it!" she said in disgust. "Remember who you are!"

He stood, a strange expression on his face, pride and surprise mingling together.

She lifted the amulet and began to speak.

"Don't!" cried a voice behind her.

She spun around. It was Eldred Cooley. Beside him stood Zenobia. She held Brick in her arms.

"You must not do this," said Cooley sternly.

Guptas howled in despair.

17

JUDGE AND JURY

"**N**ever trust a demon," said Eldred Cooley. He glared at Guptas so fiercely that for a moment Marilyn thought he might actually attack the creature.

Zenobia broke the tension by speaking. "Marilyn, are you and Kyle all right?"

Marilyn nodded. "How did you get here?"

"Brick."

Kyle laughed. "You mean that cat is actually good for something?"

"Cats are good for a great deal more than most people realize," said Cooley sternly. "Their ability to track down demons is one of the reasons they were highly valued in the ancient world. It's interesting," he said, turning to Zenobia. "You would think they would have lost the ability over the last several thousand years, since there was no use for it."

"Stick to the point, Eldred," she replied tartly.

"The point right now," he said, turning back to Marilyn, "is how to dispose of that creature you have gained control of."

"Why can't I just let him go?"

Cooley looked at her incredulously. "Do you really want to release such a monstrosity on the modern world?"

"He's had a difficult life," said Marilyn defensively.

Cooley roared with laughter. "Let him go free and you'll find out what difficult is. How do you know he had a difficult life? Did he tell you? He is a master of lies. I repeat: never trust a demon."

"He didn't tell us," said Kyle. "He showed us."

Zenobia dropped Brick, who strolled over to sniff at Guptas. "What do you mean, he showed you?"

"Well, he took us back in time...."

"He touched your minds!" cried Cooley. "Oh, we've got trouble, Zenobia. Lord only knows what he's done to these two kids. They could be completely under his control."

"No!" shouted Guptas.

The sudden shout caused Brick—who had been trying without success to catch a scent from the demon's image—to jump a foot into the air. When he landed he hissed and arched his back.

"I wouldn't do that to them," said Guptas firmly. He made a little slashing motion at the cat, which scurried over to hide behind Marilyn.

"It is pointless for you to say anything," said Cooley, "since we can't believe a word of it anyway."

"Use your brain, you old fool! What is the curse that was laid on me? I cannot be freed of the amulet until someone trusts me enough to let me out. What good would it do me to put them in my power? I could gain obedience, maybe even acceptance. But never true trust. I could never break the binding that way."

"Don't try to use your persuasive ways on me," said Cooley. "I'm too wise for that."

Guptas made a noise of disgust, then vanished.

"Now see what you've done!" said Marilyn.

Cooley was at her side before she finished speaking. Positioning himself in front of her, he began to stare into her eyes. It reminded Marilyn uncomfortably of the meeting in the cavern, when the old demon had looked at Guptas the same way. She shivered.

"I can't tell for certain," he muttered to Zenobia, who was standing at his side. "But I think she's all right."

"Of course I'm all right!" snapped Marilyn, pushing at his hand. Her arm passed through his, and she suddenly remembered that she was dealing with a ghost.

"This is too much," she said.

Kyle came over, holding the cat. "Where are we, sir?"

Cooley turned to him. "Somewhere at the edge of your world. When the last Suleiman left the castle, he pushed it over some magical border, to move it away from the world we know."

"Then what would it hurt to let Guptas free here? It's not as if we'd be letting him go in the real world."

"Other than the fact that he might kill you instantly, you should be able to see that he can transport himself

149

between our world and this castle with no trouble. He'd be back on earth raising hell in no time flat. No, there is no way around it. He must be destroyed."

"I'll bet you support the death penalty, too," said Kyle, scratching Brick between the ears.

"I won't destroy him," said Marilyn flatly.

"Marilyn, be reasonable," said Zenobia. "He's an evil creature. Look what he did to me!"

"He didn't mean to," said Marilyn uncertainly. "He just wanted you to give him the amulet."

"Why?" cried Cooley, pouncing like a cat that had spotted a mouse. "Why did he want the amulet back?"

"Because I was afraid she might be as much of a fool as you were!" roared Guptas, suddenly reappearing beside them.

Marilyn was sure that if Cooley hadn't been a ghost, he would have gone pale at that moment.

"The owner of the amulet has power over me," continued Guptas. "I don't like that, so I don't want anyone to own the amulet. I don't want anyone to control me. Most of all, I want to be free. But it was clear you had poisoned the woman's mind against me. If I couldn't get her to free me, I wanted at least to be free of her control. I never meant for her to die. I was terrified when her heart gave out. I had had no idea that might happen. You people are much weaker than the Suleimans."

"And me," said Cooley. "What about what you did to me?"

"You," said Guptas simply, "deserved to die. But I didn't do it. It was your own greed that did you in."

"What do you mean?" cried Cooley. "I ordered you to lead me to something valuable in this castle." He stopped and looked around him, then added defensively, "Because I wanted to prove to Zenobia what kind of possibilities I had uncovered."

"You've been here before?" gasped Zenobia.

"Of course. This creature led me to a valuable artifact, all right. But it was a trap. When he took me back to my hotel room and I opened the thing—"

"When you opened it, you found death," said Guptas.

"That's right!" shouted Cooley. He turned to the others. "He admits he tricked me! He showed me a precious box, but inside was some curse of the Suleimans."

Even now, as a spirit, the memory made him shudder. "When I opened the box, a hideous centipede scuttled out. It was a great purplish thing, mottled and twice as long as my hand. It slithered up my sleeve." His eyes grew wide with remembered horror. "It ran up my shirt, and while I was trying to tear open my collar—it bit me."

"It had a very powerful poison," said Guptas softly.

"You see!" screamed Cooley. "I asked him for a treasure, and he gave me death!"

For a moment no one said a word. Then Zenobia began to chuckle.

Guptas smiled. "I see you understand."

Comprehension dawned in Cooley's face. "You tricked me," he repeated bitterly.

"Not at all," said Guptas. "You merely leapt to conclusions. That box was a mere trifle for the Suleimans. The treasure was inside. You asked for something valuable, and I gave you the most precious thing

I could think of, the thing I have longed for for ten thousand years. I gave you death."

Cooley was furious. "Give me that amulet!" he said, snatching at Marilyn's hand. His fingers passed right through hers, and he made a gesture of impatience.

"It's hers by right," said Guptas calmly. "You might take it from her, but it will do you no good. The amulet can be stolen, but its power must pass freely."

"Marilyn," said Cooley, forcing himself to be calm, "please give me the amulet. This creature must be dealt with now."

"No," said Marilyn. Her voice was shaking.

"Now, listen here, young lady—"

"Eldred, shut up!" said Zenobia sharply.

To Marilyn's surprise, Cooley backed off like a whipped dog.

"Marilyn, be reasonable," said Zenobia. "This creature is evil. He is a demon!"

"*Half* demon," said Marilyn.

"Well, that's interesting," said Zenobia, raising a ghostly eyebrow. "But it doesn't make any difference. In his heart he is wicked. And he is powerful. All the time the amulet lay in the desert, the world was safe from him." She glanced at Cooley. "Far better the amulet should have remained there," she said pointedly. "But it didn't. It was brought out into the world. And now it is an unbelievable menace. If you do not free Guptas, somehow, someday, someone else will. And when that happens, I fear the whole world will pay."

She paused for a moment, then touched her niece's cheek with a hand that wasn't really there. Marilyn shivered at the sensation.

"It isn't fair," said Zenobia. "But it has come down to you. You must decide for everyone."

"So I'm judge and jury," said Marilyn softly.

"That's right," said Zenobia. "No matter what Eldred thinks, we cannot force you to make this decision."

"What do *you* think I should do?"

"I'm not certain," said Zenobia. Her face was troubled. "In a way, I could say it makes no difference to me. After all, what happens to the world now is little of my concern. But I don't want to see innocent people suffer."

"Is he so guilty?" asked Marilyn. "He didn't ask to be born. Do you know his story?"

"Do you believe it?" asked Zenobia. "And even if you do, does it make any difference? He is too powerful—and he is a creature out of time. Once the world could hold him, because there were others with power great enough to keep him in check. But free him now and you unleash an uncontrollable force. There is no one left who can master him, no safe place to put him. He can wreak unimaginable destruction."

Marilyn turned away from her aunt. "Kyle?" she whispered.

Kyle looked at her hopelessly. "I don't know what to tell you. I think Guptas got a bum deal. But I sure don't want him walking the streets of Kennituck Falls at night."

Marilyn went to the window and stared out at the great peaks surrounding them. The air was cool. Glancing down, she could see a break in the clouds, and the ground, incredibly far away. She leaned her head on the sill and tried to think, but her mind was whirling with fear, with anger, with sorrow.

"Why me?" she whispered. "Why do I have to make such a decision?"

The amulet was warm in her hand.

She stood up. "Guptas, I want to see you!"

At once the demon appeared.

"Do you have anything to say?" she asked.

Cooley started to protest. Zenobia cut him off.

Guptas looked around the circle of faces. Marilyn could sense a great weariness in him.

"I have been imprisoned for thousands of years," he said at last. "My world has vanished, and I have no home. I am a slave to whoever holds the amulet."

He turned to Marilyn and looked directly into her eyes. "I want to be free. If you can't free me from the amulet, then free me from life."

He stepped closer to her.

"Let me go, or let me die."

"I thought you couldn't die," she said, her throat tight.

He looked away. His voice little more than a whisper, he said, "There's a way. If you're willing."

18

JOURNEY INTO FEAR

When she thought about it afterward, Marilyn was never certain how much time passed before she spoke again.

She studied the faces around her. Kyle, sweet and gentle, seemed very sad. She wondered what he was thinking. Cooley was fidgeting, chewing his ghostly lips, fighting to keep his mouth shut. Zenobia's eyes were filled with pity. And Guptas looked blank; there was nothing to be read in his face.

Her grip on the amulet tightened until the edges of it were cutting into her hand. She held it pressed against her chest. Closing her eyes, she could feel a tear trickle under her lashes. At last she whispered, "Guptas, I can't do it. I can't free you."

The demon nodded. "So be it."

She opened her eyes. "What do I do now?"

"You kill me."

"I can't do that, either!"

Guptas grinned, a hideous smile filled with fangs. "It's easier than you think. You simply destroy the amulet."

"I tried that," said Zenobia. "Remember?"

He laughed, a harsh, short sound. "I remember. It was pathetic. There is only one way to destroy the amulet, and that is in the forge where it was made."

"Where is that?" asked Marilyn.

"Below us. Deep in the bowels of the castle."

"Make him take us there," said Cooley.

"Shut up!" snapped Zenobia and Marilyn together.

Silence fell over the great hall. Brick came and rubbed against Marilyn's legs. "Will you show me the way?" she asked at last.

Guptas nodded.

Marilyn sighed. "Then let's go."

She couldn't hear it.

She couldn't see it. (Several times, when she thought it was close, she spun around to try, but found nothing.)

Even so, she was certain it was there, following them; some force, some *power* she did not understand.

She had no idea how she knew it was there, but the knowledge of it was driving her to distraction.

"What are you?" she wanted to scream, but resisted, for fear the others would think she was crazy.

They had been walking for hours. At least, it seemed that way to her. With the image of Guptas leading the way, they had left the Hall of the Kings through a secret door behind the throne, entering a world of twisting passages that the demon threaded as if it had been only yesterday when he last walked them.

The sensation of being followed would not go away.

"Do you feel anything strange?" she asked Kyle at one point.

"*Everything* is strange here," he answered.

She gave up and kept to herself what the rational part of her mind insisted was a mere nervous reaction to the insanity that had enveloped them.

She tried to pay attention to the sights around her, telling herself this was a place no other human eyes had ever seen.

It was strange, but strangely beautiful—all out of proportion to her senses, the doors and ceilings built for the great race of the Suleimans. But it was in perfect condition, as if not a moment had passed from the day Guptas's father had sealed the place and left it to the ages. She saw no decay, no dust. The strange carvings in the doorsills were without nicks or chips. The floors in the winding halls gleamed as if they had been polished yesterday.

Each room and corridor had been treated as if it were a work of art. Even as they penetrated deep into the hidden heart of the castle, they found breathtaking tapestries adorning the walls.

She lost count of the rooms they passed. Once in a while Guptas stopped to point through a door, saying, "That's where the king came to be alone" or "This was where they sent me to be punished when I was little."

Marilyn began to have an odd sense of the demon's

life, of a quiet domesticity that seemed oddly incongruous for such a creature.

As they went deeper into the castle, they left the bright areas behind. Here there were no more windows—only strange glowing stones set in the ceiling, stones that cast an eerie light over the halls through which they wandered.

Guptas's comments on the rooms grew stranger: "Here is where the king met his wizards. Here is where the demons came to perform their ceremonies."

"Ceremonies?" asked Zenobia, ever curious.

"I cannot speak of them," he replied.

"How do we know he won't lead us into some kind of trap?" Zenobia had asked earlier.

"That's simple enough," Cooley had said. "Marilyn can compel him to lead us safely. Remember, he is still bound by the amulet."

"He'll lead us safely," said Marilyn.

The moment the words left her mouth, she caught her breath and wondered what would happen: Without intending to, she had shown some trust in Guptas. Would that be enough to release him?

She waited nervously, but nothing seemed to change.

She began to wonder what was happening inside her. How much did she believe in the ancient demon after all? Would her emotions betray her and free him against her will?

She wished they would reach the forge.

And then what, Sparks? Can you really destroy the amulet, knowing that it will mean killing Guptas? You know that demon better than you've ever known any living creature. You've been inside his mind. You've experienced his life. You've felt his pain.

Can you really destroy him?

She backed away from the question. It was too much for her to deal with at the moment.

The sense that something was following them increased. She reached up to stroke Brick, who was riding on her shoulders. The cat's black-and-white tail flicked back and forth.

Ahead of her Guptas stopped. His tail lashed warily from side to side, much like the cat's.

"What is it?" she asked.

"I'm not certain," he growled. He turned restlessly, a worried look on his face. "I sense dan—"

Before he could finish, the floor gave way beneath her.

Marilyn screamed. She felt a ripping sensation on her shoulders and realized, in some corner of her mind, that it came from Brick's claws. The cat had jumped away, using her as a launching pad.

She hit something solid, and all the breath was knocked out of her.

Forced into silence, as soon as she caught her breath she began to scream again, because she was in a darkness deeper than anything she had ever experienced. It was as if something had swallowed the sun, had swallowed all the light that ever existed.

"Be quiet!" snapped Guptas.

"I can't stand the dark!" she sobbed.

He turned on a light. She didn't know how he did it, but she almost wished he hadn't, because the first thing she saw was so horrible it made Guptas look almost pretty by comparison.

159

The monster sat in a corner. It was obscenely bloated, a dripping mound of flesh with an almost human face and a score of scaly tentacles sprouting from its body. It blinked for a moment when Guptas turned on the light. Then it began to smile.

Welcome, it whispered in her mind.

Marilyn began to inch away.

Oh, don't do that! I'm very hungry. It chuckled softly—a bubbling, slimy sound that made her skin crawl. *I've been waiting a long, long time for someone to step into my little trap.*

As it spoke, a tentacle slithered across the floor and wrapped around her leg. At its touch, her skin began to burn. An odor of death rose from the tentacle's slimy casing.

"Let her go!" roared Guptas.

Her attacker shrank back against the wall for a moment, then sent another tentacle lashing out to wrap around the demon. It made a loop about Guptas. But closed in on itself, passing through the illusion of the demon's presence.

Marilyn beat at the tentacle that held her leg. She could feel blisters erupt on her hand where she struck it. The creature only tightened its grip.

Suddenly she heard a clattering noise. A small cloud of dust erupted to her right. When it cleared she saw Kyle standing near her, looking slightly dazed. He looked around, and the blood drained from his face.

The creature struck out at him. Kyle jumped, avoiding the tentacle, and grabbed a shard of the broken floor that littered the area around them. He slashed at the tentacle that held Marilyn, severing it with one stroke.

The creature howled in rage. The severed tentacle began spurting a green fluid that fell in steaming gouts around her.

"Marilyn, get out of here!" yelled Kyle.

A dozen tentacles shot toward him. But the creature was confused, disoriented by its pain, and Kyle was able to jump away from the attack.

"I'll hold him off!" he shouted. "You get out!"

"Follow me!" cried Guptas, racing past Marilyn. She scrambled to her feet, but looked back when she heard Kyle cry out in pain.

The creature had managed to snare him with one of its tentacles. Now several other tentacles were snaking in his direction.

Though Kyle was screaming, he was still fighting, slashing with the piece of flooring at the tentacle that held him. Each time he struck at the monster it gasped, its cries merging with Kyle's screams in horrible chords of anguish.

"Wait!" Marilyn cried to Guptas. "Wait!"

Guptas stopped. She dashed back and stomped as hard as she could on the tentacle that was holding Kyle. The sickening squashiness beneath her heel made her stomach lurch. The creature shrieked, but loosened its grip on Kyle, who pulled himself free and scrambled backward.

"Come on!" She grabbed him by the hand and they raced after Guptas.

Behind them the creature howled in rage, thrashing its tentacles, one of which reached far enough to lash against the back of Marilyn's leg.

The burning pain spurred her to even greater speed. Letting go of Kyle's hand, she ran on, gasping and panting, every breath cutting into her like a sword of fire. Following Guptas, she raced through tunnels that led to other tunnels, and tunnels beyond that.

Finally, unable to go a step farther, she collapsed against a wall, gasping for breath.

With a jolt, she realized the strange, unseen presence she had sensed earlier was still with them.

What was it?

Seeking comfort, she reached for Kyle's hand, then cried out in horror.

He was gone.

She called his name over and over, but there was no answer.

Turning her face to the wall, she began to sob.

19

SULEIMAN'S FORGE

"Guptas! Where are we?"

The demon shook his head. "I'm not certain."

"What do you mean? This is your home!"

"Of course. But there are miles and miles of corridors and tunnels beneath the castle. Unless you have some kind of landmark, or have been following a pattern, when you get to the lower levels there is no way to tell one place from another."

She looked at him suspiciously. "Did you go get us lost on purpose?"

An evil smile crept over the demon's face. "Free me and I'll take you back to the others."

"I can command you to take me back!"

"It won't do you any good," he said sadly. "I don't know the way."

She looked confused. "Then why did you just say you could do it?"

He shrugged. "It was worth a try."

"Trying to trick me like that won't do much to prove you're trustworthy!" she said angrily.

"What difference does it make now?" he shouted back. "Why should I be trustworthy when you're going to destroy me?"

"It was what you wanted," said Marilyn, feeling guilty.

"I would have preferred freedom."

"I would have preferred never knowing you. I guess we can't have everything." She turned in a circle, then muttered, "What do I do now?"

"I don't know."

"I was talking to myself!"

The demon made a face and disappeared.

"Guptas! Get back out here!"

He reappeared, looking sullen. *Better watch it, Sparks,* she thought to herself. *When you're trapped in the bottom of an ancient castle with a demon, you don't want to make an enemy out of him. Better to have a friend.*

Which raised a question:

"You tried to save me from that creature," she said. "Why?"

Guptas turned away from her. "I like you."

She began to laugh. "You want to know something weird? I'm starting to like you, too."

The corridors seemed to wind endlessly through the dark. Unlike the upper floors, there were no glowing stones here to light the way. The only illumination came from some small magic Guptas worked in order to keep Marilyn from total panic, causing himself to glow enough that he could light the way for them.

The sense of some presence hovering near them remained strong within her.

Marilyn wondered where the others were. Was Kyle lost, too—without even a demon to guide him?

"What was that thing that tried to kill us?" she asked once as they wandered along a particularly winding corridor.

Guptas shrugged. "A mistake of some kind. The Suleimans used to experiment with magic quite a bit. They made a lot of wonderful things, and many others better left unthought of. That thing was undoubtedly some wizard's work that escaped and was lurking here in the tunnels years before my father sealed the castle. Some of those things exist only to eat. They just sleep until something edible shows up. They can last for centuries that way." He thought for a moment, then added, "Or it might have been a punishment of some kind."

"A punishment for us?"

"No. For whoever that used to be."

Marilyn shuddered, and decided not to ask for details.

They had passed through several more tunnels when Guptas gave a cry of triumph. He had led them into a chamber where several passages came together. The floor of the chamber was carved with various symbols, and Guptas had knelt to examine them.

"I've got it!" he said triumphantly. "I can get us to the forge!"

"That's good," said Marilyn in a small voice. She was bone weary. Her shoulder ached where Brick had scratched it, and the places where the monster's tentacles had seared her skin were blistered and throbbing with pain.

Even with all that, she could have gone on. But the final horror had just sunk in: When they reached the forge, she would have to destroy Guptas. And once she had done that (if she *could* do it), she would be all alone, in the bowels of the castle, in the final darkness.

Unless by some miracle the others could find her, she and Guptas would die together.

The first thing they noticed was the smell. It reminded Marilyn of the air after a thunderstorm. Guptas said it was the smell of power.

Then they heard the dull roar of it. Soon the corridor was no longer cool, the stones Marilyn lay her hand against no longer moist.

Ahead they could see a flicker of light.

"Come on!" cried Guptas. "This is it!"

He raced along the corridor, almost scampering in his glee.

"Wait!" called Marilyn, who was far too tired for scampering.

Guptas turned and waited, shifting impatiently from one foot to the other.

"I don't understand," said Marilyn. "Why are you in such a hurry to get here?"

"This was my father's special place."

The demon's smile faded, yet his face looked serene. "This is where he came to work—and to be alone. But sometimes he brought me with him." Guptas was looking in her direction, but she could tell he was lost in his memories, seeing a better time. "Those were the best days for me. When we were in court, or with other people, I was his shame, his embarrassment. He only kept me at his side then for two reasons."

Guptas fell silent.

"What were the reasons?" asked Marilyn gently.

"One was his sense of responsibility. The fact that I existed appalled him. But he would not deny it, nor hide from it. He accepted the burden of his mistake."

"And the other?"

Guptas sighed. "I was a warning against pride. By keeping me at his side, he was faced every moment with the fact of his own imperfection.

"But down here it was different. In the court, in the castle, people tolerated me, grudgingly, as the king's offspring, whatever I was. They tolerated me because they had to. But my demon blood disgusted them, and I knew that.

"My father would never show that he cared for me in front of them. But when he brought me down here, when he came to work, then he would talk to me like a son, telling me things I needed to know, and things that he thought." Guptas turned away. "He treated me as if I were ... human."

To her astonishment, Marilyn realized that Guptas's shoulders were shaking, as if he was weeping. She felt an urge to reach out to the demon, hold him for just a moment and tell him it was all right.

But she knew that if she tried, her arms would pass right through him.

He turned and walked toward the light.

A moment later, when they entered the forging area, they both cried out in astonishment.

"So, this was how it ended," murmured Guptas.

Marilyn wondered vaguely what he meant, but was too caught up in examining the room to ask.

The place was huge. Not as big as the Hall of the Kings, of course, but larger than any other room of her experience.

In the center was a pit of fire, surrounded by a stone rim a little higher than her waist. It was at least twenty feet across, filled with dancing flames of all colors. They seemed to operate on a cycle, flickering softly about three feet higher than the rim for a few moments, then roaring some twenty feet into the air, casting out a surge of heat and light that reached the farthest corners of the chamber.

Stone tables as tall as her head were arranged around the forge, littered with tools and scraps of metal. Other tools dangled from the ceiling, far beyond her reach, but just right, she assumed, for a Suleiman.

She found something attractive, almost seductive, about the flames. She felt an urge to run to them, thrust her hands among them, even fling herself into the pit. She shook herself and forced her eyes away from the forge.

She cried out in horror. A demon was about to attack her! Almost instantly she realized what it really was, and felt silly. The ebb and surge of the flames was casting strange shadows around the chamber. What she had seen, feared, was merely a statue—cleverly wrought, but a statue nonetheless—of a demon on the attack. Its face was contorted with rage. It held a deadly looking ax above its head, ready to strike. The flicker of the flames almost made it seem alive.

She crossed tentatively to it and reached out her hand.

"Amazing, isn't it?" asked Guptas. She jumped, and drew her hand back.

"You scared me." She turned to him. Looking past him, she noticed that the room was filled with the statues. "These are fantastic. Did your father make them?"

"You might say that."

"What do you mean?"

"They aren't statues, if that's what you're thinking."

An explanation began to nag at Marilyn's brain, but she fought to ignore it.

"What are they?" she asked warily, hoping the idea she was not able to press back was wrong.

"Demons," replied Guptas. "My other people." He looked around. "This is where my father fought his last battle. It makes sense. He could have lured them to the forge—for there were things they wanted from him that he kept here. Then when he got them here, he used his power to turn them into stone." Guptas stroked the stone demon with his claws. "It's not an easy spell. I imagine doing this roomful almost killed him."

His voice held a strange tone that made Marilyn uneasy. She began to edge away from him.

"It's an odd spell," he continued. His voice was

crafty now, and his tail was twitching nervously. "Father told me about it once."

"Guptas?"

"Difficult to cast, but not hard to break."

The demon turned to her. His eyes glittering with evil, he asked, "How would you like to meet my family?"

20

NOW LET DESTRUCTION REIGN

Marilyn felt her insides lurch. "You wouldn't," she whispered in horror.

Guptas caressed the stone demon with his claws. He had a faraway look in his eyes. "Why not?"

"Because you're not that way."

He crossed to another statue. The light still cast by his body caused the hideous features to spring out of the darkness. They made Marilyn shudder.

Guptas seemed to consider her statement for a moment. "I think maybe I *am* that way," he said at last.

"But they were wicked!"

"I am, too."

"No! I don't believe that."

He pounced on the statement. "Then why won't you free me from the amulet?"

She felt as if she had been struck dumb. She could think of no reasonable answer for his question.

"I don't know," she said at last. "Maybe it's because you scare me."

A momentary look of sorrow crossed his face. "I scare everyone," he said. "So I must be wicked."

"No! No, you can't say that. People just aren't ... aren't used to something like you. They're afraid of what they don't know."

Guptas looked at her. The flicker in his eyes seemed to match the flames in Suleiman's forge, as if they were somehow connected. "I'm afraid, Marilyn. It's been ten thousand years. And now you're going to destroy me. Do you think I'm not afraid? Do you think I don't wonder what will happen next? My father had a soul. My mother didn't. What about me? What will happen to me when you throw that amulet into the forge? Will I be gone forever? Will I meet my father again?" He looked at her with haunted, burning eyes. "Or will I roast in some forgotten hell?"

He reached out for her. "Can you tell me, Marilyn? Can you tell me what happens next?"

The amulet seemed to be burning in her hand. She glanced at it. The red stone in its center was flickering in unison with Suleiman's forge, with Guptas's eyes.

She shook her head. "I don't know," she whispered. "I don't know anything anymore."

Guptas sighed. In the silence that followed, Marilyn again sensed that other presence, watching, waiting. The rhythmic flare of the forge spread eerie colors and dancing shadows through the room, smearing the floor, the walls, the frozen demons with shades of fire and darkness.

She felt as though she were being crushed, as if the great mountain they had wound their way into was slowly grinding her to dust.

Something warm and soft rubbed against her leg, and she leaped to her feet, screaming.

It was Brick.

Kyle came racing into the room. "Thank goodness we found you! I thought you were gone for good!"

Zenobia and Eldred Cooley shimmered into sight behind him.

"How did you get here?" asked Marilyn.

"We found Kyle wandering in the tunnels just beyond where you fell," said Zenobia. "Then Brick brought us here. As Eldred told you, a cat can sense demons."

Marilyn was in Kyle's arms, leaning against his chest, feeling safe for the first time since they tumbled through the floor. "I thought I had lost you," he whispered. "I was terrified."

The peaceful moment ended abruptly.

"What is that creature doing here?" demanded Cooley. "Why haven't you destroyed him yet? Are you insane?"

"I don't—"

Those words were all she could get out. Guptas was on his feet, roaring with anger.

"That's enough! You're right, Eldred Cooley. Never trust a demon! I'll be what you want! I'll prove you're right! But you and your people will be the ones to pay. Because my family and I will pursue you, even beyond the grave. We'll terrorize the living, and we'll haunt the dead. And it will be on your head, Cooley. You are the one who drove me to this."

"Your family!" Cooley laughed. The laugh died on his lips as he looked around the room and realized what the shapes scattered across the floor really were.

Guptas had leaped to the edge of the forge. Standing on the stone rim, he raised his arms and began to speak. The flames shot up behind him, stretching to twice the height they had reached before, responding to the power and the magic now unleashed.

Light the color of blood filled the room. The statues sprang out in hideous detail—dozens of raging creatures, intent on death and destruction.

"Karra Nakken Re-Suleiman Karras!" roared Guptas.

The flames surged behind him. He threw back his head and roared with laughter, raising his great claws to the ceiling. "KARRA NAKKEN RE-SULEIMAN KARRAS!"

"Stop him!" cried Cooley. "Stop him! If he frees them now, they could destroy the world!"

"Marilyn!" cried Kyle, shaking her. "Marilyn, use the amulet!"

Marilyn shook her head as if she were coming out of a daze. The amulet was pulsing in her hand, throbbing with power. She held it up; light and fire seemed to drip along her forearm.

"Guptas!" she cried. "By this amulet, I command you to stop!"

The last words were buried by a sound like stone grinding on stone, and her heart sank.

She was too late.

Turning in the direction of the sound, she saw that the demon nearest them was changing. Cracks ran over its surface. A reddish tint began to replace the gray of stone.

Slowly it began to twist its head in their direction. More cracks appeared, then vanished as stone turned to flesh. Most horrible of all, the dead stone eyes glazed over, seemed to shatter like breaking glass, then blazed into life—flickering with the fire of the forge, the fire of the amulet.

The sound of stone on stone was repeated all around them. A guttural murmur of some ancient, forbidden language finding tongue again began to fill the hall.

"Look out!" cried Zenobia as the demon nearest them lunged forward, slashing at them with its ax.

Kyle and Marilyn leaped away, but not fast enough. The blade slashed across the side of her leg, laying it open to the bone, then sank into the floor behind her. As she screamed in pain and shock, the creature struggled to free its weapon so it could strike again.

An angry screech sliced the air behind her. She knew that sound. It was Brick!

She turned in time to see the cat plucked from the floor by one of the demons. Writhing in its grasp, Brick lashed out with one claw and tore open the creature's eye. It split with a hissing sound and liquid fire began to pour down the demon's cheek. Furious, it threw Brick aside. The cat struck the wall and slid to the floor, senseless.

Then Marilyn could see no more, because Kyle flung her to the floor, too. Holding her tight against him, he rolled under the biggest of the stone tables.

They were barely beneath it when a curved blade slashed against the top, cutting right into the stone.

Suddenly an evil face appeared below the edge of the table. A wicked smile split its hideous features.

Another appeared beside it, and then another.

Kyle and Marilyn huddled together and pulled back from the edge. They heard a hissing behind them. Turning, she saw two more of the creatures peering in at them from that side.

"Put your back to mine!" said Kyle. "Get as close to me as you can."

Another face appeared at the end of the table, and a scaly hand reached in for them.

A demon grabbed her arm from the other side. She smashed its hand with the amulet. The demon let go, screaming in agony. Her scream mingled with his, seeming to fill the room.

Marilyn continued screaming. This was no mirage, like Guptas. These creatures were real, and out for blood.

The sound of Kyle crying out behind her brought her to her senses. Turning, she saw that one of the demons had grabbed his ankle and was pulling him from under the table. Marilyn wrapped her arms around him and found herself engaged in a desperate tug-of-war.

A pair of scaly hands wrapped about her leg and began dragging her in the opposite direction. Another pair grabbed her other leg. Her grip on Kyle was slipping. He was screaming now, too, as a dozen evil faces glared in at them, fire in their eyes, steaming saliva dripping from their hungry mouths.

Suddenly Guptas was there, roaring in anger. "Let her go! Let her go!" he cried, slashing out at the demons.

It did no good. His arms, mere illusions, passed through them like moonlight through glass.

"I didn't mean to do it!" he moaned, his voice thick with sorrow and remorse. "I didn't mean to do it!"

A vicious wrench at her legs tore Marilyn's hands from Kyle, and she found herself in the open, outside the table. Somewhere behind her she could hear Kyle screaming.

"The amulet!" cried Guptas. "Use the amulet!"

Marilyn wrenched her hand free of the demon that was holding it. The amulet blazed with light.

"Stop!" she cried.

The demons drew back a bit.

"Stop!" she repeated.

An angry murmur rose from the horde. A set of claws slashed at her arm but missed, as if their owner didn't dare actually strike her.

"Stop!" she commanded a third time, scrambling to her feet as she did.

The demons drew back, forming a wary circle around her.

Kyle was still screaming. With a shout Marilyn broke through the circle of demons. Another circle had formed at the other end of the table. She thrust her way into it, holding the amulet before her like a shield.

Kyle, bleeding in a dozen places, looked up at her. His eyes were glazed with terror.

"Let go of him!" she screamed.

The amulet blazed, grew so hot she almost dropped it, and the demons pulled back.

She reached down to Kyle, still holding the amulet

before her, turning warily this way and that to keep the crowd of demons at bay.

He took her hand and staggered to his feet.

The demons grouped themselves around the two teens, muttering nervously, angrily.

Marilyn could feel herself connected with the amulet, feel the flow of her strength into it, and through it. Though it was holding the creatures at bay, it was draining her as it did. She knew she wouldn't last much longer.

As if sensing this, the demons began to press forward.

Holding the amulet above her, as a lone traveler might hold a torch to ward off wolves, Marilyn backed warily away from them.

They pressed slowly forward, seeming to push against some invisible wall she was creating.

Her heart was pounding against her ribs like some caged animal. The wound on her leg was throbbing, and she was still losing blood. Her head felt light. She feared she was about to faint. But she knew if she faltered for even a moment, she and Kyle were dead.

She felt something against her back, and realized it was the rim of the forge. Together, without speaking, they slid up onto it.

The flames behind them seared their backs.

There was nowhere left to go.

The demons drew closer.

"Marilyn!" cried Guptas. "You can't hold them off much longer. Free me! Free me and I will fight for you!"

"Don't be insane!" shrieked Cooley. "If you let him

loose now, it's the end of everything! He's their leader. They'll be invincible."

The demon horde inched forward. Marilyn could feel her control weakening. The flames roaring behind her seemed to be sapping her strength. Her head was throbbing. She couldn't think.

"Let me out!" cried Guptas again. "Marilyn, let me fight for you!"

Marilyn looked at the demon, then at Cooley. Between them the demon horde, held barely in check by her waning strength, muttered and crouched, waiting to leap, eager to tear her to shreds.

I'm ready to die, she thought. But then she felt Kyle beside her, his arms around her. She couldn't think about his death. She couldn't let that happen.

Her head spun with exhaustion. She staggered and almost fell backward into the flames. It was only a matter of moments before she would lose her grip and the horde would attack.

"Hold on, Marilyn," whispered Kyle, tightening his grip and trying to steady her. "Hold on!"

It wasn't enough. The demons were beating down her resistance. Each of them had its fiery eyes boring into her, willing her to die. They began to chant, some guttural cry that had no meaning but seemed to beat the little remaining strength out of her brain.

She could feel herself wavering.

"Now, Marilyn!" cried Guptas. "Free me now before it's too late!"

The demons were winning. Binding them was like trying to hold water in a sieve.

The chant grew louder. One of the demons made a sudden push forward. Another followed him.

She was losing control.

"Now!" cried Guptas.

"Don't be a fool!" screamed Cooley. "He'll kill you first!"

She stepped back and almost slipped over the rim of the forge. An image burst into her head: Guptas, explaining why he had defended her from the creature in the tunnel. His words whispered again in her mind: *I like you.*

Her grip on the amulet tightened.

"I trust you," she whispered. "Guptas, I trust you. Come forth and protect me."

The demons screamed and lunged forward.

The flames roared up behind her.

She collapsed into Kyle's arms.

And as they struggled to keep their balance on the edge of the inferno, Guptas, the son of Suleiman, returned to the flesh for the first time in ten thousand years.

21

THE HANDS OF
THE KING

Marilyn lost her balance and pitched forward, dragging Kyle with her. They struck the floor and were immediately engulfed by a wave of attacking demons.

Shrieking, crying, clawing, the monsters piled on the two teenagers like sharks in a feeding frenzy.

Marilyn, barely conscious, was aware of their claws tearing at her skin. At the same time she sensed that the creatures were, by their very numbers, slowed in their intent to kill her and Kyle immediately.

The confusion bought them only a few seconds of life.

Those few seconds were enough. Beyond the babble of the demons, she could hear a deep-throated roar, a cry of rage tempered by a strange joy.

Then she felt the demons being pulled away

from her, lifted and flung into the air like scraps of paper.

Guptas appeared above them, his face contorted with a fierce ecstasy.

"Ten thousand years!" he cried. "Ten thousand years, and finally free!"

He grabbed a demon in each hand and smashed their skulls together, then flung them forward into the forge.

The flames roared explosively, shot up, and scorched the ceiling as the cries of the dying demons filled the room.

Guptas's tail swept behind him, knocking the demons off their feet.

"It was you!" he cried. "You! I listened to you, I helped you, and everything went wrong! Never again! Never again!"

He lashed out, his great arms sending the smaller demons flying to the right and left. Marilyn and Kyle edged away from the fray. Suddenly Zenobia was at their side.

"Over there," she whispered, pointing to a fallen table. "You'll be safer there."

They scurried along the side of the forge and scrambled behind the table.

On the other side they could hear the battle raging. Unable to resist, they peered over the edge and cried out in despair.

Guptas, larger and stronger than any of the others, had had the advantage when he attacked them. But now their sheer numbers were working against him. They were attacking from all sides, climbing on his back, pulling at his legs, slashing at him with whatever weapons they could lay their hands on.

"Off!" he roared, tearing them from his body and sending them flying into the forge.

The flames were soaring, eagerly devouring every demon that landed in their midst.

"Guptas!"

The voice that rang out was strong and powerful. The fighting stopped. Marilyn cried out in horror and surprise.

It was the old demon—the one who had urged Guptas to give the signal for the rebellion in the Hall of the Kings. Though cracked with age, his voice was powerful, commanding.

"Guptas, stop this foolishness. You are one of us. Destroy those meddling children. Then lead us back to the world. To the *world*. You are the greatest among us. You can be our king. Guptas, lead us to the world again!"

"Don't listen to him," whispered Marilyn. "Guptas, don't listen to him!"

The old demon had locked eyes with Guptas. "Be our king," he whispered. "Don't be a fool. Don't betray us. There is no place for you but with us, no friends for you but us, no hope for you but us. Destroy them, and take your place as our king!"

Guptas stood as if entranced.

"Guptas!" cried the demon nearest him. "Guptas the king!"

The others took up the chant. "Guptas the king! Guptas the king!"

"You were born to rule!" cried the old demon. "Your mother was a queen among demons. Your father was king of the Suleimans. There was never another like you. There was never another Guptas! You will be greater than any king that ever reigned. The world will be yours!"

"You see!" shrieked Cooley. "You see what will happen, you young fool? You've given him the world!"

"Eldred, shut up!" said Zenobia.

"King of the world," whispered Guptas.

Marilyn dragged herself from behind the table. "Don't listen to him," she begged. "Guptas, don't listen to him!" She staggered toward him. "Guptas, don't betray me!"

The demon closest to her grabbed her about the waist. Snarling with fury, he dragged her toward the forge. His claws tore into her flesh.

"Guptas!" she screamed. "Save me!"

The demon had her at the rim. She could feel the heat and fury of the flames as her captor lifted her over the edge.

Kyle started for the forge and was immediately tackled by a dozen demons. He hit the floor with a bone-jarring crash.

"Guptas!" he cried desperately. "Fight for her!"

Marilyn beat at the scaly back of the demon clutching her. "Guptas!" she screamed. "Guptas, I need you!"

Her tears fell to the rim of the forge, sizzling instantly into steam. "Guptas!" She was weeping now as much for him as for herself. "Guptas, I trusted you! Fight for me!"

The demon who held her, small but powerful, raised her above his head. She clung to his hard arms, screaming in terror, as he tried to throw her into the flames.

Guptas began to roar. It started deep in his throat and came rumbling up like a volcano erupting, until his anger shook the very walls around them.

"Let her go!" he roared, at the same moment launching himself through the air to grab her from the demon's arms. "Let ... her ... GO!"

He wrenched Marilyn free, tucked her safely under one arm, and with the other picked up the demon and threw it into the forge.

The flames roared gratefully.

"Back!" cried Guptas. "Back, all of you!"

"Destroy the traitor!" cried the old demon. "Guptas must die!"

With a cry of rage the demons surged forward. Guptas placed Marilyn behind him, against the wall of the forge, and stood to guard her against the onslaught. But their numbers were too great. Though demon after demon went sailing over his shoulder and into the flames, it seemed there were always more coming. Guptas was bleeding from a dozen places, and then a dozen more. His sizzling black blood etched its way into the floor.

He was staggering, weakening from the punishment.

And then, so suddenly it was a shock, the demons were gone.

All but one. The old demon who had urged Guptas into his first betrayal.

"Traitor!" hissed the demon. "Fool! What will you gain for this? Nothing!"

He spat in Guptas's face.

Guptas reached forward.

"My grandfather," he whispered. "Father of my mother, king of lies, agent of hate, maker of war. I have waited too long to kill you."

"You never will," sneered the old demon.

"You are wrong," said Guptas simply. "The time has come for you to pay at last. It was all your fault, wasn't it? Everything that happened from the moment you urged my mother to deceive the king. The lies, the betrayal, the destruction—all of it is on your shoulders."

He reached forward. But his strength was gone. Arms spasming, he fell to the floor and lay there without moving.

"Guptas," said the old demon, kicking at him, and Marilyn could hear a note of regret in his voice. "Guptas the Fool, who could have ruled the world."

Raising his eyes, he glared at Marilyn. "You ruined it all," he whispered bitterly. "I think it's time for you to die."

Marilyn pressed back against the rim of the forge. The old demon stepped over Guptas and took her by the neck. His claws began to sink into her skin.

"That's enough," said a voice behind them.

The demon turned around, then began to scream.

Marilyn looked up in astonishment.

Among the litter of demons, looking down at them, stood Suleiman, father of Guptas.

"Give me the amulet," he said. His voice was quiet, strong, gentle, ancient, filled with sorrow. He extended his arm. Marilyn reached up and laid the amulet in his palm. It seemed oddly tiny in his great hand.

"No!" screamed the old demon. "Great king, do not do this. No! No! No!"

"Silence!" said Suleiman.

Closing his massive fingers over the amulet, he spoke softly, in some ancient language. A great crack of something like thunder reverberated through the chamber.

The old demon vanished.

Smoke curled from between the king's fingers. He opened his hand, gazed at the amulet for a moment, then tossed it into the forge.

The explosion knocked Marilyn to her knees.

The flames returned to normal. By their flickering light she watched as the king knelt to gather his battered son into his arms.

Guptas stirred in his grasp. "Father," he whispered.

"I should have loved you better," said the king sadly as he cradled Guptas against his chest.

After a moment the king lifted his head to look at Marilyn. Tears shimmered at the corners of his eyes. "Thank you," he said softly. "Without your trust, my son would have been doomed forever."

He looked around the room and spotted Kyle, who was quietly trying to bear the agony of his many wounds.

"Tell your friend to come before me," said Suleiman. The shadow of a smile flickered over his face. "And bring me your cat, as well."

Mystified, Marilyn gestured to Kyle, who had forced himself to his knees.

"I can't," he whispered. "I can't move."

"I'll help," she said. "Just wait."

She limped to the wall where Brick lay and lifted him gently from the floor. He was still breathing, but his body was badly broken. He opened one eye and tried to yowl in protest. The sound was pathetically weak.

"Poor baby," whispered Marilyn. Cradling the cat gently in her arms, she went to Kyle. "Put your arm on my shoulder," she said, kneeling beside him.

He struggled to his feet.

Together they crossed to the king.

Suleiman knelt and laid Guptas gently down beside him. "This much I can do for you," he said softly to Marilyn. He took Brick from her arms and held the cat cupped in his enormous hands. He closed his eyes. Brick stiffened for a moment, yowled almost in anger, then sat up, blinking, absurdly small on the king's palm.

He looked up, yowled this time in fright, and jumped back into Marilyn's arms.

Suleiman smiled. "Now you," he said to Kyle.

Kyle stepped forward. The king took him in his great arms. Like Brick, Kyle yelled out. And, like Brick, his wounds were healed. He touched himself in amazement. "Thank you," he said awkwardly.

Suleiman held Marilyn and healed her, too; healed the burns, the slash of the ax, the bruises that covered her body. And, a little, he healed the wounds of her spirit, the fear that lingered within.

After he set her down, he gathered Guptas into his arms once more. The demon stirred, then opened his eyes. With an effort that was clearly painful, he reached out his hand to Marilyn.

She stepped forward and took it. The scaly flesh was warm and dry, surprisingly pleasant to the touch.

"Thank you," he whispered. "Thank you for trusting me."

Marilyn squeezed his hand. "What will happen to him now?" she asked, looking up at the king.

"He will come to be with me." Suleiman looked around the room. "As for you, you should all go home now. Some of you have a lot to learn," he added, looking pointedly at Eldred Cooley.

"I'd love to go home," said Marilyn. "But how do we get there without Guptas?"

The king looked at her in astonishment. "What do you have a cat for?" he asked.

And then he was gone, taking his son with him.

Epilogue

Marilyn sat between Kyle and Alicia at the funeral home, listening to the preacher talk about Zenobia. She looked around. She still couldn't believe she and Kyle were in one piece, much less that they had managed to get this place back in shape in time to get out while it was still dark last night.

Getting Zenobia's body back into her coffin had been the worst part, of course. Once they had managed that, Marilyn had tried to arrange the flowers so no one would notice that the amulet was missing.

Marilyn looked up and suppressed a smile. Zenobia was sitting on the end of her coffin, looking at the minister as if she couldn't believe her ears.

"They always spout such nonsense," she had said

to Marilyn on the way home last night. "I can't wait to hear what he has to say about me."

Now, seeing that Marilyn was looking at her, Zenobia mouthed a single word: "Baloney!"

Marilyn snorted, then tried to turn the sound into a sob.

Alicia dug her in the ribs. Kyle squeezed her hand. They all stood for the hymn.

Twelve hours later Marilyn was sitting in her bed, telling Brick what a great cat he was for getting them all back, when Zenobia walked through her closed door.

Marilyn smiled. "I was hoping you would come."

"It's just to say good-bye."

Marilyn frowned. "Do you have to go?"

Zenobia nodded. "Afraid so. There's so much to do. I can't tell you all about it. But trust me, it's exciting."

"The last adventure?" asked Marilyn, trying to smile.

"The biggest," said Zenobia. "If they would just let me have a cigar, I'd be in Heaven."

SPIRIT WORLD
RESTLESS SPIRITS

Bruce Coville

Lisa Burton and her little sister Carrie can't wait to leave Sayers Island. The weather is terrible and they're bored stiff. But one rainy afternoon their grandmother teaches them 'automatic writing' to pass the time – and now the girls can't stop . . .

But the fun soon turns to terror as angry ghosts confuse the living with the dead and, unless Lisa can find a way to bring peace to the restless spirits, the ghosts will claim the ultimate price for tampering with the unknown – her sister . . .

SPIRIT WORLD
SPIRITS AND SPELLS

Bruce Coville

Trying out their new haunted house game, Spirits and Spells, in a real old haunted house seemed like a good idea to Tansy, Travis and their friends. But that was before they found out what was in the attic . . . and the basement . . . and everywhere in between . . .

Now they must play the game as though their lives depend on it – because they do . . . .

Another Hodder Children's book

SPIRIT WORLD
EYES OF THE TAROT

Bruce Coville

When Bonnie McBurnie begins to use the ancient deck of tarot cards she found in her grandmother's attic, she taps into a power unlike anything she's ever imagined.

Soon the ancient forces of the tarot begin to haunt Bonnie's life, forcing her to face a fearful secret buried in her own past – and the terrifying wrath of a powerful sorceror who has been waiting centuries for his chance to return.

Can Bonnie master the cards – or will their strange power destroy not only her, but everyone she loves?

ALIENS ATE MY HOMEWORK

Bruce Coville

Do you have problems telling lies?
Can you only speak the truth – no matter
how silly?
Then you'll know how Rod felt when his
teacher asked about his science project –
because he could only tell her the truth:
'Aliens ate my homework, Miss Maloney!'

Of course, nobody believes Rod, so nobody
bothers to ask where the aliens come from.
Just as well – because Rod is helping
Madame Pong and the crazy crew of the
Ferkel on a very secret mission . . .

ORDER FORM

Bruce Coville

0 340 71458 1	Spirit World 1: Restless Spirits	£3.99	❑
0 340 71459 X	Spirit World 2: Spirits and Spells	£3.99	❑
0 340 71460 3	Spirit World 3: Eyes of the Tarot	£3.99	❑
0 340 71461 1	Spirit World 4: Creature of Fire	£3.99	❑
0 340 65115 6	Aliens Ate my Homework	£3.99	❑
0 340 65116 4	I Left my Sneakers in Dimension X	£3.99	❑
0 340 65355 8	Aliens Stole my Dad	£3.99	❑
0 340 63593 2	Goblins in the Castle	£3.99	❑

All Hodder Children's books are available at your local bookshop or newsagent, or can be ordered direct from the publisher. Just tick the titles you want and fill in the form below. Prices and availability subject to change without notice.

Hodder Children's Books, Cash Sales Department, Bookpoint, 39 Milton Park, Abingdon, OXON, OX14 4TD, UK. If you have a credit card, our call centre team would be delighted to take your order by telephone. Our direct line is 01235 400414 (lines open 9.00 am–6.00 pm Monday to Saturday, 24 hour message answering service). Alternatively you can send a fax on 01235 400454.

Or enclose a cheque or postal order made payable to Bookpoint Ltd to the value of the cover price and allow the following for postage and packing:
UK & BFPO – £1.00 for the first book, 50p for the second book, and 30p for each additional book ordered up to a maximum charge of £3.00.
OVERSEAS & EIRE – £2.00 for the first book, £1.00 for the second book, and 50p for each additional book.

Name..

Address..

....

....

If you would prefer to pay by credit card, please complete:
Please debit my Visa/Access/Diner's Card/American Express (delete as applicable) card no:

Signature...

ExpiryDate..

ORDER FORM

More H Supernatural title to look out for from Hodder Children's Books

0 340 68076 8	NIGHT PEOPLE *Maggie Pearson*	£3.99	❑
0 340 69371 1	THE BLOODING *Patricia Windsor*	£3.99	❑
0 340 68300 7	COMPANIONS OF THE NIGHT *Vivian Vande Velde*	£3.99	❑
0 340 68656 1	LOOK FOR ME BY MOONLIGHT *Mary Downing Hahn*	£3.99	❑
0 340 68331 7	THE GRAVE-DIGGER *Hugh Scott*	£3.99	❑
0 340 68751 7	NIGHT WORLD 1: SECRET VAMPIRE *Lisa J Smith*	£3.99	❑

All Hodder Children's books are available at your local bookshop or newsagent, or can be ordered direct from the publisher. Just tick the titles you want and fill in the form below. Prices and availability subject to change without notice.

Hodder Children's Books, Cash Sales Department, Bookpoint, 39 Milton Park, Abingdon, OXON, OX14 4TD, UK. If you have a credit card, our call centre team would be delighted to take your order by telephone. Our direct line is 01235 400414 (lines open 9.00 am–6.00 pm Monday to Saturday, 24 hour message answering service). Alternatively you can send a fax on 01235 400454.

Or enclose a cheque or postal order made payable to Bookpoint Ltd to the value of the cover price and allow the following for postage and packing:
UK & BFPO – £1.00 for the first book, 50p for the second book, and 30p for each additional book ordered up to a maximum charge of £3.00.
OVERSEAS & EIRE – £2.00 for the first book, £1.00 for the second book, and 50p for each additional book.

Name...

Address...

....

....

If you would prefer to pay by credit card, please complete:
Please debit my Visa/Access/Diner's Card/American Express (delete as applicable) card no:

Signature...